LOGICS OF WORLDS

Also available from Continuum:

LOGICS OF WORLDS

BEING AND EVENT, 2

Alain Badiou

Translated by Alberto Toscano

continuum

This work is published with the support of the French Ministry of Culture – Centre National du Livre.

Liberté • Égalité • Fraternité
RÉPUBLIQUE FRANÇAISE

Continuum

Continuum International Publishing Group
The Tower Building   80 Maiden Lane
11 York Road   Suite 704
London SE1 7NX   New York NY 10038
www.continuumbooks.com

Originally published in French as *Logiques des mondes* © Editions du Seuil, 2006

This English language translation © Continuum 2009

British Library Cataloguing in Publication Data
A catalogue record for this book is available from the British Library.

ISBN-10: HB: 0–8264–9470–6
ISBN-13: HB: 978–0–8264–9470–2

Library of Congress Cataloging-in-Publication Data
Badiou, Alain.
[Logiques des mondes. English]
Logics of worlds / Alain Badiou ; translated by Alberto Toscano. p. cm.
Includes bibliographical references (p.   ) and index.
ISBN 978–0–8264–9470–2
1. Ontology. 2. Subjectivity. 3. Truth. I. Title.

B2430.B273L6413 2009
194—dc22

2008036972

Typeset by RefineCatch Limited, Bungay, Suffolk
Printed and bound in Great Britain by
MPG Books Ltd, Bodmin, Cornwall

To Françoise Badiou

Contents

Translator's Note

For Alain Badiou, the writing of philosophy is constantly obliged to span two ostensibly incompatible registers, that of mathematical formalization and that of poetic diction. Badiou's steadfast opposition to the philosophical supremacy of meaning—that is, his attempt to resurrect rationalism against the many faces of finitude—requires the cooperation of these two conditions of philosophy, poem and matheme. Among many other things, *Logics of Worlds* is also the invention of a new articulation between poetic evocation, coupled here with a good dose of narrative art, and rigorous formalized speculation. To the extent of my abilities, I have tried in this translation to stay true to the rationalist imperative of transmissibility—which would seem to tend towards the nullification of human speech—without diminishing the often remarkable ways in which Badiou musters his own linguistic resources, and those of several literary canons, to coax the reader into joining his protracted war against those who wish life to be sundered from the Idea and consigned, without remainder, to this mortal coil. Accordingly, I have worked to make the act of translation as unobtrusive as possible, keeping editorial interventions or bracketed original terms to a minimum and, when forced to choose, opting for accuracy over elegance. In the notes, I have directly replaced French references with their English counterparts, avoiding cumbersome interpolations, and have always modified translations or made my own when required to do so by the detail of Badiou's argument. Throughout, I have complied with Badiou's practice of providing references to titles alone, leaving out page numbers.

Both responding to a host of objections that were levied against this book's predecessor, *Being and Event*—namely its brusque treatment of the question of relation—and returning to theoretical preoccupations that long predated that book (topology, the dialectic), *Logics of Worlds* articulates a novel and vigorously counter-intuitive variation on a hallowed philosophical theme: the relations between being and appearing. Unless otherwise noted, I have handled the difference between *être* and *étant* simply by stressing the discreteness or individuation of the latter. Thus, *être-multiple* is simply 'multiple-being', while *étant-multiple* is 'a multiple-being'. *Être-là*, Badiou's term for situated being, and the nearest French rendering of *Dasein*, I have simply translated as being-there—though Badiou often evokes Heidegger, with some irreverence, it is rather Hegel's *Dasein* (translated by Miller as 'determinate being') that is at stake here (see Book II, Section 2). Badiou employs two main terms for the inscription of the pure multiple in different worlds, *apparaître* and *apparition*. Though he eschews any hard and fast distinction between the two, I have rendered the first with 'appearing', to denote the entire domain of worldliness and to connote the act or operation thereof, and the second by 'appearance', broadly in the sense of an instance of appearing. Among Badiou's radical redefinitions of fundamental philosophical notions, we find an attempt to rethink negation with the resources provided by contemporary logic. In Book II, Section 1, he introduces the concept of *envers*. I have opted for 'reverse' to retain the topological resonances of the term, as in 'the other side'. Having said this, the most difficult work of 'translation' will be the reader's, faced with seemingly familiar or identifiable notions—such as object, phenomenon, transcendental, world, etc.—which are here profoundly recast, with both speculative and polemical intent.

For the translation of logical and mathematical terms, I have been lucky to be able to rely on Anindya Bhattacharyya, a fine reader of Badiou and one of the few people I know capable of engaging his work directly on the formal terrain. I have thus learned that a *sous-groupe distingué* is a 'normal subgroup', a *majorant* is an 'upper bound', a *minorant* is a 'lower bound' and so on. Needless to say, any terminological problems remaining are my responsibility alone.

Badiou has been well served by his translators. Three of them—Ray Brassier, Oliver Feltham and Peter Hallward—comrades and friends as well as accomplished interpreters of his work, have been of immense help when my linguistic forces ebbed, or when Badiou confronted me with a particularly forbidding marriage of the poem and the matheme. I was also fortunate to be able to consult Justin Clemens's fine translation of the scholium to Book I, as published in *Parrhesia*. I also wish to thank Maricarmen Rodriguez, the Spanish translator of *Logics of Worlds*, for her meticulous inventory of the errata in the first French edition. I am grateful to Clare Carlisle for having kindly provided me with the Kierkegaard references. Nina Power, Chris Connery, Quentin Meillassoux, Lorenzo Chiesa, Thomas Nail, Stathis Kouvelakis and Sebastian Budgen also played their part in the preparation of this book. Finally, I'd like to thank Alain Badiou for instigating and accompanying, with a kind of benevolent mischief, this inhuman and sense-less task—the only kind worth carrying out.

Preface

1. DEMOCRATIC MATERIALISM AND MATERIALIST DIALECTIC

What do we all think, today? What do I think when I'm not monitoring myself? Or rather, what is our (my) natural belief? 'Natural', of course, in keeping with the rule of an inculcated nature. A belief is all the more natural to the extent that its imposition or inculcation is freely sought out—and serves our immediate designs. Today, natural belief is condensed in a single statement:

There are only bodies and languages.

This statement is the axiom of contemporary conviction. I propose to name this conviction *democratic materialism*. Why?

Democratic *materialism*. The individual as fashioned by the contemporary world recognizes the objective existence of bodies alone. Who today would speak of the separability of our immortal soul, other than to conform to a certain rhetoric? Who does not *de facto* subscribe, in the pragmatism of desires and the obviousness of commerce, to the dogma of our finitude, of our carnal exposition to enjoyment, suffering and death? Take one symptom among many: the most inventive artists—choreographers,

1

painters, video makers—track the manifestness of bodies, of their desiring and machinic life, their intimacy and their nudity, their embraces and their ordeals. They all adjust the fettered, quartered and soiled body to the fantasy and the dream. They all impose upon the visible the dissection of bodies bombarded by the tumult of the universe. Aesthetic theory simply tags along. A random example: a letter from Toni Negri to Raúl Sanchez, from 15 December 1999. There, we read the following:

> Today the body is not just a subject which produces and which—because it produces art—shows us the paradigm of production in general, the power of life: the body is now a machine in which production and art inscribe themselves. That is what we postmoderns know.

'Postmodern' is one of the possible names for contemporary democratic materialism. Negri is right about what the postmoderns 'know': the body is the only concrete instance for productive individuals aspiring to enjoyment. Man, under the sway of the 'power of life', is an animal convinced that the law of the body harbours the secret of his hope.

In order to validate the equation 'existence = individual = body', contemporary *doxa* must valiantly reduce humanity to an overstretched vision of animality. 'Human rights' are the same as the rights of the living. The humanist protection of all living bodies: this is the norm of contemporary materialism. Today, this norm has a scientific name, 'bioethics', whose progressive reverse borrows its name from Foucault: 'biopolitics'. Our materialism is therefore the materialism of life. It is a bio-materialism.

Moreover, it is essentially a *democratic* materialism. That is because the contemporary consensus, in recognizing the plurality of languages, presupposes their juridical equality. Hence, the assimilation of humanity to animality culminates in the identification of the human animal with the diversity of its sub-species and the democratic rights that inhere in this diversity. This time, the progressive reverse borrows its name from Deleuze: 'minoritarianism'. Communities and cultures, colours and pigments, religions and clergies, uses and customs, disparate sexualities, public intimacies and the publicity of the intimate: everything and everyone deserves to be recognized and protected by the law.

Having said that, democratic materialism does stipulate a global halting-point for its multiform tolerance. A language that does not recognize the universal juridical and normative equality of languages does not deserve to benefit from this equality. A language that aims to regulate all other languages and to govern all bodies will be called dictatorial and totalitarian.

What it then requires is not tolerance, but a 'right of intervention': legal, international, and, if needs be, military. Bodies will have to pay for their excesses of language.

This book employs a fair amount of science, as you might have guessed, in its somewhat fastidious examination of democratic materialism, which is in the process of becoming the enveloping ideology for this new century. What name can we give to the theoretical ideal under whose aegis this examination is carried out? Endorsing an aristocratic idealism has tempted many a good mind. Often under the shelter provided by a communist vocabulary, this was the stance taken by the surrealists, and later by Guy Debord and his nihilist heirs: to found the secret society of the surviving creators. It is also the speculative vow of the best of the Heideggerian legacy: practically to safeguard, in the cloister of writings wherein the question abides, the possibility of a Return. However, since such a preservation—which sustains the hope that the intellectual and existential splendours of the past will not be abolished—has no chance of being effective, it cannot partake in the creation of a concept for the coming times. The struggle of nostalgias, often waged as a war against decadence, is not only endowed—as it already is in Nietzsche—with a martial and 'critical' image, it is also marked by a kind of delectable bitterness. All the same, it is always already lost. And though there exists a poetics of the defeat, there is no philosophy of defeat. Philosophy, in its very essence, elaborates the means of saying 'Yes!' to the previously unknown thoughts that hesitate to become the truths that they are.

But, if we refuse to counter 'democratic materialism' with its formal contrary, which is indeed 'aristocratic idealism', what will be our (insufficient) name? After much hesitation, I have decided to name *materialist dialectic* the ideological atmosphere in which my philosophical undertaking conveys its most extreme tension.

What a way to conjure up a phrase from the realm of the dead! Wasn't my teacher Louis Althusser, more than thirty years ago, among the last nobly to make use of the phrase 'dialectical materialism', not without some misgivings? Didn't Stalin—no longer what he once was, even qua exemplary state criminal (a career in which he's been overtaken by Hitler in the last few years), though still a tactless reference—codify, under the heading *Dialectical and Historical Materialism*, the most formalist rules of a communist subjectivity, the source of whose paradoxical radiance no one can locate any longer? What is one to do with such a black sun? A

3

'beheaded sun', to quote Aimé Césaire? Does the inversion of the terms—turning materialism into the adjective—suffice to protect me from the fatal accusation of archaism?

Let's agree that by 'democratic' (or 'Western', it's the same thing) we are to understand the simultaneous maintenance and dissolution of symbolic or juridical multiplicity into real duality. For example: the Cold War of democracies against totalitarianism, the semi-cold war of the free world against terrorism, or the linguistic and police war of civilized countries against Islamist archaism. Let's agree that by 'dialectic', following Hegel, we are to understand that the essence of all difference is the third term that marks the gap between the two others. It is then legitimate to counter democratic materialism—this sovereignty of the Two (bodies and languages)—with a materialist dialectic, if by 'materialist dialectic' we understand the following statement, in which the Three supplements the reality of the Two:

There are only bodies and languages, except that there are truths.

One will recognize here the style of my teacher Mallarmé: nothing has taken place but the place, except, on high, perhaps, a Constellation. I cross out, nevertheless, 'on high' and 'perhaps'. The 'there are truths', which serves as an objection to the dualist axiomatic of democratic materialism (the law protects all bodies, arranged under all the compatible languages), is for me the initial empirical evidence. There is no doubt whatsoever concerning the existence of truths, which are not bodies, languages, or combinations of the two. And this evidence is materialist, since it does not require any splitting of worlds, any intelligible place, any 'height'. In our worlds, such as they are, truths advance. These truths are incorporeal bodies, languages devoid of meaning, generic infinites, unconditioned supplements. They become and remain suspended, like the poet's conscience, 'between the void and the pure event'.

It's worth paying attention to the syntax, which sets the axiom of the materialist dialectic apart from that of democratic materialism—namely the 'except that', whose Mallarméan character I underlined. This syntax suggests that we are dealing neither with an addition (truths as simple supplements to bodies and languages) nor with a synthesis (truths as the self-revelation of bodies seized by languages). Truths exist as exceptions to what there is. We admit therefore that 'what there is'—that which makes up the structure of worlds—is well and truly a mixture of bodies and languages. But there isn't only what there is. And 'truths' is the (philosophical) name of what interpolates itself into the continuity of the 'there is'.

In a certain sense, the materialist dialectic is identical to democratic materialism; to that extent they are indeed both materialisms, even if, by a nuance that cannot be neglected, what the second substantializes, the first treats as an adjective. Yes, there are only bodies and languages. Nothing exists by way of a separable 'soul', 'life', 'spiritual principle', etc. But in another sense, the materialist dialectic—centred on the exception that truths inflict on what there is through the interpolation of a 'there is what there is not'—differs entirely from democratic materialism.

In Descartes, we find an intuition of the same order regarding the ontological status of truths. We know that Descartes gives the name of 'substance' to the general form of being as really existing. 'What there is' is substance. Every 'thing' is substance: it is figure and movement in extended substance; it is idea in thinking substance. This is why Descartes's doctrine is commonly identified with dualism: the substantial 'there is' is divided into thought and extension, which in man means: soul and body.

Nevertheless, in paragraph 48 of the *Principles of Philosophy*, we see that substance dualism is subordinated to a more fundamental distinction. This distinction is the one between things (what there is, that is to say substance, either thinking or extended) and truths:

> I distinguish everything that falls under our cognition into two genera: the first contains all the things endowed with some existence, and the other all the truths that are nothing outside of our thought.

What a remarkable text! It recognizes the wholly exceptional, onto-logical and logical status of truths. Truths are without existence. Is that to say they do not exist at all? Far from it. Truths have no *substantial* existence. That is how we must understand the declaration that they 'are nothing outside of our thought'. In paragraph 49, Descartes specifies that this criterion designates the formal universality of truths, and therefore their logical existence, which is nothing other than a certain kind of intensity:

> For instance, when we think that something cannot be made out of nothing, we do not believe that this proposition is an existing thing or the property of some thing. Rather, we treat it as an eternal truth that has its seat in our thinking, and which is called a common notion or maxim. Likewise, when we are told that it is impossible for something to be and not to be at the same time, that what has been done cannot be undone, that he who thinks cannot stop being or existing whilst he

thinks, and numerous other similar statements, we recognise that these are only truths, and not things.

Note that the crux of the cogito (the induction of existence through the act of thought) is a truth in this sense. This means that a truth is what thought goes on presenting even when the regime of the thing is suspended (by doubt). A truth is thus what insists in exception to the forms of the 'there is'.

Descartes is not a dualist merely in the sense conferred to this term by the opposition it draws between 'intellectual' things, that is 'intelligent substances, or rather properties belonging to these substances', and 'corporeal' things, that is 'bodies, or rather properties belonging to these bodies'. Descartes is a dualist at a far more essential level, which alone sustains the demonstrative machinery of his philosophy: the level at which things (intellectual and/or corporeal) and truths (whose mode of being is to (in)exist) are distinguished. It is necessary to pay careful attention to the fact that unlike 'things', be they souls, truths are immediately universal and in a very precise sense indubitable. Consider the following passage, which also links truths to the infinite of their (in)existence:

> There is such a great number of [truths] that it would not be easy to draw up a list of all of them; but it is also unnecessary, since we cannot fail to know them when the occasion for thinking about them arises.

And it is true that a truth is an exception to what there is, if we consider that, when given the 'occasion' to encounter it, we immediately recognize it as such. We can see in what sense Descartes thinks the Three (and not only the Two). His own axiom can in fact be stated as follows: 'There are only (contingent) corporeal and intellectual things, except that there are (eternal) truths'. Like every genuine philosopher, Descartes registers, at the point where ontology and logic rub up against each another, the necessity of what we have chosen to call 'materialist dialectic'.

The idea that the type of being of truths is identifiable beyond the empirical manifestness of their existence was one of the principal stakes of my 1988 book *Being and Event*. In that text I established, condensing an extensive analytic of the forms of being, that truths are generic multiplicities: no linguistic predicate allows them to be discerned, no proposition can explicitly designate them. Furthermore, I explained why it is legitimate to call 'subject' the local existence of the process that unfolds these generic multiplicities (the formula was: 'A subject is a point of truth').

It is not a question here of returning to these results, which undermine the linguistic, relativist and neo-sceptical parenthesis of contemporary academic philosophy—a philosophy which is at bottom the sophisticated handmaiden of democratic materialism. These results ground the comprehensive possibility of a prospective metaphysics capable of enveloping today's actions and drawing strength, tomorrow, from what these actions will produce. Such a metaphysics is a component of the new materialist dialectic.

I would like to underscore that, by an entirely different, even opposed, path—that of a vitalist analytic of undifferentiated bodies—Deleuze too sought to create the conditions for a contemporary metaphysics. In this sense, he embodied one of the orientations of the materialist dialectic, as shown by his dogged resistance to the devastating inroads made by democratic materialism. Let's not forget his declaration that when the philosopher hears the words 'democratic debate', he turns and runs. This is because Deleuze's intuitive conception of the concept presupposed the survey of its components at infinite speed. This infinite speed of thought is effectively incompatible with democratic debate. In a general sense, the materialist dialectic opposes the real infinity of truths to the principle of finitude which is deducible from democratic maxims. For example, one can say:

A truth affirms the infinite right of its consequences, with no regard for what opposes them.

Deleuze was a free and fervent advocate of this affirmation of the infinite rights of thought—an affirmation that had to clear a path for itself against the connivance of the phenomenological tradition, always too pious (Heidegger included), and the analytic tradition, always too sceptical (Wittgenstein included). The enduring leitmotiv of this connivance is finitude, or 'modesty'. One is never modest enough when it comes either to exposing oneself to the transcendence of the destiny of Being, or to gaining awareness that our language games give us no access to the mystical beyond where the meaning of life is decided.

The materialist dialectic only exists to the extent that it ploughs the gap which separates it, on its right flank, from the diktats of authenticity, and on its left, from the humilities of Critique. If the compound effects of the two French traditions—respectively that of Brunschvicg (mathematizing idealism) and Bergson (vitalist mysticism), the one passing through Cavaillès, Lautman, Desanti, Althusser, Lacan and myself, the other through

Canguilhem, Foucault, Simondon and Deleuze—allow this new century not to be devastated by modesty, philosophy will not have been useless.

To produce, in the world such as it is, new forms to shelter the pride of the inhuman—that is what justifies us. So it is important that by 'materialist dialectic' we understand the deployment of a critique of every critique. To have done, if possible, with the watered-down Kant of limits, rights and unknowables. To affirm, with Mao Tse-tung (why not?): 'We will come to know everything that we did not know before'. In brief, to affirm this other variant of the axiom of the materialist dialectic:

Every world is capable of producing its own truth within itself.

But the ontological break, whether mathematizing or vitalist, does not suffice. We must also establish that the mode of appearing of truths is singular and that it plots out subjective operations whose complexity is not even broached in the purely ontological treatment of *Being and Event*. What the 1988 book did at the level of pure being—determining the ontological type of truths and the abstract form of the subject that activates them—this book aims to do at the level of being-there, or of appearing, or of worlds. In this respect, *Logics of Worlds* stands to *Being and Event* as Hegel's *Phenomenology of Spirit* stands to his *Science of Logic*, even though the chronological order is inverted: an immanent grasp of the parameters of being-there, a local survey of the figures of the true and of the subject, and not a deductive analytic of the forms of being.

In this task we are guided—as Hegel was in the context created by the French Revolution and the Napoleonic wars—by a contemporary conjuncture which, believing itself to possess a stable, guaranteed foundation (democratic materialism) wages against the evidence of truths an incessant propaganda war. We are all familiar with the signifiers that punctuate this war: 'modesty', 'teamwork', 'fragmentary', 'finitude', 'respect for the other', 'ethics', 'self-expression', 'balance', 'pragmatism', 'cultures'. . . All of these are encapsulated in an anthropological, and consequently restricted, variant of the axiom of democratic materialism, a variant that may be formulated as follows:

There are only individuals and communities.

The thinking of the quartet comprising being, appearing, truths and the subject—a thinking whose construction is carried out in this book—opposes to this statement the maxim of the materialist dialectic:

The universality of truths rests on subjective forms that cannot be either individual or communitarian.

Or:

To the extent that it is the subject of a truth, a subject subtracts itself from every community and destroys every individuation.

2. FOR A DIDACTICS OF ETERNAL TRUTHS

I have said that for me the existence of exceptions (or truths) to the simple 'there is' of bodies and languages takes the form of a primary evidence. The theoretical trajectory that organizes *Logics of Worlds* examines the constitution, in singular worlds, of the appearing of truths, and therefore of what grounds the evidence of their existence. I demonstrate that the appearing of truths is that of wholly singular bodies (post-eventual bodies), which compose the multiple materiality wherein special formalisms (subjective formalisms) are set out.

However, it is not a bad idea to attempt from the outset a (still unfounded) distribution of this evidence of the existence of truths; to explicate why, simply by considering the invariance existing across otherwise disparate worlds, we can oppose the relativism and denial of any hierarchy of ideas which democratic materialism implies. Here it is merely a question of describing, through the mediation of some examples, the sufficient effect of truths, to the extent that, once they have appeared, they compose an atemporal meta-history. This pure didactics aims to show that positions of exception exist, even if it is impossible to deduce from them their necessity or to empirically experience their difference from opinions. This didactics, as we know, is the crux of Plato's first dialogues, and subsequently of the whole of non-critical philosophy. Starting from any situation whatever, one indicates, under the progressively clear name of Idea, that there is indeed something other than bodies and languages. For the Idea is not a body in the sense of an immediate given (this is what must be gleaned from the opposition between the sensible and the intelligible), nor is it a language or a name (as declared in the *Cratylus*: 'We philosophers, we start from things, not words').

Of course, I give the name 'truths' to real processes which, as subtracted as they may be from the pragmatic opposition of bodies and languages, are nonetheless in the world. I insist, since this is the very problem that this book is concerned with: truths not only *are*, they *appear*. It is here and now

9

that the aleatory third term (subject-truths) supplements the two others (multiplicities and languages). The materialist dialectic is an ideology of immanence. However, it was with good reason that in my *Manifesto for Philosophy* (1989) I said that what is demanded of us is a 'Platonic gesture': to overcome democratic sophistry by detecting every Subject which participates in an exceptional truth-process. The four examples provided below should be considered as so many sketches of such a gesture. All four aim to indicate what an eternal truth is through the variation of its instances: the multiplicity of its (re)creations in distinct worlds. Each example elucidates both the theme of the multiplicity of worlds (which becomes, in Book II, the transcendental logic of being-there, or theory of the object) and that of the bodies-of-truth, such as, constructed in a world and bearing its mark, they let themselves be identified at a distance (from another world) as universal, or trans-worldly. It is a question of presenting, in each of the orders in which it is set forth, the 'except that' of truths and of the subjects that these truths elicit.

3. MATHEMATICAL EXAMPLE: NUMBERS

We draw our first example from elementary deductive algebra.

In everything that follows, by 'number' we understand a natural whole number $(1, 2, 3, \ldots, n, \ldots)$. We will take for granted that the reader is familiar with the operations of addition $(n + m)$ and multiplication $(n \cdot m)$ as definable over numbers. We then say that a number p is divisible by a number q if there exists a third number n, such that $p = n \cdot q$ ('p is equal to n times q'). One can also write $p / q = n$ or $p : q = n$.

A number (other than 1) is prime if it is divisible only by itself and by the unit 1. So, 2, 3, 5 are prime, like 17 and 19, etc.; 4 (divisible by 2), 6 (divisible by 2 and 3), or 18 (divisible by 2, 3, 6 and 9) are not.

There is a simultaneously surprising and essential arithmetical theorem which can be stated in contemporary language as follows: 'There exist an infinity of prime numbers'. As far as you go in the sequence of numbers, you will always find an infinity of new numbers that are divisible only by themselves and by 1. Thus the number 1,238,926,361,552,897 is prime, but there is an infinity of primes after it.

This theorem takes an even more paradoxical contemporary form, which is the following: 'There are as many prime numbers as numbers'. We effectively know, after Cantor, how to compare distinct infinite sets. In order to do this, it is necessary to find out if there exists between the two sets a bi-univocal correspondence: you match each element of the first set to an element of the second, such that to two different elements there correspond two different elements and the procedure is exhaustive (all the elements of the first set are linked to all the elements of the second).

Let's suppose that there is an infinite sequence of prime numbers. Let's match the first number, which is 1, to 2, the smallest prime number; then the second number, which is 2, to the smallest prime number greater than 2, which is 3; then 3 to the smallest prime number greater than 3, which is 5; then 4 to the prime number 7 and so on:

Numbers	Prime numbers
1	2
2	3
3	5
4	7
5	11
6	13
7	17
8	19
. . .	. . .
. . .	. . .

We obviously have a bi-univocal correspondence between numbers and prime numbers. There are therefore as many prime numbers as numbers tout court.

Such a statement seems to herald the triumph of the relativist, the pragmatist partisan of an irreconcilable multiplicity of cultures. Why? Because saying 'there is an infinity of prime numbers', just like saying 'there are as many prime numbers as numbers', is for an ancient Greek, even a mathematician, to speak in an entirely unintelligible jargon. First of all, no infinite set can exist for such a Greek, because everything that is really thinkable is finite. There exist only sequences that continue. Secondly, what is contained in some thing is less than that thing. This can be stated axiomatically (it is one of the explicit formal principles in Euclid's *Elements*): 'The whole is greater than the part'. Now, prime numbers are a part of numbers. Therefore there are less prime numbers than numbers.

As you can see, this might lend credence to the notion that anthropological relativism should extend to the purported absolute truth of mathematics. Given that there are only languages, it will be affirmed that in the final analysis 'prime numbers' does not have the same meaning in Euclid's Greek language as it does in ours, since an ancient Greek could not even comprehend what is said about prime numbers in the modern language. In effect, in Peyrard's 1819 literal translation of the *Elements*, the crucial statement about the sequence of prime numbers is formulated in a vocabulary which differs entirely from that of the infinite. This is Proposition 20 of Book 9: 'Prime numbers are more than any assigned multitude of prime numbers'.

Truth be told, even the definitions on the basis of which the theorem is demonstrated are very different for the Greeks and for us. Thus, the general notion of divisibility is articulated in terms of the part, the large, the small and measure. Consider definition 5 of book 7 of the *Elements*: 'A number is the part of a number, the smaller of the greater, when the smaller measures the greater'. None of these terms is really present in the modern definition. The anthropology of cultures, which is a very important branch of democratic materialism, can argue here that scientific continuity traverses whole zones of mere homonymy.

Does it follow that everything is culture, including mathematics? That universality is but a fiction? And perhaps an imperialist, or even totalitarian fiction? We will use the same example to affirm, on the contrary:

–that an eternal truth is enveloped by different conceptual and linguistic contexts (by what we shall call, beginning with Book II, different 'worlds');
–that a subject of the same type finds itself implicated in the demonstrative procedure, whether it be Greek or contemporary (whether it belongs the world 'Greek mathematics' or the world 'mathematics after Cantor').

The key point is that the truth underlying the infinity of prime numbers is not so much this infinity itself, as what it allows one to decipher about the structure of numbers: namely, that they are all composed of prime numbers, which are like the 'atomic' (indecomposable) constituents of numericality. In effect, every number may be written as the product of powers of prime numbers (this is its 'decomposition into prime factors').

For example, the number 11664 is equal to $2^4 \cdot 3^6$. But you can apply this remark to the powers themselves. Thus, $4 = 2^2$ and $6 = 2 \cdot 3$. So that, in the end, we have $11664 = 2^{2^2} \cdot 3^{2 \times 3}$, a formula in which only prime numbers appear.

This structural reasoning is so significant that it has governed the entire development of modern abstract algebra (a development that we will consider from another angle in Book VII). Given any operational domain whatever, constituted of 'objects' over which it is possible to define operations akin to addition and multiplication, can one find within it the equivalent of prime numbers? Is it possible, in the same way, to decompose objects with the help of 'primitive' objects? Here we have the origin (since Gauss) of the crucial theory of prime ideals in a ring. Regarding this process—this extraction of the structural forms latent in the conduct of numerical operations—it is clear that there is advance, triumph, new ideas and so on, but it is just as clear that Greek arithmetic is immanent to this movement.

In the decisive absence of truly operative numerical and literal notations, and hampered by their fetishism of ontological finitude, the Greeks of course only thought through part of the problem. They were incapable of clearly identifying the general form of the decomposition of a number into prime factors. Nevertheless, they grasped the essential: prime numbers are always implicated in the multiplicative composition of a non-prime number. That is the famous Proposition 31 of Book 7: 'Every composite number is measured by some prime number'. This, according to our symbolism, means that given any number n, there always exists a prime number p which divides n.

It is not an exaggeration to say that this is a 'contact' [*touché*] with the essence of number and its calculable texture, which the most contemporary of arithmetical or algebraic statements envelop and unfold in novel conceptual and linguistic contexts—new worlds—without ever 'overcoming' or abolishing it. This is what we do not hesitate to call an eternal truth—or an example of what the Greek Archimedes proudly declared to have discovered, that is 'properties inherent to [the] nature [of mathematical objects], forever existing within them, and nonetheless ignored by those that have come before me'.

The second part of Archimedes' declaration is as important as the first. As eternal as it may be, a mathematical truth must nevertheless *appear* for its eternity to be effective. Now, the process of this appearance is a demonstration, which supposes a subject (as Archimedes says, my predecessors, or me).

But, setting all psychology aside, what is the subject of a demonstrative invention, from which follows the unfolding of an eternal mathematical truth? It is what links a formalism to a material body (a body of writing in the mathematical case). This formalism exhibits and makes explicit an indefinitely subjectivizable constraint relative to the body of writing in question.

If you grant the definition of number and the associated definitions, you must accept that 'every composite number is measured by some prime number'. If you grant that 'every composite number is measured by some prime number', you must accept that 'prime numbers are more than any assigned multitude of prime numbers' (or that there is an infinity of them).

What's remarkable is that the mathematical subjective type committed to the constraint is invariant. In other words, you can take up the position to which the Greek mathematical text constrains you without needing to modify the general subjective system of the places-of-constraint. Likewise, you can love a tragedy by Aeschylus *because* you incorporate yourself into the tragedies of Claudel; or evaluate the political import of the Chinese text from 81 BC, *Discourses on Salt and Iron*, without ceasing to be a revolutionary of the seventies of the twentieth century; or, as a contemporary lover, share the agonies of Dido forsaken by Aeneas.

How does Euclid pass from the initial definitions (multiple of a number, prime numbers, etc.) to the chief structural proposition (every number is divisible by a prime number)? Through a procedure of 'finite descent' which is suited to the underlying structure of numbers. If n is composite, it is measured by a number p_1 other than 1 (if it was only measured by 1, it would be prime). We thus have $n = p_1 \cdot q_1$ (definition of 'measured by'). We then repeat the question for p_1. If p_1 is prime, we're good, since it divides (measures) n. If not, we have $p_1 = p_2 \cdot q_2$, but then $n = p_2 \cdot q_2 \cdot q_1$, and p_2 divides n. If p_2 is prime, we're good. If not, we have $p_2 = p_3 \cdot q_3$, and p_3 divides n. If p_3 is prime, etc.

But we have: $\ldots p_4 < p_3 < p_2 < p_1$. This descent must stop, because p_1 is a finite number. And it can only stop on a prime number. Therefore there exists a prime p_r, with $n = p_r q_r \cdot p_{r-1} q_{r-1} \cdot \ldots \cdot q_1$. This p_r prime divides n, QED.

The subject that informs the writing and is constrained by it is here of a constructive type: it links itself to a descending algorithm, which comes up against a halting point in which the announced result inscribes itself. This subjective type is as eternal as its explicit result, and it may be encountered in the process of all kinds of non-mathematical truths: the situation enters into a progressive reduction, until it reaches a constituent that cannot be absorbed by the reduction.

Now, how does Euclid move from the aforementioned result to our inaugural statement about the infinity of prime numbers? Through an entirely different procedure, that of apagogical argument or reductio ad absurdum, which is suited in this case to the negative formulation of the result (if there is an infinity of prime numbers, there *isn't* a finite quantity of prime numbers, which is in essence Euclid's own formulation).

Suppose there exist N prime numbers, N being a (finite) whole number. Consider the product of these N prime numbers: $p_1 \cdot p_2 \cdot \ldots \cdot p_r \cdot \ldots \cdot p_N$. Let's call it P, and let's consider the number $P + 1$. $P + 1$ cannot be a prime. That is because it is greater than all the prime numbers which, by our hypothesis, are contained in the product $p_1 \cdot p_2 \cdot \ldots \cdot p_N = P$, and which are therefore all already smaller than P, and a fortiori of $P + 1$. Therefore $P + 1$ is a composite number. It follows that it is divisible by a prime number (according to the fundamental property demonstrated by 'descent'). It is therefore certain that there exists a p prime with $(P + 1) = p \cdot q_1$. But every prime number divides P, which, by our hypothesis, is the product of all prime numbers. We thus also have $P = p \cdot q_2$. Finally, we get:

$$(P + 1) - P = p \cdot q_1 - p \cdot q_2 = p(q_1 - q_2)$$

That is:

$$1 = p(q_1 - q_2)$$

This means that p divides 1, which is entirely impossible. Therefore, the initial hypothesis must be rejected: prime numbers do not form a finite set.

This time, the subject that informs the proof and links up to it is a non-constructive subject. Developing a supposition, it comes up against a point of the impossible (here, a prime number must divide 1) which obliges it to deny the supposition. This procedure does not positively construct the infinity of prime numbers (or the prime number greater than the given quantity). It shows that the opposite supposition is impossible (that of a finite number of prime numbers, that of a maximal prime). This subjective figure too is eternal: examining the situation in accordance with a determinate concept, one perceives a real point in this situation which demands that one choose between the maintenance of the concept and that of the situation.

It is true that we thereby presume that a subject does not want the situation to be annihilated. It will sacrifice its concept to it. This is indeed what constitutes a subject of truth: it holds that a concept is only valid to the extent that it supports a truth of the situation. In this sense, it is a subject consistent with the materialist dialectic. A subject in conformity with democratic materialism may instead be nihilist: it prefers itself to every situation. We shall see (Book I) that such a subject must abandon every logic that is productive or faithful to the situation and endorse either the formalism of the reactive subject or that of the obscure subject.

When all is said and done, rejecting the reductio ad absurdum is an ideological choice with vast consequences. This confirms that mathematics, far from being an abstract exercise that no one needs to be vitally pre-occupied with, is a subjective analyser of the highest calibre. The hostility that increasingly surrounds mathematics—too distant, they say, from 'practice' or 'concrete life'—is but one sign among many of the nihilist orientation that little by little is corrupting all the subjects bowed under the rule of democratic materialism. This is something that Plato, requiring of his future guardians ten years of stubborn study of geometry, was the first to really perceive. It was one and the same thing for him to have to formulate this requirement and to criticise mercilessly what the democratic form of the state had become in Athens during and after the interminable war against Sparta.

4. ARTISTIC EXAMPLE: HORSES

Let's consider four images in which horses play a preponderant role, images separated by almost 30,000 years. On the one hand, the horse drawn with a white line and the 'panel of horses' in black, both in the Chauvet cave. On the other, two scenes by Picasso (1929 and 1939), the first drawn in grey, in which two horses drag a third dead horse, the second in which a human silhouette masters two horses, one of them held by its bridle. Here too, everything separates these two moments of representation. Picasso, who could not have been inspired by the Master of the Chauvet cave, unknown at that time, certainly gave abundant proof of his knowledge in matters of rupestral art—especially his taurine images, like the black, vaguely Cretan silhouettes of 1945. But this knowledge establishes an immediate reflexive distance vis-à-vis the Master of the Chauvet cave, because Picasso's virtuosity is plainly also a virtuosity in the mastery of a long history, which includes, if not the Chauvet-atelier, at least the ones, from ten or fifteen thousand years later, of Altamira or Lascaux. The effects of this distance are such that the relativist may declare victory once again. Namely, he will say that Picasso's horses, with their stylized heads and the geometric treatment of their legs, are only comprehensible as modern operations carried out on 'realist' horses. Classical painters sought to depict volume, musculature and momentum. Picasso instead manipulates primitive 'naivety'—including that of pre-historical models—to turn the horse into the sign of a decorative power, rearing up and almost wrenched away from its vital evidence. Whence the contradictory combination of the beasts' raised heads, which seem to strain after some celestial rescue, and the systematically ponderous power of their rumps and hooves. They are like angelic percherons. And they respond, in their 'rearing', as slow as it is violent, to a kind of desperate call.

The horses of the Chauvet-atelier are on the contrary icons of submission. Hunter's images, without doubt: all the horses lower their heads, as though captive, and what at once imposes itself on the gaze is their vast forehead, just below the mane. Nothing is more striking than the alignment (yet another perspectival effect!) of the four heads in the so-called 'panel of the horses'. It is tempting to say that they are arranged in keeping with a mysterious hierarchy, which is that of stature—the heads diminish from left to right—but also of tint (from clear to black), and especially of the gaze: we move from a kind of sleepy stupor towards the fixed intensity of the smallest one. And it is indeed this exposed, submitted and intensely visible demeanour which is essential and not, as in Picasso, the gestures that tell the story of a conflict or a call. Besides, the horse outlined in white, whose full silhouette we can behold, has legs that are far too spindly and a lean rump. Contrary to the rural innocence that Picasso discerns in these animals, the artists of the Chauvet-atelier see in them the precarious fixation, by the artist-hunter, of a conquered savageness, of a beauty both proffered and secretly dominated.

It follows that 'horse' does not have the same meaning in the two cases. The objectivity of the animal signifies very little with respect to the complete modification of the context, with a gap of almost thirty thousand years. How indeed are we to compare the almost inexplicable mimetic activity of these small groups of hunters—from our perspective almost completely destitute, and who we must imagine as relentlessly covering the walls of their cave with intense images, in the oscillating light of fires or torches—with an artist who inherited an immense and manifest history, the most famous of all artists, who invented forms or reworked the existing ones for the pleasure of painting-thought, in an atelier where all the achievements of chemistry and technology served his work? What's more, for the former, animals, such as the horses, are that in the midst of which they live: their partners, their adversaries, their food. The distance is not so great between the menaced wanderers that the hunters themselves are and the animals that they watch, hunt, observe day and night—extracting from them these magnificent painted signs that journey all the way to us, untouched by millennia. For Picasso instead, animals are nothing more than the indices of a declining peasant and pre-technological world (whence their innocence and their appeal). Or they are figures already caught in the spectacle, and thus pre-formed for drawing, like the bulls and horses of the corridas that so fascinated the painter.

We can thus say that these 'horses' are by no means the same. The Master of the Chauvet cave exalts—doubtless in order to consolidate a difficult dominating distance—the pure forms of a life which he partakes in. Picasso, for his part, can only cite these forms, because he is already withdrawn from any veritable access to their living substrate. If he appears to have revived, for these citations, the monumental style of the bygone hunters, it is at the service of an opposite signification: nostalgia and vain invocation, where there used to be commonality and praise.

Nevertheless, I contend that it is indeed an invariant theme, an eternal truth, which is at work between the Master of the Chauvet cave and Picasso. Of course, this theme does not envelop its own variation, and everything we have just said about the meaning of the horses remains correct: they belong to essentially distinct worlds. In fact, because it is subtracted from variation, the theme of the horse renders it perceivable. It explains on its own why we are immediately seized by the beauty, which is in a sense without appeal, of the works of the Chauvet-atelier, and also why the analogy with Picasso imposes itself upon us, beyond its reflexive dimension, as well as beyond Picasso's knowledge of these pre-historic stylizations. We simultaneously think the multiplicity of worlds and the invariance of the truths that appear at distinct points in this multiplicity.

What does this invariance consist in? Suppose that you entertain a relation of thought to animals that makes them into stable components of the world under consideration: there is the horse, the rhinoceros, the lion. . . Now suppose that the empirical and vital diversity of individual living beings is subordinated to this stability. The animal is then an intelligible paradigm and its representation is the clearest possible mark of what an Idea is. That is because the animal as type (or name) is a clear cut in the formless continuity of sensorial experience. It brings together a flagrant organic unity with the always recognizable character of its specific form.

This means that—as in the Platonic myth, but in reverse—to paint an animal on the wall of a cave is to flee the cave so as to ascend towards the light of the Idea. This is what Plato feigns not to see: the image, here, is the opposite of the shadow. It attests the Idea in the varied invariance of its pictorial sign. Far from being the descent of the Idea into the sensible, it is the sensible creation of the Idea. 'This is a horse'—that is what the Master of the Chauvet cave says. And since he says it at a remove from any visibility of a living horse, he *avers* the horse as what exists eternally for thought.

This entails technical consequences entirely opposed to those borne by the desire—which is equally profound and creative—to present to the gaze-thought a horse in the splendour of its musculature and the brilliant detail of its coat. The main consequence is that as far as the representation of the horse is concerned, everything is a matter of the line. The drawing must inscribe the intelligible cut, the separate contemplation of the Horse which is presented by all drawn horses. But this contemplation—which avers the Horse in accordance with the unity of the idea—is a raw intuition. It is only fixed by the sureness of the line, which is not retouched. In a single gesture, a single stroke, the artist must separate the Horse at the same time as he draws a horse. Just as—thus confirming the universality of this truth—Chinese draughtsmen seek, through strenuous training, to capture in a single stroke of the brush the indiscernibility between this buffalo and the Buffalo, between a cat and the Cat's Grin.

Here we cannot but concur with Malraux. For instance, when he writes (in his *Anti-memoirs*):

[. . .] art is not a reliance of peoples on the ephemeral, on their houses and their furniture, but on the Truth they have created, step by step. It does not depend on the grave, but on the eternal.

The eternal Truth that Picasso ultimately alludes to with his customary virtuosity can be simply stated as follows: in painting, the animal is the occasion to signal, through the certainty of the separating line alone, that between the Idea and existence, between the type and the case, I can create, and therefore think, the point that remains indiscernible. That is why, opposed as they may be in what concerns the meaning of their appearance in pictorial worlds devoid of common measure, the horses of the Chauvet-atelier and those of Picasso are also the same. Consider the dominance of contour; the singular relation between the triangle of the heads and the cylinder of the necks; the painstaking effort to register the blend of sweetness and absence in these animals' gaze: this entire formal apparatus converges on the givenness to the gaze-thought of the irreducibility of the Horse, its resistance to any dissolution into the formless, its intelligible singularity. We can thus confidently say that what the Master of the Chauvet cave initiated, thirty thousand years ago (of course, he might have been the student of yet another master, who we know nothing about: there is no origin), is also what abides, or what we abide within, and which Picasso reminds us about: it is not only amid things, or bodies, that we live and speak. It is in the transport of the True, in which it sometimes happens we are required to partake.

A famous cynic thought he was laughing behind Plato's back by saying: 'I do see some horses, but I see no Horseness'. In the immense progression of pictorial creations, from the hunter with his torch to the modern millionaire, it is indeed Horseness, and nothing else, which we see.

5. POLITICAL EXAMPLE: THE STATE REVOLUTIONARY (EQUALITY AND TERROR)

This example will combine the temporal gap (between 81 BC and 1975) and the geographical one (it comes from China).

Ten years after the seizure of power by the Chinese communists, in the years 1958–59, bitter debates arise in the Party over the country's development, the socialist economy, the transition to communism. Some years later, these debates will lead to the turmoil of the Cultural Revolution. It is altogether striking that, in Mao Tse-tung's work during this period, the critique of Stalin occupies a very important place, as if, in order to find a new path, it was necessary to return to the balance-sheet of the USSR's collectivization in the thirties. It is even more striking that this confrontation between the Stalin of the thirties to the fifties and Mao at the threshold of the sixties evokes, down to its very detail, an infinitely older quarrel: the one that took place in 81 BC in China between the Legalists and the Confucian conservatives after the death of the emperor Wu—a quarrel which is recorded in the great Chinese classic (obviously written by a Confucian), the *Discourses on Salt and Iron*. This reference is immediately intertwined with the revolutionary history of contemporary China, given that in 1973 a campaign was launched which jointly vituperated Lin

Biao—a Party potentate, leader of the Cultural Revolution, Mao's one-time designated successor and probably murdered in 1971—and Confucius. This campaign drew on the ancient Legalists, and proposed a new reading of the *Discourses*, whose watchword was that 'Lin Biao and Confucius are two badgers on the same hill'.

The *Discourse* is an astonishing text in which, before the emperor Zhao, the (Legalist) Great Secretary endures the questioning of the (Confucian) scholars on all the crucial subjects of state politics, from the function of the laws to the strictures of foreign policy, via the public monopoly over the trade of salt and iron.

Today we can circulate between:

- –the minutes of a political reunion dating more than two thousand years;
- –*Economic Problems of Socialism in the USSR*, a text in which Stalin, at the very beginning of the fifties, confirms his abiding orientations;
- –two series of considerations by Mao regarding Stalin's text: a speech from November 1953 and some marginal annotations from 1959;
- –the convulsions of the Cultural Revolution at the beginning of the seventies.

This circulation spans enormous historical and cultural differences. We traverse disjoined worlds, incommensurable appearances, different logics. What is there in common between the Chinese Empire undergoing its centralization, the post-war Stalin, and the Mao of the 'Great Leap Forward', and then of the Red Guards and the Great Proletarian Cultural Revolution? Nothing, save for a kind of matrix of state politics which is clearly invariant; a transversal public truth that may be designated as follows: a truly political administration of the state subordinates all economic laws to voluntary representations, fights for equality, and combines, where the people are concerned, confidence and terror.

This immanent articulation of will, equality, confidence and terror can be read in the proposals of the Legalists and of Mao. It is rejected in the proposals of the Confucians and of Stalin, which inscribe inequality into the objective laws of becoming. It follows that this articulation is an invariant Idea concerning the problem of the state. This Idea displays the subordination of the state to politics (the 'revolutionary' vision in the broad sense). It fights against the administrative principle, which subordinates politics to the statist laws of reality, in other words against the passive or conservative vision of the decisions of the state. But, in a more essential

21

sense, one can see in this entire immense temporal arc that thought, confronted with the state's logic of decision, must argue on the basis of consequences and that, in so doing, it delineates a subjective figure that detaches itself from the conservative figure. The argument from consequences is valid for all the four points whose invariance structures a revolutionary vision of the state (will, equality, confidence, terror). I will now show this in what concerns political will and the principle of confidence.

The Confucian scholars explicitly declare that 'if laws and customs fall into obsolescence, they must be restored [. . .] what is the use of changing them?' Against this subjectivity of restoration, or reaction, the (Legalist) Secretary of the Prime Minister affirms the positive material consequences of an ideological rupture:

> If it was necessary to blindly follow Antiquity without changing anything, perpetuating all the institutions of our fathers without modifying them in any way, culture would have never been able to burnish the old rustic ways and we would still be using wooden carts.

Similarly, Mao rises up against Stalin's objectivism. He argues that Stalin 'wants only technology and cadres' and only deals with the 'knowledge of the laws'. He neither indicates 'how to become the masters of these laws', nor does he sufficiently illuminate 'the subjective activism of the Party and the masses'. In truth, Mao indicts Stalin for a veritable depoliticization of the will:

> All of this relates to the superstructure, that is to ideology. Stalin speaks only of the economy; he does not deal with politics.

This depoliticization must be envisaged in terms of its most remote consequences: the transition to communism, the only source of legitimacy for the authority of the socialist state. Without a political break, without the will to abolish 'the old rules and the old systems', the transition to communism is illusory. As Mao never tires of repeating, in a key formula: 'Without a communist movement, it is impossible to advance into communism'. Only a will inhabited by its consequences can politically overcome the objective inertia of the state. In refusing such a risk, Stalin 'has not found the good method and the good path which lead from capitalism to socialism and from socialism to communism.'

In truth, if Stalin does not want 'subjective activism' or—it's the same thing—a 'communist movement', it is by dint of his systematic distrust of the great mass of the people, who are still peasants. Mao repeats it unceasingly: in the writings of Stalin, one 'discerns great mistrust towards the peasants'. The Stalinist conception entails that 'the state exerts an asphyxiating control over the peasantry'. In brief: 'His fundamental error derives from [. . .] not having enough confidence in the peasantry'. But here too it is the principle of consequences that authorizes a judgment: without confidence in the peasants, the socialist movement is impracticable, everything is fettered and everything is dead.

This is because Mao founds a relation, unexplored before him, between the future of the socialist process and the confidence placed in the peasants. Because he entertains distrust, 'Stalin does not approach the problem in terms of its future development'. Seen from the standpoint of politics and its consequences, the development of collective property, including its capacity to produce commodities, is not a goal in itself, or an economic necessity. It aims to serve the constitution of a popular politics, of a real alliance internal to the communist movement, which alone is capable of guaranteeing that the transition to property will be in the hands of the entire people:

> The maintenance of commodity-production inherited from the system of collective property aims to consolidate the alliance between workers and peasants.

We can see here the outline of that truth for the sake of whose deployment Mao and his partisans waged, between 1965 and 1975, their last battle. This truth is the following: political decision is not fettered by the economy. It must, as a subjective and future-oriented principle, subordinate to itself the laws of the present. This principle is called 'confidence in the masses'. Now, this is also what is advocated by the Legalist advisors of the emperor Wu, despite their constant appeals to implacable law and repression; even though, quite obviously, the stakes of confidence are entirely different, or even opposed. The Confucian scholars defend the immutable cycle of peasant production and oppose all novelties in artisanship and trade. They argue that all is well when 'the people devotes itself body and soul to agricultural tasks'. The Great Secretary retorts with a vibrant encomium for commercial circulation, voicing complete confidence in the multiform development of exchange. Here is an admirable monologue:

> If you leave the capital to travel through peaks and valleys in all directions, through the fiefs and principalities, you will not find a single

large and handsome city that is not traversed from one end to the other by great avenues, swarming with traders and grocers, brimming over with all kinds of products. The wise know how to profit from the seasons, and the skilful how to exploit natural riches. The superior man knows how to draw advantage from others; the mediocre man knows only how to make use of himself. [. . .] How could agriculture suffice to enrich the country, and why would the system of the communal field alone have the privilege of procuring the people what it needs?

In these lines, we can make out a singular correlation between will and confidence, rupture and consent. It constitutes the kernel of a trans-temporal political truth, of which Mao's meditations on Stalin of 1959 and the Great Secretary's diatribes against the Confucians in 81 BC are instances: forms of its appearing in separate worlds. But what is worthy of note is the fact that there corresponds, to these totally distinct or even opposed instances of a kernel of truth, a recognizable subjective type, that of the state revolutionary. This type too may be read through the four terms of the generic correlation (will, equality, confidence and terror). I will show this now with regard to the classical pair equality/terror, discontinuous instances of which we could also find in the likes of Robespierre or Thomas Müntzer.

The Legalist advisors of the emperor Wu are known for their apologia for the most ferocious repression in the implacable application of laws:

The law must be implacable in order not to be arbitrary, it must be inexorable in order to inspire respect. These are the considerations that presided over the elaboration of the penal code: one does not flout laws that mark with red-hot iron the slightest of crimes.

The Confucian scholars counter this repressive formalism with the classical morality of motive:

Penal laws must above all take motives into account. Those who stray from legality but whose motives are pure deserve to be pardoned.

We can witness the appearance here, with regard to the problem of repressive exigencies, of a correlation between formalism and a revolutionary vision of the state, on the one hand, and the morality of motive and a conservative vision, on the other. The Confucians subject politics to prescriptions whose value derives from their longevity. The sovereign must above all 'respect the established rites'. The Legalists desire a state activism, even at the price of a forcing of situations. This opposition is still at work in

Mao's reactions to the *Manual of Political Economy* published by the Soviets under Khrushchev, at the height of the post-Stalinist 'thaw'. The manual recalls that under communism, taking into account the existence of hostile exterior powers, the state endures. But it adds that 'the nature and forms of the state will be determined by the particular features of the communist system', which comes down to assigning the form of the state to something other than itself. Against this, as a good revolutionary formalist, Mao thunders:

By nature, the state is a machine whose purpose is to oppress hostile forces. Even if internal forces that need to be oppressed no longer exist, the oppressive nature of the state will not have changed with respect to hostile external forces. When one speaks of the form of the state, this means nothing other than an army, prisons, arrests, executions, etc. As long as imperialism exists, in what sense could the form of the state differ with the advent of communism?

As we've known ever since Robespierre and Saint-Just, the central category of state revolutionary formalism is terror—whether the word is pronounced or not. But it is essential to understand that terror is the projection onto the state of a subjective maxim, the egalitarian maxim. As Hegel saw (to then 'overcome' what in his eyes was its purely negative dimension), terror is nothing but the abstract upshot of a consideration required by every revolution. Since the situation is marked by an absolute antagonism, it is imperative to maintain:

–that every individual is identical to his or her political choice;
–that non-choice is a (reactive) choice;
–that (political) life, having taken the form of civil war, is also the exposure to death;
–that, in the end, all individuals of a determinate political camp can be substituted with one another: the living take the place of the dead.

It is then possible to understand how the Legalist Great Secretary is capable of combining an absolute authoritarianism with a principled egalitarianism. It is true, on the one hand (the formula is hard to forget) that 'the law must be such as to give the feeling that one is on the verge of an abyss'. But the real goal is to forbid inequalities, to suppress speculators, hoarders and factions. Without terror, the natural movement of things lies in the dissidence of the power of the rich. State revolutionary subjectivity, built on confidence in the real movement of politicized consciences and the exaltation of will, brings together terrorist antagonism and the consequences of equality. As the Great Secretary says:

> When one does not keep the ambition of the great families in check, it is like with branches which, having become too heavy, end up breaking the trunk. Potentates take control of natural resources.

It is then that the 'powerful will be favoured to the detriment of the meek and the assets of the state will fall into the hands of brigands'.

We are reminded here of Robespierre's cry at the Convention, on 9 Thermidor: 'The Republic is lost! The brigands triumph!' That's because behind this type of political terror lies the desire for equality. The Legalists know perfectly well that 'there is no equality without the redistribution of riches'. State revolutionary subjectivity is identified as an implacable struggle against the factions that arise from wealth or hereditary privilege. Mao's language is no different, including when he's dealing with the hereditary privileges reconstituted by the power of the Communist Party. The action of the revolutionary state aims to 'eliminate, on a daily basis, the laws and powers of the bourgeoisie'. That is why one should 'send cadres to the countryside to work in experimental farms', because it is 'one of the methods to transform the system of hierarchy'. If the Party becomes an aristocracy, state revolutionary subjectivity is done for:

> The children of our cadres worry us greatly. They have no experience of life and society. But they act arrogantly and have a very obvious superiority complex. We must educate them so that they do not depend on their parents or on the martyrs of the revolution, but only on themselves.

Equality means that everyone is referred back to their choice, and not to their position. That is what links a political truth to the instance of decision, which always establishes itself in concrete situations, point by point.

Having reached this point, the reader may imagine that he or she has hit up against a contradiction. Haven't I persistently upheld two theses proposed and developed by Sylvain Lazarus, which are essential to the politics of which we are both militants, that of the Organisation Politique: first, the thesis of the separation between the state and politics; second, the thesis of the rare and sequential character of politics? Doesn't the figure of the 'state revolutionary' directly oppose the first of these theses, and the idea of the eternity or invariance of this figure—and more generally of political truths—stand against the second? I have devoted a long note, which is to be found in the section entitled 'Notes, Commentaries and Digressions', to this question. It establishes not only that there is no contradiction on this point between Lazarus and me, but also that the two fundamental theses in question are both presupposed and sublimated in the philosophical context in which I (re)cast them.

We can now confidently draw some conclusions regarding the general characteristics of the truths of politics, which are also those of the historical sequences (and thus of the worlds, or logics of appearing) in which the radical will that aims at an emancipation of humanity as a whole is affirmed.

1. All these truths articulate four determinations: will (against socio-economic necessity), equality (against the established hierarchies of power or wealth), confidence (against anti-popular suspicion or the fear of the masses), authority or terror (against the 'natural' free play of competition). This is the generic kernel of a political truth of this type.

2. Each determination is measured up against the consequences of its inscription in an effective world. This principle of consequence, which alone temporalizes an instance of politics, knots together the four determinations. For example, wanting the real of an egalitarian maxim implies a formally authoritarian exercise of confidence in the political capacity of workers. This is the whole content of what was once referred to as the dictatorship of the proletariat. This movement is nothing other than the 'Marxist' instance of a real (or corporeal, we would say) knotting together of the four determinations.

3. There exists a subjective form which is adequate to the different instances of the generic kernel of truths. For example, the figure of the state revolutionary (Robespierre, Lenin, Mao. . .), which is distinct from that of the mass rebel (Spartacus, Müntzer or Tupac Amaru).

4. The singularity of instances (the multiple of truths) accounts for their appearance in a historically determinate world. They can only do this to the extent that a subjective form is 'carried', in the phenomenon of this world, by an organized material multiplicity. This is the very question of the political body: Leninist party, Red Army, etc.

Becoming of consequences, generic articulation, identifiable subjective figure, visible body. . . these are the predicates of a truth whose invariance is deployed through the moments which allow its fragmented creation to appear in disparate worlds.

6. AMOROUS EXAMPLE: FROM VIRGIL TO BERLIOZ

Once again following Plato—the one of the *Symposium* after the one of the *Republic*—we will show that amorous intensity too creates transtemporal and trans-worldly truths, truths that bear on the power of the Two.

Democratic materialism, which constantly relies on historical relativism, has disputed the universality of love, reducing the form of sexed relations to entirely distinct cultural configurations. Take for instance the famous thesis by Denis de Rougemont, which portrays passion-love as a mediaeval invention. Recently, some have tried to deny the existence, in the world of ancient Greece, of an autonomous sexual pleasure associated with the man/woman relation, thus making pederasty into the only paradigm in that domain. Regarding this second point, even a distracted reading of the searing subjective effects on men of the sexual strike of their spouses, as imagined by Aristophanes in his *Lysistrata, or the Assembly of Women*, allows one to conclude straightaway—if it were necessary!—that so-called 'heterosexual' desire and pleasure are universal. Regarding the first point, the poems of Sappho, figures such Andromacus or Medea, the episode of Dido and Aeneas in the *Aeneid*—all provide ample indication that, beyond the forms of its declaration, which in effect vary considerably, love is an experience of truth and as such is always identifiable, whatever the historical context may be. Of course, equally decisive proofs may be adduced at this point, which are even more remote in space or time. Let us simply mention the Japanese testimonies of Lady Murasaki's *The Tale of Gengi*, or the melodramas of Chikamatsu. Even the objection according to which passion, for the Greeks or Romans, is an attribute of women alone cannot hold, considering the proliferation of literary testimonies that suggest the opposite. It suffices to read Virgil's descriptions of Aeneas, 'groaning, his soul ravaged by his great love'.

Let us linger for a while with Virgil, regarding the traits that singularize the trans-temporal value of an amorous truth. In Book IV of the *Aeneid*, the poet stages the first night of love between Dido and Aeneas. To begin with, we reencounter here all the features of truths which we had extracted from our preceding examples (mathematical, artistic and political):

–material traces:

> Lightning torches flare and the high sky bears witness to the wedding.

–subjective break:

> Even now they [Dido and Aeneas] warm the winter, long as it lasts, with obscene desire, oblivious to their kingdoms, abject thralls of lust.

–the work of consequences:

> This was the first day of her death, the first of grief, the cause of it all.

–excess over any particular language:

> The flame keeps gnawing into her tender marrow hour by hour and deep in her heart the silent wound lives on. Dido burns with love—the tragic queen. She wanders in frenzy through her city streets.

–latent eternity:

> DIDO: When icy death has severed my body from its breath, then my ghost will stalk you through the world!

> AENEAS: I shall never deny what you deserve, my queen, never regret my memories of Dido, not while I can recall myself and draw the breath of life.

But we also find, in the density of the poem—as well as in its prosodic and musical metamorphosis, invented, twenty centuries later, by the genius of Berlioz in *The Trojans*—two other singular traits through which the discontinuous singularity of truths manifests itself: their infinity and the transfiguration into the Idea of the most banal, most anonymous, aspect of a situation. This is what I called, in *Being and Event*, the genericity of the True.

The artifice through which Virgil poetically conveys that true love, measureless love, is the sign of the infinite (in the ancient context: the sign of an action of the Immortals) is simultaneously mythological and theatrical.

It is mythological to the extent that Dido's passion for Aeneas is also a machination by Venus, who wishes to fasten her son Aeneas to Carthage in order to protect him from the plotting of Juno. We are thus told that the amorous scene, reflected as truth, is always vaster than itself. In the poem, it affixes the Two of the lovers to the historical destiny commanded by the conflict of the goddesses. This harrowing love is somehow framed by the action of the Immortals, but loses nothing of its independence (Dido is on her way to falling in love with Aeneas well before the arrival of Cupid, child and messenger of Venus). Rather, it thereby acquires a legendary force, an aura of destiny. This is an aura which, moreover, is already legible in the immediate love of the mortals. The meeting of Dido and Aeneas in effect juxtaposes two exceptional beauties, immanent to love. That of Aeneas:

> His streaming hair braided with pliant laurel leaves entwined in twists of gold, and arrows clash on his shoulders. So no less swiftly Aeneas strides forward now and his face shines with a glory like the god's.

And that of Dido:

> And there her proud, mettlesome charger prances in gold and royal purple, pawing with thunder-hoofs, champing a foam-flecked bit. At last she comes, with a great retinue crowding round the queen who wears a Tyrian cloak with rich embroidered fringe. Her quiver is gold, her hair drawn up in a golden torque and a golden buckle clasps her purple robe in folds.

These appearances elevate the Two of love to the height of the Immortal goddesses who prescribe its destiny. They initiate a theatralization, whose goal is also to signify the infinite excess over itself of love qua truth. This theatralization surrounds the episodes with a finely wrought décor, in which the amorous scene inscribes itself as the creation of a world. After divine infinity comes visible, or cosmic, infinity. This intensity of the sensible can even influence the arrangement of a banquet offered to her heroic guest by the woman who is already in love with him:

> Within the palace all is decked with adornments, lavish, regal splendour. In the central hall they are setting out a banquet, draping the gorgeous purple, intricately worked, heaping the board with grand displays of silver and gold engraved with her fathers' valiant deeds, a long, unending series of captains and commands, traced through a line of heroes since her country's birth.

But the cosmic exposition of the passionate Two is also nature itself, the scene of the hunt in the valleys ('Once the huntsmen have reached the trackless lairs aloft in the foothills'), which precedes the famous storm that envelops the lovers' quenched desire:

The skies have begun to rumble, peals of thunder first and the storm breaking next, a cloudburst pelting hail. [. . .] Dido and Troy's commander make their way to the same cave for shelter now.

With regard to this storm, it is notable that Berlioz's romanticism matches Virgil's vision precisely, bearing witness once again to the fact that the universality of truths allows itself to be recognized beyond the radical discontinuity of their advent into the logic of appearing. The love duet in Act IV of the *Trojans* is in fact preceded and almost propelled in the opera by a long symphonic fragment, a kind of splendid overture which encapsulates the hunt and the storm in an orchestral style so innovative that its syncopations and percussive pulsations evoke Gershwin's usage of jazz. So it is that, in order to regain the power of the Roman poet's ellipses, the music of the nineteenth century, enlightened by the intuition of love, is obliged to presage that of the twentieth. Yet more proof that truths, beyond History, weave their discontinuities along a delicate alloy of anticipations and retroactions. This is indeed how Berlioz equals himself to Virgil in what concerns the encrustation of love's radiances in the cosmic décor which signifies love's power of truth.

As for the infinite virtuality of amorous intensity, Berlioz depicts it in the libretto by means of a powerful intuition, which is that of representing every love—and particularly that of Dido and Aeneas—as a metonymy of all other loves. The music will thus intertwine the tender praise of the Night—and we know what Wagner makes of this in *Tristan and Isolde*—with a long series of comparisons between this night and other nights of love.

On the side of nocturnal ecstasy:

Night of drunkenness and infinite ecstasy
Blond Phoebe, great stars in her retinue,
Shine upon us your blessed glow;
Flowers of the heavens, smile upon immortal love.[1]

On the side of comparisons:

Through such a night, mad with love and joy
Troilus came to wait at the feet of the walls of Troy
For the beautiful Cressida.

Through such a night the chaste Diana
At last shed her diaphanous veil
Before the eyes of Endymion.[2]

The mixture of long interlaced chromatic melodies and vibrant evocations exhibits love in its excessive truth, in what it says about the power of the Two beyond the self-regarding enjoyment of each and every one.

The paradox of this type of truth is doubtless that love is both an exceptional infinity of existence—creating the caesura of the One through the evental energy of an encounter—and the ideal becoming of an ordinary emotion, of an anonymous grasp of this existence. Who has not experienced that at the peak of love, one is both beyond oneself and entirely reduced to the pure, anonymous exposure of one's life? The power of the Two is to carve out an existence, a body, a banal individuality, directly on the sky of Ideas. Virgil and Berlioz knew well this immediate idealization of what has only existed in you, at your scale, and which counters infinite theatralization through the majesty of everyday life. This woman 'reduced to tears, again, attempting to pray again, bending, again, beneath love, her beseeching fierceness' is by no means incompatible with the proud queen, golden on her ceremonial horse. Love is this disjunctive synthesis, as Deleuze would put it, between infinite expansion and anonymous stagnation. Ontologically, every truth is an infinite but also generic fragment of the world in which it comes to be. Berlioz voices it after his own fashion, from out of the despair of the lover, again employing the motif of the night:

Farewell, my people, farewell! Farewell revered shore,
You who once welcomed me, beseeching;
Farewell, beautiful African sky, stars that I beheld
In nights of drunkenness and infinite ecstasy,
Never again shall I see you, my run is over.[3]

But the one who expresses it most intensely is without doubt Thomas Mann in *Death in Venice*—superbly relayed by Visconti in the film of the same name. At the water's edge, Aschenbach's unpredictable passion for the young Tadzio attains this direct and sensible intuition of the Idea:

Separated from terra firma by a gulf of water, separated from his companions by his capricious pride, he ambled, his sight unfettered and perfectly aloof from the rest, his hair in the wind, down there, in the sea and the wind, upright before the misty infinite.

Through the separating power of the Two, love illuminates the anonymous existence harboured by this 'unfettered sight'—in this case the gaze of the dying Aschenbach. This is what—in yet another diagonal connection, this time through the arts rather than through time or cultures—Visconti transcribes in cinema, by means of a kind of solar distance or calm bedazzlement, as though Tadzio, his finger aloft, pointed a dying Platonist, above the sea and through the sole grace of love, towards the horizon of his intelligible world.

7. DISTINCTIVE FEATURES OF TRUTHS, PERSUASIVE FEATURES OF FREEDOM

Let's sum up the properties which permit us to say that certain productions, in worlds that are otherwise disparate, are marked by this disparateness only to the very extent that they are exceptions to it. Though their materiality, their 'bodies' as we would say, are composed only of the elements of the world, these truths—that is the name that philosophy has always reserved for them—nonetheless exhibit a type of universality that those elements, drawn from worldly particularity, cannot sustain on their own.

1. Produced in a measurable or counted empirical time, a truth is nevertheless eternal, to the extent that, grasped from any other point of time or any other particular world, the fact that it constitutes an exception remains fully intelligible.

2. Though generally inscribed in a particular language, or relying on this language for the isolation of the objects that it uses or (re)produces, a truth is trans-linguistic, insofar as the general form of thought that gives access to it is separable from every specifiable language.

3. A truth presupposes an organically closed set of material traces; with respect to their consistency, these traces do not refer to the empirical uses of a world but to a frontal change, which has affected (at least) one object of this world. We can thus say that the trace presupposed by every truth is the trace of an event.

4. These traces are linked to an operative figure, which we call a subject. We could say that a subject is an operative disposition of the traces of the event and of what they deploy in a world.

5. A truth articulates and evaluates its components on the basis of consequences and not of mere givenness.

6. Starting from the articulation of consequences, a truth elicits subjects-forms which are like instances of an invariant matrix of articulation.

7. A truth is both infinite and generic. It is a radical exception as well as an elevation of anonymous existence to the Idea.

These properties legitimate the 'except that' which grounds, against the dominant sophistry (of democratic materialism), the ideological space (or materialist dialectic) of a contemporary metaphysics.

Where the materialist dialectic advocates the correlation of truths and subjects, democratic materialism promotes the correlation of life and individuals. This opposition is also one between two conceptions of freedom. For democratic materialism, freedom is plainly definable as the (negative) rule of what there is. There is freedom if no language forbids individual bodies which are marked by it from deploying their own capacities. Or again, languages let bodies actualize their vital resources. Incidentally, this is why under democratic materialism sexual freedom is the paradigm of every freedom. Such freedom is in effect unmistakably placed at the point of articulation between desires (bodies), on the one hand, and linguistic, interdictory or stimulating legislations, on the other. The individual must be accorded the right to 'live his or her sexuality' as he or she sees fit. The other freedoms will necessarily follow. And it's true that they do follow, if we consider every freedom in terms of the model it adopts with regard to sex: the non-interdiction of the uses that an individual may make, in private, of the body that inscribes him or her in the world.

It turns out, however, that in the materialist dialectic, in which freedom is defined in an entirely different manner, this paradigm is no longer tenable. In effect, it is not a matter of the bond—of prohibition, tolerance or validation—that languages entertain with the virtuality of bodies. It is a matter of knowing if and how a body participates, through languages, in the exception of a truth. We can put it like this: being free does not pertain to the register of relation (between bodies and languages) but directly to that of incorporation (to a truth). This means that freedom presupposes that a new body appear in the world. The subjective forms of incorporation made possible by this unprecedented body—itself articulated upon a break, or causing a break—define the nuances of freedom. As a consequence, sexuality is deposed from its paradigmatic position—without thereby becoming, as in certain religious moralities, a counter-paradigm. Reduced to a purely ordinary activity, it makes room for the four great figures of the 'except that': love (which, once it exists, subordinates sexuality to itself), politics (of emancipation), art and science.

The category of life is fundamental to democratic materialism. In my view, it was by conceding too much to it that Deleuze—having started from the project of upholding the chances of a metaphysics against contemporary sophistry—came to tolerate the fact that most of his concepts were sucked up, so to speak, by the *doxa* of the body, desire, affect, networks, the multitude, nomadism and enjoyment into which a whole contemporary 'politics' sinks, as if into a poor man's Spinozism.

Why is 'life'—and its derivatives ('forms of life', 'constituent life', 'artistic life' and so on)—a major signifier of democratic materialism? Major to the point that at the level of pure opinion 'to succeed in life' is today without a doubt the only imperative that everyone understands. That is because 'life' designates every empirical correlation between body and language. And the norm of life is, quite naturally, that the genealogy of languages be adequate to the power of bodies. Accordingly, what democratic materialism calls 'knowledge', or even 'philosophy', is always a blend of a genealogy of symbolic forms and a virtual (or desiring) theory of bodies. It is this blend, systematized by Foucault, which may be called a linguistic anthropology, and which serves as the practical regime of knowledges under democratic materialism.

Does this mean that materialist dialectics must renounce any use of the word 'life'? My idea is rather—at the cost, it's true, of a spectacular displacement—to bring this word back to the centre of philosophical thinking, in the guise of a methodical response to the question 'What is it to live?' But, in order to do this, we must obviously explore the considerable retroactive pressure which the 'except that' of truths exerts on the very definition of the word 'body'. *The most significant stake of* Logics of Worlds *is without doubt that of producing a new definition of bodies, understood as bodies-of-truth, or subjectivizable bodies. This definition forbids any capture by the hegemony of democratic materialism.*

Then, and only then, will it be possible conclusively to elucidate a definition of life which is more or less the following: To live is to participate, point by point, in the organization of a new body, in which a faithful subjective formalism comes to take root.

8. BODY, APPEARING, GREATER LOGIC

The resolution of the problem of the body, which is in essence the problem of the appearance of truths, instigates an immense detour, in the sense given to this term by Plato: the detour as a mode of appropriation in thought of the thing itself. Why? Because it is a matter of bringing the status of appearing to thought. A body is really nothing but that which, bearing a subjective form, confers upon a truth, in a world, the phenomenal status of its objectivity.

When dealing with truths in *Being and Event*, I only treated the form of their being: like everything that is, truths are pure multiplicities (or multiples without One); but they are multiplicities of a definite type, which, following the mathematician Paul Cohen, I proposed to call generic multiplicities. To be extremely brief, given a world (I spoke then of 'situation'), a generic multiplicity is an 'anonymous' part of this world, a part that corresponds to no explicit predicate. A generic part is identical to the whole situation in the following sense: the elements of this part—the components of a truth—have their being, or their belonging to the situation, as their only assignable property. The being of a truth is the genre of being of its being.

I shall not revisit all of this. But my problem is now that of drawing the question of truths into a very different axiomatic, which is that of the singularity of the worlds in which truths appear. In *Being and Event*, I did not interrogate the fact that every givenness of being takes the form of a situation. We could say that the realization of being-qua-being as being-there-in-a-world is granted as though it were a property of being itself. But this (Hegelian) thesis can only be defended if one attributes to being the *telos* of its appearing. Only if, basically, one agrees that it is of the essence of being to bring about worlds in which its truth manifests itself.

If we abandon all hope of finalising the true or of incorporating it to being as becoming, if being is nothing but indifferent multiplicity, then the status of what appears 'in truth'—the corporeal (or objective) upsurge of a truth in such and such a world—requires a separate investigation. At the heart of this investigation we find the question of the consistency of worlds (or the manifestness of being-there), a question that neither the ontology of multiplicities nor the examination of the generic form of truths is capable of answering. It is only by examining the general conditions of the inscription of a multiplicity in a world, and consequently by exposing to the thinkable the very category of 'world', that we can hope finally to know: first, what the effectiveness of appearing is; then, how to grasp, in their upsurge and unfolding, the singularity of those phenomenal exceptions—the truths on which the possibility of living depends.

This demand governs the entire organization of *Logics of Worlds*. It also prescribes its equilibriums. We could effectively say that the question on which the exception that grounds the break of the materialist dialectic with democratic materialism depends is that of *objectivity*. A truth, such that a subject formalizes its active body in a determinate world, does not let itself be dissolved in its generic being. There is an irreducible insistence in its appearing, which also means that it takes place among the objects of a world. But what is an object? It could be said that the most complex and perhaps most innovative argument in this book is aimed at finding a new definition of the object, and therefore of the objective status of the existence of a truth. I claim in fact entirely to recast the concept of object, in contrast to the empiricist (Hume) and critical (Kant and Husserl) heritage that still commands its usage today. No surprise then that this proud project takes up a considerable amount of the book. At the same time, as radical as this project may be, and even though its complete logic is worked through in minute detail, it is not my real aim. In effect, I subordinate the logic of appearing, objects and worlds to the trans-worldly affirmation of subjects faithful to a truth.

The path of the materialist dialectic organizes the contrast between the complexity of materialism (logic of appearing or theory of the object) and the intensity of the dialectic (the living incorporation into truth-procedures).

In order to open up this path, I begin by assuming that the thorniest of problems, the 'physics' of life, has been resolved by the theory of the evental upsurge of a body; given this assumption, I describe the subjective types capable of taking possession of such bodies. That is the content of Book I, which is a metaphysics in the strict sense: it proceeds as though physics already existed. The advantage of this approach is that we can immediately see the (subjective) forms of 'life' that the materialist dialectic lays claim to, which are the forms of a subject-of-truth (or of its denial, or of its occultation). This study obviously remains formal as long as the problem of bodies, of the worldly materiality of subjects-of-truth, has not been treated. Given that a subjectivizable body is a new body, this problem requires that one know what the 'appearance' of a body means, and there-fore, more generally, that one elucidate what appearing, and therefore objectivity, may be.

A fundamental thesis must be inserted at this point, a thesis whose argument and detailed exposition occupy the whole central section of *Logics of Worlds*: just as being qua being is thought by mathematics (a position that is argued for throughout *Being and Event*), so appearing, or being-there-in-a-world, is thought by logic. Or, more precisely: 'logic' and 'consistency of appearing' are one and the same thing. Or again: a theory of the object is a logical theory, wholly alien to any doctrine of representation or reference. Hence the fact that Books II, III and IV are all included under the heading 'Greater Logic'. These Books make entirely explicit what a world is, what an object of this world is and what a relation between objects is. This is all correlated to purely logical constructions, which are homogeneous to the theory of categories and 'absorb' logic as commonly understood (predicative or linguistic logic).

I think I may say that, just as *Being and Event* drastically transformed the ontology of truths by putting it under the condition of the Cantor-event and of the mathematical theory of the multiple, so *Logics of Worlds* drastically transforms the articulation of the transcendental and the empirical, by putting it under the condition of the Grothendieck-event (or of Eilenberg, or Mac Lane, or Lawvere. . .) and of the logical theory of sheaves. If *Logics of Worlds* deserves the subtitle *Being and Event, 2*, it is to the extent that the traversal of a world by a truth, initially grasped in its type of being, this time finds itself objectivated in its appearing, and to the extent that its incorporation into a world unfolds the true in its logical consistency.

But the method is far from being the same in the two cases. The systematic meditations of *Being and Event* are followed here by the intertwining of examples and calculations, directly staging the consistent complexity of worlds. As infinitely diversified figures of being-there, worlds effectively absorb the infinite nuances of qualitative intensities into a transcendental framework whose operations are invariant. We can fully account for these nuances of appearing only through the mediation of examples drawn from varied worlds, and from the invariance of transcendental operations; that is, by contrasting the coherence of the examples and the transparency of forms.

What we are attempting here is a *calculated phenomenology*. The method employed in these examples can in fact be related to a phenomenology, but only to an objective phenomenology. This means that the consistency of what one speaks about (an opera, a painting, a landscape, a novel, a scientific construction, a political episode. . .) must be allowed to emerge by neutralising, not its real existence as in Husserl, but on the contrary its intentional or lived dimension. In doing so, we grasp the equivalence between appearing and logic through a pure description, a description without a subject. This 'letting-emerge' simply seeks to locally test the logical resistance of being-there, and to immediately universalize this resistance in the concept, only to then filter all of this through the sieve of formalization.

The usage of mathematical formalisms in *Logics of Worlds* is very different from the one found in *Being and Event*. This difference is the one between being-qua-being, whose real principle is the inconsistency of the pure multiple (or multiple without One), and appearing, or being-there-in-a-world, whose principle is to consist. We can also say that this is the difference between *onto*-logy and onto-*logy*. The mathematics of being as such consists in forcing a consistency, so that inconsistency will expose itself to thought. The mathematics of appearing consists in detecting, beneath the qualitative disorder of worlds, the logic that holds together the differences of existence and intensity. This time, it is consistency that demands to be exhibited. Hence a style of formalization that is both more geometrical and more calculating, at the boundary between a topology of localizations and an algebra of forms of order. In comparison, ontological formalization is more conceptual and axiomatic: it examines and unfolds decisions of thought whose impact is very general. Let us say that ontology requires a deeper comprehension of formalisms, while the Greater Logic requires a more vigilant tracking of consecutions. But the discipline of forms must be accepted. It is the condition of truth, to the extent that the acceptation of truth is detached from the ordinariness of meaning. As Lacan says, '*mathematical* par excellence', means 'transmissible outside of meaning'. I have not taken care to guarantee at every point a continuity between the two projects. Some ontological reminders will suffice, together with the guarantee of the homogeneity of the pure theory of the multiple across the two books. Problems of connection and continuity do remain, namely between 'generic procedure' and 'intra-worldly consequences of the existence of an inexistent'. I leave them for another time, or for others to solve.

In any case, once we are in possession of a Greater Logic, of a completed theory of worlds and objects, it is possible to examine on its own terms the question of change, especially the question of radical change, or of the event. As we shall see, there are very important modifications with regard to what is said about this point in *Being and Event*, though these differences too are not thematized at length. This new theory of change and its varieties takes up Book V.

One can intuitively grasp that a creative practice relates a subject to articulated figures of experience, leading to a resolution of hitherto unperceived difficulties. The language I propose to elucidate this aspect of a truth-process is that of the *points* in a world: by formalising a new body, a subject-of-truth treats points of a world, and a truth proceeds point by point. But we must obtain a clear idea of what a point is, on the basis of rigorous criteria regarding appearing, the world and the object, as set out in Books II to IV. That is the aim of Book VI.

We are then in possession of everything we need to answer our initial question—'What is a body?'—thereby tracing a decisive line of demarcation from democratic materialism. This is done in Book VII. The delicate part of this construction is the one which, having articulated body and event, opens up the problem of truths by *organizing* the body, point by point: everything is then recapitulated and clarified. Over the entire span of the existence of worlds—and not only in political action—the incorporation into the True is a question of organization. The Conclusion deals with the consequences of this book's trajectory (from subjective metaphysics to the physics of bodies, via the Greater Logic and the thinking of change) in terms of what philosophy proposes to humanity as a whole, once, in such and such a circumstance, it finds itself asking what is it to live. To live, that is, 'as an Immortal'.

Notes

1. *Nuit d'ivresse et d'extase infinie / Blonde Phoebé, grands astres de sa cour, / Versez sur nous votre lueur bénie; / Fleurs des cieux, souriez à l'immortel amour.*
2. *Par une telle nuit, fou d'amour et de joie / Troïlus vint attendre aux pieds des murs de Troie / La belle Cressida. / Par une telle nuit la pudique Diane / Laissa tomber enfin son voile diaphane / Aux yeux d'Endymion.*
3. *Adieu, mon peuple, adieu! adieu, rivage vénéré, / Toi qui jadis m'accueillit suppliante; / Adieu, beau ciel d'Afrique, astres que j'admirai / Aux nuits d'ivresse et d'extase infinie, / Je ne vous verrai plus, ma carrière est finie.*

Technical Note

1. Starting with Book II, each argument is presented in two different ways: conceptually (meaning without any formalism and, each time, with examples) and formally (with symbolisms and, if necessary, schemata and calculus). Objective phenomenology and written transparency.

2. Starting with Book II, concepts are also (re)presented through the study of texts extracted from the works of Hegel, Kant, Leibniz, Deleuze, Kierkegaard and Lacan.

3. After Book IV, under the title 'General Appendix to the Greater Logic', one will find a list of propositions (from 0 to 11) utilized in the formal arguments in Books II to IV, and reutilized in some of the demonstrations in Books V to VII.

4. Internal references to the text are coded in the following manner: the Book in Roman numerals, the Section and subsection in Arabic numerals. Thus: II.1.7 (Book II, Section 1, Subsection 7).

5. There are no footnotes or endnotes as such. However, remarks, coded in the same manner as the internal references, are provided after the Conclusion under the title 'Notes, Commentaries and Digressions'. Readers who pose themselves questions can turn to them and see. It's not entirely certain, however, that they shall find there the answers they seek.

6. After those Notes, one will find a summary of 'The 66 Statements of Logics of Worlds', followed by a 'Dictionary of Concepts' and a 'Dictionary of Symbols'.

7. An index provides a list of all the proper names that figure in the text, to the extent that there's good reason to think we are dealing with real rather than fictional persons.

8. An iconography is the indispensable complement to the Preface (Figures 1–4), Book III (Figure 5) and Book VI (Figure 6).

BOOK I
Formal Theory of the Subject (Meta-physics)

1. INTRODUCTION

The intellectual strategy that governs Book I is the following: to show from the outset that which is only fully intelligible at the end. In effect, what is a singular subject? It is the active (or corporeal, or organic) bearer of the dialectical overcoming of simple materialism. The materialist dialectic says: 'There are only bodies and languages, except that there are truths'. The 'except that' *exists* qua subject. In other words, if a body avers itself capable of producing effects that exceed the bodies–languages system (and such effects are called truths), this body will be said to be subjectivated. Let us insist on what could be termed the syntactical induction of the subject. Its mark is certainly not to be found in pronouns—the 'I' or 'we' of first persons. Rather, it is in the 'aside from', the 'except that', the 'but for' through which the fragile scintillation of what has no place to be makes its incision in the unbroken phrasing of a world.

'What has no place to be' should be taken in both possible senses: as that which, according to the transcendental law of the world (or of the appearing of beings), should not be; but also as that which subtracts itself (out of place) from the worldly localization of multiplicities, from the place of being, in other words, from being-there. Borne by an active intra-worldly body, a subject prescribes the effects of this body and their consequences by introducing a cut and a tension into the organization of places.

So I was not mistaken, more than twenty years ago, in my *Theory of the Subject*, to organize—in my jargon of the time—the dialectic of the 'splace' [*esplace*] (or, in more sober terms, of worlds) and the 'outplace' [*horlieu*] (or of the subjects that truths induce as the form of a body). Except that I cut straight to the dialectic, without drawing—in a Greater Logic—all the consequences of the obligatory materialism, of which I declared at the time, obscurely conscious of its compactness, that it was like the black sheep in the herd of ideas. That truths are required to appear bodily [*en-corps*] and to do so over again [*encore*]: that was the problem whose breadth I was yet unable to gauge. It is now clear to me that the dialectical thinking of a singular subject presupposes the knowledge of what an efficacious body is, and of what a logical and material excess with regard to the bodies–languages system might be. In short, it presupposes mastery not only of the ontology of truths, but of what makes truths appear in a world: the style of their deployment; the starkness of their imposition on the laws of what locally surrounds them; everything whose existence is summed up by the term 'subject', once its syntax is that of exception.

How are we to embark on the exposition of such a dialectic, since for the time being we are ignorant of the first principles of the logic of appearing, and don't even know what a world is, what an object is and therefore even less what a body is? Well, it's possible to start speaking of the subject at once, because the theory of the subject is essentially formal.

Let me explain.

A subject always presents itself as that which formalizes the effects of a body in accordance with a certain logic, whether productive or counter-productive. Thus a communist party, in the twenties or thirties, was a subjectivated political body which, faced with worker and popular situations, produced effects—effects that were sometimes interpretable as advances towards the construction of a public revolutionary consciousness (like the commitment to support the anti-colonial war waged in the Rif by Abd el-Krim), or as reactive effects (like the anti-leftist fight of the French Communist Party between May 68 and the elections of 1974) or as disastrous liquidating effects (like the practices of the German Communist Party at the beginning of the thirties). Alternatively, we could consider a sequence of musical works—say those of the great Viennese composers between Schönberg's *Pierrot Lunaire* (1912) and Webern's *Last Cantata* (1943)—as constructing a subjectivated artistic body which, in the context of tonal music's patent impotence, produces systemic effects of rupture together with the sedimentation of a new sensibility (brevity, the importance of silence, the unity of parameters, the breakdown of the musical 'story', etc.). It is clear then that the subject is that which imposes the legibility of a unified orientation onto the multiplicity of bodies. The body is a composite element of the world; the subject is what fixes in the body the secret of the effects it produces.

That is why we can present the figures of the subject right away, without yet possessing the means to think the effective or concrete becoming of a historically determinate subject, which in order to be thought requires a description of the body that functions as its support. We call this presentation of figures, which is indifferent to corporeal particularities, the formal theory of the subject. The fact that the theory of the subject is *formal* means that 'subject' designates a system of forms and operations. The material support of this system is a body, and the production of this ensemble—the formalism borne by a body—is either a truth (faithful subject), a denial of truth (reactive subject) or an occultation of truth (obscure subject).

The aim of Book I is to sketch a presentation of the formalism, in particular to define and symbolize the operations and then account for the typology (faithful subject, reactive subject, obscure subject). We shall defer the very difficult question of bodies, which presupposes the entirety of the Greater Logic (Books II–IV), the theory of real change (Book V) and the theory of formal decision or of transcendental 'points' (Book VI). Regarding bodies, for the time being we will simply presuppose their existence and nature, questions which will be elucidated, at the cost of some very hard work, in Book VII. Equally, even though a subject is ultimately nothing but the local agent of a truth, we will only sketch the doctrine of truths, whose detailed articulation is provided in other texts—above all, of course, in *Being and Event*. It follows that it is the subject-form which is really at stake here. In order to think this form it suffices to assume that the subjective formalism supported by a body is that which exposes a truth in the world. Having said that, we will succinctly present some subjective *modalities*. We will cross the three subjective figures with the four truth-procedures (love, science, art, politics).

The declaration that there is a (formal) theory of the subject is to be taken in the strong sense: of the subject, there can only be a theory. 'Subject' is the nominal index of a concept that must be constructed in a singular field of thought, in this case philosophy. In the end, to affirm that there must be a formal theory of the subject is to oppose the three (dominant) determinations of the concept of the subject:

1. 'Subject' would designate a register of experience, a schema for the conscious distribution of the reflexive and the non-reflexive; this thesis

conjoins subject and consciousness and is deployed today as phenomenology.

2. 'Subject' would be a category of morality. This category would (tautologically) designate the imperative, for every 'subject', to consider every other subject as a subject. It is only retroactively, and in an uncertain fashion, that this normative category becomes theoretical. Today, this is the conclusion reached by all varieties of neo-Kantianism.

3. 'Subject' would be an ideological fiction, an imaginary through which the apparatuses of the State designate (in Althusser's terms, 'interpellate') individuals.

In all three cases, there is no room for an independent, formal theory of the subject.

If the subject really is a reflexive schema, it is an immediate and irrefutable givenness and our task is to describe its immediacy in terms appropriate to an experience. But in an experience, the passive element—that which comes to be prior to any construction—cannot be subsumed by a formal concept. On the contrary, it is formal concepts that presuppose a passive givenness, since they are subordinated to the synthetic organization of the given.

Turning to the subject as a moral category, it is clear that it belongs to the register of the norm. In that regard, it can be what is at stake in a form, for example the imperative ('Respect, in every individual, the human subject that he or she is'); but it cannot be the form itself. Besides, it is clear today, as I recalled in the preface, that this conception of the subject flattens it onto the empirical manifestness of the living body. What deserves respect is the animal body as such. The forms are only the forms of this respect.

Finally, if subject is an ideological construct, its form is body-less, a pure rhetorical determination appropriate to a state command. It is possible here to speak of a materialist formalism. And in effect, for Althusser and his heirs, 'subject' is the central determination of idealisms. To sum up: in the phenomenological case, the subject is too immediate; in the ethical case, it is too corporeal (or 'biopolitical'); and in the ideological case, it is too formal.

We must recognize that we are indebted to Lacan—in the wake of Freud, but also of Descartes—for having paved the way for a formal theory of the subject whose basis is materialist; it was indeed by opposing himself to phenomenology, to Kant and to a certain structuralism, that Lacan could stay the course.

The absolute starting point is that a theory of the subject cannot be the theory of an object. That is indeed why it is only theoretical (its only empirical content is metaphorical) and tends towards the formal. That the subject is not an object does not forbid but rather requires not only that it have a being, but also that it have an appearing. Nevertheless, in Book I we are only dealing with the *typical forms* of this appearance. The appearing of the subject, which is its logic, is the fundamental stake of the whole of *Logics of Worlds*. We need to keep in mind that in the absence of a complete theory of bodies the only thing that we are assuming about the subject is its pure act: to endow an efficacious body with an appropriate formalism. This comes down to saying that we are speaking here, under the name of 'subject', only of the forms of formalism.

I would gladly place this paradoxical enterprise, which aims to articulate the form of what is but the act of a form, between two statements by Pindar. First, from the ode *Olympian 1*: 'The noise of mortals outstrips true speech'. Meaning that, at the service of truths, the subject-form (the 'noise of mortals') is nonetheless a kind of outstripping, a vaulting over each singular truth in the direction of something like an exposition of the power of the True. Secondly, from *Nemean 6*: 'Even so in one point we resemble, whether as great spirit or nature, Immortals'. Meaning that, being but a form and qua form—in the sense of the Platonic idea—the subject is immortal. In sum, we oscillate between a restrictive (or conditioned) construction and an amplifying (or unconditioned) exposition. The subject is structure, absolutely, but the subjective, as affirmation of structure, is more than a structure. It is a figure (or a system of figures) which always 'says' more than the combinations that support it. We will call *operations* the schemata that fix the subject-structure. There are four operations: the bar, the consequence (or implication), erasure (the diagonal bar) and negation. The appearance of a fifth, negation, is a matter of effects more than of acts. We will call *destinations* the schemata tied to the figures of the subject. There are four destinations: production, denial, occultation and resurrection. Throughout, we presuppose that in the 'world' where the subject unfolds its form there is:

–an event, which has left a trace. We will write this trace ε. The theory of the event and the trace can be found in Book V, but it is only intelligible if we presuppose the whole of logic (transcendental, object, relation), that is the totality of Books II to IV;

–a body issued from the event, which we will write C. The theory of the body occupies the whole of Book VII (the last), which in turn presumes a rather exhaustive grasp of Books II to VI.

As you can see, what is 'difficult' is not the subject, but the body. Physics is always more difficult than meta-physics. This (impending) difficulty is not an obstacle for the moment. The fact that the theory of the subject can be formal effectively means that we need not know from the outset what a body is, nor even that it exists; nor do we need to know, with the requisite rigour, the nature of events. It is enough for us to suppose that a real rupture has taken place in the world, a rupture which we will call an event, together with a trace of this rupture, ε, and finally a body C, correlated to ε (only existing as a body under the condition of the evental trace). The formal theory of the subject is then, under condition of ε and C (trace and body), a theory of operations (figures) and destinations (acts).

2. REFERENTS AND OPERATIONS OF THE FAITHFUL SUBJECT

We have affirmed that the theory of the subject is not descriptive (phenomenology), nor is it a practical experimentation (moralism) nor is it an instance of materialist critique (imaginary, ideology). We are therefore compelled to say that the theory of the subject is axiomatic. It cannot be deduced, because it is the affirmation of its own form. But neither can it be experimented. Its thought is decided on the horizon of an irrefutable empirical dimension which we illustrated in the preface: there are truths, and there must be an active and identifiable form of their production (but also of what hinders or annuls this production). The name of this form is *subject*. Saying 'subject' or saying 'subject with regard to truth' is redundant. For there is a subject only as the subject of a truth, at the service of this truth, of its denial or of its occultation. Therefore 'subject' is a category of the materialist dialectic. Democratic materialism only knows individuals and communities, that is to say passive bodies, but it knows no subjects.

That is the directly ideological meaning of the post-Heideggerian deconstruction, under the epithet 'metaphysical', of the category of subject: to prepare a democracy without a (political) subject, to deliver individuals over to the serial organization of identities or to the confrontation with the desolation of their enjoyment. In the France of the sixties only Sartre (in a reactive mode) and Lacan (in an inventive mode) refused to play a part in this drama. Consequently, both found themselves faced with the dialectic between subject (as structure) and subjectivation (as act). What does the subject subjectivate? As we've said, the subject comes to the place of the 'except that'. But this syntactical determination does not elucidate the subject's formal relation to the body that supports it.

Let's consider things more analytically.

We have the trace of the event, and we have a body. Is the subject the 'subjectivation' of a link between the physics of the body and the name (or trace) of the event? For example, let's suppose that following the revolt of a handful of gladiators around Spartacus, in 73 BC, the slaves—or rather *some* slaves, albeit in great numbers—form a body, instead of being dispersed into packs. Let's agree that the trace of the revolt-event is the statement 'We slaves, we want to return home'. Is the subject-form the operation whereby the new 'body' of the slaves (their army and its offshoots) connects to its trace?

In a sense, yes. It is indeed this conjunction that governs the strategies of Spartacus—strategies that happen to be fatal. First, to seek a passage towards the north, a border of the Roman Republic; then, to go south in order to commandeer some ships and leave Italy. These strategies are the subjective form borne by the body which is determined by the statement 'We slaves, we want to return home'. But in another sense, the answer is no. That is because the subjective identity which is fashioned in and by these military movements is not identical with them; it passes through operations of a different kind, which constitute subjective deliberation, division and production. First of all, the slaves 'as a body' (as an army) move in a new present; for they are no longer slaves. Thus they show (to the other slaves) that it is possible, for a slave, no longer to be a slave, and to do so *in the present*. Hence the growth, which soon becomes menacing, of this body. This institution of the possible as present is typically a subjective production. Its materiality is constituted by the consequences drawn day after day from the event's course, that is from a principle *indexed to the possible*: 'We slaves, we want to *and can* return home'.

These consequences affect and reorganize the body by treating successive points within the situation. By 'point', we understand here simply what confronts the global situation with singular choices, with decisions that involve the 'yes' and the 'no'. Is it really necessary to march south, or to attack Rome? To confront the legions, or evade them? To invent a new discipline, or to imitate regular armies? These oppositions, and how they are treated, gauge the efficacy of the slaves gathered together into a fighting body; ultimately, they unfold the subjective formalism that this body is capable of bearing. In this sense, a subject exists, as the localization of a truth, *to the extent it affirms that it holds a certain number of points*. That is why the treatment of points is the becoming-true of the subject, at the same time as it serves to filter the aptitudes of bodies.

We will call *present*, and write π, the set of consequences of the evental trace, as realized by the successive treatment of points.

Besides the conjunction of the body and the trace, the subject is a relation to the present, which is effective to the extent that the body possesses the subjective aptitudes for this relation, that is, once it disposes of or is able to impose some *organs of the present*. Take, for instance, the specialized military detachments that the slaves, led by Spartacus, try to constitute in their midst in order to face the Roman cavalry. This is why we say that the elements of the body are incorporated into the evental present. This is obvious if one considers, for example, a slave who escapes in order to enlist in Spartacus's troops. What he thereby joins is, empirically speaking, an army. But in subjective terms, it is the realization in the present of a hitherto unknown possibility. In this sense it is indeed into the present, into the new present, that the escaped slave incorporates himself. It is clear that the body here is subjectivated to the extent that it subordinates itself to the novelty of the possible (the content of the statement 'We slaves, we want to and can return home'). This amounts to a subordination of the body to the trace, but solely in view of an incorporation into the present, which can also be understood as a production of consequences: the greater the number of escaped slaves, the more the Spartacus-subject amplifies and changes in kind, and the more its capacity to treat multiple points increases.

We now need symbols to denote the body, the trace, consequence (qua operation) and the present (qua result). We must also denote subordination, or the oriented conjunction, which is ultimately essential. We have already written the trace as ε, the body as C and the present as π. We will symbolize the consequence by '$\Rightarrow$' and subordination by '—' (the bar). But we're not done. Since the body is only subjectivated to the extent that, decision by decision, it treats some points, we must indicate that a body is never entirely in the present. It is divided into, on the one hand, an efficacious region, an organ appropriate to the point being treated, and, on the other, a vast component which, with regard to this point, is inert or even negative. If, for example, the slaves confront the Roman cavalry, the small disciplined detachment readied for this task is incorporated into the present, but the general disorder of the remainder, with its multiplicity of languages (Gauls, Greeks, Jews. . .), the presence of women, its rivalry between improvised leaders, drags the whole towards the termination or impracticability of the new possible. Nevertheless, in different circumstances—for instance, the organization in the encampment of a new form of civic life—this order-less multiplicity, this unheard of and improvised cosmopolitanism, will be an inestimable resource, offset by the arrogance of well-trained detachments of gladiators. In other words, notwithstanding its subjection to the generality of the principle derived from the trace, the body is always divided by the points it treats. We will mark this important feature, on which Lacan rightly insisted, with erasure, the diagonal bar or slash, '/', which is the writing of the cleavage: under its subjectivated form, the body is therefore inscribed as '$\not\subset$'.

We can now formalize what we said about the enlisted slave. Qua pure subjective form, we have a body under erasure (the army in the process of formation, but which remains without unity) subordinated to the trace ('We slaves . . .'), but only in view of an incorporation into the present, which is always a consequence (this risky battle against the new legions which one must decide upon or refuse to wage). And these consequences, which treat some major points in the Roman historical world, found a new truth in the present: that the fate of the wretched of the earth is never a law of nature, and that it can, if only for the duration of a few battles, be revoked.

The foregoing can be summarized in the matheme of the faithful subject

$$\frac{\varepsilon}{\not\subset} \Rightarrow \pi$$

It is important to understand that the faithful subject as such is not contained in any of the letters of its matheme, but that it is the formula as a whole. It is a formula in which a divided (and new) body becomes, under the bar, something like the active unconscious of a trace of the event—an activity which, by exploring the consequences of what has happened, engenders the expansion of the present and exposes, fragment by fragment, a truth. Such a subject realizes itself in the production of consequences, which is why it can be called faithful—faithful to ε and thus to that vanished event of which ε is the trace. The product of this fidelity is the new present which welcomes, point by point, the new truth. We could also say that it is the subject in the present.

This subject is faithful to the trace, and thus to the event, since the division of its body falls under the bar, so that the present may finally come to be in which it will rise up in its own light.

3. DEDUCTION OF THE REACTIVE SUBJECT: REACTIONARY NOVELTIES

Let's consider the great mass of slaves who did not join Spartacus and his armies. The customary interpretation of their subjective disposition is that they retain within themselves the laws of the old world: you're a slave, resign yourself or seek a legal redress (make your master appreciate you so much that he will free you). I too shared for a long time the conviction that what resists the new is the old. Mao, in his subtle structural investigation of the difference between antagonistic contradictions (bourgeoisie/ proletariat) and contradictions among the people (workers/peasants), accorded an important place in the latter to 'the struggle of the new against the old'. As the prototypical component of the basic people, the slaves are nonetheless divided, by the initiative of the gladiators, between those who incorporate themselves to the evental present (the new) and those who do not believe in it, who resist its call (the old).

But this view of things underestimates what I think we must term *reactionary novelties*. In order to resist the call of the new, it is still necessary to create arguments of resistance appropriate to the novelty itself. From this point of view, every reactive disposition is the contemporary of the present to which it reacts. Of course, it categorically refuses to incorporate itself to this present. It sees the body—like a conservative slave sees the army of Spartacus—and refuses to be one of its elements. But it is caught up in a subjective formalism that is not, and cannot be, the pure permanence of the old.

In my own experience, I saw how, at the end of the sixties, the *nouveaux philosophes*, with André Glucksmann at their helm, concocted an intellectual apparatus destined to legitimate the brutal reactionary reversal which followed the red sequence that had begun in the middle of the sixties, a sequence whose name in China was 'Cultural Revolution', in the USA refusal of the Vietnam war and in France 'May 68'.

Of course, there was nothing new about the general form of the reactive constructions purveyed by the *nouveaux philosophes*. It amounted to saying that the true political contradiction is not the one that opposes revolution to the imperialist order, but democracy to dictatorship (totalitarianism). That is what American ideologues had been proclaiming loud and clear for at least thirty years. But the intellectual ambience, the style of the arguments, the humanitarian pathos, the inclusion of democratic moralism into a philosophical genealogy—all of this was the contemporary of the leftism of the time, all of this was new. In a nutshell, only erstwhile Maoists, like Glucksmann and the *nouveaux philosophes*, could dress up this old pirate's flag in the gaudy colours of the day. But this innovative tint was aimed at fatally weakening the Maoist episode, at *extinguishing* its lights, at serving, in the name of democracy and human rights, a counter-revolutionary restoration, an unbridled capitalism and, finally, the brutal hegemony of the USA. Which is to say that there aren't just reactionary novelties, but also a subjective form appropriate to producing the consequences of such novelty. It is not in the least irrelevant to note that, almost thirty years after the irruption of the *nouvelle philosophie*, Glucksmann has rushed to defend the invasion of Iraq by Bush's troops in singularly violent tones. In his own way, he is devoted to the present: in order to deny its creative virtue, he must daily nourish journalism with new sophisms.

So there exists, besides the faithful subject, a reactive subject. Obviously, it includes an operator of negation, of which we have yet to make use: the conservative slave denies that an efficacious body can be the unconscious material of a maxim of rebellion, and the *nouveaux philosophes* deny that emancipation can transit through the avatars of communist revolution. So it is really the 'no to the event', as the negation of its trace, which is the dominant instance (over the bar) of the reactive subject-form. If we write negation as '$\neg$', we get something like:

$$\frac{\neg \varepsilon}{(\quad)}$$

But the reactive figure cannot be encapsulated by this negation. It is not a pure negation of the eventual trace, since it also claims to produce something—and even, frequently under the cloak of modernity, to produce some kind of present. Needless to say, this present is not the affirmative and glorious present of the faithful subject. It is a measured present, a negative present, a present 'a little less worse' than the past, if only because it resisted the catastrophic temptation which the reactive subject declares is contained in the event. We will call it an *extinguished present*. And in order to denote it we will employ a double bar, the double bar of extinction: '$=$'.

For example, a conservative slave will find justification for his attitude in the minuscule ameliorations that will result, as a reward for his inaction, from the intense fear felt by his master at the sight of the first victories of Spartacus. These ameliorations, which are small novelties, will bear out his perception that he is partaking in the new era, while wisely avoiding incorporating himself into it. He will belong to a lustreless form of the present. Obviously, the terrible outcome of the sequence—thousands of rebels crucified all along the route that led the triumphant Crassus to Rome—will confirm and magnify the conviction that the genuine path of universally acceptable novelties, the 'realist' path, passes through the negation of the evental trace and the thoroughgoing repression of everything that resembles the subjective form whose name is Spartacus. We could say that the present which the reactive subject lays claim to is a confused present, divided between the disastrous consequences of post-evental subjective production and their reasonable counter-effect; between what's been done, and what—having refused any incorporation into this doing—one has merely received. And even when all that this amounts to is a reasonable survival, is it not still preferable to total failure and torment? Accordingly, we can write $\bar{\pi}$, with the double bar of extinction, the present that reactive subjectivity declares to be producing.

The matheme of the reactive subject therefore consists in inscribing the following: when the law of the negation of any trace of the event imposes itself, the form of the faithful subject passes under the bar, and the production of the present exposes its deletion.

$$\frac{\neg\,\varepsilon}{\dfrac{\varepsilon}{\not{\phi}}\Rightarrow\pi}\Rightarrow \bar{\pi}$$

Two things should be noted. First, that the body is held at the furthest distance from the (negative) declaration that founds the reactive subject. In effect, it is held under a double bar, as if the statement 'No, not this!' shouldn't even touch on the proscribed body. After all, that is what one imagines the Roman police demanded from the terrorized conservative slaves: that they affirm having no relation, not even a mental one, to Spartacus's troops; and that they prove this, if at all possible, by acting as informants and participating in raids and torture. The second remark is that the form of the faithful subject nonetheless remains the unconscious of the reactive subject. It is this form which is under the bar, authorising the production of the extinguished present, the weak present; this form also positively bears the trace ε, without the negation of which the reactive subject would be incapable of appearing. In effect, without declaring it, and often without telling himself as much, the terrorized conservative slave is well aware that everything which will happen to him—including the erased present of the 'ameliorations' that he hangs onto—is perturbed by the insurrection of the friends of Spartacus. In this sense, he unconsciously subordinates $\bar{\pi}$ to π. His own contemporaneousness is thus dictated to him by what he rejects and fights—just as the unquestionable contemporaneousness of the Vichy militiaman, between 1940 and 1944, was dictated to him, not by the Nazis or Pétain, but by the existence of the fighters of the Resistance.

There exists an unintentional but perfectly didactic theorist of reactive subjectivity: François Furet, historian of the French Revolution and author, in the same vein, of a bad book on the 'subjective' history of communism and communists (*The Past of an Illusion*). Furet's whole enterprise aims to show that since in the long run the results of the French Revolution were identical or even inferior to (needless to say, according to his own economistic and democratic criteria) those of the European countries which avoided such a trauma, this revolution is fundamentally contingent and pointless. In other words, Furet denies that the connection between the event, its trace and the 'sans-culotte' body bears any relation whatsoever to the production of the present. He pretends that the present π can be obtained without ε. Were we to believe him, we would thus get something like this:

$$\neg\varepsilon \Rightarrow \pi$$

But it is clear that Furet's 'demonstrations' depend on two sleights of hand. First, the logic of the result requires the weak present, the extinguished present, in place of the strong present set off by the revolutionary sequence. Did Robespierre understand by Virtue only the respect of commercial contracts? Is it the case that, when he spoke of institutions, Saint-Just had in mind our threadbare parliamentarianism, or its English forebear, which, as a good disciple of Rousseau, he despised? Of course not. Furet's underlying schema is thus clearly the following:

$$\neg\varepsilon \Rightarrow \bar{\pi}$$

Besides, as a historian, and in a sense despite himself, Furet is well aware that the evental trace ε is active only to the extent that it relies on the popular revolutionary body and those astonishing efficacious bodies which were the Convention, the Jacobin Club and the revolutionary army. Accordingly, what he intends to submit to critical revision (what he will drag under the bar, in a position of subordination) is well and truly the productivity in the present which is manifested by this body under the injunction of maxims ('Virtue or Terror', 'The government will remain revolutionary until the peace').

In the end, we re-encounter the matheme of the reactive subject in full. In this whole affair, the role played by the difference between the active present (π) and the extinguished present ($\bar{\pi}$) is evident. It is striking that it was vis-à-vis this difference that Glucksmann, from the beginning of his reactive undertaking—bizarrely dubbed 'new philosophy' (but as we've said, in a certain respect it was new)—forged the instruments of his intervention. Glucksmann's pivotal thesis is effectively that every willing of the Good leads to disaster and that the correct line is always that of the resistance against Evil. Let's pass over the circularity: Evil is above all communist totalitarianism, the effect of a willing of the True gone astray. So the (genuine) Good consists in resisting the willing of the Good. This circularity can be easily grasped: what is evil is the revolution; the fact that a body is under the affirmative jurisdiction of an event, that $\cent$ falls under ε. For Glucksmann, the present engendered by the $\varepsilon/\cent$ relation is necessarily monstrous. The genuine Good resides in a different production, which represses the first relation, under the aegis of the explicit negation of what grounds that relation. This production is undoubtedly rather pallid, rather extinguished and often merely amounts to a restoration of the pre-revolutionary state of things. It is $\bar{\pi}$ and not π. No matter, what we have there is the Good as a resistance against Evil, under the pure form of the reactive subject.

4. THE OBSCURE SUBJECT: FULL BODY AND OCCULTATION OF THE PRESENT

What relation can a patrician of ancient Rome entertain with the alarming news that beset him regarding the slaves' revolt? Or a Vendean bishop learning of the dethronement and imprisonment of the king? It cannot be a question, as in the case of the frightened slave or of François Furet, of a simple reactive subjectivity, which denies the creative power of the event in favour of a deleted present. We are obviously required to conceive an abolition of the new present, considered in its entirety as malevolent and *de jure* inexistent. It is the present itself that falls under the bar and it does this as the effect of a sovereign action, invoked by the subject in his prayers, lamentations or curses.

We obviously obtain a schema of the following kind:

The production is neither that of the present nor of its deletion, but instead that of the descent of this present into the night of non-exposition. Is this to say that all we have here is a return to the past? Once again, we need to offer a twofold answer. In part, the answer is obviously yes. What the patricians and bishops want is no doubt the pure and simple conservation of the previous order. In this sense, the past is illuminated for them by the night of the present. But, on the other hand, this night must be produced under the entirely new conditions which are displayed in the world by the rebel body and its emblem. The obscurity into which the newly produced present must be enclosed is engineered by an obscurantism of a new type. For example, it is futile to try to genealogically elucidate contemporary political Islamism. This is particularly true of its ultra-reactionary variants, which rival Westerners for the fruits of the oil map through unprecedented criminal means. This political Islamism represents a new instrumentalization of religion—from which it does not derive by any natural (or 'rational') lineage—with the purpose of occulting the post-socialist present and countering the fragmentary attempts through which emancipation is being reinvented by means of a full Tradition or Law. From this point of view, political Islamism is absolutely contemporary, both to the faithful subjects that produce the present of political experimentation and to the reactive subjects that busy themselves with denying that ruptures are necessary in order to invent a humanity worthy of the name—reactive subjects that parade the established order as the miraculous bearer of an uninterrupted emancipation. Political Islamism is simply one of the subjectivated names of today's obscurantism.

That is why, besides the form of the faithful subject and that of the reactive subject, we must give the *obscure* subject its rightful place.

In the panic sown by Spartacus and his troops, the patrician—and the Vendean bishop, and the Islamist conspirator, and the fascist of the thirties—systematically resorts to the invocation of a full and pure transcendent Body, an ahistorical or anti-eventual body (City, God,

Race. . .) from which it follows that the trace will be denied (here, the labour of the reactive subject is useful to the obscure subject) and, as a consequence, the real body, the divided body, will also be suppressed. Invoked by the priests (the imams, the leaders. . .), the essential Body has the power to reduce to silence that which affirms the event, thus forbidding the real body from existing.

Transcendent power tries to produce a double effect, which can be given a fictional expression in the figure of a Roman notable. First of all, he will say, it is entirely false that the slaves want to and can return home. Furthermore, there is no legitimate body that can be the bearer of this false statement. The army of Spartacus must therefore be annihilated, the City will see to it. This double annihilation, both spiritual and material—which explains why so many priests have blessed so many troops of butchers—is itself exposed within appearing, above that which is occulted, namely the present as such.

If we write as C (without erasure) the full body whose transcendence covers the occultation of the present, we obtain the matheme of the obscure subject:

$$\frac{C \Rightarrow (\neg \varepsilon \Rightarrow \neg \varphi)}{\pi}$$

One can see how this matheme articulates the paradox of an occultation of the present which is itself in the present. Materially, we have the radical novelties which are ε and C. But they are wrested from their creative subjective form (ε/φ, the faithful subject) and thereby exposed in appearing to their total negation—of a propagandistic type for ε, of a military or police-like kind for φ (for the examples we've chosen). The most important foreseeable effect of this is the occultation of ε as truth.

Without question, the obscure subject crucially calls upon an atemporal fetish: the incorruptible and indivisible over-body, be it City, God or Race. Similarly, Fate for love, the True without admissible image for art and Revelation for science correspond to the three types of obscure subject which are possessive fusion, iconoclasm and obscurantism. But the goal of the obscure subject is to make this fetish the contemporary of the present that demands to be occulted. For example, the sole function of the God of conspiratorial Islamism is to occult the present of the rational politics of emancipation among people, by dislocating the unity of their statements and their militant bodies. This is done in order to fight for local supremacy with 'Western' powers, without in any way contributing to political invention. In this sense, C only enters the scene so that the often violent negation of $\cent$ can serve as the appearing of that which is occulted, the emancipatory present π. The fictive transcendent body legitimates the fact that the (visible) destruction of the evental body consigns the pure present which was woven by the faithful subject, point by point, to the invisible and the inoperative.

The reader will find in Section 8 some additional considerations on the operations of the obscure subject. The crucial thing here is to gauge the gap between reactive formalism and obscure formalism. As violent as it may be, reaction conserves the form of the faithful subject as its articulated unconscious. It does not propose to abolish the present, only to show that the faithful break (which it calls 'violence' or 'terrorism') is useless for engendering a moderate, that is to say extinguished present (a present that reaction calls 'modern'). Moreover, this instance of the subject is itself borne by the debris of bodies: frightened and deserting slaves, renegades of revolutionary groups, avant-garde artists recycled into academicism, old scientists now blind to the movements of their science, lovers suffocated by conjugal routine.

Things stand differently for the obscure subject. That is because it is the present which is directly its unconscious, its lethal disturbance, while it de-articulates in appearing the formal data of fidelity. The monstrous full Body to which it gives fictional shape is the atemporal filling of the abolished present. Thus, what bears this body is directly linked to the past, even if the becoming of the obscure subject also crushes this past in the name of the sacrifice of the present: veterans of lost wars, failed artists, intellectuals perverted by bitterness, dried-up matrons, illiterate muscle-bound youths, shopkeepers ruined by Capital, desperate unemployed workers, rancid couples, bachelor informants, academicians envious of the success of poets, atrabilious professors, xenophobes of all stripes, Mafiosi greedy for decorations, vicious priests and cuckolded husbands. To this hodgepodge of ordinary existence the obscure subject offers the chance of a new destiny, under the incomprehensible but salvific sign of an absolute body, whose only demand is that one serves it by nurturing everywhere and at all times the hatred of every living thought, every transparent language and every uncertain becoming.

The theory of the subject thus contains three distinct formal arrangements. Of course, the general subjective field is necessarily inaugurated by a faithful subject, so that the point-by-point work of consequences may be visible as pure present. But generally, from the first signs that we have been accorded the gift of a present, the reactive and obscure subjects are already at work, as rivals and accomplices in weakening the substance of this present or occulting its appearance.

5. THE FOUR SUBJECTIVE DESTINATIONS

To sum up, there are three figures of the subject: faithful, reactive, obscure. They are so many formal arrangements of the letters ε, C and π (the trace, the body, the present) and the signs —, /, ¬, = and ⇒ (the bar, erasure, negation, extinction and consequence). These arrangements formalize the subjective figure, without thereby designating its synthetic usage, since the required operations—for instance negation or implication—are included in this formalization.

Having said that, we have seen how the effective concern of a figure of the subject is the present as such. The faithful subject organizes its *production*, the reactive subject its *denial* (in the guise of its deletion) and the obscure subject its *occultation* (the passage under the bar). We call *destination* of a subjective figure this synthetic operation in which the subject reveals itself as the contemporary of the eventual present, without necessarily incorporating itself into it.

Must we therefore conclude that by 'subject' we will understand, under the condition of a trace and a body, that which is destined to produce a present, to deny it or to occult it? Yes, of course, save that a supernumerary destination is at play if we no longer examine each figure separately, but rather consider the complexity of the subjective field in its historical scansion. We are referring to resurrection (of a truth), which we must now introduce.

To begin with, we should note that the contemporaneousness of a figure of the reactive or obscure type depends on the minimal production of a present by a faithful figure. From a subjective point of view, it is not because there is reaction that there is revolution, it is because there is revolution that there is reaction. We thereby eliminate from the living subjective field the whole 'left-wing' tradition which believes that a progressive politics 'fights against oppression'. But we also eliminate, for example, a certain modernist tradition which believes that the criterion for art is the 'subversion' of established forms, to say nothing of those who wish to articulate amorous truth onto the fantasy of a sexual emancipation (against 'taboos', patriarchy, etc.). Let's say that the destinations proceed in a certain order (production → denial → occultation), for reasons that formalism makes altogether clear: the denial of the present supposes its production, and its occultation supposes a formula of denial.

For example, the *nouveaux philosophes*, who denied the present of communism (in its ideal sense) and preached resignation to capitalist-parliamentarianism, could only exist because of the revolutionary activism of an entire generation between 1966 and 1976. And the occultation of every real becoming by the US government and the 'Islamists' (two faces or two names of the same obscure God) could only take place on a terrain prepared by the denial of political communism. Formally, in order to have $\neg\,\varepsilon$, one needs ε; to have π, it is useful to have π; to inscribe $C \Rightarrow (\neg\varepsilon \Rightarrow \neg\varphi)$, one requires φ, and so on. One might then believe that the schema for the figural destinations is the following:

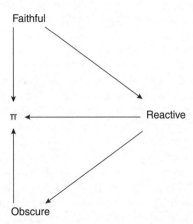

If this schema is incomplete, it is because the formal excess makes us forget what the present is a present *of*: of a truth, whose exposition in appearing is operated by the subject, or of which the subject is the active logical form. But this truth itself abides in the multiform materiality in which it is constructed as the generic part of a world. Now, a fragment of truth inserted under the bar by the machinery of the obscure can be extracted from it at any instant.

No one can doubt that the revolt of Spartacus is the event which originates for the ancient world a maxim of emancipation in the present tense (the slave wants to and can decide to be free to return home). Equally, no one can doubt that—weakened by the denial of too many fearful slaves (reactive subject) and finally annihilated in the name of the transcendent rules of the City (of which slavery is a natural state)—for the masses of slaves this present succumbs to a practical oblivion lasting many centuries. Does that mean that it's disappeared for good, and that a truth, as eternal as it may be, can also, having been created in history, slip back into nothingness? Not so. Think of the first victorious slave revolt, the one led by the astounding Toussaint-Louverture in the Western part of Santo Domingo (the part that is today called Haiti). This is the revolt which made the principle of the abolition of slavery real, which conferred upon blacks the status of citizens, and which, in the exhilarating context of the French Revolution, created the first state led by former black slaves. In sum, the revolution that fully freed the black slaves of Santo Domingo constitutes a new present for the maxim of emancipation that motivates Spartacus's comrades: 'The slaves want to and can, through their own movement, decide to be free'. And this time, the white owners will be unable to re-establish their power.

Now, what happens on 1 April 1796, when the governor Laveaux—an energetic partisan of the emancipation of the slaves—gathers together the people of Cap, together with the army of insurgent blacks, to offset the counter-revolutionary manoeuvres of certain mulattoes, by and large supported and financed by the English? Laveaux calls Toussaint-Louverture to his side, names him 'deputy governor' and finally, and above all, calls him 'the black Spartacus'. French revolutionary leaders were men nourished on Greek and Roman history. Laveaux was no different, and neither was Sonthonax, also a great friend of Toussaint-Louverture. Of course, in January 1794, the Convention, during a memorable session, had decreed the abolition of slavery in all the territories over which it had jurisdiction; consequently, all the men living in the colonies, without distinction of colour, were decreed citizens and enjoyed all the rights guaranteed by the Constitution. But Laveaux and Sonthonax, faced with a violent and complex situation in which foreign powers intervened militarily, months before, and answering only to themselves, had already taken the decision to declare the abolition of slavery then and there. And it is in this context that they saluted the 'black Spartacus', the revolutionary leader of the slaves about to be liberated, and the future founder of a free state.

More than a century later, when in 1919 the communist insurgents of Berlin, led by Karl Liebknecht and Rosa Luxemburg, brandished the name of 'Spartakus' and called themselves 'Spartakists', they too made it so that the 'forgetting' (or failure) of the slave insurrection was itself forgotten and its maxim restored—to the point that the sordid assassination of the two leaders by the shock troops of the 'socialist' Noske (Luxemburg was battered with rifle-butts, her body thrown into the canal, Liebknecht shot and dumped in a morgue) echoes the thousands crucified on the Roman roads.

As proof of this reappropriation in the following decades, one will refer to the denial of the affirmative sense of the revolt in the subtly reactive portrait that Arthur Koestler makes of Spartacus. We know that Koestler— a kind of Glucksmann of the forties with some talent to boot—after having been a Stalinist agent during the Spanish war, projects into his novels his personal about turn and becomes the literary specialist of anti-communism. The first of his renegade novels, *The Gladiators* (1939), translated into French in 1945 under the title *Spartacus*, portrays a slave leader placed somewhere between Lenin and Stalin. In order to introduce a modicum of order into his own camp—a sort of utopian city whose tormented leader he represents—he is in fact forced to use the Romans' methods and in the end to order the public crucifixion of dissident slaves. This interpretation is answered in the fifties by Howard Fast's affirmative novel, *Spartacus*, revived by the film which Stanley Kubrick drew from it, in which Kirk Douglas plays the hero in a moving humanist version of the story.

It is clear that political truth, fragmentarily borne by Spartacus and interminably occulted by the bloody triumph of Crassus and Pompey, is here dragged under the bar only to be re-exposed in the appearing of modern communist convictions and their denial; just as it was in Santo Domingo, in the global exhilaration provoked by the application, during the French Revolution, of universal egalitarian principles. This means that, together with the truth of which it is the correlate ('Slavery is not natural'), the subject whose name is 'Spartacus' travels from world to world through the centuries. Ancient Spartacus, black Spartacus, red Spartacus.

We will call this destination, which reactivates a subject in another logic of its appearing-in-truth, *resurrection*. Of course, a resurrection presupposes a new world, which generates the context for a new event, a new trace, a new body—in short, a truth-procedure under whose rule the occulted fragment places itself after having been extracted from its occultation.

Another striking example is to be found in the prodigious mathematical discoveries of Archimedes, who, from out of the discipline of geometry, anticipated the differential and integral calculus in formally impeccable writings. It is pretty much certain that in the West (the Arab history of the question is far more complex)—in particular because they were subjected during the entire scholastic period to Aristotle's obscure hostility to Platonic 'mathematism'—these writings (from the third century BC, let's not forget) became unreadable, in a very precise sense: they were in discord with all the subjective formalisms, and it was therefore impossible to articulate them to the present. But in the sixteenth and seventeenth centuries the reading of Archimedes illuminated the revitalization of mathematics, and later of physics. It is no exaggeration to say that, intersecting the reconstitution of an essential Platonism, for example that of Galileo ('The world is written in a mathematical language'), the writings of Archimedes served in their own right to instruct numerous generations of scientists. This gap of almost twenty centuries is cause for thought and chimes with what I said in the preface: every truth is eternal; of no truth can it be said, under the pretext that its historical world has disintegrated, that it is lost forever. That which suspends the consequences of a truth cannot simply amount to a change in the rules of appearing. An act is needed, of denial or occultation. And this act is always captive to a subjective figure. But what an act has done in the world, what a subjective figure has engineered, can be undone in another world by another act, which articulates another figure. Galileo's production in physics, or the production of Pascal or Fermat in mathematics, inscribe into the textual body that bears the trace of the new an entire reactivation, an entire updating to the present of this denied and occulted Archimedes, of whom there only remained, like inalterable objects, some opaque jottings. Therefore we will say that every faithful subject can also reincorporate into the eventual present the fragment of truth whose bygone present had sunk under the bar of occultation. It is this reincorporation that we call resurrection. What we are dealing with is a supplementary destination of subjective forms.

With regard to every genuine present, one can rightfully hope that a new present, by activating de-occultation, will make that present's lost radiance appear at the salvific surface of a body.

Accordingly, the complete schema of figures and destinations is this:

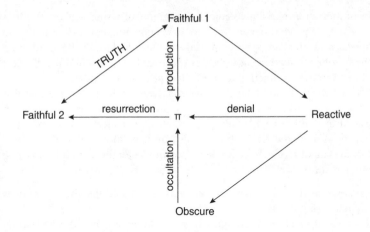

Taken in its entirety, the schema of figures and destinations is thus a circulation of the present, which is to say an empirical historicization of the eternity of truths.

6. THE FINAL QUESTION

There is one point in all of this that remains entirely to be elucidated: the body. Employed twice, as erased body (faithful form) and as full body (obscure form), the body remains an enigma. We fully understand that within appearing it is that which bears and exhibits the subjective formalism. How it bears it is not the question. It can do so as the active natural unconscious of the trace (faithful subject), at the furthest reaches of its reactive negation (reactive subject) or under the effect of a violent negation (obscure subject). But what a body is, that is something which remains to be settled. Of course, like everything that is, a body is certainly a multiple. But we cannot rest content with this weak determination. The attributes of a body-of-truth must be capable of serving as the basis for thinking the visibility of the True in the manifestness of a world, point by point. Furthermore, in order to produce this visibility, there must exist traits of separation, cohesion, synthetic unity, in short, organicity. For the time being, however, we do not have the faintest idea of how such traits could exist and be thinkable. We should add that with regard to this point, the spontaneous conception of democratic materialism (a body is the living institution of a marketable enjoyment and/or of a spectacular suffering) is of no help whatsoever. Such a conception immediately flattens the appearing of the body onto empirical and individual forms. It ignores both the ontological dimension of bodies (pure multiplicities) and their logical dimension (transcendental cohesion of appearing-in-a-world).

It is clear that the materialist dialectic, when it thinks a subjectivizable body, refers only in exceptional cases to the form of an animal body, to an organism endowed with biological identity. A subjectivizable body can equally well be the army of Spartacus, the semantics of a poem, the historical state of an algebraic problem. . . Our idea of the subject is anything but 'bio-subjective'. But in every case we must be able to think:

– the compatibility between the elements of the multiple that this body is in its being;
– the synthetic unity through which this multiple, unified in appearing (or as a 'worldly' phenomenon), is also unified in its being;
– the appropriateness of the parts of the body for the treatment of such and such a point (and, while we're at it, what a point is);
– the local efficacy of the body's organs.

Let's reiterate these criteria for our canonical example:

– In the world 'Rome in the first century BC', how do the slaves in revolt manage to put together an army?
– What is the new principle of command whereby this army can be designated as the 'army of Spartacus' (and of some others)?
– How are the specialized detachments of this army immanently organized?
– What are the strengths and weaknesses of the military body of the slaves, point by point?

Obviously, in order to find formal (and not empirical) answers to these questions we must establish the *logic* of the body: rules of compatibility among its elements, real synthesis exhibited in appearing, dominant terms, efficacious parts or organs. . .

But what is logic in an ontology of multiplicities? And how can logic envelop the real change instigated by an event? It is not difficult to understand why a long series of intervening steps is needed in order to answer this question. Nothing less is required of us than establishing what a contemporary Greater Logic can be.

Before immersing ourselves in this task, and passing some new and intricate philosophical milestones, it is worth outlining those facets of a subject that pertain to the typical modes of a truth-procedure. In so doing we link back to arguments we have already made, especially in *Being and Event*.

7. TRUTH-PROCEDURES AND FIGURES OF THE SUBJECT

The formal character of the theory of the subject entails that it does not qualify its terms, save through the didactic detour of examples. Such qualification depends on the singularity of the world, on the event that perturbs this world's transcendental laws, on the observable unruliness in the appearance of objects, on the nature of the trace wherein the vanished event endures and, finally, on what is capable of incorporating itself into the present under the sign of this trace. As we know, all of this makes up a truth-procedure, which is activated in its becoming by a subject, that is by a body behaving as the support for a formalism. Subjective formalism is always invested in a world, in the sense that, borne by a real body, it proceeds according to the inaugural determinations of a truth. A complete classification of subjective formalisms therefore requires, if at all possible, a classification of the types of truth, and not just the classification, which we have constructed, of the figures of the subject. For example, once we know that ε is an egalitarian maxim ('Like everybody else has a right to do, we slaves want to and can return home') and that C is a body of combat (the army of Spartacus), we grasp the idea that the faithful subject of this episode is of a political nature. In order to be completely certain of this we need to see from what angle the procedure inscribes itself into the world of the Roman Republic. It becomes rapidly clear that what is at stake is the maximal tension between, on the one hand, the exposition of people's life—in this instance the slaves and the affirmative thoughts that they manage to formulate—and, on the other, the state, whose power has no particular regard for this kind of affirmation. This distance between the power of the state and people's possible affirmative thinking possesses the characteristic of being errant or without measure.

It will be easier to understand this if we refer to that dimension of the state represented by the contemporary capitalist economy. Everybody knows that one must bend before its laws and its inflexible power (one must be 'realist' and 'modern', and 'make reforms', meaning: destroy public services and position everything within the circuits of Capital), but it is also clear that this notorious power is devoid of any fixed measure. It is like a superpower without a concept. We could say that the world in which there appears such a power (the state)—a measureless power which is infinitely distant from any affirmative capacity of the mass of people— is a world in which political sites can exist. If it is of a political type, an event-site (whose complete theory will be presented in Book V) is a local disruption of the relation between the mass of people and the state. What endures from such a site is a trace, a fixed measure of the power of the state, a halting-point (for thought) to the errant character of this power. If the world we start from is indeed the gap between simple exposition or presentation (let's say a multiple A) and a statist representation (let's say St (A)), whose superpower with regard to A is measureless, and if the event has as its trace a fixed measure of this superpower, say:

$$(\text{Pow } (\text{St } (A)) = a)$$

then every body referred to ε is the bearer of a political subjective formalism. This is obviously the case in the example of Spartacus. The initial world, that of the stables of gladiators, organizes the deliberate and gratuitous (we are speaking of games, after all) sacrifice of the lives of slaves in the name of the City. With regard to what the gladiators can think (beyond their 'profession'), the public power that licences such sacrifices is placed at an incommensurable distance. The revolt of Spartacus and his friends leaves as its trace the fact that this power is measurable and indeed measured: one can dare to confront Roman legions and triumph over them. This lies at the origin of the way in which the different subjective figures that constitute themselves in Italy between 73 and 71 BC are qualified politically: the faithful subject, borne by the army of Spartacus; the reactive subject, borne by the immense mass of conservative slaves; the obscure subject, placed under the murderous sign of the City and her gods, crucifying thousands of the vanquished so that even the memory of the present which was created over the course of two years by the slaves' uprising be abolished.

The resurrection of this present—as enacted by Rosa Luxemburg, Howard Fast and so many other activists of the communist movement— is itself also political. Of course, it reincorporates what the old obscure subject had occulted. But it can only do this under the condition of a new egalitarian maxim, created for eternity in the bourgeois world of the nineteenth century. This maxim is: 'Proletarians of the world, unite!'

It is not my intention here to go into the (often complex) details pertaining to the typology of truth-procedures and the intersection of this typology with that of the figures of the subject. I have done so—doubtless with varying degrees of success (I did not yet have access to a Greater Logic)—for artistic truths in my *Handbook of Inaesthetics* (original, 1998), political truths in *Metapolitics* (1998), amorous truths in *Conditions* (1992), mathematical or ontological truths in *Court traité d'ontologie transitoire* (1998; English translation, *Briefings on Existence*) and *Number and Numbers* (1990).

A preliminary remark is warranted about the contingency of types of truths. A truth-procedure has nothing to do with the limits of the human species, our 'consciousness', our 'finitude', our 'faculties' and other determinations of democratic materialism. If we think such a procedure in terms of its formal determinations alone—in the same way that we think the laws of the material world through mathematical formalism—we find sequences of signs (A, ε, C, π) and various relations $(-, /, \Rightarrow, \neg, =)$, arranged in a productive or counter-productive manner, without ever needing to pass through human 'lived experience'. In fact, a truth is that by which 'we', of the human species, are committed to a trans-specific procedure, a procedure which opens us to the possibility of being Immortals. A truth is thus undoubtedly an experience of the inhuman. Nevertheless, the fact that it is from 'our' point of view that (in philosophy) the theory of truths and subjective figures is formulated comes at a price: we cannot know if the types of truths that we experience are the only possible ones. Either other species, unknown to us, or even our own species, in another phase of its history (for instance, as transformed by genetic engineering), could perhaps have access to types of truths of which we have no idea, and not even an image.

The fact is that today—and on this point things haven't budged since Plato—we only know four types of truths: science (mathematics and physics), love, politics and the arts. We can compare this situation to Spinoza's statement about the attributes of Substance (the 'expressions' of God): without doubt, Spinoza says, there is an infinity of attributes, but we humans know only two, thought and extension. For our part, we will say that there are perhaps an infinity of types of truths but we humans only know four.

But we do truly know them. So that even if some typical expressions of the true evade us, our relation to truths is absolute. If, as is appropriate and as has always been done, we call 'Immortal' that which attains absolutely to some truth, 'we', of the human species, have the power to be Immortals.

This power is in no way undermined by the fact that there may be other means, unknown to us, of becoming Immortals.

8. TYPOLOGY

Let us now consider, very concisely, the classificatory articulations of the four types of truths in their relation to the figures of the subject. In every case, the faithful subject is nothing but the activation of the present of the truth under consideration. Therefore it has no name other than that of the procedure itself. The other figures receive particular names, depending on the procedures.

a. Political subjects. We have already discussed the gist of this point: the world exposes a variant of the gap between the state and the affirmative capacity of the mass of people, between A (presentation) and St (A) (representation). The superpower of St (A) is errant. The event fixes it: $\varepsilon \Rightarrow$ {St $(A) = a$}. A body comes to be constructed under the injunction of ε, which always takes the form of an organization. Articulated point by point, the subjectivated body permits the production of a present, which we can call, to borrow a concept from Sylvain Lazarus, a 'historical mode of politics'. Empirically speaking, this is a political sequence (73–71 BC for Spartacus, 1905–17 for Bolshevism, 1792–94 for the Jacobins, 1965–68 for the Cultural Revolution in China. . .).

The reactive subject carries the reactionary inventions of the sequence (the new form of the resistance to the new) into the heart of the people [*le peuple*] or of people in general [*les gens*]. For a long time, this has taken the name of *reaction*. The names of reaction are sometimes typical of the sequence, for instance 'Thermidorian' for the French Revolution, or 'modern revisionists' for the Chinese Cultural Revolution.

The obscure subject engineers the destruction of the body: the appropriate word is *fascism*, in a broader sense than the fascism of the thirties. One will speak of generic fascism to describe the destruction of the organized body through which the construction of the present (of the sequence) had previously passed.

The line of analysis of the other procedures proceeds in the same way: singularity of the world, event, trace, body, production, reactive subject, obscure subject.

b. Artistic subjects. In the case of artistic truths, the world exhibits a singular form of tension between the intensity of the sensible and the tranquillity of form. The event is a break in the established regime of this tension. The trace ε of this break is to be found in the fact that what seemed to partake of the formless is grasped as form, whether globally (cubism in 1912–13) or through a local excess (baroque distortions from Tintoretto to Caravaggio, passing through El Greco). The formula would therefore be of the following type: $\neg f \Rightarrow f$. A body comes to be constituted under the sign of ε; this body is a set of works, of effective realizations which treat, point by point, the consequences of the new capacity to inform the sensible, constituting within the visible something akin to a school. The production of the present is that of an artistic configuration (serialism in music after Webern, the classical style between Haydn and Beethoven, or lyrical montage in cinema, from Griffith to Welles, passing through Murnau, Eisenstein and Stroheim).

From the interior of a configuration, the reactive subject organizes the denial of that configuration's formal novelty, treating it as a simple de-formation of admitted forms, rather than as a dynamic broadening of in-formation [*mise en forme*]. It is a mixture of conservatism and partial imitation, as in all the impressionists of the twentieth century or the cubists of the thirties; this mixture will be referred to as *academicism*, noting that every new configuration is accompanied by a new academicism.

The obscure subject aims at the destruction of the works that comprise the body of the faithful artistic subject, which it perceives as a formless abomination and wishes to destroy in the name of its fiction of the sublime Body, the Body of the divine or of purity. We go from the pagan statues hammered by the Christians to the gigantic Buddhas blown up by the Taliban, via the Nazi auto-da-fes (against 'degenerate' art) and, more inconspicuously, the disappearance into storage facilities of what has fallen out of fashion. The obscure subject is essentially *iconoclastic*.

c. Amorous subjects. The world of an amorous truth makes appear an absolute Two, a profound incompatibility, an energetic separation. Its formula would be $m \perp f$: there is no relation between the sexes. Usually, the sexes are like two different species (this is after all Lacan's expression). The event (the amorous encounter) triggers the upsurge of a scene of the Two, encapsulated in the statement that these two species have something in common, a 'universal object' in which they both participate. We could say that in this case the statement ε is: 'There exists u such that m and f

73

participate in u'. Or, more formally, $(\exists u)\ [u \leq f$ and $u \leq m]$. However, no one knows what u is, only its existence is affirmed—this is the famous and manifest contingency of the amorous encounter. The body which comes to be constituted is thus a bi-sexed body, tied together by the enigmatic u. This body can be referred to as *couple*, provided we unburden this notion from any legal connotation. The production is that of an *enchanted existence* in which the truth of the Two is fulfilled in an asocial fashion.

Rooting itself in the possibilities of enchanted existence, the reactive subject works towards their abstract legalization, their reduction to routine, their submission to guarantees and contracts. Its tendency is to reduce the pure present of love to the mutilated present of the family. The most common name of this subject, through which the couple of the infinite power of the Two becomes familialist, is *conjugality*.

The obscure subject submits love to the fatal ordeal of a single fusional Body, an absolute knowledge of all things. It rejects the idea that the $m \perp f$ disjunction is only undermined by the object u, by the encounter. It demands an integrated originary destiny and consequently can only see a future for love in the chronic extortion of a detailed allegiance, a perpetual confession. Its vision of love is a *destined* one. Beyond conjugality, which it instrumentalizes (like the obscure subject always does with respect to the reactive subject), it institutes a deadly possessive reciprocity. Following *Tristan and Isolde*, Wagner's decisive poem on the obscure subject of love, which in the name of a fictive body turns the enchanted present into night, we can call this subject *fusion*.

d. Scientific subjects. A world of science is the pure exposition of appearing as such, posited, not in its givenness, but in its schema (in the laws or formulas of being-there). The only thing which testifies that this exposition has been attained is the fact that the concepts in which it is set out are mathematizable. 'Mathematizable' means submitted to the literal power of inferences, and therefore entirely indifferent to naturalness as well as to the multiplicity of languages. This criterion is self-evident, if we recall that mathematics is the exposition of being qua being, and therefore of *that which* comes to appear. Accordingly, every real thinking of appearing, by grasping it in the pure being of its appearing, amounts to extending to appearing the (mathematical) modalities of the thinking of being.

We could say that a relevant world for the sciences is given by a certain border between what is already subjected to literal inferences (and to the artificial setups of experimentation, which are machinic literalities) and what seems recalcitrant to them. An event is a sudden general displacement of this border, and the trace retains this displacement in the following form: an abstract disposition of the world, say **m**, which was like the non-subjected ground of literalization, emerges into symbolic transparency. It is impossible to conceal the patent kinship with the play of traces in art: the trace of a scientific event is of the form $\neg\, l(\mathbf{m}) \Rightarrow l(\mathbf{m})$. This is usually clouded by the fact that in art what is at stake is the sensible and the variance of its forms, while in science it is the intelligibility of the world and the invariance of its equations. Science thereby proves to be the reverse of art, which explains the spectacular isomorphism between their evental traces.

The body that is constituted to sustain, after the upsurge of ε, the consequences of a mathematico-experimental modification, takes the name of *results* (principles, laws, theorems . . .), whose consistent entanglement exposes within appearing everything that gathers around ε . The complete present which is engendered, point by point (difficulty by difficulty), by the faithful subject whose formalism is borne by the consistency of the initial results, is commonly named a (new) *theory*.

From the interior of the movement of theory, the reactive subject proposes the didactic alignment of this movement onto the previous principles, in the guise of a fortuitous complement. The reactive subject filters the incorporation of becoming into the present of science according to the epistemological grids of transmission, which it has inherited from the pre-evental period. That is why this subject can take the name of *pedagogism*: it believes it can reduce the new to the continuation of the old. A particular form of pedagogism, which conforms to the spirit of democratic materialism, is the accretion of results laid out on the same plane in accordance with the old empiricist concept of result, so that the absence of discrimination renders the present illegible. What is thereby proposed is an atonic exposition of the sciences, whose real norm, in the final analysis, cannot be any other than that of the profits which are expected of them (their lucrative 'applications').

The obscure subject aims to ruin the body of the sciences through the general appeal to a humanist fetish (or a religious one: it's the same thing) whose exigencies scientific abstraction would have obliterated. The disintegration of the components of the faithful subject is carried out here by incorporating questions devoid of any scientific meaning, entirely heterogeneous questions like ones regarding the 'morality' of such and such a result, or the 'sense of humanity' that we would need to reinject into theories, laws and the control of their consequences. Since science is a particularly inhuman truth-procedure, this kind of summons—armed with redoubtable ethics committees appointed by the state—can only aim at the decomposition of statements and the ruin of the literal or experimental bodies that bear them. This surveillance of the sciences by the priests of the day has always received the very appropriate name of *obscurantism*.

Two final considerations.

First of all, the global production of the faithful subject of the four types of truths, or the name of their present (sequence, configuration, enchantment and theory) must not lead us to lose sight of the local signs of this present, the immediate and immanent experience that one is participating, be it in an elementary fashion, in the becoming of a truth, in a creative subject-body. In their content, these signs are new intra-worldly relations; in their anthropological form, they are affects. It is thus that a political sequence signals its existence point by point through an *enthusiasm* for a new maxim of equality; art by the *pleasure* of a new perceptual intensity; love by the *happiness* of a new existential intensity; science by the *joy* of new enlightenment.

The fourth destination, resurrection, is itself also singularized by its truth-content. In politics, resurrection brings to light the egalitarian invariants of every sequence, what some time ago I called, in *De l'idéologie* (Maspero, 1976), *communist invariants*. In art, it authorizes the explosive (and creative) forms of *neo-classicism*: the imitation of the Ancients in French tragedy; the 'Romanity' of David in painting; Berlioz's return to Gluck; the lessons drawn by Ravel from the clavicembalists of the eighteenth century; the cosmological aim, reminiscent of Lucretius, of Guyotat's finest books; and so on. In love, resurrection takes the form of a second encounter, of an enchantment recaptured at the point in which it had been obscured, where routine and possession had obliterated it. This is the whole subject, admirably registered by Stanley Cavell, of the 'comedies of re-marriage' in the American cinema of the forties. Finally, in the sciences, it is always in the midst of a renaissance that the subtle theories which a scholastic approach had rendered inoperative are reincorporated.

We can summarize this entire elliptical trajectory in two tables, which themselves remain elliptical.

Table 1.1: Truth procedures and their singular activation

TRUTHS	ONTOLOGICAL GROUND (A)	EVENTAL TRACE (ε)	BODY ($\cent$)	(LOCAL) PRESENT	AFFECT	(GLOBAL) PRESENT (π)
Politics	State and people (representation and presentation) $A < \mathrm{St}\,(A)$	Fixation of the superpower of the state $\varepsilon \Rightarrow (\mathrm{St}\,(A) = a)$	Organization	New egalitarian maxim	Enthusiasm	Sequence
Arts	Sensible intensity and tranquillity of forms $S \leftrightarrow f$	What was formless can become form $\neg f \to f$	Work	New perceptual intensity	Pleasure	Configuration
Love	Sexed disjunction $m \perp f$	Indeterminate object (encounter) $(\exists u)[m \leq u \text{ and } f \leq u]$	(Bi-sexed) couple	New existential intensity	Happiness	Enchantment
Science	Boundary between the world grasped or not grasped by the letter $\mathrm{l}(\mathbf{m}) \mid \neg \mathrm{l}(\mathbf{m})$	What rebelled against the letter submits itself to it $\neg \mathrm{l}(\mathbf{m}) \to \mathrm{l}(\mathbf{m})$	Result (law, theory, principles ...)	New enlightenment	Joy	Theory

Table 1.2: Figures and destinations of the subject, crossed with types of truths

	POLITICS	ARTS	LOVE	SCIENCE
Denial	Reaction	Academicism	Conjugality	Pedagogism
Occultation	Fascism	Iconoclasm	Possessive fusion	Obscurantism
Resurrection	Communist invariants	Neo-classicism	Second encounter	Renaissance

Note: The faithful subjective figure motivates the connections in Table 1.1, whose destination is the production of the present. We recall here the three other subjective destinations: denial (reactive subject), occultation (obscure subject), resurrection (faithful subject 2).

SCHOLIUM
A Musical Variant of the Metaphysics of the Subject

Having laid out the metaphysics of the subject, we can now offer a distilled, if slightly altered, version of it.

We begin directly with the underlying ontological components: world and event—the latter breaking with the presentational logic of the former. The subjective form is then assigned to a localization in being which is ambiguous. On the one hand, the subject is only a set of the world's elements, and therefore an object in the scene on which the world presents multiplicities; on the other, the subject orients this object—in terms of the effects it is capable of producing—in a direction that stems from an event. The subject can therefore be said to be the only known form of a conceivable 'compromise' between the phenomenal persistence of a world and its eventual rearrangement.

We will call 'body' the worldly dimension of the subject and 'trace' that which, on the basis of the event, determines the active orientation of the body. A subject is therefore a formal synthesis between the statics of the body and its dynamics, between its composition and its effectuation.

The thirteen points that follow organize these givens.

1. A subject is an indirect and creative relation between an event and a world.

Let us choose as a 'world' German music at the end of the nineteenth century and the beginning of the twentieth: the final effects of Wagner—suspended between virtuoso burlesque and exaggeratedly sublime adagios—in Mahler's symphonies and lieder, some passages in Bruckner's symphonies, Richard Strauss before his neo-classical turn, the early Schönberg (*Gurrelieder*, or *Pelleas und Mélisande*, or *Transfigured Night*), the very first Korngold. . . The event is the Schönberg-event, namely that which breaks the history of music in two by affirming the possibility of a sonic world no longer ruled by the tonal system. This event is as laborious as it is radical, taking nearly twenty years to affirm itself and disappear. We pass in effect from the atonality of his *String Quartet no. 2* (1908) to the organized serialism of *Variations for Orchestra* (1926), via the systematic dodecaphonism of the *5 Pieces for Piano* (1923). All this time was required simply for the painful opening of a new music-world, about which Schönberg wrote that it would assure 'the supremacy of German music for the next 100 years'.

2. In the context of a becoming-subject, the event (whose entire being lies in disappearing) is represented by a trace; the world (which as such does not allow for any subject) is represented by a body.

Literally, the trace will be what allows itself to be extracted from Schönberg's pieces as an abstract formula of organization for the twelve constitutive tones. In place of the system of scales and of the fundamental harmonies of a tonality, there will be the free choice of a succession of distinct notes, fixing the order in which these notes should appear or be combined, a succession that is called a series. The serial organization of the twelve sounds is also named 'dodecaphonism' to indicate that the twelve tones of the old chromatic scale (C, $C\sharp$, D, $D\sharp$, E, F, $F\sharp$, G, $G\sharp$, A, $A\sharp$, B) are no longer hierarchically ordered by tonal construction and the laws of classical harmony. Instead, they are treated equally, according to a principle of succession which is chosen as the underlying structure for a given work. This serial organization refers the notes back to their internal organization alone, to their reciprocal relations in a determinate sonic space. As Schönberg puts it, the musician works with 'twelve notes that only relate to one another'.

But the trace of the event is not identical to the dodecaphonic or serial technique. As is almost always the case, it consists of a statement in the form of a prescription, of which technique is one consequence (among others). In this instance, the statement would be: 'An organization of sounds may exist which is capable of defining a musical universe on a basis which is entirely subtracted from classical tonality'. The body is the effective existence of musical pieces, of works that are written and performed, and which attempt to construct a universe conforming to the imperative harboured by the trace.

3. A subject is the general orientation of the effects of the body in conformity with the demands of the trace. It is therefore the form-in-trace of the effects of the body.

Our subject will be the becoming of a dodecaphonic or serial music, that is of a music that legislates over musical parameters—and first of all over the permissible succession of notes—on the basis of rules unrelated to the permissible harmonies of tonality or the academic progressions of modulation. What is at stake here, under the name of 'subject', is the history of a new form, as it is incorporated in works.

4. The real of a subject resides in the consequences (consequences in a world) of the relation, which constitutes this subject, between a trace and a body.

The history of serial music between Schönberg's *Variations for Orchestra* (1926) and, let's say, the first version of Pierre Boulez's *Répons* (1981) is not an anarchic history. It treats a sequence of problems, comes up against obstacles ('points', of which more below), extends its domain, fights against enemies. This history is coextensive with the existence of a subject (often bizarrely named 'contemporary music'). It realizes a system of consequences of the initial given: a trace (a new imperative for the musical organization of sounds) formally inscribed in a body (the actual suite of works). If it became saturated within nearly a half-century, this is not because it failed; it is because every subject, albeit internally infinite, constitutes a sequence whose temporal limits can be fixed after the fact. This is also true of the new musical subject. Its possibilities are intrinsically infinite. But towards the end of the 1970s, its 'corporeal' capacities, those that could inscribe themselves in the dimension of the work, were increasingly restricted. It was no longer really possible to find 'interesting' deployments, significant mutations, local completions. It is thus that an infinite subject reaches its *finition*.

5. With regard to a given group of consequences which conform to the imperative of the trace, it practically always happens that a part of the body is available or useful, while another is passive, or even harmful. Consequently, every subjectivizable body is split (crossed out).

Within the development of 'contemporary music', that is, of the only thing that in the twentieth century merited the name of 'music'—if we grant that music is an art and not that which some minister subjects to the demands of gruelling festivals—the serial organization of pitches (the rule for the succession of notes in the chromatic scale) is a rule that easily sanctions a global form. But pitch is only one of three local characteristics of the note in a given musical universe. The two others are duration and timbre. But the serial handling of durations and timbres raises formidable problems. It becomes rapidly evident that the contemporary treatment of durations, and therefore of rhythms, passes through Stravinsky (*The Rite of Spring*) and Bartók (*Music for Strings, Percussion and Celesta*), neither of whom are incorporated in dodecaphonic or serial music. The importance of Messiaen in this whole story is also considerable (the invention and theory of 'non-retrogradable' rhythms). Now, even though he had shown, in his *Four Studies in Rhythm* (1950), that he was capable of practicing a serialism extended to all musical parameters, due to his attachment to themes and his use of classical harmony Messiaen could not be fully considered as one of the names of the subject 'serial music'. Thus the treatment of the question of rhythm follows a trajectory which does not coincide with serialism. Likewise, the question of timbre, though it is rigorously tackled by Schönberg (in his theory of the 'melody of timbres') and above all by Webern, nevertheless has pre-serial origins, especially in Debussy—in this regard a 'founding father' of the same rank as Schönberg. Between the two wars, via Varèse and again Messiaen, the question of timbre followed a complex line. Later, it also provided the grounds for the break with Boulez's 'structural' orientations and the contestation of the legacy of serialism which was carried out by the French group *L'Itinéraire* (Gérard Grisey, Michaël Levinas, Tristan Murail. . .). We can thus say that, at least in terms of some of its developments, the musical body 'serialism' found itself split between pure written form and auditory sensation. To borrow from Lacan, in today's music timbre effectively names 'that which does not stop not being written' [*ce qui ne cesse pas de ne pas s'écrire*].

6. There exist two kinds of consequences, and therefore two modalities of the subject. The first takes the form of continuous adjustments within the old world, of local adaptations of the new subject to the objects and relations of that world. The second deals with closures imposed by the world; situations where the complexity of identities and differences brutally comes down, for the subject, to the exigency of a choice between two possibilities and two alone. The first modality is an opening: it continually opens up a new possible closest to the possibilities of the old world. The second modality—which we will study in detail in Book VI—is a point. In the first case, the subject presents itself as an infinite negotiation with the world, whose structures it stretches and opens. In the second case, it presents itself both as a decision—whose localization is imposed by the impossibility of the open—and as the obligatory forcing of the possible.

If, as Berg was able to do—for example in his violin concerto, known as *To the Memory of an Angel* (1935)—you treat a series almost as a recognizable melodic segment, you make it possible for it to serve a double function within the architecture of the work: on the one hand, as a substitute for tonal modulations, it ensures the overall homogeneity of the piece; but, on the other, its recurrence can be heard as a theme, thereby reconnecting with a major principle of tonal composition. In this case, one will say that the (serial) subject opens a negotiation with the old (tonal) world. If, on the contrary, as Webern did with genius in *Variations for Orchestra* (1940), you extend the series to durations, or even timbres, so that no element is either developed or returns, and the exposition is concentrated into a few seconds, it becomes entirely impossible to identify a segment in accordance with the classical model of the theme. The new musical universe then forcefully imposes itself through an alternative: either an unprecedented musical effect persuades you that the creative event is what takes the subject to the edge of silence; or it is impossible to grasp the coherence of a construction and everything is scattered—as if the only thing that existed were a mere punctuation without text. Berg is an inspired negotiator of openings to the old world, which is why he is the most 'popular' of the three Viennese, and also the one who is capable of installing the new music in the particularly impure realm of opera. Webern is only interested in points, in the gentle forcing of what presents itself as absolutely closed, in irrevocable choice. The former incorporated himself into the subject 'serial music' in the guise of a dazzling game, a fertile transaction. The latter instead embodies within it the mystique of decision.

7. *A subject is a sequence involving continuities and discontinuities, openings and points. The 'and' incarnates itself as subject. Or again, it is em-bodied [Ou encore (en-corps)]: A subject is the conjunctive form of a body.*

It suffices to say that 'Berg' and 'Webern' are only two names for sequential components of the subject 'serial music'. Accordingly, the genius of openings (theatrical continuities) and that of points (mystical discontinuities) are both incorporated into the same subject. Were it otherwise, we wouldn't know whether the Schönberg-event really consti-tuted a caesura in the world 'tonal music at the beginning of the twentieth century', since its consequences might then reveal themselves to be too narrow or incapable of successfully treating difficult strategic points. The local antinomy of 'Berg' and 'Webern', which is internal to the subject, constitutes the essential proof of 'Schönberg'; just as, in the case of the subject that Charles Rosen has named the 'classical style', the names 'Mozart' and 'Beethoven' prove with quasi-mathematical rigour that what inaugurally presented itself under the name 'Haydn' was an event.

8. The sequential construction of a subject is easier in moments of opening, but the subject is then often a weak subject. This construction is more difficult when it is necessary to cross points; but the subject is then much sturdier.

Allow me a commonsense remark. If, like Berg, you subtly negotiate with the theatricality (or lyricism) inherited from the post-Wagnerian facet of the old world, the construction of the sequential subject 'music wrested from tonality' is easier, the public less restive and consensus more rapidly obtained. Berg's operas are today repertory classics. That the subject which is thereby deployed in the openings of the old world remains fragile can be seen from the fact that Berg gradually multiplied his concessions (the purely tonal resolutions in *Lulu* and the violin concerto) and, above all, from the fact that he did not open the way to the resolute continuation of this subject, to the unpredictable multiplication of the effects of the musical body newly installed in the world. Berg is a towering musician, but he is almost always referred to in order to justify reactive movements internal to the sequence. If on the contrary, like Webern, you work on points, and therefore on the discontinuous peaks of the becoming-subject, you are faced with considerable difficulties. For a long time, you're deemed to be an esoteric or abstract musician, but it is you who opens up the future, you in the name of whom the constructive dimension of the new sonic world will be generalized and consolidated.

9. A new world is subjectively created, point by point.

This is a variation on the theme introduced in point 8. The treatment of continuities (openings) creates, bit by bit, zones of relative indiscernibility between the effects of the subjectivized body and the 'normal' objects of the world. Ultimately these are zones of indiscernibility between the trace (which orients the body) and the body's objective or worldly composition—that is, zones where event and world are superimposed in a confused becoming. Consider those (René Leibowitz, for example) who in the 1940s thought that victory was assured, and that dodecaphonism could be 'academicized'. Only the delicate crossing, through non-negotiable decisions, of some strategic points testifies to novelty. It does so by breaking apart what academicization misrepresented as an established result. The Darmstadt generation (Boulez, Nono, Stockhausen. . .) will noisily call attention to this in the 1950s, against the Schönbergian dogma itself.

10. The generic name of a subjective construction is 'truth'.

In fact, only the serial sequence opened by the Schönberg-event pronounces the truth of the post-Wagnerian musical world of the end of the nineteenth and beginning of the twentieth century. This truth is unfolded point by point, and is not contained in any single formula. But it is possible to say that in every domain (harmony, themes, rhythms, global forms, timbres. . .) it indicates that the dominant phenomena of the old world effectuate an extensive distortion of the classical style, ultimately realizing what could be termed its structural totalization, which is also akin to an emotional saturation, an anxious and ultimately hopeless search for the effect. It follows that serial music—the truth of the classical style which has reached the saturation of its effects—is the systematic exploration, within the sonic universe, of what counts as a counter-effect. The fact that this music is so often regarded as inaudible or unlistenable is due to this genius for disappointment. No doubt, it would be pointless for it to allow to be heard once again what the old world had declared suited to the ears of the human animal. The truth of a world is not a simple object of this world, since it supplements the world with a subject in which the power of a body and the destiny of a trace intersect. How can one make the truth of the audible heard without passing through the in-audible? It is like wanting truth to be 'human', when it is its in-humanity which assures its existence.

That said, the asceticism of the serial universe has been overstated. In no way does it forbid great rhythmic, harmonic and orchestral gestures—whether they operate dramatically as counters to the techniques of effect, as in the brutal successions of *forte* and *pianissimo* in Boulez, or whether they organize the contamination of music by an unfathomable silence, as is so often the case in Webern.

The essential point to grasp is that there is no contemporary understanding of the classical style and its becoming-romantic, no eternal and therefore current truth of the musical subject initiated by the Haydn-event, which does not pass through an incorporation into the serial sequence, and therefore into the subject commonly named 'contemporary music'. Those, and they are many, who declare that they only love the classical style (or the romantic, the subject is the same) and are repelled by serial music can certainly possess a knowledge of what they love, but they remain ignorant of its truth. Is this truth barren? It's a matter of usage and continuation. It is necessary to add one's own listening, patiently, to the body of the new music. Pleasure will come, as an additional bonus. Love ('I don't really love this . . .'), which is a distinct truth-procedure, should not be taken into account. For, as Lacan reminds us with his customary bluntness, the theme of a 'love of truth' should be left to religious obscurantism and to the philosophies that lose their way within it. In order to desire our incorporation into the subject of any truth whatever, it suffices that this truth be eternal. Accordingly, through the discipline demanded by participating in a truth, the human animal will be accorded the chance—whose barrenness is of little significance—of an Immortal becoming.

11. Four affects signal the incorporation of a human animal into a subjective truth-process. The first testifies to the desire for a Great Point, a decisive discontinuity that will institute the new world in a single blow, and complete the subject. We will call it terror. The second testifies to the fear of points, the retreat before the obscurity of the discontinuous, of everything that imposes a choice without guarantee between two hypotheses. To put it otherwise, this affect signals the desire for a continuity, for a monotonous shelter. We will call it anxiety. The third affirms the acceptance of the plurality of points, of the fact that discontinuities are at once inexorable and multiform. We will call it courage. The fourth affirms the desire for the subject to be a constant intrication of points and openings. With respect to the pre-eminence of becoming-subject, it affirms the equivalence of what is continuous and negotiated, on the one hand, and of what is discontinuous and violent, on the other. These are merely subjective modalities, which depend on the construction of the subject in a world and on the capacities of the body to produce effects within it. They are not to be hierarchically ordered. War can have as much value as peace, negotiation as much as struggle, violence as much as gentleness. This affect, whereby the categories of the act are subordinated to the contingency of worlds, we will call justice.

At the beginning of the 1950s, Pierre Boulez's terrorism was promptly pilloried. It's true that he cared little for the 'French music' of the inter-war period, conceiving his role as that of a censor and condemning his adversaries to nullity. Yes, we can say that in his inflexible will to incorporate music in France into a subject that in Austria and Germany was already half a century old, Boulez didn't hesitate to introduce a certain dose of terror into his public polemics. Even his writing was not exempt from this, as witness his 1952 *Structures* (for two pianos): integral serialism, violent discursivity; the counter-effect pushed to the extreme.

The anxiety of those who, while admitting the necessity of a new subjective division and welcoming the coming power of serialism, did not want to break with the prior universe, taking for granted the existence of a single music-world, may be detected in the amusing bluster of belated advocates (Stravinsky's conversion to dodecaphonism, initiated by the ballet *Agon*, dates from 1957. . .), as well as in the negotiated constructions of a Dutilleux, the most inventive of those who continue to follow in Berg's wake (listen, for example, to the 1965 *Métaboles*). We can see that 'anxiety' is to be understood here as a creative affect, to the extent that this creation is still governed by the opening rather than by the abruptness of points.

The courage of a Webern lies in seeking out those points whose outcome the new music-world must prove itself capable of deciding in all of that world's directions. To do this, he devotes the crux of a given piece to a given point, and it is easy to see how each piece enacts a pure choice with regard to rhythms, timbres, the construction of the whole and so on. Webern's elliptical side (like Mallarmé's in poetry) stems from the fact that a work need not stretch beyond the exposition of what it decides at the point at which it has arrived.

We could say that Boulez learnt about justice, between 1950 and 1980, insofar as he acquired the power to slacken the abruptness of the construction when needed and to develop his own openings without brutally denying them through a heterogeneous point—all the while relaunching his oeuvre through concentrated decisions, when chance demands to be 'vanquished word by word'.

12. To oppose the value of courage and justice to the 'Evil' of anxiety and terror is to succumb to mere opinion. All the affects are necessary in order for the incorporation of a human animal to unfold in a subjective process, so that the grace of being Immortal may be accorded to this animal, in the discipline of a Subject and the construction of a truth.

No more than Boulez could or should have avoided a certain dose of terror in pulling so-called 'French music' from the mud, could he have had a creative future outside of an apprenticeship in justice. The creative singularity of Dutilleux derives from the invention, at the edges of the subject (at the margins of its body), of what one could call a stifled anxiety (whence the remarkable aerial radiance of his writing). Webern is nothing but courage.

'Terror!,' they will say. Not in politics, in any case, where against crimes of state we have no other recourse than human rights; nor in pure abstraction, in mathematics for example.

On the contrary. We know political terror. There is also a terror of the matheme. The fact that one impinges on living bodies while the other concerns established thoughts only allows us to infer the greater harm of the first if we hold that life, suffering and finitude are the only absolute marks of existence. That would imply that there exists no eternal truth into the construction of which the living being can incorporate itself—sometimes, it is true, at the cost of his or her life. A consistent conclusion of democratic materialism.

Without any particular joy, the materialist dialectic will work under the assumption that no political subject has yet attained the eternity of the truth which it unfolds without moments of terror. For, as Saint-Just asked: 'What do those who want neither Virtue nor Terror want?' His answer is well known: they want corruption—another name for the failure of the subject.

The materialist dialectic will also propose some remarks drawn from the history of sciences. From the 1930s, acknowledging the lag in French mathematics after the bloodbath of World War I, young geniuses like Weil, Cartan and Dieudonné undertook something like a total refoundation of the mathematical setup, integrating all the crucial creations of their time: set theory, structural algebra, topology, differential geometry, Lie algebras, etc. For at least twenty years, this gargantuan collective project, which took the name 'Bourbaki', justifiably exercised an effect of terror on the 'old' mathematics. This terror was necessary in order to incorporate two or three new generations of mathematicians into the subjective process that had been opened up on a grand scale at the end of the nineteenth century (even if anticipated by Riemann, Galois or even Gauss).

None of that which overcomes finitude in the human animal, subordinating it to the eternity of the True through its incorporation into a subject in becoming, can ever happen without anxiety, courage and justice. But, as a general rule, neither can it take place without terror.

13. *When the incorporation of a human animal is at stake, the ethics of the subject, whose other name is 'ethics of truths', comes down to this: to find point by point an order of affects which authorises the continuation of the process.*

Here we cannot but cite Beckett, from the end of *The Unnamable*. In this text, the 'character' prophesies, between dereliction and justice (Beckett will later write, in *How It Is*: 'In any case we have our being in justice I have never heard anything to the contrary'). Tears of anxiety stream down his face. He wreaks unspeakable terror on himself (the bonds between truth and terror are one of Beckett's abiding concerns). The courage of infinite speech makes the prose tremble. This 'character' can then say: 'I must go on, I can't go on, I'll go on'.

Today, the music-world is negatively defined. The classical subject and its romantic avatars are entirely saturated, and it is not the plurality of 'musics'—folklore, classicism, pop, exoticism, jazz and baroque reaction in the same festive bag—which will be able to resuscitate them. But the serial subject is equally unpromising, and has been for at least twenty years. Today's musician, delivered over to the solitude of the interval—where the old coherent world of tonality together with the hard dodecaphonic world that produced its truth are scattered into unorganized bodies and vain ceremonies—can only heroically repeat, in his very works: 'I go on, in order to think and push to their paradoxical radiance the reasons that I would have for not going on'.

Foreword to Books II, III and IV

The Greater Logic

Foreword

Books II, III and IV have in common the examination of the conditions under which multiple-being can be thought in a world, and not only in its being as such. In brief, it is a matter of determining the concepts through which we apprehend the appearing, or being-there, of any multiplicity whatever. To think the multiple as multiple is the task of pure ontology. If this task is mathematical in what concerns its effectiveness, it is philosophical in its general determination. In effect, the various strands of mathematics need not identify themselves as the ontology which they nonetheless realize historically. I took on the philosophical part of pure ontology in *Being and Event*. To think the 'worldly' multiple according to its appearing, or its localization, is the task of logic, the general theory of objects and relations. It is conceived here as a Greater Logic, which entirely subsumes the lesser linguistic and grammatical logic.

To wrest logic away from the constraint of language, propositions and predication, which is merely a derivative envelope, is no doubt one of the stakes of *Logics of Worlds*. Section 4 of Book II scrupulously demonstrates that ordinary formal logic, with its syntax and semantics, is only a special case of the (transcendental) Greater Logic which is set out herein. Having said that, this demonstration is not the principal aim of the Greater Logic. Of course, its polemical advantage lies in ruining the positive claims of the entirety of so-called 'analytic' philosophies. The principal aim, as I already indicated in the preface, remains that of making possible, through a rational theory of the logic of worlds, or theory of being-there, the comprehension of change; in particular of real change, which in Book V will receive the name of event, to contrast it with the three other forms of empirical change: modification, fact and (weak) singularity. All of this paves the way for the new theory of the body-of-truth, by means of which the materialist dialectic secures a decisive advantage over democratic materialism.

This advantage warrants the toil which—as Aristotle and Hegel have taught us—is demanded of anyone who intends to expose a Greater Logic in its immanent rationality.

The plan of our own route through logic, understood as the philosophy of being-there, is the following:

– Book II exposes the fundamental properties of the transcendental world. Following a general introduction, we proceed first in a conceptual manner (Section 1) and with the help of examples, then by discussing the presentation of being-there in Hegel's *Science of Logic* (Section 2), and finally in a more formal manner (Section 3), with the aid of some mathematized reference points. We end with two sections of unequal importance: one on the status of logic in its ordinary meaning (Section 4); the other on the definition of 'classical' worlds, a category which possesses an ontological as well as a logical meaning (Section 5).

– Book III proposes a complete doctrine of being-there, in the guise of a transcendental theory of the object. This is obviously the core of the Greater Logic, all the more so to the extent that it contains the demonstration of something like a retroactive effect of appearing on being: the fact that a multiple appears in a world entails an immanent structuration of this multiple as such. Here too the reader will find an introduction, an exemplified conceptual exposition (Section 1), a discussion of the Kantian theory of the object (Section 2), a formal exposition (Section 3). Section 4 shows that death is a dimension of appearing, and not of being. Finally, a technical appendix completes three demonstrations that had been left pending in Section 3.

– Book IV elucidates what a relation is (in a determinate world, that is with regard to a determinate transcendental). Once again, it features an introduction, a conceptual exposition, the discussion of an author (Leibniz) and a formal elucidation. An appendix provides the complete demonstration of the 'second principle' of materialism.

The Greater Logic is above all an exhaustive theory concerned with the materialist thinking of worlds, or—since 'appearing' and 'logic' are one and the same—a materialist theory of the coherence of what appears. That is why in it one will find, in Sections 1 and 3 of Book III, a 'postulate of materialism' (which states that 'Every atom of appearing is real'), and then, in Sections 1 and 3 of Book IV, a 'principle of materialism', which states that 'Every world, being ontologically closed, is also logically complete'.

To grasp the requirements of a contemporary materialism without succumbing to the siren-songs of democratic materialism is a worthy enterprise in its own sake. I spared no effort in making sure that the didactic apparatus is equal to this task. The formalisms are presented and deployed without presupposing any special expertise whatsoever. And the examples, at least two for each crucial concept, make up a baroque series of distinct worlds, which may be relished in their own right: a country landscape in autumn, Paul Dukas's opera *Ariadne and Bluebeard*, a mass demonstration at Place de la République, Hubert Robert's painting *The Bathing Pool*, the history of Quebec, the structure of a galaxy. . . We can add that in Book V, in order to think change, we will draw on Rousseau's novel *The New Heloise* and on the history of the Paris Commune. In Book VI, to think the notion of point, we will turn to Sartre's theatre, Julien Gracq's novel *The Opposing Shore* and the architectural form of Brasilia. And in Book VII, to elucidate the complex notion of subjectivizable body, we will examine a poem of Valéry, the history of algebra between Cauchy and Galois, and the birth of the Red Army in the Chinese countryside in 1927.

Thus, the courage required to traverse the arid formalisms will receive, like every true crossing of the desert, its own immanent recompense.

BOOK II

Greater Logic, 1. The Transcendental

Introduction

Book II is entirely devoted to a single concept, that of the transcendental. The word 'transcendental' is warranted here because it encapsulates my recasting, with respect to *Being and Event*, of the primitive notion of 'situation', replaced here by that of 'world'. Where the earlier book followed the thread of ontology, my current undertaking, placed under the rubric of the transcendental, unravels the thread of logic. Previously, I identified situations (worlds) with their strict multiple-neutrality. I now also envisage them as the site of the being-there of beings. In *Being and Event*, I assumed the dissemination of the indifferent multiple as the ground of all that there is, and consequently affirmed the ontological non-being of relation. Without going back on this judgment, I now show that being-there as appearing-in-a-world has a relational consistency.

I have established that 'mathematics' and 'being' are one and the same thing once we submit ourselves, as every philosophy must, to the axiom of Parmenides: it is the same to think and to be. It is now a matter of showing that 'logic' and 'appearing' are also one and the same thing. 'Transcendental' names the crucial operators of this second identity. Later, we will see that this speculative equation greatly transforms the third constitutive identity of my philosophy, the one which, under the sign of eventa chance, makes 'subject' into a simple local determination of 'truth'. It effectively obliges us to mediate this determination through an entirely original theory of the subject-body.

The first three sections of Book II follow the rule of triple exposition: conceptual (and exemplifying), historical (an author) and formal. The substance of what is presented three times can also be articulated in terms of three motifs: the necessity of a transcendental organization of worlds; the exposition of the transcendental; the question of what negation is within appearing.

Since I declare that 'logic' signifies purely and simply the cohesion of appearing, I cannot avoid confronting this assertion with the astounding fortunes of logic in its usual sense (the formal regulation of statements) among those philosophies which believed they could turn the examination of language into the centre of all thought, thereby consigning philosophy to fastidious grammatical exercises. It's no mystery that in the final analysis this is a matter of bringing philosophy into the space of university discourse, a space which conservatives of every epoch have always argued it should never have left. Today, it is also quite clear that if we allow ourselves to be intimidated, philosophy will be nothing more than a scholastic quarrel between liberal grammarians and pious phenomenologists. But when it comes to logic I do not content myself with political polemic. After all, I admire the great logicians, those whom—like Gödel, Tarski or Cohen—carried out a commendable mathematical incorporation of the inherited forms of deductive fidelity. I will also carefully establish that logic, in its usual linguistic sense, is entirely reducible to transcendental operations. This will be the object of Section 4 of this Book.

We will then see—it is the object of Section 5—that the simple consideration of transcendental structures allows us to define what a classical world is, that is a world which obeys what Aristotle already considered as a major logical principle: the excluded middle. This principle declares that, given a closed statement A, when we interpret this statement in a world we necessarily have either the truth of A or that of non-A, without any third possibility. A world for which this is the case is a classical world, which is an entirely particular 'case of world'. Without going into the details, I will show that the world of ontology, that is the mathematics of the pure multiple, is classical. In the history of thought up to the present day, this point has had truly innumerable consequences.

The 'historical' companion of this Book is Hegel, the thinker par excellence of the dialectical correlation between being and being-there, between essence and existence. We will be measuring ourselves up to his *Science of Logic*.

Let's now quickly present what is at stake in each of three themes that make up the main content of the first three sections.

1. NECESSITY OF A TRANSCENDENTAL ORGANIZATION OF THE SITUATIONS OF BEING

The first section consists of a long demonstration. It is a matter of forcing thought to accept that every situation of being—every 'world'—far from being reduced to the pure multiple (which is nonetheless its being as such) contains a *transcendental organization*.

The meaning of this expression will transpire from the demonstration itself. As in Kant, we are trying to resolve a problem of possibility. Not however 'how is science possible' or 'how are synthetic judgments a priori possible' but: how is it possible that the neutrality, inconsistency and indifferent dissemination of being-qua-being comes to consist as being-there? Or: how can the essential unbinding of multiple-being give itself as a local binding and, in the end, as the stability of worlds? Why and how are there worlds rather than chaos?

As we know, for Kant the transcendental is a subjectivated construction. With good reason, we speak of a transcendental subject, which in some sense invests the cognitive power of empirical subjects. Ever since Descartes, this is the essential trait of an *idealist* philosophy: that it calls upon the subject not as a problem but as the solution to the aporias of the One (the world is nothing but formless multiplicity, but there exists a unified *Dasein* of this world). The materialist thrust of my own thought (but also paradoxically of Hegel's, as Lenin remarked in his *Notebooks*) derives from the fact that within it the subject is a late and problematic construction, and in no way the place of the solution to a problem of possibility or unity (possibility of intuitive certainty for Descartes, of synthetic judgments a priori for Kant).

The transcendental that is at stake in this book is altogether anterior to every subjective constitution, for it is an immanent given of any situation whatever. As we shall see, it is what imposes upon every situated multiplicity the constraint of a logic, which is also the law of its appearing, or the rule in accordance with which the 'there' of being-there allows the multiple to come forth as essentially bound. That every world possesses a singular transcendental organization means that, since the thinking of being cannot on its own account for the world's manifestation, the intelligibility of this manifestation must be *made possible* by immanent operations. 'Transcendental' is the name for these operations. The final maxim can be stated as follows: with regard to the inconsistency of being, 'logic' and 'appearing' are one and the same thing.

However, it does not follow, as in Kant, that being-in-itself is unknowable. On the contrary, it is absolutely knowable, or even known (historically-existing mathematics). But this knowledge of being (*onto*-logy) does not entail that of appearing (onto-*logy*). It is this disjunction which the arguments in this section attempt to force. The stages which develop this parameter have as their point of departure the impossibility of determining a being of the Whole, and finally the thesis according to which *there is no* Whole. Contrary to a Heideggerian proposition, it is irrational to evoke 'beings-as-a-whole'. It follows that every singular being [*étant*] is only manifested in its being [*être*] locally: the appearing of the being of beings [*l'être de l'étant*] is being-there. It is this necessity of the 'there' which, for a being thought in its multiple-being, entails a transcendental constitution (without subject). This constitution authorizes us to think the being as localized, to include the 'there' in the thinking of being—something that the mathematical (ontological) theory of the pure multiple, despite conveying the *whole* being of the being, does not allow. In what follows, we will call *universe* the (empty) concept of a being of the Whole. We will call *world* a 'complete' situation of being (this will be gradually elucidated). Obviously, since we show that *there is no* universe, it belongs to the essence of the world that there are several worlds, since if there were only one it would be the universe.

2. EXPOSITION OF THE TRANSCENDENTAL

'Exposition of the transcendental' signifies the description of the logical operators capable of lending coherence to appearing 'in' one of the worlds in which multiples come to be.

I write 'in' a world (in quotation marks) to indicate that we are dealing with a metaphor for the localization of multiples. As a situation of being, a world is not an empty place—akin to Newton's space—which multiple beings would come to inhabit. For a world is nothing but a logic of being-there, and it is identified with the singularity of this logic. A world articulates the cohesion of multiples around a structured operator (the transcendental).

At the core of transcendental questions lies the evaluation of the degrees of identity or difference between a multiple and itself, or between a being-there and other beings. The transcendental must therefore make possible the 'more' and the 'less'. There must exist values of identity which indicate, for a given world, to what extent a multiple-being is identical to itself or to some other being of the same world. This clearly requires that the transcendental possess an order-structure.

The other operations necessary to the cohesion of multiples in a world constitute a minimal phenomenology of abstract appearing, by which we mean what is conceptually required for appearing to be bound. We are speaking here of any appearing whatsoever in any world whatsoever. In other words, our operational phenomenology identifies the condition of possibility for the worldliness of a world, or the logic of the localization for the being-there of any being whatever.

It is very striking that this phenomenology is absolutely complete with only three operations, bound together by a simple axiomatic:

  *a.*A minimum of appearance is given.
  *b.*The possibility of conjoining the values of appearance of two multiples (and therefore of any finite number of multiples).
  *c.*The possibility of globally synthesizing the values of appearance of any number of multiples, even if there is an infinity of them.

When we say that the description of these operations makes up a complete phenomenology, we mean that the transcendental determination of the minimum, the conjunction and the envelope (or synthesis) provides everything that is needed for being-there to consist as a world.

Upon reflection, this economy of means is natural. Appearing is undoubtedly bound (and not chaotic) if I can, first, set out degrees of appearance on the basis of non-appearance (minimum); second, know what two multiples do or do not have in common when they co-appear (conjunction); and finally, if I am capable of globalising appearance in such a way that it makes sense to speak, in a given world, of a region of appearing (envelope). The form of appearing is accordingly homogeneous, so that the reciprocity between logic and appearing, and between consistency and being-there, is well-founded.

The exposition of the transcendental will thus proceed through three successive moments. The first forces upon thought the existence, in the transcendental, of a minimum. The second (finite operational domain) fixes the laws relative to the conjunction of two beings-there. Finally, the third (infinite operational domain) posits the existence of an envelope for every region of the world. A supplementary step will concern not the operations that lend consistency to appearing, but rather the consistent appearing of these operations themselves.

Keeping in mind the exceptional importance of the notion of causal bond, or necessity, in the transcendental tradition, we will conclude by showing that it is possible to derive from the three fundamental operations a measure of the correlation in a given world between the appearing of a multiple and that of another multiple. We will call this correlation dependence. In terms of the logical status of appearing, dependence interprets in a world the logical relation of implication.

3. THE ORIGIN OF NEGATION

In every transcendental theory of being-there, the question of negation is very complex. This is testified to in particular by the very dense passage that Kant devotes to the conceptualization of the 'nothing' in the *Critique of Pure Reason*, at the very end of the 'Transcendental Analytic'. Kant claims that as such the question 'is not in itself especially indispensable'. In effect, he makes do with a page and a half, opening without delay onto the Dialectic, after an absolutely impenetrable formula: 'Negation as well as the mere form of intuition are, without something real, not objects'. This suggests that appearing or phenomenality—in which everything presents itself to intuition under the form of the object—knows no negation. But the question is really far more complex. Kant has little difficulty in identifying negation on the side of the concept: there is the 'empty concept without object', which is to say that which, albeit coherent for thought, does not relate to any intuitable object, for example, the Kantian notion of the noumenon. And there is the concept that contradicts itself, like the square circle, which makes any object impossible. In these two cases, the concept points to the absence of any object: nothing appears, there is nothing there. Or, as in the case of the word 'noumenon', nothing is there but being without being-there, being out of the world. Except that Kant also wishes to extend the question of the negative to intuition, which is where things get rather awkward. He isolates the 'pure form of intuition' in its empty exercise, or designated as empty, which is to say 'without object'. This goes for the a priori forms of sensibility: time and space. Must we accord to these forms a trans-phenomenal real? Does Kant want to say that the forms of objectivity are active 'nothings'? This path is very obscure and it leads back to the theory of the faculties, to the transcendental imagination in particular. What's more, this form of the nothing is named '*ens imaginarium*'. Symmetrically—and as far as our question is concerned decisively—he posits that there are 'objects empty of a concept', that is objects designated by the concept of their lack alone. Here it seems we are touching on the negation of a real, on that which in appearing displays the negative. Moreover, in order to designate this case, Kant writes: 'Reality is *something*, negation is *nothing*, namely, a concept of the absence of an object'. The goal seems to have been attained: there is the nothing of what is, and the negative appears as a derivative intuition.

Unfortunately, Kant's concrete references are entirely disappointing: shadow, cold. . . Further on, he will unconvincingly declare: 'If light has not been given to the senses, one cannot represent darkness to oneself'. Ultimately, this subtle classification only results in the traditional paralogisms of sensation. Why would cold be more negative than heat, night than day? It seems that Kant fails to set out the appearing of the nothing under the category of '*nihil privativum*' or of 'object empty of concept'. For real lack cannot be illustrated by cold or shadow, which are themselves nothing but transcendental degrees applied to neutral objects: temperature and luminosity. The fundamental reason for this difficulty rests on the fact that appearing is in itself an affirmation, the affirmation of being-there. But how then could one define the negation of anything at all from within appearing? Of course, it is possible to think the non-apparent in a determinate world. That is indeed the aim of the first transcendental operation (the minimum). The underlying affirmation is that of a multiple, of which the only thing that will be said is that its degree of appearance in a world has a nil transcendental value. In other words, we support the negation of appearance on the being of a multiple. Once it has been ontologically identified, thanks to the order of transcendental degrees we can think the non-appearance of this multiple in such and such a world. The negation of being-there rests on the affirmative identification of being qua being.

But the non-apparent is not the apparent negation of the apparent. What we are concerned with here is the difficulty—clearly recognized by Kant himself—*of making negation appear*. Truth be told, this question has haunted philosophy from its very origins. On the basis of the impossibility for negation to come into the light of appearing, Parmenides concluded that it was a mere fiction which thought had to turn away from. Plato takes his cue from an entirely opposite fact: there is an appearing of the negative, which is nothing other than the sophist, or the lie, or Gorgias himself, with his treatise on non-being. It is therefore necessary to posit a category capable of grasping the being-there of negation, and not only, as in the

Parmenidean prohibition, the non-being-there of non-being. This may be called the first transcendental inquiry in the history of thought, culminating with the introduction, in *The Sophist*, of the Idea of the Other. However, Plato still leaves in abeyance the Other's proper mode of appearance. What I mean to say is that although he establishes that the Other allows us to think that non-being can appear, he says nothing about the way in which this appearance is effective. How does the Other, determined as a category, support the entry into appearing, not only of alterity (two different truths, for example), but of negation (the false and the true)? I can clearly see how the Other justifies the thought that this does not appear in the same way as that. A very dense passage from the *Timaeus*—concerning the fabrication by the demiurge of the soul of the world—bears on this point:

> From the substance which is indivisible and unchangeable, and from that kind of being which can be divided among bodies, he compounded a third and intermediate kind of substance, comprising the nature of the Same and that of the Other. And thus he formed it, between the indivisible element of these two realities and the divisible substance of bodies. Then, taking the three substances, he mingled them all into one form, harmonising by force the reluctant and unsociable nature of the Other into the Same. When he had mingled them with the intermediate kind of being and out of three made one, he again divided this whole into as many portions as was fitting, each portion being a compound of the Same, the Other, and the aforementioned third substance.

This text, in the form of a narration (of what, from the beginning of the *Timaeus*, Plato calls a 'plausible fable'), expressly deals with the origin of the being-there of negation. More precisely, of negation such as it is originally immanent to the soul of the world. The demiurge effectively composes this soul with a substance that comprises the Same and the Other, and which interposes itself between the indivisibility of Ideas (Idea of the Same and Idea of the Other) and the divisibility of bodies. We are at the heart of an investigation of being-there. The mixture of Same and Other (of affirmation and negation) is indeed the transcendental structure which, enabling the articulation of the indivisible and the divisible, will prepare the soul for a cosmic government of being-there.

The question then becomes: how are the Same and the Other conjoined in the substance of the soul of the world? This time, Plato's answer is disappointing: the demiurge, who like us recognizes that the Other 'reluctantly' mixes with the Same, acts 'by force'. Consequently, the origin of being-there remains assigned to an irrational moment of the narration. Plato's effort, as is often the case, only results in a fable which tells us that while the 'ontological' problem is soluble (how can we think that non-being is?), the 'phenomenological' problem (how can non-being appear?) is not.

To tease out the complexity of the problem, we can once again refer to Sartre, since the question of the effectiveness of negation is really what commands the entire construction of *Being and Nothingness*, assuring the corruption of pure being-in-itself (massive and absurd) by the nihilating penetration of the for-itself (a consciousness ontologically identical to its own freedom). Sartre's solution, as brilliant as its consequences may be (an absolutist theory of freedom), is in a certain sense tautological: negation comes to the world inasmuch as 'the world' as such supposes a constitution by the nothing. Otherwise, there would be nothing but the absurd amorphousness of being-in-itself. Therefore, negation appears because only the nothing grounds the fact that there is appearing.

The line we shall follow consists in basing the logical possibility of negation in appearing, without thereby positing that negation as such appears. In effect, the concept suited to the apparent will not be, in a given world, its negation, but what we will call its *reverse*.

The three fundamental properties of the reverse will be the following:

1. The reverse of a being-there (or, more precisely, of the measure of appearance of a multiple in a world) is in general a being-there in the same world (another measure of intensity of appearance in this world).

2. The reverse has in common with negation the fact that one can say that a being-there and its reverse do not have, in the world, anything in common (the conjunction of their degrees of intensity is nil).

3. In general, however, the reverse does not have all the properties of classical negation. In particular, the reverse of the reverse of a degree of appearance is not necessarily identical to that degree. Furthermore, the union of an apparent and its reverse is not necessarily equal to the measure of appearance of the world in its entirety.

In the end we can say that the concept of reverse supports in appearing an expanded thinking of negation, and that we only encounter classical negation for some particular transcendentals.

SECTION 1
The Concept of Transcendental

1. INEXISTENCE OF THE WHOLE

If one posits the existence of a being of the Whole, it follows, from the fact that any being thought in its being is pure multiplicity, that the Whole is a multiple. A multiple of what? A multiple of all there is. Which is to say, since 'what there is' is as such multiple, a *multiple of all multiples*.

If this multiple of *all* multiples does not count itself in its own composition, it is not the Whole. For one will have the 'true' Whole only by adding to that multiple-composition *this* identifiable supplementary multiple which is the recollection of all the other multiples.

The Whole therefore enters into its own multiple-composition. Or, the Whole presents itself as *one* of the elements that constitute it as multiple.

We will call *reflexive* a multiple which has the property of presenting itself in its own multiple-composition. Adopting an entirely classical reasoning, we have just said that if the being of the Whole is presupposed, it must be presupposed as reflexive. Or that the concept of Universe entails, with regard to its being, the predicate of reflexivity.

If there is a being of the Whole, or if (it amounts to the same) the concept of Universe is consistent, one must admit that it is consistent to attribute to certain multiples the property of reflexivity, since at least one of them possesses it, namely the Whole (which is). Moreover, we know it is consistent not to attribute it to certain multiples. Accordingly, since the set of the five pears in the fruit-bowl before me is not itself a pear, it cannot count itself in its composition (in effect, this composition only contains pears). Thus there certainly exist non-reflexive multiples.

If we now return to the Whole (to the multiple of all multiples), we can see that it is logically possible, once we suppose that it is (or that the concept of Universe consists), to divide it into two parts: on the one hand, all the reflexive multiples (there is at least one among them, the Whole itself, which as we have seen enters into the composition of the Whole); on the other, all the non-reflexive multiples (which undoubtedly are very great in number). It is therefore consistent to consider the multiple defined by the phrase 'All the non-reflexive multiples' or all the multiples which are absent from their own composition. The existence of this multiple is not in doubt, since it is a part of the Whole, whose being has been presupposed. Therefore it is presented by the Whole, which is the multiple of all multiples that are.

We thus know that within the Whole there is a multiple of *all* the non-reflexive multiples. Let us name this multiple *the Chimera*. Is the Chimera reflexive or non-reflexive? The question is relevant, since the alternative between 'reflexive' or 'non-reflexive' constitutes, as we've already said, a partition of the Whole into two. This is a partition without remainder. Given a multiple, either it presents itself (it figures in its own composition) or it does not.

Now, if the Chimera is reflexive, this means that it presents itself. It is within its own multiple-composition. But what is the Chimera? The multiple of all non-reflexive multiples. If the Chimera is among these multiples, it is because it is not reflexive. But we have just supposed that it is. Inconsistency.

Therefore, the Chimera is not reflexive. However, it is by definition the multiple of all non-reflexive multiples. If it is not reflexive, it is in this 'all', this whole, and therefore presents itself. It is reflexive. Inconsistency, once again.

Since the Chimera can be neither reflexive nor non-reflexive, and since this partition admits of no remainder, we must conclude that the Chimera is not. But its being followed necessarily from the being that was ascribed to the Whole. Therefore, the Whole has no being.

We have just reached a conclusion by way of demonstration. Is this really necessary? Wouldn't it be simpler to consider the inexistence of the Whole as self-evident? Presupposing the existence of the Whole recalls those outdated ancient conceptions of the cosmos which envisaged it as the beautiful and finite totality of the world. This is indeed what Koyré meant when he entitled his studies on the Galilean 'epistemological break': *From the Closed World to the Infinite Universe*. The argument about the 'dis-closure' of the

Whole is accordingly rooted in the Euclidean infinity of space and in the isotropic neutrality of what inhabits it.

However, there are serious objections to this purely axiomatic treatment of de-totalization.

First of all, it is being as such which we are declaring here cannot make a whole, and not the world, nature or the physical universe. It is indeed a question of establishing that every consideration of beings-as-a-whole is inconsistent. The question of the limits of the visible universe is but a secondary aspect of the ontological question of the Whole.

Furthermore, even if we only consider the world, it becomes rapidly obvious that contemporary cosmology opts for its finitude (or its closure) rather than its radical de-totalization. With the theory of the Big Bang, this cosmology even re-establishes the well-known metaphysical path which goes from the initial One (in this case, the infinitely dense 'point' of matter and its explosion) to the multiple-Whole (in this case, the galactic clusters and their composition).

That's because the infinite discussed by Koyré is still too undifferentiated to take on, with respect to the question of the Whole, the value of an irreversible break. Today we know, especially after Cantor, that the infinite can certainly be local, that it may characterize a singular being, and that it is not only—like Newton's space—the property of the global place of every thing.

In the end, the question of the Whole, which is logical or onto-logical in essence, enjoys no physical or phenomenological evidence. It calls for an argument, the very one that mathematicians discovered at the beginning of the twentieth century, and which we have reformulated here.

2. DERIVATION OF THE THINKING OF A MULTIPLE ON THE BASIS OF THAT OF ANOTHER MULTIPLE

A singular multiple is only thought to the extent that one can determine its composition (that is the elements belonging to it). The multiple that has no elements thus finds itself immediately determined: it is the Void. All the other multiples are only determined in a mediated way, by considering the provenance of their elements. Therefore, their thinkability implies that at least one multiple is determined in thought 'before them'.

As a general rule, the being of a multiple is thought on the basis of an operation which indicates how its elements originate from another being, whose determination is already effective. The axioms of the theory of the multiple (or rational ontology) aim for the most part at regulating these operations. Let us mention two classical operations. We will say that given a multiple, it is consistent to think another multiple, the elements of which are the elements of the elements of the first (this is the operation of immanent dissemination). And we will say that given a multiple, the thinkability of an other multiple the elements of which are the parts of the first is guaranteed (this is the operation of 'extraction of parts', or re-presentation).

Ultimately, it is clear that every thinkable being is drawn from operations first applied to the void alone. A multiple will be all the more complex the longer the operational chain which, on the basis of the void, leads to its determination. The degree of complexity is technically measurable: this is the theory of 'ontological rank'.

If there was a being of the Whole, we could undoubtedly separate out any multiple from it by taking into account the properties that singularize it. Moreover, there would be a universal place of multiple-beings, on the basis of which both the existence of what is and the relations between beings would be set out. In particular, predicative separation would uniformly determine multiplicities through their identification and differentiation within the Whole. But, as we have just seen, there is no Whole. Therefore, there is no uniform procedure of identification and differentiation of what is. The thinking of any multiple whatever is always local, inasmuch as it is derived from singular multiples, and is not inscribed in any multiple whose referential value would be absolutely general.

Let us consider things from a slightly different angle. From the fact that there is no Whole it follows that every multiple-being enters into the composition of other multiples, without this plural (the others) ever being able to fold back upon a singular (the Other). For if all multiples were elements of one Other, that would be the Whole. But since the concept of Universe inconsists, as vast as the multiple in which a singular multiple is inscribed may be, there exist others, not enveloped by the first, in which this multiple is also inscribed.

In the end, there is no possible uniformity among the derivations of the thinkability of multiples, nor a place of the Other in which they could all be situated. The identifications and relations of multiples are always local.

We will say that a multiple, related to a localization of its identity and of its relations with other multiples, is a being [*étant*] (to distinguish it from its pure multiple-being, which is the being of its being [*son pur être-multiple, qui est l'être de son être*]).

As for a local site of the identification of beings, we will call it, in what is still a rather vague sense, a world.

In other words, in the context of the operations of thought whereby the identity of a multiple is guaranteed on the basis of its relations with other multiples, we call 'being' [*étant*] the multiple thus identified, and 'world', relative to the operations in question, the multiple-place in which these operations operate. We will also say that the identified multiple is a 'being of the world'.

3. A BEING IS THINKABLE ONLY INSOFAR AS IT BELONGS TO A WORLD

The thinkability of a being, if it is not the Void, follows from two things: (at least) one other being, whose being is guaranteed, and (at least) one operation which justifies thought in passing from this other being to the one whose identity needs to be established. But the operation presumes that the space in which it is exercised—the (implicit) multiple within which the operational passage takes place—is itself presentable. In other words, one can say that the identity of a being is guaranteed, always in a local sense, on the basis of that of another being. Ultimately, this is because there is no Whole. But what is the place of the local, if there is no Whole? This place is without doubt where operation operates. We are guaranteed one point in this place: the other being (or other beings) on the basis of which the operation (or operations) give access to the identity of the new being. And the being which is thus guaranteed in its being names another point within the place. Between these two points lies the operational passage, with the place as such as its background.

In the end, what indicates the place is the operation. But what localizes an operation? By definition, it is a world (for that operation). The place where operation happens without leaving it is the place where a being attains its identity—its relative consistency. Thus, a being is only exposed to the thinkable to the extent that—invisibly, in the guise of an operation that localizes it—it names, within a world, a new point. In so doing, it appears in that world.

We can now think what the situation of a being is.

We call 'situation of being' for a singular being, the world in which it inscribes a local procedure of access to its identity on the basis of other beings.

It is clear that, as long as it is, a being is situated by, or appears in, a world.

We speak of a situation of being for a being because it would be ambiguous, and ultimately mistaken, to speak too quickly about *the* world of a being. It goes without saying, after all, that a being, abstractly determined in its being as a pure multiplicity, can appear in different worlds. It would be absurd to think that there is an intrinsic link between a given multiple and a given world. The 'worlding' of a (formal) being, which is its being-there or appearing, is ultimately a logical operation: the access to a local guarantee of its identity. This operation may be produced in numerous different ways, and it may imply entirely distinct worlds as the grounds for the further operations it elicits. Not only is there a plurality of worlds, but the same multiple—the 'same' ontologically—in general co-belongs to different worlds.

In particular, man is the animal that appears in a very great number of worlds. Empirically, we could even say it is nothing but this: the being which, among all those whose being we acknowledge, appears most multiply. The human animal is the being of the thousand logics. Since it is capable of entering into the composition of a subject of truth, the human animal can even contribute to the appearance of a (generic) being for such and such a world. That is, it is capable of including itself in the move from appearance (the plurality of worlds, logical construction) back towards being (the pure multiple, universality), and it can do this with regard to a virtually unlimited number of worlds.

This notwithstanding, the human animal cannot hope for a worldly proliferation as exhaustive as that of its principal competitor: the void. Since the void is the only immediate being, it follows that it figures in any world whatsoever. In its absence, no operation can have a starting point in being, that is to say, no operation can operate. Without the void there is no world, if by 'world' we understand the closed place of an operation. Conversely, where something operates [*où ça opère*]—that is, where there is world—the void can be attested.

Ultimately, man is the animal that desires the worldly ubiquity of the void. It is—as a logical power—the *voided* animal. This is the elusive One of its infinite appearances.

The difficulty of this theme (the worldly multiplicity of a unity of being) stems from the following: when a being is thought in its pure form of being, un-situated except in intrinsic ontology (mathematics), we are not taking into account the possibility that it has of belonging to different situations (to different worlds). The identity of a multiple is considered strictly from the vantage point of its multiple composition. Of course, as we've already remarked, this composition is itself thought only in a mediated sense—save in the case of the pure void. In the consistency of its being, this composition is validated only by a derivation on the basis of multiple-beings whose being is itself guaranteed. And the derivations are in turn regulated by axioms. But the possibility for a being to be situated in heterogeneous worlds is not reducible to the mediated or derived character of every assertion regarding its being.

Let us consider, for example, some singular human animals—let's say Ariadne and Bluebeard. We are familiar with the world-fable in which they are given following Perrault's tale: a lord kidnaps and murders some women. The last of them, doubtless because her relationship to the situation is different, discovers the truth and (depending on the version) flees or gets Bluebeard killed. In short, she interrupts the series of feminine fates. In Perrault's tale, this woman, who is also the Other-woman of the series, is anonymous (only her sister is accorded the grace of a proper name, 'Anna, my sister Anna . . .'). In Bartók's brief and dense opera, *Bluebeard's Castle*, her name is Judith. And in Maeterlinck's piece, *Ariadne and Bluebeard*, adapted by Paul Dukas into a magnificent but almost unknown opera, it is Ariadne.

One shouldn't be surprised that we are taking the opera by Maeterlinck–Dukas as an example of the logic of appearing. The opera is essentially about the visibility of deliverance, about the fact that it is not enough for freedom to be (in this case under the name and the acts of Ariadne), but that freedom must also appear, in particular to those who are deprived of it. Such is the case for the five wives of Bluebeard, who do not wish to be freed. This is so even though Ariadne frees them *de facto* (but not subjectively); and despite the fact that, at the beginning of the fable, she sings this astonishing maxim: 'First, one must disobey: it's the first duty when the order is menacing and refuses to explain itself'.

In a brilliant and friendly commentary on *Ariadne and Bluebeard*, Olivier Messiaen, who was Paul Dukas's respectful student, underscores one of the heroine's replies: 'My poor, poor sisters! Why then do you want to be freed, if you so adore your darkness?' Messiaen then compares this call directed at the submitted women to St. John's famous sentence: 'The light shines in the darkness and the darkness has not understood'. What is at stake in this musical fable, from beginning to end, are the relations between true-being (Ariadne) and its appearance (Bluebeard's castle, the other women). How does the light make itself present, in a world transcendentally regulated by the powers of darkness? It is possible to follow the intellectualized sensorial aspect of this problem all throughout the second act, which, in the orchestral score and the soaring vocals of Ariadne, constitutes a terrible ascent towards the light and something like the manifestation of a becoming-manifest of being, a vibrant localization of being-free in the palace of servitude.

But let's start with some simple remarks. First of all, the proper names 'Ariadne' and 'Bluebeard' convey the capacity for appearing in altogether discontinuous narrative, musical or scenic situations: Ariadne before knowing Bluebeard, the encounter between Ariadne and Bluebeard, Ariadne leaving the castle, Bluebeard the murderer, Bluebeard the child, Ariadne freeing the captives, Bluebeard and Ariadne in the sexual domain, etc. This capacity is in no way regulated by the set of genealogical constructions required in order to fix within the real the referent of these proper names. Of course, the vicissitudes that affect the two characters from one world to another presuppose that, under the proper names, a genealogical invariance authorizes the thinking of the same. But this 'same' does not appear; it is strictly reduced to the names. Appearing is always the transit of a world; in turn, the world logically regulates that which shows itself within it qua being-there. Similarly, the set N of whole natural numbers, once the procedure of succession that authorizes its concept is given, does not by itself indicate that it can be either the transcendent infinite place of finite calculations, or a discrete subset of the continuum, or the reservoir of signs for the numbering of this book's pages, or what allows one to know which candidate holds the majority in presidential elections, or something else altogether. These are indeed, ontologically, the 'same' whole numbers, which simply means that, if I reconstruct their concept on the basis of rational ontology, I will obtain the same ontological assertions in every case. But this constructive invariance is made absent, except in the assumed univocity of signs, when the numbers appear in properly incomparable situations.

It is therefore certain that the identity of a being grasped in the efficacy of its appearing includes something other than the ontological or mathematical construction of its multiple-being. But what? The answer is: a logic, through which every being finds itself constrained and deployed once it appears locally, and its being is accordingly affirmed as being-there.

What does it really mean for a singular being to be there, once its being (a pure mathematical multiplicity) does not prescribe anything about this 'there' to which it is consigned? It necessarily means the following:

    *a.*Differing from itself. Being-there is not 'the same' as being-qua-being. It is not the same, because the thinking of being-qua-being does not envelop the thinking of being-there.

    *b.*Differing from other beings of the same world. Being-there is indeed this being [*étant*] which (ontologically) is not an other; and its inscription with others in this world cannot abolish this differentiation. On one hand, the differentiated identity of a being cannot account on its own for the appearing of this being in a world. But on the other hand, the identity of a world can no more account on its own for the differentiated being of what appears.

The key to thinking appearing, when it comes to a singular being, lies in being able to determine, at one and the same time, the self-difference which makes it so that being-there is not being-qua-being, and the difference from others which makes it so that being-there, or the law of the world which is shared by these others, does not abolish being-qua-being.

If appearing is a logic, it is because it is nothing but the coding of these differences, world by world.

The logic of the tale thus amounts to explicating in which sense, situation by situation—love, sex, death, the futile preaching of freedom—Ariadne is something other than 'Ariadne', Bluebeard something other than 'Bluebeard'; but also how Ariadne is something other than Bluebeard's other wives, even though she is also one of them, and Bluebeard something other than a maniac, even though he is traversed by his repetitive choice, and so on. The tale can only attain consistency to the extent that this logic is effective, so that we know that Ariadne is 'herself', and differs from Sélysette, from Ygraine, from Mélisande, from Bellangère and from Alladine (in the opera, these are the other women in the series, who are not dead and who refuse to be freed by Ariadne); but also that she differs from herself once she has been assigned to the world of the tale. The same can be said of 327, to the extent that when it is numbering a page or a certain quantity of voters it is indeed that mathematically constructible number, but also isn't, no more than it is 328, which nevertheless, lying right next to it, shares its fate: to appear on the pages of this book.

Since a being, once worlded, is and is not what it is, and since it differs from those beings which, in an identical manner, are of its world, it follows that differences (and identities) in appearing are a matter of more or less. The logic of appearing necessarily regulates degrees of difference, of a being with respect to itself and of the same with respect to others. These degrees bear witness to the marking of a multiple-being by its coming-into-situation in a world. The consistency of this coming is guaranteed by the fact that the connections of identities and differences are logically regulated. Appearing in a given world is never chaotic.

For its part, ontological identity does not entail any difference with itself, nor any degree of difference with regard to another. A pure multiple is entirely identified by its immanent composition, so that it is meaningless to say that it is 'more or less' identical to itself. If it differs from an other, be it by a single element in an infinity thereof, it differs absolutely.

That goes to show that the ontological determination of beings and the logic of being-there (of beings in situation, or of appearing-in-a-world) are profoundly distinct. QED.

4. APPEARING AND THE TRANSCENDENTAL

We will call 'appearing' that which, of a mathematical multiple, is caught in a situated relational network (a world), such that this multiple comes to being-there, or to the status of being-in-a-world [étant-dans-un-monde]. It is then possible to say that this being is more or less different from another being belonging to the same world. We will call 'transcendental' the operational set which allows us to make sense of the 'more or less' of identities and differences in a determinate world.

We posit that the logic of appearing is a transcendental algebra for the evaluation of the identities and differences that constitute the worldly place of the being-there of a being.

The necessity of this algebra follows from everything that we've argued up to this point. Unless we suppose that appearing is chaotic—a supposition dispelled at once by the undeniable existence of a thinking of beings—there must be a logic for appearing, capable of linking together in the world evaluations of identity which are no longer supported by the rigid extensional identity of pure multiples (that is, by the being-in-itself of beings). As we know immediately, every world pronounces upon degrees of identity and difference, without there being any acceptable reason to believe that these degrees, insofar as they are intelligible, depend on any 'subject' whatsoever, or even on the existence of the human animal. We know from an indisputable source that such and such a world precedes the existence of our species, and that, just like 'our' worlds, it stipulated identities and differences, and had the power to deploy the appearing of innumerable beings. This is what Quentin Meillassoux calls 'the fossil's argument': the irrefutable materialist argument that interrupts the ideal-ist (and empiricist) apparatus of 'consciousness' and the 'object'. The world of the dinosaurs existed, it deployed the infinite multiplicity of the being-there of beings, millions of years before it could be a question of a consciousness or a subject, empirical as well as transcendental. To deny this point is to flaunt a rampant idealist axiomatic. It is clear that there is no need of a consciousness to testify that beings are obliged to appear, that is, to abide there, under the logic of a world. Appearing, though irreducible to pure being (which is accessible to thinking only through mathematics), is nonetheless what beings must endure, once the Whole is impossible, in order for their being to be guaranteed: beings must always manifest themselves locally, without any possible recollection of the innumerable worlds of this manifestation. The logic of a world is what regulates this necessity, by affecting a being with a variable degree of identity (and consequently of difference) to the other beings of the same world.

This requires that in the situation there exist a scale of these degrees—the transcendental of the situation—and that every being is in a world only to the extent that it is indexed to this transcendental.

This indexing immediately concerns the double difference to which we already referred. First of all, in a given world, what is the degree of identity of a being to another being in the same world? Furthermore, what happens in this world to the identity of a being to its own being? The transcendental organization of a world is the protocol of response to these questions. Accordingly, it fixes the moving singularity of the being-there of a being in a determinate world.

If, for example, I ask in what sense Ariadne is similar to Bluebeard's other victims, I must be able to respond with an evaluative nuance—she is reflexively what the others are blindly—which is available in the organiza-tion of the story, or in its language, or (in the Maeterlinck–Dukas version) in the music, considered as the transcendental of the (aesthetic) situation in question. Inversely, the other women (Sélysette, Ygraine, Mélisande, Bellangère and Alladine) form a series; they can be substituted with one another in their relationship to Bluebeard: they are transcendentally identical, which is what marks their 'choral' treatment in the opera, their very weak musical identification. Following the same order of ideas, I immediately know how to evaluate Bluebeard in love with Ariadne in terms of his lag with respect to himself (he finds it impossible to treat Ariadne like the other women, and thus stands outside of what is implied by the referential being of the name 'Bluebeard'). Within the opera there is something of a cipher for this lag, to be found in an extravagant element: for the duration of the last act, Bluebeard remains on the stage, but does not sing a single note or speak a single word. This is truly the limit value (which is in fact exactly minimal) of an operatic transcendental: Bluebeard is absent from himself.

Likewise I know that between the number 327 and the number 328, if assigned to the pages of a book, there is of course a difference which is in a sense absolute; but I also know that viewed 'as pages' they are very close, perhaps numbering variants of the same theme—or even a dull repetition—so that it makes sense, in the world instituted by the reading of the book, to say (this being the transcendental evaluation proper to that book) that the numbers 327 and 328 are almost identical. This time we are dealing with the maximal value of what a transcendental can inflict, in terms of identity, on the appearance of numbers.

Consequently, the value of the identities and differences of a being to itself and of a being to others varies transcendentally between an almost nil identity and a total identity, between absolute difference and indifference.

It is therefore clear in what sense we call *transcendental* that which authorizes a local (or intra-worldly) evaluation of identities and differences. To grasp the singularity of this usage of the word 'transcendental', we should note that, as in Kant, it concerns a question of possibility; but also that we are only dealing with local dispositions, and not with a universal theory of differences. To put it very simply: there are many transcendentals; the intra-worldly regulation of difference is itself differentiated. This is one of the main reasons why it is impossible here to argue from a unified 'centre' of transcendental organization, such as the Subject is for Kant.

Historically, the first great example of what could be called a transcendental inquiry ('How is difference possible?') was proposed by Plato in *The Sophist*. Let us take, he tells us, two crucial Ideas ('supreme genera')—movement and rest, for example. What does it mean to say that these two Ideas are not identical? Since what permits the intelligibility of movement and rest is precisely their Idea, it is entirely impossible to respond to the question about their ideal difference in terms of the supposed acknowledgment of an empirical difference (the evidence that a body in movement is not at rest). A possible solution is to rely upon a third great Idea, inherited from Parmenides, which seems to address the problem of difference. This is the Idea of the Same, which supports the operation of the identification of beings, ideas included (any being whatever is the same as itself). Couldn't one say that movement and rest are different because the Same does not subsume them simultaneously? It is at this point that Plato makes a remarkable decision, a truly transcendental decision. He decides that difference cannot be thought as the simple absence of identity. It is in the wake of this decision, in the face of its ineluctable consequences (the existence of non-being), that Plato breaks with Parmenides: contrary to what is argued by the Eleatic philosopher, the law of being makes it impossible for Plato to think difference solely with the aid of Idea of the same. There must be a proper Idea of difference, an Idea that is not reducible to the negation of the Idea of the same. Plato names this Idea 'the Other'. On the basis of this Idea, saying that movement is other than rest involves an underlying *affirmation* in thought (that of the existence of the Other, and ultimately that of the existence of non-being) instead of merely signifying that movement is not identical to rest.

The Platonic transcendental configuration is constituted by the triplet of being, the Same, and the Other, supreme genera that allow access to the thinking of identity and difference within any configuration of thought. Whatever name is given to it, as soon as a positivity of difference is registered, as soon as one refuses to posit that difference is nothing but the negation of identity, we are dealing in fact with a transcendental disposition. This is what Plato declares by 'doubling' the Same with the existence of the Other.

What Plato, Kant and my own proposal have in common is the acknowledgment that the rational comprehension of differences in being-there (that is, of intra-worldly differences) is not deducible from the ontological identity of the beings in question. This is because ontological identity says nothing about the localization of beings. Plato says: simply in order to think the difference between movement and rest, I cannot be satisfied with a Parmenidean interpretation which refers every entity to its self-identity. I cannot limit myself to the path of the Same, the truth of which is nevertheless beyond dispute. I will therefore introduce a diagonal operator: the Other. Kant says: the thing-in-itself cannot account either for the diversity of phenomena or for the unity of the phenomenal world. I will therefore introduce a singular operator, the transcendental subject, which binds experience in its objects. And I say: the mathematical theory of the pure multiple doubtlessly exhausts the question of the being of a being, except for the fact that its appearing—logically localized by its relations to other beings—is not ontologically deducible. We therefore need a special logical machinery to account for the intra-worldly cohesion of appearing.

I have decided to put my trust in this lineage by reprising the old word 'transcendental', now detached from its constitutive and subjective value.

5. IT MUST BE POSSIBLE TO THINK, IN A WORLD, WHAT DOES NOT APPEAR WITHIN THAT WORLD

There are numerous ways in which this point could be argued. The most immediate is that, presuming that it is impossible to think the non-appearance of a being in a given world, it would be necessary that every being be thinkable as appearing within it. This would entail that said world localizes every being. Consequently, this would be the Universe or the Whole, the impossibility of which we have already established.

We can also argue on the basis that the thinking of being-there necessarily includes the possibility of a 'not-being-there', without which it would be identical to the thinking of being-qua-being. For this possibility to be transcendentally effective, a zero degree of appearing must be capable of exposition. In other words, for appearing to be consistent requires the existence of a transcendental marking of non-appearing, or a logical mark of non-appearance. The thinkability of non-appearance rests on this marking, which is the intra-worldly index of the not-there of a multiple.

Finally, we can say that the evaluation of the degree of identity or difference between two beings would be ineffective if these degrees were themselves not situated on the basis of their minimum. That two beings are strongly identical in a determinate world makes sense to the extent that the transcendental measure of this identity is 'large'. But 'large' in turn is meaningless unless referred to 'less large' and finally to 'nil', which in designating zero-identity also authorizes a thinking of absolute difference. Thus, the necessity of a minimal degree of identity in the end stems from the fact that worlds are in general not Parmenidean (which is instead the case for being as such, or the ontological—that is mathematical—situation): they admit of absolute differences, which are thinkable within appearing only insofar as non-appearing is also thinkable.

These three arguments sanction the conclusion that there exists, for every world, a transcendental measure of the not-apparent-in-this-world, which is obviously a minimum (a sort of zero) within the order of the evaluations of appearing.

Let us keep in mind, however, that strictly speaking a transcendental measure always bears on the identity or difference of two beings in a determinate world. When we speak of an 'evaluation of appearing', as we've been doing from the start, this is only for the sake of expediency. For *what is measured or evaluated by the transcendental organization of a world is in fact the degree of intensity of the difference of appearance of two beings in this world, and not an intensity of appearance considered 'in itself'.*

Insofar as the transcendental is concerned, it follows that the thinking of the non-apparent comes down to saying that the identity between an ontologically determinate being and every being that really appears in a world is minimal (in other words, nil for what is internal to this world). Since it is identical to nothing that appears within a world, or (which amounts to the same) absolutely different from everything that appears within it, it can be said of this being that it does not appear within the given world. It is not there. This means that to the extent that its being is attested and therefore localized, this takes place somewhere else (in another world), not there.

Since this book has less than 700 pages, 721 does not appear within it, because none of the numbers that collate its paginated substance can be said to be, even in a weak sense, identical to 721, with regard to this book qua world.

This consideration is not arithmetical (ontological). We have already noted that, after all, two arithmetically differentiated pages—445 and 446, for example—can, by dint of their sterile and repetitive side, be considered as transcendentally 'very identical' from the perspective of the world that the book constitutes. The transcendental can bring forth intra-worldly identities from absolute ontological differences. This is all the more so in that it plays upon degrees of identity (whence the intelligibility of the localization of beings): my two arguments are 'close', pages 445 and 446 'repeat one another', and so on.

But as concerns page 721, it is not in the book in the following sense: no page is capable of being, whether strongly or feebly, identical to page 721. To put it in other terms: supposing that one wants to force page 721 to be co-thinkable in and for the world that this book is, one can at most say that the transcendental measure of the identity between '721' and every page of this book-world—itself in particular—is nil (minimal). One will conclude that the number 721 does not appear in this world.

The delicate point is that it is always through an evaluation of minimal identity that I can pronounce on the non-apparent. It makes no sense to transform the judgment 'Such and such a being is not there' into an ontological judgment. There is no being of the not-being-there. What I can say about such a being, with respect to its localization—with respect to its situation of being—is that its identity to such and such a being of this situation or this world is minimal, that is nil according to the transcendental of this world. Appearing, that is the local or worldly attestation of a being, is logical through and through, which is to say relational. It follows that the non-apparent conveys a nil degree of relation, and never a non-being pure and simple.

If I forcibly suppose that a very beautiful woman—Ava Gardner, let's say—partakes in the world of the cloistered (or dead?) wives of Bluebeard, it is on the basis of the eventual nullity of her identity to the series of spouses (her identity to Sélysette, Ygraine, Mélisande, Bellangère and Alladine has the minimum as its measure), but also of the zero degree of her identity to the other-woman of the series (Ariadne), that I will conclude that she does not appear within that world—not on the grounds of the supposed ontological absurdity of her marriage with Bluebeard. An absurdity which moreover would have been undercut had she come to play the role of Ariadne in Maeterlinck's opera, in which case it would have indeed been necessary—in accordance with the transcendental of the theatre-world—to pronounce oneself, via her performance, on the degree of identity between 'her' and Ariadne, and therefore on her apparent-interiority to the scenic version of the tale. This problem was already posed by Maeterlinck's mistress, Georgette Leblanc, about whom we can legitimately ask if, and to what extent, she is identical to Ariadne, since she claimed to have been her model and even her genuine creator—in particular when Ariadne acknowledges (in an admirable aria penned by Dukas) that most women do not want to be freed. This identity is all the more strongly affirmed in that Georgette Leblanc, a singer, created the role of Ariadne after having been refused that of Mélisande in Debussy's opera—something that wounded her greatly. So it makes sense to say that the degree of identity between (the fictional) Ariadne and (the real) Georgette Leblanc is very high.

This is how the question of a non-nil degree of identity between Georgette Leblanc and Ava Gardner could have arisen, how it could have come to be there, in a logically instituted worldly connection between writing, love, music, theatre and cinema. If this is not so, it is because, in every attested world, the transcendental identity between Ava Gardner and Bluebeard's women takes the minimal value prescribed by that world.

It also follows from this that there is an absolute difference between the matador Luis Miguel Dominguin (Ava Gardner's notorious lover) and Bluebeard. At least this is the case in every attested world, including in *The Barefoot Contessa*, Mankiewicz's very beautiful film, where the whole question is that of knowing if the beauty of Ava Gardner can pass unscathed from the matador to the Italian count Torlato-Favrini. The film's transcendental response is 'no'. She dies. As we shall see, to die only ever means to cease appearing, in a determinate world.

6. THE CONJUNCTION OF TWO APPARENTS IN A WORLD

One of the crucial aspects of the consistency of a world is that what sustains the co-appearance of two beings within it should be immediately legible. What does this legibility mean? In any case, that the intensity of the appearance of the 'common' part of the two beings—common in terms of appearing—allows itself to be evaluated. This part is what these two beings have in common to the extent that they are there, in this world.

In broad terms, the phenomenological or allegorical inquiry—taken here as a subjective guide and not as truth—immediately discerns three cases.

Case 1. Two beings are there, in the world, according to a necessary connection of their appearance. Take, for example, a being which is the identifying part of another. About the red leafage of ivy upon a wall in autumn, I could say that it is arguably constitutive, in this autumnal world, of the being-there of the 'ivy'—which nonetheless involves many other things, including non-apparent ones, such as its deep and tortuous roots. In this case, the transcendental measure of what the being-there of the 'ivy' and the being-there 'red-leafage-unfurled' have in common is identical to the logical value of the appearance of the 'red-leafage-unfurled', because it is the latter which identifies the former within appearing. The operation of the 'common' is in fact a sort of inclusive corroboration. A being, insofar as it is there, carries with it the apparent identity of another, which deploys it in the world as its part, but whose identifying intensity it in turn realizes.

Case 2. Two beings, in the logically structured movement of their appearing, entertain a relation with a third, which is the most evident (the 'largest') of that which they have a common reference to, once they co-appear in this world. Thus, this country house in the autumn evening and the blood-red leafage of the ivy have 'in common' the stony band which is visible near the roof as the ponderous matter of architecture, but also as the intermittent ground for the plant that creeps upon it. One will then say that the wall of the façade is what maximally conjoins the general appearing of the ivy with the appearing, made of tiles and stones, of the house.

In case 1, one of the two apparents in the autumnal world (the red leafage) was the common part of its co-appearance with the ivy. In the case under consideration, neither of the two apparents, the house or the ivy, have this function. A third term maximally underlies the other two in the stability of the world, and it is the stony wall of the façade.

Case 3. Two beings are situated in a single world, without the 'common' of their appearance itself being identifiable within appearing. Or again: the intensity of appearance of what the beings-there of the two beings have in common is nil ('nil', obviously meaning that it is indexed to the minimal value—the zero—of the transcendental). Such is the case with the red leafage there before me in the setting light of day and suddenly—behind me, on the path—the deafening noise of a motorcycle skidding on the gravel. It is not that the autumnal world has been dislocated, or split in two. It is simply the case that in this world, and in accordance with the logic that assures its consistency, the part held in common by the apparent 'red leafage' and the apparent 'rumbling of the motorcycle' does not itself appear. This means that the common part here takes the minimal value of appearance; that, since its worldly value is that of inappearing, the transcendental measure of its intensity of appearance is zero.

Allegorically grasped according to a conscious sight, the three cases can be objectivated independently of any idealist symbolism in the following way: either the conjunction of two beings-there (or the common maximal part of their appearance) is measured by the intensity of appearance of one of them; or it is measured by the intensity of appearance of a third being-there; or, finally, its measure is nil. In the first case, we will say that the worldly conjunction of two beings is *inclusive* (because the appearance of the one entails that of the other). In the second case, that the two beings have an *intercalary* worldly conjunction. In the third case, that the two beings are *disjoined*.

Inclusion, intercalation and disjunction are the three modes of conjunction, understood as the logical operation of appearing. We can already clearly glimpse the link that will be established with the transcendental measure of the intensities of appearing. The wall of the façade appears as if supported in its appearing both by the visible totality of the house and by the ivy which masks, sections and reveals it. The measure of its intensity of appearance is therefore undoubtedly comparable to that of the house and the ivy. Comparable in the sense that the differential relation between intensities is itself measured in the transcendental. In fact, we can say that the intensity of appearance of the stone wall in the autumnal world is 'less than or equal to' that of the house and that of the ivy. And it is the 'greatest' visible surface to entertain this common relation with the two other beings.

Abstractly speaking, we therefore have the following situation. Take two beings which are there in a world. Each of them has a value of appearance indexed in the transcendental of that world; this transcendental is an order-structure. The conjunction of these two beings—or the maximal common part of their being-there—is itself measured in the transcendental by the greatest value that is lesser than or equal to the two initial measurements of intensity.

Of course, it may be the case that this 'greatest value' is in fact nil (case 3). This means that no part common to the being-there of the two beings is itself there. The conjunction inappears: the two beings are disjoined.

The closer the measure of the intensity of appearance of the common part of the two apparents is to their respective values of appearance, the more the conjunction of the two beings is there in the world. The intercalary value is strong. But this value cannot exceed either of the two initial measures of intensity. If it reaches the initial measure, we have case 1, or the inclusive case. The conjunction is 'borne' by one of the two beings.

In its detail, the question of conjunction is slightly more complicated because, as we've already remarked, the transcendental values do not directly measure intensities of appearance 'in themselves', but rather differences (or identities). When we speak of the value of appearance of a being, we are really designating a sort of synthetic summary of the values of transcendental identity between this being, in this world, and all the other beings appearing in the same world. I will not directly argue that the intensity of appearance of Mélisande, one of Bluebeard's wives, is 'very weak' in the opera by Maeterlinck–Dukas. I will say instead, on the one hand, that her difference of appearance with respect to Ariadne is very large (in fact, Ariadne sings constantly, while Mélisande almost not at all), on the other, that her difference of appearance with respect to the other wives (Ygraine, Alladine, etc.) is very weak, making her appearance, in this opera-world, indistinct. The conjunction that I will define relates to this differential network. I will thus be able to ask what is the measure of the conjunction between two differences. It is this procedure that delineates the logical 'common' of appearance.

Take, for example, the very high transcendental measure of the difference between Mélisande and Ariadne, and the very weak one between Mélisande and Alladine. It is certain that the conjunction, which places the term 'Mélisande' within a double difference, will be very close to the weaker of the two (the one between Mélisande and Alladine). Ultimately, this means that the order of magnitude of the appearance of Mélisande in this world is such that, taken according to her co-appearance with Ariadne, it is barely modified. On the contrary, the transcendental measure of Ariadne's appearing is so enveloping that, taken according to its conjunction with any of the other women, it is drastically reduced. What has power has little in common with what appears weakly: weakness can only offer its weakness to the 'common'.

These conjunctive paths of the transcendental cohesion of worlds could also be approached in terms of identity. If, for example, we say that pages 445 and 446 of this book-world are almost identical (since they reiterate the same argument), and if instead pages 446 and 245 are identical only in a very weak sense (there is a brutal caesura in the argument), the conjunction of the two transcendental measures of identity (445/446 and 446/245) will certainly make the lowest value appear. In the end, this will mean that pages 445 and 245 too are identical in a very weak sense.

All of this suggests that the logical stability of a world deploys conjoined identifying (or differential) networks; the conjunctions themselves being deployed from the minimal value (disjunction) up to maximal values (inclusion), via the whole spectrum—which depends on the singularity of the transcendental order—of the intermediate values (intercalation).

7. REGIONAL STABILITY OF WORLDS: THE ENVELOPE

Let us take up again, in line with our method of so-called objective phenomenology, the example of disjunction (that is, the conjunction equal to the minimum of appearing). At the moment when I'm lost in the contemplation of the wall inundated by the autumnal red of the ivy, behind me, on the gravel of the path, a motorcycle is taking off. Its noise, whilst being there in the world, is conjoined to my vision only by the nil value of appearing. To put it otherwise, in this world, the being-there noise-of-the-motorcycle has 'nothing to do' [*rien à voir*] with the being-there 'unfurled-red' of the ivy on the wall.

But I said that it's a question of the nil value of a conjunction, and not of a dislocation of the world. The world deploys the inappearance in a world of some One of the two beings-there, and not the appearance of a being (the motorcycle) in a world other than the one which is already there. It's now time to substantiate this point.

In truth, the orientation of the space—fixed by the path leading to the façade, the trees bordering it, the house as that which this path moves towards—envelops both the red of the ivy and my gaze (or body), as well as the entire invisible background which nevertheless leads towards it, and finally also the noise of the skidding motorcycle. So that if I turn around, it's not because I imagine, between the world and the incongruous noise that disjoins itself from the red of autumn, a sort of abyss between two worlds. No, I simply situate my attention, until then polarized by the ivy, in a wider correlation, which includes the house, the path, the fundamental silence of the countryside, the crunch of the gravel, the motorcycle. . .

What's more, it is in the very movement that extends this correlation that I situate the nil value of conjunction between the noise of the motorcycle and the radiance of the ivy on the wall. This conjunction is nil, but it takes place in an infinite fragment of this world which dominates the two terms, as well as many others: this corner of the country in autumn, with the house, the path, the hills and the sky, which the disjunction between the motor and the pure red is powerless to separate from the clouds. Ultimately, the value of appearance of the fragment of world set forth by the sky and its clouds, the path and the house, is superior to that of all the disjunctive ingredients: ivy, house, motorcycle, gravel. This is why the synthesis of these ingredients, as carried out by the being-there of the corner of the world in which the nil conjunction is signalled, prevents this nullity from amounting to a scission of the world, that is a decomposition of the world's logic.

All of this can do without my gaze, without my consciousness, without my about turn, which registers the density of the earth under the liquidity of the sky. The regional stability of the world comes down to this: if you take a random fragment of a given world, the beings which are there in this fragment possess—both with respect to themselves and relative to one other—differential degrees of appearance indexed to the transcendental order of this world. The fact that nothing which appears within this fragment, including its disjunctions (those conjunctions whose value is nil), can sunder the unity of the world means that the logic of the world guarantees the existence of a synthetic value subsuming all the degrees of appearance of the beings that co-appear in this fragment.

We call 'envelope' of a part of the world that being whose differential value of appearance is the synthetic value adequate to that part.

The systematic existence of the envelope presupposes that given any collection of degrees (those which measure the intensity of appearance of beings in a part of the world), the transcendental order contains a degree superior or equal to all the degrees in the collection (it subsumes them all), which is also the smallest degree to enjoy this property (it 'grips', as closely as possible, the collection of degrees assigned to the different beings-there of the part in question).

Such is the case for the elementary experience that has served us as our guide. When I turn around to check that the noise of the world is indeed 'of this world', that its site of appearance is there, despite it bearing no relation to the ivy on the wall, I am not obliged to summon the entire planet, or the sky all the way to the horizon, or even the curve of the hills on the edge of darkness. It is enough to integrate the dominant of a worldly fragment capable of absorbing the motor/ivy disjunction within the logical consistency of appearing. This fragment (the avenue, some trees, the façade. . .) possesses a value of appearance sufficient to guarantee the co-appearance of the disjoined terms within the same world. About this fragment, we will say that its value is that of the envelope of the beings—rigorously speaking, of the degree of appearance of the beings—which constitute its completeness as being-there. This envelope refers to the smallest value of appearance capable of dominating the values of the beings in question (the house, the gravel of the path, the red of the ivy, the noise of the skidding motorcycle, the shade of the trees, etc.).

In the final scene of the opera that serves as our guide, Ariadne, having untied Bluebeard, who lies defeated and speechless, prepares to go 'over there, where they still await me'. She asks the others if they wish to leave with her. They all refuse: Sélysette and Mélisande, after hesitating; Ygraine, without even turning her head; Bellangère, curtly; Alladine, sobbing. They all prefer their servitude to the man. Ariadne then calls on the entire opening of the world. She sings these magnificent lines:

The moon and the stars illuminate all paths. The forest and the sea call us from afar and daybreak perches on the vaults of the azure, to show us a world awash with hope.

It is truly the power of the envelope that is enacted here, confronting the feeble values of conservatism in the castle which opens onto the unlimited night. The music swells, Ariadne's voice glides on the treble, and all the other protagonists—the defeated Bluebeard, his five wives, the villagers—are signified in a decisive and precise fashion by this lyrical transport which is addressed to them collectively. This is what guarantees the artistic consistency of this finale, even though in it no conflict is resolved, no drama unravelled, no destiny sealed. Ariadne's visitation of Bluebeard's castle will simply have served to establish, in the magnificence of song, that beyond every figure and every destiny, beyond things that persevere in their appearing, there is what envelops them and turns them, for all time, into a bound moment of artistic semblance, a fascinating operatic fragment.

8. THE CONJUNCTION BETWEEN A BEING-THERE AND A REGION OF ITS WORLD

When, distracted from my contemplation of the wall awash with the red of the ivy by the incongruous noise of the motorcycle skidding on the gravel, I turn, and the global unity of the fragment of the world in question reconstitutes itself, enveloping its disparate ingredients, I'm really dealing with the conjunction between the unexpected noise and the fragmentary totality (the house, the autumn evening) to which the noise at first seemed altogether alien. The phenomenological question is simple: in terms of intensity of appearance, what is the value of the conjunction? Not, as before, the conjunction between the noise of the motorcycle and another singular apparent (the red unfurled on the wall), but the conjunction between this noise and the global apparent, the pre-existing envelope which is this fragment of autumnal world. The answer is that this value depends on the one that measures the conjunction between the noise and all the enveloped apparents, taken one by one. Let's suppose, for example, that in the autumn evening one can already repeatedly hear—interrupted, but always recommencing—the mewling of a chainsaw, coming from the forest that blankets the hills. Now, the sudden noise of the motorcycle, whose conjunction with the red of the ivy is measured by the transcendental zero, will entertain with this periodic hum a conjunction which might be weak but is not nil. Moreover, this noise will doubtlessly be con-joined, in my immediate memory, to a value which in this instance is distinctly higher, to a previous passage of the motorcycle—not skidding, fast, forgotten almost at once—which the present noise revives, in a pairing that the new unity of this fragment of world must envelop.

The envelope designates the value of appearance of a region of the world as being superior to all the degrees of appearance it contains. As superior, in particular, to all the conjunctions it contains. Were we to ask ourselves about the value, as being-there, of the conjunction between the noise of the skidding motorcycle and the fragment of autumn set forth in front of the house, we would in any case be obliged to consider all the singular conjunctions (the wall and the ivy, the motorcycle and the chainsaw, the second and first passage of the motorcycle. . .) and to posit that the new envelope is the one suited to all of them. Accordingly, the envelope will have to be superior to the minimum (to zero)—the value of the con-junction of the noise and the ivy—since the value of the other conjunctions (the motorcycle and chainsaw, for instance) is not nil, and the envelope dominates all the local conjunctions.

In conceptual terms, we will simply say that the value of the conjunction between an apparent and an envelope is the value of the envelope of all the local conjunctions between this apparent and all the apparents of the envelope in question, taken one by one.

The density of this formula no doubt demands another example. In our opera-world, what is the value of the conjunction between Bluebeard and that which envelops the series of his five wives (Sélysette, Ygraine, Mélisande, Bellangère and Alladine)? Obviously, it depends on the value of the relation between Bluebeard and each of his five wives. The opera's thesis is that this relation is almost invariable, regardless of the wife (after all, that is why the five wives are hardly discernible). Consequently, since the value of the conjunction between Bluebeard and the serial envelope of this region of the world ('Bluebeard's wives') is the envelope of the con-junction between Bluebeard and each of them, this value in turn will not differ greatly from the average value of these conjunctions: since they are near to one another, the one which dominates them in the 'closest' way—and which is the highest among them (the opera suggests that it is the link Bluebeard/Alladine)—is in turn near to all the others.

If we now take into account the fragment of world that comprises the five wives and Ariadne, the situation becomes more complex. What the opera effectively maintains, including in its musical score, is that no common measure exists between the Bluebeard/Ariadne conjunction and the five others. We can't even say that this conjunction is 'stronger' than the others. Were that the case, the conjunction between Bluebeard and the envelope of the series of the six wives would have turned out to be equal to the highest of the local conjunctions, the conjunction with Ariadne. But in actual fact, in the differential network of the opera-world, Ariadne and the other wives are not ordered; they are incomparable. All of a sudden we need to look for a term that would dominate the five very close conjunctions (Bluebeard/Sélysette, Bluebeard/Mélisande, etc.), as well as the incomparable conjunction Bluebeard/Ariadne. The opera's finale shows that this dominant term is femininity as such, the unstable dialectical admixture of servitude and freedom. It is this admixture, materialized by Ariadne's departure as well as by the abiding of the others, which envelops all the singular conjunctions between Bluebeard and his wives, and finally, through the encompassing power of the orchestra, which functions as the envelope for the entire opera.

9. DEPENDENCE: THE MEASURE OF THE LINK BETWEEN TWO BEINGS IN A WORLD

In the introduction to this Book, we announced that the system of operations comprising the minimum, the conjunction and the envelope was phenomenologically complete. This principle of completeness comes down to the supposition that every logical relation within appearing, that is every mode of consistency of being-there, can be derived from the three fundamental operations.

Objective phenomenology, which serves here as our expository principle—somewhat like Aristotle's logic served Kant in the *Critique of Pure Reason*—makes much of relations of causality or dependence of the following type: if such and such an apparent is in a world with a strong degree of existence, then such and such another apparent equally insists within that world. Or, conversely: if such and such a being-there manifests itself, it prohibits such and such another being-there from insisting in the world. And finally, if Socrates is a man, he is mortal. Thus, the chromatic power of the ivy upon the wall weakens, in what concerns colour, the givenness in limestone of the wall of the façade. Or again, the intensity of Ariadne's presence imposes, by way of contrast, a certain monotony on the song of Bluebeard's five wives.

Can we exhibit the support for this type of connection—physical causality or, in formal logic, implication—on the basis of the three operations that constitute transcendental algebra? The answer is positive.

We will now introduce a derived transcendental operation, *dependence*, which will serve as the support for causal connections in appearing, as well as for the famous implication of formal logic. *The 'dependence' of an apparent B with regard to another apparent A, is the apparent with the greatest intensity that can be conjoined to the second whilst remaining beneath the intensity of the first. Dependence is thus the envelope of those beings-there whose conjunction with A remains lesser in value than their conjunction with B.* The stronger the dependence of B with regard to A, the greater the envelope. This means that there are beings whose degree of appearance is very high in the world under consideration, yet whose conjunction with A remains inferior to B.

Let's consider once again the red ivy on the wall and the house in the setting sun. It's clear, for instance, that the wall of the façade, conjoined to the ivy that creeps upon it, produces an intensity which remains inferior to that of the house as a whole. Consequently, this wall will enter into the dependence of the house with regard to the ivy. But we can also consider the gilded inclination of the tiles above the ivy: its chromatic conjunction with the ivy is not nil, remaining included in—and therefore inferior to—the intensity of appearance of the house as a whole. The dependence of the house with regard to the ivy will envelop these two terms (the wall, the roof) and many others. Accordingly, even the distant mewling of the chainsaw will be part of it. For, as we've said, its conjunction with the red of the ivy was equal to the minimum, and the minimum, the measure of the inapparent, is surely inferior to the house's value of appearance.

In fact, for a reason that only the stark light of formalization will fully elucidate, the dependence of the being-there 'house' with regard to the being-there 'red ivy' will be the envelope of the entire autumnal world.

Is the word 'dependence' pertinent here? Definitely. For if a being B 'strongly' depends on A—which is to say that the transcendental measure of dependence is high—it is because it is possible to conjoin 'almost' the entire world to A whilst nevertheless remaining beneath the value of appearance of B. In brief, if something quite general holds for A, then it holds a fortiori for B, since B is considerably more enveloping than A. Thus, what holds (in terms of global appearing) for the ivy—one can see it from afar, it is bathed in the evening's rays, etc.—necessarily holds for the house, whose dependence with regard to the ivy is very high (maximal, in fact). 'Dependence' signifies that the predicative or descriptive situation of A holds almost entirely for B, once the transcendental value of dependence is high.

We can therefore anticipate some obvious properties of dependence. In particular, that the dependence of a degree of intensity with regard to itself is maximal; since the predicative situation of a being A is *absolutely* its own, the value of this 'tautological' dependence must perforce be maximal. The formal exposition will deduce this property, along with some others, from the sole concept of dependence.

Besides dependence, another crucial derivation concerns negation. Of course, we have already introduced a measure of the inapparent as such: the minimum. But are we in a position to derive, on the basis of our three operations, the means to think, in a world, the negation of a being-there of that world? The question deserves a complete discussion in its own right.

10. THE REVERSE OF AN APPARENT IN THE WORLD

We will show that given the degree of appearance of a being, we can define the reverse of this degree, and therefore the support for logical negation— or negation *in appearing*—as the simple consequence of our three fundamental operations.

First of all, what is a degree of appearance which is 'external' to another given degree? It is a degree whose conjunction with the given degree is equal to zero (to the minimum)—for instance, the degree of appearance of the motorcycle noise with regard to that of the red of the ivy.

But what is the region of the world external to a given apparent? It is the region that gathers together all those apparents whose degree of appearance is external to the degree of appearance of the initial being-there—for instance, with regard to the red on the autumnal wall, the disparate collection comprising the degrees of noise of the skidding motorcycle, the trees on the hill behind me, the periodic mewling of the chainsaw, perhaps even the whiteness of the gravel, or the fleeting form of a cloud, and so on. But the stony wall, too bound up with the ivy, or the roof-tiles just above, gilded by the setting sun, certainly do not belong to the same region: these givens are not 'without relation' to the colour of the ivy; their conjunction with it does not amount to nil.

Finally, once we have the disparate set of beings that are there in the world but which in terms of their appearing have nothing in common with the scarlet ivy, what synthesizes their degrees of appearance, and dominates as closely as possible all their measures? The envelope of this set. In other words, that being whose degree of appearance is greater than or equal to those of all the beings that are phenomenologically alien to the initial being (in the case at hand, the ivy). This envelope will be what prescribes the reverse of the ivy, in the world 'an autumn evening in the country'.

We will call 'reverse' of the degree of appearance of a being-there in a world, the envelope of the region of the world constituted by all the beings-there whose conjunction with the first takes the value of zero (the minimum).

Given an apparent in the world (the gravel, the trees, the cloud, the mewling of the chainsaw. . .), its conjunction with the scarlet ivy is always transcendentally measurable. We always know whether its value is or is not the minimum, a minimum whose existence is required by every transcendental order. Finally, given all the beings whose conjunction with the ivy is nil, the existence of the envelope of this singular region of the world is guaranteed by the principle of the regional stability of worlds. Now, this envelope is by definition the reverse of the scarlet ivy. So it's clear that the existence of the reverse of a being is really a logical consequence of the three fundamental parameters of being-there: minimality, conjunction and the envelope.

It's remarkable that what will serve to sustain negation in the order of appearing is the first consequence of the transcendental operations, and by no means an initial given. Negation, in the extended and 'positive' form of the existence of the reverse of a being, is a result. We can say that as soon as we are dealing with the being of the being of being-there, that is with the being of appearing as bound to the logic of a world, it follows that the reverse of a being exists, in the sense that there exists a degree of appearance 'contrary' to its own.

Once again, it's worth following this derivation closely.

Take the character of Ariadne, at the very end of *Ariadne and Bluebeard*, when she leaves by herself—the other wives having refused to be freed from the bind of love and slavery that fastens them to Bluebeard. At this moment in the opera, what is the reverse of Ariadne? Bluebeard, more fascinated than ever by the splendid freedom of the one he failed to enslave, maintains a silence about which it can be argued that it is interior to the explosion of the feminine song, so that the value of the conjunction Bluebeard/Ariadne is certainly not nil. The conjunction with Ariadne of the surrounding villagers—who have captured and then freed Bluebeard, who no longer obey anyone but Ariadne and tell her: 'Lady, truly, you are too beautiful, it's not possible . . .'—is certainly not equal to zero either. The Midwife is like an exotic part of Ariadne herself, her body without concept. In fact, at the very moment of the extreme declaration of freedom—when Ariadne sings 'See, the door is open and the countryside is blue'—those who subjectively have nothing in common with Ariadne, who make up her exterior, her absolutely heterogeneous feminine 'ground', are Bluebeard's women, who can only think the relationship to man through the categories of conservation and identity. In so doing, they display their radical foreignness to the imperative which Ariadne imposes on the new feminine world—the world that opens up, contemporaneous with Freud, at the beginning of the century (the opera dates from 1906). Bluebeard's women show this foreignness through refusal, silence or anxiety. It is musically clear then that the reverse of Ariadne's triumphal song, which the men (the villagers and Bluebeard) paradoxically identify with, is to be sought in the group comprising the five wives: Ygraine, Mélisande, Bellangère, Sélysette and Alladine. And since the envelope of the group of the five wives is given—as we've already noted—by the degree of existence of Alladine, which is very slightly superior to the degree of the four others, we can conclude the following: in the world of the opera's finale the reverse of Ariadne is Alladine.

The proof is provided in the staging of this preferential negation. I quote from the very end of the libretto:

ARIADNE: Will I go alone, Alladine?

At the sound of these words, Alladine runs to Ariadne, throws herself in her arms, and, wracked by convulsive sobs, holds her tightly and feverishly for a long while.

Ariadne embraces her in turn and, gently disentangling herself, still in tears, says:

Stay too, Alladine . . . Goodbye, be happy . . .

She moves away, followed by the Midwife.—The wives look at one other, then look at Bluebeard, slowly raising his head.—Silence.

We can see that the opera-world reaches its silent border, or its surge just before the silence, when the solitude of this woman, Ariadne, tearfully separates itself from its feminine reverse.

Dukas, who wrote a strange and vaguely sarcastic synopsis of his own opera, published in 1936 after his death, possessed an altogether precise awareness that the group of Bluebeard's five wives constituted the negative of Ariadne. As he wrote, Ariadne's relationship to these wives is 'clear if one is willing to reflect that it rests on a *radical* [emphasis in the text] opposition, and that the whole subject is based on Ariadne's confusion of her own desire for freedom in love with the little need of it felt by her companions, born slaves of the desire of their opulent tormentor'. And he adds, referring to the final scene we've just quoted: 'It is there that the absolute opposition between Ariadne and her companions will become pathetic, as the freedom that she had dreamed for them all gives way'.

Dukas will express the fact that Alladine synthesizes this feminine reverse of Ariadne, this absolute and latent negation, in a manner suited to the effects of the art of music: he writes that Alladine, at the moment of separation, is indeed 'the most touching'.

11. THERE EXISTS A MAXIMAL DEGREE OF APPEARANCE IN A WORLD

This is a consequence that combines the (axiomatic) existence of a minimum, responsible for measuring the non-appearance of a being in a world, and the (derived) existence of the reverse of a given transcendental degree. What can the measure of the degree of appearance which is the reverse of the minimal degree effectively be? What is the value of the reverse of the inapparent? Well, its value is that of the apparent as such, the indubitable apparent; in short, the apparent whose being-there in the world is attested absolutely. Such a degree is necessarily maximal. This is because there cannot be a degree of appearance greater than the one which validates appearance as such.

The transcendental maximum is attributed to the being which is absolutely there. For example, the number 1033 inappears with regard to the pagination of this book. Its transcendental value in the world 'pages of this book' is nil. If we look for the reverse of this measure, we will first find all those pages which themselves are in the book, and whose conjunction with 1033 is consequently and necessarily nil (they cannot discuss the same thing, contradict it, repeat it, etc.), because it is not of the book. But what envelops all the numbers of the book's pages? It is its 'number of pages', which is really the number assigned to its last page. Let's say that it's 650. We can then clearly see that the reverse of the minimum of appearance, assigned as 'zero-in-terms-of-the-book' to the number 1033, is none other than 650, the maximum number of pages of the book. In fact, 650 is the 'number of the book' in the sense that every number lesser than or equal to 650 marks a page. It is the transcendental maximum of pagination and the reverse of the minimum, which instead indexes every number that is not of the book (in fact, every number greater than 650).

The existence of a maximum (deduced here as the reverse of the minimum) is a worldly principle of stability. Appearing is never endlessly amendable; there is no infinite ascension towards the light of being-there. The maximum of appearance distributes, unto the beings indexed to it, the calm and equitable certainty of their worldliness.

This is also because there is no Universe, only worlds. In each and every world, the immanent existence of a maximal value for the transcendental degrees signals that *this* world is never *the* world. A world's power of localization is determinate: if a multiple appears in this world, there is an absolute degree of this appearance; this degree marks the being of being-there for a world.

12. WHAT IS THE REVERSE OF THE MAXIMAL DEGREE OF APPEARANCE?

This point is undoubtedly better clarified by formal exposition than by the artifices of phenomenology (see numbers 9 and 10 in Section 3). It is none-theless interesting to approach the problem via the following remark: the conjunction between the maximum—the existence of which we have just established—and any transcendental degree is equal to the latter. That the reverse of the maximum is the minimum is simply a consequence of this remark.

Take the world 'end of an autumn afternoon in the country'. The degree of maximal appearance measures appearance as such, namely the entire world to the extent that it brings forth a measure of appearing. We can say that the maximum degree fixes the 'there' of being-there in its fixed certainty. In short, this is the measure of the autumnal envelopment of the entire scene, its absolute appearing, without the cut provided by any kind of witness. What the poets try to name as the 'atmospheric' quality of the landscape, or painters as its general tonality, here subsumes the singular chromatic gradations and the repetition of lights.

It is obvious that what this enveloping generality has in common with a singular being-there of the world is precisely that this being is there, with the intensity proper to its appearing. Thus the red of the ivy, which the setting sun strikes horizontally, is an intense figure of the world. But if we relate this intensity to the entire autumnal scene that includes it, if we conjoin it to this total resource of appearing, it is simply identified, repeated and restored to itself. So it's true that the conjunction between a singular intensity of appearance and the maximal intensity does nothing but return the initial intensity. Conjoined to the autumn, the ivy is its red, already-there as 'ivy-in-autumn'.

Likewise, in the finale of the opera, we know that the femininity-song that detaches itself from Ariadne in the layers of music, after the sad 'be happy' which she directs to the voluntary servitude of the other wives, is the supreme measure of artistic appearing in this opera-world. Accordingly, once they are related back to this element which envelops all the dramatic and aesthetic components of the spectacle, once they are conjoined to its transcendence, which carries the ecstatic and grave timbre of the orchestra, the wives, Ariadne and Bluebeard are merely the captive repetition of their own there-identity, the scattered material for a global supremacy which is at last declared.

The equation *The conjunction of the maximum and of a degree is equal to that degree* is therefore phenomenologically limpid. But this means that the fact that the reverse of the supreme measure (of the maximum transcendental degree) is the inapparent is a matter of course. For this reverse, by definition, must have nothing in common with that of which it is the reverse; its conjunction with the maximum must be nil. But this conjunction, as we have just seen, is nothing but the reverse itself. It is therefore the degree of appearance in the world of the reverse which is nil; it is the reverse that inappears in that world.

How could anything at all within the opera not bear any relation to the ecstatic finale, when all the ingredients of the work—themes, voices, meaning, characters—relate to it and insist within it with their latent identity? Only what has never appeared in this opera can entertain with its finale a conjunction equal to zero. Therefore, the only transcendental degree able to provide a figure for the reverse of the heavens opened up by Dukas's orchestra in this final moment is indeed the minimal degree.

It is therefore certain that in any transcendental the reverse of the maximum is the minimum.

SECTION 2
Hegel

---

1. HEGEL AND THE QUESTION OF THE WHOLE

Hegel is without the shadow of a doubt the philosopher who has pushed furthest the interiorization of Totality into even the slightest movement of thought. One could argue that whereas we launch a transcendental theory of worlds by saying 'There is no Whole', Hegel guarantees the inception of the dialectical odyssey by positing that 'There is nothing but the Whole'. It is immensely interesting to examine the consequences of an axiom so radically opposed to the inaugural axiom of this book. But this interest cannot reside in a simple extrinsic comparison, or in a comparison of results. What is decisive is following the Hegelian idea in its movement, that is at the very moment in which it explicitly governs the method of thinking. This alone will allow us, in the name of the materialist dialectic, to do justice to our father: the master of the 'idealist' dialectic.

In our case, the inexistence of the Whole fragments the exposition into concepts which, as tightly linked as they may be, all tell us that situations, or worlds, are disjoined, or that the only truth is a local one. All of this culminates in the complex question of the plurality of eternal truths, which is the question of the (infinite) plurality of subjectivizable bodies, in the (infinite) plurality of worlds. For Hegel, totality as self-realization is the unity of the True. The True is 'self-becoming' and must be thought 'not only as substance, but also and at the same time as subject'. This means that the True collects its immanent determinations—the stages of its total unfolding—in what Hegel calls 'the absolute Idea'. If the challenge for us is not to slip into relativism (since there are truths), for Hegel, since truth is the Whole, it is not to slip either into the (subjective) mysticism of the One or into the (objective) dogmatism of Substance. Regarding the first, whose main representative is Schelling, he will say that the one 'who wants to find himself beyond and immediately within the absolute has no other knowledge in front of him than that of the empty negative, the abstract infinite'. Of the second, whose principal representative is Spinoza, he will say that it remains 'an extrinsic thinking'. Of course, Spinoza's 'simple and truthful insight'—that 'determinacy is negation'—'grounds the absolute unity of substance'. Spinoza saw perfectly that every thought must presuppose the Whole as containing determinations in itself, by self-negation. But he failed to grasp the *subjective* absoluteness of the Whole, which alone guarantees integral immanence: 'His substance does not itself contain the absolute form, and the knowing of this substance is not an immanent knowing'.

Ultimately, the Hegelian challenge can be summed up in three principles:

–The only truth is that of the Whole.
–The Whole is a self-unfolding, and not an absolute-unity external to the subject,
–The Whole is the immanent arrival of its own concept.

This means that the thought of the Whole is the effectuation of the Whole itself. Consequently, what displays the Whole within thought is nothing other than the path of thinking, that is its method. Hegel is the methodical thinker of the Whole. It is indeed with regard to this point that he brings his immense metaphysico-ontological book, the *Science of Logic*, to a close:

The method is the pure concept that relates itself only to itself; it is therefore the *simple self-relation* that is *being*. But now it is also *fulfilled being*, the *concept that comprehends* itself, being as the *concrete* and also absolutely *intensive* totality. In conclusion there remains only this to be said about this Idea, that in it, first, the *science of logic* has grasped its own concept. In the sphere of *being*, the beginning of its *content*, its concept appears as a knowing in a subjective reflection external to that content. But in the Idea of absolute cognition the concept has become the Idea's own content. The Idea is itself the pure concept that has itself for subject matter and which, in running itself as subject matter through the totality of its determinations, develops itself into the whole of its reality, into the system of Science, and concludes by apprehending this process of comprehending itself, thereby superseding its standing as content and subject matter and cognising the concept of Science.

I think this text calls for three remarks.

1. Against the idea (which I uphold) of a philosophy always conditioned by external truths (mathematical, poetic, political, etc.), Hegel pushes to the extreme the idea of an unconditionally autonomous speculation: 'the pure concept that has itself for subject matter' articulates straightaway, in its simple (and empty) form, the initial category, that of being. To place philosophy under the immanent authority of the Whole is also to render both possible and necessary its auto-foundation, since philosophy must be the exposition *of* the Whole, identical to the Whole *as* exposition (of itself).

2. However, the movement of this auto-foundation goes from (apparent) exteriority to (true) interiority. The beginning, because it is not yet the Whole, seems alien to the concept: 'In [. . .] *being* [. . .] its concept appears as a knowing [. . .] external to that content'. But through successive subsumptions, thinking appropriates the movement of the Whole as its own being, its own identity: 'in the Idea of absolute cognition the concept has become the Idea's own content'. The absolute idea is 'itself the pure concept that has itself for subject matter and which [runs] itself [. . .] through the totality of its determinations [. . .] into the system of Science'. What's more, it is not only the exposition of this system, it is its completed reflection, and it ends up 'cognising the concept of Science'.

We can see here that the axiom of the Whole leads to a figure of thought as the saturation of conceptual determinations—from the exterior towards the interior, from exposition towards reflection, from form towards content—as we gradually come to possess, in Hegel's vocabulary, 'fulfilled being' and the 'concept comprehending itself'. This is absolutely opposed to the axiomatic and egalitarian consequences of the absence of the Whole. For us it is impossible to rank worlds hierarchically, or to saturate the dissemination of multiple-beings. For Hegel, the Whole is also a norm, and it provides the measure of where thought finds itself, configuring Science as system.

Of course, we share with Hegel a conviction about the identity of being and thought. But for us this identity is a local occurrence and not a totalized result. We also share with Hegel the conviction regarding a universality of the True. But for us this universality is guaranteed by the singularity of truth-events, and not by the view that the Whole is the history of its immanent reflection.

3. Hegel's first word is 'being as concrete totality'. The axiom of the Whole distributes thought between purely abstract universality and the 'absolutely *intensive*' which characterizes the concrete; between the Whole as form and the Whole as internalized content. As we shall see, the theorem of the non-Whole distributes thought in an entirely different way, in accordance with a threefold division: the thinking of the multiple (mathematical ontology), the thinking of appearing (logic of worlds) and true-thinking (post-evental procedures borne by the subject-body).

Of course, triplicity is also a major Hegelian theme. But it is what we could call the triple of the Whole: the immediate, or the-thing-according-to-its-being; mediation, or the-thing-according-to-its-essence; the overcoming of mediation, or the-thing-according-to-its-concept. Or again: the beginning (the Whole as the pure edge of thought), patience (the negative labour of internalization), the result (the Whole in and for itself).

The triple of the non-Whole, which we advocate, is as follows: indifferent multiplicities, or ontological unbinding; worlds of appearing, or the logical link; truth-procedures, or subjective eternity.

Hegel remarks that the complete thinking of the triple of the Whole makes four. This is because the Whole itself, as immediacy-of-the-result, still lies beyond its own dialectical construction. Likewise, so that truths (the third term, thought) may supplement worlds (the second term, logic), whose being is the pure multiple (the first term, ontology), we need a vanishing cause, which is the exact opposite of the Whole: an abolished flash, which we call the event, and which is the fourth term.

2. BEING-THERE AND LOGIC OF THE WORLD

Hegel thinks with an altogether unique incisiveness the correlation between, on one hand, the local externalization of being (being-there) and, on the other, the logic of determination, understood as the coherent figure of the situation of being. This is one of the first dialectical moments of the *Science of Logic*, one of those moments that fix the very style of thinking.

First of all, what is being-there? It is being as determined by its coupling with what it is not. Just as for us a multiple-being separates itself from its pure being once it is assigned to a world, for Hegel being-there 'is not simple being, but being-there'. A gap is then established between pure being ('simple being') and being-there; this gap stems from the fact that being is determined by that which, within it, is not it, and therefore by non-being: 'According to its becoming, being-there is in general being with non-being, but in such a way that this non-being is assumed in its simple unity with being; being-there is determinate being in general'. We can pursue this parallel further. For us, once it is posited—not only in the mathematical rigidity of its multiple-being, but also in and through its worldly localization—a being is given simultaneously as that which is other than itself and as that which is other than others. Whence the necessity of a logic that integrates these differentiations and lends them consistency. For Hegel too the immanent emergence of determination—that is of a negation specific to a being-there—means that being-there becomes being-other. On this point, Hegel's text is truly remarkable:

> Non-being-there is not pure nothing; for it is a nothing *as nothing of being-there*. And this negation grasps being-there itself; but in the latter it is unified with being. Consequently, non-being-there is itself a being; it is *not-being-there as a being*. But a not-being-there as a being is itself being-there. At the same time, however, *this second being-there* is not being-there in the same way as before; for it is just as much not-being-there; being-there as not-being-there; being there as the nothing of itself, so that this nothing of itself is equally being-there.—Or being-there is essentially *being-other*.

Of course, the assertion that being-there is 'essentially being-other' requires a logical arrangement that will lead—via the exemplary dialectic between being-for-another-thing and being-in-itself—towards the concept of reality. Reality is in effect the moment of the unity of being-in-itself and of being-other, or the moment in which determinate being has in itself the ontological support of every difference from the other, what Hegel calls being-for-another-thing. For us too, a 'real' being is the one which, appearing locally (in a world), is at the same time its own multiple-identity—as thought by rational ontology—and the various degrees of its difference from the other beings in the same world. So we agree with Hegel that the moment of the reality of a being is that in which being, locally effectuated as being-there, is identity with itself and with others, as well as difference from itself and from others. Hegel proposes a superb formula, which declares that 'Being-there as reality is the differentiation of itself into being-in-itself and being-for-another-thing'.

The title of Hegel's book alone suffices to prove that what ultimately regulates all this is a logic—the logic of the actuality of being. We can add to it the affirmation according to which, on the basis of this being-there, 'determinacy will no longer detach itself from being', for (this is the decisive point) 'the true that now finds itself as the ground is this unity of non-being with being'. For our part, what is effectively exposed to thought in the (transcendental) logic of the appearing of beings is the rule-governed play of multiple-being 'in itself' with its variable differentiation. Logic, qua consistency of appearing, organizes the aleatory unity, under the law of the world, between the mathematics of the multiple and the local evaluation of the multiple's relations both to itself and to others.

If the agreement between our thinking and Hegel's is so manifest here, it is obviously because for him being-there remains a category that is still far from being saturated, standing at a considerable remove from the internalization of the Whole. As so often, we will admire in Hegel the power of local dialectics, the precision of the logical fragments in which he articulates some fundamental concepts (in this instance, being-there and being-for-another).

We could also have anchored our comparison in the dialectic of the phenomenon, rather than in that of being-there. Unlike us, Hegel does not identify being-there (the initial determination of being) with appearing (which for him is a determination of essence). Nonetheless, the logical constraint that leads from being-there to reality is practically the same as the one that leads from appearing to 'the essential relation'. Just as we posit that the logical legislation of appearing is the constitution of the singularity of a world, Hegel posits:

1. that essence appears, and becomes real appearance;
2. that law is essentially appearing.

This idea is a profound one, and we take inspiration from it. We must understand that appearing, albeit contingent with regard to the multiple-composition of beings, is absolutely real; and that the essence of this real is purely logical.

However, unlike Hegel, we do not posit the existence of 'kingdom of laws', and even less that 'the world that is in and for itself is the totality of existence; there is nothing else outside of it'. For us, it is of the essence of

146

the world not to be the totality of existence, and to endure the existence of an infinity of other worlds outside of itself.

3. HEGEL CANNOT ALLOW A MINIMAL DETERMINATION

For Hegel, there can neither be a minimal (or nil) determination of the identity between two beings, nor an absolute difference between two beings. On this point Hegel's doctrine is thus diametrically opposed to ours, which instead articulates the absolute intra-worldly difference between two beings onto the 'nil' measure of their identity. This opposition between the logic of the idealist dialectic and the logic of the materialist dialectic is illuminating because it is constructive, like every opposition (*Gegensatz*) is for Hegel. For him opposition is in effect nothing less than 'the unity of identity and diversity'.

The question of a minimum of identity between two beings, or between a being and itself, is meaningless for a thinking that assumes the Whole, for if there is a Whole there is no non-apparent as such. A being can fail to appear in a given world, but it is not thinkable for it not to appear in the Whole. This is why Hegel always insists on the immanence and proximity of the absolute in any being whatever. This means that the being-there of every being consists in having to appear as a moment of the Whole. For Hegel, appearing never measures zero.

Of course, it can vary in intensity. But beneath this variation of appearing there is always a fixed determination which affirms the thing as such in accordance with the Whole.

Consider this passage, at once clear-cut and subtle, which is preoccupied with the concept of magnitude:

A magnitude is usually defined as that which can be *increased* or *diminished*. But to increase means to make the magnitude *more*, to decrease, to make the magnitude *less*. In this there lies a *difference* of magnitude as such from itself and magnitude would thus be that of which the magnitude can be altered. The definition thus proves itself to be inept in so far as the same term is used in it which was to have been defined. [. . .] In that imperfect expression, however, one cannot fail to recognize the main point involved, namely the indifference of the change, so that the change's own *more* and *less*, its indifference to itself, lies in its very concept.

The difficulty here derives directly from the inexistence of a minimal degree, which would permit the determination of what possesses an effective magnitude. Hegel is then obliged to posit that the essence of change in magnitude is Magnitude as the element 'in itself' of change. Or, that far from taking root in the localized prescription of a minimum, degrees of intensity (the more or the less) constitute the surface of change, understood as the immanent power of the Whole within each thing. For my part, I subordinate appearance as such to the transcendental measure of the identities between a being and all the other beings that are-there in a determinate world. Hegel instead subordinates this measure (the more/less, *Mehr/Minder*) to the absoluteness of the Whole, which in each thing governs its change and raises it up to the concept.

For me, the degree of appearance of a being has its real in minimality (the zero), which alone authorizes the consideration of its magnitude. For Hegel, on the contrary, the degree has its real in the (qualitative) change that attests to the existence of the Whole; consequently, there is no conceivable minimum of identity.

Now, that there exists in every world an absolute difference between beings (in the sense of a nil measure of the intra-worldly identity of these beings or a minimal degree of identity of their being-there) is something which again Hegel is not going to allow. He calls this thesis (which he considers to be false) 'the proposition of diversity'. It declares that 'There are no two things which are perfectly equal'. In his eyes the essence of this thesis is to produce its own 'dissolution and nullity'. Here is Hegel's refutation:

> This involves the dissolution and nullity of the *proposition of diversity*. Two things are not perfectly equal; so they are at once equal and unequal; equal, simply because they are things, or just two, without further qualification—for each is a thing and a one, no less than the other—but they are unequal *ex hypothesi*. We are therefore presented with this determination, that both moments, equality and inequality, are diverse in *One and the same thing*, or that the difference, while falling asunder, is at the same time one and the same relation. It has therefore passed over into *opposition*.

We encounter here the classical dialectical movement whereby Hegel sublates identity in and by difference itself. From the inequality between two things we derive the immanent equality for which this inequality exists. For example, things only display their difference to the extent that each is One by differentiating itself from the other, and therefore, from this angle, is the same as the other.

This is what the clause of minimality, as the first moment of the phenomenology of being-there, makes impossible for us. Of course, we do not adopt, any more than Hegel, 'the proposition of diversity'. It is possible that in a determinate world two beings may appear as absolutely equal. But neither do we undertake a sublation of the One of the two beings; we do not exhibit anything as 'One and the same thing'. It might turn out that in a given world two beings will appear as absolutely unequal. There can be Twos-without-One (as we have established elsewhere, this is the great problem of amorous truths).

In effect, the clause of the non-being of the Whole irreparably disjoins the logic of being-there (degrees of identity, theory of relations) from the ontology of the pure multiple (mathematics of sets). Hegel's aim, as prescribed by the axiom of the Whole, is on the contrary to corroborate the unified onto-logical character of any given category (in this instance, the equality of beings).

4. THE APPEARING OF NEGATION

Hegel confronts with his customary vigour the centuries-old problem whose obscurity we have already underscored: what becomes, not of the negation of being, but of the negation of being-there? How can negation appear? What is negation, not in the guise of nothingness, but in that of a non-being in a world, in accordance with the logic of that world? In Hegel's post-Kantian vocabulary, the most radical form of this question will be the following: what becomes of the phenomenal character of the negation of a phenomenon?

For Hegel, the phenomenon is 'essence in its existence'; that is, in our own vocabulary, a being-determined-in-its-being (a pure multiplicity) insofar as it is there, in a world. The negation of a phenomenon thus understood will amount to an essential negation of existence. We can easily observe how Hegel will make the fact that essence is internal but also alien to the phenomenon (because the phenomenon is essence, but only insofar as the essence exists) 'work' within the phenomenon itself. We will thus see the inessential side of phenomenality (existence as pure external diversity) enter into contradiction with the essence whose phenomenon is existence, the immanent unity of this diversity. Thus the negation of the phenomenon will be its subsisting-as-one *within* existential diversity. This is what Hegel calls the *law* of the phenomenon.

We have the solution of the problem: the phenomenal negation of the phenomenon is that every phenomenon has a law. It is clear that (as with our concept of the reverse) negation itself remains a positive and intra-worldly given.

Here is Hegel's comment on the negative passage from phenomenal diversity to the unity of law:

> The phenomenon is at first existence as *negative* self-mediation, so that the existent is mediated with itself through *its own non-subsistence*, through an other, and, again, through the *non-subsistence of this other*. In this is contained *first*, the mere appearing and disappearing of both, the unessential phenomenon; *secondly*, also their *permanence* or *law*; for *each* of the two *exists* in this sublating of the other; and their positedness as their negativity is at the same time the *identical, positive* positedness of both. This permanent subsistence which the phenomenon has in law, is therefore, conformable to its determination, opposed, *in the first place*, to the *immediacy* of being which existence has.

It is obvious that the phenomenon, as the non-subsisting of essence, is nothing but 'appearing and disappearing'. But as a result it sustains as its internal other the permanence of the essence of which it is the existence. This specific negation of phenomenal non-subsisting by the permanence within it of the essence is the law. Not simply essence, but essence having become the law of the phenomenon, and thus the positivity of its appearing–disappearing.

Accordingly, the sunstruck ivy in the autumn evening is the pure phenomenon for the essential 'autumn' it harbours within it, autumn as the compulsory chemistry of the leaves. Its appearing-red is undoubtedly the inessential aspect of this vegetable chemistry, but it also attests to its permanence as the invariable negation of its own fleetingness. Lastly, the autumnal law of plants—the chemistry which dictates that at a given temperature a given pigmentation of the leafage is necessary—is the immanent negation on the wall of the house of the phenomenon 'red of the ivy'. It is the invisible invariable of the fleetingness of the visible. As Hegel says, 'the kingdom of laws is the reproduction *at rest* of the phenomenal world'.

What must be granted to Hegel may be summarized in two points:

1. The negation of a phenomenon cannot be its annihilation. This negation must itself be phenomenal, or it must be a negation *of* the phenomenon. It must concern the apparent in appearing, its existence, and not unfold as a simple suppression of its being.

In the positivity of the law of the phenomenon, Hegel perceives intra-worldly negation. I am obviously proposing an entirely different concept, that of the reverse of a being-there. Or, more precisely: the reverse of a transcendental degree of appearance. But we agree on the affirmative reality of 'negation', as soon as one decides to operate according to a logic of appearing. There is a being-there of the reverse, just as there is a being-there of the law. Law and reverse have nothing to do with nothingness.

2. Phenomenal negation is not classical. In particular, the negation of the negation does not equal affirmation. For Hegel, law is the negation of the phenomenon, but the negation of the law does not restore the phenomenon. In the *Science of Logic* this second negation opens in fact onto the concept of actuality.

Similarly, if Alladine is the reverse of Ariadne, the reverse of Alladine is not Ariadne. Rather, as we suggested, it is femininity-song grasped in its own right.

The similarities, however, stop here. For in Hegel the negation of the phenomenon is nothing but the effectuation of the contradiction which constitutes its immediacy. If law arises as the negation of the phenomenon, if, as he says, 'the phenomenon finds its contrary in the law, which is its negative unity', it is ultimately because the phenomenon harbours the contradiction of essence and existence. The law is the unity of essence returning via negation into the dispersion of its own existence. For Hegel there is an appearing of negation because appearing, or existence, is internally its other, essence. In other words, negation is there, since the 'there' is already negation.

This axiomatic solution, which puts the negative at the very origin of appearing, cannot satisfy us. As I've said, negation for us is not primitive but derivative. The reverse is a concept constructed on the basis of three great transcendental operations: the minimum, the conjunction and the envelope.

It follows that the existence of the reverse of a degree of appearance has nothing to do with an immanent dialectic between being and being-there, or between essence and existence. Alladine is the reverse of Ariadne due to the logic of that singular world which is the opera *Ariadne and Bluebeard*, and could not be directly derived from Ariadne's being-in-itself. More generally, the reverse of an apparent is a singular worldly exteriority whose envelope we determine, and which cannot be derived from the consideration of the being-there taken in terms of its pure multiple being. In other words, the reverse is indeed a logical category (and therefore relative to the worldliness of beings); it is not an ontological category (linked to the intrinsic multiple composition of beings, or, if you will, to the mathematical world).

Notwithstanding its great conceptual beauty, we cannot second the declaration that opens the section of the *Science of Logic* entitled 'The World of Appearance and the World-in-Itself':

> The existent world tranquilly raises itself to the realm of laws; the null content of its varied being-there has its subsistence in an *other*; its subsistence is therefore its dissolution. But in this other the phenomenal also coincides *with itself*; thus the phenomenon in its changing is also an enduring, and its positedness is law.

No, the phenomenal world does not 'raise itself' to any realm whatsoever, its 'varied being-there' has no separate subsistence which would amount to its negative effectuation. Existence stems solely from the contingent logic of a world which nothing sublates, and in which—in the guise of the reverse—negation appears as pure exteriority.

From the red of the ivy spread out on the wall, we will never obtain—even as its law—the autumnal shadow on the hills, which envelops the ivy's transcendental reverse.

SECTION 3
Algebra of the Transcendental

1. INEXISTENCE OF THE WHOLE: TO AFFIRM THE EXISTENCE
OF A SET OF ALL SETS IS INTRINSICALLY CONTRADICTORY

Since the formal thinking of entities has been accomplished in mathematics as set theory, establishing the inexistence of a total being means demonstrating, on the basis of the axiomatic of this theory, that a set of all sets cannot exist. 'Set of all sets' is in effect the mathematical concept of the Whole.

As the well-versed reader will have already recognized in the conceptual exposition of this point, at the core of this demonstration lies Russell's paradox, which concerns the division between sets that are elements of themselves (such that $(a \in a)$) and those that are not: $\neg (a \in a)$.

This paradox, communicated to Frege by Russell in 1902, has a far more general impact than the one which bears on the Whole, or on the inconsistency of the concept of universe. In effect, it means that *it is not true that to a well-defined concept there necessarily corresponds the set of the objects which fall under this concept*. This acts as a (real) obstacle to the sovereignty of language: to a well-defined predicate, which consists within language, there may only correspond a real inconsistency (a deficit of multiple-being).

To demonstrate this, we consider the predicate 'not being an element of oneself', which we will write P_p ('p' for 'paradoxical'). The definition is written as follows:

$$P_p (a) \leftrightarrow \neg (a \in a)$$

This predicate is perfectly clear, devoid of formal deficiencies. Suppose there exists a set (a being) that effectuates this concept. It will be the set M_p of all the sets that have the property P_p. Therefore, it will be the set of all the sets which are not elements of themselves, or non-reflexive sets. Therefore:

$$\text{(I)} \quad (a \in M_p) \leftrightarrow P_p(a) \leftrightarrow \neg(a \in a)$$

We then show that M_p can neither be an element of itself nor can it not be an element of itself. It suffices to apply the equivalences from (I) above, as postulated for any a, to the multiple M_p. We then get:

$$(M_p \in M_p) \leftrightarrow P_p(M_p) \leftrightarrow \neg(M_p \in M_p)$$

The equivalence thereby obtained between a statement ($M_p \in M_p$) and its negation ($\neg(M_p \in M_p)$) is an explicit formal contradiction. It ruins any logical consistency whatsoever. Therefore, M_p cannot be. This means that the predicate P_p has no extension, not even an empty [*vide*] extension (since the void [*vide*] is a set). In terms of what exists, multiple-being does not follow from language. The real of being breaks with predicative consistency.

The inexistence of the Whole is thus a consequence. For if the Whole exists, there must exist, as a subset of the Whole, the set M_p of those multiples which satisfy the property P_p, that is to say those multiples a such that $\neg(a \in a)$. This stems from a fundamental axiom, the axiom of separation or Zermelo axiom.

The axiom of separation draws the conceptual consequences from Russell's paradox. This paradox shows that one cannot pass directly from a predicate to the multiple of the beings that fall under this predicate. Keeping this in mind, we introduce an ontological condition: *given a set and a predicate*, there exists the subset of this set comprising the elements that fall under the predicate. You no longer say: given P, there exists M_p such that $(a \in M_p) \leftrightarrow P_p(a)$. That would make the entirety of language inconsistent (Russell's paradox). You say instead: given (any) E and P, there always exists $E_p \subseteq E$ such that $(a \in E_p) \leftrightarrow P(a)$. You can separate in E all the $a \in E$ which fall under the predicate P. There is a 'there is' which is given with P: the set E. The paradox then ceases to function.

Unless, of course, you force the existence of a total set U. Then the property '$\neg(a \in a)$' separates, in U, all the a's that have this property, and the paradox once again ruins all consistency. Formally speaking, if U is the set of all sets:

$\exists M_p \, [(\forall a) \, [(a \in U) \to (\neg \, (a \in a) \leftrightarrow (a \in M_p)]]$ ax. sep.

$M_p \in U$ U is total

$(M_p \in M_p) \leftrightarrow \neg \, (M_p \in M_p)$ consequence

The last formula is an explicit contradiction, which ruins language. We must therefore posit that M_p does not exist. Since M_p is derived from U through the legitimate axiom of separation, this means that U does not exist.

This completes the formal demonstration of the inexistence of the Whole.

2. FUNCTION OF APPEARING AND FORMAL DEFINITION OF THE TRANSCENDENTAL

Ontologically, a multiple cannot differ 'more or less' from another. A multiple is only identical to itself, and it is a law of being-qua-being (the axiom of extension) that the slightest local difference—for example one which concerns a single element amid an infinity of others—entails an absolute global difference.

The axiom of extension declares that two multiple-beings are equal if and only if they have *exactly* the same multiple composition, and therefore the same elements. In formal terms:

$$(a = \beta) \leftrightarrow \forall x[(x \in a) \leftrightarrow (x \in \beta)]$$

A contrario, the existence of a single element that belongs to the one but not the other entails that the two beings are absolutely distinct:

$$\exists x \, [(x \in a) \text{ and } \neg \, (x \in \beta)] \to \neg \, (a \in \beta)$$

It also follows that if two beings are globally different, there certainly exists at least one element of the one that is not an element of the other (this will turn out to be of crucial importance). Therefore there exists a *local* difference, or difference 'in a point', which can serve to test the global or absolute difference between the two beings.

This means that the ontological theory of difference circulates univocally between the local and the global. Every difference in a point entails the absolute difference of two beings. And every absolute difference implies that there exists at least one difference in one point. In particular, there can be no purely global difference, meaning that in being as such there is no purely intensive or qualitative differentiation.

But the same cannot be said in terms of appearing. It is clear that multiples in situation can differ more or less, resemble one another, be nearer or farther and so on. It is thus necessary to admit that what governs appearing is not the ontological composition of a particular being (a multiple) but rather the relational evaluations which are determined by the situation and which localize that being within it. Unlike the legislation of the pure multiple, these evaluations do not always identify local difference with global difference. They are not ontological. That is why *we will give the name 'logic' to the laws of the relational network which determine the worldly appearing of multiple-being*. Every world possesses its own logic, which is the legislation of appearing, or of the 'there' of being-there.

The minimal requirement for every localization is being able to determine a degree of identity (or non-identity) between an element a and an element β, when both are deemed to belong to the same world. We therefore have good reason to think that in every world there exists what we will call a *function of appearing*, which, given two elements of that world, measures their degree of identity. We will write the function of appearing as **Id** (a, β). It designates the extent to which, in terms of the logic of the world, we can say that the multiples a and β appear identical.

The function of appearing is the first transcendental indexing: it is a question of knowing what is the degree of identity between two beings of the same world, that is the degree according to which these two beings *appear identical*.

But what are the values of the function of appearing? What *measures* the degree of identity between two appearances of multiplicities? Here too there is no general or totalizing answer. The scale of evaluation of appearing, and thus the logic of a world, depends on the singularity of that world itself. What we can say is that in every world such a scale exists, and it is this scale that we call the transcendental.

Like everything that is, the transcendental is a multiple, which obviously belongs to the situation of being of which it is the transcendental. But this multiple is endowed with a structure which authorizes the fact that on its basis one can set out the values (the degrees) of identity between the multiples that belong to the situation, that one can establish the value of the function of appearing **Id** (a, β), whatever a and β may be.

This structure has properties that vary depending on the worlds. But it also possesses general invariant properties, without which it could not operate. There is a general mathematics of the transcendental, which we will develop below.

The idea—a very simple one—is that in every world, given two beings α and β which are there, there exists a value p of **Id** (α, β). To say that **Id** $(\alpha, \beta) = p$ means that, *with regard to their appearing in that world*, the beings α and β—which remain perfectly and univocally determined in their multiple composition—are identical 'to the p degree', or are p-identical. The essential requirement then is that the degrees p are held in an order-structure, so that for instance it can make sense to say that in a fixed referential world, α is more identical to β than to γ. In formal terms, if **Id** $(\alpha, \beta) = p$ and **Id** $(\alpha, \gamma) = q$, this means that $p > q$.

Note that saying 'it makes sense to say that α is more identical to β than to γ' does not indicate an obligation: the relation of identity from α to β may also not be comparable to the relation of identity from α to γ: order is not necessarily total. For the time being, it suffices to keep in mind that the logic of appearing presents itself as an order and that transcendental operations present themselves as indexings of beings on the algebraic and topological resources harboured by this order.

3. EQUIVALENCE-STRUCTURE AND ORDER-STRUCTURE

It is useful to recall here what an order is. After all, the transcendental makes possible evaluations and comparisons, composing a scale of measurement for the more or less, and the simplest abstract form of such a power is the order-relation—in other words, that which allows us to say that a given element α is 'greater than' (or placed 'higher' on the scale of comparison, or of superior intensity, etc.) than another element β.

To get a good grasp of the essence of the order-relation, it is helpful to compare it to another primitive relation, the one that establishes the strict (or rigid) identity between two elements. This is called the equivalence-relation. It axiomatically decrees the identity (equivalence) between two elements α and β in the following fashion:

a. An element α is always identical with itself (reflexivity).
b. If α is identical to β, and β to γ, then α is identical to γ (transitivity).
c. If α is identical to β, then β is identical to α (symmetry).

Note that the relationship of equivalence decrees a rigorous symmetry, which is formalized by the appropriately-named 'axiom of symmetry'. In this relationship, the relation between an element and another is the same as the relation between this element and the first. That is why the equivalence-relation is used most frequently in order to sanction the *substitution* of β for a in a formula, once we know that β is equivalent to a. We could even say that our three axioms (reflexivity, transitivity and symmetry) are axioms of substitutability.

But this entails that the very essence of relation, the essence of every differentiated evaluation or of every comparison, is not yet captured by the 'relation' of equivalence. For a comparative evaluation always presumes that we are able to contrast really distinct elements, which is to say non-substitutable elements. For this to be the case, we must reject the third axiom, the one that declares the symmetry of the linked elements. Basically, the order-relation is the result of this rejection. It is 'like' the equivalence-relation, with the proviso that it replaces symmetry with antisymmetry.

The order-relation assumes that difference is axiomatically perceivable. Of course, the fact that a term is linked to itself can constitute a primitive given. Likewise, the ability for the relation to transit (in the sense that if $a = \beta$ and $\beta = \gamma$ then $a = \gamma$) is a useful property of expansion. We will therefore retain reflexivity and transitivity. But in the end it is there where two terms cannot be substituted in terms of what links them that the relationship between relation and singularity is affirmed and that differentiated evaluations become possible. We will thus explicitly reject symmetry.

A relation between elements of a set A is an order-relation, written $\leq$, if it obeys the following three axiomatic dispositions:

a. Reflexivity: $x \leq x$.
b. Transitivity: $[(x \leq y)$ and $(y \leq z)] \to (x \leq z)]$.
c. Antisymmetry: $[(x \leq y)$ and $(y \leq x)] \to (x = y)]$.

Antisymmetry is what distinguishes order from equivalence, and what allows us truly to enter the domain of the relation between non-substitutable singularities. In the (order-)relation that x entertains with y, the element x cannot trade places with y unless these two elements are rigorously 'the same'. The order-relation is really the very first inscription of a demand of the Other, inasmuch as the places that it establishes (before $\leq$ or after $\leq$) are in general not exchangeable. Reflexivity and transitivity are Cartesian dispositions: self-relation and order of reasons. But they are properties that also pertain to identity or equivalence. The order-relation retains these Cartesian properties. But with antisymmetry it formalizes a certain type of non-substitutability.

For the sake of intuitive ease, and since we have comparisons in mind, $x \leq y$ may be read in one of the two following ways: 'x is lesser than or equal to y' or 'y is greater than or equal to x'. We could even say 'smaller than' or 'bigger than'. But we should bear in mind that the dialectic of the great and the small in no way subsumes the entire, axiomatically established field of the order-relation. These are merely ways of reading the symbolism; the essence of the order-relation is comparison 'in itself'.

The concept of an order-relation does not contain the fact that it links together all the elements of the base set A. That is why, in the general case, a set endowed with an order-relation is called a *partially-ordered set*, or POS. In a POS, there are three possible cases for any two elements x and y: either $x \leq y$, or $y \leq x$, or neither $x \leq y$ nor $y \leq x$. In the third case, we say that x and y are *incomparable* (or not linked).

Relation is said to be *total* in the particular case in which two elements taken at random are always comparable: we have either $x \leq y$ or $y \leq x$.

Every transcendental T of a given world is a partially-ordered set (a POS), with the proviso that in certain worlds, which are in point of fact very special, the transcendental is the bearer of a total order-relation.

What we could call the ontology of the transcendental is summed up by the existence, in every world, of a POS.

4. FIRST TRANSCENDENTAL OPERATION: THE MINIMUM OR ZERO

The formalization of the exposition of the transcendental, or formal presentation of the fundamental operations that make the cohesion of appearing possible, takes the form of particular properties of an order-structure, because this type of structure lies at the base of every transcendental.

The existence of a minimum—of a degree zero of magnitude—is a very simple property.

From now on, let T (for 'transcendental') stand for a set endowed with an order-relation written as $\leq$. This relation obeys the three axioms of order: reflexivity, transitivity and antisymmetry. It is a question of formalizing the reasonable idea according to which the transcendental T, which serves as the support for evaluations of intensity in that which appears, is capable of establishing a *nil intensity*.

Of course, nil or zero are determinations relative to a world, and therefore to the transcendental of that world. In the order of appearing (or of logic), it is meaningless to speak of a nil intensity in itself. We know that in the order of being there exists an intrinsic vacuity, that of the empty set or set of nothing, which is in itself the minimum multiple. But the empty set is really a name that only takes on meaning in a very particular situation, the ontological situation, which is mathematics as it has been historically developed. In that situation, 'empty set' or $\varnothing$ is the proper name of being-qua-being. With regard to that which appears in a given world, all that we can hope is to be able transcendentally to evaluate a *minimal* intensity. Obviously, for one inhabiting this world, such a minimum will equal zero, because no intensity will be known which is inferior to this minimum. But for the logician of appearing this minimum will be relative to the transcendental in question.

We therefore posit that the transcendental T of any situation implies a minimum for the order that structures T. Let us call this minimum μ. We are dealing with an element such that, for every element p of T, we have $\mu \leq p$ (μ is 'lesser than' every element p of T).

A really remarkable point, though it is deductively very simple, is the *uniqueness* of the minimum. The demonstration of this uniqueness is an almost immediate consequence of the axiom of antisymmetry. This means that it truly inheres in the order-structure, whose principal feature is antisymmetry.

Suppose that μ and μ' are both minimum. It follows, by the definition of the minimum, which is to be inferior to every other element of the transcendental, that $\mu \leq \mu'$ and $\mu' \leq \mu$. The axiom of antisymmetry demands that μ and μ' be the same, or that $\mu = \mu'$.

Here then is our first phenomenological motif correlated to the One: from the existence of a capacity for a degree zero of identity in appearing it follows that this degree is in every case unique. There exists, in general, an infinity of measures of appearance, but only one of non-appearance.

5. SECOND TRANSCENDENTAL OPERATION: CONJUNCTION

The formalization of the phenomenological idea of conjunction elucidates its concept, at the same time as it details its purely algebraic nature. As we have seen, the underlying phenomenal idea is to express what two beings have in common, to the extent that they co-appear in a world. More precisely, it is a question of that which appears as being common to two apparents. The transcendental translation of the 'common' of two apparents, and therefore the operator of conjunction, passes through the comparison of their intensities of appearance on the basis of the order-structure of the transcendental. Given the measure of the intensities of appearance (that is of the differentials of appearance) of two beings which are there in this world, we ascertain the intensity of appearance of that which is maximally common to them *in the world in question*. In order for the transcendental to operate in this direction, it is simply necessary that, given two degrees of its order, there always exists the degree that is immediately 'enveloped' by the two others; that is, the greatest degree that the two others simultaneously dominate.

For any POS (in this case, for a transcendental T), this idea can be realized in the following way: given two elements p and q of T, that is two transcendental degrees, *we suppose that there always exists an element (written as $p \cap q$) which is the greatest of all those which are lesser than both p and q*. In other terms, if $r \leq p$ and $r \leq q$ (r is lesser than or equal to p and q), we have on the one hand $p \cap q \leq p$ and $p \cap q \leq q$ ($p \cap q$ is also lesser than p and q), and on the other hand $r \leq p \cap q$ ($p \cap q$ is greater than or equal to every r that has this property). If such a $p \cap q$ exists, we say that it is the conjunction of p and q.

As with the minimum μ, the fact that for a given p and q their conjunction is unique is an immediate consequence of the axiom of antisymmetry.

We can see that in the transcendental T, the conjunction, that is $p \cap q$, measures the degree of appearance 'immediately inferior' to the degrees p and q. That is why it is invoked as a measure of what is in common to two beings which co-appear in world if the differential of intensity with regard to their appearing is measured by p and q. We can still call the operation $p \cap q$ 'conjunction' even if it does not pertain to beings-there as such, but to the transcendental measures of appearing, which ground its logical bond.

On the basis of the operation $\cap$, it is interesting to formalize the three cases that have served us as phenomenological guides for the introduction of conjunction.

In case 1, that of the red foliage of the ivy and of the ivy as a whole, we accepted that the manifestness of the being-there of the latter, in the rural world of autumn, carries that of the former. If then, drawing on the resources of the transcendental and its order-structure, we agree to assign value q to the appearing of the ivy and value p to that of the red foliage, we have the following transcendental ordering, which expresses the subordination of manifestations: $p \leq q$. We conclude from this that the value of appearance of what the two have in common is p itself, that is $p \cap q = p$. This is certain, by the definition of $\cap$. For p is lesser than or equal both to p (by $p \leq p$, the axiom of reflexivity of the order-relation) and to q (by the subordination of manifestations). And it is certainly the greatest in this case, for if another were greater than it, that is greater than p, it could obviously not be lesser than both q and p. Finally, $p \cap q = p$.

What's more, the link between the subordination $p \leq q$ and the conjunctive equation $p \cap q = p$ is even tighter. We have just shown that if $p \leq q$, then $p \cap q = p$. But the reciprocal is also true: if $p \cap q = p$, then $p \leq q$. That is because the definition of $p \cap q$ dictates that $p \cap q \leq q$. So if $p \cap q = p$, we have $p \leq q$.

We can then see that the transcendental order, which authorizes the comparison of intensities of appearance in a world, and conjunction, which exhibits the degree of appearing of what two apparents have in common, are linked by the equivalence $p \leq q \leftrightarrow (p \cap q = p)$. This equivalence will be used so often in what follows that it warrants a name. We will call it proposition P.0.

With proposition P.0 in hand, it would be perfectly possible to begin the exposition of the transcendental with an axiomatic of conjunction, and to make order into an induced structure, utilizing the equivalence above as a definition of this order. This would highlight the relational and operational immediacy of appearing, but at the price of the genuine intelligibility of its logic and of the more secure path which leads to this logic on the basis of the ontology of the multiple.

In case 2, that of the red foliage of the ivy and the visible architecture of the house, we indicated that it is a third term, the stone wall, which appears as the greatest visible surface that enters into the composition of the being-there of the two other terms. If t is the transcendental indexing of this wall, p that of the red foliage and q that of the house, we obviously have $t \leq p$ and $t \leq q$, since t is the greatest degree of the transcendental to entertain this double relationship. We will then simply have $t = p \cap q$, with t differing from both p and q.

Finally in case 3, that of the wall of the house covered by the red foliage and the noise of the motorcycle, there is—as we saw—a disjunction, meaning that the greatest apparent that these two beings-there have in common is the zero of the transcendental of the countryside in autumn. If, as we resolved, we write this zero as μ (marking the minimum of appearing in the world in question), the value of the wall of the house as p, and that of the motorcycle starting up as q, we can inscribe the nil conjunction in the following equation: $p \cap q = \mu$.

Since they are the two first fundamental givens of the structure of the transcendental, it is useful to consider a little more closely the relations between the operation of conjunction and the existence of the minimum (we will soon explicate the third and last of these givens, the envelope). We have just seen that if $p \cap q = \mu$ it is possible to say that p and q are disjoined values. We can add that the conjunction of anything whatsoever with a being whose value of appearance in a world is the minimum is in turn equal to the minimum. In effect, the minimum marks the non-apparent in a world. Obviously, what such a non-apparent has in common in the order of appearing with anything whatsoever cannot appear either. Whatever the transcendental value p may be, we necessarily have the equation $p \cap \mu = \mu$.

6. THIRD TRANSCENDENTAL OPERATION: THE ENVELOPE

The analytical determination of the elements p and q, taken in their common appearing, is expressed by the conjunction $p \cap q$ (the degree of intensity situated just below the degrees p and q). But in order to construct logic as the legislation of appearing, we need a synthetic determination. The intuitive phenomenal idea, which we outlined above, is to express, through a single intensity, the entire intensity contained by a fragment or part of a world; but also to express it with the greatest precision, to grasp this sum of intensities as closely as possible. It is a matter of finding the intensity of appearance of an element that *envelops*—this is the term we proposed—the global appearance of the part in question. Or again, to establish the degree of appearance immediately greater than that of every element contained by this part.

The phenomenological intuition can be formalized as follows: let **m** be a world, and T its transcendental. Consider the subset B of the transcendental which represents all the intensities of appearance of the fragment of the world in question. If $S \subseteq \mathbf{m}$ is this fragment (this finite or infinite part) of the world and if T is the transcendental of this world, $B \subseteq T$ will be that part of the transcendental which contains all the measures of intensity of appearance for the elements of the part S.

For instance, if S is the corner of countryside in the autumn with the house, the ivy, the driveway, the noise of the motorcycle and so on, B will

163

be the set of the intensities of appearance of all these beings, from the red unfurling of the plant on the wall to the shadows of evening by the trees, via the white of the gravel, or the harsh skidding of the wheels of the motorcycle, or the slant of the roof tiles beneath the sky. We will then directly look for a measure of intensity that envelops all these intensities. In brief, this will be the intensity of appearance of all this 'taken together', with a change in scale. Something like a fragment of the autumn itself.

Let's suppose that there exists at least one element t of T which is larger than (greater than or equal to) all the elements of B. In other words, if $b \in B$, then $b \leq t$. We will say that t is an *upper bound* of B. For instance, we can imagine that the atmosphere of the autumn evening, already seized by the luminous rupture which opposes the shadows to the red splendour of the wall—like the sign of the coming cold in the declining light of day—dominates all the ingredients of the fragment of the world in question. Accordingly, the transcendental measure of its appearing is greater than that of all these ingredients, and thus greater than all the elements of B.

Let's now suppose that there exists an element u which is the *least of all the upper bounds of B*. In other words, u is an upper bound of B, and if t is another upper bound of B, we have $u \leq t$. This can indeed be the atmosphere of which we spoke, but strictly related—fastened, as it were—to the local fragment of the world. The play of shadows and light, of the silent background and the wail—as it operates there, before this house, on this path, and not farther, towards the horizon. The element u is the envelope of B, that is a degree of intensity which dominates all the degrees belonging to B, but as closely as possible. We say that B is a *territory* for u. Using the terminology somewhat improperly, we could even say that the situational fragment S, whose intensities of appearance are added up by B, is enveloped by the intensity u, or by every element whose intensity of appearance is u. Or again, that the intensity u has the part S of the world as its territory.

If the envelope u exists for a subset B of the transcendental T, by the axiom of antisymmetry it is unique.

We therefore pose that, *in a transcendental T, every collection of degrees of intensity, and thus every subset B of T, admits of an envelope u. Or that there always exists a u for which B is a territory.*

This property can be envisaged as a property of phenomenal completeness. We are capable of thinking (of measuring) the envelope (the intensive synthesis) of every phenomenal presentation, whatever its ontological character may be.

In general, we will write $u = \Sigma B$ to indicate that u is the envelope of B, or that B is a territory for u.

B can be defined by a certain property of elements of T. For example, B can be 'all the elements of T that have the property P'. We can then imagine we are looking for the envelope of a fragment of the world all of whose intensities are lesser than that of the red of the ivy. Or that P is the property 'being a degree of intensity lesser than that of the red of the ivy'. We will then write $B = \{q \in T/P\,(q)\}$. This reads: 'B is the set of the elements q of T that possess the property P'.

In this case the envelope of B will be written as: $u = \Sigma\{q/P(q)\}$.

We can then see very plainly that u is the element of T:

- which is greater than or equal to all the elements q of T that have property P (upper bound);
- lesser than or equal to every element t which, like itself, is greater than or equal to all the elements q with property P (least upper bound).

A particular case is the one in which B is reduced to two elements, p and q. An upper bound is then simply an element t greater than both p and q. And the envelope is the least upper bound, that is the smallest of all the elements greater than or equal to both p and q. It is called the union of p and q, and is generally written $p \cup q$. Since in a transcendental there exists the envelope of every subset B of T, it is obvious that the union of p and q always exists.

7. CONJUNCTION OF A BEING-THERE AND AN ENVELOPE: DISTRIBUTIVITY OF $\cap$ WITH REGARD TO Σ

The formalization is here extremely illuminating, because it shows that the subordination of the phenomenological motif of conjunction to that of the envelope issues quite straightforwardly into a classical algebraic property: the distributivity of the operation of conjunction (the operation $\cap$) with regard to the operation of envelope (the operation Σ).

Let O be the opera-world *Ariadne and Bluebeard* by Maeterlinck–Dukas. Let us write $f_1, f_2, \ldots, f_5$ the five wives of Bluebeard and F the fragment of the world 'Bluebeard's wives', that is $F = \{f_1, f_2, \ldots, f_5\}$. The envelope of F will be written ΣF. In fact, this envelope is the wife of Bluebeard with the greatest differential intensity of the five, that is Alladine. But that's not important here. Our question, if *bb* designates Bluebeard himself, is to know the value of his conjunction with the envelope 'Bluebeard's wives'.

Let us accordingly write this conjunction as $bb \cap \Sigma F$. What we saw in the conceptual exposition is that its value is that of the envelope of all the local conjunctions—in this case, the envelope of Bluebeard's conjunctions with each of his five wives, that is:

$$bb \cap \Sigma F = \Sigma\{bb \cap f_1, bb \cap f_2, \ldots, bb \cap f_5\}$$

In a general sense, we will pose that the relation between the local (or finite) operator $\cap$ and the global envelope Σ is one of *distributivity*. What an element and an envelope have in common is the envelope of what this element and all the elements that the envelope envelops have in common. This is written as follows:

$$p \cap \Sigma B = \Sigma\{(p \cap x)/x \in B\}$$

Let us spell it out: the conjunction of an element p and the envelope of a subset B is equal to the envelope of the subset T comprising all the conjunctions of p with all the elements x of B.

8. TRANSCENDENTAL ALGEBRA

We can now summarize what a transcendental structure is.

1. Let **m** be a world. In this world, there always exists a being $T \in$ **m** which is called the *transcendental* of the world. The elements of T are often called *degrees*, because they measure the degree of identity between two beings which appear in the world in question.

2. *Order*. T is a set endowed with an order-structure, that is a relation $\leq$, which obeys the following axioms:

    a. $x \leq x$ reflexivity
    b. $[(x \leq y) \text{ and } (y \leq z)] \rightarrow (x \leq z)$ transitivity
    c. $[(x \leq y) \text{ and } (y \leq x)] \rightarrow (x = y)$ antisymmetry

We read $x \leq y$ as 'the degree x is lesser than or equal to the degree y'.
Or: 'the degree y is greater than or equal to the degree x'.

3. *Minimum*. There exists in T a minimal degree μ, which is lesser than or equal to every element of T:

$$(\forall x)\ (\mu \leq x)$$

The degree μ is often called the zero degree or nil degree (of the world in question).

4. *Conjunction*. Given two degrees of T, p and q, there exists the degree $p \cap q$, which is the greatest degree to be simultaneously lesser than or equal to both p and q. We call $p \cap q$ the *conjunction* of p and q.

5. *Envelope*. Let B be any set of degrees of T. Therefore, $B \subseteq T$. There always exists in T a degree, written ΣB, which is the smallest of all the degrees that are greater than or equal to all the elements of B. We call the degree ΣB the *envelope* of B. We also say that B is a *territory* for ΣB.

If B only comprises two degrees, say p and q, the envelope of B is called the union of p and q, and it is written $p \cup q$.

6. *Distributivity*. Let B be a part of T ($B \subseteq T$) and d a degree. The conjunction of d and the envelope of B is equal to the envelope of the conjunctions of d and of each of the elements of B. That is:

$$d \cap \Sigma B = \Sigma \{d \cap x / x \in B\}$$

With these properties of the order T, we can see to the requirements of a comprehensive formalization of appearing. As will be clear in what follows, this structure of the transcendental makes possible a complete formal phenomenology—that is a complete logic of being-there.

A structure conforming to points 2 to 6 above is known to logicians by the name of *complete Heyting algebra*. In English, in the recent literature, it is often called a 'locale'.

9. DEFINITIONS AND PROPERTIES OF THE REVERSE OF A TRANSCENDENTAL DEGREE

The formalization of the reverse follows clearly from our conceptualization. It reveals the extent to which the concept of the reverse—and thus of negation—is an operational synthesis of the axiomatic givens of the transcendental order.

As we said, the reverse of a being-there is the envelope of that region of the world constituted by all the beings-there of the same world which are disjoined from the initial being-there.

Take a degree p of a transcendental T. A degree disjoined from p is a degree q whose conjunction with p is nil. We then have the following equation: $p \cap q = \mu$. The set of degrees with this property is written as follows: $\{q \mid p \cap q = \mu\}$—that is the set of q's whose conjunction with p has the minimal value. Lastly, the envelope of this set (and thus the reverse of p) is written: $\Sigma\{q/p \cap q = \mu\}$. It is the smallest degree in T which is greater than or equal to all the degrees q such that $p \cap q = \mu$.

The notation for the reverse of p will be $\neg\, p$. Its definition is written as follows:

$$\neg\, p = \Sigma\{q/p \cap q = \mu\}$$

It is clear that $\neg\, p$ combines alterity, or foreignness ($p \cap q = \mu$), with maximality (the operation Σ). It designates the maximal alterity, which is why its role is to be the bearer of negative connections in appearing.

The two main formal properties of the reverse can be easily demonstrated through simple calculus.

a. The conjunction of a degree and its reverse is always equal to the minimum. In formal terms: $p \cap \neg\, p = \mu$.

$p \cap \neg\, p = p \cap \Sigma\{q/p \cap q = \mu\}$ def. of $\neg\, p$

$p \cap \neg\, p = \Sigma\{p \cap q/p \cap q = \mu\}$ distributivity

But the envelope of all the terms equal to μ is obviously μ itself. Therefore $p \cap \neg\, p = \mu$.

Accordingly, at the end of Dukas's opera, the conjunction of Ariadne and her reverse Alladine is reduced to mere tears, the nothingness of all affirmation.

Even the ill-equipped logician will recognize in this formula a variant of the principle of non-contradiction. That an apparent and its maximal 'other' have a nil conjunction can also be put in the following way: the statement 'A and non-A' has no value (it is always false). Appearing, as the logic of being-there, abides by this principle.

b. The reverse of the reverse of a degree is always greater than or equal to that degree itself. In formal terms: $p \leq \neg\,\neg\, p$.

$\neg\,\neg\, p = \Sigma\{q/q \cap \neg\, p = \mu\}$ def. of the reverse

But we have just seen that $p \cap \neg\, p = \mu$. Therefore p is part of those q's such that $q \cap \neg\, p = \mu$. And since $\neg\,\neg\, p$ must be greater than or equal to all these q's (the definition of Σ), it follows that $p \leq \neg\,\neg\, p$.

Supposing that Alladine, the reverse of Ariadne, in turn possesses a reverse, such a reverse cannot have a value less than that of Ariadne herself. This reverse is the pure musical power of Ariadne, the song of Ariadne detached from Ariadne, her femininity-song, whose value in the opera is very high.

In this result concerning the reverse of the reverse, we can also recognize an aspect of that logical law of so-called double negation—to wit that the negation of the negation of a statement has at least as much value as that statement itself. Or, that not-not-A is certainly not 'less true' than A.

Having said that, we need to insert here a remark of considerable importance. In classical logic, we learn that not-not-A has exactly the same truth-value as A. The negation of the negation is equivalent to affirmation. Here it is not so. In general (in a given transcendental) it is not the case that $\neg \neg p \leq p$. Most of the time, it is not true that the reverse of the reverse of p is lesser than or equal to p. That is not deducible from the fundamental structures of the transcendental. If $\neg \neg p \leq p$ were the case, since we have $p \leq \neg \neg p$, antisymmetry would mean that $\neg \neg p = p$. We would then be confronted with the 'classical' case, in which the reverse of the reverse, the verso of the verso, is nothing but the initial element, the recto. In accordance with a trivial logical interpretation, we can put it as follows: the logic of appearing is not necessarily a classical logic, because the negation of the negation is not always equal to affirmation.

A world (and there are such worlds) in which the transcendental is such that the reverse of the reverse of every degree is equal to that degree can legitimately be called a classical world.

But we are particularly interested in one case: what is the value of the reverse of a minimum? In logic, the minimum of truth is the false. And the negation of the false is the true, which, if we can put it that way, is the maximum in terms of truth-values. But we have not (yet) formally defined a maximum within the transcendental order.

10. IN EVERY TRANSCENDENTAL, THE REVERSE OF THE MINIMUM μ IS A MAXIMAL DEGREE OF APPEARANCE (M) FOR THE WORLD WHOSE LOGIC IS GOVERNED BY THAT TRANSCENDENTAL

We wish to establish, for every degree p of a transcendental T whose minimum is μ, that the degree p remains lesser than or equal to the reverse of μ, that is $\neg \mu$. In other words, whatever $p \in T$ may be, we need to have $p \leq \neg \mu$. Hence:

$$\neg \mu = \Sigma\{q \mid q \cap \mu = \mu\} \qquad \text{def. of } \neg$$

But, as we have seen, one of the obvious properties of μ is that for *every* q, we have $q \cap \mu = \mu$ (the value of the conjunction with zero is zero). It follows that $\neg \mu$ is the envelope of the transcendental T as a whole, or: $\neg \mu = \Sigma T$.

But the definition of the operation Σ demands that ΣT is greater than or equal to every element of T, and thus to every degree of this transcendental. So it is indeed true that, whatever $p \in T$ may be, we have $p \leq \neg \mu$.

The degree $\neg \mu$ is thus maximal in T. What's more, by the axiom of antisymmetry, it is certainly the only one to be maximal. Henceforth we will designate by M the maximal degree of any transcendental.

We can now establish the fundamental properties of the minimum and the maximum with regard to the reverse (and thus with regard to negation):

The reverse of the reverse of the minimal degree is equal to that degree. Likewise, the reverse of the reverse of the maximal degree is equal to the maximal degree. In these particular cases, double negation is equivalent to affirmation. Formally, $\neg \neg \mu = \mu$, and $\neg \neg M = M$. With regard to double negation, the minimum and the maximum behave in a classical manner.

The demonstration can be carried out as follows:

a. We have just seen that $\neg \mu = M$ (by definition). Therefore, we also have $\neg \neg \mu = \neg M$.

In proposition P.0 we showed, with regard to conjunction, that $p \leq q$ is strictly equivalent to $p \cap q = p$. We know that $p \leq M$ is always the case, since M is the maximal degree. Therefore, it is always the case that $p \cap M = p$.

Now, by the definition of $\neg$, we know that:

$$\neg M = \Sigma\{q \mid q \cap M = \mu\}.$$

By virtue of the preceding remark, which decrees that $q \cap M = q$, this entails that:

$$\neg \neg \mu = \neg M = \Sigma\{q \mid q = \mu\} = \Sigma \{\mu\} = \mu.$$

b. From the above equations, it follows that $\neg \neg M = \neg \mu$. But, by definition, $\neg \mu = M$. Therefore $\neg \neg M = M$.

11. DEFINITION AND PROPERTIES OF THE DEPENDENCE OF ONE TRANSCENDENTAL ON ANOTHER

Let p and q be two elements of T. Let us consider the subset B of T so defined: 'All the elements t of T whose conjunction with p is inferior to q'. This is written: $B = \{t \mid p \cap t \leq q\}$. Note that B is never empty, since $p \cap q \leq q$, and that B consequently has as its elements at least q, $p \cap q$, and, of course, the minimum μ.

The conceptual determination of dependence leads us to recognize that it is nothing other than the envelope of B. Let us therefore pose that *the dependence of a degree q with regard to a degree p is the envelope of all the degrees t such that $t \cap p \leq q$.*

We will write the dependence of q with regard to p as $p \Rightarrow q$. The formal definition is:

$$p \Rightarrow q = \Sigma\{t/p \cap t \leq q\}$$

Let us recall the idea that underlies this definition. The envelope of B above is (in fact) the largest element t such that $p \cap t \leq q$. In other words, we are dealing with the greatest 'piece' that can be connected to p while remaining 'close' to q. What have here is thus a measure of the degree of dependence of q with regard to p, or of the degree of possible causal proximity between p and q. Or again, in another vocabulary: the largest degree of intensity which, when combined to the one measured by p, remains inferior to the intensity measured by q.

It is important to note that, once p and q are fixed, the dependence $p \Rightarrow q$ is itself a fixed term of T, and not a relation between p and q. This means that $p \Rightarrow q$ is the fixed result of the envelope-operation given by $\Sigma \{t/p \cap t \leq q\}$, an operation which concerns p and q.

We will now show that if $p \leq q$, then the dependence of q with regard to p has the maximal value in T. This is written: $p \Rightarrow q = M$. This is the case of the wall of the façade, whose degree of appearance is inferior to that of the red ivy it supports. Hence, everything that can be said about the wall's power of appearing will a fortiori be said about the ivy. Consequently, to go from the degree of appearance of the wall and of what it harbours in appearing to that of the ivy is a logical movement which enjoys the maximal value.

Here is a demonstration:

Whatever t may be, we have $p \cap t \leq p$ (definition of $\cap$). If now $p \leq q$, whatever t may be, we have $p \cap t \leq q$ (transitivity of $\leq$). It follows that the subset $B = \{t/p \cap t \leq q\}$ is equal to T as a whole (because every $t \in T$ has the property which defines the elements of B). Its envelope is accordingly the maximum M, which has been defined as the envelope of T. But the envelope of B is, by definition, the dependence of q with regard to p. It is thus established that if $p \leq q$, then $p \Rightarrow q = M$.

We can immediately derive from this remark a foreseeable property: *the dependence of p with regard to itself is maximal.* In effect, we always have $p \leq p$ (reflexivity). Therefore $(p \Rightarrow p) = M$.

In actual fact, the connection between a maximal dependence and a transcendental subordination of the degrees of appearance is even tighter than this. We can in effect demonstrate the reciprocal of the above property: if the dependence of q with regard to p has the maximum value, then $p \leq q$.

If in effect $p \Rightarrow q = M$, since $p \Rightarrow q$ is the greatest t such that $p \cap t \leq q$, we necessarily have $p \cap M \leq q$. But $p \cap M = p$. Therefore, $p \leq q$.

We observe that the value of dependence for two ordered transcendental degrees is evident at least in terms of *the direction of order*: if $p \leq q$, then $(p \Rightarrow q) = M$. This is the case for classical categorial inclusions. If 'man' is a subset of 'mortals'—which indicates a transcendental subordination—then the implication that leads from 'Socrates is a man' to 'Socrates is mortal' is absolutely true.

The cases of nuanced, non-classical dependence will concern in particular those beings-there whose degrees of appearance are incomparable.

SECTION 4
Greater Logic and Ordinary Logic

We will show that, for a given world, logic in its usual sense—that is the formal calculus of propositions and predicates—receives its truth-values and the meaning of its operators from the transcendental of that world alone. In this sense, logic is nothing but the linguistic transcription of certain rules of coherence of being-there. There is no logic but the logics of worlds.

If we consider that 'Greater Logic' is basically tantamount to 'transcendental logic', and 'ordinary logic' to 'formal logic', then the title of this section evokes that of a famous book by Husserl. The comparison is not absurd. Husserl tried to ground the operations of logic—which in his time was being mathematically formalized—on a network of conscious intentionalities whose constituent value justifies connecting them to the Kantian transcendental tradition. For my part, I would like to establish that, for a given world, the transcendental which regulates the intensity of appearance of beings within it—and therefore that world's logic of appearing—is also the key to logic in its usual linguistic sense, to the extent that such a logic comes to establish itself in the world in question. Both Husserl and I try to subordinate formal logic to transcendental operations. But ultimately the terms are reversed. I regard the usual linguistic interpretation of logic as an entirely secondary anthropomorphic subjectivism, which must itself be accounted for by the intrinsic constitution of being-there. Husserl, on the contrary, only discerns the ultimate seriousness of all logic once the (conscious) subjective basis of formal operations has been constituted. For the phenomenologist, the real is in the final analysis consciousness. For me, consciousness is at best a distant effect of real assemblages and their evental caesura, and the subject is through and through—as the examination of its forms in Book I showed—not constituent, as it is for Husserl, but constituted. Constituted by a truth. Finally, for both Husserl and I logic is of course essentially transcendental. But for Husserl this means that in order to be grasped scientifically it must be referred to a theory of the constitutive acts of consciousness, while for me it depends on an ontological theory of the situations of being. Of course, this theory identifies some fundamental operations of binding within appearing: the conjunction and the envelope. But these operations are indifferent to every subject, and only require the arrival, there, of multiple-beings.

We can clearly see, with regard to this point, the opposition between the materialist dialectic and the two academic traditions that today lay claim to supremacy: phenomenology and analytical philosophy. These two currents both require a constituent assertion about the originariness of language. And both concur in seeing, whether in rhetoric or logic—or in any case in the intentional forms of the control of syntagms—the schema of this originariness. The materialist dialectic undermines this schema, replacing it with the pre-linguistic operations which ground the consistency of appearing. As a consequence, logic, formal logic included, not to mention rhetoric, all appear for what they are: derivative constructions, whose detailed study is a matter for anthropology.

To establish that the entirety of academic or linguistic formal logic may be recast in terms of transcendental operations, it suffices to show that ordinary logical connections (*A or B, A and B, A implies B*), logical negation (*not-A*), quantifiers (*for every x, x* has the property *P*; *there exists* an *x* which has the property *P*)—that all of this is only a transcendental manipulation of terms and operations that we have already inventoried: the minimum, the maximum, the conjunction and the envelope. This will provide us with a syntactical legitimation. We must also show that truth-values (the true, the false)—but if needs be also all kinds of possible nuances of these values, what are usually termed modalities, like the necessary, the probable, the true-in-certain-cases-but-not-always, the possibly-true, the ineluctably-certain, the notoriously-false-except-there-are-exceptions, etc.—are similarly representable by transcendental operators. This will in turn provide us with a semantic legitimation.

Basically, we will show that in a determinate world where it is supposed that ordinary logic must be thought and interpreted, the true is represented by the maximal degree of appearance, the false by the minimal degree and the modal values by other degrees, if such degrees exist in the transcendental of the world in question. We will also show that the connector 'and' is represented by the conjunction, the existential quantifier by the envelope (in its complete sense), negation by the reverse, implication by dependence, and the connector 'or' by the envelope (of two degrees) or union. These are exercises that pertain to a semi-formal exposition.

This undertaking will be completed by a consideration of the universal quantifier which, like the reverse, can be deduced from originary transcendental operations.

1. SEMANTICS: TRUTH-VALUES

As we announced, we will proceed in accordance with a semi-formal regime.

Consider an elementary predicative statement of the type $P(x)$, to be read as: 'x has the property P'; suppose moreover that this statement is referred back to a determinate world, whose transcendental is T. Here the letter x designates a variable, a being of the world taken at random. Since we are dealing with a variable, we do not know whether it possesses the property in question or not. That is why an expression such as $P(x)$ will be called *open*: its value (true, false, probable, not very probable, etc.) effectively depends on the *determinate* term which is substituted for x. The variable x will instead be called *free*.

Now, if the letter 'a' designates a determinate being-there, in other words if 'a' is the proper name of an apparent, then we should be able to know whether this apparent possesses the property P or not. In this case, we say that $P(a)$ is a *closed* expression. As for a, it is called (by contrast with the variable x) a *constant*. Therein lies the entire difference between the out-of-context phrase 'this thing is red'—whose truth-value is unknowable in the absence of information about what thing we're dealing with—and the phrase referred to the autumnal world 'the ivy is red', which is true.

Let us now suppose that we are in possession of a language with variables ($x, y, \ldots$), constants ($a, b, c, \ldots$) and predicates ($P, Q, R, \ldots$). We can interpret the statements constructed in this language in a transcendental T as follows:

1. If $P(a)$ is true, we will assign it the value M (the maximum in T).

2. If $P(a)$ is false, we will assign it the value μ (the minimum in T).

3. If there exist, in the transcendental of the world in question, elements other than μ and M, let's say p, then $P(a) = p$ signifies that the statement, neither true nor false, has an 'intermediate' value, for example 'a strong possibility of being true', 'true in some particular cases, but more often false' and so on.

This is the case for example with 'the gravel of the path is grey' which, in absolute terms, is neither true nor false, since, though this gravel is white, the statement can be true if it has rained, if I see the path in the mist and so on.

2. SYNTAX: CONJUNCTION ('AND'), IMPLICATION ('IF . . . THEN'), NEGATION, ALTERNATIVE ('OR')

The structure of the transcendental, as expounded in Sections 1 and 3 of Book II, will help us to interpret logical connections.

1. What is the value of $[P(a)$ and $Q(b)]$, which consists in simultaneously affirming $P(a)$ and $Q(b)$? Intuitively, it is clear that $[P(a)$ and $Q(b)]$ is true insofar as a possesses the property P and b also possesses the property Q. If even one of the two does not clearly possess the property, for instance if $Q(b)$ is false, then $[P(a)$ and $Q(b)]$ is certainly false. Generalizing, we can say that $[P(a)$ and $Q(b)]$ cannot be more true than the one of the two which has the weakest truth-value, if these values are comparable. Thus, if $P(a)$ is true but $Q(b)$ is only probable, the conjunction of the two is merely probable.

So it is entirely reasonable to interpret the value of $[P(a)$ and $Q(b)]$ as being, in the transcendental, the conjunction of the presumed values of $P(a)$ and $Q(b)$. In effect, the conjunction of p and q, that is $p \cap q$, is the greatest of all those which are lesser than or equal to p and q. If, for example, $P(a) = M$ and $Q(b) = M$ (both are true), then $[P(a)$ and $Q(b)]$ will have the value $M \cap M = M$. If $P(a) = M$ and $Q(b) = \mu$, then $[P(a)$ and $Q(b)] = M \cap \mu = \mu$, because M denotes the true and μ the false.

Now, if $P(a) = M$ (true) and $Q(b) = p$ (probable), then $[P(a)$ and $Q(b)] = M \cap p = p$, because $p \leq M$ in every transcendental (applying P.0).

2. The question of implication follows the same pattern and naturally leads to its interpretation in terms of dependence, as defined above.

Intuitively, the fact that $P(a)$ implies $Q(b)$ signifies only that the truth of $P(a)$ compulsorily entails the truth of $Q(b)$. In natural language, this is said 'if $P(a)$, then $Q(b)$'. This point is validated by the operator $p \Rightarrow q$ (the dependence) of a transcendental.

Let's suppose that $P(A) = M$ and that $[P(a) \Rightarrow Q(b)] = M$. We will verify that $Q(b) = M$, and we will then have the interpretation of dependence in terms of implication.

We know (see subsection 11 above) that if $[P(a) \Rightarrow Q(b)] = M$, we necessarily have $P(a) \leq Q(b)$. But it is then required, since $P(a) = M$, that $Q(b) = M$.

The mediaevals already noted that *ex falso sequitur quodlibet* (anything whatsoever follows from the false), meaning that if $P(a)$ is false, the implication of $Q(b)$ by $P(a)$ is always true, whatever $Q(b)$ may be. This is also valid in a transcendental. It is easily shown that if $p = \mu$, then $(p \Rightarrow q) = M$, whatever q may be: if $p = \mu$, then $p \leq q$, from which we infer that $(p \Rightarrow q) = M$.

To cover the general case, we will pose from the get-go that the value of '$P(a)$ implies $Q(b)$' is $p \Rightarrow q$, if p is the value of $P(a)$ and q that of $Q(b)$. We could say that (transcendental) dependence interprets (logical) implication.

3. Let us now deal with negation, or the value 'non-$P(a)$' for the world in question. The reader will have already understood that we will interpret it using the reverse of the value of $P(a)$. This does not throw up any particular problem. The value of 'the ivy is not red' will be the value of the reverse of the degree of appearance assigned to the red of the ivy. If, as we assumed, in the autumnal world the ivy is effectively red, its degree of appearance being maximal, that is M, and since, as we established, the reverse of M is μ, the final value of 'the ivy is not red' is minimal. We will therefore conclude that in this world the statement is false. It is worth noting however that, unless we know the particulars of a transcendental, we cannot predict what follows from the negation of statements whose value is intermediate. For example, 'the gravel is not grey' will indeed be worth the reverse of the value assigned to 'the gravel is grey'. But if we suppose that this value is p, we have no general rule allowing us to know the value of $\neg p$. The only certainty is that the conjunction of p and $\neg p$ is worth the minimum μ, as we demonstrated in Section 3.

4. Let us briefly discuss the alternative, the connector 'or', whose classical interpretation is that 'A or B' is true if A is true, or B is true, or both. In fact, we can consider it as a particular (finite) case of the envelope. Take, for

example, two apparents, say the ivy and the tile roof of the house. Consider the property 'being of a colour that contains violet'. The two apparents in question neither truly validate this property nor absolutely reject it. We could say that if a is the ivy, b is the tile roof and P the property in question, the truth-value of $P(a)$ will be intermediate, say p, and the value of $P(b)$ too, say q. What can we say then about the value of '$P(a)$ or $P(b)$'? It is entirely reasonable to assign it the value immediately superior to that of $P(a)$ and of $P(b)$, or simultaneously equal to both if they are equal to one another. This value is provided by the envelope of the set constituted by the degrees p and q. In effect, the connector 'or' designates a complex phrase which is true 'in measure' of the highest value of its components. We will then pose that when $P(a)$ has the value p and $P(b)$ the value q, the value of '$P(a)$ or $P(b)$' is $\Sigma\{p, q\}$. We can easily recognize here the classical case in which if either p or q has the value M—meaning 'true'—then $\Sigma\{p, q\}$ certainly has the value M, because the envelope must be greater than or equal to that of which it is the envelope.

To conform with classical notation we have already decided to write $\Sigma\{p, q\}$ in the form $p \cup q$ and to call it the union of the degrees p and q.

Just as we remarked that it is not always true, in the transcendental of a given world $\mathbf{m}$, that the negation of the negation is the same thing as affirmation, it is important here to note that it is no more true in general, in a given world, that the union of a degree and its reverse is always worth the maximum M. In other words, the equation $p \cup \neg\, p = M$ is not a transcendental law. This means that we cannot take for granted that, in every world, the statement '$P(a)$ or non-$P(a)$' is true. This is only the case for classical worlds, of which we will speak in Section 5.

3. THE EXISTENTIAL QUANTIFIER

Let us enhance our language, by allowing expressions such as 'there exists an x such that $P(x)$', or 'at least one x possesses property P', expressions which are often formalized by $\exists x(Px)$.

How is this to be interpreted in a transcendental T? For all the constants of our language $(a, b, c, \ldots)$ and for a predicate P, we have in T truth-values corresponding to $P(a)$, $P(b)$, $P(c)$, $\ldots$ These are for example the values attributed to the statements 'the ivy is red', 'the gravel is red', 'the noise of the motorcycle is red' and so on. These values form a subset, let's call it A_p, of T (with $A_p \subseteq T$). In other words, for all of our determinate terms designated by the proper names a, b, c, ... (the constants), we know whether they have the property P, don't have it, perhaps have it, probably don't have it, etc. And these values make up a subset of T, which is A_p.

Consider the envelope of A_p, that is ΣA_p. It designates the smallest of the elements of T greater than or equal to all the elements of A_p. In other words, it designates the 'maximal' value of all the statements $P(a)$, $P(b)$, etc. We can say that ΣA_p designates a truth-value 'at least as large' as all those assigned to $P(a)$, $P(b)$, ... Consequently, there exists an x which has the property P to the measure of ΣA_p, or 'to the degree fixed' by ΣA_p.

We will therefore pose that the value of 'there exists an x such that $P(x)$' is ΣA_p. This value, of course, pertains to T, that is to the world **m** of which T is the transcendental. This value is justified by the fact that for every a we have:

$$\text{value of } P(a) \leq \Sigma A_p$$

This means: ΣA_p designates 'at least as much' truth as that assigned to $P(a)$, if a is the constant which P fits 'the most'.

If, in particular, there exists an a which possesses property P absolutely, or if a designates an entity that possesses the property designated by P—meaning that $P(a)$ is true, just as 'the ivy is red' is true in the autumnal world; if we thus have $P(a) = M$, M belongs to A_p (which is the collection of all the values of statements of the type $P(a)$). But then $\Sigma A_p = M$, which can be interpreted as follows:

$$\exists x\, P(x) = M$$

So, there exists an x such that $P(x)$. In our case, at least the ivy, meaning that in the autumnal world the following existential judgment is true: there indeed exists an apparent which has the property of being red.

We can thus see how (in what is still a very informal fashion) the existential quantifier, $\exists$, may be interpreted as an envelope in the transcendental: the value of 'there exists an x' is the envelope whose domain for the interpretation of x's is the territory.

We finally have at our disposal a possible projection of the logical connectors into a transcendental: *and* (conjunction), *implies* (implication), *no* (negation), *or* (alternative) and *there exists* (existential quantifier). These projections are in turn correlated with assignations of truth-value to elementary statements of the type $P(a)$. These values necessarily include μ (the false) and M (the true), but they may include others, depending on the transcendental in question. Grasped in terms of this function, T can be called a *logical space*.

4. THE UNIVERSAL QUANTIFIER

We have yet to tackle the question of universal statements of the type 'every x has property P', or $\forall x\, P(x)$. What is at stake is the interpretation of the universal quantifier—for instance as it features in the statement: 'Every apparent [in this autumnal world] is marked by a kind of sadness'.

We will take a somewhat technical detour, but its intuitive sense should quickly become evident. Consider a subset A of elements of T ($A \subseteq T$), and let the set B be defined as follows: 'all the elements of T which are smaller than all the elements of A'. We can call B the set of the lower bounds of A. In other words, if for every element y of A, x is such that $x \leq y$, then x is an element of B. Or:

$$B = \{x / y \in A \rightarrow x \leq y\}$$

Note that B is never empty, since the minimum μ is undoubtedly inferior to all the elements of A. Since we are in a transcendental, there exists ΣB, the envelope of B. This ΣB is by definition the smallest element of T which is larger than all the elements of B (which are in turn smaller than all the elements y of A). We will show that ΣB is itself also smaller than all the elements of A.

Let a be an element of A. The axiom of distributivity gives us:

$$a \cap \Sigma B = \Sigma\{a \cap x / x \in B\}$$

But, by the definition of B (the set of the lower bounds of A), and because a is an element of A, we have $a \geq x$ for every $x \in B$. This means that a is an upper bound of B, and that it is therefore greater than or equal to the envelope of B (the smallest of the upper bounds by definition). Accordingly, for every a of A, we have $\Sigma B \leq a$, meaning that ΣB, the envelope of all the lower bounds of A, is also a lower bound of A: the largest of the lower bounds of A. We will write it ΠA.

Let us now consider the set of values assigned in T to statements of the type $P(x)$. That is, to the values of $P(a)$, $P(b)$, . . ., for all the constants a, b, . . . For example, the values for the statements 'the hills on the horizon are marked by a great sadness', 'the noise of the motorcycle is marked by a great sadness', etc.

As above, let A_p be this set (such that $A_p \subseteq T$). The degree ΠA_p is lesser than or equal to all the values assigned in T to statements of the type $P(a)$, and it is the largest to have this property. In brief, every statement of the type $P(a)$ is 'at least as true' as the degree of truth fixed by ΠA_p. Whatever the constant a may be, the statement $P(a)$ has a degree of truth which is at least equal to ΠA_p, and ΠA_p is the largest value to have this property. This means that *all the terms* have the property P at least to the degree fixed by ΠA_p.

We can therefore argue that the truth-value of $\forall x\, P(x)$ is set by ΠA_p.

If, for example, 'for every x, $P(x)$' is absolutely true—in the world of autumn, all the apparents are effectively marked by a great sadness—this means that $P(a) = M$, whatever the constant a may be. In this case $A_p = \{M\}$ (no $P(a)$ has a value other than M). But it is obvious then that $\Pi A_p = M$, which is the projection onto T of the fact that $\forall x\, P(x)$ is true.

If there exists a constant a (be it only one) which is such that $P(a)$ is absolutely false—the glorious red of the ivy is not at all sad, but on the contrary a radiant sign of joy—we have $P(a) = \mu$. But then $\mu \in A_p$. And since ΠA_p is inferior to every element of A_p, we have $\Pi A_p \leq \mu$, and therefore $\Pi A_p = \mu$. This time we are dealing with the projection of the fact that 'for every x, $P(x)$' is absolutely false: a single case (here named by the constant a, the ivy) counts as an objection to the universal totalization, since the existent named by a does not have the property P.

Of course, there may be intermediary cases, in which $\Pi A_p = p$. For instance if nothing, not even the ivy, is truly joyous, or absolutely negates the predicate 'sadness'—without by that token suggesting that everything is sad, or that there is a universal validation for this glumness of things. In this case, we will say that 'for every x, $P(x)$' is only true to the degree p (strongly, but not totally, etc.).

Finally, the operator Π (the global union, or counter-envelope) is a coherent interpretation of the universal quantifier.

It was in order to keep the exposition as simple as possible that we only mentioned predicative formulas, of the type $P(x)$. We could equally well have envisaged relational forms, of the type $\Re(x, y)$, such as 'x is situated to the right of y'. It is possible to give a value to this type of statement in a transcendental on the basis of constants. One will ask, for instance, what is the value of $\Re(a, b)$. One can then use the operations $\cap$ and Σ (for example) to give a value to 'and' or to 'there exists'.

The absolutely general and non-naïve presentation of these kinds of things, employing relations with n terms, preoccupies numerous logicians.

It is replete with extraordinarily bothersome subtleties of notation, especially when it is a question of dealing in detail with quantifiers. In effect, if you try to establish the protocol of evaluation for formulas of the type 'for all x's, there exists y such that for all z's we have $\Re(x, y, z)$', that is $(\forall x)(\exists y)(\forall z)\ [\Re(x, y, z)]$, you need to be very careful! Even more so if you wish to elucidate the case of a given formula. But it can be done.

For the time being our only aim is to delineate how a transcendental is 'readable' as a logical space, and to bring formal logic back to its true essence: a transcendental algebra. As we shall see, this is an algebra which is also—and perhaps more essentially—a topology. This shouldn't elicit surprise, since a world is never anything other than a machine to localize being.

SECTION 5
Classical Worlds

---

1. WHAT IS A CLASSICAL WORLD?

We have already indicated that, in a given transcendental, it is not true in general that the reverse of the reverse of a being-there is that being itself. We know only that the reverse of the reverse of a being-there is a transcendental value greater than or equal to the value assigned to that being. In logical terminology, it is not true in general (or in every world in which logical connectors are interpreted), that the negation of the negation is equivalent to affirmation. A world whose transcendental is such that this equivalence effectively holds is a classical world. This stems from the fact that the logics which allow both the principle of non-contradiction and the 'law of double negation' are called classical, as against intuitionist and para-consistent logics.

The idea of classical logic also refers to a separate property, the famous principle of the excluded middle: given a closed proposition p, either p or non-p is true, there is no third possibility. A classical logic simultaneously validates the principle of the excluded middle and the principle of non-contradiction (the truth of the statement p and that of the statement non-p cannot be given at the same time). An intuitionist logic validates the principle of non-contradiction, but not the principle of the excluded middle. A para-consistent logic validates the principle of the excluded middle, but not the general form of the principle of non-contradiction. In each case, we are dealing with important variations in the definition and the meaning of the operator of negation.

The excluded middle is certainly not a valid principle in every world, or for every transcendental. Objective phenomenology provides a wonderful illustration of this point. If I consider the ivy on the wall as the sun sets, and I examine the statement 'the red of the ivy continues to shine forth', I can clearly see that this statement is not absolutely true, at least not in the duration that it implies. Nor is it absolutely false, since, over a brief initial period, when the oblique radiance of the sun has yet to fade too much, the statement enjoys a certain validity. In the end the statement is neither true (it does not take the maximal value in the transcendental in question) nor is it false (it does not take the minimal value). In the world in question it does not satisfy the principle of the excluded middle. We have already noted that this world also does not validate the 'law' of double negation: the reverse of the reverse of the transcendental intensity of appearance of the noise of the motorcycle is not necessarily this selfsame noise. The world of the house in the autumn evening is not classical, in the sense that it validates neither double negation nor the excluded middle.

Let us now consider an entirely artificial world (it is doubtful whether we can really speak of a world in this instance), the one composed by Bluebeard and just one of his five wives, let's say Mélisande. If, in terms of intensities of appearance, the reverse of the one is the other, we immediately see that this tiny world is classical. For the reverse of the reverse of Bluebeard, for example, is the reverse of Mélisande, that is Bluebeard himself. And if I declare—another example—that 'every being is sexed', I can verify that this is indeed the case for Bluebeard and Mélisande, and I will unambiguously conclude that this proposition is true in the world that they constitute. Likewise if I say 'there exists a woman'.

In passing we can note the solidarity between the 'law' of double negation and the 'principle' of the excluded middle. They always seem to be co-validated in a classical world. If we examine matters from the standpoint of non-classical worlds, this solidarity is pretty intuitive. For if a proposition—let's say 'there exists a woman'—does not obey in a given world the excluded middle, this means for instance that the existence of a woman in this world is such that, though it is impossible to cast doubt upon it, it is nevertheless excessive to declare it as absolutely certain. In such a world, we could say that a woman semi-exists. Let ϕ be the value accorded to semi-existence, that is to the statement 'a woman exists', in the transcendental of such a world. Moreover, the value of the statement 'there exists no woman' is, as we have seen, the minimum μ, since it is impossible to cast doubt on this existence. By virtue of the semantic rules outlined in Section 4, the transcendental value of 'there exists no woman' is the reverse of the value assigned to 'there exists a woman'. Consequently, the reverse of ϕ is μ. It follows that the reverse of the reverse of ϕ is the reverse of μ, which is perforce the maximum M, and thus cannot be ϕ. Finally, we can see that the reverse of the reverse of the value assigned to the semi-existence of women in the world under consideration is by no means equal to this value itself: the non-validity of the excluded middle entails the non-value of the 'law' of double negation.

Further on, we will demonstrate the strict equivalence between the two statements (excluded middle and double negation), both of which are necessarily validated by every classical world.

A fundamental example of a classical world is ontology, or the theory of the pure multiple, or historical mathematics. This is essentially because a set is defined extensionally: a set is identified with the collection of its elements. This definition really only acquires meaning if one rigorously accepts the following principle: given an element, either it belongs to a set, or it does not. There is no third possibility.

In effect, the transcendental of ontology is reduced to two elements, capable of discriminating between belonging and non-belonging. These elements are the minimum, which indexes non-belonging, and the maximum, which indexes belonging.

2. TRANSCENDENTAL PROPERTIES OF THE WORLD OF ONTOLOGY

Take any two beings, and call them 1 and 0. If we posit the order $0 \leq 1$, we will see that the two-element set $\{0, 1\}$ possesses a transcendental structure. We will call this transcendental T_0.

The minimum of T_0 is clearly 0.

The conjunction of 0 and 1 in T_0 is obviously 0.

All in all, T_0 has four subsets: the singleton $\{0\}$, the singleton $\{1\}$, T_0, and lastly, the empty set. The envelopes of these subsets are respectively 0, 1, 1 and 0 (this is a good exercise concerning the intuition of envelopes).

One can easily see that the reverse of 0 is 1 (which is thus the maximum) and that the reverse of 1 is 0.

If a world has T_0 as its transcendental, it is clear that in this world there exist only two values of appearance for any element x of said world. The one is maximal (1), meaning that x appears absolutely, the other minimal (0), meaning, as the degree zero always does, the non-appearance of x. This is indeed what makes T_0 into a minimal transcendental: it decides, without the least nuance, between appearance and non-appearance. In so doing, it simply reiterates the founding discrimination of Parmenidean ontology, namely that being excludes non-being.

The classicism of T_0 is particularly evident in what concerns both the double negation and the excluded middle.

On the one hand, since $\neg 1 = 0$, we have $\neg\neg 1 = \neg 0 = 1$.

On the other, since $\neg 0 = 1$, we get $\neg\neg 0 = 0$.

The transcendental T_0 thereby validates the 'law' of double negation.

An important preliminary remark is called for before we deal with the excluded middle. That the choice between p and $\neg p$ is exclusive means that if we totalize these two choices, we have the totality of possible choices. In other words, the sum of the value of p and the value of $\neg p$ is necessarily the maximal value; otherwise there would need to be, besides p and $\neg p$, a further third value, which we presupposed there is not (*excluded* middle).

But, what does addition (or totalization) mean within a transcendental structure? Obviously, we are dealing with the envelope, the synthetic operation par excellence. And the envelope of just two transcendental degrees is nothing other than their union, which is written $p \cup q$. So, if a transcendental validates the principle of the excluded middle, it is because in this transcendental—letting M denote the maximum—we always have the equation $p \cup \neg p = M$.

Now, it is certain that in T_0: $0 \cup \neg 0 = 0 \cup 1 = 1$.

Likewise, $1 \cup \neg 1 = 1 \cup 0 = 1$.

And since 1 is the maximum, we're good: T_0 validates the excluded middle.

We have thus established that the transcendental of the world of ontology is classical. This is something that throughout the history of philosophy has entailed the general conviction regarding the classicism of every world. So that when a world was evidently not classical in the order of appearing, the only choice was between discrediting this world (it was non-true, or illusory) or sceptically discrediting ontological consistency itself.

The truth is that there exist non-classical transcendentals which are heterogeneous to the logical rule of ontology, and which nonetheless guarantee appearing a fully experienceable logical consistency in the worlds that they structure. The fact that being-there is ruled by another logic than that of its being does not at all mean that it introduces the least inconsistency into being.

Every world consists. 'Logic' and 'appearing' are one and the same thing.

3. FORMAL PROPERTIES OF CLASSICAL WORLDS

We will now demonstrate the formal equivalence between the excluded middle and the 'law' of double negation. We will thereby characterize classical worlds as worlds whose transcendental validates one of these two statements, and consequently both.

We will even add a third, which will serve us as a kind of mediation.

Consider the formal equation $\neg p = \mu$, which stipulates that the reverse of p is equal to the minimum. In every case, this equation has a solution, which is that $p = M$ (the maximum). We effectively know that in every transcendental the reverse of the maximum is the minimum. Regardless of what transcendental we are dealing with, we thus have $\neg M = \mu$, which is in a sense the universal solution of the equation. But is it the only solution? Not at all. Above, we proposed an example of another solution, that of the semi-existence of women in a given world, whose value, written ϕ, was such that $\neg\phi = \mu$, even though ϕ differs from M. In non-classical worlds, it is entirely possible that $\neg p = \mu$, even though p differs from M.

Note that in the transcendental of the (classical) world of ontology, that is T_0, the equation in question has the maximum as its sole solution. In effect, in that world, if $\neg p = 0$, it is necessary that $p = 1$, for only $\neg 1 = 0$ (in effect, $\neg 0 = 1$, and there is nothing in this transcendental save for 1 and 0).

We thus have at our disposal three properties which in every case are those of T_0:

–the 'law' of double negation, or $\neg\neg p = p$;
–the 'principle' of the excluded middle, or $p \cup \neg p = M$;
–the equation $\neg p = \mu$ has only one solution, which is M.

We can demonstrate that these three properties are equivalent, and that therefore any of the three, if it is validated by a transcendental, is sufficient in order to conclude that every world whose intensities of appearance are regulated by this transcendental is, like the world of ontology, a classical world.

Two statements are equivalent if each is the consequence of the other. In other words, a and β are equivalent if a implies β ($a \rightarrow \beta$) and β implies a ($\beta \rightarrow a$). This is why equivalence is written as a double implication (its most common symbol is $\leftrightarrow$). A moment of reflection will show the reader that if one wishes to demonstrate the equivalence of three (or more) statements one can proceed as follows: one demonstrates that the first statement implies the second, the second implies the third and so on. Then one shows that the last implies the first. That is exactly what we do for the three aforementioned properties. We leave the details of this calculus for the appendix. They show that the three properties (double negation, excluded middle and uniqueness of the solution of the equation $\neg p = \mu$) are equivalent.

A transcendental that verifies any of these three properties—and consequently the two others—will be said to be 'Boolean'.

A classical world is a world whose transcendental is Boolean.

APPENDIX

Demonstration of the Equivalence of the Three Characteristic Properties of a Classical World

---

We wish to establish that the following three properties are equivalent:

Double negation : $\neg\,\neg\, p = p$.
Excluded middle: $p \cup \neg\, p = M$.
The equation $\neg\, p = \mu$ only has M as a solution.

1. First of all, we will show that in a transcendental T, if $p \cup \neg\, p = M$, then $\neg\,\neg\, p = p$.

$\neg\, p \cup p = M$	hypothesis
$\neg\,\neg\, p \cap (\neg\, p \cup p) = \neg\,\neg\, p \cap M = \neg\,\neg\, p$	application
$(\neg\,\neg\, p \cap \neg\, p) \cup (\neg\,\neg\, p \cap p) = \neg\,\neg\, p$	distributivity
$\mu \cup (\neg\,\neg\, p \cap p) = \neg\,\neg\, p$	$\neg\,\neg\, p \cap \neg\, p = \mu$
$\neg\,\neg\, p \cap p = \neg\,\neg\, p$	for every x, $\mu \cup x = x$
$\neg\,\neg\, p \leq p$	P.0
$p \leq \neg\,\neg\, p$	Section 3
$p = \neg\,\neg\, p$	antisymmetry

2. We then show that in a transcendental T, if $\neg\,\neg\, p = p$, then the equation $\neg\, p = \mu$ has as its only solution $p = M$.

$\neg\, p = \mu$	presupposed equation
$\neg\,\neg\, p = \neg\, \mu$	consequence
$\neg\,\neg\, p = M$	def. of M
$p = M$	hypothesis $\neg\,\neg\, p = p$

3. Finally, we show that in a transcendental T, if the equation $\neg\, p = \mu$ has $p = M$ as its only solution, then for every p we have $p \cup \neg\, p = M$.

We will establish that $\neg(p \cup \neg p)$ is equal to the minimum μ in every transcendental. It will follow that if in a transcendental every equation of the type $\neg p = \mu$ has as its only solution $p = M$, then $p \cup \neg p = M$.

$$\neg(p \cup \neg p) = \Sigma\{t \, / \, t \cap (p \cup \neg p) = \mu\} \qquad \text{def. of } \neg$$
$$\neg(p \cup \neg p) = \Sigma\{t \, / \, (t \cap p) \cup (t \cap \neg p) = \mu\} \qquad \text{distributivity}$$

But the definition of the union $\cup$ of two elements r and s—the smallest of the elements superior to both r and s—obviously implies that if $r \cup s = \mu$, it is because both r and s are equal to μ. Finally, we get:

$$\neg(p \cup \neg p) = \Sigma\{t \, / \, (t \cap p) = \mu \text{ and } (t \cap \neg p) = \mu\}$$

Because the t's in the above formula must fulfil $t \cap p = \mu$, it follows that they are lesser than or equal to $\neg p$, which, being the envelope of all the t's that verify this equality, is superior or equal to all of them. We thus have $t \leq \neg p$. And because these t's must fulfil $t \cap \neg p = \mu$, it follows, for the same reason, that $t \leq \neg \neg p$. But then, by the definition of the conjunction $\cap$ of $\neg p$ and $\neg \neg p$, that we must have $t \leq \neg p \cap \neg \neg p$. Now, the conjunction of an element, here $\neg p$, and of its reverse is equal to the minimum (cf. Section 3). Therefore $t \leq \mu$, meaning that $t = \mu$.

Finally, $\neg(p \cup \neg p)$ is equal, in every transcendental T, to the envelope of a subset all of whose terms are equal to μ, that is to the envelope of the subset $\{\mu\}$. We have already remarked that such an envelope is in turn equal to μ.

If our transcendental of reference verifies the property 'the equation $\neg p = \mu$ has as its only solution $p = M$', since in every transcendental $\neg(p \cup \neg p) = \mu$, it follows, in this particular case, that $p \cup \neg p = M$.

BOOK III
Greater Logic, 2. The Object

Introduction

This book proposes an entirely new concept of what an object is. We are obviously dealing with the moment of the One in our analysis. That is because by 'object' we must understand that which counts as one within appearing, or that which authorizes us to speak of *this* being-there as inflexibly being 'itself'.

The main novelty of this approach is that the notion of object is entirely independent from that of subject. Of course, from Book I onwards, we introduced and accorded their rightful force and significance to the joint themes of truths and subjective formalisms. We shall return to them in Book VII, under the rubric of the doctrine of the body. But these exemplary 'non-objects' (the subject-form and the truth-procedure) directly depend on the objective laws of change and not on those of appearing. The concept of the object pertains instead to the analytic of being-there and, like the transcendental, it does not presuppose any subject.

Having already sketched, in a purely formal theory, a doctrine of the pre-objective dimensions of the subject, we will thus move to the construction of a subject-less object. Within the complete theory of subjects-of-truth, this construction inserts itself between metaphysics (formal subjective types) and physics (theory of subjectivizable bodies). It is, therefore, the principal logical moment of the materialist dialectic. Only a logic of the object, as the unit of appearing-in-a-world, effectively allows the subjective formalisms to find support in that which serves as their objective dimension: the body, which supports the appearing and duration of every subject, making intelligible the idea that an eternal truth can be created in a particular world.

So our trajectory can be summed up as follows: (object-less) subjective formalism, (subject-less) object and objectivity of the subject (bodies). It inscribes into the logic of appearing the generic becoming of truths which *Being and Event* had treated within the bounds of the ontology of the pure multiple.

This goes to show the extent to which we take our distance from Kant—the master, after Descartes and Hume, when it comes to the *immediate* subject–object correlation as the unsurpassable horizon of every cognition. In the extension to this Book, Kant will thus serve as our interlocutor, in particular through those intensely debated passages which he devotes in the first two editions of the *Critique of Pure Reason* to what he calls the 'deduction of the pure concepts of understanding'.

The construction of the concept of the object obviously takes its cue from the results of Book II. Throughout, it presupposes the situation of being of beings in the form of a world, and therefore of the transcendental of that world. The argument will thus take the following form. First, we define the indexing of a given multiple-being on the transcendental of a world. This indexing is one and the same as the appearance of this being in that world; it is what localizes the being of that being in the guise of *a* being-there-in-a-world.

Basically, indexing is a function which links every difference immanent to the multiple to its intensity of appearance in the world. With regard to this point, the formal exposition is as simple and clear as it can be: if x and y are two elements of a being A, and T is the transcendental of the world in question, indexing is an identity-function $\mathbf{Id}(x, y)$ which measures in T the degree of 'apparent' identity between x and y. In other words, if $\mathbf{Id}(x, y) = p$, it means that x and y are 'identical to the p degree' with regard to their power of appearance in the world. The result of this transcendental evaluation of differences is what we call the *phenomenon*. It is noteworthy that within the space of phenomenality, it is possible exhaustively to examine the question of existence as a question which is entirely distinct from that of being. That is why the conceptual and formal study of existence follows immediately after that of the phenomenon and comes before that of the object. At that stage, it is effectively a question of appearing as a pure logic (of the phenomenon, of existence), because transcendental algebra legislates over worldly differences; but it is not yet a question of the object, or of objectivity, for we still lack the means to account for the real of the One.

This is because, in order to be able to say of a multiple, that it objectivates itself in a world (and not merely that one can register an existence within that world), one still needs to ascertain that there is an effective link between multiple-being and the transcendental schemata of its appearance—or of its existence. At the end of the logical process of the worldly regulation of differences, under what condition can we affirm that it is indeed this ontologically determinate multiple which is there as an object-of-the-world? On this point, our question is entirely parallel to the one posed by Kant in a crucial passage of the *Critique*, a passage entitled 'Refutation of Idealism', to which he chose to give the particularly dogmatic form of a 'theorem'. It is a matter for him of establishing that 'our *inner experience* [. . .] is possible only under the presupposition of outer experience', and that, therefore, there exist 'objects in space outside me'.

Since we posit that appearing has nothing to do with a subject (whether empirical or transcendental), naming instead the logic of being-there, we clearly cannot oppose an inner to an outer experience. In fact, no experience whatsoever is involved. But we are obliged to establish that an object is indeed the being-there of an ontologically determinate being; or that the logic of appearing does not exhaustively constitute the intelligibility of objects, which also presupposes an ontological halting point that is at the basis of appearing as the determination of objects-in-the-world.

The simple rigorous formulation of the problem requires a detour whose necessity can be easily explained. What is a being grasped in its being? A pure multiple. What is its (ontological) determination? It is the set of elements belonging to it. Therefore, if the object is the localization in a world of a determinate multiple, and if this localization is not a constitution, there must exist a logical clause that links the nature of the object to the elements of the multiple-being of which it is the objectivation.

This clause presupposes an analysis of the object into its components, carried out up to the point where it is sutured to the analysis of the multiple into its elements. In other words, we must:

a. identify, within appearing, what a component (in fact, a part) of the transcendental indexing of a being is;

b. identify the minimal form (which we will term atomic) of these components;

c. find (or posit) an intelligible intersection between an 'atom of appearing' and an 'atom of being', that is between a minimal component of what is given as localized in a world, and the elementary composition of the multiple-being which underlies this givenness.

We are here inside a materialist axiomatic which presupposes that there exists an obligatory point of articulation between the logic of appearing and the ontology of the multiple. No world is such that its transcendental power can entirely de-realize the ontology of the multiple. The One (or atomicity) is the point of ontological articulation.

Once in possession of this logical-materialist clause, we can define what an object is. The inquiry will then orient itself towards the subtle logic of the (onto-logical) One, what we call atomic logic.

The main argument consists in moving back from being-there to being-in-itself, in order to establish that every objectivation is a kind of transcendental marking of beings. Technically speaking, this means that on the basis of the transcendental appearance of objects in a world, we can think singular features of the beings 'themselves', to the extent that these beings underlie objects. These features will be organized around three fundamental operators. The first, of a topological kind, is the localization of an element (ontology) or of an atom (logic of appearing) on a transcendental degree. The second, which is more algebraic, is a relation of (worldly) 'compatibility' between two elements of a multiple-being. The third is an order-relation which is directly defined on the elements of a being (a multiple that appears in a world). This relation amounts to the projection onto being of the fundamental feature of the transcendental (the partial order-structure). At an intuitive level, these three operators indicate that no multiple comes out unscathed from its appearance in a world. If it is there—in such and such a world—it exposes itself 'in person' to a singular intelligibility, which is not conveyed by its pure ontological composition. It is thus that capabilities for internal harmony, regional localization or hierarchy come to appear in the inmost organization of a being, simply by virtue of being objectivated in such and such a world and under such and such a transcendental prescription.

It happens to that which appears that it is otherwise thinkable in its being.

This new intelligibility of beings according to the objects that they have become in a world reaches its apex when it is demonstrated that a being itself may, under certain conditions, be synthesized (enveloped), and therefore be ascribed a unity other than the one that counts its pure multiplicity as one. Everything happens as if appearance in a world endowed pure multiplicity—for the 'time' it takes to exist in a world—with a form of homogeneity that can be inscribed in its being. This (demonstrable) result—which shows that appearing infects being to the extent being comes to take place in a world—is so striking that I have named it the 'fundamental theorem of atomic logic'.

If one is willing to bolster one's confidence in the mathematics of objectivity, it is possible to take even further the thinking of the logico-ontological, of the chiasmus between the mathematics of being and the logic of appearing. But one then needs to equip oneself with a more topological intuition and to treat the degrees of the transcendental as operators of the localization of multiple-beings. We can observe a fundamental correlation between the transcendental and certain forms of coherence internal to the multiple-being constructing itself under our very eyes, little by little. To use the technical language of contemporary mathematics, this correlation is a *sheaf*. There is a sheaf of appearing towards being—that is the last word on the question. We only provide the details of the construction for the curious, the cognoscenti or the resilient. A large scholium is devoted to it at the very end of this Book.

Beyond the thematic or methodological divisions (in particular the distinction between the conceptual expositions and the more formal developments), this book comprises three main arguments corresponding to the aforementioned contents.

1. Transcendental indexing of multiple-beings. This argument concludes with the pre-objective concepts of phenomenon and existence.

2. Analytic of phenomena and definition of the object on the basis of the properties of transcendental indexing: phenomenal components and ultimately atoms are identified within the object. It is then possible to provide a materialist definition of the object, under the sign of the One.

3. Algebraic markers, in being, of its appearing: localization, compatibility and order. The envelope of a pure multiplicity: the advent, according to appearing, of Unity as the retroaction of the being-qua-object on the being-in-its-being.

The complete form of the general synthesis (the transcendental functor) constitutes a supernumerary argument.

Without a doubt, due to the extreme rigorousness of the chains of reasoning, the formal exposition is here often more illuminating than the didactic phenomenology that precedes it. This exposition is self-sufficient. However, we have shunted to the appendix, alongside the construction of the transcendental functor, some intermediary demonstrations.

The last section is devoted to the question of death. Following in Spinoza's footsteps, we shall see that this is a purely logical question. This section is a prolongation of the formal theory of existence.

SECTION 1
For a New Thinking of the Object

1. TRANSCENDENTAL INDEXING: THE PHENOMENON

Take a world, for instance the slow constitution of a demonstration at the Place de la République. Since the demonstration brings together very disparate political forces and organizations, we will ask ourselves how these forces and organizations appear in the gradual filling of the esplanade by thousands of people. An 'ontological eye' only sees a rather indistinct multiple: men and women, banner poles, discussions, sound checks, newspaper vendors... But it is not this indistinct multiple which really has the power to appear in the singular process of a demonstration, in the world 'demonstration in the making'. For a more phenomenological eye, there are significant differences, which alone can really articulate the place, the people, the newspapers, the banners, and the slogans in the world in question. For instance, two loudspeakers, heard from a distance, seem to bellow identically. The 'loudspeaker-fact' does not allow difference to appear at all. Similarly, two groups of very young people—high-school students?—have identical ways of treading on the mud with their suction-cup trainers (it has recently rained), of laughing or of speaking too fast, swallowing vowels as though they were scalding chestnuts. But already a flag of a certain red over here, and one of a certain black over there, tell us—let's make this hypothesis—that once again the demo-appearing has brought together those bitter and fraternal adversaries, the heirs of Lenin and those of Bakunin. Farther away, those lean gentlemen, busily intent on their phones, could very well be agents from the intelligence service of the Ministry of the Interior, a compulsory fragment of what appears in such a world. And those big girls over there, many of them African, leaning against the statue? Employees of a fast-food restaurant? Let's not forget the statue itself which, holding its timeless olive branch above this agitation, seems a little too benedictory, a little too certain of being above all this, like the Republic is in France.

To the extent that these multiple-beings partake in the world, they differ more or less. When all is said and done, the innumerable joy of their strong identities (loudspeakers, steps, clapping, ranks. . .) and of their equally pronounced differences (the red or black flags, the snaking cops, the cadence of the African djembe drums over against the miserabilist slogans of threadbare unions, and so on) is that which constitutes the world as the being-there of the people and things which are incessantly intermingled within it.

We still need to think through the 'worldly' unity of all these differences which set forth the appearing of the demonstration.

We call *function of appearing* that which measures the identity of appearance of two beings in a world. To this end, we assume that a transcendental exists in this demonstration's situation of being, with all the operational properties that we have already accorded to the transcendental. It is this transcendental which fixes the values of identity between any two beings of the world. To every pair of beings which belong to this world is ascribed a transcendental degree, which measures the identity of the two beings in appearing. If this degree is p, we will say that they are 'p-identical'. If this degree is the maximum M, that they are absolutely identical. If it is the minimum, μ, that they are entirely different, and so on. It is this attribution to every pair of beings of a transcendental degree that we call 'function of appearing' or 'transcendental indexing'.

For example, the groups of young high-school students are sufficiently indistinct in their pre-demonstration behaviour that, given two of these groups (those of the Lycée Buffon and those of the Lycée Michelet, for instance), it is tempting to say that their identity is equal to the maximum of the transcendental order. On the contrary, we could believe in the utter non-identity of the post-Bolshevik red flags and the post-Kronstadt black flags. Must we assert that the function of appearing evaluates their identity to be the zero of the transcendental? Today, that would be very excessive. There's no love lost, of course, but they are always stuck together. It will be prudent to suppose that their identity has a weak but non-nil value; that it is measured by a degree which is certainly close to the minimum, but not equal to it.

This is how the phenomenon of each of the beings that comes to localize itself in the world 'demonstration at Place de la République' is constituted, as an infinite network of evaluations of identities (and therefore of differences).

Take a red flag, for example: if we consider it as a phenomenon, it will have been differentially compared not only with the black flags, of course, but with other red flags—perhaps this time the transcendental indexing of identity approaches the maximum—and finally, with everything that appears in the way of emblems, placards, banners and graffiti, but also as the absence of such emblems. Like this closed shuttered window on the fourth floor of an affluent apartment building, which, overlooking the crowd, seems to be saying that it is the bearer of a hostile absence, of non-appearing in this variegated world, that it is irreducibly refractory to the flags of disorder, so that in all likelihood we have a nil transcendental value for the identity between the window and any of the red flags.

Given any being appearing in a world, *we call 'phenomenon' of this being the complete system of the transcendental evaluation of its identity to all the beings that co-appear in this world.*

As we can see, transcendental indexing is the key to the phenomenon as the infinite system of differential identifications.

In order for phenomenal constitution to remain consistent, do we need to think through some rules that govern a function of appearing? For sure, and we shall see why.

Consider a singular differential network: on the right of the republican statue which blesses everyone, a group of bearded guys and women with dreadlocks coagulates around a black flag. Further to the right, some gaunt moustachioed Kurds, like mountain kings descended onto the plains, unfold a banner vituperating the crimes of the Turkish army. Two multiplicities thus come to appear in the demonstration-world. It is clear that the transcendental indexing of these two beings—the Kurds and the anarchists—has an intermediate value, between minimum and maximum. That is because neither do the anarchists absolutely differ from the Kurds, considering their common desire to appear untamed, nor are they entirely identical, as indicated, for instance, by the opposition between the red of the banner and the black of the flags. But above all, this value is independent of the order in which we consider the beings in question.

We can insert here a remark on objective phenomenology, which we have referred to several times as one of our methods, and which we already distinguished from intentional phenomenology in the preface. From the point of view of a supposed consciousness, one will say that the intentional act of discrimination between the group of anarchists and that of the Kurds must take place in a definite temporal order: a conscious gaze shifts from the one to the other and recapitulates phenomenal difference, inscribing into language the temporalized movement of evaluation. If we suspend any reference to intentional consciousness, there only subsists the immediate veridicality of an evaluation of identity, of the kind 'the group of Kurds and the group of anarchists are identical to the p degree'. This evaluation cannot retain any reference whatsoever to time or temporal order, for the chief reason that no time is implied in the transcendental indexing of being-there. Time here is only a parasite introduced by the metaphorical or didactic usage of vulgar phenomenology. Objective phenomenology comes down to suppressing this parasitism by retaining only the identitarian or differential result of the trajectory that is imputed to a consciousness. It will, therefore, settle on a determinate transcendental value in the world 'demonstration at the Place de la République' for that which connects and differentiates the group of Kurds and the group of anarchists, without it being possible to assign an order to this value.

This can be put more simply: the function of transcendental indexing is symmetrical, in that the value of identity of two beings-there is the same, whatever the order in which they are inscribed.

Let us now complicate the situation somewhat, by envisaging even farther to the right, towards the Avenue de la République, a third group coming together, visibly composed of striking postmen, recognizable by the blue-yellow work jacket they have donned so that everyone may identify them. In this case, the differential network comprises three multiple-beings: the anarchists, the Kurds and the postmen. These beings are all grasped in the birth of their appearance in the world in question, in the progressive legibility of their being-there. The rule of symmetry, which we already established, means that we also have three transcendental indexings: the one scrutinized earlier, of the identity of the anarchists and the Kurds, that of the Kurds and the postmen and finally that of the postmen and the anarchists. Is there a transcendental rule that operates on this triplet? Certainly there is. This rule stems from the fact that there always exists a transcendental evaluation of 'what there is in common' to two given evaluations. This is the transcendental operator of conjunction. Accordingly, the group of anarchists and the group of Kurds—who co-appear in the world—both make appear their will to inspire fear, the fierce mask of the rebel. On the other hand, the group of Kurds and that of the postmen both make the uniform (or uniformity) appear as the external sign of belonging. All the Kurds wear a grey outfit and all the postmen wear the blue jacket with yellow piping. Finally, the group of anarchists and the group of postmen share a very recognizable 'French' air, the same masculine conceit, at once congenial and weak, arrogant and puerile, projected into slogans which are made somewhat ridiculous by their chumminess, like 'Ant, fist, anarchist!', on one side, and 'Pot-pot, pot-post, popo—post-man!', on the other.

Keeping in mind that no temporal order interferes with the evaluations, we can clearly see that what grounds the shared identity between postmen and anarchists could not be weaker, less given in appearing, than the conjunction of what supports the identity between anarchists and Kurds, on the one hand, and between the Kurds and the postmen, on the other. In other words, the intensity of appearance in the world 'demonstration at Place de la République', of sartorial uniformity (common to the Kurds and the postmen) is certainly at least as strong as the conjunction of the fierce posture (common to the Kurds and the anarchists) and a comic-masculine-French demeanour (common to the anarchists and the postmen). Otherwise it would mean that moving from what is in common to one group and another, to what is in common between the latter and a third group would produce an intensity of appearance lesser than what the first and the third have in common, which is obviously impossible. This is because the intensity of co-appearance of the Kurds and the anarchists, joined to that of the anarchists and the postmen, can only diminish or equal, but certainly never surpass the intensity of co-appearance which can be directly registered between the Kurds and the postmen. The intervention of a third term cannot augment the intensity of co-appearance because it exposes the first two terms to the differential filter of a supplementary singularity.

This means that the conjunction of the transcendental degree which measures the identity between the Kurds and the anarchists and of the one which measures the identity between anarchists and postmen gives a transcendental value, which is always lesser than or equal to the one which measures the identity between the Kurds and the postmen.

This rule testifies to a kind of triangular inequality of the transcendental conjunction, as applied to identitarian evaluations: the degree of identity between two beings x and y, conjoined to the degree of identity between y and z remains bound by the identity between x and z.

The phenomenon is ultimately governed by two laws.

1. *Symmetry*. In the construction of the phenomenon of a being, the identitarian relationship to another being also participates in the construction of the phenomenon of this second being. Thus what differentiates the black flag from the red flag is identical to what differentiates the red flag from the black flag.

2. *Triangular inequality*. If we take an evaluation which, by involving a second being, participates in the construction of the phenomenon of the first being, and conjoin it to an evaluation which, by involving a third being, participates in the construction of the phenomenon of the second, the initial evaluation remains lesser than or equal to the identity-evaluation of the first being and the third—which in turn participates in the construction of the phenomenon of the first being. Thus, to the extent that the intensity of appearance of the fierce attitude sums up the conjunctive co-appearance of the Kurds and the anarchists, and the somewhat Frenchy look that of the anarchists and the postmen, we can say that the intensity of appearance accorded to the 'fierce-Frenchy' complex cannot exceed that of the sartorial uniformity which recapitulates the co-appearance of the Kurds and the postmen.

Symmetry and triangular inequality are the necessary laws for every transcendental indexing.

2. THE PHENOMENON: SECOND APPROACH

Let us consider the painting by Hubert Robert, *The Bathing Pool* (see Figure 5). Treating it as a world, we can easily find within it the transcendental construction of phenomena. The whole question of pictorial assemblage in effect amounts to distributing identities and differences according to the degrees which prescribe the drawing of forms, the spectrum of colours, the overall lighting and so on. This invisible prescription is the work of the painter in the succession of his gestures (a certain brushstroke, then another. . .), but it only exists in the completed space of the canvas as the transcendental which organizes its appearing. It will be noted in passing that this point is indifferent to the figurative or abstract character of the artwork in question. In every case, the temporal construction as the amassing of artistic decisions is ultimately recapitulated as the transcendental of a closed visibility. In this regard, it can only be recognized, from painting to painting, as the painter's particular style. Style is understood here as something like the family resemblance of the transcendentals.

Let us glean from Hubert Robert's painting the features already discerned in the example of the demonstration at Place de la République.

1. The identity-function operates conjointly on the forms, colours, representative indices and so on. It is easy to see, for instance, that the columns of the central round temple must both be harmoniously similar and nevertheless distinct. Thus the blueness of the columns in the background is intended to bear their distance with regard to those in the foreground, but also their identity with regard to the variation in lighting (were the temple to turn, it is the two bronzed columns in the foreground that would become blurred and bluish). We can find another example of this (coloured) differentiation in formal identity: wrapped by the shadow of the trees, the columns on the far left are almost black. The work here consists in obtaining, in the transcendental field of style, an effect of strong identity, which is nevertheless not maximal, since the columns appear as distinct, not only individually (one can opt to count them), but in groups (gilded columns in the foreground, lighter on the right, bluish towards the background, black on the left. . .). Similarly, in the demonstration, the anarchist and Kurdish flags were more distinct by virtue of their local ascription than in terms of their symbolic appearance (the black and the red). The same remark can be made in what concerns the four fountains, giving forth the water, which doubtlessly comes from the centre of the earth, into the pool with the nude women. On the right and left, we see two statue plinths which hold the gushing mouths of the bronze lions and in the centre, two plinths for flower beds. In every case, the play of discordant symmetries establishes the transcendental solidity of these small waterfalls. The statue on the right is masculine, the one on the left feminine. On the right there is a light shadow, on the left a background of light yellow flowers and so on. We could say that the white water is born here in accordance with a subtle transcendental network of identities which figurative differences serve rather to exalt than to deny (no doubt inscribing all of this into the genre of neo-classicism).

2. We can verify that the differences in degree of appearance are not prescribed by the exteriority of the gaze. Of course, the gaze is presupposed as facing the painting, at a distance that must be neither too great nor too little. But just as nothing in the demonstration-world as a place of being-there required that the consideration of the group of postmen precede that of the high-school students, equally, under the verdant arch that half-

buries the old temple—doubtlessly devoted to Venus, as the central statue indicates, its blanched stone blessing the nudities beneath—nothing obliges us to examine the woman drying her legs on the left, or the pale red dress of her servant, before the two women who are still in the water. The play of identities is vaguely erotic; it makes disrobing into the invisible gesture common to the naked woman and the one who has clothed herself again. This gesture is testified by the clothes laid against one of the fountains. It transcendentally organizes the degree of identity of the sitting woman on the left and the two bathers. It puts in abeyance the function of the six (clothed) women in the background, above the steps of the temple. We can now reconstruct the rules of every transcendental indexing (of every function of appearing).

Symmetry. The degree of 'gestural' identity between the nude bathing women and the woman sitting on the left does not depend on the order in which one considers these two fragments of the painting. In every case, the distance between clothed and nude is what 'measures' appearing here.

Transitivity. If I consider the three groups—the two nude women in the water, the draped woman drying herself on the left and the clothed women at the top of the steps of the temple—I can clearly see that the degree of identity between the nude and the draped (which is strong, borne by the invisible disrobing), taken in conjunction with the degree of identity between the draped and the clothed in the background (obviously weaker, since the motif of disrobing is absent from it), remains in the end lesser than the degree of identity between the nude and the clothed. Why? Because this last transcendental degree no longer passes in any way through the allusion to the gesture (disrobing), since, if we can put it this way, it is filled by the pure pictorial force of an immediately recognizable motif, that of the opposition-conjunction between the nude and the dressed. Paradoxically, from a pictorial standpoint, the nude is more identical to the clothed, through a direct relation, than it could be through the detour of gesture to the draped. That is because the latent referent of the identification is not the same. Under the effect of the interpolation of an unconnected idea (the operation of disrobing), the detour through the draped weakens the simple force of the motif of the nude, which can only be thought in its contrasting appearance vis-à-vis that of clothing.

Let us speak in the language of predicates. The conjunction of the degree that measures the identity of the nude and the draped, and of the one that measures the conjunction of the draped and the clothed remains lesser than or equal to the degree that measures the identity of the nude and the clothed.

As we can see, the transcendental of the painting requires the function of identity to be both symmetrical and transitive.

All of this articulates the appearing of the neo-classical nostalgia of the ruins, in its singular coupling with a kind of natural covering, a verdant interment, which is itself summoned to be nothing but an arch for the triplet of the nude, disrobing and clothing, whereby the observer is also, willy-nilly, a libertine voyeur. Through the deception of the fountains, the world is here the juncture between the eroticism of the eighteenth century and a pre-romanticism that mimics antiquity. And what appears in this world, the phenomenon of the nude, or of the fountains, is constructed within it as the rule-governed intertwining of differential evaluations.

3. EXISTENCE

We have called the 'phenomenon' of a multiple-being, relative to the world in which it appears, the giving of the degrees of identity that measure its relationship of appearance to all the other beings of the same world (or, more precisely, of the same object-of-the-world).

This definition is relative and by no means rests, at least in an immediate sense, on the intensity of appearance of a being in a world. Take, for example, the statue on the left in Hubert Robert's painting. We can see that its relation of identity to the painting's two other statues (the one at the centre of the temple and the one atop the fountain on the left) indicates that it is the most 'discrete' of the three, being neither the Venus that watches over the nude women, like the statue of the temple, nor exalted by the golden light, like the statue on the left. We can also grasp the rotating network of identities between the statues and the living women. There are three statues, just as there are three groups of women (the nude ones in the water, the draped one and her servant on the water's edge and the clothed ones at the top of the steps), but the spatial correspondences—the pictorial being-there—are crossed; the Venus in the background, right next to the clothed women, actually watches over the bathers. The statue on the right overhangs the bathers, but shares with the clothed women a kind of penumbra or blurriness. Finally, the draped woman leans on the plinth of the statue of the left, and it is indeed this statue that she is in dialogue with, inasmuch as, just like her, the sculpture is an allusion to the terrestrial character of nudity. We can observe the round-robin of similarities in the painting-world, but the intensity of appearance of a given figure, or of a given luminous area, is not directly accessible in it. Take the foliage below the leaning tree on the left, which serves as the background for the statue: gilded, stretched, almost reduced to luminous dust, it appears intensely, even though its relations of identity to the libertine scene, the ancient round temple and the gushing waters seem to be entirely tangential.

We need to take into account the identitarian manifestness of the foliage, the clearing that it sets out on the left of the painting, even though the temple is already leaning to this side. This force of appearance simply measures the degree of self-identity of the golden-green foliage, taken as the punctuation of a place in the world (in this case, the left bottom corner of the canvas). It is clear, in effect, that the more the relation of self-identity of a being is transcendentally elevated, the more this being affirms its belonging to the world in question, and the more it testifies to the force of its being-there-in-this-world. The more, in brief, it exists-in-the-world, which is to say it appears more intensely within it.

Given a world and a function of appearing whose values lie in the transcendental of this world, we will call 'existence' of a being x which appears in this world the transcendental degree assigned to the self-identity of x. Thus defined, existence is not a category of being (of mathematics), it is a category of appearing (of logic). In particular, 'to exist' has no meaning in itself. In agreement with one of Sartre's insights, who borrows it from Heidegger, but also from Kierkegaard or even Pascal, 'to exist' can only be said relatively to a world. In effect, existence is nothing but a transcendental degree. It indicates the intensity of appearance of a multiple-being in a determinate world, and this intensity is by no means prescribed by the pure multiple composition of the being in question.

So what does the existence of a group of high-school students from the Lycée Buffon mean in the demonstration that's shaping up at Place de la République? Only that this gathering that the students form little by little, around their banner ('Buffon buffets the buffoons') is sufficiently constituted and identifiable for the measure of its identity (its self-relation) relative to the world of the demonstration, to be undoubtedly transcendentally high—something which obviously cannot be deduced from a mere collection of high-school students. Conversely, if one tries, in Hubert Robert's painting, to count as one the central ensemble comprising the Venus of the temple, the connected column and the clothed women, one comes up against a dissemination of appearing, a self-relation whose intensity is weak. As a being-there in the painting-world, this multiple exists weakly (unlike, for example, the group formed by the two nude bathers and the fountain that their clothes are thrown upon). This proves that it is not spatial separation that matters here, but rather existence, as transcendentally constituted by the pictorial logic.

The existence of an element can be understood as the ascription to this element of a transcendental degree. In effect, the identity-value of any x to itself is a function which assigns to this x the degree of that identity. We can thus speak of existence as a transcendental degree, and therefore see how existence unfolds, like these degrees themselves, between the minimum and the maximum.

If the existence of x takes the maximum value in the transcendental, it means that x exists absolutely in the world in question. This is the case for the statue of the Republic in the world of the demonstration—fearless, compact and benedictory, bestowing its capital signifier unto the place, it appears there devoid of nuances or weaknesses. One will say the same of the round temple in the painting-world, just as of the bathers, and even of the combination of the two, the internal connection of an Antiquity in ruins and an affluent eroticism—with the proviso that 'existing absolutely in a world' means 'appearing in it with the highest degree of intensity which is possible in this world'.

If the existence of x takes the minimal value in the transcendental, it is because x inexists absolutely in the world in question. Consider, for instance a robust proletarian detachment from the Renault factory in Flins, awaited by the demonstrators, anticipated by the unfortunate placard held aloft by a maudlin beanpole ('You will pay for your Flins!') but, unlike the high-school students or the Kurds, entirely unformed and lacking—at least at this moment in the world I'm telling you about. Likewise, a living male, whether nude or clothed, is the essential absent from Hubert Robert's libertine painting. Without a doubt, the masculine sex inexists for the painting because it is the eye whose gaze the painting awaits; but were this eye to be included, a different world would be at stake, another regime of appearing than the one enclosed by the edges of the canvas.

Finally, if the existence of x has an intermediary function, it is because the being x under consideration exists 'to a certain degree', which is neither 'absolute' existence (the maximal intensity of appearance or degree of self-identity) nor definite inexistence (minimal intensity of appearance). This is the case for the group of postmen, which is recognizable but ill-constituted, always on the verge of dissolving; or the forest in the very background of the painting, behind the temple or towards the right, reduced to a blue-green so faint that it communicates vertically, in an almost uninterrupted way, with the clouds in the sky, under a light which, on high, yet again gilded, recalls the gold dust above the bathers. This forest certainly exists, but according to a degree of self-identity which has been considerably weakened by the pictorial logic of the backgrounds.

We will now establish a fundamental property of existence: in a given world, a being cannot appear to be more identical to another being than it is to itself. Existence governs difference.

This property is a theorem of existence, which we will demonstrate in the formal exposition of Section 3 of this Book; we may nevertheless phenomenologically legitimate it without the least difficulty.

Consider, for instance, the aleatory identity of the group of librarians in the demonstration-world. They number only three—two of whom are ready to flee—and have all come to demand that the state set the price of art books; we can certainly argue that this 'group', by dint of its inconsistency, has a strong transcendental identity to the almost inexistent 'group' of the workers from the Renault factory in Flins. It is nevertheless excluded that this identity be a phenomenon of greater intensity than that of the appearance of the group of librarians. This is because the differential phenomenal intensity of the librarians and the Flins workers—as derisory components of the demonstration—includes, in terms of appearing, the existence of these two groups.

Likewise, the statue of Venus at the centre of the round temple, as well as the two women who seem to be contemplating this statue, partake of a tonality which is comparable to the clothes of the bathers abandoned beside one of the fountains. The phenomenon of both includes this identity of tone as a rather elevated transcendental degree. But each of the terms naturally takes upon itself that which grounds the elevation of this degree, namely a fairly polished whiteness, incorporating it into the evaluation of its own necessity of appearance in the painting, and therefore into its own existence. It follows that the transcendental degree which measures the intensity of the statue, just as the one which measures that of the two women or the clothes, cannot be lesser than the transcendental measure of their identity.

Lastly, the evaluation of the degree of identity between two beings of the same world remains lesser than or equal to the evaluation of existence of each of these beings; once again, one exists at least as much as one is identical to another.

Let us nevertheless retain the essential aspect: if the being of a being-there, its pure multiple form, is (mathematically) thinkable as an onto-logical invariant, the existence of this being is conversely a transcendental given, relative to the laws of appearing in a determinate world. Existence is a logical concept and not, like being, an ontological one. That existence subsumes difference (through its transcendental degree) does not make existence into the One of appearing. The fact that existence is not a form of being does not make it into the unitary form of appearing. As purely phenomenal, existence precedes the object and does not constitute it. The thinking of objectivity (or the of the One of appearing) requires another speculative detour.

4. ANALYTIC OF PHENOMENA: COMPONENT AND ATOM OF APPEARING

Let us assume an established set (in the ontological sense, a pure multiple) which appears in a determinate world. For example, the group of anarchists in the demonstration, considered as an abstract collection of individuals, or the set of columns of the round temple in the painting, considered as a denumerable repetitive series (at least in principle). To the extent that such multiples appear, they are elementarily indexed on the transcendental of a world. Accordingly, one can measure the (high) degree of identity between these two expertly badly shaven and black-clad anarchists, while, grasped pictorially, the columns at the front of the temple, massive and orange in colour, only achieve their serial identity to those in the background through the perspectival means of difference (their far greater size) and the chromatic means of the *sfumato* (the background columns are lost in the sylvan blue). All this transcenden-tally consists to the extent that the function of appearing assigns degrees to the identity of any two elements in the sets ('the anarchos' or 'the old temple').

The first question to pose is whether we can analyze the sets from the point of view of their appearing, to discern the being-there of certain parts of these sets. Ontologically (according to being qua being), we know that every set has subsets or parts. But can one also logically discern 'com-ponents' of a given phenomenon? For example, it does indeed seem that the background columns—in which the golden tint of the stone is prisoner of the vague-blue—are, within the painting, a component of the appearance of the old temple. But what could be the rigorous concept of such an analytic of parts?

This first question is only there to set the stage for a second one, which asks whether this supposedly practicable analysis allows for a halting point, something like a minimal component of every being-there.

Ontologically, there exists a double stopping point. On the one hand, only the empty set, which is an obligatory part of every pure multiple, does not admit of any part other than itself. On the other, given an element a of any multiple A, the singleton of a, written $\{a\}$, that is the set whose sole element is a, is like a 'minimal' part of A, in the sense that this part is prescribed by an element (a) whose belonging to A this part counts as one.

Logically, or according to appearing, is there a halting point for the analytic decomposition of beings-in-a-world? It does indeed seem that, if we're dealing with the group of anarchists, a given singular individual, who tries very hard to look menacing, is a non-decomposable component of what ultimately appears as the 'anarchos-in-the-demonstration'.

These phenomenological indications nevertheless remain indecisive as long as we have not reconstructed the concept of a component of appearing, or a minimal component, on the basis of the transcendental indexing of multiples that are there in a world.

Ultimately, what matters for us is knowing whether appearing admits of an instance of the One, or of the one-at-most [*un-au-plus*]. In a determinate world, is there a minimal threshold of appearing, on the hither side of which there is nothing there? This is the old question of perceptual atomicity, which the empiricists unceasingly reworked and which every doctrine of cerebral localizations, as sophisticated as it may be (as in contemporary neurosciences), re-encounters as the cross it must bear: what is the unit of counting of appearing or of the cerebral trace that corresponds to it? What is the factual and/or worldly atom of a perceptual apprehension? What is the *point* of appearance which is either the inducer of the phenomenon (on the side of what appears) or is induced by the phenomenon (on the side of mental reception)? For our part, it is a matter neither of perception nor of the brain, but of knowing whether one can make sense—once the world and its transcendental have been set—of a minimal unit of appearing-in-this-world.

Such a minimality only exists here as a correspondence between the elements-there of the world and the transcendental. This is the case for the transcendental value, with regard to the group of anarchists, of the menacing individual; or for the value, with regard to the temple, of the practically invisible columns on the left background of the temple. We sense that in these cases we are indeed on the analytical edge of appearing. But what is the concept of this edge, to the extent that it still retains the unity of an appearance?

Consider a function of the set which we took as our referent at the outset (the anarchists, the temple. . .) to the transcendental, that is a function which associates a transcendental degree to every element of the set. Such a function may be intuitively interpreted as the degree according to which an element belongs to a component of appearing of the initial set. Let's suppose, for example, that the function associates to the columns of the temple the maximal value if they are very clearly outlined and golden or orange, the minimal value if they are black, and an intermediate value if they are not obviously either the one or the other, dissipating their light into the sylvan blue. We can plainly see how this function will separate out, within the apparent-set 'the columns of the temple', the two columns of the foreground, as taking the maximal value of belonging to a component. Conversely, the columns on the left will be excluded from this component, their degree of belonging being minimal. The columns on the right will be treated as mixed, since they belong to the component 'to a certain degree', just like those in the background, but to a lesser degree.

We will call 'phenomenal component' a function of a being-there-in-a-world on the transcendental of this world. If the function has degree p, as its value for an element of the being-there under consideration, this means that the element belongs 'to the p degree' to the component defined by the function. The elements that 'absolutely' compose the phenomenal component are those to which the function assigns the maximal transcendental degree.

Let's take another example. In the world 'demonstration', among the members of the nebula marching alongside the militant cluster of the anarchos, the function may assign the maximal value to those who are (1) dressed in black jackets and have a menacing air, (2) echo the slogans of the anarchos ('Destroy the wage! A guaranteed income for everyone existing!'), (3) carry a black flag, (4) taunt the Trotskyists and (5) throw stones at bank windows. The function will assign a value slightly less than the maximum to those who have only four of these properties, a weaker one to those who have only three, an even lesser one to those who have just two, a very weak one to those who have only one, and finally the minimal value to those who have none, or who have a property which is in absolute contradiction with one of the five (like waving a red flag or sicking the stewards on any stone-thrower). We can thus see how the maximal value will outline the 'hard' component of the anarchist nebula, and the intermediate values will identify less determinate components.

We can now identify the features of an atomic phenomenal component. It suffices to postulate the following: if a being-there x belongs absolutely to the component, then another being-there y can only belong absolutely to it if x and y are, with regard to their appearing, absolutely identical. To put it otherwise, if x and y are not absolutely identical in appearing and x belongs absolutely to the component, then y does not belong absolutely to this component. Given these conditions, it is clear that the component can 'absolutely' contain at most one element.

The 'at most' is crucial here. In the order of being, we spontaneously call atom a multiple which has a single element and which is, in this sense, indivisible (it cannot be divided into disjoined parts). But we are not in the order of being. We start from the formal discernment of the phenomenal components of the world and we ask ourselves what can come to the world, or come to appearing-in-a-world, under this component. It will certainly be atomic if two apparents come to appear within it only in exchange for their strict intra-worldly identity. But it will also be atomic if no apparent can come to appear within it absolutely, since in that case the phenomenal component is exclusive to the multiple, already being exclusive to the one. That is why an atom of appearing is a phenomenal component such that, if an apparent absolutely establishes itself within it in the world, then every other apparent which comes under this case will be identical to the first ('identical' in the sense of appearing, that is of transcendental indexing). The atom in appearing, or in the logical (rather than ontological) sense, is not 'one and only one, which is indivisible' but 'if one, not more than one and if not none'.

Take, for example, in the painting-world, the component prescribed by 'applying the colour red to an important surface'. The only apparent in the painting which answers to this condition is the dress of the woman sitting against the central pillar of the temple. This is not to say that it is the only phenomenal index of red within the painting-world. There are the red flowers in the two basins, the pale red dress of the draped woman's servant and other flowers of a very dark red on the bush which is in the very foreground on the lower left of the canvas. . . But we can nevertheless say that the component 'red applied to the surface' is atomic, in that only one apparent maximally validates this predicate.

If we now prescribe another component for 'displaying the masculine sex', it is evident that no apparent can associate a maximal value of appearance to this predicate. Of course, within the painting, the statue on the right represents a male hero, and in this sense validates the component to a certain degree. But aside from the haziness that envelops this statue, a drape veils the organ, so that this degree is by no means maximal. It automatically follows that this component is atomic. This does not mean that it is integrally empty; the statue may be said to belong to it. Rather, it means that 'not displaying the masculine sex' is not phenomenally applicable in the same manner to all the apparents of the painting. It is thus that the statue displays and veils it at the same time, so that it cannot be said that it does not display it at all. It displays it, yes, with a differential degree which is not absolute, but which is also not nil. Let us say that this apparent is p-male-sex, that is 'displaying the male organ to the p degree'. It will, therefore, figure in the component in question, but only to the p degree. Conversely, the dresses carelessly thrown against the fountain testify that no male is witnessing the scene, that the women are among themselves and need not take any particular precaution when they disrobe. One will say that these dresses only belong to the component to the minimal degree, which in the world in question means not at all. Lastly, the component prescribed by 'displaying the male sex' is atomic because it undoubtedly contains at least one apparent which figures within it to the p degree, but none which belong to it absolutely.

Let us insist on the fact that uniqueness is here uniqueness in appearing. It may very well happen that two ontologically distinct multiple-beings belong to the same atomic component—that they are elements of the same atom. Let's suppose, for example, that in the demonstration-world we only accept groups, that is political pluralities, as beings-there—which after all does justice to the collective phenomenality of such a world. It may well then turn out that the hard kernel of the anarchists constitutes an atom, in that the functional properties which identify it within appearing (outfits, demeanour, slogans. . .) do not allow one to take the analysis further and identify an extra-hard core of the hard. It may even be the case that the transcendental logic of the demonstration, which is political visibility, elicits the 'worldly' inseparability of the hard anarchists from Montreuil and those of Saint-Denis, whatever their banners may be up to. Of course, they are distinct in their geographical provenance and their disparate bodies. But when it comes to the political logic of appearing, they are identical, and can therefore be co-presented in the atom 'hard anarchists'. In terms of that political logic, they do not make up a multiplicity according to their being-there, as distinct as they may be in terms of being-qua-being.

We can carry out the same exercise with regard to the possible atomicity of the columns of the temple in the painting. The two columns in the foreground are sufficiently identical in their pictorial execution to enter into an atom of appearance—'typical Roman column'—from which conversely will be excluded all the fading or romanticized blue columns of the background, as well as the black columns (purely 'functional', or charged with holding up the whole) on the left side.

It turns out, therefore, that an atom of appearing can be an ontologically multiple phenomenal component. It is enough for the logic of appearing to prescribe the identity-in-the-world of its elements for its atomicity to be acknowledged.

We can analyze the property of atomicity on the basis of difference as well as on the basis of identity. For example, we can isolate in Hubert Robert's painting a component that obeys the pictorial prescription 'trace a green, black and yellow diagonal starting from the bottom left of the painting'. It is plain that only the great tree, leaning and interrupted, the symbol of the verdant burial of the ruins, belongs in the painting to this component. If we consider one of the inapparent columns on the temple's left we can indeed say that its identity to the tree—standing sumptuously in the foreground as the natural elision of all of ancient culture—is nil, that its pictorial value is zero. It obviously follows that belonging to the component 'coloured diagonal', which is absolute for the tree, is nil for the column. The fact that this is true for every ingredient of the painting which differs absolutely from the great tree indicates that the component 'coloured diagonal' is atomic (in absolute terms, it only contains the tree).

Abstractly speaking, we can put it as follows: if the transcendental evaluation of the identity of two apparents in a world is the minimal degree, that is if these two apparents are absolutely different within the world in question, and if, moreover, one of the two apparents belongs absolutely to an atomic component, then the second apparent does not belong absolutely to this component.

Finally, we call 'atom of appearing' a component of a being A which appears in a world such that, if two ontologically distinct elements of A, x and y, both belong absolutely to this component, then x and y are absolutely identical in the world. Conversely, if x and y are not absolutely identical, and x belongs absolutely to the component, then y does not belong absolutely to it.

5. REAL ATOMS

Take an element (in the ontological sense) of a multiple A appearing in a world, for example one of the columns of the set 'round temple' in the painting. Let us call this element 'c'. The phenomenon of c is, beside c 'itself' (as pure multiple), the set of degrees which give a value to the identity of c and x, where x covers all the possible intensities of the world. In other words, we are considering the set of values which identify c in terms of its others, but also in terms of itself, since in the phenomenon c we will have the degree that measures the identity of c to itself, a degree which is nothing other than the existence of c.

Let us restrict the phenomenon of c to the set 'temple'. We will then say in particular that if c_1, c_2, etc. are the other columns of the temple, the degrees of identity of c_1, c_2, etc. to c participate in the phenomenon of c, considered here in terms of a referential multiple (the temple). Now, and this is a crucial remark, the phenomenal function thus restricted—which assigns to every column of the temple its degree of identity to another column or to itself—is an atom for the appearing of the temple or a minimal component of this appearing. Why? First of all, it is clear that once c is set, the phenomenal function in question is a function of the multiple 'temple' to the transcendental—to each value of a being x of the temple there indeed corresponds a degree of T, which is the value of its identity to the column c. We know, for example, that if c is the column in the left foreground and c_1 its neighbour to the right, the function has a high transcendental value. Conversely, if c_6 is the column visible in the background towards the right, the function has a weak value. So this function undeniably identifies a phenomenal component of the temple.

But what happens if an element belongs absolutely to this component? Let us pose, for example, as we have already done, that in pictorial terms the two columns in the foreground are identical in their appearing (the transcendental indexing of their identity has the maximal value). Supposing that another component, let's say column c_2 just to the right of c_1, is itself also just a typical Roman column, we will likewise have a maximal value for its identity to c. We can then be sure that the beings c_1 and c_2 are also maximally identical, because two apparents which are absolutely identical to a third are doubtless obliged to be identical to one another.

We can thus see that the phenomenal function in question (the degree of identity to column c) defines an atom of appearing of the temple, since, first of all, it identifies a phenomenal component and secondly, it is such that if two apparents belong absolutely to this component it means they are transcendentally identical. In order to satisfy absolute belonging, a clause of uniqueness is indeed required.

The consequence of this point is the following: *Given a multiple A which appears in a world, every element 'a' of A identifies an atom of appearing, via the function of A to T defined above by the degree of identity of every element x of A to the singular element 'a'. Such an atom will be said to be 'real'.*

Let us gauge the importance of the existence of real atoms; it attests to the appearance, in appearing, of the being of appearing. For every pure multiplicity *A* led to be there in a world, we are certain that to the onto-logical composition of *A* (the elementary belonging of the multiple *a* to the multiple *A*) there corresponds its logical composition (an atomic com-ponent of its being-there-in-this-world). We encounter in this point another ontological connection which, unlike the Kantian dualism of the phenomenon and the noumenon, anchors the logic of appearing—at the fine point of the One—in the ontology of formal multiplicities.

The question that must then be addressed is that of the validity of the reciprocal. It turns out that every constitutive element of a worldly being prescribes an atom of appearing. Is it true, reciprocally, that every atom of appearing is prescribed by an element of a multiple that appears? In other words, at the point of the One or of uniqueness is there identity, or total suture, between the logic of appearing and the ontology of the multiple?

We will answer 'yes', thereby positing, to borrow an image from Lacan, that the One (the atom) is the quilting point of appearing within being. We are dealing here with a postulate, which we will call the 'postulate of materialism', that can be simply stated as follows: *every atom of appearing is real*. Or, in more technical terms: given an atomic function between a mul-tiple and the transcendental of a world—that is a component of the appear-ing of this multiple which comprises at most an element (in the sense of 'absolute' belonging)—there always exists a (mathematical) element of this multiple which identifies this (logical) atom (or atom of appearing).

Let us first of all examine this materialist requirement in light of objec-tive phenomenology. We have said that such and such an individual, marked by all the characteristic signs of the anarchist as publicly represen-tative, identifies as atomic the component determined by the function 'flaunting the five insignia of the hardcore anarchist'. Now, an individual is, for the group of anarchists, an element of the pure multiple that this group is. The reciprocal will be the following: given any atomic component of the group of anarchists, it will ultimately be identified by an individual of the group. This reciprocal is obviously quite likely if we hold that, when all is said and done, aside from the void there is only the multiple. But it is not a mandatory consequence of the logic of appearing. Let us say that it provides its materialist version.

We have reached the point of a speculative decision, for which there is no transcendental deduction. This decision excludes that appearing may be rooted in something virtual. In effect it requires that an actual dimension of the multiple (of ontological composition) be involved in the identification of every unit of appearing. There where the one appears, the One is. This explains why appearing, there where it is One, cannot be other than it is. In an elementary sense, there is an 'it's like that' of what appears where the 'it's' is an 'it's one'. For the postulate of materialism ('every atom is real') requires that the 'it's one' be sustained by some one-that-is [*un-qui-est*]. It will not be in vain to refer to it as the *unease* [*l'inquiet*], to the extent that it is indeed there where logic draws its consistency from the onto-logical that thought can enter into its most fecund unease [*in-quiétude*] (the one-who-studies [*l'un-qui-étudie*]).

Let us restate the materialist requirement in a more sophisticated form. 'To impose the idea of a vertical symmetry' defines, it seems, a virtual (invisible) component of Hubert Robert's painting. The sole element of this component would be the line—which is not figured as such in the forms and colours—which divides the surface into two areas of equal size. The materialist postulate will say: 'yes, this atomic component exists'. But it is prescribed by the column of the temple which is placed exactly at the centre of the painting (the one at whose foot the clothed women are to be found); this column is the real element of the apparent-multiplicity 'round temple'. Every apparent, which, situated centrally and vertically disposed like this column, is in this respect, transcendentally identical to it, will co-participate in the atomic component. To put it otherwise, the transcendental name of this atom in the world of the painting is the column, to the extent that the column assigns that which is identical-in-appearing to it to the atom 'vertical axis'. The significance of the axiom of materialism is evident: it demands that what is atomically counted as one in appearing already have been counted as one in being. What we mean to say is that it has already been counted—and therefore can always be counted (the ontological laws of the count are inflexible)—among the elements of a multiple which appears in the place in question within appearing (within such a world).

The one of appearing is the being-one of one which appears. The one appears [*paraît*] to the extent that it is the one of that which, in appearing, appear-is [*par-est*].

At the conclusion of this analysis, which is both regressive (the definition of transcendental operations) and progressive (finding a real stopping-point in atomic components), we are now ready to define what an object is.

6. DEFINITION OF AN OBJECT

Given a world, we call object of the world the couple formed by a multiple and a transcendental indexing of this multiple, under the condition that all the atoms of appearing whose referent is the multiple in question are its real atoms.

For example, the group of anarchists is an object of the world 'demonstration at Place de la République' in as much as:

a. its visibility as an identifiable political group is guaranteed by a transcendental indexing adequate to the world in question (that is by collective indices);

b. every atomic component of the group is ultimately identifiable by an individual of the group (it is prescribed by a transcendental identity to this individual).

Similarly, the round temple is an object of Hubert Robert's painting to the extent that its consistency is guaranteed by pictorial operations that make it appear as it does (forms, perspectives, contrasts, etc.), but also because every instance of the One in this appearing (a vertical axis, for instance) is sutured to the elementary composition of the apparent multiplicities (one of the fourteen or fifteen columns, for instance).

In an abstract sense, it should be underscored that an object is jointly given by a conceptual couple (a multiple and a transcendental indexing) and a materialist prescription about the One (every atom is real). It is therefore neither a substantial given (since the appearing of a multiple *A* presupposes a transcendental indexing which varies according to the worlds and may also vary within the same world) nor a purely fictional given (since every one-effect in appearing is prescribed by a real element of what appears).

The object is an ontological category par excellence. It is fully logical, in that it designates being as being-there. 'Appearing' is nothing else, for a being—initially conceived in its being as pure multiple—than a becoming-object. But 'object' is also a fully ontological category, in that it only composes its atoms of appearing—or stopping-points-according-to-the-One of the there-multiple—in accordance with the mathematical law of belonging, or of pure presentation.

The only inflexible truth regarding the intimate decomposition of the worldly fiction of being-there is that of being-qua-being. The object objects to the transcendental fiction, which it nevertheless is, the 'fixion' of the One in being.

7. ATOMIC LOGIC, 1: THE LOCALIZATION OF THE ONE

The postulate of materialism authorizes us to consider an element of a multiple which appears in a world in two different ways: either as 'itself', this singular element that belongs (in the ontological sense) to the initial multiple, or as that which defines, within appearing, a real atom. In the first sense, the element depends solely on the pure (mathematical) thinking of the multiple. In the second sense, it is related, not only to this multiple, but to its transcendental indexing. It is therefore a dimension of the object, or of the objectivation of the multiple, and not only of the multiple-being of the being-that-appears.

From now on, we will freely speak of any element whatsoever as an element of the object or, even more abstractly, as an object-element. This expression is an ontological one, taking 'element' from the doctrine of being and 'object' from that of appearing. It designates a real element of a multiple, to the extent that this element identifies an atom of appearing, and therefore an atomic object-component.

We call 'atomic logic' the theory of the relations which are thinkable between the elements of an object. We will see that this logic inscribes the transcendental into multiple-being itself.

What we are moving towards is the retroaction of appearing on being. The concept of the object is pivotal to this retroaction. What is at stake is knowing what becomes of a pure multiple once it will be there, in the world. This means asking what happens to a being in its being, insofar as it becomes an object, the material form of localization in the world. What of being thought in the feedback-effect of its appearing? Or, what are the ontological consequences of logical apprehension?

From the fact that such and such an individual has been grasped by the identity-evaluations of the world 'demonstration'—for example as the generic or maximal figure of the group of anarchists—what follows in terms of its intrinsic multiple-determination and its capacity to pass through other registers of appearing? Or, from the fact that such and such a patch of colour—a white both gilded and polished—is assigned by Hubert Robert to the two nude women bathing in the fountain, what follows with regard to the pictorial and trans-pictorial doublet of nudity and femininity? And what happens to the possible usages of the polished-gilded white?

This point is essential for the following reason. Later, we will see that an event, in affecting a world, always has a local rearrangement of the transcendental of this world as its effect. This modification of the conditions of appearing may be seen as an alteration of objectivity, or of what an object in the world is. The problem is then that of knowing to what degree this transformation of objectivity affects the beings of this world in their very being. We already know that becoming-subject is precisely such a retro-action—namely concerning particular human animals—of the evental modifications of objectivity. The precondition for becoming a subject in a determinate world is that the logic of the object be unsettled. This tells us the importance of the general identification of the effects on multiple-being of its worldly objectivation.

An object is no doubt a figure of appearing (a multiple and its transcendental indexing), but its atomic composition is real. That which will define the counter-effect on the multiple (the real, the being) of its appearance as an object necessarily concerns its atomic composition, since it is this composition that 'carries' the real's mark on the object. The entire question thus comes down to examining what it means for an atom of appearing to be 'there', in this world. These are the precise stakes of atomic logic, which is the heart of the Greater Logic.

In a general sense, an atom is a certain rule-governed relationship between an element a of a multiple A and the transcendental of a world. A real atom is basically a function whose values are transcendental degrees. If an atom is real it is because the function is operationally prescribed by an element a of the multiple A, in the sense that, whatever x may be, the transcendental of the function for x is identical to the degree of identity between this x and a.

The postulate of materialism is that every atom is real. It follows that the logic of atoms of appearing ultimately concerns a certain type of correlation between the elements of a multiple A and the transcendental degrees, which are themselves elements of the transcendental T. The essence of this correlation is the localization of A in a world, conceived as the logical capture of its being. The fact that, for example, the group of anarchists is, under the postulate of materialism, really there in the world 'demonstration' may be reduced in the final analysis to a certain relationship between the individuals (elements) of the group and the transcendental which evaluates the effective degree of appearing of the beings in this world.

At this level, the topological approach is the most pertinent one. The atom is ontological to the extent that it is shared between the multiple composition of a being (the individuals of the group of anarchists, the columns of the round temple. . .) and the transcendental values of localization and intensity that may be assigned to this composition ('absolutely typical of the anarchists', 'indexing a vertical axis of the painting', etc.).

The very close formal bonds that unite the concept of the transcendental to that of topology will be elucidated in Book VI, which is devoted to the theory of the 'points' of a transcendental. For the time being, it suffices to consider—somewhat metaphorically—a degree of the transcendental as a power of localization. We thus circulate between the (rather global) register of appearing and the (rather local) register of being-there, keeping in mind that the profound unity of these two registers lies in their co-belonging to logic, that is to the transcendental.

Given a world, let us arbitrarily choose a transcendental degree. We can then ask what an atom of appearing is relative to this degree. Consider the atom prescribed by 'marking the vertical axis of the painting', relative to a weak degree of pictorial intensity—for example the one that corresponds to the presence of the colour 'bright blue', which is merely evoked, at the feet of the fountain on the left, by a piece of the draped woman's dress. What is the transcendental measure of this assignation of the atom to a particular degree (a localization)? Given a being that may be registered in the world, this assignation will be obtained by taking what there is in common between the value of the atom for this being and the degree in question. For example, the value of the atom 'marking the vertical axis' has the maximum value for the column of the temple which is on the right foreground. The degree assigned to the appearing of the bright blue is very close to the minimum (this colour is 'almost not there', or 'there by way of allusion'). What appears in common to the two, localizing the atom according to this degree (or this instance of the there-in-the-world), is obviously the conjunction of the two values. Now, the conjunction of the maximum and of any other degree is equal to the latter. We will thus say, in this particular case, that, for the being 'column in front on the right', the assignation of the atom to the localization 'place of the bright blue in the painting-world' is equal to this localization.

In a general sense, *we will call 'localization of an atom on a transcendental degree' the function which associates, to every being of the world, the conjunction of the degree of belonging of this being to the atom, on one hand, and of the assigned degree, on the other*.

It appears then that every assignation of an atom to a degree—every localization—is itself an atom. Mastering the intuition of this point is both very important and rather difficult. In essence, it means that an atom which is 'relativized' to a particular localization gives us a new atom.

Recall that if a being is 'absolutely' in an atomic component (like the column in front and to the right in the atomic component 'marking the vertical axis'), another being can only be absolutely in the component if it is transcendentally identical to the first (if it is indiscernible from the first from the standpoint of appearing). The localization of the atom on a degree p retains this property. It does so negatively, since in general it is impossible for there not to be a being which provides the localized atom with its maximal value. In effect, for a localized atom, the greatest possible value of belonging is localization. It is a constitutive property of conjunction that it is lesser than or equal to the two conjoined terms. Therefore, a given being cannot lend the conjunction of an atomic value and a degree a value greater than this degree. It follows that the value of the atom 'marking the vertical axis of the painting', localized on the degree which evaluates the 'bright blue' in the painting-world, cannot surpass this (weak) degree. In particular, it is out of the question that a being gives the maximal value to this localization. This means that there exists no being in the painting that can 'absolutely' belong to the localized atom. That is what makes this localization into an atom. Since an atom requires only that one being *at most* belong to it absolutely, every component that no being can occupy 'absolutely' is an atom. We will here make full use of the remark made earlier in Subsection 5 (on real atoms): in the order of appearing, a component that is not occupied absolutely by any apparent is atomic. It follows, in general, that the localization of an atom on a transcendental degree is in effect an atom.

The sole exception is obviously localization on the maximal degree. To illustrate this case, we'll consider an inverted variant of the previous example. Take the component of the painting-world prescribed by 'applying the red to an important surface'. It is atomic because only the dress on the steps belongs absolutely to this component. If we now localize this atom on the maximal degree, we obtain, for a given being, the conjunction between the degree assigned to this being by 'applying red' and the maximal degree. But the conjunction of a given degree and the maximum is the degree in question. We thus formally possess the maximal value for the only being which absolutely validates 'applying red over an important surface', that is the dress on the steps. This proves that the conjunction in question is indeed an atom.

Consequently, every localization of an atom on a transcendental degree is an atom. But, by the postulate of materialism, every atom is real. A given atom is prescribed by an element (in the ontological sense) of a multiple A of the world. Let 'a' be this element. If this atom is localized by a degree, we have a new atom, which in turn must be prescribed by an element b of the multiple in question. We will say that b is a localization of a. Thus, through the mediation of the transcendental, we define a relation that is immanent to the multiple. We thus have the sketch of a retroaction of appearing onto being. Since A appears in a world where the transcendental is established, it follows that some elements of A are localizations of other elements of the same multiple. We may, for example, say that, having been localized on the degree of intensity assigned to the red dress on the steps, the column on the front right of the temple is transcendentally linked to every element of the painting that possesses this degree. That is indeed a relation immanent to the 'pictorial' beings that may be registered on the surface of the canvas.

Let us restate this definition more explicitly: *Take an object presented in a world. Let an element 'a' of the multiple 'A' be the underlying being of this object. And let 'p' be a transcendental degree. We will say that an element 'b' of A is the 'localization of a on p' if b prescribes the real atom resulting from the localization on the degree p of the atom prescribed by element a.*

8. ATOMIC LOGIC, 2: COMPATIBILITY AND ORDER

At this point in our discussion, it is very important to emphasize once again that localization is a relation between elements of A, and therefore a relation that directly structures the being of the multiple. Of course, this relation depends on the logic of the world in which the multiple appears. But in the retroaction of this logic, we are indeed dealing with an organizational (or relational) grasp of being-qua-being. In the last of our examples, the pictorial logic feeds back on the neutrality of what is there, so that it makes sense to speak of a relation between the red dress and the column of the temple, or in the demonstration-world, of a relation between such and such an individual and such and such another.

On the basis of this primitive relation between two elements of a multiple-being such as it appears in a world, we will try to set out a *relational form of being-there* capable of lending consistency to the multiple in the space of its appearing, so that ultimately there is a solidarity between the ontological count as one of a given region of multiplicity and the logical synthesis of the same region.

It is imperative to understand the nature of the problem which is basically the one that Kant designated with the barbarous name of 'originary synthetic unity of apperception' and which he was ultimately incapable of resolving, since he was unable to think through the (mathematical) rationality of ontology itself. It is a question of showing that, as great as the gap may be between the pure presentation of being in the mathematics of multiplicity, on one hand, and the logic of identity which prescribes the consistency of a world, on the other, a twofold system of connections exists between them.

– At the point of the One, under the concept of atom of appearing, and assuming the postulate of materialism, we can see that the smallest component of being-there is prescribed by a real element of the multiple that appears. This is an analytical quilting point between being as such and being-there, or the appearing of any being whatever.

– In global terms, and by means of the retroaction of transcendental logic on the multiple composition of what appears, there exist relations immanent to any being which is inscribed in a world. These relations ultimately authorize us (under certain conditions) to conceptualize the synthetic unity of a multiple that appears, a unity that is correlated to the existential analysis of the multiple in question. This unity is at one and the same time dependent on the multiple-composition of the being, that is on its being, and on the transcendental, that is on the laws of appearing. This is exactly what Kant searched for in vain: an ontico-transcendental synthesis.

This synthesis is ultimately realizable in the form of a relation, which is itself global, between the structure of the transcendental and the structure that is retroactively assignable to the multiple insofar as the latter appears in such and such a world. For profound theoretical reasons, we will from now on refer to this global relation as the *transcendental functor*.

The aim of what follows is to specify the steps in the construction of the transcendental functor as operator of regional ontological consistency. It is clear that in this domain formal presentation reigns supreme. We are merely trying to introduce the reader to it. Let us start with a very simple consideration. We are looking for the connections between logic and ontology, between the transcendental and multiplicities. What is the primordial link between an element x of a multiple that appears in a world and a particular degree p of the transcendental of this world? Existence. In effect, to every element x of an object, there corresponds the transcendental degree p which evaluates its existence. It is therefore possible to conceive of an existence as a power of localization, since it is a transcendental degree. For example, if we identify the existence of the column on the front right of the temple in the painting-world, we can say that it has the power to localize the diagonal traced by the shadow that hangs over the fountain. Here the column is evidently conceived as an atomic component of the temple-object, and the tree as a real point of the atom prescribed by 'tracing a diagonal from the left bottom corner of the painting towards its middle upper part'. Since the existence of the column is a transcendental degree (which is in fact very close to the maximum), we possess the new atom which has been obtained by the localization on this existence of the real atom prescribed by the tree. The melancholic and natural inclination of the tree is in some sense straightened up by its measurable conjunction with the potent existence—both ancient and vertical—of the column. The precarious verdant time is measured by the eternal time of art.

Given two real elements of the appearing-world, we can localize the one on the existence of the other. We thereby obtain an atom which, by virtue of the postulate of materialism, is necessarily real. But the construction can be inverted. For example, we may consider the localization of the column of the temple on the existence of the leaning tree, which gives us another atom. In this case, it is the time of ancient art, the solemn time of the ruin, which is measured by the natural and transitory force of existence of the old tree whose roots can no longer manage to keep straight. The relational idea is then the following: if two symmetrical localizations are equal, one will say that the real elements are transcendentally compatible. In other words, *given an object that appears in a world, we will say that two (real) elements of this object are 'compatible' if the localization of the one on the existence of the other is equal to the localization of the latter on the existence of the former.*

In the demonstration-world, let us choose the atom represented by a typical anarchist. Let us suppose that we localize it on the existence of a postman marching all alone on the sidewalk. This means that we express what there is in common between the functional value of a given element 'grasped' by the anarchist—what is the degree of identity to the anarchist of this nurse who has insisted in coming dressed in her white veil?—and the existence of the postman, which all in all is rather evasive, since he does not present himself as a component of a consistent subgroup. Is the product of this evaluation equal to its symmetric counterpart? The latter is the functional value of the nurse grasped by the solitary postman—to what extent does she share his solitude?—in its conjunction with the solid existence of the typical anarchist. Inequality is likely and one will accordingly conclude that the typical anarchist and the stray postman are incompatible in the world in question. This ultimately expresses a kind of existential disjunction which is internal to co-appearance in the world. Inversely, compatibility means not only that two beings co-appear in the same world, but moreover that they enjoy a kind of existential kinship within it, since if each operates atomically in its conjunction with the existence of the other, the result of the two operations is exactly the same atom.

We are here in possession of an operator of similarity which acts retro-actively on the elementary composition of a multiplicity, to the extent that this multiplicity appears in a world. We can now make sense of expressions such as 'the column on the front right of the temple, grasped in its being, is scarcely compatible with the draped woman's blue dress', or, transporting ourselves to Place de la République, 'the solitary postman ambling on the sidewalk is compatible with the veiled nurse'.

To wield an operator of synthesis, or a function of unity, we must bring relations internal to beings even closer to the structure of the transcendental. What in effect is the transcendental paradigm of synthesis? It is the envelope, which measures the consistency of a region of appearing, whether finite or infinite. But in order to construct the synthetic concept of the envelope, we require the analytic concept of order. It just so happens that we are now capable of directly defining an order-relation over the 'atomized' elements of such and such a multiple-in-the-world.

The principle behind this definition is simple. We begin by considering two compatible elements—the solitary postman and the veiled nurse, or the two columns on the front right and left of the round temple. If, and only if, the existence of one of these elements is lesser than or equal to that of the other (this inequality is decided in accordance with the transcendental order, since every existence is a degree), we will say that the being-there of the first is lesser than or equal to the being-there of the second. Or, in somewhat more formal terms: *An element of an object of the world possesses a type of being-there which is lesser than that of another being if the two are compatible and if the degree of existence of the first is lesser than the degree of existence of the second.*

If we suppose that the intensity of political existence of the solitary postman on the sidewalk is lesser than the one (which is already not very high) of the nurse, who at least promenades her disorientation on the road, we will say, since these two elements of the demonstration-world are compatible, that the being-there of the postman is lesser than that of the nurse—the fact that we are really dealing with an order-relation is intuitively clear. Note that even though this elementary ordering of the objects of the world obviously implies an inequality of existence— existence is, in effect, the immediate link between the intensity of appearance of a being-there in a world and the hierarchy of transcendental degrees—it nevertheless cannot be reduced to such an inequality, since in addition it is necessary that the elements thereby ordered are also compatible. And compatibility is a localizing or topological relation.

In the formal exposition, we will show moreover that it is possible directly to define the order-relation between elements of an object on the basis of existence and the function of appearing, without needing explicitly to pass through compatibility. Hence elementary order over objects has a purely transcendental essence. But it also has a topological essence, since it is possible to define this order on the basis of localization, as we indicate in the formal exposition and demonstrate in the appendix. Finally, this order is a 'total' concept. It prepares real synthesis.

9. ATOMIC LOGIC, 3: REAL SYNTHESIS

To obtain the real synthesis of an object or of an objective region we simply need to apply to the objective order the approach which allowed us to define the envelope of the transcendental degrees. Consider an objective region, for example the set constituted by the almost hidden or invisible columns of the round temple. Suppose, which is far from evident, that all the columns of the temple are compatible. It follows from the definition of objective order that they are ontologically ordered by their degree of pictorial existence. We can then ask whether there exists, for the objective order, a least upper bound for our initial set. In this example, the answer is pretty clear. As pale and bluish as it might be, the column at the back, which is largely visible behind the central statue, placed between the two columns at the front which establish the vertical axis, nevertheless possesses, with regard to other 'hidden' columns, an indisputable pictorial manifestness. Since its degree of existence is immediately superior to that of the others, it unquestionably guarantees their real synthesis. We can really say that this column holds up the entire invisible or not-so-visible part of the temple. We can thus see that the envelope of an objective zone for the order-relation sustains the unity of the being-there, or of the object, beyond the inequalities in its appearing.

Under precise conditions—namely those of compatibility—we are thus constructing here a unity of being for the object, or at least for certain objective zones. The key point of the retroaction of appearing on being is that it is possible in this way to reunify the multiple composition of a being. What was counted as one in being, disseminating this One in the nuances of appearing, may come to be unitarily recounted to the extent that its relational consistency is averred.

SECTION 2
Kant

Thought precedes all possible determinate ordering of representations.

Kant is without doubt the creator in philosophy of the notion of object. Broadly speaking, he calls 'object' that which represents a unity of representation in experience. It is clear then that the word 'object' designates the local outcome of the confrontation between receptivity ('something' is given to me in intuition) and constituent spontaneity (I structure this given by means of subjective operators with a universal value, which together make up the transcendental). In my own conception, there is neither reception nor constitution, because the transcendental—no more and no less than the pure multiple—is an intrinsic determination of being, which I call appearing, or being-there. One could then think that the comparison with Kant is out of place, and that there is only a homonymy in our respective uses of the word 'object'. For Kant, the object is the result of the synthetic operation of consciousness:

The transcendental unity of apperception is that unity through which all the manifold given in an intuition is united in a concept of the object.

For me, the object is the appearing of a multiple-being in a determinate world, and its concept (transcendental indexing, real atoms...) does not imply any subject. But the question is far more complicated. Why? Because the notion of object crystallizes the ambiguities present in Kant's undertaking. In brief, it is the point of undecidability between the empirical and the transcendental, between receptivity and spontaneity and between objective and subjective. Now, in my own undertaking, and under the condition of the postulate of materialism, the word 'object' also designates a point of conjunction or reversibility between the ontological (belonging to a multiple) and the logical (transcendental indexing), between the invariance of the multiple and the variation of its worldly exposition. What's more, in both cases this reversibility—or this contact between two modes of the existence of the 'there is'—takes place under the aegis of the One. What is undoubtedly Kant's most important statement in the 'Transcendental Analytic', the one which he goes so far as to call 'the supreme principle of all synthetic judgments', is the following:

Every object stands under the necessary conditions of synthetic unity of the manifold of intuition in a possible experience.

But my own postulate of materialism also indicates that every object, when it comes to the possibility of its appearance in a world, is subject to the synthetic condition of a reality of atoms. Of course, we part ways on the word 'experience'. But it is nonetheless important to understand that by 'possible experience' Kant designates the general correlate of objectivity, relating it to a synthesis—to a function of the One, as I would put it in my own vocabulary—which precedes any actual intuition:

Without that original reference of these concepts to possible experience wherein all objects of cognition occur, their reference to any object whatsoever would be quite incomprehensible.

In brief, the empirico-transcendental undecidability of the notion of object is expressed here by its division into 'object in general', which is really the pure form of the object, and the 'any object whatsoever' [*object quelconque*] which is really given—as phenomenon—in an intuition. This is why Kant asks 'whether a priori concepts do not also serve as antecedent conditions under which alone anything can be, if not intuited, yet thought as object in general'. My goal too is not that of making visible what is known in a world, but that of thinking appearing or the worldliness of any world whatsoever—whence the affinity with the Kantian idea of possible experience. We could say that possible experience, the place of the thinking of an object 'in general', is the same thing as the possible world, the place in which atomic unity is what makes the object in general legible.

The rapprochement is even more significant if we refer to the first edition of the *Critique of Pure Reason*. In that edition, the onto-logical ambivalence of the object takes the particularly striking form of the opposition between a transcendental object and an empirical object. Kant begins by reiterating that it is 'only when we have thus produced synthetic unity in the manifold of intuition that we are in a position to say that we know the object', which indeed corresponds to the synthetic value that we accord to the transcendental functor. But, having announced that now 'we are in a position to determine more adequately our concept of an object in general', Kant—in a passage that is as famous as it is obscure—opposes the formally indistinct character of the 'non-empirical' object = X to the determination of the intuited object:

> The pure concept of this transcendental object, which in reality throughout all our knowledge is always one and the same, is what can alone confer upon all our empirical concepts in general relation to an object, that is, objective reality. This concept cannot contain any determinate intuition, and therefore refers only to that unity which must be met with in any manifold of knowledge which stands in relation to an object.

It is very striking to see that the necessity of the transcendental object, as the logical condition of empirical objects, is nothing other than the pure capacity for unity (it 'refers only to that unity'). Similarly, in my own trajectory, the thinking of the object 'in general', as the transcendental indexing of a multiple-being, designates the local consistency of appearing, in its possible connection with the pure multiple. In both cases, we are dealing with what Kant calls—precisely with respect to the 'object in general'—'a simple logical form without content', and which I designate as the point in which the reciprocity between appearing and logic shows itself.

This gives us the following correlations:

KANT	BADIOU
Possible experience	Possible world
Unity of self-consciousness	Structural unity of the transcendental of a world
Transcendental object = X	General (or logical) form of the objectivity of appearing
Synthetic unity	Postulate of the real one (of atoms)
Empirical object	Unity of appearing in an actual world

Starting from this table, we can construct a definition of the object common to Kant and me: the object is what is counted as one in appearing. In this regard, it is equivocally distributed between the transcendental (the logical form of its consistency) and 'reality'—this reality being for Kant the empirical (phenomenality as received in intuition) and for me multiple-being (the in-itself received in thought). This is because the test of the One in appearing is also the test of what *one* being-there is. This means that what is counted as one must stem both from being and from the structures of the transcendental as forms of the 'there'. Or again, in Kant's vocabulary, that receptivity and spontaneity intersect in the object; or in mine that the ontological and the logical do so.

Since the analogy concerns the point of undecidability between the transcendental and its other (the empirical for Kant, being-qua-being for me), it should be no surprise that it can extend to notions that pertain to either of the two domains. This is the case for the notions of degree of appearing, existence and lastly thought (which is here distinguished from cognition [*connaissance*]).

1. Transcendental degree

I have argued that the very essence of the transcendental of a world lies in setting the degree or intensity of the differences (or identities) of what comes to appear in that world. Let us accept for a moment that we can read the Kantian term 'intuition' as designating not a 'subjective' faculty but the space of appearing as such, or that by which the appearing of being is appearing. This gives us a very precise correspondence between the theme of a transcendental degree and what Kant calls the 'axioms of intuition' and the 'anticipations of perception'. The principle of the axioms of intuition is the following:

All intuitions are extensive magnitudes.

And that of the anticipations of perception is:

In all phenomena, the real—which is an object of sensation—has intensive magnitude, that is, a degree.

In fact my conception fuses together, in the guise of a general algebra of order, 'extensive magnitude' and 'intensive magnitude'. The resources of modern algebra and topology—obviously unknown to Kant—justify enveloping the two notions in the single one of 'transcendental degree', provided we accord it, aside from the general form of order, the minimum, the conjunction and the envelope. It remains that Kant saw perfectly well that it is of the essence of the phenomenon to be given as nuance or variation. Were the object itself to be conceived outside of this possible variation (what I call the transcendental indexing of a pure multiple) it would for Kant be withdrawn from every unity in appearing and given over to an elementary chaos. This is because the consciousness of the synthetic unity of homogeneous diversity within intuition in general—to the extent that it first makes possible the representation of an object—is the concept of a magnitude (a quantum). Likewise, Kant saw that appearing—though he regrettably indexes it to sensation—is nonetheless assigned to an intensive correlation, which places it between a minimal and a positive evaluation:

> Every sensation, however, is capable of diminution, so that it can decrease and gradually vanish. There is therefore a continuity of many possible intermediate sensations, the difference between any two of which is always smaller than the difference between the given sensation and zero or complete negation. [. . .]
>
> A magnitude which is apprehended only as unity, and in which multiplicity can be represented only through approximation to negation = 0, I entitle an intensive magnitude. Every reality in the phenomenon has therefore intensive magnitude or degree.

These lines clearly indicate that for Kant the concept of the object is subordinated to grasping the transcendental as governing ordered variations. Moreover, that is why he calls the pure understanding—which recapitulates transcendental operations in terms of subjective capacity— the faculty of rules, just as for me the transcendental is the formal regulation of identities, on the basis of a certain number of operations such as conjunction or the envelope.

But we cannot say that Kant proposes a truly innovative conception of the degree, whether intensive or extensive. Despite the reluctance of commentators to underscore this point, in the elaboration of his concepts Kant betrays a patent insufficiency when it comes to the mastery of the mathematics of his time, both in terms of usage and of pure and simple acquaintance. In particular, his conception of the infinite and consequently of quantitative evaluations is outmoded. In this regard, he is far inferior not only to Descartes and Leibniz, who are great mathematicians, but to Malebranche or Hegel. The latter knew and discussed in detail, in the *Logic*, the treatises of Lagrange and the conceptions of Euler, while Kant's thought does not venture much farther than the most elementary, or even most approximate, notions of arithmetic, geometry or analysis. In this respect, he resembles Spinoza: very respectful of the mathematical paradigm, but too far from it to be philosophically able to treat contemporary authors. It does not seem that the Kantian transcendental, reliant as it is on the old logic of Aristotle, makes room, in the inner workings of the categorial construction, for novelties as gripping as the recreation of arithmetic by Gauss, the stabilization of analysis by d'Alembert or Euler's multiform inventions—all Kant's contemporaries. In a nutshell, there is a kind of mathematical childishness in Kant, which is probably the other side of his provincial religiosity.

Consider two well-known examples. In the introduction to the *Critique*, the 'demonstration' of the fact that 'mathematical judgments are all synthetic' relies heavily on the remark about $7 + 5 = 12$, to wit that it is undoubtedly a synthetic judgment, since 'the concept of twelve is by no means already thought merely by my thinking of that unification of 7 and 5, and no matter how long I analyze my concept of such a possible sum I will still not find 12 in it'. Following which, Kant makes a rather pitiful use of the intuition of the fingers of the hand to pass from 7 to 12. Much further on, he will also say, speaking of the concept of magnitude, that mathematics 'looks for its consistency and meaning in number, and for the latter in the fingers, the grains of the calculating tablet, or in lines and points placed under the eyes'. This is to imprison the 'intuition' of mathematical structures in a naïve empiricism which it has been their obvious aim, ever since the Greeks, to overturn.

Truth be told, Kant's crucial remark on 'synthesis' in $7 + 5 = 12$ is totally hollow. We certainly don't need to wait for Peano's axiomatization of elementary arithmetic to be persuaded of its vacuity. Almost a century earlier, objecting to some Cartesians who took the judgment 'two plus two makes four' as an example of clear and distinct knowledge through intuition (and hence as synthetic knowledge), Leibniz argued for the purely analytical character of this equality, proposing its demonstration 'through definitions whose possibility is recognized', a demonstration essentially identical to that of modern logicians. What's more, this is not the only 'detail' on which Kant, believing himself to be demolishing the 'dogmatism' of Leibniz's metaphysics, was surpassed by the formal anticipations harboured by that supposed dogmatism.

Let's consider another example. Kant's proposed 'proof' of the principle of the axioms of intuition assumes that an extensive magnitude is one 'in which the representation of the parts makes possible the representation of the whole'. If that were so, whole numbers wouldn't constitute an extensive field at all! For the definition of their totality is very simple (the first limit ordinal), while defining what precisely is a part (any subset whatsoever of whole numbers) and how many are there is a problem that remains undecidable today (theorems of Gödel and Cohen). Descartes, by posing that the idea of the infinite is clearer than that of the finite, Leibniz, by posing the principle of continuity, or Hegel, by posing that the active essence of the finite is the infinite and not the opposite, are all closer to the mathematical real than Kant. It is clear then that when it comes to the problem of defining a magnitude, Kant's conceptual technique remains rather crass. However, if we stick to the question of the transcendental constitution of the object, we can say that the Kantian conception, which makes appearing into the place of variable and rule-governed intensities, is very apt.

2. Existence

I have posed that existence is nothing other than the degree of self-identity of a multiple-being, such as it is established by a transcendental indexing. With regard to the multiple-being as thought in its being, it follows that its existence is contingent, since it depends—as a measurable intensity—on the world where the being, which is said to exist, appears. This contingency of existence is crucial for Kant, because it intervenes as a determination of the transcendental operation itself. This operation is effectively defined as 'the application of the pure concepts of the understanding to possible experience'. In my vocabulary—and obviously with no reference to any 'application'—this can be put as follows: the logical constitution of pure appearing, the indexing of a pure multiple on a worldly transcendental. But, just as with the object, Kant will immediately distinguish within this operation its properly transcendental or a priori facet from its receptive or empirical one.

It (synthesis or the operation) is concerned partly with the mere intuition of an appearance in general, partly with its existence.

Now, the a priori conditions of intuition are purely transcendental, and in this respect they are necessary. I will express myself as follows: the laws of the transcendental (order, minimum, conjunction, envelope) and the axioms of transcendental indexing (symmetry and triangular inequality for the conjunction) are effectively necessary for being to come to be as being-there. The conditions 'for the existence of the objects of a possible empirical intuition' are instead contingent. In conformity with the earlier table outlining conceptual correspondences, I would put this in the following way: the fact that such and such multiple-beings appear in such and such a world is contingent with regard to the transcendental laws of appearing. But the fact that a multiple-being effectively appears in a world depends on its degree of self-identity in that world. Similarly, for Kant, existence is simply the continuity in appearing of what allows itself to be counted as one under the name of 'substance'; this is the entire content of what he calls the first 'analogy of experience', which states:

> In all change of appearances substance is permanent.

That is because this 'permanence' is nothing other than the fact of being there, in the field of experience. As Kant explicitly writes:

> This permanence is, however, simply the mode in which we represent to ourselves the existence of things (in the phenomenon).

We will leave aside the idealist motif of representation and agree with Kant that existence is nothing other than the degree of identity (of permanence) of a being 'in the phenomenon' (according to being-there-in-a-world).

3. Thought

To carry out a transcendental inquiry (that of Plato on the Idea of the other, of Descartes on existence, of Kant on the possibility of synthetic judgment, of Husserl on perception...), it is always necessary to distinguish the element in which the inquiry proceeds from the one which is at stake in the inquiry. Accordingly, at the beginning of the investigation, there is a separation which isolates something like a pure thought, from which one has withdrawn everything which will nonetheless serve as the object of the announced inquiry. Thus Plato must separate himself from Parmenides and identify thought otherwise than through its pure coextension with being. Descartes, through hyperbolic doubt, and Husserl, through the transcendental *épochè*, separate immanent reflection from any positing of the object. Similarly, Kant distinguishes thought (the element in which transcendental philosophy advances) from cognition (which determines particular objects). For my part, I distinguish speculative metaontology from mathematical ontology, and mathematical ontology from the logic of appearing. But, more fundamentally, I also distinguish thought (the subjective figure of truths) from knowledge (the predicative organization of truth-effects). This distinction is constant in the transcendental inquiry I am carrying out here, because it is a question of designating and activating, within disparate knowledges (vulgar phenomenology or taught mathematics), the dimension of thought which authorizes the updating of their formal axiomatic.

We will thus fully concede to Kant, not only the distinction between thought and cognition, but also a kind of antecedence of transcendental thought over the contingent singularity of being-there. There must be concepts a priori 'as conditions under which alone something is not intuited, but thought as an object in general'. There must exist a formal identification of the object, such as it is constituted in its worldly being-there, or such as it appears. And this identification is thought—as Kant remarkably puts it—with respect to transcendental operators as such. In my own terms, it is with respect to transcendental algebra. In Kant's, it is with respect to pure categories:

> Now when this condition (of sensible intuition) has been omitted from the pure category, it can contain nothing but the logical function for bringing the manifold under a concept. By means of this function or form of the concept, thus taken by itself, we cannot in any way know and distinguish what object comes under it, since we have abstracted from the sensible condition through which alone objects can come under it.

However, in the context of its general validity for both Kant and I, the exact usage of the word 'thought' introduces an essential divergence. For Kant, in effect, thinking by pure concepts has no relation whatsoever to a determinate real. Thought is here identical to an (empty) form. Transcendental categories 'are nothing but forms of thought, which contain the merely logical faculty of uniting a priori in one consciousness the manifold given in intuition'. I will concede to Kant that the power of thought of transcendental categories is of a logical nature, because the consistency of appearing is the logic of being qua being-there. But I will absolutely not concede to him that by 'logic' we must only understand the undetermined, or the empty form of the possible. In the first edition, Kant wrote the following, which is a little clearer:

A pure use of the category is indeed possible, that is, without contradiction; but it has no objective validity, since the category is not then being applied to any intuition so as to impart to it the unity of an object. For, the category is a mere function of thought through which no object is given to me and by which I merely think that which may be given in intuition.

The expression 'function of thought' is interesting. Unlike Kant, I argue in effect that such a function is an object for thought, in the sense that it is not through different faculties (for example understanding and sensibility) that we are given functions and the values or arguments of functions, but through the single generic capacity of thought. To say that transcendental operators, taken as such, only relate to the empty form of the object in general, or to the indistinct character of possible objects, is to forget that the determination of the object takes place in thought, by the elucidation of its multiple-being (pure mathematics) as well as by the logic of its being-there (transcendental logic, subsuming formal logic). So that appearing, which is the place of the object, is—for thought—in the same real relation with its transcendental organization as pure being is with its mathematical organization.

Kant is right to note the following:

> [. . .] if I leave aside all intuition, the form of thought still remains, that is the manner of determining an object for the manifold of a possible intuition.

This is what makes the idea of a noumenal (rather than simply phenomenal) being of objects rational in his eyes, albeit in a purely regulative and restrictive sense. That is because the form of thought does not extend beyond the limits of sensibility. What Kant does not see is that thought is nothing other than the capacity synthetically to think the noumenal and the phenomenal; or—and this will be the Hegelian ambition—to determine being as being-there.

Perhaps in the end, beyond even his obscurantist attachment to pious moralism—which supposes the hole of ignorance in the real—Kant is a victim of his unreasoned academic attachment (which is also pre-Leibnizian, or even pre-Cartesian) to the formal logic inherited from Aristotle. The thematic of the 'empty form' presupposes the originary distinction between analytic judgments, which are devoid of content (and are only addressed, if we remain with the scholastic heritage, by logic), and

synthetic judgments (which ultimately call for a transcendental constitution of experience). I have instead shown, in Section 4 of Book II, that
formal (or analytic) logic is a simple derivation of transcendental (or
synthetic) logic. Accordingly, in the creative activity of a thought we
should never distinguish between its form and its content. Kant takes great
pains to avoid what he regards as a chimera: the existence in us of an
'intellectual intuition' which would give us access to the in-itself of objects,
or to their noumenal dimension. But by showing that the intuition of an
object presupposes that one has thought the transcendental concept of an
object 'in general', he skirts the truth, which is to be found precisely in the
overturning of Kant's prudence: the concept of object designates the point
where phenomenon and noumenon are indistinguishable, the point of
reciprocity between the logical and the onto-logical.

Every object is the being-there or the being of a being.

SECTION 3
Atomic Logic

The formal exposition of concepts such as 'function of appearing' (or 'transcendental indexing'), 'phenomenon', 'atom of appearing' and so on, has the virtue of clarifying the coherence of the logical laws of being-there. One has the feeling of advancing in accordance with a line of reasoning which imposes pertinent materialist restrictions (like the one which decrees that every atom is real) on a general logic (that of the relation between multiplicities and a transcendental order). Then one 'reascends' from appearing to being by studying how the atomic composition of an object affects the multiple-being that underlies this object. This approach culminates in the demonstration that, under certain conditions, every (real, ontological) part of a multiple A possesses a unique envelope. This means, contrary to Kant's conclusions, that appearing authorizes real syntheses. The fact that every multiple is required to appear in the singularity of a world does not by any means render a science of being-there impossible.

1. FUNCTION OF APPEARING

Let A be a set (that is a pure multiplicity, a pure form of being as such). We suppose that this multiple A appears in a world **m** whose transcendental is T. We will call 'function of appearing' an indexing of A on the transcendental T thus defined: it is a function $\mathbf{Id}(x, y)$—to be read as 'degree of identity of x and y'—which to every pair $\{x, y\}$ of elements of A makes correspond an element p of T.

We have seen that the intuitive idea is that the measure of the identity between the elements x and y of A, such as they appear in the world $\mathbf{m}$, is set by the element p of the transcendental which is assigned to the pair $\{x, y\}$ by the function $\mathbf{Id}$. The fact that T has an order-structure is what authorizes both this measure of (phenomenal) identity and the comparison between these measures. One can then say that x appears more or less identical, or similar, to y.

For example, if $\mathbf{Id}(x, y) = M$ (as we saw in II.3.10, M is the maximum of T), we will say that x and y are 'as identical as they can be'. From the interior of the world of which T is the transcendental, this means that x and y are absolutely identical. If instead $\mathbf{Id}(x, y) = \mu$ (the minimum), we can say that, relative to T and therefore to the world in which x and y appear, these two elements are absolutely non-identical, or absolutely different. Lastly, if $\mathbf{Id}(x, y) = p$, with p as 'intermediate', that is $\mu < p < M$, we will say that x and y are 'p-identical', or that the measure of their identity is p.

In order for $\mathbf{Id}$ to support the idea of identity in a coherent fashion, we impose two axioms on it, axioms which are very similar to those governing the equivalence-relation. In brief, the degree of identity of x and y is the same as that of y and x (axiom of symmetry) and the conjunction of the degree of identity of x and y with the degree of identity of y and z remains lesser than or equal to the degree of identity of x and z. We are dealing with a kind of transitivity: if x is identical to y in the measure p, and y is identical to z in the measure q, x is at least as identical to z as that which indicates the degree that 'conjoins' p and q, namely $p \cap q$. The formula also bears an affinity, despite some inversions, with the triangular inequality characteristic of metric spaces: the sum of the two sides of a triangle is greater than the third side.

The formal notation is as follows:

$$\text{Ax. } \mathbf{Id}.1\text{: } \mathbf{Id}(x, y) = \mathbf{Id}(y, x)$$

$$\text{Ax. } \mathbf{Id}.2\text{: } \mathbf{Id}(x, y) \cap \mathbf{Id}(y, z) \leq \mathbf{Id}(x, z)$$

Note that we are leaving out reflexivity, which is nevertheless the first axiom of the equivalence-relation. This is because we do not want a rigid concept of identity. Though the latter may fit the determination of multiple-being as such, it does not suit its appearance or its localization, which demands the availability of degrees of identity and difference.

The axiom of rigid (or reflexive) identity would be written as follows: $\mathbf{Id}(x, x) = M$. It would indicate that it is in an absolute sense (according to the maximum of T) than an element x is identical to itself. This is certainly true if one wishes to speak of the identity 'in itself' of the pure multiple x. But we are concerned with the appearing of x in the world **m**, and therefore with the degree according to which the element x appears in this situation. We will measure this degree of appearance of x in **m** by the value in the transcendental of the function **Id**(x, x). That will then lead us to the concept of existence.

2. THE PHENOMENON

Given a fixed element of A, let's say $a \in A$, *we call 'phenomenon of a relative to A' (in the world* **m** *in question) the set of values of the function of appearing* **Id**(a, x) *for all the x's which co-appear with a in the set A.* In other words, for $x_1 \in A$, $x_2 \in A$, ..., $x_a \in A$, ..., we have the transcendental values of the identity of a to $x_1, x_2, \ldots, x_a, \ldots$, defined by **Id**$(a, x_1)$, **Id**$(a, x_2)$, ..., **Id**$(a, x_a)$, ... The set formed by 'a' and all the transcendental degrees constitutes the phenomenon of 'a' (relative to A). We will write this as follows:

$$\Phi(a/A) = \{a, [\textbf{Id}(a, x_1), \textbf{Id}(a, x_2), \ldots, \textbf{Id}(a, x_a), \ldots]/x_a \in A\}$$

It is important to note that we are not directly considering the presentation of a in the world, but rather that of a in a multiple A presented in the world. This is what is implied in the whole conceptual discussion around the examination of the identity, for example, of a young anarchist in the group of anarchists, under their black flag, and this same examination in terms of his phenomenal belonging to the world 'demonstration at Place de la République'. As we saw, what interests us is the phenomenon of this young anarchist to the extent that he differentiates himself from those who co-appear with him under the same black flag. Since at first he only appears as a 'young anarchist', his true phenomenal identity is what distinguishes him from the other anarchists. We will thus posit that the identity-referent is A (the set of anarchists), and that the phenomenon of the singular young anarchist, say a, is the sum of its degrees of identity to the other elements of A, that is to the other anarchists.

Of course, we may consider ampler or more restricted sets. But the formal precaution always tells us to inscribe appearance in a world under the sign of a referential multiple, guaranteed to be an element (in the ontological sense) of the world in question. The referent A is at bottom nothing but a guarantee of being-in-the-world for the appearing of its elements. That is why we introduced a formal definition of the phenomenon which passes through the referent $A \in$ **m**.

Note that the phenomenon of a is in the end the couple formed by a itself, on the one hand, and a set of transcendental degrees, on the other. That's what makes phenomenon into a ontologico-transcendental notion, since a 'itself' is none other than a in the sense of multiple-being (a as element of A), while a collection of transcendental degrees obviously depends on the transcendental T, that is on the world in question and on that which organizes the logic of appearing within it.

3. EXISTENCE

We will call *degree of existence of x* in the set A, and thus in the world **m**, the value taken by the function $\mathbf{Id}(x, x)$ in the transcendental of this world. Accordingly, for a given multiple, existence is the degree according to which it is identical to itself *to the extent that it appears in the world*. We insisted in the conceptual exposition on the fact that existence is relative to a world and that its concept is that of a measure, or a degree.

Let us now sum up the conceptual parameters.

The intuitive idea is that a multiple-being x has more phenomenal existence in the world, the more it vigorously affirms its identity within it. Hence the reflexive relation of the function of appearing, that is $\mathbf{Id}(x, x)$, provides a good evaluation of a being's power of appearance. Therefore, if $\mathbf{Id}(x, x) = M$ (the maximum), we will hold that x exists absolutely (relative to A, and thus to **m** and the transcendental T). While if, for every A (which belongs to the world), $\mathbf{Id}(x, x) = \mu$ (the minimum), we can say that x does not exist at all (in this world) or that x inexists for **m**. To express this interpretation symbolically, we will write $\mathbf{E}x$ instead of $\mathbf{Id}(x, x)$ and we will read this expression as 'existence of x', nevertheless keeping in mind the two things:

–$\mathbf{E}x$ is not at all an absolute term, because it depends not only on the transcendental T, but on the function of appearing that indexes on the transcendental the multiple A of which x is an element.

–$\mathbf{E}x$ is a transcendental degree, and therefore an element of T.

An immediate property of the function of appearing is the following: the degree of identity between two elements x and y is lesser than or equal to the degree of existence of x and the degree of existence of y. One cannot be 'more identical' to another than one is to oneself. In other words, the force of a relation cannot trump the degree of existence of the related terms. We will call this property P.1. We have justified it at the conceptual level but we can deduce it here as a theorem of existence. In fact, it is an immediate consequence of the axioms of the function of appearing. All we require is a brief elementary calculus, which illustrates to perfection the usage of these axioms:

Demonstration of P.1:

$\mathbf{Id}(x, y) \cap \mathbf{Id}(y, x) \leq \mathbf{Id}(x, x)$	axiom $\mathbf{Id}.2$
$\mathbf{Id}(y, x) = \mathbf{Id}(x, y)$	axiom $\mathbf{Id}.1$
$\mathbf{Id}(x, y) \cap \mathbf{Id}(x, y) \leq \mathbf{E}x$	consequence and def. of $\mathbf{E}x$
$\mathbf{Id}(x, y) \leq \mathbf{E}x$	$p \cap p = p$

For the same reasons, $\mathbf{Id}\ (x, y) \leq \mathbf{E}y$. It follows that:

$$\mathbf{Id}(x, y) \leq \mathbf{E}x \cap \mathbf{E}y \qquad \text{def. of } \cap$$

An important consequence of this theorem of existence is that if an element x inexists in a world $\mathbf{m}$, say if $\mathbf{E}x = \mu$ (from the point of view of appearing x is absolutely non-identical to itself), then the identity of x to any apparent of the same world, let's say y, can similarly only be nil. That is because $\mathbf{Id}(x, y) \leq \mathbf{E}x$ in this case becomes $\mathbf{Id}(x, y) = \mu$. This means that what inexists in a world is not identical in it to anything (or rather, it does not let any identity to another appear).

4. PHENOMENAL COMPONENT AND ATOM OF APPEARING

Take a set A which appears in a world $\mathbf{m}$ whose transcendental is T. A 'phenomenal component' of A is a function that associates a transcendental degree p to every element x of A. In other words if π is the function in question of A to T, we get, for every x of A, a degree p such that $\pi(x) = p$.

The underlying intuitive idea is that $\pi(x) = p$ measures the degree according to which the element x belongs to the component of A whose characteristic operator is π. For example, if for a given $x \in A$ we have $\pi(x) = M$ (the maximum), we can say that x belongs 'absolutely' to the component constructed by the function π. If $\pi(x) = \mu$ (the minimum), we will say that x does belong to the component in the least. If $\pi(x) = p$, we will say that x p-belongs to it: it is in this phenomenal component of a 'in the measure p'. We have offered some significant examples of these differences of belonging to a component, with regard to the set 'group of anarchos' in the world 'demonstration', or 'columns of the temple' in the world 'painting by Hubert Robert'.

We will now define some minimal components for a set A which supports a phenomenon. In the order of appearing, such a component is the point of the One below which no appearance is possible any longer.

We call atomic object-component, or simply 'atom', an object-component which, intuitively, has at most one element in the following sense: if there is an element of A about which it can be said that it belongs absolutely to the component, there is only one. This means that every other element that belongs to the component absolutely is identical, within appearing, to the first (the function of appearing has the maximum value M when it evaluates the identity of the two elements in question).

Take for instance, two entirely generic individual anarchists, or two columns of the temple in the foreground: they validate an atomic component given by functions of the type 'being an anarchist truly typical of the set of anarchists' or 'being a clearly delineated temple column, more orange than blue'. It is not that, in ontological terms, there is only a single multiple that can validate these features (or that gives to the function the value M). Rather, it is that, from the standpoint of appearing in the world in question, if there are several multiples that do this (two columns, a hundred anarchists), they are phenomenally identical. We are indeed dealing with an atom of appearing.

The whole point is to correctly code the function that identifies the component, so as to prescribe the atomic simplicity of its composition. From now on we will write $a(x)$ every function which identifies a component, since we are principally concerned with atomic components.

First of all, to allow the function $a(x)$ to coherently support the general idea of a phenomenal component, or of a sub-phenomenon of the phenomenon of A, we impose the following axiom on it:

$$\text{Ax. } a.1: a(x) \cap \mathbf{Id}(x, y) \leq a(y)$$

This axiom indicates that the degree of belonging of y to any object-component, whether atomic or otherwise, cannot be lesser than its degree of identity to x combined with its degree of belonging to the component of this x. In other words, if x belongs 'strongly' to the component identified by the function $a(x)$, and if y is 'very identical' to x, y must itself belong very strongly to this component.

Let's take some significant particular cases. If x belongs absolutely to the phenomenal component, this means that $a(x) = M$. Let's suppose that the degree of identity $\mathbf{Id}(x, y)$ of y to x is measured by p. The axiom $a.1$ then tells us that $M \cap p \leq a(y)$. Since $M \cap p = p$, this means that $p \leq a(y)$. We can indeed verify that the degree of belonging of y to the component, a degree measured by $a(y)$, must in every case be at least equal to its identity to x, measured by p.

Let us now suppose that y does not at all belong to the component identified by the function a – as is the case with the carrier of the red flag with its hammer and sickle vis-à-vis the component 'hardcore anarchists' of the group of anarchists in the demonstration-world. We then have $a(y) = \mu$. The axiom dictates that, whatever x may be, we have $a(x) \cap \mathbf{Id}(x, y) = \mu$. If in particular x belongs absolutely to the component of hardcore anarchists, that is if we have $a(x) = M$, it necessarily follows that $\mathbf{Id}(x, y) = \mu$, since $M \cap \mu = \mu$. This means that the identity in the appearing of the demonstration-world between a hardcore anarchist, on one hand, and a carrier of a hammer and sickle flag, on the other, is nil, whatever their ontological similarities may otherwise be, or even their pure and simple identity in the appearing of another world (a world for instance in which 'being young' would instantly ground a powerful identity in appearing, say the world suggested by an old persons' home).

The first axiom in fact holds for every phenomenal component. The second identifies the atomic components:

$$\text{Ax. } a.2\text{: } a(x) \cap a(y) \leq \mathbf{Id}(x, y)$$

This axiom clearly indicates that the 'conjoined' degree of belonging of x and y to the component identified by the function a depends on the degree of identity of x and y. That is what will 'atomize' every component which obeys the axiom. The aim is to make it impossible for two different elements to both belong 'absolutely' to an atomic component. Suppose that x and y are absolutely distinct. Their degree of identity in the world is nil, which we here write as $\mathbf{Id}(x, y) = \mu$. It follows that, if x belongs absolutely to the component—in other words if $a(x) = M$—then y does not belong to it at all, that is $a(y) = \mu$. The axiom effectively dictates that $a(x) \cap a(y) \leq \mu$. Which, if $a(x) = M$, means that $a(y) = \mu$. The axiom prescribes that two absolutely distinct elements cannot both belong 'absolutely' to the same atomic component. In this sense, an atom is indeed a simple component (or marked by the One).

5. REAL ATOM AND POSTULATE OF MATERIALISM

A fundamental remark is now called for. For $a \in A$, or for a being-component of A (an element of the multiple A in the ontological sense), we can define a function $a(x)$ which is an atom. It suffices to posit that this functions associates to every $x \in A$, the transcendental measure of the identity of x and a. That is, $a(x) = \mathbf{Id}\,(a, x)$. Hence, to associate to every column of the round temple its degree of identity to a fixed column, say c, is an atomic function, say $c(x)$, of the set 'temple' to the transcendental of the painting by Hubert Robert.

To establish that every function $a(x)$ thus defined on the basis of a real element a of the referent-set A determines an atom of appearing, it suffices to verify the two aforementioned axioms of atoms.

1. $a(x)$ verifies axiom $\alpha.1$:

$a(x) \cap \mathbf{Id}(x, y) = \mathbf{Id}(a, x) \cap \mathbf{Id}\,(x, y)$	def. of $a(x)$
$\mathbf{Id}(a, x) \cap \mathbf{Id}\,(x, y) \leq \mathbf{Id}\,(a, y)$	axiom $\mathbf{Id}.2$
$a(x) \cap \mathbf{Id}\,(x, y) \leq \mathbf{Id}\,(a, y)$	consequence
$a(x) \cap \mathbf{Id}\,(x, y) \leq a(y)$	def. of $a(y)$

2. $a(x)$ verifies axiom $\alpha.2$:

$a(x) \cap a(y) = \mathbf{Id}(a, x) \cap \mathbf{Id}\,(a, y)$	def. of $a(x)$ and $a(y)$
$\mathbf{Id}(a, x) \cap \mathbf{Id}\,(a, y) = \mathbf{Id}(x, a) \cap \mathbf{Id}(a, y)$	axiom $\mathbf{Id}.1$
$\mathbf{Id}(x, a) \cap \mathbf{Id}(a, y) \leq \mathbf{Id}(x, y)$	axiom $\mathbf{Id}.2$
$a(x) \cap a(y) \leq \mathbf{Id}\,(x, y)$	def. of $a(x)$ and $a(y)$

In such a case, the atomic phenomenal component $a(x)$ is entirely determined in appearing—on the basis of the function of appearing $\mathbf{Id}$—by a being-component, the element $a \in A$. The elementary real (in the ontological sense) prescribes atomicity in appearing (in the sense of the logic of the world).

If a given atom, defined by the function $a(x)$, is identical to a single atom of the type $a(x)$—in other words, if there exists a single $a \in A$ such that for every $x \in A$ we have $\alpha(x) = a(x) = \mathbf{Id}(a, x)$—we will say that the atom $\alpha(x)$ is real.

A real atom is a phenomenal component, that is a kind of sub-apparent of the referential apparent which, on one hand, is an atomic component (it is simple, or non-decomposable), and on the other, is strictly determined by an underlying element $a \in A$, which is its ontological substructure. At the point of a real atom, being and appearing conjoin under the sign of the One.

It only remains to formulate our 'postulate of materialism', which authorizes a definition of the object. As we know, this postulate says: every atom is real. It is directly opposed to the Bergsonist or Deleuzean presupposition of the primacy of the virtual. In effect, it stipulates that the virtuality of an apparent's appearing in such and such a world is always rooted in its *actual* ontological composition.

6. DEFINITION OF THE OBJECT

Under the condition of the postulate of materialism, we are now able to provide a precise technical definition of what an object in a world is.

*By 'object' we understand the couple formed by a multiple A and a transcendental indexing **Id**, a couple which is written (A, **Id**), under the condition that that every atom of which A is the support be real; in other words, that every atomic component of the appearing of A be equivalent to a real atom **Id**(a, x) prescribed by an element a of A.*

We must make sure that the ontological connection does not elide the difference between the two registers. That every atom of appearing is real clearly means that it is prescribed by an element a of A, and therefore by the ontological composition of A. It does not follow from this that two ontologically different elements a and b prescribe different atoms. 'Atom' is a concept of objectivity, hence of appearing, and its laws of difference are not the same as those of ontological difference. For example, we said that the atomic component 'having all the features of a typical anarchist' was prescribed, in the demonstration-world, by an individual of the group of anarchists. But two individuals of this group can perfectly well prescribe the same atom, provided that both are typical or generic anarchists, and are thus, in what concerns the political appearing of the groups in the demonstration, perfectly identical.

The formalism allows us to establish in which cases two different elements prescribe the same atom. At bottom, the atomic partitive functions $a(x)$ and $b(x)$ (meaning **Id**(a, x) and **Id**(b, x)) are the same if the elements a and b have the same degree of existence and if the degree of their identity is precisely the degree of their existence. This result is profoundly significant. It indicates that our two anarchists are both typical if their intensity of existence is the same (if one of the two were effectively less present in the world, he would embody to a lesser degree the attributes of the exemplary anarchist) and if this intensity of existence regulates their identity (they are exactly as identical as they exist, or being typical, they are as identical to themselves in this typicality as they are identical to every equally typical individual).

What follows is the demonstration of this point, which sums up certain properties of transcendental indexing. We call this proposition P.2.

– Direct proposition (we suppose that the atoms are identical and show that they possess the property of equality between their existence and their degree of identity):

$\mathbf{Id}(a, x) = \mathbf{Id}(b, x)$	real atoms are equal
$\mathbf{Id}(a, a) = \mathbf{Id}(b, a)$	consequence (if $x = a$)
$\mathbf{Id}(a, b) = \mathbf{Id}(b, b)$	consequence (if $x = b$)
$\mathbf{Id}(a, b) = \mathbf{Id}(b, a)$	axiom $\mathbf{Id}.1$
$\mathbf{Id}(a, a) = \mathbf{Id}(b, b) = \mathbf{Id}(a, b)$	consequence
$\mathbf{E}a = \mathbf{E}b = \mathbf{Id}(a, b)$	def. of $\mathbf{E}$

– Reciprocal proposition (we suppose that $\mathbf{E}a = \mathbf{E}b = \mathbf{Id}(a, b)$ and show that the atoms are equal):

$\mathbf{Id}(a, x) \cap \mathbf{Id}(a, b) \leq \mathbf{Id}(b, x)$	axiom $\mathbf{Id}.2$
$\mathbf{Id}(a, x) \cap \mathbf{E}a \leq \mathbf{Id}(b, x)$	hypothesis ($\mathbf{Id}(a, b) = \mathbf{E}a$)
$\mathbf{Id}(a, x) \leq \mathbf{E}a$	by P.1
$\mathbf{Id}(a, x) \cap \mathbf{E}a = \mathbf{Id}(a, x)$	by P.0
$\mathbf{Id}(a, x) \leq \mathbf{Id}(b, x)$ (I)	consequence

The same exact calculus can be made by permuting a and b (starting this time with $\mathbf{Id}(b, x) \cap \mathbf{Id}(b\,a) \leq \mathbf{Id}(a, x)$). The result of this permutation is

$\mathbf{Id}(b, x) \leq \mathbf{Id}(a, x)$ (II)

Through anti-symmetry, the contrast between (I) and (II) gives us the following: $\mathbf{Id}(a, x) = \mathbf{Id}(b, x)$, that is by the definition of real atoms, $a(x) = b(x)$, or $a = b$.

7. ATOMIC LOGIC, 1: LOCALIZATIONS

Up until now we have made use, above all, of qualitative metaphors: a transcendental degree measures the intensity according to which a given being appears in a world. Little by little, we will explore a more fundamental determination, the one contained in the expression 'being-there', whose character is topological. Since a world is essentially the place of appearing, a transcendental degree is the index of a localization in the place, of a singular 'there' prescribed by the general logic of the place.

Letting ourselves be guided by this localizing comprehension of transcendental degrees, we can return to the definition of atoms, and finally of objects.

Take a phenomenal component $\pi(x)$. We have seen that, in global terms, it is a function of a multiple A on the transcendental of the world. How do we move from the global to the local? We can try to localize this component or object-part in the transcendental by considering $\pi(x) \cap p$, that is 'what $\pi(x)$ is worth in p' or 'what $\pi(x)$ and the point p have in common'. This can also be interpreted in the following terms: what appears in common between the degree according to which x belongs to the component in question and the degree p? An intensity of appearance in an objective region of the world is thereby localized on p. This allows us in some sense to analyze the object-components in terms of a local decomposition of the spectrum of intensities. We will also be confronted with the inverse problem (a problem of 'stitching'): given a local analysis of the components of an object, can we reconstitute the object as a whole?

Since the most fundamental components of an object are the atoms of appearing, what matters to us is of course the local analysis of atoms. And since, by virtue of the postulate of materialism, every atom of an object is real, we must investigate the localization of a real atom.

The basic definition for this analytic-synthetic argument is the following: *We call 'localization of a (real) atom on p', and write as $a \upharpoonright p$, the function of A (to which a belongs) to the transcendental T which is defined, for every x of A, by $a(x) \cap p$.* Let us again recall in passing that $a(x)$ is nothing other than $\mathbf{Id}(a, x)$, and that with increasing frequency we will end up, once every ambiguity has been put aside, simply writing it as a.

The fundamental remark for the conduct of this entire argument is therefore provided by the very simple proposition which establishes that every localization of an atom is an atom.

We must therefore demonstrate that if $a(x)$ is an atom of A, and if we write the function $a(x) \cap p$ as $(a \upharpoonright p)(x)$, then this function is an atom. Following our notational conventions we can write that $a \upharpoonright p$ is an atom.

We simply need to verify that the function $(a \upharpoonright p)(x)$ corroborates the two axioms of the atomic components, which were established in Subsection 4 above.

–Axiom α.1. We must show that:

$$(a \restriction p)(x) \cap \mathbf{Id}(x, y) \le (a \restriction p)(y)$$

$a(x) \cap \mathbf{Id}(x, y) \le a(y)$	ax. α.1: a is an atom
$a(x) \cap p \cap \mathbf{Id}(x, y) \le a(y) \cap p$	consequence
$(a \restriction p)(x) \cap \mathbf{Id}(x, y) \le (a \restriction p)(y)$	def. of $a \restriction p$

–Axiom α.2. We must show that:

$$(a \restriction p)(x) \cap (a \restriction p)(y) \le \mathbf{Id}(x, y)$$

$a(x) \cap a(y) \le \mathbf{Id}(x, y)$	ax. α.2: a is an atom
$[a(x) \cap p] \cap [a(y) \cap p] \le \mathbf{Id}(x, y)$	$q \cap p \le q$
$(a \restriction p)(x) \cap (a \restriction p)(y) \le \mathbf{Id}(x, y)$	def. of $a \restriction p$

We can therefore see that the global analysis of objects—of which real atoms are the foundation, at the same time that they guarantee the connection between the logic of appearing and the mathematics of being—can issue into a local analysis without losing its guiding thread. Localized by an element of the transcendental, an atom remains an atom.

If $a(x)$ is a (real) atom, there always exists an $a \in A$ such that $\mathbf{Id}(a, x) = a(x)$. That is indeed why we grant ourselves the right to designate every atom of the object $(A, \mathbf{Id})$ with the name—say a—of the element of A which identifies it. We have just seen that, since a is in this sense an atom, $a \restriction p$ is also an atom. The postulate of materialism demands then that there exists $b \in A$ such that $(a \restriction p)(x) = \mathbf{Id}(b, x)$. Bestowing being on what before was only an operation, we will call b *the localization of a on p*, and write $b = a \restriction p$. This notation is onto-topological: it 'topologizes' the multiple a on the basis of transcendental localizations. We should not lose sight of the fact that, in technical terms, this notation actually means: $\mathbf{Id}(b, x) = \mathbf{Id}(a, x) \cap p$.

Thus, $b = a \restriction p$ is a relation between elements of A, which can be read as 'the element b is the transcendental localization of the element a, relative to the degree p'. We are thus very much on the path which consists in retrogressing from the transcendental constitution of appearing towards the ontological constitution of what appears. Or, to put it otherwise, we move from the object—the mode of appearing of a multiple-being in a world—to something like a structuration of the multiple as such.

The subsequent sections systematically explore this path, by defining a general form of the relation 'of proximity' between elements of an object, and then an order-relation between these elements.

8. ATOMIC LOGIC, 2: COMPATIBILITY

Let us define the so-called relation of compatibility between elements of an object $(A, \mathbf{Id})$. *We will say that two elements of A, say a and b, are 'compatible' (relative to a world* $\mathbf{m}$*, to the transcendental T of this world, and to the transcendental indexing* $\mathbf{Id}$ *of A on T), if the localization of a on the degree of existence of b is equal to the localization of b on the degree of existence of a.* In formal terms, designating the relation of compatibility with ‡, we have the following:

$$a \ddagger b \leftrightarrow [a \restriction \mathbf{E}b = b \restriction \mathbf{E}a]$$

This relation expresses an existential kinship in appearing between the elements, a and b, grasped in the atomic dimension which they prescribe. It is as 'names of atoms' that a and b are mentioned here. We should always be able to recall that a, for example, is identified with the atomic component $\mathbf{Id}(a, x)$, and that a notation such as $a \restriction \mathbf{E}b$ actually designates the (atomic) object-component which is the function $a(x) \cap \mathbf{E}b$, in which $\mathbf{E}b$ is a transcendental degree, the one that measures the intensity of existence of b. Lastly, compatibility expresses the fact that a and b are transcendentally 'of the same kind', to the extent that each is localized on the existence of the other. Accordingly, in the demonstration-world, the group of anarchists, localized on the degree of existence of the group of Kurds, is equal to the group of Kurds localized on the degree of existence of the anarchists. In effect, that which appears of the common part of existence of the two groups, or the coexistence of the two groups, is more or less identical to their degree of identity. In more empirical terms, we can say that their coexistence in the demonstration is made manifest by the strong formal identity of their presentation (the desire to appear menacing, their superficial machismo, etc.). Thus, when we express the difference between a given element of the demonstration and the group of anarchists, on the one hand, and the difference between the same element and the group of Kurds, on the other, we obtain equality by reciprocally localizing these differences on the existence of the other group. That is why we will say that the two groups—or rather the generic atomic components of these two groups (the typical anarchist and Kurd)—are compatible within appearing.

We will now treat this remark with due rigour by showing that it follows from the definition of compatibility that what is 'common' to the existence of a and the existence of b (namely the conjunction of their existential degrees) is in fact equal to their degree of identity. This will be expressed as follows: the atoms a and b are compatible if they coexist in the exact measure that they are identical. This is Proposition P.3.

Let us note first of all that Proposition P.1 tells us that:

$$\mathbf{Id}\ (a,\ b) \leq \mathbf{E}a \cap \mathbf{E}b$$

(this is the proposition 'one cannot be more identical to another than one is to oneself'). We will show that if a is compatible with b, then $\mathbf{E}a \cap \mathbf{E}b \leq \mathbf{Id}$ $(a,\ b)$ (this means 'two compatible elements cannot be more identical to themselves than they are to one another'). Consequently, in accordance with anti-symmetry, $\mathbf{E}a \cap \mathbf{E}b = \mathbf{Id}(a,\ b)$.

We return at the beginning to the functional notation of atoms (that is $a(x)$ rather than a), in order to make the demonstration clearer.

$a(x)\ \lceil\ \mathbf{E}b = b(x)\ \lceil\ \mathbf{E}a$	hypothesis: $a \ddagger b$
$\mathbf{Id}(a,\ x)\ \lceil\ \mathbf{E}b = \mathbf{Id}(b,\ x)\ \lceil\ \mathbf{E}a$	def. of $a(x)$ and $b(x)$
$\mathbf{Id}(a,\ b)\ \lceil\ \mathbf{E}b = \mathbf{Id}(b,\ b)\ \lceil\ \mathbf{E}a$	case $x = b$
$\mathbf{Id}(a,\ b) \cap \mathbf{E}b = \mathbf{E}b \cap \mathbf{E}a$	def. of $\lceil$ and $\mathbf{E}$
$\mathbf{Id}(a,\ b) \cap \mathbf{E}a \cap \mathbf{E}b = \mathbf{E}a \cap \mathbf{E}b$	consequence
$\mathbf{E}a \cap \mathbf{E}b \leq \mathbf{Id}\ (a,\ b)$	by P.0

It is therefore true that compatibility (atomic equality through reciprocal localization on existences) entails that the 'common' of degrees of existence is equal to the degree of identity of the terms in question. But the relation is stronger. We can, in effect, demonstrate the reciprocal: if the common of existences is equal to the degree of identity, if the coexistence of the two terms has the same exact measure as their identity in appearing, then these two terms are compatible (all of this passes through the atoms of appearing prescribed by these two terms, according to the world and the transcendental of reference). Finally—and this is Proposition P.3—the equation $\mathbf{E}a \cap \mathbf{E}b = \mathbf{Id}(a,\ b)$ can serve as a definition for $a \ddagger b$.

The somewhat technical demonstration of this reciprocal is left to the appendix of this chapter for the enthusiasts, who I hope will be numerous, especially since the indispensable calculus will be accompanied by some supplementary phenomenological considerations.

The great interest of all this lies in showing that the compatibility between two elements—which in a multiple is a relation brought about by its appearing in a world—admits of two equivalent definitions. The first, of a topological character, goes through the reciprocal localization of each of the two elements on the degree of existence of the other, and the recognition of the equality of these two localizations. There is an equality in the being-there of the two elements to the extent that each is grasped 'according' to the existence of the other. The second, of an algebraic character, says that the measure of the coexistence of the two elements is strictly equal to their degree of identity. In both cases, compatibility concerns the atoms prescribed by the elements as well as their degrees of existence. We may thus conclude that compatibility is a kind of affinity in appearing, borne by the underlying relations between the atoms' power of the One, on one hand, and the intensity of existence of the real elements that prescribe these atoms in the world in question, on the other.

9. ATOMIC LOGIC, 3: ORDER

In order to expound the properties of order, we will take some distance from the conceptual presentation. We have directly linked order in being-there to compatibility, by defining it as the inequality of degrees of existence between two compatible elements (grasped as atoms). We will see that a very simple formal definition of ontological order is possible, one that no longer directly implies either localization or compatibility, but relates to the fundamental categories of appearing—existence and identity—such that we may speak of a transcendental definition. We will in effect demonstrate that the relation of a to b, which inscribes the fact that the existence of a is equal to its degree of identity to b, is an order-relation. *We will say that $a < b$ if a exists exactly as much as it is identical to b, that is if $\mathbf{E}a = \mathbf{Id}(a, b)$.* The structuration of the multiple here takes place through an immediate retroaction of what legislates over appearing.

The proposition which tells us that the relation in question is indeed an order-relation, and that it is identical to the articulation of compatibility and the inequality of existence, will be referred to as proposition P.4.

Following proposition P.1, we know that a cannot exist less than it is identical to b (we always have $\mathbf{Id}(a, b) \leq \mathbf{E}a$). It suffices then to show that a also cannot exist more than it is identical to b in order to be certain (this is the meaning of anti-symmetry) that the degree of existence of a is equal to its degree of identity to b.

In formal terms, it is thus a question of establishing the following:

1. That the relation $\mathbf{E}a \leq \mathbf{Id}(a, b)$ is equivalent to the one which we proposed in the conceptual exposition, namely the combination of $a \ddagger b$ and $\mathbf{E}a \leq \mathbf{E}b$.

2. That the relation $\mathbf{E}a = \mathbf{Id}(a, b)$ is indeed an order-relation (reflexive, transitive and antisymmetrical) between the elements a and b.

Let's start with the equivalence of the relations.

– *Direct proposition*. We suppose that $\mathbf{E}a \leq \mathbf{Id}(a, b)$ and prove the truth of $a \ddagger b$ and $\mathbf{E}a \leq \mathbf{E}b$.

$\mathbf{Id}(a, b) \leq \mathbf{E}b$	P.1
$\mathbf{E}a \leq \mathbf{Id}(a, b)$	hypothesis
$\mathbf{E}a \leq \mathbf{E}b$ (I)	transitivity of $\leq$
$\mathbf{E}a \cap \mathbf{E}b \leq \mathbf{Id}(a, b)$	$p \cap q \leq p$
$a \ddagger b$ (II)	by P.3

– *Reciprocal proposition*. We suppose that $a \ddagger b$ and $\mathbf{E}a \leq \mathbf{E}b$, and we demonstrate that if this is the case then $\mathbf{E}a \leq \mathbf{Id}(a, b)$.

$\mathbf{E}a \leq \mathbf{E}b$	hypothesis
$\mathbf{E}a \cap \mathbf{E}b = \mathbf{E}a$	by P.0
$\mathbf{E}a \cap \mathbf{E}b \leq \mathbf{Id}(a, b)$	hypothesis $a \ddagger b$
$\mathbf{E}a \leq \mathbf{Id}(a, b)$	consequence

Let us now show that the relation between the object-elements—a and b—in the form $\mathbf{E}a = \mathbf{Id}(a, b)$ is indeed an order-relation, which we will write as $<$ from now on.

– *Reflexivity*. We undoubtedly have $a < a$, since, given the definition of $\mathbf{E}$, $\mathbf{E}a = \mathbf{Id}(a, a)$ is nothing other than $\mathbf{E}a = \mathbf{E}a$.

– *Transitivity*. Let's suppose that we have $a < b$ and $b < c$. We can show that $a < c$ in the following way:

$\mathbf{E}a = \mathbf{Id}(a, b)$ (I)	$a < b$
$\mathbf{E}b = \mathbf{Id}(b, c)$	$b < c$
$\mathbf{E}a \cap \mathbf{E}b = \mathbf{Id}(a, b) \cap \mathbf{Id}(b, c)$	consequence
$\mathbf{Id}(a, b) \cap \mathbf{Id}(b, c) \leq \mathbf{Id}(a, c)$	ax. $\mathbf{Id}$.2
$\mathbf{E}a \cap \mathbf{E}b \leq \mathbf{Id}(a, c)$ (II)	consequence
$\mathbf{Id}(a, b) \leq \mathbf{E}b$	by P.1
$\mathbf{E}a \leq \mathbf{E}b$	consequence by (I)
$\mathbf{E}a \cap \mathbf{E}b = \mathbf{E}a$	by P.0
$\mathbf{E}a \leq \mathbf{Id}(a, c)$	consequence by (II)
$a < c$	def. of $<$

– *Anti-symmetry*. Let's suppose that we have $a < b$ and $b < a$. We need to show that $a = b$. But watch out! We must be on guard here against the ontological amphiboly, the double reference of the letters 'a' and 'b'. The equality $a = b$ that we're dealing with is not the ontological identity of the elements a and b considered in their pure multiple-being. It is the identity in appearing, or the purely logical identity, of the atoms $a(x)$ and $b(x)$ prescribed by the elements a and b.

One of the fundamental conditions which makes it possible for two atoms that are prescribed by two elements, which might turn out to be distinct in their being, nevertheless to be equal in appearing (equal as atomic object-components), is nothing other than Proposition P.2. The atoms $a(x)$ and $b(x)$ are equal—meaning that the functions $\mathbf{Id}(a, x)$ and $\mathbf{Id}(b, x)$ take the same transcendental values for all x's—if and only if $\mathbf{E}a = \mathbf{E}b = \mathbf{Id}(a, b)$. Now, if $a < b$, then by definition $\mathbf{E}a = \mathbf{Id}(a, b)$ and if moreover $b < a$, it follows that $\mathbf{E}b = \mathbf{Id}(b, a)$. Thus the atoms are indeed the same.

This establishes that the relation $\mathbf{E}a = \mathbf{Id}(a, b)$ is an order-relation. This relation retroactively projects the transcendental constitution of a world, which is originally an order, onto the elements of a multiple which appears in this world. For example, in the painting-world of Hubert Robert, one will say that, grasped in its being, the blue dress of the draped woman, thrown against the fountain on the left, is 'inferior in being-there' to the column in front on the right (the one that 'realizes' the atom of median verticality), if it is true that the value of pictorial existence of the blue of the dress is equal to the degree of identity between this coming of the blue into the world and the vertical power of the column. This equality is probable, because though the amplitude of existence of the dress is weak in scope, the same can be said of the degree of identity between the lateral and decorative aspect of this blue patch, on the one hand, and the constructive power of the temple column, on the other. In the appearing that is transcendentally organized by the conscious and unconscious ordering of the painter's gestures, that which supports with its being the coloured value 'bright blue', is of lesser importance than that which imposes the vertical axis and symmetry. That is also why the painting, in its very being, is more architectural than symphonic.

10. ATOMIC LOGIC, 4: THE RELATION BETWEEN RELATIONS

What is the link between the relation of compatibility ($\ddagger$), the order-relation ($<$) and the operation of localization ($\lceil$)? A theory of intra-objective relations must also be capable of being a theory of the relation between relations. This is especially so to the extent that we can consider localization as essentially topological, compatibility (in its second definition, provided by P.3) as essentially algebraic, and the order-relation (as introduced here) as purely transcendental. Whence the fact that the bond between these relations explores and connects different types of thought.

Regarding compatibility, we already know that it subsumes order. In effect, we demonstrated earlier that if $a < b$, then $a \ddagger b$. This subsumption will introduce us to a thoroughly classical relational connection: the similarity between two terms placed in an identical dependence with regard to a third. If in effect two object-elements undergo the same domination, they are related in terms of their being-in-the-world. Thus, in the demonstration-world, a postman on the brink of deserting and an entirely isolated worker from the Renault Flins factory may have very few objective traits in common. But they will share the fact that their weak manifest existence is almost equal to their weak identity to—let's say—the thundering figure at the head of the anarchist procession. Whence, with regard to the atomicity of the predicate 'bellowing somewhat lewd slogans'—an atomicity prescribed in the real by the character in question— an identical subordination of the postman and the worker according to the ontological order. In the logic of appearing, which is here the logic of the demonstration, the beings-there of the postman and the worker are compatible, insofar as their existences are both measurable by their very weak identity to every ostentatious demonstrator.

In formal terms, the common feature elicited by a shared ontological inferiority turns out to be compatibility. It amounts to a harmonious organization of the relations induced in the multiple by its becoming-object.

We will show that if a and b are both dominated by c—in the sense that it is simultaneously true that $a < c$ and $b < c$—then a and b are compatible ($a \ddagger b$). We will call this as Proposition P. 5.

$a < c$ and $b < c$	hypothesis
$\mathbf{E}a \leq \mathbf{Id}(a, c)$ and $\mathbf{E}b \leq \mathbf{Id}(b, c)$	def. of $<$
$\mathbf{E}a \cap \mathbf{E}b \leq \mathbf{Id}(a, c) \cap \mathbf{Id}(c, b)$	consequence and ax. $\mathbf{Id}.1$
$\mathbf{Id}(a, c) \cap \mathbf{Id}(c, b) \leq \mathbf{Id}(a, b)$	ax. $\mathbf{Id}.2$
$\mathbf{E}a \cap \mathbf{E}b \leq \mathbf{Id}(a, b)$	transitivity of $\leq$
$a \ddagger b$	by P.3

Proposition P.5 is extremely important. It effectively shows that if, in a multiple that appears, one of the elements (say, the atom of appearing prescribed by this element) 'dominates' a part, in the sense that it is an upper bound (by <) of all the elements belonging to this part, we can affirm that all these elements are compatible in pairs (by ‡). This indicates the force of, as well as the precondition for, the retroactive synthesis of a multiple-being by the transcendental logic of the world wherein it appears.

Now, what can we say about the link between order and localization? Here too, an equivalence exists between possible definitions. We can in effect posit that a is inferior to b if a (considered as an atom) is equal to the localization of b on the existence of a, that is $a = b \ulcorner \mathbf{E}a$. The fact that this definition is equivalent to the other two we have already encountered—algebraic ($a \ddagger b$ and $\mathbf{E}a \leq \mathbf{E}b$) and transcendental ($\mathbf{E}a = \mathbf{Id}(a, b)$)—is demonstrated in the Appendix to Book III, whose reading I once again recommend. This reading makes it effectively possible to anticipate the final arguments of this section, which contain what we will call the fundamental theorem of appearing. On the background of the intimate identity between being and being-there, this theorem knots together the topological, algebraic and transcendental orientations of thought.

11. ATOMIC LOGIC, 5: REAL SYNTHESIS

We have clearly defined the relational structures (localization, compatibility and order) that affect multiple-beings once these beings are thought in the retroaction of their becoming-object. Our aim is to show that, under certain conditions, certain objects or regions of objectivity can support a real synthesis in the following sense: there exists an envelope of the order-relation <, that is a least upper bound of the objective region considered for this relation. This envelope obviously assigns to the object—conceived here as a collection of atoms and therefore (by virtue of the postulate of materialism) thought in its multiple-being—a unity of a new type. In short, the latter is a retroaction of the logic of appearing on the ontology of the multiple. This unity is really ontological.

The precondition for the existence of ontological synthesis may be directly deduced from Proposition P.5. Let B be a part of an object $(A, \mathbf{Id})$. Let's suppose that B can be unified, and therefore that there is an envelope for the relation <. Let ε be this envelope. Since every envelope is an upper bound, we know that for two elements—say b and b'—of B, we have $b < \varepsilon$

and $b' < \varepsilon$. P.5 then decrees the compatibility between b and b'. In other words, only an object or an objective region whose elements (in the onto-logical sense) are compatible in pairs can have an envelope and thus be the object of a real synthesis in the world.

We will now demonstrate that if an objective region of the world is such that its elements are compatible in pairs, then it allows for a real synthesis. We will thus have entirely resolved the problem of the ontological One. For this demonstration, we require a supplementary property of com-patibility, a property that lets us pass from the relational structure which is immanent to the object to the transcendental determinations of the world, and in particular to the status of identity. This property is of great interest in its own right. It effectively establishes a connection between the compatibility of two elements b and b' of a multiple B and the atomic composition of an object, of which B is the underlying multiple. This is already an ontological link or a correlation between the pure presentation of the multiple and the legislation of appearing. It is obviously constructed on the basis of the postulate of materialism. This remarkable property is expressed as follows: if b and b' are two compatible elements of B, and we write $b(x)$ and $b'(x)$ the atoms corresponding to b and b', for two given elements x and y of B, we will always have $b(x) \cap b'(y) \leq \mathbf{Id}\ (x, y)$. We will call it P.6.

To clarify the meaning and importance of P.6, note the following: if $\mathbf{Id}(x, y) = \mu$, that is if the degree of identity between x and y is minimal (which, in a situation, means that it is nil, or that x and y are absolutely different), in order that, in any case, b and b' may be compatible, the aforementioned statement prescribes that $b(x) \cap b'(y) = \mu$. In particular, if x is 'absolutely' in the atomic component b—in other words if $b\ (x) = M$—then y must be absolutely absent from the atomic component b', that is $b'(y) = \mu$. Other-wise, we could not have $b(x) \cap b'(y) = \mu$. This means that if the atomic components b and b' are compatible, they cannot accept into their com-position totally non-identical elements. If, conversely, $b(x) \cap b'(y) = M$, this means that $b(x) = b'(y) = M$, and therefore that x and y are absolutely elements of, respectively, the atomic components b and b'. The compati-bility between b and b' consequently demands that $\mathbf{Id}(x, y) = M$, that is the absolute identity of x and y. This means that if b and b' are compatible, they can 'absolutely' accept into their composition (ontologically) different elements x and y, provided that these elements are 'absolutely' identical in appearing, or qua beings-there.

I leave the (very instructive) demonstration of P.6 for the appendix.

Taking this result as given, we are now in a position to demonstrate the *fundamental theorem of atomic logic*.

The fundamental theorem of atomic logic

Given an objective region B of the support-set A of an object $(A, \textbf{Id})$, if the elements of B are compatible in pairs there exists an envelope ε of B for the ontological order-relation $<$ defined on the object.

To mark out this theorem, namely in the scholium devoted to the transcendental functor, we will give it the far too modest name of 'Proposition P.7'.

The demonstration of the theorem depends on a fundamental lemma, which we will call lemma Ψ, and which is in actual fact, the construction of the envelope of B in the guise of an atom. We begin, as always, from an object $(A, \textbf{Id})$ and we consider it as an (ontological) part of A, that is $B \subseteq A$. We thus have the lemma Ψ:

If the elements of B are compatible in pairs, the function of A in the transcendental T defined by the equation

$$\pi(x) = \Sigma\{\textbf{Id}(b, x) \mathbin{/} b \in B\}$$

is an atom.

Let us reflect on what this function represents. Given an element x of set A, it considers *all* the degrees of identity between this x and *all* the elements of the subset B. In other words, it 'situates' the element x in relation to the objective region B. This situation is synthesized by the envelope Σ, which fixes with the greatest possible accuracy the maximum of the degrees of identity in question. Ultimately, $\pi(x)$ means something like 'the greatest identitarian proximity between x and the elements of B', or 'the highest degree of identity through which x approaches that which composes B'.

The tremendous importance of this construction lies in the fact that it provides the means for comparing an isolated element to a subset or an objective region on the basis of the measure of the greater or lesser identity between this element and the elements of the subset in question. However, it sets a precondition for this comparison to result in a well-determined measure: that the elements of B be compatible in pairs. Considering the algebraic definition of compatibility (Proposition P.3), this amounts to saying that, when taken in pairs, the degree of existence of elements cannot exceed their degree of identity. We may accordingly affirm that B is an existentially homogeneous subset, to the extent that within it existential disparities [*écarts d'existence*] cannot outstrip differences. Nothing exists within B whose existence is not regulated by its networks of identity to the other elements. The lemma thus comes down to saying that every existentially homogeneous subset authorizes the construction of a singular atom, about which the theorem will subsequently show that it is indeed an envelope for B, and thus the point-like synthesis of an objective region.

Here is the demonstration of lemma Ψ. It is a question of verifying that the function $\pi(x)$ corroborates the two axioms $\alpha.1$ and $\alpha.2$ of the atomic phenomenal components.

Under the constant condition of considering all the $b \in B$, we have the following:

$\mathbf{Id}(x, y) \cap \Sigma\{\mathbf{Id}(b, x)\} = \Sigma\{\mathbf{Id}(x, y) \cap \mathbf{Id}(b, x)\}$	distributivity
$\mathbf{Id}(x, y) \cap \mathbf{Id}(b, x) \leq \mathbf{Id}(b, y)$	ax. $\mathbf{Id}.1$ and $\mathbf{Id}.2$
$\Sigma\{\mathbf{Id}(x, y) \cap \mathbf{Id}(b, x)\} \leq \Sigma\{\mathbf{Id}(b, y)\}$	consequence
$\mathbf{Id}(x, y) \cap \pi(x) \leq \pi(y)$	def. of π

This last statement is the Axiom $\alpha.1$ (for π).

Take now any two elements of A, say x and y. The definition of the function π gives us:

$$\pi(x) \cap \pi(y) = \Sigma\{\mathbf{Id}(b, x) \cap \mathbf{Id}(b', y) \mid b \in B \text{ and } b' \in B\}$$

But since we made the hypothesis that that the elements of B are compatible in pairs, b and b'—which are two non-descript [*quelconques*] (or 'generic') elements of B—are compatible. We may therefore apply the result contained in Proposition P.5. That is:

$$\mathbf{Id}(b, x) \cap \mathbf{Id}(b', y) \leq \mathbf{Id}(x, y)$$

It follows that $\mathbf{Id}(x, y)$ is greater than all the elements of the type $\mathbf{Id}(b, x) \cap \mathbf{Id}(b', y)$ contained in the bracket which is used above to write $\pi(x) \cap \pi(y)$—these elements are successively obtained when b and b' are run through set B. $\mathbf{Id}(x, y)$ is thus an upper bound for all these elements. But the envelope is by definition the least upper bound. It follows that this envelope must be lesser than or equal to $\mathbf{Id}(x, y)$. But the envelope is none other than $\pi(x) \cap \pi(y)$. So we ultimately get the following:

$$\pi(x) \cap \pi(y) \leq \mathbf{Id}(x, y)$$

Which is exactly Axiom α.2 of the atomic components.

It is thereby proven that the function $\pi(x)$ is an atom. Accordingly, there exists a real element which prescribes this atom. Let us call this element ε. That ε prescribes π means that, for a given x of A, its degree of identity to ε is the same transcendental degree as $\pi(x)$.

We will now show that ε is the envelope of B for the ontological order-relation $<$, thereby establishing Proposition P.7. We proceed in two stages. First, we establish that ε is an upper bound of B. Then, under the condition of a lemma bearing on the existence of ε—which we will consequently name e(Ψ)—that it is the least upper bound.

The element ε is the upper bound of all the $b \in B$:

$$\mathbf{Id}(\varepsilon, x) = \Sigma\{\mathbf{Id}(b, x) \mid b \in B\} \qquad\qquad \varepsilon \text{ prescribes the atom } \pi$$

This equation means that, having set an $x \in A$, we have $\mathbf{Id}(b, x) \leq \mathbf{Id}(\varepsilon, x)$. This is because $\mathbf{Id}(\varepsilon, x)$, the envelope of all the $\mathbf{Id}(b, x)$, is the upper bound of all of them. In particular, in the case where $x = b$, we get the following:

$\mathbf{Id}(b, b) \leq \mathbf{Id}(\varepsilon, b)$	see above
$\mathbf{E}b \leq \mathbf{Id}(\varepsilon, b)$	from $\mathbf{E}$
$b < \varepsilon$	by P.4

What is the 'value' of the existence of ε? The answer to this question—lemma e(Ψ)—is very revealing. The existence of ε is indeed the envelope (in the transcendental sense) of the set of degrees constituted by the existential values of the elements of B. Consequently,

$$\mathbf{E}\varepsilon = \Sigma\{\mathbf{E}b \mid b \in B\}$$

The demonstration of lemma e(Ψ) is as follows, with b as any element of B:

$b < \varepsilon$	ε is an upper bound of B
$\mathbf{E}b = \mathbf{Id}(\varepsilon, b)$ (I)	def. of $<$
$\mathbf{Id}(\varepsilon, x) = \pi(x) = \Sigma\{\mathbf{Id}(b, x) \mid b \in B\}$	def. of ε
$\mathbf{Id}(\varepsilon, \varepsilon) = \Sigma\{\mathbf{Id}(b, \varepsilon) \mid b \in B\}$	case $x = \varepsilon$
$\mathbf{E}\varepsilon = \Sigma\{\mathbf{Id}(\varepsilon, b) \mid b \in B\}$ (II)	def. of $\mathbf{E}$ and ax. $\mathbf{Id}.1$
$\mathbf{E}\varepsilon = \Sigma\{\mathbf{E}b \mid b \in B\}$	by (I) and (II)

With this result in hand, we may conclude by demonstrating that ε is indeed the least upper bound of B. Here is how:

Let c be an upper bound of B. For every $b \in B$, we have $b < c$. We get:

$b < c$	hypothesis
$\mathbf{E}b = \mathbf{Id}(b, c)$	def. of $<$
$\Sigma\{\mathbf{E}b \mid b \in B\} = \Sigma\{\mathbf{Id}(b, c) \mid b \in B\}$ (I)	consequence
$\mathbf{Id}(\varepsilon, c) = \Sigma\{\mathbf{Id}(b, c) \mid b \in B\}$	def. of ε; case $x = c$
$\mathbf{E}\varepsilon = \Sigma\{\mathbf{E}b \mid b \in B\}$ (II)	lemma e(Ψ) above
$\mathbf{E}\varepsilon = \mathbf{Id}(\varepsilon, c)$	I and II
$\varepsilon < c$	def. of $<$

Finally, the element ε, defined as prescribing the atom $\pi(\mathrm{x})$, is indeed the least upper bound of B. It is thus, for the relation $<$, an envelope of B, thereby guaranteeing the real synthesis of B for the world in question. Proposition P.7, or the fundamental theorem of atomic logic, has been demonstrated.

We will recall once again that this ontological synthesis can only be constructed if the elements of B are compatible in pairs. Only in that case is the function $\pi(\mathrm{x}) = \Sigma\{\mathbf{Id}(b, x) \mid b \in B\}$ an atom and only then does it identify a real element of B.

SECTION 4
Existence and Death

1. EXISTENCE AND DEATH ACCORDING TO
PHENOMENOLOGY AND VITALISM

There is a secret philosophical complicity between the theories that root meaning in the intentionalities of consciousness (to cut to the chase, let's call these the phenomenological orientations) and those, by all appearances entirely inimical, which make life into the active name of being (let's call these the vitalisms: Nietzsche, Bergson and Deleuze). This complicity rests on the axiomatic assumption of a term which has the power to transcend the states that deploy or unfold it, such that every singularity of being can be rigorously thought only in the most refined possible description of the unique act that constitutes and relates it to the One, of which it is a transitory mode. Of course, the One-term is in one case intentional consciousness, whose real figures are constituent acts, and in the other the power or élan of inorganic life, of which organisms—and in the end all actual singularities—are the evanescent modalities. But the movement of thought is the same, positing on the edges of the in-existent (the free nothingness of consciousness, the chaotic formlessness of life as such) a kind of over-existence whose creative activity is unfolded by the infinite multiplicity of what is (states of consciousness or figures of the subject, on the one hand, and living individuals, on the other). To exist then means to be in the constituent movement of originary over-existence. In other words, to exist is *to be constituted* (by consciousness or life).

But to be constituted *also means to be nihilated* [*néantisé*]. The constituent act only reveals its over-existence in the deposition (the precariousness, the mortality) of that which it constitutes. A state of consciousness is ultimately nothing but its dissolution in time, which is why Husserl directed his investigations towards an infinite description of the temporal flux as such. 'Internal time-consciousness', which is the passage of death through constituted consciousness, exemplarily affirms the over-existence (the timelessness) of constituent consciousness. Similarly, the death of a singular life is the necessary proof of the infinite power of life.

We can thus say that the term common to phenomenology and vitalism—to Husserl and Bergson, Sartre and Deleuze—is death, as the attestation of finite existence, which is simply a modality of an infinite over-existence, or of a power of the One which we only experience through its reverse; through the passive limitation of everything that this power has deigned to constitute, or, as Leibniz would say, to fulgurate.

Basically, in both cases, the guarantee of the One as constituent power (*natura naturans*, in Spinoza's terminology) is the mortality or finitude of the multiple as a constituted configuration (*natura naturae*: states of consciousness, actual individuals). Death alone is proof of life. Finitude alone is proof of the transcendental constitution of experience. In both cases, a secularized or sublimated God operates in the background, the over-existent broker of being. One may call Him Life, or—like Spinoza—Substance or Consciousness. We're always dealing with Him, this underlying infinite whose terrestrial writing is death.

To unshackle existence down here from its mortal correlation requires that it should be axiomatically wrested from the phenomenological constitution of experience as well as from the Nietzschean naming of being as life. To think existence *without finitude*—that is the liberatory imperative, which extricates existence from the ultimate signifier of its submission, death. It is true, as Hegel said, that the life of the spirit (which is to say, free life) is the one that 'holds fast to what is dead'. It means that life is indifferent to death. This is the life which does not measure up its actuality either to the transcendental constitution of experience or to the chaotic sovereignty of life.

Under what conditions is existence—our existence, the only one that we can bear witness to and think—that of an Immortal? This is—on this point at least, Plato and Aristotle were in agreement—the only question of which it can be said that it pertains to philosophy, and to philosophy alone.

2. AXIOMATIC OF EXISTENCE AND LOGIC OF DEATH

In this book, we have offered a rigorous definition of existence. The existence of a given multiple, relative to a world, is the degree according to which it appears as identical to itself in that world. In formal terms, the existence of a being ε, relative to the world $\mathbf{m}$, is the value of the transcendental indexing $\mathbf{Id}(\varepsilon, \varepsilon)$ in the transcendental of that world.

Let us reiterate the key points. If $\mathbf{Id}(\varepsilon, \varepsilon) = M$ (the self-identity of the appearing of ε is maximal), then ε exists absolutely in the world $\mathbf{m}$. In other words, the existence of ε is coextensive with its being. If instead $\mathbf{Id}(\varepsilon, \varepsilon) = \mu$, the existence of ε in the world $\mathbf{m}$ is nil; ε inexists in $\mathbf{m}$. This means that its existence is totally uncoupled from its being. There will also be intermediate cases, in which the element ε exists 'to a certain extent'.

It is crucial to remember that existence is not as such a category of being, but a category of appearing; a being only exists according to its being-there. And this existence is that of a *degree* of existence, situated between inexistence and absolute existence. Existence is both a logical and an intensive concept. It is this double status which makes it possible to rethink death.

There is an initial temptation to say that a being is dead when, in the world one is referring to, its degree of existence is minimal, or when it inexists in that world. To affirm of a being ε that it is dead would amount to acknowledging that we have the equation: $\mathbf{Id}(\varepsilon, \varepsilon) = \mu$. This also means that death is absolute non-self-identity, the loss of that logical minimum of existence which is represented by a non-nil value of identity. But this would be to overlook that death is something other than inexistence. Death *happens* [*survient*]. And it necessarily happens to an existent. Therein lies the profundity of the canonical truism: 'Fifteen minutes before his death, he was still alive'. This truism is immune to derision, since we experience its truth with bewilderment and pain when we find ourselves besides the dying. Thus death is the coming to be of a minimal value of existence for a being endowed with a positive evaluation of its identity. In formal terms, we can speak of the death of being ε when we 'pass' from the existential equation $\mathbf{Id}(\varepsilon, \varepsilon) = p$ (where p is a non-minimal value, that is $p \neq \mu$) to the equation $\mathbf{Id}(\varepsilon, \varepsilon) = \mu$.

Just like existence, death is not a category of being. It is a category of appearing, or, more precisely, of the becoming of appearing. To put it otherwise, death is a logical rather than an ontological concept. All that can be affirmed about 'dying' is that it is an affection of appearing, which leads from a situated existence that can be positively evaluated (even if it is not maximal) to a minimal existence, an existence that is nil *relatively to the world*. Besides, to speak of nil 'in itself' makes no sense for a given multiple. Only the empty set may be said to be ontologically nil, since, whether presented or not, it is never exposed to death, nor even to the passage from one degree of existence to another. The whole problem is to know what this 'passage' consists in. To fully understand this point, we require nothing short of a theory of natural multiples, accompanied by a theory of the event. We will make do with two remarks.

1. The passage from a value of identity or existence to another cannot be an immanent effect of the being under consideration. That is because this being has no other immanence to the situation, and consequently to its own identity, than its degree of existence. The passage necessarily results from an exterior cause which affects, whether locally or globally, the logical evaluations, or the legislation of appearing. In other words, what comes to pass with death is an exterior change in the function of appearing of a given multiple. This change is always imposed upon the dying being, and this imposition is contingent.

The right formula is Spinoza's: 'No thing can be destroyed except through an external cause'. It is impossible to say of a being that it is 'mortal', if by this we understand that it is internally necessary for it to die. At most we can accept that death is possible for it, in the sense that an abrupt change in the function of appearing may befall it and that this change may amount to a minimization of its identity, and thus of its degree of existence.

2. Consequently, it is vain to meditate upon death, for as Spinoza also declared: 'A free man thinks of nothing less than of death, and his wisdom is a meditation on life, not on death'. That is because death is merely a consequence. Thought must instead turn towards the event on which the local alteration of the functions of appearing depended.

Considered outside of any dependence on a supernumerary event, dying, just like existing, is a mode of being-there, and therefore a purely logical correlation.

APPENDIX
Three Demonstrations

1. ON COMPATIBILITY: ALGEBRAIC AND TOPOLOGICAL DEFINITIONS

In the formal exposition (Section 3), we showed that the topological definition of compatibility on the basis of localization ($a \between b$ means that ($a \upharpoonright \mathbf{E}b = b \upharpoonright \mathbf{E}a$)) implied that $\mathbf{E}a \cap \mathbf{E}b = \mathbf{Id}(a, b)$—a more algebraic formula. We declared that it was possible to demonstrate the reciprocal, thereby establishing the equivalence of the two approaches. Here is the demonstration of that reciprocal.

Let's begin with a useful lemma about localizations. It expresses the following idea: if I localize an element a (and therefore the real atom prescribed by this element) on the degree of its identity to an element b, I will obtain the same thing as I would if I localized b on this same identity (which is also the identity of b to a, by virtue of the symmetrical character of identities, contained in the axiom $\mathbf{Id}.1$). Thus the typical anarchist, referred back to his degree of identity to the typical Kurd, is the same thing as the typical Kurd, referred back to his degree of identity to the typical anarchist.

In formal terms, it's a matter of establishing that $a \upharpoonright \mathbf{Id}(a, b) = b \upharpoonright \mathbf{Id}(a, b)$. Let's call this result lemma A. Here is its demonstration.

Let's posit that $g = a \upharpoonright \mathbf{Id}(a, b)$, and $h = b \upharpoonright \mathbf{Id}(a, b)$. We will also write $a(x)$ for the real atomic function $\mathbf{Id}(a, x)$ and $b(x)$ for the atomic function $\mathbf{Id}(b, x)$. We then get the following:

$$g(x) = a(x) \cap \mathbf{Id}(a, b) = a(x) \cap a(b) \qquad \text{def. of } \upharpoonright \text{ and of the atom } a(x)$$
$$a(x) \cap a(b) \leq \mathbf{Id}(b, x) \qquad \text{Axiom } \alpha.2$$

271

$g(x) \leq \mathbf{Id}(b, x)$	consequence
$g(x) \leq b(x)$	def. of $b(x)$
$g(x) \leq \mathbf{Id}(a, b)$	first line and def. of $\cap$
$g(x) \leq b(x) \cap \mathbf{Id}(a, b)$	def. of $\cap$
$g(x) \leq h(x)$	def. of h

An exactly symmetrical reasoning, in which at the outset $g(x)$ is replaced by $h(x)$, results in $h(x) \leq g(x)$. By dint of anti-symmetry, we have $g(x) = h(x)$. That is, as intended, $a \restriction \mathbf{Id}(a, b) = b \restriction \mathbf{Id}(a, b)$. Lemma A has been demonstrated.

In the same register, a technical lemma (lemma B) shows that the localization of an element on the conjunction of two degrees is equal to the localization of this element on the first degree, itself localized on the second. That is:

$$a \restriction (p \cap q) = (a \restriction p) \restriction q.$$

The following is the demonstration of lemma B, which the reader could usefully anticipate as an exercise:

$((a \restriction p) \restriction q)(x) = (\mathbf{Id}(a, x) \cap p) \cap q$	def. of $\restriction$
$\mathbf{Id}(a, x) \cap (p \cap q) = a \restriction (p \cap q)$	def. of $\restriction$
$((a \restriction p) \restriction q)(x) = a \restriction (p \cap q)(x)$	consequence
$(a \restriction p) \restriction q = a \restriction (p \cap q)$	notational convention

From lemma B we can draw another—phenomenologically interesting—consideration. Take an atom of appearing (for example, a typical anarchist in the demonstration-world). Let's suppose that it is localized on what there is in common between the existence of the element that prescribes it and the existence of another element (for example, a typical postman). It is then as if it had been localized only on the existence of the second element (the postman). This follows from the fact that the localization of an atom on its own existence (the existence of the element that prescribes it) is identical to this element (to this atom). Accordingly, in its localization on the common appearing of these two existences, the existence of an element in its own right is not taken into account. If you localize a typical anarchist (bearded, vociferating, etc.) on what is in common between his existence and that of a typical postman (dressed in blue and yellow, wearing his union badge, etc.) you only need to take into account the existence of the postman. Formally, this is expressed as follows: $a \restriction (\mathbf{E}a \cap \mathbf{E}b) = a \restriction \mathbf{E}b$. Let's call this result lemma C. Here is its very suggestive demonstration:

$a \lceil \mathbf{E}a(x) = \mathbf{Id}(a, x) \cap \mathbf{E}a$ (I)	def. of $\lceil$
$\mathbf{Id}(a, x) \leq \mathbf{E}a$	by P.1
$\mathbf{Id}(a, x) \cap \mathbf{E}a = \mathbf{Id}(a, x)$ (II)	by P.0
$a \lceil \mathbf{E}a(x) = \mathbf{Id}(a, x)$	(I) and (II)
$a \lceil \mathbf{E}a = a$ (III)	notational convention
$a \lceil (p \cap q) = (a \lceil p) \cap q$	lemma B
$a \lceil (\mathbf{E}a \cap \mathbf{E}b) = (a \lceil \mathbf{E}a) \cap \mathbf{E}b$	application
$a \lceil (\mathbf{E}a \cap \mathbf{E}b) = a \lceil \mathbf{E}b$	by (III)

As we announced earlier, we are now in the position to prove the reciprocal: if the measure of the coexistence of two elements is equal to that of their identity, they are compatible. This completes the demonstration of P.3.

$a \lceil \mathbf{Id}(a, b) = b \lceil \mathbf{Id}(a, b)$	lemma A above
$\mathbf{Id}(a, b) = \mathbf{E}a \cap \mathbf{E}b$	hypothesis
$a \lceil (\mathbf{E}a \cap \mathbf{E}b) = b \lceil (\mathbf{E}a \cap \mathbf{E}b)$	consequence
$a \lceil \mathbf{E}b = b \lceil \mathbf{E}a$	lemma C above
$a \ddagger b$	def. of $\ddagger$

2. TOPOLOGICAL DEFINITION OF THE ONTO-LOGICAL ORDER <

We announced earlier that in the end three equivalent definitions of the onto-logical order < can be provided: the definition of an algebraic kind, given in the conceptual exposition (we have $a < b$ when a is compatible with b and $\mathbf{E}a \leq \mathbf{E}b$); the transcendental definition given in the formal exposition (we have $a < b$ when the existence of a is equal to its identity with b); and finally a directly topological definition: we have $a < b$ when the atom prescribed by a is equal to the localization of b on the existence of a, that is $a = b \lceil \mathbf{E}a$.

We will now supply the complete proof of the equivalence between the topological definition and the transcendental definition. We need to demonstrate that $[(\mathbf{E}a = \mathbf{Id}(a, b)) \leftrightarrow (a = b \lceil \mathbf{E}a)]$. Note the free circulation between the use of letters (a or b) to designate elements, in the ontological sense, and to designate atoms, in the logical sense.

The proof makes use of the lemmas demonstrated in Subsection 1 of this appendix.

– *Direct proposition*. The transcendental definition implies the topological definition.

$$a \, ⌠ \, \mathbf{Id}(a, b) = b \, ⌠ \, \mathbf{Id}(a, b) \qquad \text{lemma } A \text{ above}$$
$$\mathbf{E}a = \mathbf{Id}(a, b) \qquad \text{transcendental def. of } <$$
$$a \, ⌠ \, \mathbf{E}a = b \, ⌠ \, \mathbf{E}a \qquad \text{consequence}$$
$$a \, ⌠ \, \mathbf{E}a = a \qquad \text{(III) in the proof of lemma } C$$
$$a = b \, ⌠ \, \mathbf{E}a \qquad \text{consequence}$$

– *Reciprocal proposition*. The topological definition implies the transcendental definition.

We start with a technical lemma on localizations, whose conceptual self-evidence is guaranteed, if we only reflect on it for an instant. Let's call it lemma D. Lemma D affirms that the existence of a localization of a on degree p is equal to the conjunction of the existence of a and of this degree. That is, $\mathbf{E}(a \, ⌠ \, p) = \mathbf{E}a \cap p$. Here is the demonstration. Let's posit (following the postulate of materialism) that $b = a \, ⌠ \, p$. It follows that:

$$\mathbf{Id}(b, x) = \mathbf{Id}(a, x) \cap p \qquad \text{def. of } b$$
$$\mathbf{Id}(b, b) = \mathbf{Id}(a, b) \cap p \qquad \text{case } x = b$$
$$\mathbf{E}b = \mathbf{Id}(a, b) \cap p \quad \text{(I)} \qquad \text{def. of } \mathbf{E}$$
$$\mathbf{Id}(b, a) = \mathbf{Id}(a, a) \cap p \qquad \text{case } x = a$$
$$\mathbf{Id}(a, b) = \mathbf{E}a \cap p \qquad \text{def. of } \mathbf{E} \text{ and ax. } \mathbf{Id}.1$$
$$\mathbf{E}b = \mathbf{E}a \cap p \cap p \qquad \text{by (I)}$$
$$\mathbf{E}(a \, ⌠ \, p) = \mathbf{E}a \cap p \qquad \text{def. of } b \text{ and } p \cap p = p$$

To prove our reciprocal—that the topological definition of $<$ entails the transcendental definition—we will first of all establish that this topological definition implies the compatibility between a and b (an expected result but one that is nevertheless interesting in its own right). Here is how.

$$a = b \, ⌠ \, \mathbf{E}a \quad \text{(I)} \qquad \text{topological def. of } <$$
$$\mathbf{E}a = \mathbf{E}(b \, ⌠ \, \mathbf{E}a) \qquad \text{consequence}$$
$$\mathbf{E}a = \mathbf{E}b \cap \mathbf{E}a \quad \text{(II)} \qquad \text{lemma } D \text{ above}$$
$$a \, ⌠ \, \mathbf{E}b = (b \, ⌠ \, \mathbf{E}a) \, ⌠ \, \mathbf{E}b \qquad \text{by (I)}$$
$$a \, ⌠ \, \mathbf{E}b = b \, ⌠ \, (\mathbf{E}a \cap \mathbf{E}b) \qquad \text{lemma } B \text{ above}$$
$$a \, ⌠ \, \mathbf{E}b = b \, ⌠ \, \mathbf{E}a \qquad \text{by (II)}$$
$$a \ddagger b \qquad \text{def. of compatibility}$$

But if $a \ddagger b$, we know, by P.3, that $\mathbf{E}a \cap \mathbf{E}b = \mathbf{Id}(a, b)$. And since we also know, by (II) in the above proof, that $\mathbf{E}a \cap \mathbf{E}b = \mathbf{E}a$, we finally have $\mathbf{E}a = \mathbf{Id}(a, b)$, which is the transcendental definition of $<$.

3. DEMONSTRATION OF PROPOSITION P.6

It is a question of establishing that if b and b' are compatible, then for every pair of elements of the referential multiple A—say x and y—we have $b(x) \cap b'(y) \leq \mathbf{Id}(x, y)$.

A proof can be written as follows (recall that $b(x)$ is a way of writing the atom b, whose exact definition, which we reprise hereafter, is $\mathbf{Id}(b, x)$).

$\mathbf{Id}(b, x) \leq \mathbf{E}b$ and $\mathbf{Id}(b', y) \leq \mathbf{E}b'$	P.1
$\mathbf{Id}(b, x) = \mathbf{Id}(b, x) \cap \mathbf{E}b$	by P.0
$\mathbf{Id}(b', y) = \mathbf{Id}(b', y) \cap \mathbf{E}b'$	by P.0
$\mathbf{Id}(b, x) \cap \mathbf{Id}(b', y) = \mathbf{Id}(b, x) \cap \mathbf{Id}(b', y) \cap \mathbf{E}b \cap \mathbf{E}b'$	consequence
$\mathbf{E}b \cap \mathbf{E}b' = \mathbf{Id}(b, b')$	$b \ddagger b'$ and P.3
$\mathbf{Id}(b, x) \cap \mathbf{Id}(b', y) = \mathbf{Id}(b, x) \cap \mathbf{Id}(b', y) \cap \mathbf{Id}(b, b')$	consequence
$\mathbf{Id}(b, b') \cap \mathbf{Id}(b, x) \leq \mathbf{Id}(b', x)$	ax. $\mathbf{Id}$.1 and ax. $\mathbf{Id}$.2
$\mathbf{Id}(b, x) \cap \mathbf{Id}(b', y) \leq \mathbf{Id}(b', x) \cap \mathbf{Id}(b', y)$	consequence
$\mathbf{Id}(b', x) \cap \mathbf{Id}(b', y) \leq \mathbf{Id}(x, y)$	ax. $\mathbf{Id}$.1 and ax. $\mathbf{Id}$.2
$\mathbf{Id}(b, x) \cap \mathbf{Id}(b', y) \leq \mathbf{Id}(x, y)$	consequence
$b(x) \cap b'(y) \leq \mathbf{Id}(x, y)$	notation for real atoms

A SCHOLIUM AS IMPRESSIVE AS IT IS SUBTLE

The Transcendental Functor

1. OBJECTIVE PHENOMENOLOGY OF THE EXISTENTIAL
ANALYSIS OF AN OBJECT AND OF THE CONSTRUCTION
OF THE TRANSCENDENTAL FUNCTOR

In Section 3 of Book III we began by reasoning locally: localization of an atom, compatibility between two elements, onto-logical order. We worked on atomic components of objects, that is on the One-in-the-world, which, as the postulate of materialism tells us, always intersects some One-in-being. We then proceeded regionally—real synthesis, by envelopment, of a region of appearing. Under a condition of compatibility, we showed that a real element guarantees the synthetic cohesion of the objective region. This is the fundamental theorem of atomic logic.

We now come to the global analysis of an object. Take, for example, the round temple in Hubert Robert's painting. How are we to carry out, in the Cartesian sense, its (transcendental) decomposition into clear and distinct parts? The most immediate foothold is to be found in existence, the degree of existence of the columns. We can always regroup the (real) elements of the object by degrees of existence. We thereby associate to every degree p the subset of the object composed of elements that have the degree of existence p. Let us agree that the three fully visible columns in the foreground have the maximal degree of existence, while the entirely concealed columns in the left background possess a very weak degree of existence. The columns in the right background have an intermediate degree of existence, and so on. It is clear how, on the basis of the transcendental, we slice up the temple-object into rigorously homogeneous existential strata.

What we have here is a kind of operator, which associates to every degree of the transcendental the set of the elements of the object whose common characteristic is that their existence is measured by this degree. We call this operator the *transcendental functor of the object*.

Likewise, we shall see how the transcendental functor of the group of postmen analyzes this group into strata according to their degree of properly protesting existence. Accordingly, those who repeat the slogans, who hold up the banner, who, wearing blue and yellow, are really attired as postmen, and so on, will be collectively assigned by the functor to a very high degree of existence, while the one who goes it alone, dragging his heels along the gutter, will be pinned—along with his brethren in native timidity—to a degree of existence on the edge of nothingness.

The transcendental functor is not exactly a function, since it does not associate to transcendental degrees elements of the object, but rather sub-sets, such as 'columns concealed by the foliage' or 'the most protesting postmen'. In order to carry out the existential analysis of an object fully, we would first like to find a procedure that associates to a transcendental degree an element that is the 'representative' of its existential class. Thus, to an almost maximal degree there would correspond this exemplarily protesting postman, while to a very weak degree there would correspond the one who, manifestly panicking on the sidewalk, tries to vanish into the becalming flow of passers-by. Most of all, we also want this analysis to respect syntheses. This last point is extremely profound. We know that given a set of transcendental degrees, there always exists, as a kind of synthetic punctuality, the envelope of this set. Suppose that we succeed in 'representing' in an object such and such a degree by a typical element, endowed precisely with this degree of existence. That would give us something like a selective existential analysis of the object. For example, to four different transcendental degrees, spread out between the minimum and the maximum, there corresponds a single column of the temple, which is exemplary in its way of making the degree exist pictorially. The set of degrees obviously admits of an envelope for the order-relation that organizes the transcendental. But does the group of columns also admit of an envelope, acting as a real synthesis for the order-relation that structures the elements of an object in the retroaction of their appearing? Or better, is the synthetic term really the one that corresponds, through the procedure of typical selection, to the degree that acts as an envelope in the transcendental?

If the answer to all these questions is positive, it will mean that, on the basis of a set of transcendental degrees, the existential analysis of an object can select some typical existents, and that the unity of these existents corresponds to the enveloping unity of the degrees. We will thereby have obtained a kind of projection of the laws of the transcendental onto the existential (and real) analysis of the object.

Let us try to provide an image of this projection. We'll take as our object the group of postmen, with its hardcore (high degree of existence), its anonymous rank-and-file, its margins (weak degree) and so on. For every degree that measures an existence, we select a typical 'representative'. We then have a kind of internal metonymy of the object: a maximal existent (this particularly visible 'leader'), a minimal existent (the postman adrift on the sidewalk), an 'average' existent for every nuanced existential stratum of this average. If the real synthetic unity of this metonymic group (perhaps the leader himself, whose degree of existence presupposes that of the others) corresponds to the envelope of the degrees (perhaps, in this case, the maximal degree), then the transcendental functor may be said to be 'faithful'. The question is then: can faithful functors exist?

The answer to the question, exemplified in the next subsection and rigorously constructed in the final formal demonstration, is both restrictive and overabundant.

It is restrictive, because we will only attain our aims if the selective metonymy of the object (the choice of typical representatives of a class of existence) gives us a subset of the object all of whose elements are compatible in pairs. The question will then be whether the bellowing leader of the blue-and-yellow postmen and the drifter on the sidewalk are compatible, in the sense of that real relation which we will recall is stated as follows: the localization of the former on the existence of the latter is equal to the localization of the latter on the existence of the former.

It is overabundant because, under this condition of compatibility, we get as an additional benefit the following remarkable phenomenon: each typical element of each existential stratum is the localization of the synthetic element of the corresponding existential degree. Accordingly, if we presuppose the compatibility of all the representative elements of each degree of existence that is assignable to the postmen, each of these elements—for example the timid fugitive—is equal to the localization on its degree of existence (in this instance, almost nothing) of the term that carries out the real synthesis of the subset 'postmen' and which in this case is the over-visible leader. What's more, this term is itself the projection of the formal synthesis of the degrees, which is obtained, in the transcendental, by the envelope. To put it otherwise, if you localize the great ruddy postman who leads the group on the degree of existence of the fugitive running along the gutters, you will get, as the resulting atom, this fugitive himself (the function that assigns to every x of the group its degree of identity to this fugitive). When the condition of compatibility authorizes it, we thus have a topological synthesis that underlies the transcendental functor.

It is the highest possible feat of thinking to recover, in being as it is affected by its appearing—as though appearing were projected onto being on the basis of the transcendental—the power of the One and of global localization, of which this selfsame appearing seemed bound to dispossess it.

2. EXAMPLE OF A FUNCTOR: LOGICAL EVALUATION OF A BATTLE

Classical military clashes, unlike the 'total' wars of the twentieth century, may be considered as works, and therefore as closed worlds. We will try here to describe the transcendental functor of the battle of Gaugamela (1 October 331 BC) in which Alexander irrevocably destroyed the Persian army and the power of Darius III.

Generally speaking, the transcendental of a battle supports the differential evaluation of the capacity for combat of the different subsets of the two opposing armies. For example, at a given moment of the clash, what is the value of the units of heavy cavalry deployed by Darius on his left flank, under the command of Bessus (who, after the rout, will murder Darius), or by Alexander, both on his left flank (commanded by Parmenion, later assassinated by Alexander) and his right flank (the famous 'Companions', around Alexander himself)? Do Darius's new weapons, 200 scythed chariots and 15 elephants (employed for the first time in history) lead to a qualitative advantage? Are the 2,000 Greek mercenaries providing support to the 2,000 members of Darius's royal guard able to withstand the impact of the 12,000 soldiers-strong Macedonian phalanx, armed with the fearsome sarissa, a spear more than 4 m in length? Needless to say, these evaluations also concern more enveloping multiples. What is the military significance of Darius's mass levy of 50,000 peasants from the vicinity? Note that this 'vicinity' is right in the middle of modern Iraq, 30 km from Mosul. But let's move on. . . To what extent is the crushing numerical superiority of the Persian cavalry (35,000 horsemen against around 7,000) diminished by the fact that it comprises 20 or so different nationalities? In the end, all these differential intensities come down to the transcendental synthesis which assigns a degree of local combative intensity to predefined units, like the Armenian heavy cavalry on the far right of the Persian line or the second reserve line deployed by Alexander behind the phalanx, and so on. This degree dynamically gathers together factors such as number, armament, determination, position in the line, portion of the terrain occupied and mobility. The generals try to anticipate its assignation through reconnoitring, entrenchments or reorganizations of the army's arrangement [*dispositif*].

Let's consider two striking examples from the battle of Gaugamela. Darius orders the levelling out of the central area of the battlefield, so that the scythed chariots may manoeuvre with ease. Alexander is largely aware of this plan, through prisoner interrogations and reconnoitring patrols, which he insists in taking part in. His riposte is cunning—to approach Darius, he opts for an oblique formation. Instead of presenting himself in line, front against front, he advances his right flank towards Darius's left, and leaves his own left flank set back. Moreover, to compensate for the latter move and thwart a breakthrough by the chariots, he doubles his line of heavy infantry in depth.

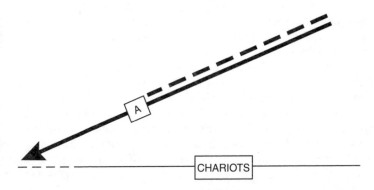

The Persians are forced to stretch their line to the left in order not to be enveloped. But if they shift this line too much, the chariots will no longer benefit from the primed terrain. Therefore, they must attack Alexander's right. In doing so, they create a break in their own infantry on the centre-left and a charge from Alexander's cavalry displaces them.

Through his manoeuvre (the oblique formation and the sliding along his enemy's left) Alexander clearly aims to weaken the combat capacity of the

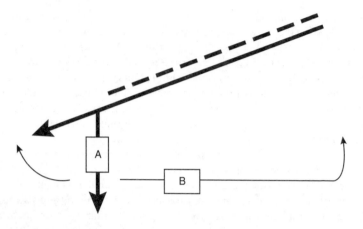

Persian heavy infantry, using Darius's reinforcement of the manoeuvring capacity of his chariots against him. It is in this sense that every military strategy exploits the differential intensities of the 'battle-world', linking the occupation of space by combat units to intellectual speculations on the transcendental of that world.

We will thus define the functor as follows: integrating the incessant modifications introduced by action itself, it assigns to a degree of intensity—a degree of combat capacity—those subsets of the opposing armies which effectively possess this capacity. We have just seen how when the Persians are forced to initiate combat on their left, their heavy infantry on the centre-left corresponds to an intensity which is markedly weaker than that of the heavy infantry placed on the Macedonian right, because its line is excessively stretched, while Alexander's cavalry, charging against it, remains compact. However, more or less at the same moment, the Persian cavalry launches itself all the way to the right, against the Macedonian left which the oblique formation has set back. It manages to isolate two units of the phalanx and, penetrating the breach, to carry out a raid behind the lines all the way to the field camp, thereby paralyzing any advance by the Macedonian left flank.

We could say that to such a configuration there corresponds, in terms of the functor, the assignation to the right flank of a transcendental value of existence that is markedly higher than that of the Macedonians' left flank. Of course, we could describe the action of the functor with respect to the totality of the components of the two armies and their development. For

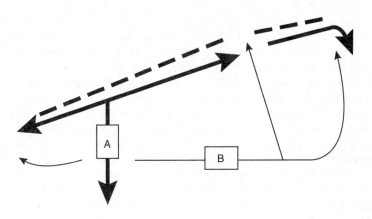

example, the partial looting of the field camp in the raid behind the lines by the Persian heavy cavalry (in actual fact comprising Albanians, Sacesinians and Hyrcanians) signifies the attribution of the multiplicity 'Macedonian reserves and materials' to a weakened degree of existence, while the multiple 'Albanian cavalry' corresponds to a high degree of combative existence.

It is clear at this stage that a crucial part of the arrangement [*dispositif*] of each army—or even of the two entire armies viewed as parts of the 'battle-world'—corresponds to a set of transcendental degrees. For example, the Macedonian right corresponds through the functor to a gradation of degrees going from a very high-combat capacity (the dislocation of the Persian front in its centre-left) to a median capacity (the resistance front-against-front on the far left of the line); while the Persian army in its entirety corresponds to very disparate degrees, going from extreme weakness (the attack of scythed chariots which hasn't had any effect, the centre-left is being routed) to almost maximal degrees (the cavalry charge behind Macedonian lines). We should recall in passing that in general these degrees are only partially ordered—in a battle there exist resources that remain incomparable.

Let's agree in any case to call (transcendental) *territories* these sets of degrees (of combat capacity). We can see that to such territories there correspond, through the functor, parts of the world (Macedonian right flank, reserves, Persian army, Albanian cavalry, etc.). It is these parts which actually constitute the significant objects of the battle-world. They correspond to territories within the degrees of local military capacity which transcendentally govern the battle. Of course, these objects are modified by the becoming of this world, which is also the mobility of its appearance. Every world can effectively be considered as the sum of its modifications (we shall examine this point in Book V).

Alexander radically modifies the situation of near-stalemate at Gaugamela (illustrated by the diagram above) through two decisive manoeuvres. The first, prepared ever since the initial approach, counters the incursion of the enemy cavalry with the second line of the phalanx as well as with reserves of light troops, quashing any of its intended consequences. The second, which is instead improvised, is a horse charge by Alexander himself with the heavy cavalry of his Companions, which crosses the entire battlefield behind the Persian lines to fly to the rescue of its threatened right flank.

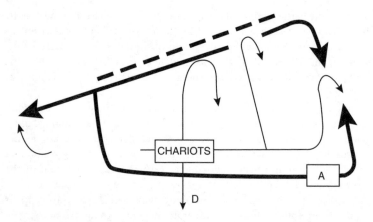

At the end of these movements, the Persian army comes undone, so that the transcendental values of its combat capacity uniformly tend towards the minimum. This effectively signals the disappearance of the battle-world as such, which is terminated by Alexander's complete victory.

Integrating into our account the dynamic of the world, which is the real of appearance and determines the extension of the functor, let us now concentrate on one object, corresponding to a territory of transcendental degrees—namely the centre of Darius's setup [*dispositif*], which includes the Greek mercenaries, the royal guard, the elephants, the scythed chariots, the Hyrcanian cavalry (on the right) and the Indian cavalry (on the left). Note that in general to a fixed degree of the territory there correspond several elements of an object: all those which have the same intensity of combative existence in the becoming of the battle. The object 'centre of the Persian army' is not exempt from this rule. The Greek mercenaries and the royal guard in the end synthesize the same average-weak degree. Valorous at the onset of the clash, they find themselves out of their depth and flee with the king once the news of Alexander's breakthrough and the failure of the chariot charge is confirmed. The Hyrcanian cavalry corresponds to a high degree of existence, as testified by its vigorous resistance when Alexander—in the midst of his charge across the battle-field to support his right—attacks it from the rear. Sixty Companions are killed. It shares this intensity of appearance in the battle with the archers placed in front of the line, who valiantly assure the protection of the charioteers.

In order to organize the analysis of the functor, we will choose for the elements of the object 'centre of the Persian army' a 'typical' representative of each degree of the corresponding territory. This element will be typical in the sense that with regard to the becoming of the appearance of the object in the battle-world, the global importance of its existence is greater than that of elements with the same existential intensity. For example, if we take the archers and the Hyrcanian cavalry, which correspond through the functor to the same (rather high) transcendental degree, which are more important in terms of the becoming of the centre of the Persian army? The cavalry, undoubtedly. The archers perfectly fulfil their function as protectors of the scythed chariots, but the chariots turn out to be a false good idea. On the contrary, the dogged resistance of the Hyrcanian cavalry takes Alexander by surprise, and, had it lasted a little longer, it could have led to the rout of the Macedonian right. It is therefore this cavalry which we'll consider as 'typical' of the combative intensity which characterized it. Likewise, if neither the scythed chariots nor the elephants, despite their novelty, influence the outcome of the conflict (they were not the 'weapons of mass destruction' the Persians imagined . . .), it is the chariots which we will choose to represent the (weak) degree of combat capacity that they have in common. That is because the chariots were the essential ingredient in Darius's battle-plan and their failure has a disastrous effect on the morale of the whole centre, beginning with that of Darius himself. The elephants—in any case few in number—were just an extra. The chariots will thus be the typical element of the object 'centre of the Persian army', corresponding through the functor to the weak transcendental degree which characterized them in the battle-world.

Lastly, to each degree of the territory, there corresponds just one 'typical' element of the object. We thereby obtain what we will call a projection of the transcendental on the object.

Does there exist then an element of this object which may be considered as globally typical—namely an object which has a synthetic value, an envelope-value, with regard to the objective appearing of the multiple in the world? In the case in question, does there exist an element of the object 'centre of the Persian army' which subordinates all the others to itself in terms of the destiny of the object as a whole within the battle-world? We know that the Persian centre collapses long before the almost victorious cavalry, on the right, ends up giving ground. Is an element of this centre perfectly representative of this rout, signalled by the premature flight of the king? Without a doubt, the answer is yes. The failure of the scythed chariots is the key to the (material, but above all moral) collapse of the Persian general staff around Darius. Let's not forget that it was for the chariots that Darius decides to have the battlefield levelled; that for that very reason, and on the basis of information gleaned by his impressive intelligence services, Alexander chooses to advance in an oblique formation, deploying his phalanx on two ranks and drawing the Persian line towards their left, hoping to displace it vis-à-vis the primed terrain. Consequently, the Persians are forced to commit their cavalry prematurely on the left flank and stretch their line, allowing the Macedonians' central strike-force, the 2,100 Companions, to plunge into the breach. It is therefore certain that of all the elements of the object 'centre of the Persian army', such as it appears in the battle-world 'Gaugamela', the element 'scythed chariot' possesses a synthetic value with regard to all the others. It is this element which, in the main, decides the subsequent modifications of the object up to its terminal minimization.

To sum up:

1. The transcendental functor of the battle-world makes a degree of combat capacity correspond to the organic sub-multiples of each army (phalanxes, cavalry regiments, archers, chariots, etc.) which possess this capacity.

2. This ascription naturally incorporates the becoming of the battle, its complete mobile appearance. The degree to which a military unit corresponds is the combat capacity such as it is effectively manifest in the duration of its engagement.

3. An object is a sub-multiple of an army correlated to the degrees that

the functor assigns to the elements of this sub-multiple, degrees which in turn constitute a territory within the transcendental.

4. In general, it is possible to correlate a typical element of the object under consideration to a degree of the territory. This element exemplarily manifests the combat capacity set by the degree in question, from the standpoint of the becoming of the object (consistency, advance, collapse, flight. . .) in the battle-world.

5. This correlation between a transcendental territory and a collection of typical elements of an object is called a projection.

6. The projection may in turn be synthesized or enveloped by a globally typical element, which in actual fact decides the destiny of the object in the battle-world.

This analysis moves from the transcendental (evaluation of local combat capacities, territories) back to the multiple (objects of the battle-world), by determining an immanent synthesis of the multiple itself, that is the element of an object which decides upon the ultimate appearance of this object in a determinate world.

To conclude, it's worth noting that there does seem to be a formal precondition for the successful completion of the analysis. In effect, why have we been able to say that the element 'scythed chariots' was in the position of a synthesis, or an envelope, for the object 'centre of the Persian army' in the battle-world 'Gaugamela'? Because it was the essential ingredient in a strategic calculation that subordinates the other elements of the object to it. In effect, if the elite troops (Greek mercenaries and royal guards) occupied this position in space, it is because in principle they were to advance into the breach opened by the chariots on the primed terrain; if the archers were a little in front, it was in order to protect the charioteers; if the best heavy cavalry flanked the centre on its left and right, it's because it needed to protect the advance of the infantry behind the chariots, and so on. In other words, all the elements of the object, in their spatial disposition and differential evaluations, were compatible with one another. They were under the sway of a battle-plan which articulated them all with the supposedly decisive action of the 200 scythed chariots. We will accordingly add a seventh analytical point:

7. It is on the proviso of their mutual compatibility that the elements of the object selected in a projection to represent the degree of a territory are synthesized by one among them.

The irony, in the case of the battle-world of Gaugamela, is that the fate of the object 'Persian army' was decided, in the direction of rout and obliteration, by the very multiple—the chariots—around which the compatibility of a victorious presupposition had been constructed. But we have shown that it is just here that Alexander's genius lies. The oblique formation, the two ranks of heavy infantry, the slide to the left, the gap and the charge—Alexander undertakes the undoing of the real synthesis to which Darius had subordinated the evaluations of intensity of his own military arrangement. Once the element that played the role of envelope is no longer operative, we witness the alteration of the whole of appearing, namely the collapse of the Persian army.

This reveals the extent to which military genius is really the genius of the transcendental functor; the genius of the ascent from the measures of intensity towards the effectiveness of opposing masses, the genius of the undoing of real syntheses and their conversion into inconsistency, into the rout of unbound multiplicities.

But it is also the genius of appearing. This explains why in the long run the great captains—Alexander, Hannibal, Napoleon—are always defeated. We are left with their works, the battles, which we do not cease to contemplate, because they have the immaterial status—both universal and local—of truths.

That is because, conceived in terms of the transcendental functor, these battle-worlds are just one among the innumerable localizations of a statement whose profundity is unrivalled. This statement concerns nothing less than the correlation between the syntheses of appearing (the envelopes of transcendental degrees) and the possibility of syntheses of being (the envelopes of order that can be directly constituted on the multiplicities that appear).

In the case in question, this statement takes the following form: From every projection, onto a group of real military units, of a set of degrees evaluating the combat capacities in a determinate battle-world, we can extract a projection onto typical representatives of these units. The only condition is that these typical units be rendered mutually compatible by an ordered battle-plan. So not only does a representative military unit correspond to each degree of combat capacity, but these units are synthesized or enveloped by one among them, which decides on the fate of the object as a whole within the battle.

In abstract terms, one will say the following: Take an object that is there in a world. For every set of transcendental degrees, we can define a projection on the object which makes each degree correspond to a single real element of the multiple underlying that object. If these elements are compatible with one another, they are enveloped by an element of the object that guarantees their synthesis according to the ontological order immanent to the multiple, in correspondence with the envelope that synthesizes the degrees in the transcendental of the world.

The functor thereby guarantees the intelligibility of reascending from the transcendental synthesis in appearing back to the real synthesis in multiple-being.

3. FORMAL DEMONSTRATION: EXISTENCE OF THE TRANSCENDENTAL FUNCTOR

We wish to obtain the most complete possible global results regarding the inmost constitution of being-there in the retroaction of its appearing. Under a condition of compatibility, we shall see that the synthetic capacity of the transcendental (the envelope) can be projected, term by term, onto the multiple composition which is the being of every object.

We will thus start from the transcendental, and 'reascend' towards multiple-being. If we have an object $(A, \mathbf{Id})$, it makes sense to associate to an element p of the transcendental *all* the elements of A which have the degree of existence p. One thereby undertakes an existential analysis of the object which, as the transcendental 'scanning' progresses, carves out from it disjoined parts whose appearing is homogeneous (all the elements of a part have the same degree of existence). With regard to the object 'centre of the Persian army', we encountered this type of procedure, which regroups the military units according to their effectively manifested combat capacity. Accordingly, to the maximum M would correspond the part of A composed of all the x's such that $\mathbf{E}x = M$, namely the x's which exist absolutely in the appearing of A. Or to μ would correspond all the x's of A which inexist in its appearing.

We called this analysis of the strata of existence of an object its transcendental functor. The 'transcendental functor' of the object $(A, \mathbf{Id})$, written $\mathbf{F}A$, associates to every element p of T the part of A composed of x's such that $\mathbf{E}x = p$. That is,

$$\mathbf{F}A(p) = \{x/x \in A \text{ and } \mathbf{E}x = p\}$$

We observe that the correlation guaranteed by $\mathbf{F}A$ takes place from an element of the transcendental T towards a subset of A. The transcendental functor is the schema for a thinking that seizes hold of objects analytically, according to the existential stratification of their appearing. This thinking localizes the object (the appearing of the pure multiple) on the basis of, and within, the transcendental—just as we localized in the battle-world the multiples that appeared within it (cavalry, archers, etc.) on the basis of their combat capacity.

What happens to the values of the transcendental functor $\mathbf{F}A$ if $q \leq p$? What is the correlation between $\mathbf{F}A(p)$ and $\mathbf{F}A(q)$? This point is fundamental, because it concerns the link between the constitutive relation of the transcendental (order) and the existential analysis of the object. It bears on the relationship between the existentially homogeneous strata of the object, viewed from the vantage point of the order-structure of the transcendental.

Let $y \in \mathbf{F}A(p)$. By definition, this means that $\mathbf{E}y = p$. Take the localization on q of the atom prescribed by y, that is $y \lceil q$. An easy technical result regarding localizations, which we demonstrated in the first part of the appendix under the name of lemma D, tells us that $\mathbf{E}(a \lceil p) = \mathbf{E}a \cap p$. Hence $\mathbf{E}(y \lceil q) = \mathbf{E}y \cap q$. But since y is in the existential stratum p, it turns out that $\mathbf{E}(y \lceil q) = p \cap q$. Now, if $q \leq p$, by the inexhaustible P.0, $q \cap p = q$. In this case, consequently, $\mathbf{E}(y \lceil q) = q$, and therefore $(y \lceil q) \in \mathbf{F}A(q)$. Finally, if $q \leq p$, every element of $\mathbf{F}A(p)$ localized on q belongs to $\mathbf{F}A(q)$. Positing that $\phi_q(y) = y \lceil q$, we get the commutative diagram below:

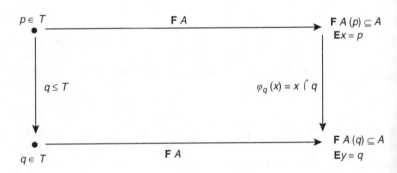

We will verify that the functor $\mathbf{F}A$ is endowed with some very remarkable properties. In fact, it harbours the possibility of a synthesis of existential analysis. It enacts what, following the topologists, we could call a recollement (or sticking back together) of transcendental analysis.

To forge ahead, let's further topologize our examination of the transcendental. To do this, we will take the elements of T from a different vantage point than the one of their strict belonging to T. We will grasp them in their synthetic, or enveloping, function. Recall that, in Sections 1 and 3 of Book II, we termed *territory* of p every part of T of which p is the envelope. The set of the territories of p is written as follows: $\{\Theta / \Theta \subseteq T$ and $p = \Sigma\Theta\}$. A territory, Θ, is that whose global appearing p is capable of measuring synthetically.

Our problem is then the following: can one synthesize an existential analysis which is carried out on the basis of a territory in T? This is the moment in the analysis when we reascend, for instance, from a set of the measures of combat capacity towards the military units that effectively appear in the battle. Let's suppose that a territory, Θ, has been fixed for p. Let $(A, \mathbf{Id})$ be an object and $\mathbf{F}A$ the transcendental functor of this object. To each element q of the territory ($q \in \Theta$) corresponds an existential stratum of the object A, such that $\mathbf{F}A(q) = \{x / \mathbf{E}x = q\}$. We could say that the functor associates to the territory Θ a collection of parts of the object, a collection each member of which, $\mathbf{F}A(q)$, is homogeneous in terms of its degree of appearing (or of existence).

We wish to pass analytically from this collection of parts of A to a collection of elements of A, in such a way that a part of the object is associated to the territory Θ. This part would in some sense be the projection of territory Θ into the very being of the object, with the added virtue that each element of the projection would represent a degree of existence. To put it in other terms, given an element q of the territory, we wish to select in $\mathbf{F}A(q)$ *one* element x_q of A, such that $\mathbf{E}x_q = q$ (or $x_q \in \mathbf{F}A(q)$). As q traverses the territory Θ, the collection of x_q's thereby selected would be a part of A 'representative' of the territory in terms of existential analysis, since all the x_q's have different degrees of existence. This is what we did when, treating the object 'centre of the Persian army' according to the functor, we chose a 'typical' element of a given combat capacity: the chariots rather than the elephants, the Hyrcanian cavalry rather than the archers and so on. The territory is thus 'projected' onto the object.

Since Θ is a territory for p ($p = \Sigma\Theta$), the analytical projection is only faithful if it is completed by a synthesis that takes place around p, or on the basis of p. But what is the transcendental projection of p? It is the functor $\mathbf{F}A$ applied to p, meaning that part of A, written $\mathbf{F}A(p)$, which brings together all the elements of A whose degree of existence is p. Here too we want to relate the association of a part of A, $\mathbf{F}A(p)$, to p (which is the synthesis of territory Θ), to the association of a single element of A to p.

This element must operate synthetically with regard to all the x_q's, which represent in A the territory Θ.

If we solve this twofold problem:

- the selection of the x_q's representing the elements of the territory Θ (analysis);
- the determination a single element $\varepsilon \in \mathbf{F}A(p)$ which takes a collectivizing position with regard to the x_q's (synthesis);

we will have truly achieved the transcendental thinking of the object from a topological point of view (p and its territories).

In terms of synthesis, this idea clearly follows from the examination of the diagram given earlier. In effect, the correlation between $\mathbf{F}A(p)$ and $\mathbf{F}A(q)$ rests entirely on the function ϕ, which associates $y \lceil q$ to $y \in \mathbf{F}A(p)$. Let's suppose that our analytical (or representative) problem has been resolved—an element x_q of $\mathbf{F}A(q)$ is associated to each element q of a territory Θ. Our synthetic problem will be resolved if we find in $\mathbf{F}A(p)$ a single element ε such that, for every $q \in \Theta$ and every element x_q of $\mathbf{F}A(q)$ associated to q, we get $\varepsilon \lceil q = x_q$. In other words, we want it to be the case that when one scans territory Θ—when $\mathbf{F}A(q)$ is associated to every element q and an element x_q has been selected in each part $\mathbf{F}A(q)$—then, for the invariable element ε, we get, for every q, $\varepsilon \lceil q = x_q$, and furthermore ε is the envelope of the x_q's for the ontological order $<$. As a result, ε guarantees a comprehensive grasp of the unity of the multiple qua being-there in terms of localization, since $\varepsilon \lceil q = x_q$; in terms of compatibility, since $x_q \ddagger x_{q'}$; in terms of order, since $x_q < \varepsilon$.

This means that ε carries out in A the recollection of the x_q's, just as, in the transcendental, p carries out the recollection of the territory Θ. Analysis and synthesis are projected, via the functor, from the transcendental into the object. We saw how in the battle-world the element 'scythed chariots' occupied the synthetic position. It was the ε-term of the object 'centre of the Persian army'.

Let us now suppose that, in the general case, we can equally resolve the problem—there exists a synthetic ε. For $q \in \Theta$ and $q' \in \Theta$, we have selected x_q and $x_{q'}$ in $\mathbf{F}A(q)$ and $\mathbf{F}A(q')$. By definition, we know that

$$\mathbf{E}x_q = q, \ \mathbf{E}x_{q'} = q', \ \varepsilon \lceil q = x_q, \ \varepsilon \lceil q' = x_{q'}$$

But then, using a minor lemma (lemma B) demonstrated in the appendix, we get the following:

$$x_q \ \lceil \ \mathbf{E}x_{q'} = (\varepsilon \ \lceil \ q) \ \lceil \ q' = \varepsilon \ \lceil \ (q \cap q') \qquad \text{lemma } B$$

$$x_{q'} \ \lceil \ \mathbf{E}x_q = (\varepsilon \ \lceil \ q') \ \lceil \ q = \varepsilon \ \lceil \ (q' \cap q) \qquad \text{lemma } B$$

$$x_q \ \lceil \ \mathbf{E}x_{q'} = x_{q'} \ \lceil \ \mathbf{E}x_q \qquad p \cap q = q \cap p$$

$$x_q \ddagger x_{q'} \ (x_q \text{ and } x_{q'} \text{ are compatible}) \qquad \text{def. of } \ddagger$$

This point is crucial—if the synthesis of a territory Θ by a point p of the transcendental can be projected into the object, then the elements $x_{q'}$, which 'represent' the transcendental in the object, are compatible in pairs.

Let's recall (Proposition P.3) a more algebraic definition of compatibility:

$$\mathbf{E}x_q \cap \mathbf{E}x_{q'} = \mathbf{Id}(x_q, x_{q'})$$

This means that the degree of existence 'common' to x_q and to $x_{q'}$—that is their maximal 'common' existence (the conjunction of $\mathbf{E}x_q$ and $\mathbf{E}x_{q'}$)—cannot exceed the measure of their difference. Being compatible means that two elements coexist just as much as, and no more than, they differ. It is only on this condition of compatibility that we can hope fully to solve the problem of the transcendental projection, or to accomplish the retroaction on pure being of the synthetic capacity of the transcendental. Similarly, we remarked that the synthetic value of the element 'scythed chariots' presupposed a rule of compatibility; the one implied by Darius' battle-plan.

Let us now reformulate our question.

Let Θ be a territory for p. We will call 'projective representation' of Θ the association, to every element $q \in \Theta$, of an element x_q of $\mathbf{F}A(q)$ (therefore of an element x_q of A such that $\mathbf{E}x_q = q$). We will say that a projective representation is 'coherent' if, for every pair $q \in \Theta$ and $q' \in \Theta$, we get $x_q \ddagger x_{q'}$ (x_q and $x_{q'}$ are compatible).

We ask whether, under these conditions, it is possible to find in $\mathbf{F}A(p)$ a single element ε (hence $\mathbf{E}\varepsilon = p$) which takes a synthetic position for a given coherent representation. This means that for every $q \in \Theta$, the localization of ε in q is x_q (hence $\varepsilon \ \lceil \ q = x_q$), and that ε is the envelope of the x_q's (for $<$) just as p is the envelope of the $q \in \Theta$ (for $\leq$).

The answer is positive. The proposition that follows is a kind of summing up of all of our efforts, and its philosophical meaning, which this scholium has simply sketched, is pretty much inexhaustible. It conveys the complete form of the ontological constitution of worlds.

Complete form of the onto-logy of worlds

Let A be a set which ontologically underlies an object $(A, \mathbf{Id})$ in a world $\mathbf{m}$ whose transcendental is T. We write $\mathbf{F}A$ the transcendental functor of A, which associates to every element p of T the subset of A composed of all the elements of A whose degree of existence is p, that is $\mathbf{F}A(p) = \{x \mid x \in A \text{ and } \mathbf{E}x = p\}$. We call territory of p, and write as Θ, every subset of T of which p is the envelope, that is $p = \Sigma\Theta$. Finally, we call coherent projective representation of Θ the association, to every element q of Θ, of an element of $\mathbf{F}A(q)$, say x_q (we obviously have $\mathbf{E}x_q = q$) which possesses the following property: for $q \in \Theta$ and $q' \in \Theta$, the corresponding elements of $\mathbf{F}A(q)$ and $\mathbf{F}A(q')$, x_q and $x_{q'}$, are compatible with one another, that is $x_q \ddagger x_{q'}$. Under these conditions, there always exists only one element ε of $\mathbf{F}A(p)$—p being the envelope of Θ—which is such that, for every $q \in \Theta$, the localization of ε on q is uniformly equal to the element x_q of the coherent representation, that is $\varepsilon \lceil q = x_q$. This element ε is the real synthesis of the subset constituted by the x_q's, in the sense that it is their envelope for the onto-logical order-relation written as $<$.

Let's suppose that there exists a coherent projection of a territory Θ for p, and let's name this projection P. Since the elements of P (the x_q's that correspond to the elements q of Θ) are compatible in pairs (by the definition of coherence), there exists an envelope ε of P for the relation $<$, as we established in Proposition P.7.

1. To begin with, we show that $\mathbf{E}\varepsilon = p$, and that therefore, as required, $\varepsilon \in \mathbf{F}A(p)$.

We saw earlier (it was the content of lemma e(Ψ)) that $\mathbf{E}\varepsilon = \Sigma\{\mathbf{E}x_q / x_q \in P\}$. But the definition of a projective representation demands that $\mathbf{E}x_q = q$. Therefore $\mathbf{E}\varepsilon = \Sigma\{q \mid x_q \in P\}$. And since to each $q \in \Theta$ there corresponds only one x_q, and if $q \neq q'$ we get $x_q \neq x_{q'}$, it turns out that $\mathbf{E}\varepsilon = \Sigma\{q \mid q \in \Theta\}$. But since p is supposed to have Θ as its territory, we have $\Sigma\{q \mid q \in \Theta\} = p$. And therefore, when all is said and done, $\mathbf{E}\varepsilon = p$.

2. We then show that, for every $q \in \Theta$, $\varepsilon \lceil q = x_q$.

Since ε is the envelope of P, for every $x_q \in P$ we get $x_q < \varepsilon$. But the topological definition of $<$ demands that $x_q = \varepsilon \lceil \mathbf{E}x_q$, and since $\mathbf{E}x_q = q$ (because $x_q \in \mathbf{F}A(q)$), it turns out that $\varepsilon \lceil q = x_q$.

So there does indeed exist a single element ε such that $\mathbf{E}\varepsilon = p$; its localization q is, for every q, identical to the selected element x_q, whatever the selection may be, provided that the selected elements are compatible in pairs. To put it in different terms, every coherent projective representation of a transcendental territory Θ is synthesized in the pure multiple that underlies the appearance of the object by a unique element, whose degree of existence is equal to the transcendental element p of which Θ is the territory. Mathematicians, those unconscious ontologists, will say that the transcendental functor $\mathbf{F}A$ is a 'sheaf'.

The being of the object is internally organized, on the basis of the existential analysis, by syntheses that correspond to the transcendental envelopes (to the territories). This can also be expressed as follows: there exists an intelligible correlation from the transcendental towards the pure multiplicities whose being-there it regulates, the sheaf. Therefore, considering the world as a whole, we have the category of all the sheaves that go from the transcendental T towards all the objects of type $(A, \mathbf{Id})$, which are there in this world. This is among the most remarkable mathematical structures that saw the light in the 1950s and 1960s. This structure is called the 'Grothendieck topos'. A world, as a site of being-there, is a Grothendieck topos.

BOOK IV

Greater Logic, 3. Relation

Introduction

This book completes the Greater Logic, and thus what can be called the analytic part of *Logics of Worlds*. By 'analytic' I mean that the inquiry bears only on the transcendental laws of being-there, to the extent that it belongs to the being of being-there to appear or to manifest itself. It saves for later the problem of a genuine change, that is to say the possibility not only of a worldly localization of multiplicities, but of a break, a discontinuity in the protocol of the appearance of beings (or of their existence).

The analytic can also be defined as the theory of worlds, the elucidation of the most abstract laws of that which constitutes a world qua general form of appearing. It completes the mathematics of multiple-being with the logic of being-there. We may therefore also conclude that the analytic is nothing other than the *exposition* of the logic of worlds. In this regard, though it furnishes them with the objective domain of their emergence, it cannot yet attain the comprehension of the terms that singularize the materialist dialectic: truths as exceptions, and subjects as the active forms of these exceptions. That is why the Greater Logic is placed between the formal theory of the subject (metaphysics) and its material theory: the thinking of bodies (physics).

In our first step, the exposition of the objective laws that pertain to any world whatever set out the operations that make it possible for a multiplicity to come to being-there, or to be required to appear. That is the transcendental logic, properly so-called. We then constructed the concept of what comes to be as existent under transcendental conditions. That is the concept of the object, insofar as it designates the onto-logical conjunction: its support in being (onto-) is a multiplicity; its appearing, its worldly logic (-logical) is a value of intensity of appearance, or a value of existence. Lastly, the analytic of the object, considered in the subtlety of its atomic composition, comes down to four statements:

– What exists in a world is a pure multiple.
– That a multiple exists is nothing but the contingent indexing of this multiple on the transcendental. Therefore, existence is not.
– Nonetheless, having to exist (or to appear) retroactively endows being with a new consistency which is distinct from its own multiple dissemination.
– Accordingly, the non-being of existence means that it is otherwise than according to its being that being is. It is precisely the being of an object.

The object exhausts the dialectic of being and existence, which is also that of being and appearing, or that of being-there, or finally that of extensive (or mathematical) multiplicity and intensive (or logical) multiplicity. To complete the construction of the concept of 'world', we simply have to think what is given 'between' the objects. This is the problem of the co-existence in the same world (or according to the same transcendental) of a collection of objects.

This problem has a properly ontological or purely extensive facet: 'how many' objects are there in a world? What is the type of being, and therefore the type of multiplicity, of the beings that co-appear in a world? This question has haunted philosophy ever since its first tentative cosmological steps. It seems that the ancient atomists, from Democritus to Lucretius, had glimpsed the possibility of an infinite plurality of worlds. It is even possible that, under the name of 'void', they ascribed infinity to the 'ground' of being-there. Conversely, it is clear that for Aristotle the arrangement of the world is essentially finite. When it comes to the extension of the world, can we decide between the finite and the infinite? The problem persists at the heart of the Kantian dialectic, which solves it in the direction of undecidability: nothing allows the understanding to choose between the thesis of the world's essential finitude and the antithesis of its infinity in time and space. In what follows it will be clear that we reject the critical thesis of undecidability. We will propose a demonstration, not just of the infinity of every world, but of this infinity's type: the cardinal of a world is an inaccessible cardinal.

The other facet of the problem of the co-existence of objects is transcendental, or logical: what are objects for one another? Or, what is a relation?

Here, our investigation follows a cautious and somewhat restrictive path. Since the logic of objects is nothing but the legislation of appearing, it is not in effect possible to accept that relations between objects have a power of being. The definition of a relation must be strictly dependent on that of objects, not the other way around. On this point, we are in agreement with Wittgenstein who, having defined the 'state of affairs' as a 'combination of objects', posits that 'if a thing can occur in a state of affairs, the possibility of the state of affairs must be written into the thing itself'. In other words, if an object enters into combination with others, this combination is, if not implied, in any case regulated by objects. We will see that in order to obtain a clear concept of relation, it suffices to specify its dependence on objects: a relation is a connection between objective multiplicities—a function— that creates nothing in the register of intensities of existence, or in that of atomic localizations, which is not already prescribed by the regime of appearance of these multiplicities (by the objects whose ontological support they are). It is on this basis that the question of the universality of a relation poses itself. We will say that a relation is universally exposed in a world if it is clearly 'visible' from the interior of this world, in a sense which will be specified below.

We re-encounter here a classic Platonic problem. The universal part of a sensible object is its participation in the Idea. I translate this as follows: the ontological part of an object is the pure, mathematically thinkable, multiplicity that underlies it. But what could we possibly mean by the universality of a relation? This is the question treated by Plato in *The Sophist*, a question which he's forced to tackle once the figure of the sophist is identified as the master of inexact relations.

In general, we moderns are governed by the Kantian answer to this question, including in the guise of linguistic relativism. This answer is oriented towards universality as the subjective constitution of experience (the transcendental as conceived by critical idealism). Or, for the 'post-moderns', towards the negation of every universality, in favour of the free competition of sense-producing devices, namely 'cultural' ones. Obviously, this Kantian answer and its avatars cannot satisfy us Platonists. The transcendental is not subjective, nor is it as such universal (there are multiple worlds, multiple transcendentals). As for terminating the universal in favour of the democratic parity of language-games, it's out of the question.

Plato's solution is to allow the existence, as 'supreme genera', of Ideas whose intelligible content is relational, like the Idea of the Same or the Idea of the Other. This is a fertile solution. It has guided us in our presentation of the great operators of every transcendental evaluation of being-there (conjunction, envelope, etc.). But when it comes to relations between objects, or intra-worldly relations, we cannot ground their universality elsewhere than in the world in which the objects linked by these relations appear. There are no 'supreme genera' to guarantee, in something like a World of worlds, the universality of a worldly relation. But there is a way out: to extract the formal conditions that must be obeyed by a relation in order for it be considered as universally established in a determinate world. Metaphorically speaking, what this requires is the existence of a privileged point of the world from which this relation is observable, a point that is itself observable, to the extent that it makes visible the relation of every other supposed point from which one could also observe this relation. In other words, a relation is universal if its intra-worldly visibility is itself visible. It is then effectively impossible to cast doubt on its existence. Within the full extension of the world, it is a relation *for all*.

These considerations allow us to establish one of the most striking results of the analytic of worlds. We will demonstrate that every relation is universal. More precisely, we will demonstrate that the infinity of a world (its ontological characteristic) entails the universality of relations (its logical characteristic). The extensive law of multiple being subsumes the logical form of relations. Being has the last word. It already did at the level of atomic logic, where we affirmed, under the name of 'postulate of materialism', that every atom is real. That is why the universality of relations—which is itself not a postulate but a consequence—is accorded the status of 'second constitutive thesis of materialism'.

In this Book, the argument culminates in the identification, in every object, of an elementary trace of the contingency of being-there. This is the theory of the proper inexistent of an object: there is an element of the multiple underlying every object whose value of existence in the world is nil. Its link to the foregoing discussion is that every relation between objects links together the inexistent of the one to the inexistent of the other. Relations, which conserve existence, also conserve inexistence. We will see in Book V that the point of the inexistent is the measure of what can happen to a world.

SECTION 1
Worlds and Relations

---

1. THE DOUBLE DETERMINATION OF A WORLD:
ONTOLOGY AND LOGIC

On 24 July 1534, Jacques Cartier plants a cross on the spot where the small town of Gaspé, at the far east of Quebec, will later be built. He does so as the mandatory, or lieutenant, of King François I. He's obviously taking possession of something, but of what? We have to say of a world, all the more in that Cartier knew almost nothing about it—isolated, lost and believing himself to have sailed towards the shores of Asia. Four hundred and forty-two years later, we witness the victory in Canada's provincial elections of a party which has taken the name of the world that Cartier opened (and closed) with an essential sign. It is in fact René Levesque, leader of the 'Parti Québécois' (the PQ), who becomes Prime Minister. And, four years later, in 1980, his government asks the inhabitants of Quebec to grant it the power to negotiate with the federal Canadian authorities over the 'sovereignty' of Quebec. Do said inhabitants all consider themselves as 'Quebecois', in the meaning given to this term by the PQ, that is as the atomic constituents of entities all of which are part of the same world, the one that Cartier opened and closed as a Francophone and Catholic space? That's the whole question. In fact, in 1980 a clear majority votes 'no'. The demand that Quebec receive the statist dignity of the world which it declares itself to be is rejected in the name of another world which has already been validated, the Canadian federation with its Anglophone majority.

But the symbolic 'worlding' of Quebec already has a long history, from the bloody revolt of 1837 (the Patriotic Party of Pamineau against the English) to the riots against the war of 1914–18, from the admission of the French language in certain official documents (1848) to the law of 1977 which makes French into the only official language of Quebec, from the terrorism of the Front de libération du Québec (assassination of the minister Pierre Laporte in 1970) to the indecisive result of the 1995 referendum (independence is rejected by just 50.6% of voters). It must be admitted that the thinking of this tumultuous history is that of a becoming-world, or of a world-in-becoming. Under this name, 'Quebec', whether it be called a 'province' or a 'nation', there lies a complex and mobile figure, whose internal consistency authorizes that it be regarded as a world.

What then are the criteria for this identification? Objective phenomenology distinguishes right away between two types:

1. There are intrinsic determinations. In the case of the world 'Quebec', the majority use (more than 80% today) of the French language, territorial unity, population statistics (7.5 million inhabitants, a little more than 8% Anglophones, etc.), the extreme exiguousness of the populated area (90% of inhabitants on 2% of the territory), the riverine character of this area (concentrated around the Saint-Laurent), and an infinity of other possible predicates.

2. There are networks of relations. In the case of the world 'Quebec', first of all the antagonism between the Anglophone concentration of powers, economic as well as political and cultural, and the Francophone mass which is largely proletarian. But also—beneath this principal contradiction, as it were—the neo-colonial problem of the status of the aboriginal occupants, the 'Indians', as they were named by Cartier, who thought he had arrived in India. This problem is also manifest at the level of language, witness the opposition between the names of cities issued from the French colonial settlement (Sagnunay, Québec, Trois-Rivières, La Malboire. . .), with their provincial seventeenth-century air, and the wholly different linguistic provenance of the names of the towns of the great North, Kuujjuak, or Ivajivik, or those of the East where, beyond Baie-Corneau and Sept-Îles, we find Natasquan.

We can say that these relations (Anglo-French and French-Anglo-'Indian') make up a significant part of the transcendental regulation of what it is to be 'from Quebec'. It is they who already gave their unique character to Anglo-French clashes, as each of the camps tried to enlist 'Indian' groups to its service, the Hurons on the French side, the Iroquois on the English.

In a very broad sense, we will say that there is a 'world' to the extent that it is possible to identify a configuration of multiple-beings who appear 'there' and of (transcendentally regulated) relations between these beings. A world is ontologically assignable by that which appears, and logically assignable by the relations between apparents.

It will be objected that this double determination is ultimately that of being-there in general. What else is required in order to identify a world? The objection is pertinent. We need to take a step back and tackle the analysis anew.

In Section 1 of Book II, we proposed a formal definition of what a world is for a relation. The central idea is very simple: if an object is of the world and another object entertains with it the relation in question, then the second object is also of the world. We could, for example, say that with regard to the relation between an individual and a couple, designated by 'being a child of this couple', Quebec is a world, insofar as the individual will be Quebecois like his parents. Here 'relation' does not have a particular link to the transcendental, for a very simple reason: we do not yet have any idea of what a relation between objects is, if we take 'object' in its strictest meaning, namely as a multiple-being and its transcendental indexing. In fact, we must think two types of relations, in order to secure an intelligible answer to the question of what a world is:

a. the constitutive relations (or operations) of the theory of the pure multiple, or theory of being-qua-being; in effect, every world is constructed on the basis of multiple-beings, and it is important to know under what conditions these multiple-beings are globally exposed to constituting the being of a world;

b. the relations between apparents of the same world, that is to say the relations between objects.

Consider for instance 'our' galaxy (the one to which the sun and its system of planets belong). Under what relational parameters can we consider this celestial spiral 100,000 light-years in diameter (1 billion billion kilometres) as a world? After all, let's not forget that this unit of existence, as numerically considerable as it may be, with its (as a low estimate) 100 billion stars, is still only a small region of the 'local supercluster', which itself subsumes—what poetry in the unlimited!—the three clusters of Virgo, as well as those of the Cup, Leo and the Hunting Dogs.

The conditions of consistency of the galaxy as world are obviously of two kinds:

– One can unambiguously assign a given star to this galaxy and not another. Thus, the star closest to the sun, Proxima Centauri, is certainly of the same world as the sun. In a general sense, one can describe the multiple figures that compose this galaxy: billions of stars (the oldest towards the centre, the youngest in the spiralling arms), a halo of gas and dust, other dispersed constituents. This is a rough enumeration, tied to the multiple-composition of the galaxy. This enumeration is oriented in particular towards a distribution of masses (70% for the stars, 30% for the rest).

– One can think the relations, internal to galactic appearing, that link to one another the objects (stars of all types, gas clouds, planets. . .) which are transcendentally assigned to deploy themselves there, in this galaxy. These relations in their turn determine a certain differentiation and consistency for the world in question. Thus, the galaxy has a centre (the bulb, denser than the rest of the disc, and the seat of very complex movements of expansion of gases) and arms with charming names, like the main spiral arm, called Sagittarius, the internal arm of the Swan, or the external arm of Perseus. The ensemble of the disc, bulb and arms turns around the centre, according to the principles of differential rotation (the rotation speed depends on the distance from the centre). On the basis of these relative differentiations, it is possible, for example, to account for why the sun, and 'us' with it, makes a complete orbit of the galaxy, that is the orbit of 'our' world, in around 240 million years.

It is clear that two questions must orient our conceptual exposition of what a world is. First, in what operational framework should we situate the ontological enumeration of the multiple-beings summoned to appear in a determinate world? Second, what really is a relation between objects? In short, what is the appearing of a connection in appearing?

2. EVERY WORLD IS INFINITE, AND ITS TYPE OF INFINITY IS INACCESSIBLE

The statement 'the ontological measure of any world whatever is an infinite of an inaccessible type' will only be clearly understood and demonstrated in the formal exposition. Objective phenomenology can nevertheless shed light on what is at stake. Take Quebec, provisionally assumed as a world, and suppose that we have at our disposal an identifiable collection of multiple-beings which partake in the composition of this world, for instance, the cities of Montreal, Trois-Rivières and Gaspé. It seems clear that the neighbourhoods that make up these cities are also part of the Quebec-world, which can be put as follows: the elements of a multiple-being that ontologically underlies a world also ontologically underlie that world. Supposing that a street in Montreal is predominantly Anglophone, it will still be an (Anglophone) street of Quebec. Similarly, if we think that the galaxy, constituted as a world, is in the main composed of stars—that is of nuclear plants burning hydrogen to turn it into helium—we nonetheless must admit that the stars' satellites, 'cold' planets like our Earth, are also part of the multiple-being of this world. This property has a scientific name: a world is transitive, in the sense that an element of an element of the world is still of this world. Even better: given a multiple-being of a world, the collection constituted by the elements of its elements is also an element of that world. We can see this if we consider, for example, the set of all the inhabitants of all the cities in Quebec, which is the element 'urban population' of Quebec. Or all the elements of all the 'stellar systems' (stars, planets, asteroids, comets, trapped gases. . .) that compose the galaxy. These elements set forth the galactic composition in a tableau: stars of population I or II, red giants, white or brown dwarves, black holes, neutron stars, gaseous planets, gas clouds of nebulae, etc. This tableau names the diversity of the world as such and registers that this diversity, whatever the world, belongs to it. In other words, if you disseminate an (ontological) component of a world by examining the elements of its elements, the result of this dissemination, when counted as one (collected in its multiple-being), is still a component of the same world. This is the first fundamental property which pertains to the operative extension of a world thought in its being: a world makes immanent the dissemination of that which composes it. The world does not have a 'beneath' that would be external to it, a sort of pre-worldly matter. It is only a world to the extent that what composes its composition lies within its composition.

But a world doesn't have a heterogeneous 'above' either. If you bring together all the parts of a temporal moment of Quebec, as motley as this collection may be—Indians, Parti Québecois, blizzards, Anglophones, sled dogs, hydroelectric plants, maple syrup, Montreal's universal expo. . .— you get a cross-section of the complete state of Quebec and therefore what is obviously a part of the world 'Quebec'. Likewise, the parts of the solar system, including lunar attraction as a cause of tides, or the ceaseless natural decomposition of millions of cadavers of living beings, or the mind-boggling complications of Saturn's system of rings, together make up a local (and infinite) state of the galaxy, attributable as such to the world that the galaxy is. In other words, if you totalize the parts of an (ontological) component of a world, counting as one the system of these parts, you get an entity of the same world. This is the second fundamental property with regard to the operative extension of a world thought in its being: a world makes immanent every local totalization of the parts of that which composes it. Its state (the count as one of the subsets of the beings that are there) is itself in the world, and not transcendent to it. Just as there is no ultimate formless matter, so there is no principle of the state of affairs.

Neither matter (beneath) nor principle (above), a world absorbs all the multiplicities that can intelligibly be said to be internal to it.

The crucial thing to note is that this property requires the actual infinity of every world. If a world were finite, it would follow, first of all, that all the beings which enter into its composition would themselves be finite. For if one among them possessed an infinity of elements, since these elements are also elements of the world, the world would have to be infinite. For example, you can say that urban Quebec is a finite world, since it comprises, let's say, a dozen important cities. But then none of these cities can have an infinite population (whatever the concrete meaning of this expression may be) since, by virtue of the interiority to the world of every dissemination, the inhabitants of the cities are themselves also elements of the Quebec-world.

Let's suppose that world contains, on the stage of appearing, only a finite number of apparents (this number may of course be very large, for instance, 100 billion stars for a galaxy). Let us now choose one among the multiple-beings of the world which have the greatest number of elements. Let's call this element 'Betelgeuse', with reference to the giant star of the same name, which is 1,600 times greater than the sun. Of course Betelgeuse, as the reasoning in the previous paragraph shows, cannot have more elements than the world. It is only the largest finite being of the world. But the second property of worlds stops us from leaving it at that. This property tells us that the set of parts of Betelgeuse is still an element of the world. Now—this is one of Cantor's fundamental theorems—the set of parts of Betelgeuse is 'more numerous' than Betelgeuse itself. Whence a contradiction: contrary to what we assumed, Betelgeuse is not one of the biggest beings of the (supposedly finite) world.

That a finite collection has more parts than elements is easily intuited. If a Quebecois couple has four children (who are therefore all Quebecois)— let's say Luc, Mathieu, Marc and Jean—you can effortlessly see that

Luc-and-Mathieu, Luc-and-Jean, Luc-and-Marc, Mathieu-and-Marc, Mathieu-and-Jean, Marc-and-Jean, already makes six subsets which differ from the filiative quartet. When you pass from a multiple to its parts, you augment the number. And if you remain in the same world, this obviously means that no being of this world has a maximal number of elements. Ultimately, this forbids the world itself from being finite. For if you take the parts of Betelgeuse, then the parts of these parts, and so on, you create an ascending series of numbers, which will perforce surpass the (finite) number assigned to the world. That is impossible, since every composition of a being of the world is itself of the world.

The principle 'neither sub-sistence nor transcendence' ultimately results in the necessity that every world be ontologically infinite. Of course, there are 100 billion stars in the galaxy and 7.5 million inhabitants in Quebec, and these numbers, albeit noteworthy, are finite. This simply means that, to the extent that they are considered as ontologically deployed and transcendentally differentiated worlds, the galaxy and Quebec cannot in any way be reduced to their stars or their inhabitants. That much is suggested by the simple consideration of its subatomic legislation after the big-bang (or after the formation of galaxies, one billion years later), for the former, and its tumultuous pre- and post-colonial history, for the latter.

This infinite is not any infinite whatever. It is an infinite of the inaccessible type, in the following sense: you cannot construct its concept through any of the operations of ontology, such as these may be redeployed in the world. In other words, this infinite results neither from dissemination nor from the totalization of parts of a lesser quantity; since their results remain immanent to the world, the operations that concern the beneath (disseminated elementary matter) and the above (state of subsets) cannot attain or construct the degree of infinity of this world. The extension of a world remains inaccessible to the operations that open up its multiple-being and allow it to radiate. Like the Hegelian absolute, a world is the unfolding of its own infinity. But, unlike that Absolute, the world cannot internally construct the measure or the concept of the infinite that it is.

This impossibility is what assures that a world is closed, without it thereby being representable as a Whole from the interior of the scene of appearance that it constitutes. A world is closed for the operations that set out the being-qua-being of what appears within it: transitivity, dissemination, totalization of parts. Accordingly, if I apply, from the interior of a world, the laws of the expansive construction of the multiple to the multiple-beings that are transcendentally indexed in this world, I never leave it. But this does not mean that, for one who exists in this world, or who enjoys a non-nil self-identity in it, the world is totalizable, since the 'number of the world'—its type of infinity, and therefore this world itself, as thought in its multiple-being—remains inaccessible to the operations of ontology. In this sense, a world remains globally open for every local figure of its immanent composition. It is with good reason that looking at the night sky, man—that resident of the galaxy always prone to overrate his own existence—beholds the limitless opening of his world in all directions. But it is also with good reason that, informed by science, which involves ontology properly so-called (mathematics), he can say, but not really see, that the Milky Way is the galaxy viewed from its side, and that the constellations harbour, as initially undetectable traces, the radiance of other worlds. This paradoxical property of the ontology of worlds—their operational closure and immanent opening—is the proper concept of their infinity. We will sum it up by saying: every world is affected by an inaccessible closure.

3. WHAT IS A RELATION BETWEEN OBJECTS?

A relation, within appearing, is necessarily subordinated to the transcendental intensity of the apparents that it binds together. Being-there—and not relation—makes the being of appearing. This is what we could call the axiom of relations. I say 'axiom' because of the intuitive, or phenomenological, manifestness of its content: relation draws its being from what it binds together. The most rigorous formulation of the axiom could then be the following: a relation creates neither existence nor difference. Let's recall that an object, the unit of counting of appearing, is the couple formed by a multiple-being and its transcendental indexing (or function of appearing) in a determinate world. We will then call 'relation' between two objects of a given world every function of the elements of the one towards the elements of the other, such that it preserves existences and safeguards or augments identities (that is, maintains or diminishes differences).

Let's take an example from contemporary Quebec. Consider, as objects of this world, on the one hand what's left of the Indian community of the Mohawks, on the other the various echelons of government administration. In 1990, the 'Oka Crisis' establishes an intense relation between these two objects: the Mohawks barricade the site of a future golf course which would encroach on a portion of what they consider as their ancestral territory. The revolt takes a violent turn. It will feature the intervention of the Quebec Provincial Police, as well as the army, gun battles, the death of a policeman, a number of wounded. It is a decisive question to know what appeared there and constituted the relation. Should we say that the revolt of the Mohawks against the municipality of Oka, and subsequently against the provincial and federal organs of the state, is the appearance of a previously absent intensity of existence of the Indians in the Quebec-world? Or should we on the contrary contend that in terms of existence the relation only proposes that which, invisible for those who neglected it, was nonetheless a component of an object of the world? Truth be told, this question will only be completely resolved once we will see how an event changes the transcendental arrangement [*dispositif*] of a world. But a relation as such is precisely not an event. It does not transform the transcendental evaluations; it presupposes them, insofar as it too appears in the world. We will therefore maintain that the Mohawk revolt, rigorously conceived as the relation between the object 'the Mohawks' and the object 'Quebecois administration', only elicits the appearance of objective existences that are already there, even if—and this is one of the reasons for the revolt—this existence is minimized or belittled by its official counterparts. Equally, we will say that the internal differentiations deployed by the violent incidents and their outcome—on the side of the Mohawks as well as on that of the different tendencies within the administration—are legible on the basis of the relation, but are not created by it. It is not because we move from objects to relations that we can forget the proper function of appearing: to localize multiples according to a transcendental being-there, and not to bring forth multiple-being as such.

The same goes if we examine the relations between a singular object of the galaxy—say the sun—and other objects of the same world. If we write, for example, that the sun is situated 28,000 light-years away from the centre of the galaxy, or on the edges of the major spiralling arm, we define relations between this particular star and other apparents of the galaxy. But these relations can only specify the modalities of the being-there of the sun; they constitute neither its intensity of existence nor its internal protocol of differentiation. That is why, moreover, it makes sense to say that they are relations between a given object and another (the sun on one side, the galactic bulb or the spiralling arms on the other). What's more, the physics that underlies astrophysics does not stop referring relations back to ontic parameters. Its most burning current problem is without a doubt that of understanding gravitational force—a typical example of the relation between the objects of a world—in terms of the subatomic composition of these objects. And whether we are dealing with Lavoisier's assertion 'nothing is lost, nothing is created', or the principles of thermodynamics, physics does not cease declaring that relations and their laws are not themselves creative, either of existence or of difference. The multiple is always what is given.

In the end, the definition of a relation of appearing is essentially negative.

A relation is an oriented connection from one object towards another, on condition that the existential value of an element of the first object is never inferior to the value which, through this connection, corresponds to it in the second object, and that to the transcendental measure of an identity in the one there corresponds in the other a transcendental measure which also cannot be inferior.

The formal exposition will show in a particularly clear fashion that this negative definition is a conservative definition. A relation in appearing largely conserves the entire atomic logic of objects. This is quite natural. Atomic logic expresses in the very being of apparents—in objects—the conditions of their appearing. Once it has itself appeared, a link between two objects is only identifiable to the extent that the intelligibility of the objective being of what is linked remains legible, including in terms of the relation involved.

For example, that is how the Mohawk revolt lays out on the barricades atomic components of the object 'Mohawk people': singular individuals who declare, by their very presence and action, that their existence in Quebec is that of an Indian community, and that their identity to other Mohawks is consequently extremely strong. It is clear that this atomic logic—woven out of compatibilities, order and real syntheses—is activated, but not produced, by the Oka incident. Accordingly, it is this logic which will structure in the last instance the relationship to the administrations, the police and the army, and which will ultimately be projected into very delicate negotiations.

If we wish to move to a positive definition of relations, we will say: a relation between two objects is a function that conserves the atomic logic of these objects, and in particular the real synthesis which affects their being on the basis of their appearing. It is this definition in terms of conservation or invariants which we will adopt in the formal exposition.

4. LOGICAL COMPLETENESS OF A WORLD

We established above that a world is ontologically marked by an inaccessible closure. This point concerns multiple-beings as such, not objects. In the purely logical register of relations between objects, does there exist an equivalent 'closing' principle? This presupposes, once again, an operational network which allows us to say that, in a rationally defined sense, one 'does not leave' appearing, that is to say its transcendental organization, that is to say the world. We must therefore examine what becomes of the relationship between relations and the world. Or, we must think the Relation between the world—which is made up of objects and relations between objects—and relations. Broadly speaking, the logical completeness of the world will obtain if it makes sense to say that the Relation between relations is itself in the world.

On this point, Quebec will furnish us with a phenomenological metaphor. We took as our example of relation the revolt of the Mohawk Indians against the Quebecois administration over the planned construction of a golf course on their customary territory. If we consider the great emotion displayed by public opinion for the whole duration of the barricades at the golf site—two months of tensions and violent clashes—we can say that this relation, the 'Oka crisis', is itself linked to the Quebec-world in such a way that this internal visibility, expressed by the fervour of opinion, is totally immanent to this world. Not only does the direct relation between the Mohawk rebels and the Quebecois Provincial Police enjoy an objective status in the world, but the same can be said for the complex system of relations to this relation, manifest in the innumerable forms of information, taking sides, emotion, political decisions and so on. It is clear that a relation to the relation is both a relation to the objects and a relation to their connection. Thus, one Quebecois will establish with the object 'the Mohawks' a fraternal relationship of support, vituperating the intransigence of the authorities while taking a stance on the successive stages of the revolt. Another will shed bitter tears over the policeman killed in the gun battles and day after day will monitor the firmness of the government's stance over the site. If we consider these two Quebecois in turn as objects of the world, we see that they each entertain a relation to each of the objects linked together by the 'Oka incident' (the Indians and the cops, for instance) and, by the same token, a relation to this link itself, that is a relation to the relation.

The elementary figure of this arrangement is ultimately triangular. There are two initial objects, the relation that links them, and then the relation of a third object to the first two.

We will call such a triangle a diagram of the world.

If the two relations between the progressive citizen and the objects involved in the relation constitute a relation to the relation, it is because his opinion and reactions circulate through the whole triangle. Accordingly, the unconditional support for the Mohawks will entail, as the revolt progresses, a growing hostility towards the provincial authorities. This means that the trajectory 'support + Oka revolt' determines the intensity of the relation 'vituperation of the Quebecois administration'. As long as the Oka revolt lasts, whether we move from the citizen to the administration via the Mohawks or do so directly, we are always dealing with the same hostile subjective intensity. This can be put very simply: the triangular diagram is commutative. That is the fundamental abstract expression for a relation to a relation on the basis of an object. In the end, the commutative triangle above is the clear-cut expression of the subjective implication of the Quebecois citizen by the conjunctural relation which the Oka incident constituted in 1990. In this sense, it designates the co-appearance of this citizen and this relation in the Quebec-world.

Of course, a commutative triangle is an entirely elementary diagram. We can easily imagine more complex arrangements, where there is a relation to a complex of relations. Above, we invoked the figure of a reactionary Quebecois hostile to the Indians and favourable to police repression. This gives us the following diagram of the Quebec-world in 1990:

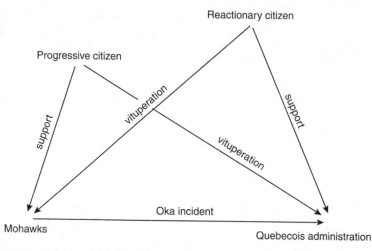

It is interesting that this diagram can be immediately completed, following the simplest laws of the world. For the progressive citizen will begin to vituperate the reactionary one, and vice versa. And this reciprocal vituperation will certainly be a relation, in that the existential intensities—the subjective political violence—will be conserved, together with the entire atomic logic of the two camps: the organizers of the opposing political positions, namely those who are superior in terms of the onto-logical relation, are precisely those who will clash on the television or in the street, compatibilities and incompatibilities will cut across families, and so on and so forth. We will then get the complete diagram (on the following page).

It is not difficult to see that this diagram remains commutative: the reactionary citizen's support for the police is intensified by having to vituperate the progressive citizen's vituperation of the selfsame police. Similarly, when he vituperates the reactionary citizen's support for the police, the progressive citizen proportionately increases his own direct vituperation of the police.

It is important to note—this anodyne remark is nonetheless crucial—that, in the context of the Oka incident, which serves as our primitive relation, the derivative relation between the progressive and the reactionary can only be vituperation, if the diagram is to remain commutative and therefore coherent. In effect, if the reactionary supports the progressive, who in turn supports the Mohawks, there follows a flagrant contradiction with the direct relation of vituperation that the reactionary entertains with

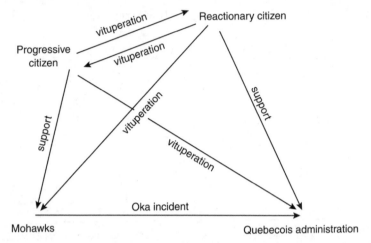

the Mohawks. The diagram will no longer be commutative. So there exists only one possible relation between the two citizens who engage themselves, according to distinct relations, in the primitive relation—at least if we preserve the idea of a coherent circulation of opinions.

This metaphorical situation will help us to construct the concept of the logical completeness of a world. *Given a relation between two objects of a world, we say that this relation is 'exposed' if there exists an object of the world such that it composes a commutative triangular diagram with the two initial objects*:

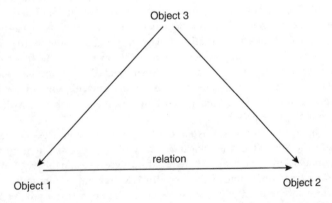

This diagram will be called an exposition of the relation, and object 3 will be called its exponent.

Thus the progressive citizen, just like the reactionary citizen, is the exponent of the relation 'Oka incident'.

We will then say that *the relation is 'universally exposed' if, given two distinct expositions of the same relation, there exists between the two exponents one and only one relation such that the diagram remains commutative*:

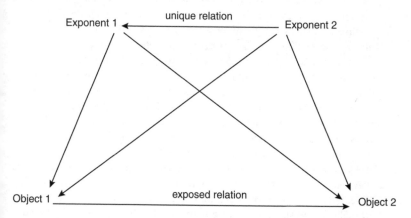

We previously noted that within the Quebec-world the relation 'Oka incident' was universally exposed. In sum, a universal exposition combines the intra-worldly grasp of a relation and a law of uniqueness. It is an intra-worldly making-evident of the connection between objects under the sign of the One.

The definition of the logical completeness of a world can then be put very simply: every relation is universally exposed. We will meditate on this definition and examine some of its consequences.

5. THE SECOND CONSTITUTIVE THESIS OF MATERIALISM: SUBORDINATION OF LOGICAL COMPLETENESS TO ONTOLOGICAL CLOSURE

The metaphor of the visible is well suited for understanding what it means to say that a relation is exposed, and we shall use it abundantly. But we should keep in mind that it is also entirely deceptive because the laws of appearing are intrinsic and do not presuppose any subject. From this point of view, the real of thought is here entirely contained in the diagrams, abstracting from every interpretation of the arrows.

Take the local intra-galactic relation that links a planet to its star (the earth to the sun, for example) in terms of the product of gravitational forces. We say that this relation appears in the galaxy-world to the extent that it is universally exposed. We call metaphor of the visible the following translation: there exists an object of this world from which the relation in question is seen as closely as possible. 'Seen' will be understood in the sense of the elementary diagram: from the object in question, one sees the planet and the star, and this 'seeing' apprehends the attractive relation between the two, for example in the form of a 'seeing' of the planetary orbit. 'As closely as possible' will be understood in the sense of the relationship between the exponents of the relation. The privileged exponent—the selected object from which one 'sees' the relation—is such that, if from another object one likewise 'sees' the orbit of the earth around the sun, then from this other object one can also see the first. This first exponent of the relation is the closest from which one 'sees' the relation, so that it too is always seen from every other point from which this relation is also visible. One may for example maintain that this 'universal' exponent is, in 'our' galaxy, the star Proxima Centauri. At 4.2 light-years from the sun, this star is sufficiently distant from the earth–sun relation for this relation to be entirely 'visible' to it, since the distance earth–sun, with its 150 million kilometres, is nothing much. But one can also say that, from every other star of the galaxy from which one can grasp the earth–sun relation, it is also possible to 'see' Proxima Centauri. It follows that Proxima Centauri universally exposes the earth–sun relation. For example, we have the elementary diagram on the opposite page.

In short, it can be noted that from the Spica of Virgo one sees the seeing of the earth–sun relation, such as it is exposed to the visible by Proxima Centauri. The metaphor of the visible thereby illustrates the logical completeness of a world: that a relation is universally exposed means that this relation is always, at a point of the world (for an object of the world), 'given to see', such that this given-to-see is itself visible for every other givenness-to-the-visible of the relation. An exposition is universal if it is itself exposed.

It must be added that universality envelops uniqueness: it is in one way alone that Proxima Centauri, as the universal exponent of the earth–sun relation, gives itself to be seen—as we are supposing—from the Spica of Virgo. If we shift the metaphor of the visible towards the more abstract

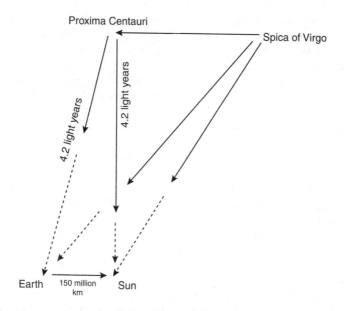

metaphor of knowledge, we will say that a relation is exposed to the extent that there exists at least one point, internal to the world, from which is it known. And we will say that it is universally exposed to the extent that there exists one and only one point of the world from which it is known as clearly and distinctly as possible.

The universal exposition of a relation is clearly an index of the dimension of the world. I must be far enough away to 'see' the totality of the relation without thereby leaving the world, which in this case means that Proxima Centauri, albeit of the same galaxy, is infinitely farther from the sun and the earth than can be expressed by the earth–sun distance. Moreover, it must also be possible for the initial exponent to be captured by the global seeing that takes place from every other exponent. This requires, in the case of the galaxy, that its global dimension be extraordinarily more size-able than the ones involved in genuinely local relations (the ones which concern, for example, a star and its planetary system). This is indeed the case, since the relationship is of the order (very approximately) of 1 to 9 billion. It is this extraordinary dimension of the galaxy (which is here numbered, and thus finite, but is internally infinite) which guarantees that local relations are universally exposed within it.

The connection between the dimension of a world and its logical completeness is in fact entirely rigorous. In the appendix to this Book, we will demonstrate the following remarkable property: from the fact that every world contains—in an ontological sense—an inaccessible infinity of objects, it follows that every relation is universally exposed within it. In other words, as far as worlds are concerned, the logical completeness of appearing is a consequence of their ontological closure. We can consider this property as the second fundamental thesis of materialism. Let's recall that the first (which we called the postulate of materialism), whose character was local, was stated as follows: every atom is real. It already expressed a certain type of subordination of appearing to being: to be sure, the object is a figure of the One in appearing, but its ultimate components, the non-decomposable units of its appearance in a world, are subject to the law of its elementary composition, and thus to the ontology of the multiple. This time we have a global thesis, which does not concern the One (the atoms) but the Infinite (the world): the global logic of appearing legislates over objects and relations between objects. Since we can establish that this logic is complete—in the sense of the universal exposition of every relation—simply due to the inaccessible infinity of a world, we can affirm here too the subordination of the main properties of appearing to the deepest determinations of multiple-being.

The proof that the logical completeness of a world is subordinated to its inaccessible infinity only attains perfect clarity in a formal exposition. However, we can give an idea of it. Between 1534 (Cartier's 'discovery') and the beginning of the seventeenth century, what will later become Quebec is simply a coastal base for cod fishing, to which can be added some incursions into the interior, linked to fur trading. That's what this 'new world' is, as seen from the kingdom of France. When, in 1608, Champlain founds a settlement colony, he aims at broadening the commercial basis, and, needless to say, evangelizing the Indians. In our terms, it is a question of expanding and stabilizing the colonial figure of this world, a world that remains very obscure for the provisional conquerors. The form taken by this stabilization is exemplarily local: a fortified residence ('L'Abitation'), the nucleus of Quebec City, which comprises an important storehouse and the dwellings of the totality of the colonists, that is, in 1608, 28 people, more than half of whom will die in less than a year. Let's consider the possible system of relations between the people shut up in the colonial Abitation and a given object presented in the obscurity of the environing world, for example, the Indians (there will be an alliance with the Huron), the animals (acquiring furs is the key to this arrange-ment), the space (the foundation of other outposts, such as Trois-Rivières in 1634), the climate (it is during the terrible winters of the North that sickness decimates L'Abitation) and so on. These relations are undoubtedly exposed, once they are all caught in the 'seeing' which is linked to the true inhabitants of the place, namely the Indians, but also, especially from the end of the seventeenth century, in the 'seeing' of the English and their Iroquois allies. The universal character of this exposition presupposes that in this fledgling colonial world there always exists an observation which is close to the small founding group, an observation furnished by the world itself on the basis of its local characteristics (around L'Abitation)—keeping in mind that the objective support for this observation (for example, the Hurons of the territory) is in turn observed by whomsoever grasps the (often precarious) state of the relations between L'Abitation and its environs. This is the case, for instance, with the English, who seek to gauge the status of the colonial implantation of the French, particularly in terms of the development of the French alliance with the Huron. It is clear then that the universality of the exposition depends entirely on the resources of the world, on its objective density. If L'Abitation is situated in such a way that all its relations with the obscurity of the world (trade, illness, alliances. . .) are 'visible' from the standpoint of this or that co-apparent in its world, this can only be on condition of an intrinsic overabundance of objects in the world. It is this overabundance that unfolds as the history of the French colonization, and thus as the history of the constitution of Quebec. And this history, which is that of the appearance of objects and relations, is ultimately the history of the universal exposition of every relation between the co-apparents of the Quebec-world.

The history of a world is nothing but the temporal figure of the universal-ity of its exposition. In the last instance, it is the unfolding of its over-abundance of being. The infinite inaccessibility of the ontological support of a world gives rise to the universal exposition of relations and therefore to the logical completeness of that world.

6. THE INEXISTENT

Every object—considered in its being as a pure multiple—is inexorably marked by the fact that in appearing in this world it could have also not appeared and, moreover, it may appear in another world. Take for instance a neutron star. Considered in its pure neutronic 'starness', namely as a very small ball of ultra-concentrated matter (no more than 10 kilometres in radius), but one with astonishing density (100 million tons per cubic centimetre!), the star is not immediately decipherable as an object of this galaxy. It is always possible to isolate its history: a massive star (with a mass greater than, say, 10 times that of the sun) travels towards a red giant, explodes, burning 100 million times brighter (these are the famous supernovas), and declines, separating, within the matter thus dispersed, on the one hand a gigantic expanding cloud, dusts and gas, a nebula, on the other a minuscule 'core' made up of neutron gas, where the void has almost disappeared, which is called a neutron star. It is possible to reconstitute the awesome nuclear complexities of this history, to approximate its successive states, to think by means of them the uncertainty of the idea of matter, to explore the organizing function of the void, and so on. All of this can be done without taking into account that a singular neutron star is always situated in a galaxy, which can in turn be registered as a world on the map of the universal sky. It is therefore necessary that, at least in one point of its appearing, the real of a neutron star attests its indifference to its worldly site. In other words, the rationality of worlds requires that the contingency of the objective composition of objects be legible in objects themselves. Or again, that in order for a multiple to be separable for thought from the world wherein it appears—just as physics can separate the theory of the neutron star from the belonging of every star of this type to a particular galaxy—the multiple must not be conveyed in full by its appearance. There is a reserve of being which, subtracted from appearance, traces within this appearance the fact that it is always contingent for such a being to appear there. We can also say that a real point of inexistence is traced in existence—which measures the degree of appearance of an object in a world—in which we can read the fact that the object as a whole could have not existed. This applies to our neutron star, about which it will be said that its atomic neutrality, or material in-difference (the fact that it no longer comprises anything but 'neutral' gas, with no void nor an identifiable atomic structure), expresses that it is partly on the way to inexistence in the galaxy where it nevertheless figures.

Generally speaking, given a world, *we will call 'proper inexistent of an object' an element of the underlying multiple whose value of existence is minimal. Or again, an element of an apparent which, relative to the transcendental indexing of this apparent, inexists in the world*. The thesis on the rationality of the contingency of worlds can then be stated as follows: every object possesses, among its elements, an inexistent.

The formal calculus will effortlessly show that, if we accept the postulate of materialism, an object only admits of a single proper inexistent. Hence, the (indisputably materialist) statement which posits that the rationality of contingency is revealed to be deducible from this postulate—a cause for considerable intellectual satisfaction. We can conceptually outline this connection. Take the proper inexistent of, say, the legislation on suffrage in Quebec between 1918 and 1950. Suffrage is 'universal' (women can vote from 1918), except that it excludes the Inuit (integrated in 1950) and other Amerindians (integrated in 1960). The object 'civic capacity of the Quebecois populations' admits as its proper inexistent, during this temporal sequence, the set of 'Indians'. This means that said 'Indians' have no electoral existence. Their appearance on the scene of the vote is nil (or indexed to the minimum). But it follows that, relative to the indexing of the object 'civic capacity of the populations', the 'Indians' have a degree of identity to every other element of the population which is also nil. This translates the evident fact that, if you have no rights (if you inexist with regard to right), your degree of identity to the one who has all the rights is nil. This is moreover a property of atomic logic: if an element of an object inexists in a world, it is only minimally identical to another element of the same object.

Now consider the function that attributes transcendental minimality to every element of the population of Quebec, thought in terms of its electoral rights. To put it otherwise, let's envisage an (imaginary) decree that would brutally abrogate all these rights. It is immediately obvious that this decree would come down to equating all populations to those which already have no rights, namely, at least between 1918 and 1950, the 'Indians'. In abstract terms, this signifies two things. First, the decree of abrogation of rights effectively defines an atom: something like an atom of legislative action, a non-decomposable decree. The object-component defined by this abrogation, namely those who have absolutely no rights, is transcendentally without parts: within right, 'to have no rights', or more precisely 'to be outside of any right', establishes a juridically non-differentiable category. Second, and in conformity with the postulate of materialism, this atom is actually prescribed by a real element of the population between 1918 and 1950: the 'Indians'. To have no rights is to be transcendentally identical to an Indian.

We can put it the other way around: the degree of identity of the

'Indians' to every element of the Quebecois population between 1918 and 1950, relative to the transcendental 'Quebec' and the referential object 'civic and political rights', is equal to the minimum of the transcendental in question. Hence, 'Indian' names a real atom (the persistently nil identity to that which it designates) which in turn represents the atomic function of the abrogation of rights. 'Indian' thus names the inexistent element of the object 'civic and political rights' with regard to the transcendental 'Quebec-between-1918-and-1950'. It is evident that this inexistence, though obviously referred to a singular object of the world, ultimately delineates a being which appears in this world at the edge of the void of appearance itself. 'Indian' designates a being which is undoubtedly (ontologically) 'of the world', but which is not absolutely in the world according to the strict logic of appearing. This can be inferred from the fact that Indians are not absolutely Quebecois, because they do not have the political rights which in the Quebec-world govern the appearing of the Quebecois citizen; but neither are they absolutely non-Quebecois, since Quebec is well and truly their transcendental site of appearance. The inexistent of an object is suspended between (ontological) being and a certain form of (logical) non-being.

We can conclude the following: given an object in a world, there exists a single element of this object which inexists in that world. It is this element that we call the proper inexistent of the object. It testifies, in the sphere of appearance, for the contingency of being-there. In this sense, its (ontological) being has (logical) non-being as its being-there.

SECTION 2
Leibniz

> The world is not only the most wonderful machine, but also [. . .] the best commonwealth.

Two formulas give us the measure of Leibniz's project. The first, taken from a letter of 1704 to Sophie-Charlotte, declares that, like Harlequin coming back from the moon, the philosopher can say: 'It is always and everywhere in all things just as it is here'.[1] The other, from a letter to Sophie of 1696: 'My fundamental meditations revolve around two things, namely unity and infinity'. Ultimately, it is a question of determining what the world must be for the infinite of its detail to be so firmly enveloped by the One that everything everywhere is the same thing.

That is why Leibniz is exemplarily a thinker of the world and of its creation by God. The world is the real testing ground for a renewed pact between the one and the infinite, a pact whose general principle lies in the 'new calculus': if a series converges on a limit, it can be thought both as the infinite detail of its terms and as the one of the limit that recapitulates it. The world is just such a series for the God that fulgurates its reality: spectacularly diverse but nonetheless grasped in its unique Reason, whose value is calculated by God, the supreme geometer. That is why it is also possible to say that each individual substance, each 'metaphysical point' of the world, is identical to the totality of the world.

In order to express this identity between the local and the global, Leibniz makes use of several kinds of images. There is the dynamic one of concentration: 'The units of substance are nothing other than different concentrations of the Universe, represented according to the different points of view which distinguish them'. There is the optical one of the mirror: each substance or monad is an 'active indivisible mirror' of the Universe. There is that of representation: 'The soul finitely represents the infinity of God'. There is that of the trace: 'Each substance possesses something infinite, to the extent that it envelops its cause, namely God; in other words, it constitutes a trace of his omniscience and omnipotence'. There is that of abbreviation: '[souls] are always images of the Universe. They are abridged worlds, fecund simplicities'. Finally, there is the one that sums up all the others, the image of expression. In order to 'express' another, a term must be constituted in total independence, it must be perfectly separable but nonetheless isomorphic to that from which it is separated. Consider these magnificent formulas:

> Each mind is as it were a world apart, sufficient unto itself, independent of all other created things, including the infinite, expressing the universe, it is as lasting, as subsistent and as absolute as the very universe of created things itself.

Let us translate this into my vocabulary: every object of the world expresses the world because it expresses its law or reason, which is like the (divine) limit of the real series of objects. We can therefore propose that, just like my own, the Leibnizian thinking of the world takes place, on the one hand, according to the ontological consideration of objects (the units of existence, which he calls monads), on the other, according to the logical consideration of their arrangement, which I call the transcendental and which Leibniz sometimes calls 'sufficient reason' and sometimes 'pre-established harmony'. One will use 'sufficient reason' if one has in mind the global character of the series of objects (monads), to the extent that they appear (or exist) in this world and not in another:

> The reason or universal determining cause that makes things be, and that makes them be this way and not otherwise, must be outside matter.

This passage tells us that the transcendental principle of being-there (or being-thus, it's the same thing) must be capable of being thought as separate from the objects whose degree of existence it establishes. Leibniz uses 'pre-established harmony' instead when he wants to think the local correlation between two terms of the same world (for example, the soul and the body). In the world, there is no possible influence of one term on another. What happens instead is that, referred to the same world, the two terms agree with regard to their deployment because they are under the same law (harmony for Leibniz, operations of the transcendental for me). Let's quote once again the philosopher's own formulations:

> There is effort in all substances; but this force is, strictly, only in the substance itself, and what follows from it in other substances is only in virtue of a 'pre-established harmony'.

Leibniz and the present work share the same orientation with respect to the theory of the world. First, the ontological entry-point into the theory is something like a metaphysical mathematics. For Leibniz, it's a question of indivisible 'points of being', or metaphysical atoms. That is because his paradigm is the differential calculus which he and Newton invented. For my part, it is pure multiplicities, because my paradigm is Cantor's set theory. Second, the logical entry-point is the indexing of real beings on a rule that sets the intensities of existence as well as the relations of identity and difference for everything that makes up the detail of appearing. As Leibniz superbly puts it: 'Besides the principle of change, there must be the detail within that which changes'. For him, this rule is the pre-established harmony, understood as a divine calculus. For me, it is the transcendental of a world, understood as the anonymous legislation of appearing.

A striking consequence, which we also have in common, is that relation thus finds itself strictly subordinated to the nature of the linked terms. As we saw, Leibniz rules out any real action from an identifiable being in the world in the direction of another being. Hence the famous negative image of the 'windowless' monad. It is true that objects exhaust their virtuality in the being-there of their effective creation and that, in their place, they are internally endowed with everything they need in order for their transcendental indexing to determine their power of appearing. This can also be put in the terms outlined in this section: a relation creates nothing, neither in the order of existence, nor in that of localization. In classical metaphysics, one can say that existence is substantial and localization accidental. But what does Leibniz say? That 'neither substance nor accident can enter a monad from without', which is indeed the principle governing my own (negative) definition of relation.

The agreement with Leibniz on the theory of being-there or of the world thus encompasses the following points:

'1. We think the world first in its being (monads, multiplicities), then in terms of the coherence of its appearing (pre-established harmony, transcendental).

2. There is nothing extrinsic about belonging to a world. Belonging is marked, in the units that constitute the world (individuals or objects), by their internal composition (effort or *conatus* in the monad; atomic composition of objects).

In the order of appearing, relation is subordinated to the linked terms, and has no creative capacity.

The extent of my agreement with Leibniz on all these matters can be shown in terms of the thinking of death. I argued at the end of Book III that death is a category of appearing (or of existence) and not a category of being. This means that in a certain sense death is not. For a determinate being, it is, on the one hand, relative to a world in which this being appears (but it may appear in another), on the other, it is the ascription to an existence of the minimal value of a transcendental. But the minimal value of a transcendental is not to be confused with nothingness. So what does Leibniz say? That a living being (an animal) is a datum of the world such that this datum has no absolute origin (it would need to emerge out of nothingness, but there is no nothingness in the world), nor irreparable end (for every being persists). Therefore death has no being:

> Since there is no first birth or entirely new generation of the animal, it follows that it will suffer no final extinction or complete death, in the strict metaphysical sense.

More precisely still, dying affects appearing, not being. Let's recall the astonishing formula:

> The things which are thought to come into being and perish merely appear and disappear.

But where do these appearances and disappearances occur? On the stage of the world, where a given being comes to figure. But it will be objected that for Leibniz there is only one world, one harmony, one divine calculus, and not, as for me, the egalitarian indifference of an infinity of worlds, constructed on distinct transcendentals. Sure, but the question is in truth more complex. For Leibniz, there is indeed a single existing (or really apparent) world, but there is an infinity of possible worlds. But these worlds are far from inexisting purely and simply. Their reality is twofold.

First, there is being in the possible; it cannot be pure nothingness. As Leibniz writes: 'there is in things that are possible, or in possibility or essence itself, a certain need for existence, or (if I may so put it) a claim to exist'. The very fact that it is possible, that it is given in its essence, means that a world 'tends by equal right towards existence'.

Second, the infinity of possible worlds has its proper ontological place, which is none other than the divine intellect: 'There is an infinite number of possible universes in the ideas of God'.

Leibniz thus grants a certain type of being to the infinite multiplicity of worlds: 'Each possible world [has] the right to claim existence in proportion to the perfection which it involves'. Leibniz is beyond doubt the thinker who has most enduringly meditated on the hypothesis of an infinite plurality of essential worlds, and on the reason or limit, in the mathematical sense, of this infinite series. He is the one who, like a science-fiction writer (Guy Lardreau has rightly paid homage to him as such) does not stop asking himself what 'other worlds' are, and how things would have turned out had Caesar not crossed the Rubicon. Yet it is true that Leibniz affirms 'that only a single [world] can exist'. Existential uniqueness offsets essential plurality. This unique world, fulgurated by God, will obviously be the one that envelops the greatest degree of perfection: the best of all possible worlds.

Gilles Deleuze already acutely noted that it is on this point that we moderns diverge from Leibniz's classical-baroque stance. For us, it is effectively indisputable that there are multiple worlds, a divergent series of worlds, and that none may claim to be the best in the absence of a transcendent norm that would sanction their comparison. That is why, once we've moved through his extraordinary analytic of the infinite and his onto-logical rigour, Leibniz ends up disappointing us. To my mind, the true content of this disappointment is the desperate retention of the power of the One. Leibniz's genius lies in having grasped that any understanding of the world rests on the infinity of objects, which is itself 'bound' by transcendental operations. But his limit lies in always wanting a convergence of series, a recapitulation of the infinite in the One—both 'from below', in the thesis of the pure monadic simplicity of beings ('The *monad* [. . .] is nothing but a simple substance, [. . .] that is to say, without parts'), and 'from above', in that which is proper to God ('God alone is the primary Unity, or original simple substance'). In Leibniz, the admirable insight about the infinite dissemination of worlds and their transcendental organization finds itself in some sense framed by two postulates: that of the 'metaphysical atoms' (closed sovereignty of the individual, on the model of the organism) and that of the transcendent One (divine architectonic).

Given these conditions, it is not surprising that Leibniz is tempted to give up on two of his greatest metaphysical decisions: the existence of the actual infinite and the non-being of relations. On the first point, the hesitation is constant, leading him for example to write, at the very beginning of *On the Ultimate Origination of Things*: 'Besides the world or aggregate of finite things we find a certain Unity'. 'Aggregate of finite things'? We witness the fragility of the Leibnizian critique of finitude, faced with the preservation of the sovereignty of the One. On the second point, in order to ensure the coherence of complex worlds, Leibniz ends up by reintroducing a connection that is both immanent and supernumerary. He no longer relies simply on the resources of multiplicity and harmony (objects and the transcendental) in order to uphold the existence of a world. This is the famous and obscure doctrine of the *vinculum substantiale*—this expression itself ('substantial bond') suggests to what extent Leibniz deemed it necessary to reconsider the inexistence of relations. There is indeed a being of this kind of relation, a 'minimal reality' which, he writes, 'adds a new substantiality [to monads]'.

With this 'adjunction to monads'—a relation that according to Leibniz is 'absolute (and hence substantial), albeit in flux with regard to what must be united'—we witness the end of the audacity with which Leibniz, relying only on the simplicity of being and transcendental regulations, separated the infinite multiplicity of worlds, as well as the infinite multiplicity of the objects in each world, both from finitude and from the obligation of ties.

Today, it is beyond Leibniz that we must recover the onto-logical correlation—without any support besides itself—between the disseminating multiplicity and the rule that objectifies its elements.

SECTION 3
Diagrams

1. ONTOLOGY OF WORLDS: INACCESSIBLE CLOSURE

The being that underlies every world is composed of multiple-beings whose being-there is realized by their indexing (or function of appearing) on the transcendental of the world in question. The question of knowing in what sense these beings are ontologically 'of the same world' comes down to examining for which constructions of multiplicities a world is closed. It is clear that the mathematical examination of an operational closure concerns the 'dimension' of the set within which one operates. If you apply to a multiple a very powerful operation and if the world is very small, it is quite likely that the result of the operation will overstep the world. For example, if you place yourself in the Quebec-world, and the operation is 'representing the layout of the city of Montreal in 200 million years', there is a good chance that you will exceed the resources of the world, since everything suggests that on this time-scale, there will be no city of Montreal, no Quebec, no Canada and not even a human species, at least in the way that we know it. The properly ontological examination of the question of the limits of a world presumes that it is possible to put forward hypotheses on the number of multiples contained in a world, and that this may be done, for the moment, in a manner entirely independent from the actual appearing of these multiples and thus from the identity-function which articulates them onto the transcendental of the world.

Of course, we saw, and we will confirm, that these hypotheses cannot strictly speaking be formulated *from the interior* of a world. This is what accounts for the fact that the closure in question remains inaccessible.

These are hypotheses made by the logician with the resources of mathematical formalization, on the basis of an entirely singular world, the world that we can call 'formal ontology of worlds'. This does not make them any less rational, insofar as they set out the appropriate criteria for every enumeration of a world.

In the theory of the pure multiple (ontology of sets), the measure of any multiple whatever is given by a cardinal number. Everybody knows the finite cardinals, which number and differentiate finite sets from the standpoint of pure quantity: one, two, three and so on. Cantor's genius lay in introducing infinite cardinals, which do in the infinite what the natural wholes do in the finite: they tell us 'how many' elements there are in a given multiple. The fundamental result of this subsection can be put simply: *every world is measured by an inaccessible infinite cardinal*. We will now sketch the demonstration in a few steps.

As we recalled in the conceptual exposition (Section 1 of Book IV), the two fundamental operations of the theory of the pure multiple are dissemination and totalization.

1. Dissemination consists in considering the set of the elements of the elements of the initial multiple. If we write this dissemination as $\cup A$, for a being A which appears in a world $\mathbf{m}$, since an element of $\cup A$ is an element of an element of A, the formal definition of $\cup A$ is:

$$x \in \cup A \leftrightarrow \exists a \, [(a \in A) \text{ and } (x \in a)]$$

It is characteristic of a world that what composes a multiple which appears in a world is also part of this world (property of transitivity of $\mathbf{m}$). Otherwise, the being of the world, its matter, would be out of the world 'from below', which is a constitutive thesis for every idealist cosmology ever since the *Timaeus*, where Plato affirmed the irrational and 'errant' character of the material cause. In a general sense, we thus have:

$$[(A \in \mathbf{m}) \text{ and } (a \in A)] \rightarrow (a \in \mathbf{m})$$

It follows from transitivity that all the elements of the elements of A indeed belong to the world $\mathbf{m}$. From the fact that a, element of A, belongs to $\mathbf{m}$, it follows that the elements x of a also belong to it. We therefore know that all the elements of $\cup A$ are elements of $\mathbf{m}$. That the world is a world for the operation of dissemination thus means that the collection of the elements of $\cup A$, that is $\cup A$ itself, is in turn an element of the world. In other words, the dissemination of every being A which appears in a world belongs (in the ontological sense, and not in the register of the object) to this world.

2. Totalization consists in counting as one the set of the parts of the initial multiple. If we write it $\mathbf{P}(A)$, since an element of $\mathbf{P}(A)$ is a part (or subset) of A, its formal definition is the following:

$$x \in \mathbf{P}(A) \leftrightarrow \exists B \,[(B \subseteq A) \text{ and } (x = B)]$$

It is characteristic of a world that the parts of a being which appears within it are also part of that world. Otherwise, the structuration of the world, that is the internal arrangement of the being of the objects appearing within it—the constitutive parts of these objects, or their ontological state—would be out of the world 'from above', which is also a constitutive thesis of every idealist cosmology, ever since Plato in the *Timaeus* affirmed that the arrangement of the world takes place on the basis of an intelligible transcendent model. For our part, we will posit that the parts of a being which is there in a world are also there in that world. In order again to avoid transcendence, in this instance the transcendence of the One, we will similarly posit that the count as one of these parts is itself in the world. The multiple constituted by all the parts of A thus belongs to every world in which A comes to appear. Therefore:

$$(A \in \mathbf{m}) \to (\mathbf{P}(A) \in \mathbf{m})$$

On the basis of these two properties, we will show that every world is infinite. The fundamental theorem used in these demonstrations is a famous theorem of Cantor, which I employed extensively in *Being and Event*, and which says that the cardinal that 'numbers' a set A is always inferior to the one that numbers the set $\mathbf{P}(A)$ of the parts of A. For the philosophical assimilation of this technical result, the reader will refer to meditations 12, 13, 14, 26 and Appendix 3 of *Being and Event*. It will suffice here to note that we call cardinality of a multiple the cardinal that numbers this multiple (that 'counts' its elements).

First of all, we show that it is impossible for a being that appears in a world (which is an element of this world in the ontological sense) to be of a magnitude equal to that of the world itself. Take the cardinal κ, which measures the dimension of $\mathbf{m}$. Suppose that $A \in \mathbf{m}$, and that the cardinality of A is also κ. By virtue of the operational closure of $\mathbf{m}$ for the operation of totalization, we know that $\mathbf{P}(A)$ also belongs to $\mathbf{m}$. By virtue of Cantor's theorem, the cardinality of $\mathbf{P}(A)$, let's say η, is greater than that of A.

We thus have $\eta > \kappa$. But the world **m** is transitive: the elements of its elements also belong to it. Therefore, the elements of $\mathbf{P}(A)$ all belong to **m**. This means that there are at least η beings in the world **m**. This is strictly impossible, since what numbers **m** is κ, and κ is indeed smaller than η. The initial hypothesis must be rejected: no being-there of **m** has the same cardinality as **m** itself. This means that the 'power' of a world is intrinsically greater than that of all the beings which ontologically compose that world.

Suppose now that a world **m** is finite. It has, let's say, n elements (its cardinality is n, a finite number). By the reasoning above, all the beings that figure in **m** have less than n elements. Therefore, there exists a maximal cardinality for the beings of this world, let's say q, with $q < n$. Take one of the beings which effectively has this maximal cardinality, say $A \in$ **m**. We know that $\mathbf{P}(A)$ is also a being in the ontological composition of **m**. But this is impossible, since the cardinality of $\mathbf{P}(A)$ is greater than that of A, that is greater than the number q, which is the maximal cardinality possible for an element of **m**. We must therefore abandon the initial hypothesis: a world **m**, once it is closed for the operation of totalization **P**, cannot be finite. In other words, the cardinality κ of every world is an infinite cardinal number, and is consequently at least equal to every first infinite cardinal, the one which measures the set of whole numbers (the series 1, 2, 3, . . ., n, $n+1$, . . . to infinity), the famous $\aleph_0$.

The inaccessible character of the infinite cardinal which measures the extension of a world simply synthesizes, in the adjective 'inaccessible', the closure of this world by the fundamental operations of ontology, a closure (or operational immanence) which is itself the consequence of the fact that no transcendence governs the intelligibility of these worlds. We observe in effect that it is impossible to 'construct' (or attain) the cardinality *of* the world on the basis of the cardinalities available *in* the world. That is the upshot of the foregoing demonstrations. Since the dissemination of a multiple belonging to **m**, like the totalization of its parts, is always made up of elements of this same **m**, and since the cardinality of an element of **m** remains lesser than that of **m** itself, it is clearly impossible to construct in a world, either from below (dissemination) or from above (totalization), anything whatsoever that may attain the numerical power of that world. So, finally, it is firmly established that the magnitude of any world whatever is only measurable by an inaccessible infinite cardinal. This is the principle of inaccessible closure that governs the ontology of worlds.

Note that 'inaccessible infinite' does not as such mean 'very large infinite'. The smallest of infinites, namely $\aleph_0$, is itself inaccessible. This is easy to grasp: the elements of $\aleph_0$ are the natural numbers, that is the finite cardinals. It is evident that, applied to finite multiples, the operations of dissemination and totalization only produce finite results. The cardinal $\aleph_0$ is therefore certainly inaccessible, for it marks the absolute caesura between the finite and the infinite. In fact, it is the number of a world: the world of whole numbers, or world of arithmetic, already thoroughly explored by the Greeks. Then again, an inaccessible cardinal greater than $\aleph_0$ must truly be gigantic. This is also easily grasped, for it would need to have the same relationship to the innumerable series of infinite cardinals as $\aleph_0$ does to the finite cardinals. In this sense, an inaccessible cardinal greater than $\aleph_0$ would carry out something like a 'finitization' of all the infinites smaller than it. Whence an almost unrepresentable power of infinity. Moreover, to affirm the existence even of a single cardinal of this kind requires a special axiom. One demonstrates—by means that exceed the present exposition—that with the ordinary axioms of the theory of the multiple it is absolutely impossible to prove the existence of such a cardinal.

Our only certainty is that a world can only be measured by an inaccessible cardinal. This also means that every 'world' that would lay claim to anything less would not be a world. This is one of the aspects of the unrelenting conceptual struggle that must be waged against the different facets of finitude. But we do not yet possess any valid means to choose between two hypotheses: either all worlds have a cardinality $\aleph_0$ (as mathematicians say, all worlds are indeed infinite, but denumerable), or there exist worlds whose inaccessible infinite cardinality is greater than $\aleph_0$. This second option has my preference, but I must confess it is only a preference. It preserves the horizon of worlds endowed with an extensive power in comparison with which the figures of the inaccessible that are known to us remain derisory.

2. FORMAL DEFINITION OF A RELATION BETWEEN OBJECTS IN A WORLD

Up to this point, we have presented the logic of appearing strictly from the standpoint of the internal composition of objects, in particular their atomic substructure. In brief, we have carried out an analytic of appearing, in the framework of the presentational unity which constitutes objectivity. As we said, the principal aim of the present Book is to define what a relation between objects is, and thereby fully to constitute the logic of appearing, not only as the structural logic of objectivity, but as *world-logic*. To abide with Kant's vocabulary, we could say that it's a question of delineating a dialectic of objectivity that inserts the logical givenness of objects into the universe of relations.

In the conceptual exposition, we defined relation as closely as possible to the essential transcendental operation: the measuring of identities and differences, including that degree of self-identity which is existence. We defined the relation between objects as an oriented connection between the beings that underlie these objects, a connection that cannot create either difference or existence. We were then able to observe that a relation conserves the atomic logic of objects. Here, we will start directly from this conservation, that is from a kind of ontologico-transcendental invariance or stability. We will posit in effect that a functional connection between objects is identifiable as a relation only to the extent that it 'conserves' the principal transcendental particularities of these objects, in particular the degrees of existence and the localizations. This means that no relation has the power to upset the real atomic substructure of appearing. There is a resistance of matter.

Let's be more precise. Take two objects, (A, α) and (B, β). We abandon here the suggestive notation for identity $(A, \mathbf{Id})$, since we must designate several distinct objects, that is several possible functions of appearing. Whence an extensive usage of Greek letters to designate the different functions of appearing assigned to the different objects. A *relation* from the object (A, α) to the object (B, β) is given in appearing if it conserves the fundamental existential and topological givens of this appearing. Otherwise the relation could not be thought as a relation between *these* objects, and *it would not appear*. It is to the precise extent that it operates through the global maintenance of the transcendental characteristics of the object, and therefore of the logical laws of appearing, that relation itself appears and can make the world consist in appearance as an (inaccessible) unity.

We have already seen (III.1 and III.3) that the main logical given associated with the object is the degree of existence of the elements of its underlying multiple-being (that is $\mathbf{E}x$) and that the main topological given is the localization of an atom on the transcendental index p. Consider, for an object, the restriction to degree p of the power of the One (of atomic projection) of its elements, written $x \restriction p$. In order for a connection from multiple A to multiple B to appear as a relation, it is thus required that it retains the degrees of existence and the localizations. On this condition, it is simplest to use the old concept of function, namely as that which makes an element of set A correspond to every element of set B. If we write $\rho(x) = y$, we must understand by this that ρ associates to every x of A one y of B, according to the rules that the singularity of the function must indicate. A relation from (A, a) to (B, β) will be a function ρ of A towards B which leaves the existences and localizations invariant. We will therefore posit that:

A 'relation' from an object (A, α) to an object (B, β) is a function ρ of set A towards set B which satisfies, for every $a \in A$:

$$\mathbf{E}\rho(\mathrm{a}) = \mathbf{E}a,$$

$$\rho(a \upharpoonright p) = \rho(a) \upharpoonright p$$

Let us recall the notational conventions: the letters a and β obey the rules for functions of appearing, which were generally written as **Id** in the previous sections. For example, $\beta[\rho(a), \rho(b)]$ designates the degree of identity of elements which, in the multiple B, correspond by the function ρ to the elements a and b of multiple A. The transcendental T is presumed as invariant, since we remain in the same world **m**, of which A and B are beings (A and B are 'there' in **m**).

Without any further ado, we can recover, on the basis of this definition (the conservation of the bases of atomic logic), the property which served as our starting-point in the conceptual exposition: a relation cannot make the terms that it connects less identical than they were to begin with. This is written as follows:

$$a(a, b) \leq \beta[\rho(a), \rho(b)], \text{ for } a \in A \text{ and } b \in A$$

In other words, a relation cannot diminish the degree of identity between two terms. The two correlates $\rho(a)$ and $\rho(b)$ are at least as identical in B as a and b are in A. Or again, no relation presents to thought differences greater than the ones given at the outset. A relation appears in a world to the extent that through it identity is conserved or reinforced, never reduced. A relation does not create difference. Here is the demonstration of this consequence (we take ρ to be a relation), which we will call Proposition P.8.

$a \upharpoonright a(a, b) = b \upharpoonright a(a, b)$	lemma A (III, appendix)
$\rho [a \upharpoonright a(a, b)] = \rho [b \upharpoonright a(a, b)]$	consequence
$\rho(a) \upharpoonright a(a, b) = \rho(b) \upharpoonright a(a, b)$	conservation of $\upharpoonright$ by ρ

This means that, for every y of B, we have:

$\beta \, [\rho(a), y] \cap a(a, b) = \beta \, [\rho(b), y] \cap a(a, b)$ def. of the real atoms and of $\int$

In particular, for $y = \rho(a)$, we get:

$\mathbf{E}\rho(a) \cap a(a, b) = \beta \, [\rho(b), \rho(a)] \cap a(a, b)$ consequence, def. of $\mathbf{E}$
$\mathbf{E}a \cap a(a, b) = \beta \, [\rho(a), \rho(b)] \cap a(a, b)$ conservation of $\mathbf{E}$ by ρ
$\mathbf{E}a \cap a(a, b) = a(a, b)$ by P.0 and P.1
$a(a, b) \cap \beta \, [\rho(a), \rho(b)] = a(a, b)$ consequence
$a(a, b) \leq \beta[\rho(a), \rho(b)]$ by P.0.

In fact, the conservative power of a relation, based on the retention of $\mathbf{E}$ and $\int$, extends to the whole transcendental structuration of the multiple which underlies the objects, meaning that the entire atomic logic is conserved. We will now show that this is the case for the two relations which are constitutive of this logic, compatibility and onto-logical order.

Proposition P.9: a relation ρ conserves the relation of compatibility. If a is compatible with b in A—in the sense, written $a \ddagger b$, of III.3.8—and if ρ is a relation between (A, a) and (B, β), then $\rho(a)$ is compatible with $\rho(b)$ in B. That is:

$$a \ddagger b \to \rho(a) \ddagger \rho(b)$$

We suppose that $a \ddagger b$. It follows that:

$a \, \int \mathbf{E}b = b \, \int \mathbf{E}a$ topological def. of $\ddagger$
$\rho(a \, \int \mathbf{E}b) = \rho(b \, \int \mathbf{E}a)$ consequence
$\rho(a) \, \int \mathbf{E}b = \rho(b) \, \int \mathbf{E}a$ conservation of $\int$ by ρ
$\rho(a) \, \int \mathbf{E}\rho(b) = \rho(b) \, \int \mathbf{E}\rho(a)$ conservation of $\mathbf{E}$ by ρ
$\rho(a) \ddagger \rho(b)$ topological def. of $\ddagger$

Proposition P.10: a relation ρ conserves the ontological order $<$, in the sense that if $a < b$, then $\rho(a) < \rho(b)$. That is $a < b \to (\rho(a) < \rho(b))$.
We suppose that $a < b$. We get:

$a \ddagger b$ hypothesis and P.4
$a \ddagger b \to \rho(a) \ddagger \rho(b)$ P.9 above
$\rho(a) \ddagger \rho(b)$ (I)   consequence
$\mathbf{E}\rho(a) = \mathbf{E}a$ and $\mathbf{E}\rho(b) = \mathbf{E}b$ conservation of $\mathbf{E}$ by ρ
$\mathbf{E}a \leq \mathbf{E}b$ hypothesis and P.4
$\mathbf{E}\rho(a) \leq \mathbf{E}\rho(b)$ (II)   consequence
$\rho(a) < \rho(b)$ (I), (II) and P.4

We can finally see the outlines of the principal characteristics of a world, grasped simultaneously in its being and its appearing.

1. We begin with a collection of multiples (sets), all of which belong to the world. This makes up the stable (and mathematically thinkable) being of every situation. We write these multiples A, B, C, etc., and the ontologist can say that $A \in \mathbf{m}$, $B \in \mathbf{m}$, etc. Furthermore, he can state the fundamental 'quantitative' property of a world, the number of $\mathbf{m}$ (the quantity of multiples appearing in $\mathbf{m}$), is an inaccessible cardinal infinite.

2. Among the multiples of $\mathbf{m}$, there is the transcendental T, endowed with a structure that is uniform in terms of its principles: partial order with minimum, conjunction of every pair of elements, envelope and distributivity of the conjunction with regard to the envelope. Obviously, T can vary considerably from one situation to the next, from the minimal Boolean algebra $T_0 = \{M, \mu\}$, all the way to very sophisticated topologies.

3. Every multiple A which appears in $\mathbf{m}$ is indexed on the transcendental by a function of appearing $\mathbf{Id}$, and the result of this indexing determines an object $(A, \mathbf{Id})$. This object has atomic components of type $\mathbf{Id}(a, x)$, where a is a real element of A.

4. Every real element a of an object A can be assigned to its degree of existence in A, that is $\mathbf{E}a$—which is actually the value of the function of appearing $\mathbf{Id}(a, a)$; and it is also localizable by an element of T, in the form of the atom $a \restriction p$ (localization of a on p) which is ontologically defined by the element b such that $b(x) = a(x) \cap p$.

5. Between two objects (A, a) and (B, β), there can exist relations, that is functions of A towards B that conserve the essential givens of appearing: intensities of existence and localizations.

6. The multiples of the situation are retroactively structured by their objectivation in appearing: compatibility, order, envelope. In particular, there exists a real synthesis of every part of a being whose elements are compatible in pairs. Relations conserve this structuration.

A world is ultimately a system of objects and relations which makes an infinite collection of pure multiples appear, and prescribes for them an atomic composition which relations leave invariant.

3. SECOND FUNDAMENTAL THESIS OF MATERIALISM: EVERY RELATION IS UNIVERSALLY EXPOSED

We will now outline—completing it in the appendix to this Book—the demonstration of the result announced in the conceptual exposition, whose importance is considerable: the logical completeness of a world is a consequence of its ontological closure.

Let's begin with the formal definitions.

We will say that a relation p between two objects (A, a) and (B, β) is exposed if there exists an object (C, γ) such that:

–There is a relation f between (C, γ) and (A, a).

–There is a relation g between (C, γ) and (B, β).

–The combination of the successive relations f then p, which from now on we will write $p \circ f$, is equal to the relation g. In other words, the relational triangle below is commutative:

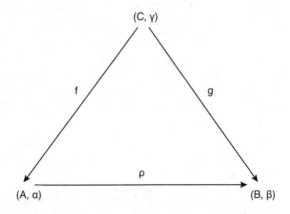

Regarding the object (C, γ), we say that it is an exponent of the relation p.

We will say that a relation p between two objects is universally exposed if there exists an exponent (U, v) of the relation p such that, for every other exponent (C, γ) of the same relation, there exists, from (C, γ) towards (U, v), a single relation that commutes the diagram which inscribes the two expositions. In other words, the following diagram is commutative (which basically means that $f \circ k = l$, and that $g \circ k = m$):

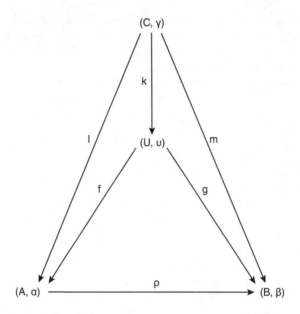

We say that a world is logically complete if every relation is universally exposed within it.

The second fundamental thesis of materialism can thus be stated as follows: from the fact that every world is ontologically closed (its type of infinity is inaccessible) we deduce that it is logically complete (every relation is universally exposed within it).

The detail of the demonstration, which recapitulates almost the entirety of the formal apparatus of the logical theory of worlds, is provided in the appendix to this Book.

Finally, from the fact that every world has an inaccessible cardinality we draw the conclusion that every relation is universally exposed.

4. THE INEXISTENT

All that is left for us to do is to formally study the construction, as an element of every multiple which appears in the world, of what we have called the proper inexistent of the multiple, which is the mark, within objectivity, of the contingency of existence.

For every object (A, δ), the function $a(x) = \mu$, which assigns to every element $x \in A$ the value μ, is an atom. We can immediately verify this, since $a(x) \cap a(y) = \mu$, and $a(x) \cap \delta(x, y) = \mu$, which corroborates the axioms α.2 and α.1 of the atomic object-components.

By virtue of the postulate of materialism, which requires that every atom be real, there exists an element of A which identifies this atom. If $\varnothing_A$ is this element, we have, for every $x \in A$, $\delta(\varnothing_A, x) = \mu$. In particular, $\mathbf{E}\varnothing_A = \delta(\varnothing_A, \varnothing_A) = \mu$. The degree of existence of $\varnothing_A$ is minimal, or transcendentally nil. Moreover, it is possible to establish that the property of inexistence characterizes the element $\varnothing_A$. Take an element $a \in A$ which we presume to inexist, meaning that $\mathbf{E}a = \mu$. We know (proposition P.1) that, for every element x of A, $\delta(a, x) \leq \mathbf{E}a$. This comes down to saying that $\delta(a, x) = \mu$. What we have there is an atom, the same one which is prescribed by $\varnothing_A$. Therefore our element a and $\varnothing_A$ are transcendentally identical.

It is interesting to note that, given two objects (A, a) and (B, β) and a relation ρ between the two, it is certain that the value of ρ for the proper inexistent of (A, a) is the proper inexistent of (B, β). To put it otherwise: $\rho(\varnothing_A) = \varnothing_B$, regardless of the nature of the relation ρ.

This is an immediate consequence of the preservation of existences by relations. In effect, it must be the case that $\mathbf{E}\rho(\varnothing_A) = \mathbf{E}\varnothing_A = \mu$. Therefore, $\rho(\varnothing_A) = \varnothing_B$, since, as we've just remarked, the nullity of existence characterizes the proper inexistent of an object. One will simply say: every relation conserves inexistence.

It is worth dwelling one last time, after its conceptual presentation, on the signification of this phantom-like element, the proper inexistent of an object. Its 'existence' is guaranteed in every object, because the minimum μ exists in every transcendental, and so too does, for every multiple A of the world (ontologically conceived), the real atom prescribed by $\varnothing_A$. However, since its degree of existence is nil and its identity to every other element of A is also nil, it is with good reason that it is called the proper inexistent of A. The functions of such a local inexistent (distinct from the empty set, which is being as non-being, and which is a global operator) are considerable. As we saw, the same may be said with regard to philosophical meditation about it. We insisted above on the fact that the inexistent testifies in an apparent for the contingency of its appearance. We will also note that it can be said of $\varnothing_A$ both that it is (in the ontological sense)—since it belongs to multiple A—and that it is not (in the logical sense), since its degree of existence in the world is nil. Adopting a Heideggerian terminology, it is then possible to say that $\varnothing_A$ is in the world a being whose being is attested, but whose existence is not. Or, a being whose beingness [*étantité*] is nil. Or again a being who happens 'there' as nothingness.

We will see in Book V that the 'sublation' of this nothingness, that is the tipping-over of a nil intensity of existence into a maximal intensity, characterizes real change. Among the numerous consequences of a jolt affecting an object of the world, such a sublation is in effect the signature of what we will call an event.

APPENDIX

Demonstration of the Second Constitutive Thesis of Materialism: The Ontological Closure of a World Implies its Logical Completeness

To give the philosophical importance of the conclusion its due, and to recapitulate the formal properties of the exposition of relations, we will now provide the full demonstration in the form of successive lemmas.

Lemma 1. Given two multiples A and B appearing in a world, the product of these two sets, that is the set constituted by all the ordered pairs of elements of A and B (in this order), must also appear in this world.

If A and B are both in a world, they are, by virtue of the property of ontological closure of worlds, on an inaccessible infinite level of multiple-being. Such a level is closed for the fundamental operations of set theory, namely ∪ (union), **P** (set of parts), as well as the separation, within a set, of the elements of this set which have a given property, provided that this property only has objects of the world as its parameters. Consequently, there exists on this level the union $A \cup B$, the set constituted by all the elements of A and all the elements of B. Again by virtue of closure, there also exists within it the set $A \cup (\mathbf{P}(A \cup B))$, composed of all the elements of A and all the elements of the set of parts of the union of A and B. Let us now consider the following well-defined property: 'to be a set with two elements, of which one is an element of A and the other a pair composed of this same element of A and any element of B'. If we note that a pair composed of an element of A and an element of B is certainly a part of the union $A \cup B$, it is possible to conclude that the property in question allows us to separate, within the set $A \cup (\mathbf{P}(A \cup B))$—present on the inaccessible infinite level in question—all the elements of the type $\{a,\{a, b\}\}$. Such an element is an ordered pair (a, b) composed of an element of A and an element of B. This means that the elements a and b are not substitutable in terms of their places: if $\{a, \{a, b\}\} = \{c, \{c, d\}\}$, then it must necessarily be the case that $a = c$ and $b = d$. I leave the demonstration of this point to the inquisitive reader. It is very instructive.

The set of all the ordered pairs (a, b) of elements of A and B is called the product, or 'Cartesian product', of the sets A and B. Since it is obtained by separation, in terms of a defined property, within a set which itself exists in the infinite level under consideration—the set $A \cup (\mathbf{P}(A \cup B))$—this product also exists on this level by virtue of the law of closure (or inaccessibility).

This can be put as follows: if A and B appear in a world, their product also appears within it. QED.

Lemma 2. Take a relation ρ given in a world between an object (A, a) and an object (B, β). There exists a multiple F_ρ whose elements are all the pairs $\{x, \rho(x)\}$ where x is an element of A and $\rho(x)$ is the element of B which corresponds to x by the relation ρ.

Since A and B are multiples appearing in the world, the product $A \cdot B$ of A and B also exists in this world (by lemma 1). Consider the well-defined property 'being an ordered pair whose first term belongs to A and whose second term is the correspondent in B of the first by the relation ρ'. This property defines a subset, which we write F_ρ, of all the ordered pairs composed of an element of A and an element of B. The set of all these pairs is none other than the product $A \cdot B$. By virtue of the inaccessible closure of a world, the set of the parts of $A \cdot B$, namely $\mathbf{P}(A \cdot B)$, appears in the world, since $A \cdot B$ appears in it. And by virtue of the transitiveness of a world, every element of $\mathbf{P}(A \cdot B)$ also appears in it. But we have just seen that F_ρ, as a subset of $A \cdot B$, is an element of the set of its parts, that is $\mathbf{P}(A \cdot B)$. Therefore, F_ρ appears in the world.

Lemma 3. Take a relation ρ of a world, between two objects (A, a) and (B, β), and let F_ρ be the set defined in lemma 2. In the world there is an object (F_ρ, υ), with the transcendental indexing υ defined as follows: if $(a, \rho(a))$ and $(a', \rho(a'))$ are two elements of F_ρ (with $a \in A$, $a' \in A$), the degree of transcendental identity of $(a, \rho(a))$ and $(a', \rho(a'))$ is defined by:

$$\upsilon \{(a, \rho(a)), (a', \rho(a'))\} = a\,(a, a') \cap \beta\,(\rho(a), \rho(a'))$$

Basically, the transcendental indexing of F_ρ is given by the conjunction of the measures of identity of the elements concerned in the pairs that compose F_ρ, measures which are taken on the basis of the transcendental indexings of A and B.

It is very important to note that we are providing this notation of the transcendental indexing of F_ρ so that its symmetry may be visible. But one can immediately simplify it by noting that

$$\alpha(a, a') \cap \beta(\rho(a), \rho(a'))$$

is in effect equal to $\alpha(a, a')$. Since ρ is a relation, it cannot create difference, which means that the degree of identity in B between $\rho(a)$ and $\rho(a')$ is at least equal to the degree of identity between a and a' in A. We thus have: $\alpha(a, a') \leq \beta(\rho(a), \rho(a'))$.

By P.0, this means that $\alpha(a, a') \cap \beta(\rho(a), \rho(a')) = \alpha(a, a')$. Finally, the transcendental indexing of F_ρ is to be written as follows:

$$\upsilon\{(a, \rho(a)), (a', \rho(a'))\} = \alpha\,(a, a')$$

We can now demonstrate, in stages, lemma 3.

That in a world there is the object (F_ρ, υ) means, first, that the multiple F_ρ appears within it (ontological condition); second, that the function υ is effectively a transcendental indexing of F_ρ (logical condition); third, that all the atoms of (F_ρ, υ) are real (materialist condition).

The first point is nothing other than lemma 2, since we suppose that A and B appear in the world. The second amounts to verifying that the function given by $\alpha(a, a')$, which defines υ, really obeys the axioms of transcendental indexings, or the functions of appearing—this is particularly trivial, since α is the transcendental indexing of A. That leaves the third point, which is dealt with by

Lemma 4. Every atom of (F_ρ, υ) is real.

Let $\varepsilon(x, \rho(x))$ be an atom of (F_ρ, υ). Consider the function ε^* of A to the transcendental T, defined by $\varepsilon^*(x) = \varepsilon(x, \rho(x))$. We will show that this function is an atom of the object (A, α). We do so by directly verifying that the function in question validates the axioms $\alpha.1$ and $\alpha.2$.

For the axiom $\alpha.1$, we must show that $\varepsilon^*(x) \cap \alpha(x, y) \leq \varepsilon^*(y)$.

$\varepsilon(x, \rho(x)) \cap \upsilon[(x, \rho(x)), (y, \rho(y))] \leq \varepsilon(y, \rho(y))$	ε, atom, validates $\alpha.1$
$\varepsilon^*(x) \cap \alpha(x, y) \leq \varepsilon^*(y)$	def. of ε^* and of υ

For the axiom $\alpha.2$, we must show that $\varepsilon^*(x) \cap \varepsilon^*(y) \leq \alpha(x, y)$.

$\varepsilon(x, \rho(x)) \cap \varepsilon(y, \rho(y)) \leq \upsilon[(x, \rho(x)), (y, \rho(y))]$	ε, atom, validates $\alpha.2$
$\varepsilon^*(x) \cap \varepsilon^*(y) \leq \alpha(x, y)$	def. of ε^* and of υ

We know that ε^* is an atom of (A, a). But we obviously assume that (A, a) is an object of the world, and therefore that every atom of (A, a) is real. So, there exists an element $c \in A$ which prescribes the atom ε^*. This means that, for every x of A, we have $\varepsilon^*(x) = a(c, x)$. We can then see that:

$$\varepsilon(x, p(x)) = a(c, x) \qquad \text{def. of } \varepsilon^*$$
$$\upsilon\,[(c, p(c)), (x, p(x))] = a(c, x) \qquad \text{def. of } \upsilon$$
$$\varepsilon(x, p(x)) = \upsilon\,[(c, p(c)), (x, p(x))] \qquad \text{consequence}$$

This shows that the atom ε of (F_p, υ) is real, since it is prescribed by the fixed element $(c, p(c))$.

To be entirely rigorous (as we have committed ourselves to be in this appendix), it is necessary to prove that the element $(c, p(c))$ is the only one to prescribe the atom ε. If another element, say $(d, p(d))$, did the same, in light of the construction above every x of A would give us the equation $a(c, x) = a(d, x)$. Which, since (A, a) is an object, means that, within the world, c and d appear identical. Uniqueness is thereby demonstrated.

Lemma 5. The object (F_p, υ) is an exponent of the relation p.

We will now define the relations f and g, respectively of the object (F_p, υ) to the object (A, a) and of the object (F_p, υ) to the object (B, β). To define a relation is above all to consider a function (in the ordinary sense) between support-sets of objects (ontological part).

The functions (in the ontological sense) are very simple. Recall that every element of F_p has the form $(a, p(a))$, with $a \in A$ and $p(a) \in B$. The function f will make the element a correspond to every pair $(a, p(a))$, while the function g will do so with $p(a)$. We can immediately note that the diagram below is commutative:

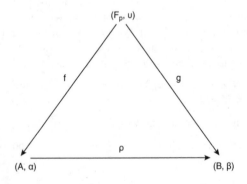

In effect, if you start from the element $(a, \rho(a))$ of F_ρ, you get, by f, the element a. To this element a, ρ correlates $\rho(a)$, which is exactly what the function g directly correlates to the initial element of F_ρ. Thus $p \circ f = g$.

Therefore, if we prove that f and g are indeed relations, we will have proven by the same token that the object (F_ρ, v) is an exponent of the relation ρ.

Let's begin with the conservations of existences. In the definitions of the two functions f and g, we can see almost immediately that, for any element $(a, \rho(a))$ of F_ρ, we have:

$$\mathbf{E}(f(a, \rho(a))) = \mathbf{E}a \qquad \text{def. of } f$$
$$\mathbf{E}(g(a, \rho(a))) = \mathbf{E}(\rho(a)) = \mathbf{E}a \qquad \text{def of } g \text{ and relation } \rho$$

We simply have to show that in (F_ρ, v) the existence of an element $(a, \rho(a))$ is itself also equal to $\mathbf{E}a$, so that f and g conserve existences. This point is not at all difficult. In effect we have (definition of the object (F_ρ, v) and definition of existence):

$$\mathbf{E}(a, \rho(a)) = v\{(a, \rho(a)), (a, \rho(a))\} = a(a, a) = \mathbf{E}a$$

Let us now show that f and g conserve localizations, in other words that $f(a \upharpoonright p) = f(a) \upharpoonright p$, and that $g(a \upharpoonright p) = g(a) \upharpoonright p$.

Since every atom of (F_ρ, v) is real, it follows that, for every element of (F_ρ, v), say $(a, \rho(a))$, and for every degree p of the transcendental, there exists an element $b \in A$ such that the atom $(a, \rho(a)) \upharpoonright p$ (localization of the element of F_ρ on p) is equal to the real atom prescribed by the element $(b, \rho(b))$. Now, if this element b is none other than $a \upharpoonright p$ (localization on p of the element a of the object (A, a)), then the functions f and g conserve localizations. Let's show first of all that this is the case for f (we must establish that $f[(a, \rho(a)) \upharpoonright p] = f(a, \rho(a)) \upharpoonright p$):

$$f[(a, \rho(a)) \upharpoonright p] = f[a \upharpoonright p, \rho(a \upharpoonright p)] \qquad \text{hypothesis } b = a \upharpoonright p$$
$$f[(a \upharpoonright p, \rho(a \upharpoonright p)] = a \upharpoonright p \qquad \text{(I)} \qquad \text{def. of } f$$
$$a \upharpoonright p = f(a, \rho(a)) \upharpoonright p \qquad \text{(II)} \qquad \text{def. of } f$$
$$f[(a, \rho(a)) \upharpoonright p] = f(a, \rho(a)) \upharpoonright p \qquad \text{(I) and (II)}$$

Let's now verify that the same goes for g (we must show that $g(a, \rho(a)) \upharpoonright p$ is the same thing as $g[(a, \rho(a)) \upharpoonright p)]$).

$$g[(a, \rho(a)) \upharpoonright p] = g[a \upharpoonright p, \rho(a \upharpoonright p)] \qquad \text{hypothesis } b = a \upharpoonright p$$
$$g[a \upharpoonright p, \rho(a \upharpoonright p)] = \rho(a \upharpoonright p) \qquad \text{def. of } g$$
$$\rho(a \upharpoonright p) = \rho(a) \upharpoonright p \qquad \rho \text{ is a relation}$$

$$g \, [(a, \, \rho(a)) \, \lceil \, p] = \rho(a) \, \lceil \, p \qquad \qquad \text{consequence}$$
$$g[(a, \, \rho(a)) \, \lceil \, p] = g(a, \, \rho(a)) \, \lceil \, p \qquad \qquad \text{def. of } g$$

All that is left for us is to demonstrate that $a \, \lceil \, p$ is indeed that atom prescribed by the localization (relative to the object F_ρ) of the element $(a, \, \rho(a))$. To do so, we return to the original definition of atoms. We must establish that, for every $x \in A$, and keeping in mind the definition of localizations, we have:

$$v[(a \, \lceil \, p, \, \rho(a \, \lceil \, p), \, (x, \, \rho(x)] = v[(a, \, \rho(a), \, (x, \, \rho(x)] \cap p$$

Therefore, keeping in mind the definition of v:

$$a(a \, \lceil \, p, \, x) = a(a(x)) \cap p$$

This is none other than the definition, in the object $(A, \, a)$, of the localization of the element a on p.

We are now confident that f and g, which conserve existences and localizations, are indeed relations, respectively between $(F_\rho, \, v)$ and $(A, \, a)$, and between $(F_\rho, \, v)$ and $(B, \, \beta)$.

Lemma 6. The relation ρ is universally exposed by the object $(F_\rho, \, v)$ and by the relations f and g.

Since we know that $(F_\rho, \, v)$, via f and g, exposes the relation ρ, it only remains to show the universal character of this exposition. We must therefore establish, for every other exponent $(C, \, \gamma)$ of ρ, the existence of a unique relation k from the object $(C, \, \gamma)$ to $(F_\rho, \, v)$ such that the schema on the following page is commutative.

Basically, it's a matter of demonstrating that there exists a unique relation k such that $f \circ k = l$ and $g \circ k = m$.

We took the object $(C, \, \gamma)$ to be an exponent of the relation ρ. This means that the triangle CAB commutes, or that $p \circ l = m$. Therefore, if we start from an element $c \in C$, we necessarily get $\rho(l(c)) = m(c)$. Consequently, the pair $(l(c), \, m(c))$ is of the type $(x, \, \rho(x))$, where x is an element of A, which means that this pair is an element of F_ρ. We are therefore justified in defining a function k between C and F_ρ in the following manner: $k(c) = (l(c), \, m(c))$. It is then evident that the triangles $CF_\rho A$ and $CF_\rho B$ commute, as required. That is because to an element c of C there corresponds, by k, $(l(c), \, m(c))$, and then, to this element, by f, there corresponds the element $l(c)$, which is the one that corresponds to c by virtue of the relation l. The same consideration demands that, starting from c, we end up with the

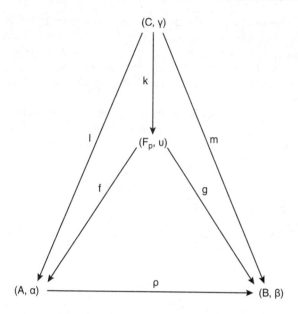

element $m(c)$ of B, whether we pass through the combination $g \circ k$ or go directly through m.

We must nevertheless make sure that k is indeed a relation, and therefore that it conserves existences and localizations. This point can be inferred from the fact that l and m are assumed to be relations, and therefore conserve existences and localizations. For example, we have the following calculus.

$k(c) = (l(c), m(c))$	def. of k
$\mathbf{E}(k(c)) = \mathbf{E}(l(c), m(c))$	consequence
$\mathbf{E}(k(c)) = \mathbf{E}(l(c))$	def. of $\mathbf{E}$ and def. of v
$\mathbf{E}l(c) = \mathbf{E}c$	l is a relation
$\mathbf{E}(k(c) = \mathbf{E}c$	consequence

Therefore the function k conserves existences. To show that it conserves localizations is done exactly in the same way, and it will be the only point that we leave as an exercise for the reader.

To conclude, it is necessary to verify that the relation k is the only one to render the schema that defines the universal exposition of ρ commutative.

351

It suffices to examine this schema attentively. If we have $l(c)$ in A, and $m(c)$ in B, and if the schema commutes, it is obviously because the corresponding element in F_p—taking the definition of f and g into account—is the element $(l(c),\ m(c))$. Accordingly, a function between C and F_p, which makes the schema commute, is of necessity defined like k: to c of C there corresponds $(l(c),\ m(c))$.

This completes the full demonstration of the second constitutive thesis of materialism: in any world whatever, every relation is universally exposed. Or again: from ontological closure, we infer logical completeness.

GENERAL APPENDIX TO THE GREATER LOGIC
The 11 Propositions

We provide here the list of the propositions used under a coded name (from P.0 to P.10) in various demonstrations. These propositions are all demonstrated, and often subsequently employed, in Book II for P.0 (the study of conjunction), in Book III for propositions P.1 to P.7 (the study of atomic logic), and finally in Book IV for the last three propositions (the formal study of relations). Some will be utilized, under their coded name, in Books V, VI and VII.

P.0. That the conjunction of x and a is equal to x is equivalent to x itself being lesser than or equal to a. Or:

$$(x \leq a) \leftrightarrow (x \cap a) = x$$

P.1. The identity of x and y is always lesser than or equal to the conjunction of the existences of x and y. Or:

$$\mathbf{Id}(x, y) \leq \mathbf{E}x \cap \mathbf{E}y$$

P.2. The atom prescribed by a is the same as the atom prescribed by b if and only if the existence of a and the existence of b are equal, and equal to their degree of identity. Or:

$$\forall x[\mathbf{Id}(a, x) = \mathbf{Id}(b, x)] \leftrightarrow (\mathbf{E}a = \mathbf{E}b = \mathbf{Id}(a, b))$$

P.3. The elements of a and b are compatible if the conjunction of their existences is equal to the degree of their identity. Or:

$$(a \ddagger b) \leftrightarrow (\mathbf{E}a \cap \mathbf{E}b = \mathbf{Id}(a, b))$$

P.4. That the existence of a is lesser than or equal to its identity to b is an order-relation between a and b. This relation is equivalent to the following:

a and *b* are compatible and the existence of *a* is lesser than or equal to that of *b*. Or:

$$(\mathbf{E}a \leq \mathbf{Id}(a, b)) \leftrightarrow ((a < b) \leftrightarrow [(a \ddagger b) \text{ and } (\mathbf{E}a \leq \mathbf{E}b)])$$

P.5. If, according to the onto-logical order <, two elements are lesser than or equal to the same third element, they are compatible with one another. Or:

$$[(b < c) \text{ and } (b' < c)] \rightarrow (b \ddagger b')$$

P.6. If two elements *b* and *b'* are compatible, the conjunction of the values of the atoms they prescribe remains, for any two elements *x* and *y*, lesser than the degree of identity between this *x* and this *y*. Or:

$$(b \ddagger b') \rightarrow [(\mathbf{Id}(b, x) \cap \mathbf{Id}(b', y)) \leq \mathbf{Id}(x, y)]$$

P.7. If all the elements of a part *B* of an object are compatible with one another, there exists an envelope of *B* for the onto-logical order-relation <. Or:

$$[(b \in B \text{ and } b' \in B) \rightarrow (b \ddagger b')] \rightarrow (\exists \varepsilon)(\varepsilon = \Sigma B)$$

P.8. A relation between two objects cannot diminish the degree of identity between two elements of these objects. Therefore, if (*A*, *a*) and (*B*, *β*) are the two objects and *ρ* the relation:

$$a(a, b) \leq \beta[\rho(a), \rho(b)], \text{ for } a \in A \text{ and } b \in A$$

P.9. A relation conserves compatibility. Or:

$$(a \ddagger b) \rightarrow [\rho(a) \ddagger \rho(b)]$$

P.10. A relation conserves onto-logical order. Or:

$$(a < b) \rightarrow [\rho(a) < \rho(b)]$$

Note

1. Leibniz's allusion is to Nolant de Fatouville's 1684 play *Arlequin, empereur dans la lune*.

BOOK V

The Four Forms of Change

Introduction

HAMM: What's happening
CLOV: Something is taking its course.

Samuel Beckett

1. THE QUESTION OF CHANGE

The transcendental analytic of being-there, or formal theory of worlds, or Greater Logic, leaves the question of change untouched. What we mean is real change, the change which imposes an effective discontinuity on the world where it takes place. We could also say that the thinking of singularity still lies ahead for us, if the word 'singularity' is taken to designate a being the thought of which cannot be reduced to that of its worldly context. A singularity is that with which a thought begins. But if this beginning is a mere consequence of the logical laws of a world, it merely appears in its place and begins—strictly speaking—nothing. Truth be told, we cannot find the means to identify change either in the order of mathematics, the thinking of being qua being, or in that of logic, the thinking of being-there or appearing. To put it bluntly: the thinking of change or of singularity is neither ontological nor transcendental.

Being, qua being, is pure multiplicity. By this token, it is absolutely immobile, in conformity with Parmenides' potent original intuition. The mathematical thinking of a multiplicity may of course envelop power or excess. It is even a law of being (theorems of Gödel and Cohen) that the parts of a multiple enjoy an unassignable or errant excess over its elements.

However, this inscription of excess or errancy takes place from within the ambit of a more essential thesis, which compels the exposition of the multiple to tolerate neither generation nor corruption. As affected as it may be by the paradoxes of its own infinity, multiple-being remains inflexibly immutable. It can never evade the potentially comprehensive visibility which exposes it to the injunctions of the matheme. Besides, the fact that the thinking of being as such is mathematical means nothing else than this: being, as integral transparency, only accords with kinds of writing which link it to axiomatic decisions and their consequences. Being is immobile because it cannot impede the deduction that illuminates its laws.

Contrary to the fiction that Parmenides proposed in order to support his admirable concept, being is not One. On the contrary, it is the inconsistency of the pure multiple. But, as Wittgenstein remarks in the *Tractatus*, pure objective multiplicity is even more immobile than the uncertain supposition of the One. Granting, according to his formula, that 'objects make up the substance of the world', one will offer as evidence that 'objects are what is unalterable and subsistent; their configuration is what is changing and unstable'. The pure thinking of being is as eternal as the multiple forms whose concept it harbours.

But neither is genuine change given to us on the side of appearing, or of the transcendental constitution of being-there, on the side, that is, of worlds. For the appearing of a being in a world is the same thing as its modifications in that world, without any discontinuity and thus any singularity being required for the deployment of these modifications. Here too Wittgenstein is a precious guide. In the *Tractatus*, he still only admits the existence of a single world. But he saw perfectly well that the general form of a world, or that which is intelligible in the worldliness of a world, is purely logical. Logic provides the essence of the proposition. But 'to give the essence of a proposition means to give the essence of all description, and thus the essence of the world'. If the essence of the world is only intelligible as the (logical) essence of description in general, it is obviously because the world is nothing other than everything which appears. 'The world is all that is the case'. Finally, the occurrences of becoming, or what Wittgenstein calls 'the totality of facts', constitute the identity of the world, and by no means its change.

In our own approach, this logical identity of a world is the transcendental indexing of a multiplicity—an object—as well as the deployment of its relations to other multiplicities which appear in that world. There is no reason to suppose that we are dealing with a fixed universe of objects and relations, from which we would have to separate out modifications. Rather, we are dealing with modifications themselves, situating the object as a multiplicity—including a temporal one—in the world and setting out the relations of this object with all the others. In particular, we accept the great relativist lessons of physics, from Galileo to Einstein and Laurent Nottale, as self-evident: the phenomenon integrates into its phenomenality the variations that constitute it over time, as well as the differences of scale that stratify its space.

If, for example, as we did in Book III, we identify as 'world' a demonstration on Place de la République, we are obviously thinking of the becoming of the crowd, from its initial gathering to its shambling dispersion along the rows of police vans. The intensities of objects and relations are measured according to a singular temporal transcendental, which objectivates in their appearing multiplicities such as 'the firm stance of the group of anarchists from one end to the other', or 'the organizing role of the rail workers' union', or 'the growing isolation of the Kurdish communists' and so on. In other words, the object absorbs, as elements of the multiplicity that it is, the modifications which include it within the time of the world, through which it only 'changes' to the extent that this 'change' *is* its appearing-in-the-world.

As long as the transcendental regulation remains identical, it is certainly possible to witness considerable variations affecting the 'same' element, just as the columns of the round temple in Hubert Robert's painting can be luminous in the foreground, or a dark blue for those that perspective relegates to the background. But these variations are nothing but the immanent movement of appearing, whose possible intensities and amplitude are prescribed by the transcendental. This is the same thing that we highlighted, in the scholium to Book III, with regard to the transcendental functor and its military exemplification: the differential assignations of intensity (of combat capacity) integrate the tactical modifications that affect the units (cavalry, archers, etc.) over the duration of the clash. We proposed the following formula: a world is the set of its modifications.

We will call 'modification' the rule-governed appearing of intensive variations which a transcendental authorizes in the world of which it is the transcendental. Modification is not change. Or better, it is only the transcendental absorption of change, that part of becoming which is constitutive of every being-there. Neither the thinking of being nor that of appearing bear witness to change, insofar as change would affect being-there, either in its being or in its 'there', in a different way than the rule which composes being-there as multiple and localizes it as object.

So what is the source of the real change that certain worlds undergo? An exception is required. An exception both to the axioms of the multiple and to the transcendental constitution of objects and relations. An exception to the laws of ontology as well as to the regulation of logical consequences. This Book is devoted to the nature and the possible forms of existence of this exception.

2. SUBVERSION OF APPEARING BY BEING: THE SITE

The trouble is obviously that 'pure being' and 'being-there' embody the absolute partition of the 'there is' as such. If change, in any case the change which is something more and other than mere modification, is possible neither as being (ontologically) nor as appearing (logically), we run the risk that it might remain purely and simply unthinkable. The general outline of the solution to this problem is the following. A change, if it is a singularity and not a simple consequence (a modification), comes about neither according to the mathematical order that grounds the thinking of the multiple nor according to the transcendental regulation that governs the coherence of appearing. Of course, there is only the being-there of multiples. But it can happen that multiple-being, which is ordinarily the support for objects, rises 'in person' to the surface of objectivity. A mixture of pure being and appearing may take place. For this to happen, it is enough that a multiple lays claim to appearing in such a way that it refers to itself, to its own transcendental indexing. In short, it is enough that a multiple comes to play a double role in a world where it appears. First, it is objectivated by the transcendental indexing of its elements. Second, it (self-)objectivates, by figuring among its own elements and by thus being caught up in the transcendental indexing of which it is the ontological support. Worldly objectivation turns this multiple into a synthesis between the objectivating (the multiple support and referent of a phenomenality) and the objectivated (belonging to the phenomenon). We call such a paradoxical being a 'site'.

3. LOGIC OF THE SITE: TOWARDS SINGULARITY

This ontological characterization of the exception which supports change is nevertheless insufficient. The self-belonging multiple—the site—is itself certainly exposed to its own transcendental indexing. But it may turn out that the degree of appearance which is thereby conferred upon it is very weak, so that the transformations of the world induced by this appearance remain altogether limited, or even inexistent. It is absolutely necessary to double the ontological characterization of the event with a logical characterization, whose starting-point resides in the existential intensity conferred upon the multiple which is marked by self-belonging.

This play between being and existence (between ontology and logic) is obviously the principal innovation, in terms of the doctrine of change, with regard to *Being and Event*. At the time, having no theory of being-there at my disposal, I effectively thought that a purely ontological characterization of the event was possible. Perspicacious readers (namely Desanti, Deleuze, Nancy and Lyotard) quickly brought to my notice that I was framing the ontological definition of 'what happens' both from below and from above. From below, by positing the existence, required by every event, of an event-site, whose formal structure I rather laboriously delineated. From above, by demanding that every event receive a name. One could then say, on the one hand, that there was in fact a 'worldly' structure of the event (its site, summoning the void of every situation), and on the other, a rather unclear transcendental structure (the name, attributed by an anonymous subject). As we shall see, I am now able fundamentally to equate 'site' and 'evental multiplicity'—thus avoiding all the banal aporias of the dialectic between structure and historicity—and that I do so without any recourse to a mysterious naming. Moreover, in place of the rigid opposition between situation and event, I unfold the nuances of transformation, from mobile–immobile modification all the way to the event properly so-called, by way of the neutrality of fact.

4. PLAN OF BOOK V

The structure of this Book is very simple. The conceptual exposition determines in successive stages the concept of event or of strong singularity—first at the ontological level (self-belonging), then at the logical level (intensity of existence and extension of consequences). The historical discussion takes place with Deleuze, the only contemporary philosopher—following in Bergson's wake—to have made the intuition of change into the crux of a renewed metaphysical programme. Bergson already regarded himself as the only genuine interlocutor of Parmenides, and above all the only one in a position to avoid the devastating effects of Zeno's paradoxes against movement on the entire tradition of conceptual philosophy. Likewise, Deleuze turned himself into the bard of divergent becomings and disjunctive syntheses. Both attempted to avoid the paradoxes of dualism (becoming/movement, essence/appearance, one/multiple, etc.) by subordinating to a pure creative virtuality—*élan vital* for Bergson, chaos for Deleuze—the segmentations attested to by the visible result. We will nonetheless conclude that by restricting the thinking of change to the vital simplicity of the One, even if this involves the (classical) precaution of thinking the One as a power of differentiation—just as was done before him by the Stoics, Spinoza, Nietzsche and Bergson—Deleuze cannot really manage to account for the *transcendental* change of worlds. It remains impossible to subsume such a change under the sign of Life, whether it is renamed as Power, Élan or Immanence. It is necessary to think discontinuity *as such*, a discontinuity that cannot be reduced to any creative univocity, as indistinct or chaotic as the concept of such a univocity may be.

We end with a rather limpid formal exposition, almost devoid of the machinery of demonstration.

SECTION 1
Simple Becoming and True Change

---

1. SUBVERSION OF APPEARING BY BEING: THE SITE

Take any world whatever. *A multiple which is an object of this world—whose elements are indexed on the transcendental of the world—is a 'site' if it happens to count itself in the referential field of its own indexing.* Or: a site is a multiple which happens to behave in the world in the same way with regard to itself as it does with regard to its elements, so that it is the ontological support of its own appearance. Even if the idea is still obscure, its content is plain: a site supports the possibility of a singularity, because it summons its being in the appearing of its own multiple composition. It makes itself, in the world, the being-there of its own being. Among other consequences, the site endows itself with an intensity of existence. A site is a being to which it happens that it exists by itself.

The question arises: is it possible to give a more concrete idea of what a site is? Does a site exist?

Let us consider the world 'Paris at the end of the Franco-Prussian war of 1870'. We are in the month of March 1871. After a semblance of resistance, spurred by their fear of proletarian and revolutionary Paris, the 'republican' bourgeois of the provisional government capitulate to Bismarck's Prussians. In order to consolidate this political 'victory'—very akin to Pétain's reactionary revenge in 1940 (better to make a deal with the external enemy than to leave oneself exposed to the internal enemy)— they compel the election, by the frightened rural world, of an Assembly with a royalist majority, an Assembly whose seat is in Bordeaux. The government, led by Thiers, is determined to profit from the circumstances in order to reduce the workers' political capacity to nothing. This is because on the Parisian side the proletariat is armed, having been mobilized during the siege of Paris in the guise of the National Guard. In theory, it even has at its disposal several hundred cannons. The Parisians' military organism is the Central Committee, on which sit the delegates of the different battalions of the National Guard, who are in turn linked to the great popular neighbourhoods of Paris—Montmartre, Belleville, and so on. We thus have a divided world, whose transcendental organization assigns intensities of political existence according to two antagonistic criteria. In what concerns legal and electoral (or representative) arrangements, it is impossible to ignore the dominance of the Assembly of rural legitimists, Thiers's capitulationist government and the officers of the regular army, who, having let themselves be thrashed by the Prussian troops without putting up much of a fight, now dream of taking it out on the Parisian workers. That is where power lies, all the more so in that it is the only power recognized by the occupier. On the side of resistance, of political invention, of French revolutionary history, we find the fecund disorder of the Parisian workers' organizations, which mix together the Central Committee of the 20 *arrondissements*, the Federation of Union Chambers, some members of the International, the local military committees, etc. In truth, the historical consistency of this world, split and unbound by the consequences of the war, rests on the prevailing conviction about the inexistence of a proletarian governmental capacity. For the vast majority of people, often including the workers' themselves, the politicized workers of Paris are incomprehensible. They are the proper inexistent of the object 'political capacity' in the uncertain world of this Spring 1871. For the bourgeois, they still exist too much, at least physically. The Paris Bourse harries the government with the following refrain: 'You will never carry out any financial operations if you do not finish once and for all with these scoundrels'. To begin with, through a seemingly straightforward imperative: the disarming of the workers, especially the recovery of the cannons, which the military committees of the National Guard have positioned all throughout Paris. It is this initiative which will turn the object 'March 18' (a day), such as it is exposed in the world 'Paris in Spring 1871', into a site. That is, it will turn it into that which exposes itself in the appearing of which it is a support.

March 18 is the first day of that enormous event, destined to guide the thinking of all revolutionaries up to the present day, an event which is called (which named itself): the Paris Commune, that is the exercise of power, in Paris, by republican or socialist political militants and armed workers' organizations, between 18 March and 28 May 1871. This sequence is brought to an end by the massacre of several tens of thousands of 'rebels' by the troops loyal to Thiers's government and the reactionary Assembly. What exactly is this beginning, March 18, as an object? The answer is: the appearance of worker-being—up until then a social symptom, the brute force of uprisings or a theoretical threat—in the space of political and governmental capacity. What takes place? Thiers orders General Aurelle de Paladines to seize the cannons from the National Guard. The coup is pulled off, around 3 a.m. in the morning, by some select detachments. By all appearances, a complete success. On the walls, it is possible to read the proclamation by Thiers and his ministers, bearing the paradoxes of a split transcendental evaluation: 'May the good citizens separate themselves from the bad and aid the public forces'. But, by 11 a.m. in the morning, the coup has utterly failed. Hundreds of women of the people, then anonymous workers and national guards acting of their own accord, encircle the soldiers. Many fraternize. The cannons are taken back. General Aurelle de Paladines is panic-stricken. The great red peril looms: 'The government calls upon you to defend your dwellings, your families, your property. Some unruly men, at the beck and call of hidden leaders, train on Paris the cannons that had been taken from the Prussians'. According to him, it's a question of 'having done with an insurrectional committee, whose members only represent communist doctrines and who would pillage Paris and bury France'. A wasted effort. Though it is devoid of an actual leadership, the rebellion spreads, occupying the whole city. Armed workers' organizations take over barracks, public buildings and finally the seat of the municipal government, the Hôtel de Ville, which under the red flag will be the place and symbol of the new power. Thiers escapes through a hidden staircase, the minister Jules Favre jumps out of a window, and the entire apparatus of government disappears, installing itself at Versailles. Paris belongs to the insurrection.

March 18 is a site because, besides everything that appears within it under the evasive transcendental of the world 'Paris in Spring 1871', it too appears, as the fulminant and entirely unpredictable beginning of a break with the very thing that regulates its appearance (though this break is still devoid of a concept). Note that 'March 18' is the title of one of the chapters of the magnificent *History of the Paris Commune of 1871* published by the militant Lissagaray in 1876. In that chapter, as one would expect, he deals with 'the women of March 18' and 'the people of March 18', thereby attesting to the inclusion of 'March 18', now become a predicate, in the evaluation of what results from the varying vicissitudes that make up that day. Through the ups and downs of March 18, Lissagaray clearly sees that, impelled by being, an immanent overturning of the law of appearing takes place. The fact that the working people of Paris, overcoming its fragmentary political formation, has thwarted a clear-cut, forcibly executed governmental act (the seizure of the cannons) ultimately entails the demand that there appear an unknown capacity, an unprecedented power. This is how 'March 18' comes to appear, under the injunction of being, as an element of the object that it is.

In effect, from the standpoint of rule-bound appearing, the possibility of a proletarian and popular governmental power purely and simply does not exist. Not even for the militant workers, who speak the language of the 'Republic' in an indefinite way. On the evening of March 18, the majority of the members of the Central Committee of the National Guard—the only effective authority of the city abandoned by its legal guardians—remain convinced that they should not sit in the Hôtel de Ville, repeating that 'they do not have a mandate to govern'. It is only with the sword of circumstances at their throat that they will end up—as Édouard Moreau (a complete nobody) will instruct them on the morning on March 19—deciding to 'hold elections, provide public services and shield the city from a surprise'. Willy-nilly, they constitute themselves into a political authority. In so doing, they include March 18, as the beginning of this authority, among the effects of March 18. It is thus necessary to understand that March 18 is a site, to the extent that it imposes itself on all the elements that contribute to its own existence as invoking 'by force', on the indistinct background of worker-being, an entirely new transcendental evaluation of the latter's intensity. Thought as an object, the site 'March 18' subverts the rules of political appearing (that is, of the logic of power) by means of the support-being 'March 18', in which the impossible possibility of worker-being is shared out.

2. ONTOLOGY OF THE SITE

In what concerns the thinking of its pure being, a site is simply a multiple to which it happens that it is an element of itself. In other words, it is that which, in the first section of Book II, we called a 'reflexive' set. We have just illustrated this 'reflexivity' with the example of March 18, a complex set of vicissitudes from which it follows that 'March 18' is instituted, in the object 'March 18', as the demand of a new political appearing, as forcing an unprecedented transcendental evaluation.

Another example will help us to grasp the paradox of this self-belonging, and the extreme precariousness—in fact, the mandatory fading—of the site. Consider the world constituted by Jean-Jacques Rousseau's novel, *The New Heloise*. As you know, this novel recounts the thwarted love between the beautiful Swiss woman Julie d'Étanges and the commoner Saint-Preux. Under her father's thumb, Julie marries the wise Monsieur de Wolmar, who—aside from organizing an exemplary kind of civilized country life in Clarens—attempts a therapy of the lovers' passion by means of forgetting. This therapy ultimately fails. As she lies dying, Julie is compelled to write—it will be her last letter—in Rousseau's marvellous musical style: 'The virtue that separated us on earth, will unite us in our eternal abode. I die in this sweet expectation. Too happy to pay with my life for the right always to love you without crime, and to tell you so once again'.

The novel distributes the intensities on a calculated background of separations. Once forbidden, love must painfully assume lack: 'I feel it, my friend, the weight of absence overpowers me'. Moreover, this is what justifies the literary form chosen by Rousseau: the epistolary novel, the novel of what traverses absence. It also means that every real encounter between Julie and Saint-Preux exposes them to the danger of desire. Accordingly, all the book's great scenes examine their infrequent reunions, in a knowing link to the pre-romantic complicity of nature. This is true of the first kiss in the copse: 'The sun begins to wane, we flee from the remaining rays into the wood'; of Julie's 'fall', after Saint-Preux's journey in the Valais mountains: 'I forgot everything, and could only remember love'; of the night of shared and sublime love, in the moment of illusory hope: 'Come then, soul of my heart, life of my life, come reunite with me'; and of the most famous of all the scenes, after Julie's marriage and Saint-Preux's voyage around the globe, in this immense moment when the lovers' bodies will never come together again, the scene of temptation during a boat trip on the lake: 'The oars' steady, monotonous noise excited me into dreaming'. Each time, these punctuations restart the novel, bearing witness to the power of love against every reasonable order, and even against every ordinary happiness. Against every order: true love is to be found in 'these divine diversions of reason, more brilliant, more sublime, stronger, a hundred times better than reason itself'; against every happiness: 'My friend, I am too happy; happiness bores me'. But at the same time, though this power of the amorous encounter might decisively change the course of the world and of the subjects who inhabit it, it does so only once it's disappeared. Rousseau is the literary wizard of this infinite trembling in which the amorous site makes the radiance of appearing coincide with its immediate revocation. Now, just as the disorganized enthusiasm of 18 March 1871 only founds the Commune to the extent that, from March 19 on, what is at stake are its extremely thorny consequences and the missing discipline they require, likewise love is born of loss and is faithful to it through 'the concurrence of souls in faraway places'.

This is because the very being of the amorous encounter, such as it subverts appearing, carries an ineluctable dose of nothingness. The twofold metaphor of this revelation of the void that lies beneath the being-there of multiplicities is, on the side of Saint-Preux, the very romantic call to the fusion of the lovers under the sign of death, as proven by the line: 'would it not be a hundred times better to see each other for a single instant and die?'; on Julie's side, it is the subtle and pondered certainty that in love there is a desiring reverie which is more essential than any reality. These incomparable melodies are well known. The first declares the glimpsed antecedence of being over appearing, in a kind of caesura of happiness: 'Woe betide anyone who has nothing left to desire! He loses everything he owns, so to speak. There's less enjoyment to be drawn from what one obtains than from what one hopes for, and one is only happy before being happy'. The second is the canticle to non-being intoned by indestructible love: 'The land of chimeras is the only one in this world worthy of being inhabited, and such is the nothingness of human affairs, that aside from the Being that exists on its own, the only beauty is in that which is not'.

This understanding of what is played out for a subject on the basis of the amorous site explores the inevitable termination of the pure self-coincidence, the paradoxical self-belonging, which gives the site its worth. The ontology of the site is entirely that of what cannot be maintained, since it is, by a reflexive violence, an exception to the laws of being, in particular of the law that forbids a multiple from being an element of itself (this is formally expressed in the axiom of foundation). Thus the amorous encounter—just like a victorious day of insurrection, for example 18 March 1871—is an exceptional form of the One, the form of what dwells in itself as whole and as an element of the whole. This form of the one is but a passage, a visitation: the laws of being close up on that which will have violated them for a flash of time. As Saint-Preux writes: 'This eternity of happiness was but an instant of my life. Time has resumed its slowness in the moments of my despair, and boredom measures in long years the unfortunate remainder of my days'.

The ontology of a site can thus be described in terms of three properties:

1. A site is a reflexive multiplicity, which belongs to itself and thereby transgresses the laws of being.
2. Because it carries out a transitory cancellation of the gap between being and being-there, a site is the instantaneous revelation of the void that haunts multiplicities.
3. A site is an ontological figure of the instant: it appears only to disappear.

3. LOGIC OF THE SITE, 1: CONSEQUENCES AND EXISTENCE

As we've said, the entirety of a doctrine of change cannot be reduced to the site. We called 'modification' the simple becoming of the objects of a world under the rule of the intensities prescribed for that world by its transcendental. There obviously exist intermediaries between simple modification and the properly evental effects of which a site is capable. The site must in fact be thought, not only in terms of the three ontological particularities that we have just accorded it, but also in the logical (or intra-worldly) deployment of its consequences. Since the site is a figure of the instant, since it only appears to disappear, true duration can only be that of consequences. The enthusiasm of 18 March 1871 undoubtedly founds the first workers' power in history. But when, on May 10, the Central Committee proclaims that in order to save 'this revolution of March 18 which it has made so beautifully' it will 'put an end to the quarrels, defeat ill will, bring an end to rivalries, ignorance and incapacity', this swaggering despair conveys something of what, for the preceding two months, had appeared in the city in terms of the distribution or envelopment of political intensities.

Having said that, what is a consequence? The subordination of formal logic to transcendental logic, whose guiding principle we have established (Book II, Section 4), licences a rigorous definition. A consequence is the logical interpretation of a relation between transcendental degrees, a relation which we called *dependence*. The dependence of a degree q with regard to a degree p is the envelope of all the degrees t whose conjunction with p remains lesser than or equal to q. Thus the measure of the entailment of q by p, written $p \Rightarrow q$, is formally equal to the envelope of all the degrees whose conjunction with p remains inferior to q. Broadly speaking, it is the degree which, conjoined with the 'entailing' degree, lies as close as possible to the entailed degree. If we move from the transcendental back to the beings that appear in a world, we can establish the value of the relation of consequence between them through the mediation of their degree of existence. If the element a of an object is such that the existence of a has value p, and if the element b of the same object exists to the degree q, we will posit that b is the consequence of a to the exact extent of the value of the entailment of q by p.

This regime of consequence in appearing is one of Rousseau's leitmotifs. In his work, the intensity of existence has a name: 'happiness'. The question of the relations of consequence in which happiness can endure is the same one which plays a central role in what he dubbed 'sensitive morality'. For example, if remembrance (or the imaginary) can have such a place in amorous happiness, it is because the intensity of existence of the idea of the beloved transcends space, so that very distant configurations of the world remain bound to it through a consequence whose transcendental value is maximal: 'Try as we may to escape what is dear to us, its image, faster than the sea and the winds, chases us to the ends of the universe, and wherever we may take ourselves we take with us that which makes us live'. Monsieur de Wolmar, Julie's cold, wise husband, will instead argue that time, in this respect different than space, diminishes, or renders minimal, existential consequences. He counts on forgetting—this name for atonic consequences—to 'cure' the original passion of Saint-Preux for his wife. For Wolmar, the value of existential consequence from the disappeared site of passion to the living present is almost nil. This subtle husband flatters himself that he is only a rival in the past tense: 'He [Saint-Preux] does not evade me as the possessor of the person he loves, but as the abductor of the one he loved'. Saint-Preux 'loved her [Julie] as he saw her, not as she was'. Ultimately, Wolmar fights the existential power of the site through the purely worldly labour of ordinary becomings: 'He loves her in the past tense: this is the truth of the enigma. Strip him of memory, and he will lose love'. Between the intensity of existence of (past) feeling and that of the (present) amicable 'sweet relation', the value of the consequence is weak, perhaps nil. Only an elevated value of this relation of consequence would be dangerous, for it would turn amicable or pacified appearing into the equivocal support of passion. Rousseau will finally conclude that Wolmar is mistaken. No more than space, time does not abolish the intensities that attach themselves to the consequences of an amorous site. But the main point to retain from this whole analysis is that consequence is a (strong or weak) relation between existences, and that therefore the degree according to which a thing is a consequence of another is never independent of the intensity of existence of these things in the world in question. Thus, to use another example, the declaration of the Central Committee of which we spoke above may be read as a thesis on consequences. It records:

– the very strong intensity of existence of the day of 18 March 1871, this 'beautiful' revolution;
– implicitly, the disastrous degree of existence of political discipline in the workers' camp two months later ('ill will', 'exhaustion', 'ignorance', 'incapacity');
– the (regrettably abstract) desire to raise the value of the consequences of the politics under way with respect to the power of existence of its disappeared origin.

The site is the appearing/disappearing of a multiple whose paradox is self-belonging. The logic of the site concerns the distribution of intensities around this disappeared point which is the site. We must therefore begin by the beginning: what is the value of existence of the site itself? We will then proceed by dealing with what this allows us to infer about consequences.

4. LOGIC OF THE SITE, 2: FACT AND SINGULARITY

Nothing, in the ontology of the site, prescribes its value of existence. An upsurge can be a barely 'perceivable' local appearance (this is merely an image, for there is no perception here). A disappearance may leave no trace. It may well happen that, ontologically affected by the marks of 'true' change (self-belonging, indication of the void and disappearance in the instant), a site may nonetheless, by virtue of its existential insignificance, differ little from a simple modification. Take Tuesday 23 May 1871. When almost the whole of Paris is at the mercy of the Versailles army rabble, who are executing workers by the thousands all over the city, and any political and military leadership has collapsed on the side of the communards, who fight barricade by barricade, the remnants of the Central Committee make their final proclamation, hurriedly posted on a few walls. It is—as Lissagaray notes with dark irony—a 'proclamation of victors'. It demands the joint dissolution of the (legal) Assembly of Versailles and the

Commune, the army's pull-out from Paris, a provisional government entrusted to delegates from the larger cities, and a mutual amnesty. How are we to characterize this sad 'Manifesto'? In its very incongruity, it cannot be reduced to the normality of becoming. Albeit in a tattered and derisory form, it still expresses the Commune's self-certainty, its correct conviction that it contains a political beginning. It is legitimate to treat this document—which the wind from the barracks will blow into the oubliettes—as a site. Having said that, in the brutal twilight of the workers' insurrection, its value of existence is very weak. What is at stake here is the singular power of the site. The Central Committee's Manifesto is undoubtedly ontologically situated in what the evental syntagm 'Paris Commune' holds together, but since in its own right it is only a sign of decomposition, of powerlessness, it leads the singularity back to the edges of the pure and simple 'normal' modification of the world.

For this not to be the case, the force of existence in the appearing of the site would have to compensate for its vanishing. Only a site whose value of existence is maximal is potentially an event. This is certainly the case, on 18 March 1871, when, led by its women, the working people of Paris stops the army from disarming the National Guard. It is the same when love imposes the power of the incomprehensible—unlike the Central Committee's 'Manifesto', which imposed the powerlessness of incomprehension. As Saint-Preux declares so fittingly: 'It is a miracle of love; the more it exceeds my reason, the more it enchants my heart, and one of the pleasures it provides me is that of not understanding it at all'. Only a complete power of existing differentiates a site from the simple network of modifications in which the law of the world persists. A site that does not exist maximally is a mere fact. Though ontologically identifiable, it is not, within appearing, logically singular.

We have called *modification* the simple becoming a world, seen from the standpoint of an object of that world. Since it is internal to the established transcendental correlations, modification does not call for a site.

We will call *fact* a site whose intensity of existence is not maximal.

We will call *singularity* a site whose intensity of existence is maximal.

We now have at our disposal three distinct degrees of change: modification, which is ontologically neutral and transcendentally regular; the fact, which is ontologically supernumerary but existentially (and thus logically) weak; singularity, which is ontologically supernumerary and whose value of appearance (or of existence) is maximal.

Note that the repressive force of the Versailles troops is accompanied by a propaganda that systematically de-singularizes the Commune, in order to present it as a monstrous set of facts, which must (forcibly) be brought back into the normal order of modification. This leads to some extraordinary statements, such as the one made in the conservative paper *Le Siècle* on 21 May 1871, in the midst of the massacres of workers: 'The social difficulty has been resolved or is on the way to being resolved'. One couldn't put it better. It is true that already on March 21, three days after the insurrection, Jules Favre had declared that Paris was in the hands of 'a handful of scoundrels, subordinating the rights of the Assembly to I don't know what bloody and rapacious ideal'. In the appearing of a world, the strategic and tactical choices move between modification, fact and singularity, because it is always a question of relating to a logical order. Without requiring instruments as horrific as those employed by the Versailles troops, it is nevertheless from a return to the placid order of modifications that Wolmar expects the 'cure' of the erstwhile lovers: through the work of time, the impassioned singularity will become a pure fact, and this fact will in turn fade into the familial and amicable contract. Monsieur de Wolmar has understood, or at least thinks he has understood, that the singular fervour of the passion that unites Julie and Saint-Preux, with its elective dimension and existential power, depends on 'so many praiseworthy things, which should be regulated rather than abolished'. To 'regulate' a singularity requires treating its consequences as though they were of the order of fact, and hence appropriate to the transcendental measure of modifications. This is why Rousseau's novel is the improbable articulation of a wild singularity and of the desire to no longer be anything but the calm agent of the modifications of a rustic and familial world. On the one hand, we have the cry of love, which exempts existence from the laws of being: 'Nature has conserved our being, and love delivers us to life'. On the other, the immobile utopia of the friends gathered in Wolmar's home: 'A small number of gentle and placid people, united by mutual needs and reciprocal goodwill, contributing in different ways to a common end: each finding in his state everything that's needed to be happy with it and not desire to leave it, they all attach themselves to this state as though that's how they'll have to spend the rest of their lives'. The sense of appearing is played out between the gentleness of regulated perpetuation (but it is in its name that the ruthless Thiers declares on 22 May 1871, in the midst of the massacres, that 'the cause of justice, order, humanity and civilization has triumphed') and the insurrection of existence (but it is because of it that Saint-Preux declares himself 'violently tempted to plunge her [Julie] with him into the waves, and to end in her arms his life and its long torments'), when what surges up puts into question the logic which makes it so that this appearing has the consistency of a world.

If it happens to a world, by dint of a site coming to be within it, to be finally situated and to arrange itself between singularity and fact, it is then up to the network of consequences to decide.

5. LOGIC OF THE SITE, 3: WEAK SINGULARITY AND STRONG SINGULARITY

Since it is characterized by a maximal intensity of existence, singularity lies farther than fact from mere immanent modification. If we are now obliged to distinguish between weak singularities and strong singularities, it is in terms of the links of consequence which the vanished site establishes with the other elements of the object that had presented it in the world. In brief, we can say that existing maximally for the duration of its appearance/disappearance confers on the site the power of a singularity—but that the *force* of a singularity lies in making its consequences, and not just itself, exist maximally. We reserve the name 'event' for a strong singularity [*singularité forte*]. The complete typology of change thus comprises four classes arranged in the following manner:

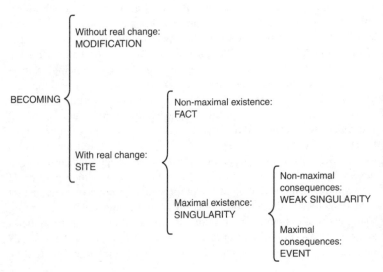

BECOMING

Without real change: MODIFICATION

With real change: SITE

Non-maximal existence: FACT

Maximal existence: SINGULARITY

Non-maximal consequences: WEAK SINGULARITY

Maximal consequences: EVENT

I will now provide a brief didactic illustration of the predicative distinction strength/weakness [*force*/faiblesse] as applied to singularities (to sites whose transcendental intensity of existence is maximal). It is evident that, in terms of how appearing is worked over by a truth, the Paris Commune, brutally crushed within two months, is nonetheless far more important than 4 September 1870, when the political regime of the Second Empire collapses and the Third Republic begins, which will last 70 years. This is not a matter of the actors involved. September 4 too involves the working people, beneath red flags, overrunning the square of the Hôtel-de-Ville and triggering the collapse of officialdom, so well recounted by Lissagaray: 'Great dignitaries, fat functionaries, vicious mamelukes, imperious ministers, solemn chamberlains, moustachioed generals, snuck out pathetically on September 4, like ham actors booed by their audience'. On the one hand, an insurrection that institutes no duration, on the other a day that changes the state. September 4 will be hijacked by bourgeois politicians, especially anxious to re-establish the order of property-owners. The Commune, Lenin's ideal referent, will instead inspire a century of revolutionary thought and thus come to deserve the famous evaluation that Marx proposed of it at the time:

Working men's Paris, with its Commune, will be for ever celebrated as the glorious harbinger of a new society. Its martyrs are enshrined in the great heart of the working class. Its exterminators history has already nailed to that eternal pillory from which all the prayers of their priest will not avail to redeem them.

Let's posit that in alignment with the general development of European states, which makes them converge on the parliamentary form, 4 September 1870 is a weak singularity. And that the Commune, by proposing to thinking a rule for emancipation, relayed by October 1917 and also by the summer of 1967 in China or the French May '68, is a strong singularity. For what counts is not only the exceptional intensity of its surging up—the fact that we are dealing with a violent episode that creates appearing—but the glorious and uncertain consequences that this upsurge, despite its vanishing, sets out.

Commencements are to be measured by the re-commencements they enable.

One could also say that the love between Julie and Saint-Preux is but a sterile passion, which it is right to renounce. What founds an entire universe—the utopia of Clarens—is instead the marriage of Julie to Monsieur de Wolmar. Rousseau himself leans towards this judgement when he reflects that 'heroism has but a vain appearance, and nothing is solid save for virtue'. But must we only take into account what is 'solid'? That which imposes upon a world the serene force of its transcendental intensity? Must one always—weak singularity—be this 'man of taste who lives to live, who knows how to enjoy himself, who seeks out true and simple pleasures and who would like to promenade himself outside his own front door'? Rousseau does not resign himself to this. Only the feeling that shakes up souls and delivers them to the infinity of the True is truly universal in its consequences, and manages to be equal to the whole world. In the torment of strong singularity one must be able to cry out: 'What is the existence of the whole world compared to the delicious sentiment that unites us?' One must be faithful to the incantations of 'sensitive morality': 'O sentiment, sentiment! Sweet life of the soul! Which is the heart of stone that you have never touched? Who is the unfortunate mortal from whom you will never wrest some tears?' Just like 4 September 1870, the origin of an interminable Republic, the irruption of Wolmar into the life of Julie—a forced irruption imposed by her father—signals the foundation of an order, the very order that Julie describes as 'the immutable and constant attachment between two honest and reasonable people who, destined to spend the rest of their days together, are happy with their fate and try to make it pleasant for one another'. Love is instead what makes truth of disorder, which is why it is the bearer of that which is indelible in the event. As Julie will confess at death's door: 'Tried as I did to stifle the first sentiment that gave me life, it concentrated itself in my heart'.

To judge if an aleatory adjunction to the world deserves to be taken, not just as a singularity beyond modifications and facts, but as an event, we must look to that portion of it which endures in the concentration, beyond itself, of its intensity.

6. LOGIC OF THE SITE, 4: EXISTENCE OF THE INEXISTENT

There is no stronger transcendental consequence than the one which makes what did not exist in a world appear within it. This is the case for the day of 18 March 1871, which puts at the centre of the political storm a collection of unknown workers, unknown even to the specialists of revolution, those surviving '48ers' who unfortunately will encumber the Commune with their bluster. Consider the first proclamation of 19 March 1871 by the Central Committee, the only organism directly accountable for the insurrection of March 18: 'Let Paris and France together lay the foundations for a Republic acclaimed along with all its consequences, for the only government which will put an end to the era of invasions and civil wars once and for all'. Who signs this unprecedented political decision? Twenty people, three quarters of whom are proletarians which the occasion alone constitutes and identifies. It's easy then for the governmental paper *L'Officiel* to ask: 'Who are the members of this committee? Are they communists, Bonapartists or Prussians?' We already encounter the inexhaustible theme of 'foreign agents'. But the consequence of the event is to bring to (a provisionally maximal) political existence the workers who were inexistent on its eve.

The strong singularity can thus be recognized by the fact that its consequence in the world is to make exist within it the proper inexistent of the object-site.

It is to a phenomenon of the same order that Julie ascribes the sudden revelation—for her, the tender, not very sensual, radiant believer—of sexual sensibility, when she faints in the arms of Saint-Preux, who she's been bold enough to beckon, one evening, into the shadows of a copse. She deems this to be a mere concession to masculine desire. But she is mistaken: 'I learnt in the copse at Clarens that I had been too confident, and that one should not accord anything to the senses when one wishes to refuse them something. An instant, a single instant set my own aflame with a fire that nothing can put out'. The subjective inexistence of sensuality is abruptly brought into existence, in the clandestine night, as the consequence of the amorous encounter.

In a more abstract fashion, we will propose the following definition: *Take a site (an object marked by self-belonging) which is a singularity (its intensity of existence, as instantaneous and evanescent as it may be, is nonetheless maximal). We will say that this site is a 'strong singularity' or an 'event' if the value of the entailment of the (nil) value of its proper inexistent by the (maximal) value of the site is itself maximal.*

This formula only seems intricate. We know (IV.1 and IV.3) that every object possesses a proper inexistent as an element (that is an element whose transcendental value of existence is minimal). We also know (II.1.4) that it is the transcendental idea of the entailment of one degree of appearance by another which supports the formal idea of implication (of consequence). We are therefore simply saying this: *The maximally true consequence of an event's (maximal) intensity of existence is the existence of the inexistent.*

Obviously, we are confronted here with a violent paradox. For if an implication is maximally true, and its antecedent is too, its consequence must also be maximally true; this leads to the untenable conclusion according to which, under the effect of an event, the inexistent of the site exists absolutely.

In effect, the unknowns of the Central Committee, politically inexistent in the world of the eve of the insurrection, exist absolutely on the very day of their appearance. The people of Paris obey their proclamations, encouraging them to occupy all public buildings, participating in the elections that they organize. Similarly, Julie's neglected sensuality imposes itself, indestructible, as a consequence of the first kiss.

The paradox can be analysed in three steps.

First of all, the principle behind this tipping-over from inexistence to absolute existence in worldly appearing is an evanescent principle. The event consumes its own power in this existential transfiguration. Neither 18 March 1871 nor the encounter between the very young Julie and her philosopher-tutor have the least stability. Their ontological precariousness, their un-founded being, dissipates itself in that which it brings to absolute existence. As Saint-Preux says: 'Of us, only our love is left'.

Furthermore, if the inexistent of the site must finally attain maximal intensity in the order of appearing, it is only to the extent that it now stands in the place of what has disappeared; its maximality is the subsisting mark of the event itself in the world. As Saint-Preux says: 'there are eternal impressions that neither time nor our attentions can efface. The wound heals but the mark remains, and this mark is a treasured seal'. The 'eternal' existence of the inexistent is the outline or statement, in the world, of the disappeared event. The proclamations of the Commune, the first workers' power in universal history, or the reign of sensibility as decreed by Julie—these are existents whose absoluteness manifests that an entirely new arrangement of its appearing, a mutation of its logic, has befallen the world. It is through the existence of the inexistent that the subversion of appearing by being, which underlies it, unfolds within appearing itself. This is the logical indication of a paradox of being: an onto-logical chimera. Of course, we recognize within it the trace of the vanished event, to which, ever since Book I, we have accorded the power to orient a subjectivizable body. Yes, this ε from which stems the subjective power of the body is nothing other than the over-existence which affects the proper inexistent of an object of the world, when this object is an event-site.

Finally, there where existence now stands, the inexistent must return.

The worldly order is not subverted to the point of being able to demand that a logical law of worlds be abolished. Every object has one proper inexistent. And if the latter sublimates itself—as the trace whence a subject proceeds—in absolute existence, another element of the site must cease to exist, in order for the law to be safeguarded and for the coherence of appearing to be ultimately preserved.

7. LOGIC OF THE SITE, 5: DESTRUCTION

Adding a conclusion to his *History of the Paris Commune of 1871* in 1896, Lissagaray makes two observations. The first is that the cabal of reactionaries and murderers of workers from 1871 is still in place. Aided by parliamentarianism it has even been augmented by 'some bourgeois pied-pipers who, disguised as democrats, assist its advances'. The second is that the people have now constituted their own force: 'Thrice [in 1792, 1848 and 1870] the French proletariat has made the Republic for others; it is now ripe for its own'. In other words, the Commune-event, begun on 18 March 1871, definitely did not have as one of its consequences the destruction of the dominant group and its politicians; but it destroyed something more important: the political subordination of the workers and the people. What was destroyed was of the order of subjective incapacity. As Lissagaray exclaims: 'Ah! The workers of the countryside and the towns are not uncertain of their capacity'. Though crushed and convulsive, the absolutization of the workers' political existence—the existence of the inexistent—nonetheless destroyed an essential form of subjection, that of proletarian political possibility to bourgeois political manoeuvring.

The fact that more than a century later this subjection has been reconstituted—or rather reinvented under the name of 'democracy'—is another story, another sequence in the troubled history of truths. What we can say is that there where an inexistent lay, the destruction of what legitimated this inexistence came to be. At the beginning of the twentieth century, what occupies the place of the dead is no longer proletarian political consciousness but—even though it doesn't know it yet—the prejudice about the natural character of classes and the millennia-old vocation of property-owners and the wealthy to wield state and social power. It is this destruction that the Paris Commune carries out for the future, even in the apparent putting to death of its own over-existence.

We can draw from this a transcendental maxim: if what was worth nothing comes, in the guise of an evental consequence, to be worth everything, then an established given of appearing is destroyed. What seemed to support the cohesion of the world is abruptly turned to nothing. Thus, if transcendental indexing is indeed the (logical) base of the world, it is with good reason that we can say, along with the Internationale: 'The earth shall rise on new foundations' [*Le monde va changer de base*].

It is only in the name of such a change that Saint-Preux declares his eternal fidelity to the sorrowful love that unites him to Julie. Of course, as he says, 'I have lost everything', but he immediately adds: 'I have only my faith left: it will be with me until the grave'. What is the content of this 'faith'? Very simply the possibility of a life in love, a possibility testified to, in an immeasurable way, by that which he was obliged to renounce; on its own, this possibility enacts the irreversible destruction of what is nevertheless a widespread and socially legitimate prejudice: the prejudice according to which two individuals are necessarily each other than the other, so that one can and must distinguish between the one and the other, between 'you' and 'me'. Having enacted, in the event of passion-love, the over-existence of sexed in-difference, Saint-Preux objects to this prejudice, in words valid for all time: 'two lovers love one another? No, "you" and "me" are words banished by their tongue; they are no longer two, they are one'.

Through the transitory creation of a new subject of truth, love irreversibly imposes the destruction of the ordinary social idea, the one that separates bodies, consigning them to their particular interests.

When the world is violently enchanted by the absolute consequences of a paradox of being, all of appearing, threatened by the local destruction of a customary evaluation, must reconstitute a different distribution of what exists and what does not. Under the pressure that being exerts on its own appearing, the world may be accorded the chance—mixing existence and destruction—of an other world. It is of this other world that the subject, once grafted onto the trace of what has happened, is eternally the prince.

SECTION 2
The Event According to Deleuze

Deleuze always paid tribute to Sartre as the one who awoke the French philosophy of the thirties and forties from its academic slumber. He thought that it all began with the 1937 article, 'The Transcendence of the Ego'. Why? Because in this text Sartre proposed the idea—I quote Deleuze—of 'an impersonal transcendental field, having the form neither of a synthetic personal consciousness nor that of a subjective identity—the subject, on the contrary, is always constituted'. I especially want to subscribe to this remark by Deleuze insofar as the theme of an impersonal transcendental field dominates the whole of my Greater Logic, in which it is effectuated as a logic of appearing or of worlds—down to the smallest technical detail.

Deleuze also notes that Sartre was prevented from thinking through all the consequences of his idea because he continued to tie the impersonal field to a self-consciousness [*conscience (de) soi*]. This is entirely correct. We can put it differently: Sartre was still concerned with the auto-unification of the transcendental. He did not expose the subject to the chance of a pure Outside. One of the names of this Outside is 'event'. That is why the event, as that to which the power of a thought devotes itself and/or that from which this power stems, has after Sartre become a term common to most contemporary philosophers. Aside from the critique of the phenomenology of consciousness, this term has been conveyed to us, on the side of truth-procedures, by the enduring impact in the twentieth century of four overlapping themes: in politics, Revolution; in love, erotic liberation; in the arts, performance; and in the sciences, the epistemological break. In philosophy, we can detect it in Wittgenstein ('The world is all that is the case') as well as in Heidegger (being as coming-to-be, *Ereignis*).

The notion is central in Deleuze, just as it is in my own endeavour. But what a contrast! The interest of this contrast is that it exposes the original ambiguity in the notion. In effect, it is a notion that contains a structural dimension (interruption as such, the appearance of a supernumerary term) and a dimension that concerns the history of life (the concentration of becoming, being as coming-to-self, promise). In the first case, the event is unbound from the One, there is separation, assumption of the void, pure non-sense; in the second, it is the play of the One, composition, intensity of plenitude, crystal (or logic) of sense. *Logic of Sense* is Deleuze's most note-worthy effort to clarify his concept of the event. He does so in the company of the Stoics. This sets the tone: the 'event' must comply with the inflexible discipline of the All, from which Stoicism takes its bearings. Between 'event' and 'fate' there must be a subjective reciprocation of sorts. I will extract from *Logic of Sense* what we could call the four Deleuzian axioms of the event:

Axiom 1. 'Unlimited-becoming becomes the event itself'.

The event is the ontological realization of the eternal truth of the One, of the infinite power of Life. It is by no means that which a void, or an astonishment, separates from what becomes. On the contrary, it is the concentration of the continuity of life, its intensification. The event is the gift of the One amid the concatenation of multiplicities. We could propose the following formula: in becomings, the event testifies to the One of which these becomings are the expression. That is why there is no contradiction between the unlimited character of becoming and the singularity of the event. The event immanently exposes the One of becomings, it makes this One become. The event is the becoming of becoming: the becoming(-One) of (unlimited) becoming.

Axiom 2. 'The event is always what has just happened, what will happen, but never what is happening'.

The event is a synthesis of past and future. In truth, as the expression of the One within becomings, it is the eternal identity of the future as a dimension of the past. For Deleuze just as for Bergson, the ontology of time does not accept any figure of separation. Furthermore, the event cannot be what lies 'between' a past and a future, between the end of one world and the beginning of another. Rather, it is encroachment and connection: it realizes the undividable continuum of Virtuality. It exhibits the unity of the passage that binds the a-little-after to the a-little-before. It is not 'what is happening', 'what is coming to pass', but that which, in what is happening, has and will become. The event speaks the being of time, or time as the continual and eternal instance of being; it does not carry out any division in time, it does not insert any intervallic void between two times. The 'event' rebuts the present as passage *and* separation, the operational paradox of becoming. This can be put in two ways: there is no present (the event is re-presented, it is the active immanence that co-presents past and future); or, everything is present (the event is living or chaotic eternity as the essence of time).

Axiom 3. 'The nature of the event is other than that of the actions and passions of the body. But it results from them'.

As the becoming of becomings, or disjunctive eternity, the event intensifies bodies, concentrating their constitutive multiplicity. Therefore it can neither be of the same kind as the actions and passions of these bodies, nor can it stand above them. The event is not identical to the bodies that it affects, but neither does it transcend what happens to them or what they do. So it also cannot be said to differ (ontologically) from bodies. Qua result, it is the differentiator of the actions and passions of bodies. For what is the One immanent to becomings, if not Becoming? Or difference, or Relation (other terms in Deleuze's lexicon). But Becoming is not an idea, it is what becomings become. Thus the event affects bodies, because it is what they make or support as an exposed synthesis. It is the advent within them of the One that they are, as a distinct nature (the virtual rather than the actual) and a homogeneous result (without them, it is not). That is the meaning to be given to the formula: 'The event is coextensive with becoming'.

We should think of the event of Life as a body without organs: its nature is other than that of living organisms, but it is only unfolded or legible as the result of the actions and passions of these organisms.

Axiom 4. 'A life is composed of the same single Event, despite all the variety of what happens to it'.

The difficult point here is not the reiteration of the One as the concentrated expression of vital unfolding. The three foregoing axioms are clear about that point. The difficulty lies in understanding the word 'composed'. The event is that which composes a life a little like a musical composition is organized by its theme. The event is not what happens to a life, but that which is in that which happens, or that which happens in that which happens. Hence there can only be one Event. Amid the disparate material of a life, the Event is the Eternal Return of the identical, the undifferentiated power of the Same: 'powerful inorganic life'. When it comes to any multiplicities whatever, it is of the essence of the Event to compose them as the One that they are, and to exhibit this unique composition in potentially infinite variations.

With these four axioms, Deleuze makes explicit his own conception of the event's ambiguity: he opts for fate. The event is not the chance-laden passage from one state of affairs to another. It is the immanent mark of the One-result of all becomings. In the multiple-that-becomes, in the in-between of those multiples which are active multiplicities, the event is the fate of the One.

It suffices to reverse the axioms—here, as in Book II, the 'reverse' is what makes negation appear—to obtain a pretty good axiomatic for what I call 'event': a site which, having appeared according to the maximal intensity, is equally capable of absolutizing in appearing what hitherto was its own proper inexistent.

Axiom 1. An event is never the concentration of vital continuity or the immanent intensification of a becoming. It is never coextensive with becoming. On the contrary, it is a pure cut in becoming made by an object of the world, through that object's auto-appearance; but it is also the supplementing of appearing through the upsurge of a trace: the old inexistent which has become an intense existence.

With regard to the continuum in the becomings of the world, there is both a lack (impossibility of auto-appearance without interrupting the authority of the mathematical laws of being and the logical laws of appearing) and an excess (impossibility of the upsurge of a maximal intensity of existence). 'Event' names the conjunction of this lack and this excess.

Axiom 2. The event cannot be the undivided encroachment of the past on the future or the eternally past being of the future. On the contrary, it is a separating evanescence, an atemporal instant which disjoins the previous state of an object (the site) from its subsequent state. We could also say that the event extracts from one time the possibility of another time. This other time, whose materiality envelops the consequences of the event, deserves the name of new present. The event is neither past nor future. It presents us with the present.

Axiom 3. The event cannot result from the actions and passion of a body, nor can it differ in kind from these actions and passions. On the contrary, an active body adequate to the new present is an effect of the event, as we shall see in detail in Book VII. We must here reverse Deleuze—in the sense that he himself, following Nietzsche, wants to reverse Plato. It is not the actions and passions of multiples which are synthesized in the event as an immanent result. It is the blow of the evental One which magnetizes multiplicities and constitutes them into subjectivizable bodies. And the trace of the event, itself incorporated into the new present, is obviously of the same nature as the actions of this body.

In a general way, we can say that Deleuze posits the One as ontological condition (chaos, the One-All, Life) and as evental result, whereas I posit that the One ontologically in-exists (the multiple is 'One-less') and is only linked to truths to the extent that it is an evental principle, and not at all a result. I cannot accept the idea that events 'are never anything but effects', to the point that Deleuze ends up calling them 'events-effects'. This is not because they are causes, or worse, 'essences'. They are acts, or actants, material principles (the site) of a truth. For Deleuze, the event is the immanent consequence of becomings or of Life. For me, the event is the immanent principle of exceptions to becoming, or Truths.

Axiom 4. There can be no composition of that which is by a single event. On the contrary, there is a de-composition of worlds by multiple event-sites.

Just as it is the separation of time, so the event is a separation from other events. Truths are multiple and multiform. They are also in exception of worlds, not the One that makes worlds chime with one another. While he denies it—arguing as he does for the idea of divergent series and incompossible worlds—Deleuze often adopts the Leibnizian principle of Harmony. The eternal and unique Event is the focal point on which the ingredients of a life converge. Beyond the 'chaosmos' in which divergent series and multifarious multiplicities are effectuated, 'nothing subsists but the Event, the Event alone, *Eventum tantum* for all the contraries, communicating with itself through its own distance, resonating through all its disjunctions'. Well, this 'resonance' has no charm for us. I affirm the dull and utterly unresonant sound of what has locally cut through the appearing of a site, and which nothing brings into harmony—or disharmony— either with itself (be it as a subsistent solitude) or with other becomings (be it as the absorption of contraries). There is not and there cannot be a

'Unique event of which all the others are fragments and shards'. The one of the truth that the event initiates presupposes its being without-One, its contingent dissemination.

As Lyotard might say, this dispute amounts to a differend. For it concerns the fundamental semantic connection of the word 'event': on the side of sense for Deleuze, on the side of truth for me. Deleuze's formula is irrevocable: 'The event, that is to say sense'. From the beginning of his book, he fashions what to my mind is a chimerical entity, an inconsistent portmanteau-word: the 'sense-event'. Incidentally, this brings him far closer than he would have wished to the linguistic turn and the great lineage of contemporary sophistry. To argue that the event belongs to the register of sense tips it over entirely onto the side of language. Consider this: 'The event is sense itself. The event belongs essentially to language, it entertains an essential relationship with language'. It would be necessary to examine in detail the dramatic reactive consequences of statements of this kind, and of many others—for instance: '[The event] is the pure expressed which signals to us in what happens'. This contains in germ the aestheticization of all things, and the expressive politics of so-called 'multitudes', in which the Master's compact thought is today dispersed. As a localized dysfunction of the transcendental of a world, the event does not possess the least sense, nor is it sense. The fact that it only abides as a trace does not entail that it must be tipped over onto the side of language. It simply opens up a space of consequences in which the body of a truth is composed. As Lacan saw, this real point is strictly speaking senseless, and its only relationship to language is to make a hole in it. This hole cannot be filled by that which, according to the transcendental laws of saying, is sayable.

Like all the philosophers of vital continuity, Deleuze cannot maintain the gap between sense, the transcendental law of appearing, and truths as exceptions. At times, he even seems to equate the two terms. He once wrote to me that he 'had no need' for the category of truth. He was perfectly right. Sense is a sufficient name for truth. But this equation gives rise to some perverse effects. Vitalist logic, which submits the actualizations of multiplicities to the law of the virtual One-All, cannot perceive the purely religious character of the simultaneous assertion that events are sense, and that they possess, as Deleuze proclaims, 'an eternal truth'. If sense effectively possesses an eternal truth, God exists, since he was never anything other than the truth of sense. Deleuze's idea of the event should have persuaded him to follow Spinoza—who he elects as 'the Christ of philosophy'—right to the end, and to name the unique Event in which becomings are diffracted as 'God'. Lacan was well aware that if you consign what happens to sense or meaning, you work towards the subjective consolidation of religion, for, as he wrote, 'the stability of religion stems from the fact that meaning is always religious'.

This latent religiosity is only too observable among those disciples of Deleuze who are busy blessing, in unbridled Capital, its supposed constitutive reverse, the 'creativity' of the multitudes. These disciples believe that they saw—that's what you call seeing—in the alter-globalization demonstrations of Seattle or Genoa, when an otherwise idle youth partook in its own way in the sinister summits of finance, the planetary Parousia of a communism of 'forms of Life'. I think that Deleuze, often sceptical vis-à-vis his own constructions once they touched on politics, would have laughed up his sleeve about all this pathos. It remains that, having conceptualized before everyone else the place of the event in the multiform procedures of thought, Deleuze was forced to reduce this place to that of what he called 'the ideal singularities that communicate in one and the same Event'. If 'singularity' is inevitable, the other words are all dubious. 'Ideal' could stand for 'eternal' if it did not excessively cloud over the real of the event. 'Communicate' could stand for 'universal', if it did not pass over the interruption of every communication which is immediately entailed by the rupture of transcendental continuity. We have already said why 'one and the same' is misleading: it turns the One-effect on bodies of the event's impact into the absorption of the event by the One of life.

Deleuze strongly underscored the nature of the philosophical combat in which the fate of the word 'event' is played out: 'A twofold struggle has as its object to stop every dogmatic confusion of the event with essence, but also every empiricist confusion of the event with the accident'. There's nothing to add. Except that, when he thinks the event as the intensified and continuous result of becoming, Deleuze is an empiricist (which after all he always claimed to be). And that, when he reabsorbs the event into the One of the 'unlimited *Aiôn*, of the Infinitive in which it subsists and insists', in the always-there of the Virtual, he has a tendency to dogmatism.

To break with empiricism is to think the event as the advent of what subtracts itself from all experience: the ontologically un-founded and the transcendentally discontinuous. To break with dogmatism is to remove the event from the ascendancy of the One. It is to subtract it from Life in order to deliver it to the stars.

SECTION 3
Formalizing the Upsurge?

1. VARIATIONS IN THE STATUS OF THE FORMAL EXPOSITIONS

In Books II, III and IV, devoted to the analytic of worlds, or to the three concepts of the Greater Logic (transcendental, object, world), the formal exposition borrows its rigorous form from the rather subtle schemata of mathematized logic (in its categorial form). This stems from the fact that the logical identity of appearing is elucidated particularly well by the theory of complete Heyting algebras, and then by those that concern the correlations between these algebras and multiplicities. More precisely, the theory of worlds relies on the remodelling—deriving in particular from the work of Grothendieck—of the relation between the thinking of place (topology) and the thinking of the multiple, algebraic structures included. This is not surprising, if you consider that being-there, which is appearing as such, is that which articulates multiplicities with regard to a localization. The fact that the formal schema for the determination of being-there is to be found in the work of the person responsible for refounding algebraic geometry—meaning the localization of structures—is pretty natural. We saw that ontological synthesis, in the retroaction on being of its transcendental localization, lets itself be thought as a sheaf, a key concept of modern algebraic geometry. All of this allowed us to double the conceptual exposition with a formal exposition assured of its concepts and consistent with certain strata of deductive mathematics.

It was not so in Book I, where the formalizations of the concept of subject were, so to speak, *sui generis*. That is also why, borrowing Lacan's term, we called them mathemes.

In this book, as in Books VI and VII, we have an intermediary situation between Book I (devoid of a para-mathematical apparatus) and the three Books of the Greater Logic (consistent with entire strata of this apparatus). Under the names of 'singularity', 'event', 'point' and 'body', from now on it will be a question of what is neither being nor appearing, neither ontology nor logic, but rather the aleatory result of what happens when appearing is unsettled by the being that it localizes. We pass from the theory of worlds to a theory of the support of subjects and the becoming of truths. This means that the formalization of the concept, even if it persists in borrowing resources from established mathematics, can no longer enjoy its previous deductive continuity; it tends to focus on formulas or diagrams whose fixation on the page does not chiefly aim to impose a demonstrative constraint, but rather to distance the concept from the ambiguities of interpretation, and to deliver it bare—according to the power of the letter alone—to its absence of sense, through which it makes truth of relation.

The formal exposition is now proof of the 'ab-sense' (to take up again Lacan's motif) visited upon the concept. That is why it must be read in a somewhat different way than when it served to uphold analytical coherence. It is effectively a kind of recapitulation, or non-interpretable summary, of the conceptual exposition.

2. ONTOLOGY OF CHANGE

Given a world **m**, we call *modification* the variations of intensity (or of appearing) that affect the elements of an object. In other words, if $(A, \mathbf{Id})$ is an object, every difference in the transcendental indexings of the elements of A is a modification of A in terms of its appearing. For instance, it is enough to know that for $x \in A$ and $y \in A$, $\mathbf{Id}(x, y) \neq M$, to corroborate that the pair $\{x, y\}$ registers a modification in the appearing of A. A fortiori, if $\mathbf{Id}(x, y) = \mu$ (x and y being absolutely different), we have an absolutely real modification in the being-there of A.

For example, in the world *The New Heloise*, we know that the cousins Claire and Julie are the two students of the 'philosopher' Saint-Preux. If we consider the small pedagogical cell comprising the three of them as an object of the book—of the world—the very first among the letters that comprise the novel tell us that Claire and Julie appear very differently in this object, from a threefold point of view: their relationship with

Saint-Preux (they both love him, but it is not the same kind of love); Saint-Preux's relationship to them (a caring big brother for Claire, a furious lover for Julie); how they consider themselves (Claire's simplicity, Julie's 'abysses'). In truth, the cousins attest to the ever-possible non-identity of young women faced with the classical problem of their education, their fundamental variability on this point. We have $\mathbf{Id}$(Julie, Claire) $\neq M$, or again $\mathbf{Id}$(Julie, Claire) $= p$, where p is very small—relations that inscribe the modification of the feminine in the object 'the tutor and his two students'. Modifications are therefore that form of change which is but the unfolding of a multiple in its appearing, in its becoming-object. We can thus write the following equation: modification = objectivation.

Let us now suppose than an object $(A, \mathbf{Id})$ of a world $\mathbf{m}$, whose transcendental is T, is suddenly affected by the self-belonging, or reflexivity, of A. It happens that $A \in A$. We will then say that the object $(A, \mathbf{Id})$ is a site.

Why do we need to say 'it happens'? Because this is not something that could *be*. In what concerns its exposition to the thinkable, the pure multiple obeys the axioms of set-theory. Now, the axiom of foundation forbids self-belonging. It is thus a law of being that no multiple may enter into its own composition. The notation $A \in A$ is that of an ontological (mathematical) impossibility. A site is therefore the sudden lifting of an axiomatic prohibition, through which the possibility of the impossible comes to be. This effectuation of the impossible can be put in the following way: a being appears under the rule of the object whose being it is. In effect, the 'it happens' makes A appear in the referential field of the object $(A, \mathbf{Id})$.

Needless to say, it is impossible to conceive any stabilization of this sudden occurrence of A in its own transcendental field or under the retroactive jurisdiction of its own objectivation. The laws of being immediately close up again on what tries to except itself from them. Self-belonging annuls itself as soon as it is forced, as soon as it happens. A site is a vanishing term: it appears only in order to disappear. The problem is to register its consequences in appearing.

3. LOGIC AND TYPOLOGY OF CHANGE

First of all, everything depends on the transcendental value or intensity of existence that will have been assigned to A, for the flash of time in which its appearing, under the form of self-belonging, coincides with its disappearing. The problem is thus to know what the value of the existence of A will have been in the time, which is not a time, of its incorporation into the object $(A, \mathbf{Id})$. The typology of change is at first dependent on the transcendental value of $\mathbf{Id}(A, A)$, or of $\mathbf{E}A$. What is the degree of intensity of the existence of the site?

We will say that the site is a fact if $\mathbf{E}A = p$, *with* $p \neq M$. This also means that, from the standpoint of the appearing that governs the object $(A, \mathbf{Id})$, the belonging of A to A is not absolute. It is only 'to the p degree' that the appearing/disappearing of A, qua element of A, has really taken place. A fact is indeed an appearing of the site, but a measured, or average, appearing.

We will say that the site is a 'singularity' if the intensity of existence of A is maximal, that is if $\mathbf{E}A = M$. For a flash of time, there was, in this case, the absolute appearance of A in the transcendental field, under its own objective reference $(A, \mathbf{Id})$.

However, the intensity of existence does not alone decide the extension of the consequences of the self-referential inscription of the site in the world in question. We will suppose that, as far as consequences are concerned, a weak singularity behaves like a modification. It only affects other beings in the canonical way, in conformity with the nature of the object.

More precisely, we can say that *a multiple-element really* (or absolutely, it's the same) *affects another element—for the same given object—if the dependence of the value of existence of the second with regard to the value of existence of the first is maximal*. Formally, if $(A, \mathbf{Id})$ is an object, with $x \in A$ and $y \in A$, we posit that:

$$\text{'}x \text{ really affects } y\text{'} \leftrightarrow [(\mathbf{E}x \Rightarrow \mathbf{E}y) = M]$$

Real affection is a form of modification. A fact must comply with this definition, it does not unsettle the regime of affections. Consequently, if A is a site, but with $\mathbf{E}A = p$ or $p \neq M$, we will have $(\mathbf{E}A \Rightarrow \mathbf{E}x) = M$ if and only if $(p \Rightarrow \mathbf{E}x) = M$ under the regular conditions of the object. But we know (II.3) that under these regular conditions we have $(p \Rightarrow \mathbf{E}x) = M$ if and only if $p \leq \mathbf{E}x$. This comes down to saying that—as in the case of modifications— a simple fact only really affects those beings whose intensity of existence is superior to its own. We can recall here that 18 March 1871 would have been a pure fact if it had really affected (impressed, mobilized, etc.) the powerful, the bourgeois, the military, but its impact on the popular and working masses had been very weak. Since, on the contrary, it aroused immense enthusiasm among ordinary people, it is entirely necessary that,

A being the singularity, we have $(\mathbf{E}A \Rightarrow \mathbf{E}x) = M$ for weak, or even nil, values of $\mathbf{E}x$.

But this is what raising the degree of existence of the singularity to the maximum cannot achieve—far from it. Of course, this is necessary in order to be able to speak of a singularity which, for an object $(A, \mathbf{Id})$, will be defined by $\mathbf{E}A = M$ (in the evanescent time of the appearing of A). But if A remains caught in the net of ordinary logic, we will have $(\mathbf{E}A \Rightarrow \mathbf{E}x) = M$ if and only if $\mathbf{E}A \leq \mathbf{E}x$, which implies that $M \leq \mathbf{E}x$ and therefore $\mathbf{E}x = M$. In general, a singularity only affects the 'absolute' elements of the object, those elements whose existence is entirely averred in objective appearing. That is its power, but it is also its obvious limit. That is why a singularity that leaves unchanged the logical law '$(\mathbf{E}A \Rightarrow \mathbf{E}x) = M$ if and only if $\mathbf{E}x = M$' will be called a *weak singularity*. The change to which a weak singularity testifies does not modify anything in the logic of being-there. We are not yet dealing with an effective change.

To think the effectiveness of change, both in the order of being (site) and in that of appearing (singularity), we must directly evaluate the efficacy *on the transcendental* of the existential value of the site. To do this, we will ask if the site is capable or not of sublating the proper inexistent of the object, generally written $\emptyset_A$ (see IV.3). This sublation means that the site affects the inexistent, just as March 18 affects the thesis of an absolute political incapacity of workers, or just as love for Saint-Preux affects in Julie the virtuous inexistence of sexual desire. If $\emptyset_A$ is the proper inexistent of the object (and we thus have $\mathbf{E}\emptyset_A = \mu$), this affection is written as follows:

$$(\mathbf{E}A \Rightarrow \mathbf{E}\emptyset_A) = M$$

We have declared that this equation is strictly impossible if A is a mere fact, which behaves like a modification. For the equation implies that $\mathbf{E}A \leq \mathbf{E}\emptyset_A$, that is $\mathbf{E}A \leq \mu$, and therefore $\mathbf{E}A = \mu$. This means that A inexists and that, contrary to the hypothesis (existence of a site), there was no subversive appearance of being-in-person in the space of appearing whose being it is.

In fact, the existential weakness of a fact prohibits any subversion of the logical laws of appearing, any sublation, by a weak singularity, of the proper inexistent of the object. If A is a singularity—and not just a fact—the equation is also formally impossible. But in this case, *it may be* that the existential power of the singularity subverts the regime of the possible. This subversion defines the strong singularity or event.

*Given an object (A, **Id**), we call* event *the appearance/disappearance of the site A provided that this site is a singularity, that is* $\mathbf{E}A = M$, *which really affects the proper inexistent of the object, that is* $(\mathbf{E}A \Rightarrow \mathbf{E}\varnothing_A) = M$.

This affection will legitimately be called a sublation of the inexistent. For it is obvious that, as soon as the vanishing of the strong singularity corroborates the above equation—which subverts the usages of logic— logic takes back its rights. Now, if $(\mathbf{E}A \Rightarrow \mathbf{E}\varnothing_A) = M$, this is because $\mathbf{E}A \leq \mathbf{E}\varnothing_A$. But if A is a strong singularity, $\mathbf{E}A = M$. We therefore have $M \leq \mathbf{E}\varnothing_A$, and finally $\mathbf{E}\varnothing_A = M$. While what we had, by virtue of the definition of the inexistent, was $\mathbf{E}\varnothing_A = \mu$.

The fundamental consequence of an event, the crucial trace left by the disappearance of the strong singularity, which is its apparent-being, is the existential absolutization of the inexistent. The inexistent was transcendentally evaluated by the minimum; it is now, in its post-evental figure, evaluated by the maximum. That which inappeared now shines like the sun. 'We have been nought, we shall be all'—that is the generic form of the evental trace, named ε in Book I, the trace whose position with regard to the body tells us on which subjective type that which comes to be under the name of truth relies.

4. TABLE OF THE FORMS OF CHANGE

The four forms of change are formally defined on the basis of three criteria: the inexistence or not of a site, the strength or weakness of a singularity, the sublation or non-sublation of the inexistent. An ontological criterion, an existential criterion and a criterion relative to consequences. We can now set out the table opposite.

5. DESTRUCTION AND RECASTING OF THE TRANSCENDENTAL

The brutal modification, under the disappearing impetus of a strong (evental) singularity, of the transcendental value of $\varnothing_A$ (the inexistent of $(A, \mathbf{Id})$), cannot leave intact the transcendental indexing of A, nor, consequently, the general regime of appearing in the world of the elements of A. Bit by bit, the whole protocol of the object will be overturned. A re-objectivation of A will have taken place, which retroactively appears as a (new) objectivation of the site.

Change [for an object $(A, \mathbf{Id})$ in a world $\mathbf{m}$]	Is A a site? $(A \in A)$	$\mathbf{E}A = ?$	$\mathbf{E}A \Rightarrow \mathbf{E}\varnothing_A = ?$ $(\mathbf{E}\varnothing_A = \mu)$
Modification	No	$\mathbf{E}A$ is not evaluated	Does not have a value
Fact	Yes	$\mathbf{E}A = p$ $(p < M)$	$\mathbf{E}A \Rightarrow \mathbf{E}\varnothing_A = \neg p$ (reverse of p) (because $p \Rightarrow \mu = \neg p$)*
Weak singularity	Yes	$\mathbf{E}A = M$	$\mathbf{E}A \Rightarrow \mathbf{E}\varnothing_A = \mu$ (because $M \Rightarrow \mu = \neg M = \mu$)**
Strong singularity (or event)	Yes	$\mathbf{E}A = M$	$\mathbf{E}A \Rightarrow \mathbf{E}\varnothing_A = M$ (subversion of the rule) $(\mathbf{E}\varnothing_A = \mu) \to (\mathbf{E}\varnothing_A = M)$

* By the definition of dependence $\Rightarrow$, we have $p \Rightarrow \mu = \Sigma(t/t \cap p = \mu)$, which is the definition of $\neg p$, the reverse of p (II.1 and II.3).

** We demonstrated (II.1 and II.3) that the reverse of M is μ. And we saw above that $M \Rightarrow \mu = \neg M$.

As a very first example, consider the inevitable death of an element.

Recall (III.5) that the death of an element x is the passage from $\mathbf{E}x = p$ to $\mathbf{E}x = \mu$, under the effect of a cause exterior to x. Consider an object $(A, \mathbf{Id})$ relative to which an event has taken place. The main effect of the appearance/disappearance of the site is the sublation of the inexistent, $\mathbf{E}\varnothing_A = M$, when previously we had $\mathbf{E}\varnothing_A = \mu$. But the formal laws of the transcendental, forced by the strong singularity, are restored as soon as the site has been dissipated (as soon as it has un-appeared). This means that there must be a proper inexistent of the object $(A, \mathbf{Id})$. And since $\varnothing_A$ ceases to inexist—rather, it exists absolutely—it is necessary that another element of A, whose value of existence was p, with $p \neq \mu$, comes to occupy the position of the inexistent. This means, if δ is that element, that we have the passage $(\mathbf{E}\delta = p) \to (\mathbf{E}\delta = \mu)$, which formalizes the death or destruction of δ. It obviously follows that the function $\mathbf{Id}$ of the object $(A, \mathbf{Id})$ is subverted, in another point than the one occupied by the inexistent $\varnothing_A$. We had $\mathbf{Id}(\delta, \delta) = p$, we now have $\mathbf{Id}(\delta, \delta) = \mu$. But most often transformations cannot stop there. For example, we always have $\mathbf{Id}(\delta, x) \leq \mathbf{E}\delta$. If $\mathbf{E}\delta = p$, this simply means that $\mathbf{Id}(\delta, x) \le p$. But once $\mathbf{E}\delta = \mu$, we must have, for every $x \in A$, $\mathbf{Id}(\delta, x) \le \mu$, that is $\mathbf{Id}(\delta, x) = \mu$.

Thus, through an inevitable death under the injunction of the event, is inaugurated the destruction of what linked the multiple A to the transcendental of the world. The opening of a space of creation requires destruction.

BOOK VI
Theory of Points

Introduction

Alarm the 'no' until it changes into a 'yes'.

Natacha Michel

We already had the chance in Book I, particularly with reference to the military decisions of Spartacus, to speak of the 'points' of a world from which a truth originates. A faithful subject is the form of a body whose organs treat a worldly situation 'point by point'. Accordingly, the objective existence of a cavalry in the Roman army works as a point for the body-of-combat of the rebellious slaves in the following way: must the point be treated by creating a cavalry that would imitate the tactical discipline of the Romans? Or should one stick with the numerical mass of the slaves, perhaps capable of 'drowning' the enemy's charges? It is clear that treating the point concerns the existence of an organ of the body and its mode of constitution on the basis of the multiplicities that compose that body. It is also clear that in the long run this treatment will decide the outcome of the battles and, therefore, the local fate of the eternal truth: 'The slaves must and can liberate themselves relying on their own forces'. In the form of an alternative, a point is a transcendental testing-ground for the appearing of a truth.

We linked this notion of point to that of decision. The point is ultimately a topological operator—a corporeal localization with regard to the transcendental—which simultaneously spaces out and conjoins the subjective (a truth-procedure) and the objective (the multiplicities that appear in a world).

Recall the formal definition employed in Book I. A point of the world (in effect, of the transcendental of a world) is that which makes appear the infinity of the nuances of a world—the variety of the degrees of intensity of appearing, the branching network of identities and differences—before that instance of the Two which is the 'yes' or 'no', affirmation or negation, surrender or refusal, commitment or indifference. . . In brief, a point is the crystallization of the infinite in the figure—which Kierkegaard called 'the Alternative'—of the 'either/or', what can also be called a choice or a decision. Even more simply, there is a 'point' when, through an operation that involves a subject and a body, the totality of the world is at stake in a game of heads or tails. Each multiple of the world is then correlated either to a 'yes' or to a 'no'.

This correlation of the infinite and the Two, the filtering of the former by the latter, has no need of a 'decider' in the psychological or anthropological sense of the term. 'Decision' is here a metaphor for a characteristic of the transcendental: the existence (or relative weakness thereof) of these kinds of appearances of the degrees of intensity of appearing before the tribunal of the alternative. We could also say, just as metaphorically, that a point in a world is that which allows an exposition to be distilled into a choice.

But these metaphors can lead us astray, concealing as they do the formal essence of the point. A point is not that which a subject-body 'freely' decides with regard to the multiplicities that appear in a world. A point is that which the transcendental of a world imposes on a subject-body, as the test on which depends the continuation in the world of the truth-process that transits through that body. A subject-body comes to face the point of the point, in the same sense that we could say it finds itself with its back to the wall. In a place of the world, the appearance of things is composed in such a way that:

1. There are only two possibilities left for the articulation in becoming of the subject and the world, via that object of the world which is the body.

2. In one way or another, one must go through the point. Of course, it is possible not to. One can, like the office clerk Bartleby in Melville's eponymous novella, 'prefer not to'. But then a truth will be sacrificed by its very subject. Betrayal.

3. Only one of the two possibilities allows for the unfolding of the subjective truth-process. The other imposes an arrest, a reflux or even destruction. Disaster.

It is clear that a point is the local test of the transcendental of a world for the subject of a truth. What's more, in its efficacy or its result, this test indiscerns the subjective metaphor ('one must decide, one must go through with it') and the objective metaphor ('there are only two possibilities and only one of them is "the right one" '). That is why we can also say that a point, as the reduction of infinite multiplicity to the Two, localizes the action of that truth to which an event has given the chance to appear in a world.

These considerations clarify the construction of this Book VI.

To begin with, a group of examples aims at lending greater precision to the formal definition of the point as a transcendental structure (reduction of the infinite to the Two), then at clarifying the ambiguity of the point, which lies between the subjective metaphors of decision (to do or not to do, everything depends on me) and the objective metaphors of localization (here there are only two possible ways of continuing, you can't do anything about it). Accordingly, this conceptual elucidation involves two important lines of argument. The first, more preoccupied with the subjective presentation, dramatizes what we could call the logical investigation of 'choice'. The second, rooted in the transcendental logic of appearing, introduces us to the localizing function of the point and to the topology that may be inferred from it.

There follows a discussion with Kierkegaard. Why? Because the question of the point of indiscernibility between the objectivity (or transcendence) of the world (or of God) and the existential constitution of consciousness is at the centre of the Kierkegaardian theory of radical choice. While we have nothing in common with a philosophy of consciousness and even less with the mysteries of despair and religious faith, we do share with Kierkegaard the following question: where is it decided that a truth is put to the test in the guise of an alternative?

Finally, the formal exposition secures all the required connections between the infinity of transcendental degrees, the power of the Two and topology. It culminates in a very beautiful theorem about appearing: the points of the transcendental of a world define a topological space. In the style of Kierkegaard, albeit secularized, this amounts to saying: where there's a choice, there's a place.

When one accepts, in the midst of the ocean of the world, to throw the dice, the Mallarméan declaration 'nothing will take place but the place' can be read as follows: 'nothing places a truth but the succession, point by point, of the choices that perpetuate it'.

SECTION 1
The Point as Choice and as Place

1. THE SCENE OF THE POINTS: THREE EXAMPLES

Let us begin with an example we already presented in Book III, a demonstration at Place de la République. Suppose we ask ourselves a global question about it, one whose answer is ultimately 'yes' or 'no'. For example, we ask ourselves if, when all is said and done, the political content of this demonstration supports the government, which we assume to be 'on the left', or whether on the contrary it contests it. At first sight the question is unclear since this popular display features organizations tied to the government as well as others, characterized as 'far left', which criticize it more or less explicitly, at least verbally, and finally others who are resolutely opposed to it, advocating a politics entirely different from its own. Within the demonstration, all of these components constitute objects (in the sense given to this term by the Greater Logic) with their own transcendental indexing which ultimately governs the existential intensity of the participants (considered here as atoms of political groupings). If we wish to obtain a 'yes' or 'no' answer to a global question concerning this complex world—as harsh as some of its slogans may be, is the demonstration a boon to the government?—it is obviously necessary to 'filter' the complex transcendental through a binary device and reduce the nuances of evaluation to the simplicity that characterizes every ultimate choice: either 1 (for yes) or 0 (for no). If we can achieve this in a coherent way, without needing to force or modify the operations of appearing, we will say that the question concerning the general tendency of the world 'demonstration'—formulated as 'Does it play for or against the government?'—is a point of that world. You can see how the point enacts a kind of abstract regrouping of the multiplicities that appear in the world. Their complex composition is subsumed under a binary simplification, which is also something like an existential densification.

Let's use the adjective 'existential' as our pivot-point in order to introduce our second example. As the theoretician of absolute freedom, the existentialist Sartre always liked to imagine situations in which the infinite complexity of nuances, the apparent chaos of the world, could be reduced to the dual purity of the choice. His theatre in particular is above all the staging of these brutal reductions of the subjective arena to a decision without either guarantee or causality, lending a figure, in the face of the density of being, to the strange transparency of nothingness. I would gladly say, in my own vocabulary, that Sartre stages the theatre of points. Consider his heroes: beyond the abstract (but already dual) experiences of Good and Evil, will Goetz, in *Lucifer and the Lord*, refuse or accept to lead the rebellious peasants? In *Dirty Hands*, will Hugo—after having murdered its well-loved leader, Hoederer—slip into the existential way out that the cynicism of the Party allows him to glimpse? Or will he affirm, in solitude, his pure freedom?

Let's explore this second example. The initial situation is murky, shifting and undecidable. We could say that the transcendental values are scattered between minimality and maximality, failing to assure the kind of historical continuity that one could rely on. First of all, did Hugo kill Hoederer for purely political reasons? Of course, he was designated for this task by the Party authorities, in agreement with the most committed militants and in conformity with the 'orthodox' line. That's because Hugo is a partisan of a revolutionary seizure of power by the Party alone, while Hoederer is used to acting independently and takes it upon himself (the Party leadership is cut off from the USSR by the war) to organize a provisional coalition with the local reactionaries. Everything seems crystal-clear: Hugo is delegated by the Party—as it turns out by Olga, the only woman Hugo admires—to liquidate the right opportunist Hoederer. However, Hugo had accepted this mission for all too subjective reasons: to confront his soul, which is that of a petit-bourgeois political journalist, with the bitter delights of the pure act. But there's a further twist: he catches his wife, Jessica, in Hoederer's arms and it is only then that he shoots, while pronouncing the opaque line: 'You have freed me'. The motive is thus unclear.

Truth be told, things are considerably more convoluted. The spectator knows that Hugo has stopped loving Jessica: 'Don't you know that our love was just a game?', he tells her in a 'conjugal' scene prior to the murder. The spectator also knows that Hugo is ready to declare a new type of love for Olga. He also sees that Hugo loves Hoederer, his mentor and paternal figure. Hoederer call Hugo 'the young one'. But above all, right after the murder, under the influence of the USSR—with which communications have been re-established—the party line changes: the alliance with the reactionary nationalists wins out. This appears to vindicate Hoederer. But, as Louis and Olga—typical representatives of Party discipline—comment: 'His attempt was premature and he was not the right man to direct such a policy'. The party leadership can thus:

    a. think that Hoederer's assassination was a good thing;
    b. adopt his policy in the aftermath, erecting statues to him;
    c. consequently deny that the murder was commissioned as a political murder, shunting responsibility for it onto an anonymous assassin;
    d. 'salvage' Hugo, provided that he follows the new line.

This gives us an idea of the unprecedented arrangement and entanglement of the values of evaluation. This world—that of the Communist Party, but also that of love, conjugality and paternity—is presented by Sartre as refractory to any choice that would command absolute commitment. We could almost say: the Communist Party and 'ordinary' private life treat a world without points, because it is a world without principles, an absolutely impure world. This is what Hoederer explains to Hugo in a well-known tirade:

> How you cling to your purity, young man! How afraid you are to soil your hands! All right, stay pure! What good will it do? Why did you join us? Purity is an idea for a yogi or a monk. You intellectuals and bourgeois anarchists use it as a pretext for doing nothing. To do nothing, to remain motionless, arms at your sides, wearing kid gloves. Well, I have dirty hands. Right up to the elbows, I've plunged them in filth and blood. But what do you hope? Do you think you can govern innocently?

In short, the world of everyday action is not the world of Ideas, of the 'yes or no', of affirmations or points. It is the variation of occasions, polymorphous impurity, the sacrifice of everything secondary to everything that is (provisionally) primary. Hugo instead will hold a point against both the Party and his own life.

Everything is staked on the word 'salvaging' [*récuperation*]. Though he is the (mandated) murderer of the one whose line has been rehabilitated, Hugo can be regarded by the Party as 'salvageable' to the extent that he has always been disciplined. But, aside from his aversion to the term ('Salvageable! What an odd word. That's a word you use for scrap, isn't it?'), in this way out offered to him by the Party, Hugo sees his own dissolution into the ambiguities of appearing. The meaning of Hoederer's murder was already equivocal (politics, love or the bitter end of both?). What's more, in order to be 'salvageable', Hugo must belatedly adopt the policy of the one he murdered and lie about the murder itself, as Olga passionately asks him to do:

> You're not even sure that you killed Hoederer. Very good, you're on the right track. You've got to go just a bit farther, that's all. Forget it; it was a nightmare. Never mention it again; not even to me. The man who killed Hoederer is dead.

In this way, the world would absorb Hugo in the simultaneous erasure of the act (he didn't do it) and of the act's meaning (if he did do it, it was for no reason). On the basis of these negative elements, Hugo will constitute a point where his subjectivity affirms itself as intrinsic truth: salvageable or unsalvageable? This is the point, Kierkegaard's 'either/or', through which the confused totality of the elements of the world is re-evaluated.

On the side of the 'salvageable', which would be represented by Hugo's acceptance of Olga's proposal, we find the first bloc of these elements: the turnabouts of politics, Hoederer's cynicism, a love's disastrous failure, mechanical disciplines, the complexities of the situation, the perpetual becoming of circumstances, the will to survive. All of this speaks in favour of historical impurity, of the choice of realism: continuing with the Party.

On the other side, we have the absoluteness of commitment, the necessary continuity of choices, a paradoxical fidelity to Hoederer ('If I renounced my deed he would become a nameless corpse, a throw-off of the party'), the decision to have done with what is already corrupted, etc. The labyrinth of appearing is thus rectified, re-activated by its projection onto an implacable duality. All of this pushes the decision onto the side of solitary rebellion.

On this basis, a simple choice—a maximal intensity—is obtained through the simple designation of one of the terms, the second. This is Hugo's final cry: 'Unsalvageable!' Doubtless this imperious Two is, in the case at hand, that of pure subjectivity, of transparency opposed to the disgusting density of the world. It nonetheless tells us what the form of a point is. Hugo evaluates the world of his existential and political situation in terms of its classification under two predicates, 'salvageable' or 'unsalvageable', and he orders this classification by according the positive value to 'unsalvageable'. We can thus say: a point is a type of function which associates, to every intensity of appearing in a world, one of the values of a set with two elements, a maximal element and a minimal element.

But it must be added that something about the world is respected in this projection. The immanent connections remain. If, for example, you put on the side of the 'salvageable' the internal violence of intra-Party relations *and* the fact that it has come around to Hoederer's policy, you must also include the part which is common these two terms: namely that the Party, after having ordered Hoederer's murder, is compelled to hide the murder and celebrate the memory of the deceased (since it has come around to his policy). The reduction of the world to a simple duality therefore respects conjunction. If, on the side of the 'unsalvageable', you have the group of objects constituted by the fidelity to Hoederer as a model of activist conviction, the disgust at opportunism and the end of the love for Jessica, you must also find there that which subjectively synthesizes these objects: Hugo's 'purity', his abstract and normative relationship to himself and ultimately the suicidal tendency of this purity. Hugo's act is thus a synthesis: in this case, the reduction respects the envelope. In other words, the intensities of appearance of a complex world are projected onto the Two of pure choice, in such a way that the transcendental operations (conjunction and envelope) are somehow preserved by the projection.

The following definition ultimately imposes itself: a point of the world is a general relation between the objective intensities of this world, on the one hand, and an instance of the Two, on the other. This relation conserves the constitutive operations of the logic of appearing (conjunction, envelope, etc.).

Having attained this definition, we can leave aside the dramatization that characterizes the Sartrean theory of freedom. The examples of points drawn from Sartre are in effect all of the same type. A free consciousness chooses its fate, always reducing the nuances of the world to the same alternative: either I affirm my freedom by assuming the freedom of others or I ratify my inner capitulation by arguing from external necessity.

I would like to offer an example which is not as reliant on psychological dramatization. In *Le Rivage des Syrtes* (translated into English as *The Opposing*

Shore), Julien Gracq presents us, under the name of Orsenna, with a historically becalmed and lethargic city, consigned to mere perpetuation. The writer's art lies in transmitting the atony of such a world, its lack of any point: in this world, no decision seems to be on the order of the day; the coastal garrisons, embodied by captain Marino, no longer experience any kind of expectation, only a melancholic inactivity of the spirit, a kind of subtle and voluptuous renunciation. In such a context, as the young Aldo finds out for himself, to say 'yes' or 'no' is meaningless. All is torpor and flight of meaning. Here is the example, accomplished in literature, of a transcendental that no duality is able to summon to the tribunal of judgement, action or becoming.

Having said that, there is a multiplication of the signs both of the resumption of the activities of the old forgotten enemy, Farghestan (maritime incidents, espionage. . .), and of a kind of diffuse spiritual excitement, a tension combining disquiet and hope. Aldo's love for Vanessa is itself carried along by this turmoil or signifies it. His discussion with an envoy from Farghestan (a very beautiful scene) knots this double series of symptoms around what will turn out to constitute a single point: should one temporize, persevering in age-old indolence and atony? Or is it necessary, against everything that seems to incline the city to serenity, to prepare for war? The envoy from Farghestan is the messenger of the fact that such a point, such an alternative, may be on the order of the day. More and more it appears that, tormented in its historical sleep, public opinion—and Aldo's opinion with it—nonetheless begins to orient itself towards a decision. Because they desire that there be a point—the only conceivable sign of vitality or activation of the transcendental of Syrtes—the people, Vanessa, Aldo, prepare themselves joyously but unconsciously for war and disaster.

But in actual fact, Orsenna's political leader, the old Danielo, has long been engineering the resumption of the war. Aldo himself was only a pawn in his game. But Danielo knows that the victory of Farghestan and the destruction of Orsenna will almost inevitably be the outcomes of a war. Why take such a risk? Towards the end of the book, he explains himself in a tense and very beautiful discussion with Aldo. 'Who lives?' must once again be an active question for the city. It is time to have done with atony. The Orsenna-world must again be capable of proposing the obligation of choice to the distressed subjects that inhabit it. In brief, there must be a point for everyone: historical slumber or war? Danielo then says the following:

When a boat is rotting on the strand, the one who pushes it out into the waves may be said to be unconcerned by its loss, but at least not by its destination.

Orsenna's path towards the abruptness of a point—there where the question of war will concentrate into a single alternative the endless and idle declensions of collective existence—concerns destiny, destination. A point is, according to the Two, the destinal possibility of a world.

2. POINT AND POWER OF LOCALIZATION

A point is only effective, as an instance of the Two, to the extent that it is localized. Accordingly, Hugo can only affirm his constitutive point ('salvageable or unsalvageable?') by grappling with the concentrated unfolding of all the differential intensities of the situation, which is to say only as *Dirty Hands* nears its denouement. In *The Opposing Shore*, Aldo can only synthesize what happens to Orsenna to the extent that the alternative—'interminable historical slumber or destruction through war'—is clarified and intensified by three great successive dialogues: with Marino, captain of chimerical cartographies, who teaches him the force of boredom; with the envoy from Farghestan, the active sign of the Other; and with Danielo, the conscious engineer of the appearing of the point. But, in a more subtle way, we could say that it is the point that localizes the body-of-truth with regard to the transcendental. To the extent that the truth of Orsenna is that of an apparent survival within a historical death, it is effectively the test of choice, as set forth by the old Danielo, which will locally corroborate this latent death by throwing the city into a war it is bound to lose. And if Hugo's truth is the absolute freedom to decide what the meaning of the world is for him, it is only at the point when he proclaims 'Unsalvageable!' that this truth attains its theatrical appearing.

A point, which dualizes the infinite, concentrates the appearing of a truth in a place of the world. Points deploy the topology of the appearing of the True.

Let's take up again for a moment the example of the battle of Gaugamela, which we explored in the scholium to Book III. A battle may abstractly be defined as a point in a war. If we accept Clausewitz's great axiom whereby war is the continuation of politics, it is indeed in a battle that an alternative (victory or defeat) in the long run decides as to the truth of a politics. But, as we said, a battle may itself be regarded as a world. In that case, its crucial episodes are themselves so many points. Take the way that Darius's decision to level the terrain at the heart of the battlefield to facilitate the manoeuvre of the scythed chariots decides on the classical point of every military engagement: enveloping along the flanks or charging at the centre. Or the way that Alexander, interiorizing the treatment of this point by Darius, opts for the oblique order and consequently for enveloping the enemy left flank, against the line formation and the central clash. In so doing, he accepts that his own left flank is set back, leaving that side relatively weak. The most clear-cut result of all these treatments of points concerns, strictly speaking, the localization in the general space of the battle of the relation between the multiples that appear within it and categories such as left, right, shifting, retreat and so on. We can say that the points fix the topology of the battle-world.

But this is merely an example of a far more general truth, which we will demonstrate formally on the basis of the degrees of the transcendental of a world. The points of a world constitute a veritable power of localization (technically speaking, a topological space).

We have already had occasion to note that the transcendental of a world, though it presents itself at an elementary level in an algebraic form (the algebra of the order-relation that governs identities and differences and therefore, in the final analysis, existence and objectivity), is actually a power of localization and consequently a topological power. The duality of philosophical designations reproduces this distinction. When we say 'logic of appearing', we privilege the coherence of the multiples that compose a world, their envelopment and the rule for the correlation of intensities of appearance. When we say 'form of being-there', we privilege instead the localization of a multiple, that which wrests it away from its simple mathematical absoluteness, inscribing it in the singularity of a worldly place.

With the notion of point we have the wherewithal to think the co-existence of these two determinations within the general logic of what allows pure being to attain its intrinsic appearing. In other words, the transition between ontology and logic is made visible when we consider the points of a world. That is why points are metaphorically the indices of a decision of thought. This anonymous decision carries out the caesura of the word onto-logy. It makes that which is appear in the interlacing of logic. To put it another way, it indicates the latent topology of being.

From an intuitive standpoint, it is clear that 'to localize' means to situate a multiple 'in the interior' of another. Or, to utilize a multiple, whose worldly position is assumed as established, to delimit the place of appearance of another multiple. Our aim is thus to think the correlation between the transcendental of a world (degrees of intensity), the topological concept of 'interior' and the point. This correlation harbours the rationality of the power of localization of points.

3. INTERIOR AND TOPOLOGICAL SPACE

First of all, we need to elucidate what a topology is. Basically, a topological space is given by a distinction, with respect to the subsets of a multiple, between a subset and its interior. A localization acts in such a way that it makes sense to speak of an element as being 'there', which is to say in the interior of a place (of a part of the initial multiple). The axiomatic deployment of what a place (or a power of localization) is consists in finding the principles of interiority.

Let's consider, for example, the city of Brasilia, artificial capital of Brazil, which we can think of as a 'pure' city, since it rose up from nothing—bare plateau in 1956, inaugurated in 1960. What does it mean to say that Brasilia is a place, a space? First of all, of course, that we know what it means to say 'living in Brasilia' or 'coming to Brasilia'. Thus there is a referential set, the set of elements that constitute Brasilia. The interior of this referential set is 'Brasilia' itself. If I am 'in the city', that is because I am part of the instantaneous composition of Brasilia; that there is a place means first of all that a multiple is given, such that its interior is identical to itself. Dealing as we are with the referential totality 'Brasilia', with the global site of localizations, we can assert the following: the interior of Brasilia *is* Brasilia.

Now, this site arranges its parts immanently. This arrangement is so deliberate in Brasilia—outlined as it was by the founder of the Brazilian school of architecture, Lucio Costa, as early as 1955—that it composes the place as a 'flat' sign that would have acquired the force of localization proper to a body. The masterplan (see Figure 6) is the development of a simple cross traced on a desert plateau in the state of Goïas. The centre is there along with the geometric definition of a point—the intersection of two straight lines. Lucio Costa simply bent the transverse on the two sides of the glorious axis, on which, under the direction of Oscar Niemeyer, all the government buildings will be erected. We thus have the schema of a bird attuned—for one like me who loves this city woven out of absences—to the clear immensity of the sky, a sky so great that when evening comes it dilates and absorbs the bird-city, immobile in the midst of nothing. In this elementary disposition of signs, the water echoes the sky: at the edge of the bird, the great lakes, north and south, redraw and reiterate, like a single shimmering curve, the built movement of the wings. The parts are then clearly identifiable as the 'avenue of the ministries' and 'monument square' (the straight central axis, oriented from northwest to southeast), 'north residence zone' and 'south residence zone' (the two wings), 'sector of individual villas' (shores of the lakes) and so on. These parts possess an obvious power of localization. Thus to be 'in' the south residence zone means to inhabit one of the buildings distributed along this wing and regrouped—in accordance with a principle that the communist architects conceived as egalitarian—into 'neighbouring units', where you can find, along the roads that form them into a grid, collective utilities, stores or schools.

Note that such an interior (of the south wing) is in turn evidently prescribed or localized by the part of which it is the interior—a lodging or utility of the south wing is a part of the south wing. We can say that the interior of the south wing is included in the multiple 'south wing'.

Similarly, the ensemble of (admirable) monuments that make up the gigantic 'Square of the Three Powers'—the seat of the government (executive), the palace of justice (judiciary), flattened onto the ground, like plates for a giant's meal, the symmetrical domes of the National Assembly and the Senate (legislative)—form the interior of the square. They are what the square localizes in space via materialized symbols. And we can obviously write that the interior of the Square of the Three Powers is included in this square.

What about the traditional algebraic operations that are applicable to space—namely the conjunction of two places and the iteration or repetition of a local trajectory—if we now apply them to the notion of interior? In other words, let's pose the following two questions:

1. Knowing the interior of two parts of a definite space, is it possible to know the interior of what these two parts have in common, of their spatial conjunction?

2. Knowing the interior of a given part, what can we say about the iteration of its comprehension? To put it otherwise: What is the interior of the interior?

If we take, for example, Brasilia's south lake and one of the rich villas bordering it, with its garden leaning towards the water, we can intuitively note that what the part 'lake' and the part 'villa' have in common is precisely the garden, for which the lake plays the role of an incorruptible horizon in an evening populated by white wading birds perching motion- lessly on the trees. But the interior of the lake, conceived as a component of the space 'Brasilia', contributes to the whole city an edge of tranquil freshness which lightens its stellar geometry. And the interior of the garden has the same function with respect to the villa. This legitimately excludes from this interior the thorny hedge that acts as a barrier and whose defensive function is turned towards the hostile stranger, towards that which is other than the intimate coolness of a residence. Consequently, when all is said and done, the interior of what the lake and the villa have in common, which is the interior of the garden, is nothing other than what the two interiors of the lake and the villa have in common, namely the function of gentleness and serenity in the direction of their boundaries.

In sum, the interior of a conjunction is the conjunction of the interiors.

This can be negatively verified if we ask what is the interior of the con- junction between the white domes of legislative power, almost touching the ground, and the vertical axis of government, of executive power. The answer is clear: this interior does not exist, it is empty. That is because the two contrasting interiors—the vertical line of the decreed order and the horizontal line of the debated and voted law—entertain no immediate spatial relationships. This crystallizes, in an architectural arrangement, the parliamentary principle of the separation of powers. It is then clear that if the interiors of two parts have nothing in common, the interior of the conjunction of these two parts is empty.

Let us now turn to the iteration of the powers of a place: does the interior of a part itself possess an interior, and if so what is it? I enter the Ministry of Foreign Affairs, by far the most beautiful of the series of ministries ranged along the 'Esplanada dos Ministerios'. I'm in the great hall, with its shards of light shining on water surfaces tessellated with water lilies. At one end, I see the strange vertical inner garden, the immense ascent under glass of a tropical plant which meshes with the official bareness. Could I be any more in the interior of this modern palace than I am already? No, it is offered to me as invisible from the outside, and now I have crossed the almost anonymous order of glass and cement to dis- cover the giant flower that this order encloses; I can only interiorize this interior and enjoy it from within. When it localizes me, the interior has

413

no other interior than itself, reiterated. The interior of the interior is the interior.

We are now in possession of four features of the interior of a part for a given referential set.

1. The interior of the referential set is none other than itself.
2. The interior of a part is included in that part.
3. The interior of the conjunction of two parts is the conjunction of their interiors.
4. The interior of the interior of a part is its interior.

These are the four axioms of the interior. One will then say that a multiple is a topology to the extent that it has been possible to define over its parts an 'interior' function that validates our four axioms. Basically, we have just shown in what sense the architecture of Brasilia can be thought of as a topological space. What is worthy of note is that every world may be considered as a topological space once it is thought in terms of the points that its transcendental imposes as a test on the appearing of a truth of that world. The expression 'being-there' here takes on its full value. Exposed to points, a truth which finds its support in a body veritably appears in a world as though the latter had always been its place.

In the evenings, as I lost myself, I often imagined—through the bay-windows of an apartment in Brasilia's south wing, in the still clarity of the sky—that the cartography of stellar signs, whose earthly lineaments the city's monuments seemed to trace, was telling me that I would be there forever. The bird stretched on the dry soil, the lunar lagoons, Niemeyer's stylized cement: everything told me that Brasilia's fragments, opened up in this way and orienting me through the night, had incorporated me into the birth of a new world.

4. THE SPACE OF POINTS, 1: POSITIVATION OF A TRANSCENDENTAL DEGREE

The demonstration of the fact that, being endowed with an interior, the points of a world form a topological space is only entirely clear in the formal exposition. We will nevertheless sketch out an intuitive presentation.

We can remark to begin with that the general idea of a link between topology and the transcendental is pretty natural. The worldly law of multiplicities is to appear in a place. It should be no surprise then that the abstract idea of place—the distinction between interior and exterior, topological spaces—is intrinsically linked to the transcendental structure that governs the intensities of appearance. That the points of a world (of a transcendental) compose a topological space is a more precise and more astonishing idea. Its general significance is the following: the power of localization of a world resides where the infinity of qualitative nuances of that world appear before the instance of the Two, which is the phenomenal figure of an 'anonymous decision'. The transit from being to being-there is validated in a world by the reduction of all the degrees of intensity to the elementary figure of the 'yes' or 'no', of the 'either this or that', in its exclusive sense.

Kant and the great names of German idealism after him had a similar intuition when they installed at the centre of their dreamy physics the duality of attraction and repulsion. This dialectical interpretation of Newton wanted to plead for matter—whether visible or invisible (the ether)—before the tribunal of an original division of force.

Let's come back for a moment to Brasilia's architecture. The transcendental of the city governs in particular the active intensities of everything that is found within it; for example, sedentariness, or privative appearance, governs the arrangement of the wings, which aside from stores feature only apartments. In the city's northwest, the potent military disposition is inscribed by the juxtaposition of the officers' residences and the Ministry of Defence, which is separate from the other ministries, and so on. Under these conditions, what is a point? It is a transversal distribution of intensities according to an allocation of space—or of its signification—which exhibits a simple division. In the case of Brasilia, it is clear that the opposition north/south, inaugurally inscribed in the masterplan, organizes what we could call a 'weak' point. That is because the voluntarist symmetry of this plan distributes the same functions (and, therefore, very similar degrees) on different edges of the Two. Thus the north wing of the bird is doubtless not as thoroughly structured by residence blocs as the south wing, but it is functionally homogeneous to it. On the contrary, the east/west opposition—which sets industry, the rail station and the military quarters on one side and the lakeshore villas and leisure clubs on the other—organizes a strong point. Likewise, the point that brings into contrast intensities of the type 'solemn appearance of the void' (the Square of the Three Powers, as a kind of terrestrial constellation) and those of the type 'peace of the trees and the waters' (the forest-like shores of the south lake), is a strong point of the city which must deal with its fearsome representative function (the State as manifested in its purity) while offering to politicians, high-ranking civil servants and ambassadors abodes capable of keeping them in this almost dead place, at least if compared to the explosive life of São Paulo.

If we now gather together all these points, we will see that they have a power of localization situated in some sense 'beneath' the transcendental. They are something like a summary of the being-there of the city; or, more precisely, they extract from its transcendental the regime of tensions or even (for a materialist dialectician) of contradictions that organizes its spatial form: representation and habitation, power and everyday life, functions of peace and functions of war, study and leisure. Because the transcendental of the city is the pure creation of a few men, all of this is inscribed in space as localized intensity and finds its measure in the points. We could equally show that the crucial clashes in a battle, which as we saw expose the political subject-body to the points of its successive decisions, present in the place (the 'field' of battle) a concentrate of war understood as a world. Thus points rather naturally provide something like the topological summary of the transcendental. They space out the world.

But if points form, in connection with the transcendental, a topological space, we must be able to define the interior of a part of the set of points. In brief, given a group of points, what is the interior of this group? And how is this interior linked to the transcendental degrees that govern appearing?

The idea—which is very profound—is the following. A point concentrates the degrees of existence, the intensities measured by the transcendental, into only two possibilities. Of these two possibilities, only one is the 'good one' for a truth-procedure that must pass through this point. Only one authorizes the continuation, and therefore the reinforcement of the actions of the subject-body in the world. All of a sudden, the transcendental degrees are in fact distributed into two classes by a given point that treats the becoming of a truth: the degrees associated with the 'good' value and those associated with the bad one.

Naturally, this bipartition changes according to the points under consideration. For example, in the procedure that impels Orsenna to redemptive war, the dreamy inertia of captain Marino, his weak existential determination, will be assigned the negative value by the global point 'historical slumber or destructive awakening'. However, in the education of the novel's hero, Aldo, Marino's melancholic views will by contrast have a positive value with regard to the point 'respecting military routine or acting in an adventurous and disordered manner'. Likewise, the oblique order adopted by Alexander against Darius at Gaugamela—setting the cavalry on his left flank far back—assigns to the degree of combative presence and valour a negative value with regard to the different point 'being exposed or not to the charge of the chariots'.

As we have seen, in the interpretation relative to a given world, the fundamental idea is to associate to a transcendental degree all the points with regard to which this degree and the multiples that index their existence within it take a positive value. If you will, all the 'good points'. Allow me a final trivial example. A low subjective intensity, or a complete composure, will take a positive value for the point 'mastering a complex negotiation or letting oneself be dominated in it'. A very marked intensity, a rage worthy of Achilles, will instead take a positive value in the case of points of the duel type (striking or being struck). This same rage would be useless in a Byzantine negotiation, and so on. To know which of the two terms of the Two is positive depends on the context. In Sartre's plays, the pure decision adequate to the affirmation of freedom takes on the positive value, while opportunistic calculations, or the submission to supposed determinisms, pass on the side of the negative. We could say that for Sartre the positivation of an intensity is the set of the points of the world that assign it to the appearance of phenomena of self-engendering or of subjective transparency. In the case of Brasilia, if we retain as orientation its symbolic value as the capital of an immense country devoid of geographical unity, we will say that the positivation of a degree brings together the points that assign it to the spatial evidence of that value. The latter is very high for the Senate or the Assembly, those austere and colossal signs of cement, weak for the sumptuous villas set back in the shadows, at the edge of the lake, radiant sites that simply affirm one of the perennial archaic traits of Brazil: the unparalleled and indefensible privileges of the wealthy.

In every case, it is possible to collect around a transcendental degree all the binary functions of the 'point' type which positivize that whose intensity of appearance this degree measures. This collection is the positivation of the degree.

5. THE SPACE OF POINTS, 2: THE INTERIOR OF A GROUP OF POINTS

If a point assigns a positive value to at least one degree of intensity—if this point is in the positivation of the degree in question—it can be argued that, in the world that one is operating with, this point actively contributes to every process that includes multiples whose intensity of existence is the degree in question. For example, the point 'approaching the enemy obliquely or frontally' ascribes a positive value to the disposition of Alexander's military units during the battle of Gaugamela. The point 'expressing the city of Brasilia as a political capital and not as the site of private fortunes' ascribes a positive value to the monuments of the Square of the Three Powers and their intensity of architectural existence, but a negative value to the private villas of the south lake, in spite of the fact that they might be consummate examples of their genre.

Speaking more generally, the 'active' parts of a group of points are constituted by the positivations. If a group of points effectively contains all the points that positivate a degree of intensity of appearing—thereby assigning a positive value to every differential intensity of appearance measured in an object of the world by this degree—one can say that this group of points activates the degree in question through the whole extension of a process in the world.

Consequently, we will call *interior* of a group of points the active part of the group, namely the union of all the positivations which are parts (or subgroups) of the group in question. The interior of a group of points is that which this group contains in terms of an integral affirmative resource in the world.

But to what extent is it legitimate to 'topologize' this resource by considering it as the interior of a set of points? Very simply, it is legitimate because the subgroup composed by all the positivations put together fulfils the characteristics of the interior, such as they have been phenomenologically outlined above. The formal demonstration is here irreplaceable, but we will provide four intuitive 'proofs' which correspond to the four fundamental characteristics of the interior of a part of a multiple. We will present them in a somewhat different order than the one used on page 414.

The verification of axiom no. 2 of the interior (the interior of a set is included in this set) is trivial. Take a group of points. Those among them which have the property of belonging to a positivation obviously form a subset included in the group. This is what we called the 'active' subset of the group, about which we said that it plays the role of interior for the group. It is clear that this interior is included in that of which it is the interior.

Next, if we consider two groups of points, the interior of the points that the two groups have in common is exactly what their interiors have in common (axiom no. 3 of the interior). The interior of the group of points shared by both groups is effectively made up of the positivations that are included in that group. It is clear that these positivations, which belong simultaneously to the two groups, belong to their interiors and thus form the common part of these interiors.

Third, the interior of the group comprising the totality of the points of a world is none other than this totality itself, just as the interior of Brasilia, if we conceive the city as a world, is identical to Brasilia (axiom no. 1 of the interior). If a point of the world is not in the interior of the set of these points, it is because it does not partake in *any* positivation, since the totality of points definitely contains as parts the totality of the positivations, which are sets of points. Accordingly, the point in question does not assign a positive value to *any* transcendental degree, to any existence or to any-thing of what appears in the world. This amounts to saying that it is not a point, since a point is that which elicits the power of the Two, introducing a binary partition in the values of appearance.

Lastly, what is the interior of the interior of a group of points? By definition, the interior is the union of a set of positivations. The interior of this interior is the union of the positivations contained in a union of positivations. In other words, it is the interior itself (axiom no. 4 of the interior).

We have thus 'demonstrated' that the active part of a group of points—what it contains in terms of positivations—does indeed define an interior of this group. This means that the points of a world are a topological space. In that which puts the power of truth of appearing to the test it is possible to decipher that this appearing is, in its essence, a *topos*: appearing, considered as the support of a truth tested by the world, is the *taking-place* of being.

As for the activation of this taking-place, we will note that everything depends in the end on the number of points in a world. This question will turn out to be fundamentally identical to that of a world's power of orientation or localization. We shall see that, if we stick with transcen-dental structures, all situations are in a certain sense, possible—from the absence of every point to the association of a point to any intensity of appearance whatsoever. A world's power of localization, as elicited by the concentration of differential intensities in a point, can vary from all to nothing.

6. ATONIC WORLDS

A world is said to be *atonic* when its transcendental is devoid of points. The existence of atonic worlds is both formally demonstrable and empirically corroborated. We have said enough to make it clear that in such worlds no faithful subjective formalism can serve as the agent of a truth, in the absence of the points that would make it possible for the efficacy of a body to confront such a truth. This explains why democratic materialism is particularly well-suited to atonic worlds. Without a point there's no truth, nothing but objects, nothing but bodies and languages. That's the kind of happiness that the advocates of democratic materialism dream of: nothing happens, but for the death that we do our best to put out of sight. Everything is organized and everything is guaranteed. One's life is managed like a business that would rationally distribute the meagre enjoyments that it's capable of. As we saw, that is indeed the maxim that holds sway on Gracq's shore of the Syrtes: nothing will happen any more, so it is impossible to decide anything.

Worlds adequate to these maxims of happiness through asthenia (and euthanasia, the perennial demand of those who hanker for a 'pointless' existence, who want to be able to 'manage' their death in the same muffled style as their life) are formally possible, as we shall show, following our literary example, through the mathematics of transcendental structures.

Empirically, it is clear that atonic worlds are simply worlds which are so ramified and nuanced—or so quiescent and homogeneous—that no instance of the Two, and consequently no figure of decision, is capable of evaluating them. The modern apologia for the 'complexity' of the world, invariably seasoned with praise for the democratic movement, is really nothing but a desire for generalized atony. Recently we have witnessed the extension to sexuality of this deep desire for atony. One of the orientations of Anglo-American gender studies advocates the abolition of the woman/ man polarity, considered as one of the instances—if not the very source— of the major metaphysical dualisms (being and appearing, one and multiple, same and other, etc.). To 'deconstruct' sexual difference as a binary opposition, to replace it with a quasi-continuous multiple of constructions of gender—this is the ideal of a sexuality finally freed from metaphysics. I will make no empirical objections to this view of things. I am very happy to accept that the figures of desire and the illuminations of fantasy unfold in the multiple—even if this multiple is infinitely more coded and monotonous than the deconstructors of gender suppose. My contention is simply that this infinite gradation, this return to multiple-being as such, does nothing but uphold, in the element of sex, the founding axiom of democratic materialism: there are only bodies and languages, there is no truth. In so doing, the 'world of sex' is established as an entirely atonic world. That is because the normative import of the difference of the sexes obviously does not lie in any biological or social imperative what-soever. What is at stake is simply the fact that sexual duality, making the multiple appear before the Two of a choice, authorizes that amorous truths be accorded the treatment of some points.

In this sense, it is indeed true that sexual orientation is not given but constructed. Or, in Simone de Beauvoir's Sartrean vocabulary, one is not born a woman (or a man), but becomes one. Sexual orientation appears *in the world of love*, this world that elsewhere I have called 'the scene of the Two'. For it belongs to the essence of this type of truth that it proposes to lovers, whoever they may be, the appearance of their becoming before a tribunal which is made up of the few points of the world of love that they themselves have declared. Conceived according to the materialist dialectic, the difference of the sexes serves as the support which makes it possible for a subjective formalism to amorously take hold of a body that an encounter has brought forth into the world—in a manner that is entirely independent of the empirical sex of those who commit themselves to it. This difference is always a break with the atony of fashionable sexualities. This leads us to the correlation—which logic fully elucidates—between atony and the impossibility of solitude (universal 'communication'). Let us call 'isolate' a non-minimal degree of positive intensity such that nothing is subordinated to it, except for the minimum. In other words, there is nothing between it and the nothing. Where everything communicates infinitely, there exists no point. Empirically, an isolate is an object whose intensity of appearance is non-decomposable. To evaluate its pertinence in a construction of truth we do not need to analyse it, to decompose it and to reduce it. It is a halting point in the world. Such a halting point attests that at least in one place the atony of the world is undermined and that one is required to decide to say 'yes' or 'no' to a truth-procedure.

For example, Goetz, in Sartre's *Lucifer and the Lord*, experiences that his world (a waning Middle Ages devastated by civil war) is really a kind of atonic chaos. He had tried in fact to make it appear before the moral duality of Good and Evil. But there is no isolate within experience capable of according to this duality the status of a veritable point. When Goetz tries to do Good, worldly multiplicities come undone, are left in tatters: the peasants refuse the gift of their lands, the leper is disgusted by the kiss, his beloved dies... Everything seems to collapse into what Sartre calls 'tourniquets': Good turns into Evil, the uncoiling of appearances accelerates, subjectivity loses its grip on any real whatsoever. This is, in our terms, formalism without a body. Finally, Goetz realizes that the only foothold is not found in the categories of conscience, but in the world's only isolate: the peasants' war. The process of this war does not call for any analytic dissolution. Neither does it appear before the abstractions of morality. It is itself its own end and requires only that one participate in it or oppose it. Thus Goetz will accept the request of the peasant leader Nasty: to put his qualities as a military leader at the service of the peasantry's disorganized bands. Nasty, for his part, knows that at least one point exists: a peasant's choice to be either a free rebel or a serf. Goetz will follow his lesson. His last words, which are typical of the labour of a point against the threatening atony of a world, will be: 'There is this war to wage, and I will wage it'.

This lesson is worth reflecting upon today, since the declaration of the atony of a world may be simply ideological. Under the cover of a programme of familial happiness devoid of history, of unreserved consumption and easy-listening euthanasia, it may mask—or even fight against—those tensions that reveal, within appearing, innumerable points worthy of being held to. To the violent promise of atony made by an armed democratic materialism, we can therefore oppose the search, in the nooks and crannies of the world, for some isolate on the basis of which it is possible to maintain that a 'yes' authorizes us to become the anonymous heroes of at least one point. To incorporate oneself into the True, it is always necessary to interrupt the banality of exchanges. Like René Char invoking the silence of Saint-Just on the 9 Thermidor, it is necessary to 'forever close the crystal shutters over *communication*'.

7. TENSED WORLDS

Though often isolates are rare, we should also keep in mind that it is equally possible for a transcendental to have as many of them as it has degrees. Such is the disposition of *tensed* worlds, which are thereby opposed to atonic worlds. So many degrees of intensity of appearance, so many possible points; decision, which is nowhere in an atonic world, is everywhere in a tensed world. This is indeed also Sartre's conviction: I can 'choose myself', that is to say freely decide my being in every situation, which is after all what I do. However, the appearing of this choice—its pure reflection—is generally not manifest. This means that, though every specific circumstance may be a point—it suffices for this to treat it in isolation, in itself, as the isolate that it is—consciousness more often than not manages to incorporate it into an atonic world. In this case, it suffices to refer it back to something other than itself, to dissolve it into the complexity of the world, drowning it in communication.

For example, Hugo and his wife Jessica discuss Hugo's mission (to liquidate Hoederer) and do not manage to agree on its meaning. We have the following dialogue:

HUGO: Jessica! I'm serious.
JESSICA: Me too.
HUGO: You are playing at being serious. You told me so yourself.
JESSICA: No. That's what you're doing.
HUGO: You've got to believe me, I beg you.
JESSICA: I'll believe you when you believe that I'm serious.
HUGO: Alright, I believe you.
JESSICA: No. You're playing at believing me.
HUGO: This can go on forever!

This is the example par excellence of the impossibility that consciousnesses often come up against when they try to overcome atony and to constitute their own becoming (in this instance their love or at least their complicity) into a sufficiently resistant isolate, capable of anchoring an active point. This dialogue is indeed typical of the values—at once ludic and desperate—into which we're cornered by the democratic injunction, so that we may become the servants of the world's atony.

But matters differ when Hoederer declares:

I'm in a hurry. I'm always in a hurry. Once I could wait. Now I can't.

He points to a tensed world, partly contradicting the overt atony of the worlds of pragmatism. In the tensed worlds, each key moment is an isolate on which one must ground a decision. That's when life, point by point, leaves you no respite, attuned as it is to the tension of everything that appears.

Many worlds are neither atonic nor tensed. Take Brasilia, for instance, tensed, following its east-west axis, between mass destitution and the sumptuousness of the lake; but atonic, following its north-south axis, in terms of the two wings of habitations. On the one hand, the corporeal tension of the bird that a political will, that of the president Kubitschek, set upon the ground; on the other hand, the egalitarian span of the dwellings, dreamed up by two communist architects, Costa and Niemeyer. Thus, between atony and tension, we wager our worlds, according to opposite imperatives: to find peace within them or to exceed, point by point, that which in these worlds merely appears.

There where I come to be, I'm only there to the point that I am.[1]

SECTION 2
Kierkegaard

> Where *eternity* is related as *futurity* to the individual in pro-
> cess of becoming, there the absolute disjunction belongs.

The exemplary anti-philosopher that Pascal is for/against Descartes and
that Rousseau is for/against Voltaire and Hume, Kierkegaard, as we know,
is for/against Hegel. Each time the same leitmotiv returns: philosophy
depletes in the concept the most precious aspect of existence, which is the
interiority of existence itself. This interiority presents itself for Pascal as
an immediate connection to the Christian miracle. For Rousseau, it takes
the shape of sensible moral conscience—the 'voice of the heart'. For
Kierkegaard, the key to existence is none other than absolute choice,
the alternative, disjunction without remainder. Or, more precisely:
Kierkegaard turns a particular point, which sums up all the others, into the
instance through which the subject comes back into himself so that he may
communicate with God. In the pure choice between two possibilities,
which are in fact two ways of relating to the world and to himself, the
subject attains the being-there of what Kierkegaard names 'subjective
truth' or 'interiority'. To quote a very beautiful formula from the *Sickness
Unto Death*: 'In wanting to be itself, in being oriented towards itself,
the Self plunges through its own transparency into the power which
posited it'.

What concerns us here is understanding the connection that Kierkegaard establishes between choice as a cut in time and the eternity of truth
as subjective truth. Or again, to fully clarify the reasons why he thinks that
having done with Hegel means reconstructing that moment of existence

when we are summoned to a radical decision, which alone—and not the laborious becoming-subject of the Absolute—constitutes us in a manner worthy of the Christian paradox. The dispute between Hegel and Kierkegaard is in effect a dispute about Christianity, and it concerns the function of decision in the constitution of Christian subjectivity. The initial insight is the same. Christianity affirms that, as Kierkegaard puts it, 'the Eternal itself appeared in a moment of time'. This is the historical essence of the Christian religion: eternity inscribed itself in the singularity of an epoch. The divergence concerns the meaning and the consequences of this 'dialectic' of time and eternity. In what way can rational thought take on the historicity of the Absolute?

The Hegelian interpretation of this violent paradox is that the Absolute cannot rest content, like Aristotle's immobile prime mover, with an ineffective or indifferent transcendence. It must itself experience a becoming-other, it must be exposed to finitude, it must bear witness to the fact that the life of Spirit 'is not the life that shrinks from death [. . .] but rather the life that endures it and maintains itself within it'. This means making use of what Kierkegaard—following others but adopting a contemptuous tone—calls the resources of mediation: God's becoming makes eternity come to be through the effective mediation of time. Or, it unfolds the eternal becoming of the concept as time. This is what gives its standing as a Hegelian axiom to the famous formula: '*Die Zeit ist der Begriff da*', time is the being-there of the concept.

For Kierkegaard, the nature of the Christian paradox is utterly different. It is a challenge addressed to the existence of each and everyone, and not a reflective theme that a deft use of dialectical mediations would externally enlist in the spectacular fusion of time and eternity. The time that is at stake in Christianity is my time, and Christian truth is of the order of what happens to me, and not of what I contemplate. That is what he vehemently argues in the *Postscript*, thus taking on, in complete fidelity to the apostle Paul, an entirely militant theory of truth:

> Only the truth which *builds up* is a truth *for you*. This is an essential predicate relating to truth as inwardness; its decisive characterization as upbuilding *for you*, that is, for the subject, is its essential difference from all objective knowledge, inasmuch as the subjectivity itself becomes part of the mark of the truth.

Hegel tells us that since God appeared in historical time, it is necessary to know the stages of the becoming-subject of the Absolute. Kierkegaard replies that for precisely the same reason, knowing is useless. It is necessary to experience the Absolute as subjective inwardness.

That is why, for Kierkegaard, there cannot exist a moment of knowledge ('absolute knowledge', in Hegel's terms) where truth is complete or present as a result. Everything commences, or recommences, with each subjective singularity. We can recognize here the pointed thrust of anti-philosophy: the philosopher imagines that he has settled the question, because he approaches the relation between time and eternity the wrong way around. The philosopher reconstructs time on the basis of eternity, while Christianity commands us to encounter eternity in our own time. The philosopher claims to know the game of life because he knows its rules. But the existential question, that is the question of truth, is not that of knowing and reproducing the rules of the game. The point is to play, to partake in the contest, and this is what the (Hegelian) philosopher avoids:

> For the philosopher, world history is ended, and he mediates. [. . .] He is outside; he is not a participant. He sits and grows old listening to the songs of the past; he has an ear for the harmonies of mediation.

In our own vocabulary, we could say that Kierkegaard vigorously maintains that thought and truth must not simply account for their being, but also for their appearing, which is to say for their existence. That the Christ came is the emblem of this demand. It is up to us to experience the coming of the True, or the True as a singular coming-to-be in a determinate world, and not just the general historicity of Truth or (in its Heideggerian version) the historiality of the concealment of Being. Thinking must also be a form of commitment in the thought that thinks. This is how Kierkegaard puts it: 'Thinking is one thing, but existing in what one thinks is another'.

It turns out that existing in what one thinks always comes down to choosing, to being confronted with an 'either/or'. In brief: to submit subjective truth to the test of a point. This test is dramatic, its affect is despair, but it is also the crossing of a threshold, the affirmative treatment of the point. This treatment is identical to the Subject's self-exposition, what Kierkegaard calls its transparency or its being-open (in this he shows a profound insight into the correlation between point and opening, that is between the corporeal construction of the True and topology or being-there). It is only in the contingent test of a point (of an absolute choice) that the subject exists in what it thinks, instead of remaining content with simply knowing what it thinks:

> The ethicist has *despaired* [. . .]; in this despair he has *chosen himself*; in and by this choice, he *becomes transparent*.

The text continues—somewhat oddly, it must be said, for those who haven't followed the existential paths of the Kierkegaard-subject—'he is a married man', for 'taking a stance against the secret character of aesthetics, he concentrates on marriage as the most profound form of transparency'. This oddity suggests that the time has come to approach the singular forms taken in Kierkegaard by the dazzling grasp of the link between truth, subject and point. We will do this in three steps:

1. clarifications on the Christian paradox;
2. doctrine of the point or of absolute choice;
3. ambiguities of the subject.

1. THE CHRISTIAN PARADOX

As we've already said, the Christian paradox (which for us is one of the possible names for the paradox of truths) is that eternity must be encountered *in* time. The thinker must at all costs avoid 'abstracting from the difficulty of thinking the eternal in becoming'. He must face up to the paradox: 'To the extent that all thought is eternal, there is a difficulty for the existent'. Those who, like Hegel, claim to elude this difficulty present genuine thought with a largely comic spectacle, a comedy in which we once again find the obsession with marriage as an ethical criterion:

> And so it is a comical sight to see a thinker who in spite of all pretensions, personally existed like a nincompoop; who did indeed marry, but without knowing love or its power, and whose marriage must, therefore, have been as impersonal as his thought; whose personal life was devoid of pathos or pathological struggles, concerned only with the question of which university offered the best livelihood.

The thought of the authentic thinker (to use Heidegger's existential jargon, which owes so much to Kierkegaard) is only effective in passion and pathetic struggle. The category of 'pathos' in fact plays a fundamental role in the overall economy of Kierkegaard's thought. The section devoted to pathos in the *Postscript* precedes and prepares the section entitled 'The Dialectical', which deals with the content of the Christian paradox, namely 'the dialectical contradiction that an eternal happiness is based on the relation to something historical'. This section on pathos clearly differentiates between three forms of pathos; we are even tempted to say between three 'figures of conscience', since it's extremely obvious that this threefold character, as anti-Hegelian as its objective may be, retains from its enemy the formalism of hierarchically ordered stages: aesthetic pathos, ethical pathos and properly Christian pathos.

Aesthetic pathos arouses the exaltation of poetic speech and of the possibilities with which such speech enchants the imagination. Inversely, ethical pathos resides entirely in action. The poet produces in speech a brilliant testimony of eternity. But ethical pathos transforms existence itself so that it may be able to receive this testimony in truth and in time:

> It does not consist in testifying about an eternal happiness, but in transforming one's existence into a testimony concerning it.

Let us note in passing that another important difference between poetic or aesthetic pathos and ethical pathos is that the former is aristocratic—it is the pathos of the genius, and thus the pathos of difference—while the latter is anyone's pathos, the pathos of the nondescript citizen:

> Poetic pathos is differential pathos, but existential pathos is poor man's pathos, pathos for every man. Every human being can act within himself, and one sometimes finds in a servant-girl the pathos which one seeks for in vain in the existence of a poet. The individual can, therefore, readily determine for himself how he stands towards an eternal happiness, or whether he has any such relationship.

If 'truth' is the name of a subjective connection constructed between existence and eternity, Kierkegaard very clearly proposes a conception of truth as always generic or anonymous. We can't but welcome the idea that the experience of the True in the existential singularity of a world is possible for everyone, without any predicative precondition; and, moreover, that it takes the form of a relation, which for us is the incorporation into the becoming of a post-eventual truth. Kierkegaard is especially close to this idea of incorporation when he argues that the experience of eternity is that of a superior passivity, of abandonment to the universal singularity of the True, which always takes the form of an encounter:

> [Any individual whatever] need only allow resignation to be visited upon his entire immediacy with all its yearnings and desires. [. . .] This visitation of the individual's immediacy means that the individual must

not have his life in his immediacy, and the significance of resignation is the consciousness of what may happen to him in life.

Once the 'visitation' of a new passivity institutes the existential pathos in which I can daily encounter eternity, I am open to the second great leap, the one through which I pass into the third stage, that of properly Christian pathos. It must be said that as a general rule in Kierkegaard's writings—just as in the final Hegelian mediation in the direction of absolute knowledge—the second leap or second choice, between ethical pathos and Christian pathos, is far more complex and obscure than the first, between aesthetico-poetic and, ethical pathos. That is because religious pathos is not, unlike ethical pathos, the passive action through which I encounter the paradox or eternity, but rather the abiding of subjectivity in the absolute paradox, in the form of the absurd affirmed and confirmed as such. The statement of Christian, albeit semi-heretic, origin—*credo quia absurdum*—is here taken to its extreme, becoming the sole form of authentic existence, existence in faith:

> *To believe* is specifically different from all other appropriation and inwardness. Faith is the objective uncertainty due to the repulsion of the absurd held fast by the passion of inwardness, which in this instance is intensified to the utmost degree. This formula fits only the believer, no one else, not a lover, not an enthusiast, not a thinker, but simply and solely the believer who is related to the absolute paradox.

We thus see that belief is the subjective form of the True, whose proper pathos is that of the absurd as the holding fast of objective uncertainty. But what does this holding fast mean? Simply that absolute choice never offers the least objective guarantee. That is the function of the point. It is the test of the true in the Alternative, the leap into a new subjective stage—but this choice does not fulfil the least promise of the real.

The objective power of the One does not guarantee the subject-body any instance of the Two.

2. DOCTRINE OF THE POINT

We should never lose sight of the fact that the Kierkegaardian doctrine of the point, in the form of his theory of the choice, operates in a definite formal framework: that of the stages of existence, which are three—

aesthetic, ethical and religious (or, more precisely, Christian). However, as Žižek has noted, what characterizes this threefold arrangement is that it never presents itself as such to the existent who chooses his existence. Every choice proposes an alternative, an 'either/or'. Either aesthetics (for example, the seduction of women through language) or ethics (the serious commitment to marriage). Either ethics (action detached from any resistance by immediate desires) or the religious (holding fast to faith in the face of the absurd). We could say that what for us takes the form of a reduction of the infinite nuances of the transcendental of a world to the rigidity of the Two is referred back by Kierkegaard to its simplest expression: the Three presents itself as Two. With that proviso, the general logic is fully that of the point.

First of all, it is only for a subject turned towards its interiority (in our terms, only for a subjectivizable body) that the alternative (the point) comes to signify a constitutive test. The laws of the world (transcendental objectivities) have no use for points and all tend towards indifference or non-choice (towards atony). To anyone who imagines (like the Hegelian philosopher in Kierkegaard's eyes) that in order to make a suitable choice it is necessary abstractly or objectively to know the laws of becoming, one will retort that to begin with abstract or objective laws is to begin from eternity. And if one begins from eternity one misses existence, or misses the present. Not having been experienced in a real choice, eternity itself then turns out to be fallacious:

> Viewed eternally, *sub specie aeterni*, in the language of abstraction, in pure thought and pure being, there is no either-or. How in the world could there be, when abstract thought has taken away the contradiction? [. . .] Like the giant who wrestled with Hercules, and who lost strength as soon as he was lifted from the ground, the either-or of contradiction is *ipso facto* nullified when it is lifted out of the sphere of the existential and introduced into the eternity of abstract thought.

Furthermore, the moment of absolute choice, and it alone, reveals subjective energy, just as we know that the activity of the faithful subject only becomes a power in the world point by point. Kierkegaard reproaches 'these people whose personality is devoid of the energy necessary passionately to say "either/or" '. He goes as far as arguing that this passion, this energy, is what grounds the possibility for the subject to encounter eternity in time:

In making a choice, it is not so much a question of choosing the right as of the energy, the earnestness, the pathos with which one chooses.

Finally, Kierkegaard understands just as we do that the decision imposed by the treatment of a point—the occurrence of the choice—is truly the moment when one has the chance of incorporating oneself into a process of truth, thus vaulting the abyss between aesthetics and ethics:

The crucial thing is not deliberation but the baptism of the will which incorporates the choice into the ethical.

Moreover, as we already indicated, in the vocabulary of transparency (though it seems that the Danish word means 'open'), Kierkegaard clearly sees that the logics of choice is a topo-logic. That is because we are dealing with different subjective localizations on which it is necessary to pronounce oneself: aesthetic or ethical, ethical or religious, aesthetic or religious. It is also a topo-logic because to choose is to triumph over what in man's soul is not open, not transparent, what forbids him from fully accessing his own interior. For 'in every man there is something which, to a certain extent, stops him from becoming entirely transparent to himself'. To move beyond this interdiction we can only rely on radical choice itself, without deliberation or delay, since deliberation and delay only prepare the way for repetition, the need to discover, 'once the choice has been made, that there is something that must be redone'. On the contrary, choice with no other possibility but choice—the point as such—purifies the soul, renders it transparent, so that even if the content of the choice is erroneous, the subject, having become co-extensive with his own interior, will be able to perceive it:

For the choice being made with the whole inwardness of his personality, his nature is purified and he himself brought into immediate relation to the eternal power whose omnipresence interpenetrates the whole of existence.

If it is energetic and unconditional, choice—as the guarantor of the connection between subjective time and eternity—localizes the subject in the element of truth:

As soon as one can get a man to stand at the crossways in such a position that there is no recourse but to choose, he will choose the right.

In sum, Kierkegaard sees perfectly well that the theory of the point is a formal or transcendental theory. That is because the apparent content of the alternative is of little import, it is the capacity to treat the point that matters, what I have called the existence of an organ for the point. In Kierkegaard's vocabulary, this means that the essence of choice is choice itself, not what is chosen:

> My either/or does not in the first instance denote the choice between good and evil; it denotes the choice whereby one chooses good *and* evil/or excludes them.

And again:

> Choice itself is decisive for the content of the personality. Through choice the personality penetrates into what has been chosen; if it does not choose, it withers.

This idea of a 'penetration' into what has been chosen is what I translate in terms of the organ that treats a point, insofar as it is indeed an 'organic' part of the body-of-truth. In the end, Kierkegaard anchors the existential contingency of eternal truths to the encounter and to the treatment of special points.

3. AMBIGUITIES OF THE SUBJECT

Without doubt, this specialization of points raises questions and affects Kierkegaard's thought with a kind of Christian limitation.

To begin with, due to its strong teleological character, the doctrine of 'stages' considerably restricts the constitutive function of points for any subject of truth whatever: only the religious stage, to the extent that it reflects the absoluteness of the Christian paradox by maintaining existence within it as its proper element, can claim to follow from the truly absolute choice. This is especially true if we consider that though the choice seems to operate 'between' stages, in fact the opposite is also true: it is through the absoluteness of choice that the stage is constituted 'in truth', which is to say, for Kierkegaard, in the transparent interiority of a subject. Kierkegaard can write: 'Thanks to my "either/or", ethics appears'. Only then can choice, or the point, which makes the final stage appear (if indeed such a stage can appear, which remains an open question), properly be called absolute. Thus, in manner very much parallel to Hegel's, what we finally get as the solution to the Christian paradox is obviously not mediation as absolute knowledge, but decision as absolute existence. In a well-known formula,

Kierkegaard affirms that 'aesthetics in a man is that by which he is immediately what he is; ethics is that by which he becomes what he becomes'. It is very tempting to say that the religious is in a man, when all is said and done, the becoming of what he is at the same time as the being of what he becomes. We would then be very close to Hegel.

This is because for Kierkegaard the subject remains essentially prisoner to the dialectic of the Same and the Other. When he writes: 'it is only in freedom that one attains the absolute', he merely offers us a tautology, since the absolute, as choice, is precisely freedom itself. And the intimate affect of this tautology is despair: I despair at having to become the absolute that I am, and thereby to become, point by point, other than myself. Finally, the essence of faith in the absolute that I am is the despair at no longer being the non-absolute that I am. This is the dialectical split of the subject, whose revelatory moment is the pure point, the alternative.

Let's follow the stages of what Sartre called 'tourniquets'.

First, choice constitutes me as absolute:

In choosing absolutely, I choose despair, and in despair I choose the absolute, for I myself am the absolute.

Second, the absolute 'myself' that I become in choice negatively realizes the non-absolute being of the self who chooses:

This self which he then chooses is infinitely concrete, for it is in fact himself, and yet it is absolutely distinct from his former self, for he has chosen it absolutely. This self did not exist previously, for it came into existence by means of the choice, and yet it did exist, for it was in fact 'himself'.

Third, the only solution that makes it possible to hold in the same place (that of choice) the subject who chooses and the (absolute) subject that choice chooses as pure choice is the archetypal and always-already-eternal intervention of God in the moment of decision:

His self is, as it were, outside of him, and it has to be acquired, and repentance is his love for this self, because he chooses it absolutely out of the hand of the eternal God.

The circle is closed. The initial problem was that of knowing how the subject-individual can treat the consequences of the Christian paradox, namely the historicity of the Absolute. Against Hegel and his concept, Kierkegaard proposes a pathetics of existence. Subordinated to choice, this pathetics constructs a Christian figure of the subject as the continual encounter of the paradox itself, that is to say of the existence of eternity in time. But this figure only holds up if it is supported by God, to the extent that his own coming has taken place in time. Man is never anything but this creature who has been granted the possibility of travelling, point by point, the inverse path of God. And he can only do so because God, beholding his despair, lets him know that despairing is the true condition of every hope.

SECTION 3
Topological Structure of the Points of a World

1. DEFINITION

Since a point is essentially the binary dramatization of the nuances of appearing, our formal aim is simple: to define a correlation between a transcendental T and a binary structure. We are already acquainted with a binary transcendental structure. This is the transcendental T_0, comprising only the degrees 1 and 0, or M and μ, which is the transcendental of the thought-world of ontology (on this point see Section 5 of Book II). We know that, endowed with the elementary order $0 \leq 1$, the set $\{0, 1\}$ is indeed a transcendental, which is classical in kind, since its structure is that of a Boolean algebra.

The idea is then the following: in order to treat in a global and binary manner a world whose transcendental is neither global nor binary, we will consider the functions that make this transcendental 'correspond' to T_0. Our aim will thus be to refer the infinite evaluation of nuances back to the simplicity of a choice. This operation is the formalization of a 'deciding'. Deciding always means filtering the infinite through the Two.

Let us note in passing that since T_0 is the transcendental of ontology, this procedure also involves projecting the complex singularity of appearing onto the simplicity of being.

We must still make sure that the dualizing projection respects the structures of the initial transcendental. If I want to obtain an evaluation of the global political meaning of *this* demonstration, as a singular world, it is necessary that, when I reduce its transcendental to the binary structure $\{0, 1\}$, I conserve the order-relations of the initial transcendental, with the extreme entanglement of existential intensities and localizing atomicities whose worldly cohesion it guarantees. Similarly Hugo, in *Dirty Hands*, conveys the totality of the articulations of a political and amorous conjuncture in the theatrical form of a suicidal choice.

The rational guarantee for this point is well-known: the operation of reduction must amount to a structural homomorphism between the initial transcendental form T and the binary transcendental T_0. What are we dealing with? Consider the general case of a correspondence between any two transcendentals. Take a function ϕ of a transcendental T towards a transcendental T'. This function is said to be a *homomorphism* if it conserves the conjunction $\cap$ and the envelope Σ. In order that this 'conservation' is clear we will write the operations constitutive of T' as $\cap'$ and Σ'. We should then get:

$$\phi(p \cap q) = \phi(p) \cap' \phi(q)$$

$$\phi(\Sigma B) = \Sigma' \{\phi(p) \mid p \in B\}$$

One also often says that ϕ is a $\cap$-Σ function of T to T', in order to indicate that it makes correspond to a conjunction the conjunction of the corresponding values, and likewise for the envelope.

A homomorphism is said to be 'surjective' if all the degrees of T' are affected by the function. In other words, if $p' \in T'$, there exists $q \in T$ such that $\phi(q) = p'$. In the case that concerns us, that of points, it is required that the correlation be surjective. We have already said as much: if to all the degrees of T_0 there corresponds a single value of T (either 1 or 0), the point does not introduce any division in the world and the Two cancels itself out in the One, which is contrary to the essence of the point. Accordingly, there always exists at least one degree p such that $\phi(p) = 1$, and at least one degree q such that $\phi(q) = 0$. Since all the values of T_0 are accordingly affected by ϕ, this function of T on T_0 is surjective. To obtain the concept of global and binary evaluation that we're looking for, it ultimately suffices to consider the surjective homomorphisms of T in the direction of T_0, the transcendental $\{0, 1\}$ of ontology. Such a function (if one exists, which as we shall see is not always the case) exposes a complex world to an evaluation or a decision by 'yes' or 'no'. Only a function of this type reduces the transcendental nuances and allows one globally to 'come to the point' of the world in question.

For example, we could say that Danielo's secret ploy to re-expose Orsenna to a radical choice (1 = war, 0 = historical slumber) is a point-function. Little by little, it connects all the components of the city's situations, particularly in the coastal garrisons of Syrtes, to the possibility of such a choice. It is to this end that Aldo is sent to the region bearing obscure orders, that Vanessa is manipulated, that provocations are allowed, such as the incursion of a small warship into the territorial waters of Farghestan, and so on. Thus, it is the elements of the world and their connections which are articulated onto a binary transcendental, which is all the stronger to the extent that it remains latent. A point is a kind of analytic mediation between the transcendental complexity of a world (its often non-classical logic) and the (always classical) imperative of binarity or decision.

Finally, the definition is the following: *Let T be any transcendental structure whatever. We call 'point' of T a surjective homomorphism of T on T_0. Or: a point of T is a surjective ∩-Σ function of T on {0, 1} considered as a transcendental.*

The two exercises that follow aim to elucidate in what sense there is a 'conservation', by a point or 'in a point', of the transcendental structures.

Ex. 1. A surjective homomorphism f (*a* ∩-Σ function) of T to T_0 conserves order. In other words: if $p \leq q$ in T, then $\phi(p) \leq' \phi(q)$ in T_0.

If ϕ is ∩-Σ, we have:

$\phi(p \cap q) = \phi(p) \cap' \phi(q)$	homomorphism
$\phi(p) = \phi(p) \cap' \phi(q)$	hypothesis $p \leq q$ and P.0
$\phi(p) \leq' \phi(q)$	P.0

Ex. 2. A surjective homomorphism conserves the minimum and the maximum. In other words: $\phi(\mu) = 0$ and $\phi(M) = 1$.

Let μ be the minimum of T. For every $q \in T$ we have $\mu \leq q$, and consequently, in light of the preceding exercise, $\phi(\mu) \leq \phi(q)$. It follows that $\phi(\mu) = 0$. If in fact $\phi(\mu) = 1$, we have $1 \leq \phi(q)$ for every q, that is $\phi(q) = 1$ for every q (since 1 is the maximum of T_0); accordingly, there exists no $p \in T$ such that $\phi(p) = 0$, and the function, not being surjective, cannot be a point.

In the case of the maximum, the reasoning is entirely similar. We can also note that by conserving the envelope, the conjunction and the minimum, a surjective homomorphism conserves the reverse. Now, M is equal, by definition, to $\neg\mu$. Therefore, a surjective homomorphism conserves the maximum.

The existence of a point for a given transcendental expresses a minimal, albeit latent, 'kinship' between this transcendental and T_0, which is the operator of appearing of ontology itself. If in effect T is 'too different' from T_0, it will be impossible to identify a surjective homomorphism between the two. If we accept that a point, as the correlation between an infinite order and a simple duality, is that by which a global decision can divide a world, we can see how the question of knowing whether a transcendental has many points or a few, or even no points at all, carries considerable consequences. This question will be clarified once we have shown, in terms of points, that being-there qua world deserves its name: this is the problem of the power of localization of points, or of points as a topological space.

2. THE INTERIOR AND ITS PROPERTIES. TOPOLOGICAL SPACE

The four axioms of the interior, empirically presented with respect to the architecture of Brasilia, will be formalized by writing as **Int** ('interior function') the function which, to each part of a given multiplicity, makes correspond its interior.

1. The interior of the referential set (of the world, if you will) is identical to that set. This means that since a world is a power of localization of the appearing of multiplicities, it is incapable of localizing itself by distinguishing its interior from its boundary or exterior. We will thus write:

A-int$_1$ $\qquad\qquad\qquad$ $\mathbf{Int}(E) = E$

2. The interior of any part is included in that part.

A-int$_2$ $\qquad\qquad\qquad$ $\mathbf{Int}(A) \subseteq A$

3. The interior of the conjunction of any two parts of the referential set is the conjunction of the interiors of these two parts.

A-int$_3$ $\qquad\qquad\qquad$ $\mathbf{Int}(A \cap B) = \mathbf{Int}(A) \cap \mathbf{Int}(B)$

4. The interior of the interior of a part is identical to its interior.

A-int$_4$ $$\mathbf{Int}(\mathbf{Int}(A)) = \mathbf{Int}(A)$$

Obviously, there may exist a great number of different **Int** functions for the same referential multiple E. This means that a multiple has many ways of being a power of localization. This is patently opposed to Aristotle's conception, according to which a thing has a 'natural' place. In the multiplicity of worlds, there cannot be any naturalness of the place. Everything that is there may find itself de-localized by another worldly power.

E is said to be a topological space when a function **Int** can be defined over the parts of E. A topological space is a power of localization in the following precise sense: in any subset of a referential space, it distinguishes the interior of this subset from its multiple-being as such. Given $A \subseteq E$, we know what it means for an element x to be situated in the interior of A. This is written: $x \in \mathbf{Int}(A)$. And since in general $\mathbf{Int}(A) \neq A$, it is evident that being localized in the interior of A (a topological property) differs from simply belonging to A (an ontological property). A topological space is a multiplicity such that the predicate 'being in', in the sense of 'being there', is separate from the predicate 'being an element of'. That is why the following theorem should cause no surprise: through the mediation of points, the transcendental of a world can (though not always, not if the world is atonic) be considered as a topological space. This is a way of reiterating that a world is the being-there of an infinite set of multiplicities.

3. THE POINTS OF A TRANSCENDENTAL FORM A TOPOLOGICAL SPACE

Our goal is to correlate the transcendental notion of point of a world and the topological notion of interior. By showing that every subset of points of a world allows for an interior, we will establish that, besides setting the possible intensities of appearance, a transcendental is indeed a power of localization. The logic of appearing is topological.

Let T be a transcendental structure. And let $\pi(T)$ be the set of its points, that is the set of the surjective $\cap$-Σ functions ϕ of T on T_0, or $\{0, 1\}$. Let's say that $\phi \in \pi(T)$ for every surjective homomorphism ϕ of T on $\{0, 1\}$.

We will associate to every element p of the transcendental T a *set* of points, written P_p, which may be read as 'positivation of p'. We are dealing with the set of points that 'give' p the value 1 (that is all ϕ such that $\phi(p)$ = 1). In formal terms:

$$P_p = \{\phi \mid \phi \in \pi(T) \text{ and } \phi(p) = 1\}$$

P_p is a set of the $\cap$-Σ functions operating between T and $\{0, 1\}$. Or, P_p is a subset of the set $\pi(T)$ of all the points of T. We thus have $P_p \subseteq \pi(T)$.

The fundamental theorem of this subsection defines, on the basis of the positivations, a topology over the set $\pi(T)$ of the points of T. We take, as the interior of a part A of $\pi(T)$ (of a given set of points), the union of all the positivations contained in that set. We then have the theorem:

Let $\pi(T)$ be the set of the points of a world (of a transcendental T). Let A be a part of $\pi(T)$. If we stipulate that the interior of A is the union of all the positivations contained in A—that is $\mathbf{Int}(A) = \cup\ (P_p\ /\ P_p \subseteq A)$—we obtain a topology. Thus defined, the function $\mathbf{Int}$ effectively obeys the four axioms A-int, or axioms of the interior.

This theorem extracts from the structure of a given transcendental—which as we will recall is founded on the order-relation alone—a structure of localization (a topology). To do this, we pass from the notion of a degree of the transcendental, which is still strictly ontological (a degree is an element of T), to that of point. The notion of point is functional: it connects each element, through a function ϕ, to that matricial form of the Two (of the 'yes or no') which is the minimal transcendental $\{0, 1\}$. The point is a 'thickening' of the element through its homomorphic projection onto the Two. This thickening is the bearer of the power of localization.

The demonstration of the theorem consists in verifying, axiom by axiom, that the function $\mathbf{Int}(A) = \cup\ (P_p\ /\ P_p \subseteq A)$ effectively conforms to the formal requirements of an interior of A, for $A \subseteq \pi(T)$.

We provide these verifications as exercises (with their solutions . . .) without following the canonical order of the axioms.

Ex. A-int$_2$. Show that $\mathbf{Int}(A) \subseteq A$ is verified by the function defined in the theorem.

By definition, $\mathbf{Int}(A)$ is the union of the positivations P_p which are parts of A. Accordingly, every element of $\mathbf{Int}(A)$ is an element of at least one P_p which possesses this property and is, therefore, an element of A. Consequently, $\mathbf{Int}(A)$ is a part of A.

> Ex. A-int$_3$. Show that the equation $\mathbf{Int}(A \cap B) = \mathbf{Int}(A) \cap \mathbf{Int}(B)$ is verified by the function defined in the theorem.

$\mathbf{Int}(A \cap B) = \cup \{P_p \mid P_p \subseteq A \cap B\}$. But the positivations P_p, which are parts of both A and B, are those P_p that belong both to the interior of A and the interior of B, since these interiors are the union of the P_p which comprise their parts. It immediately follows that $\mathbf{Int}(A \cap B) = \mathbf{Int}(A) \cap \mathbf{Int}(B)$.

> Ex. A-int$_1$. Show that $\mathbf{Int}(\pi(T)) = \pi(T)$, where $\pi(T)$ is the set of all the points (that is, the referential set), is verified by the function defined in the theorem.

The interior of $\pi(T)$ is constituted by the union of *all* the positivations, that is of all the points ϕ for which there exists at least one degree p such that $\phi(p) = 1$. If $\mathbf{Int}(\pi(T)) \neq \pi(T)$, this means that there exists a point ϕ that does not belong to any positivation. For such a supposed point, we have $\phi(p) = 0$ for every $p \in T$. This is impossible, since ϕ must be a surjective function, and must therefore take the value 1 for at least one degree of T. The hypothesis must consequently be rejected and $\mathbf{Int}(\pi(T)) = \pi(T)$.

> Ex. A-int$_4$. Show that $\mathbf{Int}(\mathbf{Int}(A)) = \mathbf{Int}(A)$ is verified by the function defined in the theorem.

$\mathbf{Int}(A)$ is the union of all the positivations P_p such that $P_p \subseteq A$. But $\mathbf{Int}(\mathbf{Int}(A))$ is in turn the union of all the positivations included in $\mathbf{Int}(A)$, that is of all the positivations included in A. This amounts to saying that $\mathbf{Int}(\mathbf{Int}(A)) = \mathbf{Int}(A)$.

By verifying the four axioms of the interior, the entity 'all the positivations included in a given set of points' authorizes us to treat the set of all the points of a world as a topology. The theorem is demonstrated.

4. FORMAL POSSIBILITY OF ATONIC WORLDS

An atonic world is a world without any points. The notion of atony can be linked to that of an isolate, thus producing the formal truth of a manifest contemporary condition: the obsession with communication and the horror of solitude imply atony. The basic theorem is the following: if the transcendental of a classical world contains no isolate, that world is atonic (it has no point).

Consider a classical transcendental T_c, which is a Boolean algebra (see II.5). We call *isolate* of T_c a degree $i \in T_c$ which has the following properties:

–i differs from the minimum μ;

–if j is strictly lesser than i, then $j = \mu$.

In other words, an isolate i does not permit any element smaller than it other than μ. It is an isolated element in the following sense: no 'complexity' separates it from the nothing. In other words, it is unanalysable into subcomponents of itself.

The fundamental theorem that leads to the consideration of atonic worlds is thus the following: *if there exists a point of T_c, there exists an isolate*. The obvious consequence of this theorem is that if a classical transcendental has no isolate, it is atonic (without points).

The demonstration is carried out in five short steps, which constitute useful revisions in what concerns transcendental structures, classical worlds and points. Let's begin with a general result, which does not involve the classicism of the world, and which establishes a link between the points and the reverse of a degree.

Lemma 1. In a given transcendental T which contains a point ϕ, let p be a degree of T. If $\phi(p) = 1$, then $\phi(\neg p) = 0$.

$p \cap \neg p = \mu$	property of $\cap$
$\phi(p \cap \neg p) = \phi(\mu) = 0$	subsection 1, Ex. 2
$\phi(p \cap \neg p) = \phi(p) \cap \phi(\neg p)$	def. of ϕ
$\phi(p) \cap \phi(\neg p) = 0$	consequence
$\phi(p) = 1$	hypothesis
$1 \cap \phi(\neg p) = 0$	consequence
$\phi(\neg p) = 0$	$1 \cap 1 = 1$

We now turn to a technical result which, outside of any reference to points, concerns the relation in a classical world (in a Boolean transcendental) between strict order and the reverse of a degree.

Lemma 2. In a transcendental T_c of a classical world, if $p < q$ (strict order, excluding $p = q$) then $\neg q < \neg p$ (also strict order).

$p < q$	hypothesis
$p \cap \neg q \leq q \cap \neg q$	consequence
$p \cap \neg q = \mu$	property of $\cap$ and def. of the minimum
$\neg q \leq \neg p$	def. of $\neg$

But if $\neg q = \neg p$, we also have $\neg\neg q = \neg\neg p$. Since the world is a classical one, this means that $p = q$, which contradicts $p < q$. Therefore, $\neg q \neq \neg p$, and we have $\neg q < \neg p$.

Lemma 3. In the transcendental T_c of a classical world, if $\neg p \leq p$, then $p = M$ (the maximum).

$\neg p \leq p$	hypothesis
$\neg p \cup p \leq p \cup p$	consequence
$M \leq p \cup p$	the world is classical
$M \leq p$	$p \cup p = p$
$p = M$	def. of M

Armed with these three results, we will construct an isolate, under the twofold condition that the world be classical and that a point exist. If the point is ϕ, this isolate is defined as the reverse of the envelope of all the degrees p such that $\phi(p) = 0$. In other words, that which comes as the 'outside' of everything that a point assigns to the negative is isolated. In the present, we see examples of this formal maxim on a daily basis: only that which excepts itself in one sense or another from the pointlessness of what is in circulation has any value.

Lemma 4. Let E_0 be the set of the degrees p of a classical transcendental such that, for the point ϕ, $\phi(p) = 0$. And let ΣE_0 be the envelope of this set. It is impossible that there exist a degree q such that $\Sigma E_0 < q < M$.

If $\Sigma E_0 < q$, it is assured that $\phi(q) = 1$, since ΣE_0 envelops all the degrees p such that $\phi(p) = 0$. By lemma 1, it follows that $\phi(\neg q) = 0$. Whence, by the definition of E_0, $\neg q \leq \Sigma E_0$. By the transitivity of the relation $\leq$, we then get $\neg q \leq q$, and consequently, because of lemma 3, $q = M$. The strict inequality $q < M$ is impossible.

Theorem. If T_c is the transcendental of a classical world and admits of a point ϕ, there exists in T_c at least one isolate.

Consider the degree $\neg \Sigma E_0$, with E_0 the same as it was in lemma 4. We will show that this degree is an isolate. Suppose in fact that it is not. Then there exists a degree q such that:

$$\mu < q < \neg \Sigma E_0 \qquad \text{strict inequalities}$$

but, by lemma 2, the consequence of this is

$$\neg\neg \Sigma E_0 < \neg q < M \qquad \text{because } \neg\mu = M$$

And since the transcendental is classical, we get (law of double negation):

$$\Sigma E_0 < \neg q < M$$

Which is what lemma 4 declares to be impossible. Consequently, the interposed degree q cannot exist and $\neg \Sigma E_0$ is an isolate.

We have thus shown that if T_c—the transcendental of a classical world—admits of a point, it also admits of an isolate. Therefore, if T_c has no isolate, it also has no point, and the world of which T_c is the transcendental is atonic, which is the result we predicted.

5. EXAMPLE OF A TENSED WORLD

A tensed world is a world which has as many points as there are degrees in its transcendental. In a way, it is the opposite of atonic worlds. Having considered the correlation between the existence of points and that of isolates, we can imagine that a tensed world has many isolates. In fact it is possible to provide several formal examples of tensed transcendental structures in which each degree of the base-set T prescribes an isolate, which in turn corresponds to a point.

The simplest thing is without doubt to consider a set E and the set $P(E)$ of its parts, as we already did in order to define topologies. $P(E)$ is the transcendental T, the degrees are the parts of E or the elements of $P(E)$. The order-relation is inclusion: $A \leq B$ means that $A \subseteq B$. The minimum is the empty set. We know in effect that $\varnothing \subseteq A$, whatever part A of E we're dealing with. The maximum is E itself, since if A is a part, we obviously have $A \subseteq E$. The conjunction is the intersection $A \cap B$. The envelope of a collection of I parts is the union of all these parts, that is $\bigcup_{i \in I} Ai$.

The reader can easily verify, if he or she so wishes, that all the axioms of a transcendental are valid for this simple structure. What then is an isolate? It is a part such that strictly speaking it has no other sub-part than the void. All the singletons, or the parts composed of a single element of E, fit the bill. In effect $\{e\}$, with $e \in E$, is indeed a part of E and this part in turn has no part other than $\varnothing$. We can already see that there are as many isolates as there are elements of E. This means that nothing stands in the way of the existence of a very large number of points: to each isolate $\{e\}$ there corresponds a very simple point ϕ (recall that a point is a function of $P(E)$ on $\{0, 1\}$):

$$\phi (A) = 1 \qquad\qquad\qquad\qquad\qquad \text{if } e \in A$$
$$\phi (A) = 0 \qquad\qquad\qquad\qquad\qquad \text{if } \neg\, (e \in A)$$

That ϕ is a point can be effortlessly verified. For example, the fact that ϕ $(A \cap B) = \phi (A) \cap (B)$ is clear, since $\phi (A \cap B) = 1$ presupposes—$\{e\}$ being the selected isolate—that $e \in (A \cap B)$, and, therefore, that $e \in A$ and $e \in B$, meaning that $\phi(A) = \phi(B) = 1$. And if $\phi (A \cap B) = 0$, it is because e does not belong to $A \cap B$. Therefore, it does not belong to one of the two. Let's say it's A. Then we have $\phi(A) = 0$, which automatically leads to:

$$\phi(A) \cap \phi(B) = 0 = \phi(A \cap B)$$

In every case, we thus have as many points as there are elements of E. A world with such a transcendental is a world 'in tension': it requires every truth-process to confront the snares of nondescript existence [*l'existence quelconque*], whose intensity, as weak as it may be, hides a point. We can invoke the world of the Resistance: every circumstance is dangerous, every encounter difficult. Everything that appears demands that we be on guard and decide. In the words of René Char, that great Resistance fighter: 'Plunge into the hollowing unknown. Force yourself to pivot.'[2]

Notes

1. *Là où je suis, je ne suis là qu'au point où j'y suis.*
2. *Enfonce-toi dans l'inconnu qui creuse. Oblige-toi à tournoyer.*

BOOK VII

What is a Body?

Introduction

This maritime moment
With all its crimes, horror, ships, people, sea, sky, clouds,
Winds, latitude and longitude, outcries
How I wish in its Allness it became my body in its Allness
Álvaro de Campos/Fernando Pessoa

With the lengthy construction of the laws of appearing and change behind us, we are now beckoned by what, for our purposes, is the 'useful' distillate of such a construction: to be able to answer the question 'What is a body?'—insofar as a body is this very singular type of object suited to serve as a support for a subjective formalism, and therefore to constitute, in a world, the agent of a possible truth. We will thereby obtain the physics adequate to our materialist dialectic: the physics of subjectivizable bodies.

Let us recall the stages of the conceptual strategy that authorizes us to conclude with this physics.

To begin with, and taking the existence of bodies for granted, we exhibited the subjective formalisms capable of being 'borne' by such bodies. This is the (formal) metaphysics of the subject, established pending a still unthought physics. It already appeared, at this pre-analytical stage, that a subjectivizable body is efficacious to the extent that it is capable of treating some *points* of the world, those occurrences of the real that summon us to the abruptness of a decision.

Since a body is the bearer of the subjective appearance of a truth, we subsequently explored the general legislation of appearing, the transcendental laws that lend meaning to the being-there of any multiple. We admired their essential simplicity. Three operations effectively suffice to account for all the types of appearing or all the possibilities of differentiation (and identity) in a determinate world: minimality, conjunction and the envelope. Or the inapparent, co-appearance and infinite synthesis.

Having constructed the transcendental legislation of worlds, we were then able to explore that which, under the presupposition of such a legality, makes it so that a multiple appears in a world as an object. The key to the doctrine of objectivity is the postulate of materialism: every object that appears in a world is composed of real atoms. On the basis of this postulate it is possible to establish a kind of structural reciprocity between being and appearing: if the elements of a multiple that are given in a world as objects are compatible according to their appearing, there exists an ontological synthesis of these elements (according to their being).

Finally, we tackled the question of the relations among objects. A restrictive but limpid definition subordinates the thinking of relation to that of the atomic composition of the objects that it relates. It is then possible to determine the universal character of a relation in a given world. This entails a remarkable property, which is materialist to the extent that it subordinates the universality of a relation to the global being of the world in which this relation is defined: we can infer from the (inaccessible) infinity of a world that every relation is universally exposed in that world.

Transcendental, object and relation—that is the content of the Greater Logic.

We were then ready to deal with real change, on the basis of the notion of site. A site is an object of the world that globally falls under the laws of differentiation and identity that it locally assigns to its own elements. It *makes itself* appear. Examining the possible consequences of the existence of a site, we can infer a crucial distinction between a fact and an event. Broadly speaking, an event is a site which is capable of making exist in a world the proper inexistent of the object that underlies the site. This tipping-over of the inapparent into appearing singularizes—in the retroaction of its logical implications—the event-site.

In order to complete, on the side of worlds, our examination of the impact of the upsurge of a subject on the fragility in becoming of a truth, in Book VI we developed the theory of points. This part of the transcendental analytic is very close to topology. In it we demonstrate that the points of a transcendental constitute a topological space. In addition, the theory of points allows us to broach the qualitative difference of worlds, since it is possible to establish that the question of points varies considerably depending on what transcendental forms are at stake (world without points or atonic worlds, worlds with 'enough points' or tensed worlds, intermediary worlds, etc.).

All that's left is for us to ask what a body is.

In order to do this, we work under the supposition that an event-site exists. We thus recapitulate the totality of the analytic in Books II to V. We are always in a world (there is a transcendental); in this world objects appear, which are atomically structured; between these objects there exist relations (or not). An object can 'become' a site. Of course, as such it vanishes without delay, but the amplitude of its consequences sometimes characterizes it as an event. And it is on condition that an event has taken place, as we shall show, that a body is constituted.

Simplifying considerably (we now recapitulate Book I): the static system of consequences of an event is a (generic) truth. The immanent agent of the production of the consequences (of a truth), or the possible agents of their denial, or that which renders their occultation possible (that which aims to erase a truth)—all of these will be called subjects. The singular object that makes up the appearing of a subject is a body. Whatever subject we may be dealing with, a body is what can bear the subjective formalism, that is to say:

–The five operations that organize its field: subordination, erasure, implication, negation and extinction, or —, /, →, ¬ and =.

–The trace of the vanished event, which is (see the end of Book V) the existence of a past inexistent, and which we write ε.

–The present, written π, which is a predicate attributable to consequences: $(\pi = \varepsilon \rightarrow (\ ))$.

–The typology of subjective figures: faithful, reactive and obscure.

–The derived operational compositions: production, denial, occultation and resurrection.

A multiple-being which bears this subjective formalism and thereby makes it appear in a world receives the name of 'body'—without ascribing to this body any organic status.

In Book I, we saw what it means to say that a body 'bears' the subjective formalism. In the fundamental operations where it is the present that is at stake, the body—which is always under erasure since it is 'marked' by the subjective formalism—may serve as the material support for the evental trace, thus lending force to the production of the present (faithful subject). It may be repressed under the two bars of subordination which are dominated by the negation of the evental trace, thereby assuring, at a distance, the materiality of an extinction of the present (reactive subject). Finally, in the guise of a fantasmatic body supposed to be under erasure, it may produce its own negation as the effect of the negation of the eventaltrace, thereby obtaining the subordination or occultation of the present (obscure subject).

Additionally, the efficacy of the subjective becoming of a body is reliant on the points of the world that it encounters.

So we must first of all answer the following question: in a world where an event-site is given, what is a body? What is the appearing of a body? Or, more precisely, what marks out a body among the objects that constitute the appearing of a world? We will then turn to the immanent determination of a body's capacities—point by point. That will permit us to show that a subjectivizable body can only exist under very rigorous transcendental and eventalconditions. We will then transit through Lacan, whose theory of the body marked by the signifier offers a first structural version of our conclusions. Lastly, the formal exposition will provide us with a limpid schema of the internal composition of a body and of the reasons and conditions of its subjective efficiency.

SECTION 1
Birth, Form and Destiny of Subjectivizable Bodies

1. BIRTH OF A BODY: FIRST DESCRIPTION

Let us take Valéry's famous poem, 'The Graveyard by the Sea' (*Le Cimetière marin*), and consider it as a world. In our terms, this poem is the story of an event. Starting with a real place (the cemetery of the southern French town of Sète, perched above the Mediterranean), the stanzas construct a simplified appearing, reduced to three objects whose degree of existence is positive, perhaps even maximal: the sea, the sun (or noon), the dead, plus an object whose degree of existence is on the edge of nothingness: the poet's consciousness.

Let us indicate the poetic form taken by these transcendental values. Before the evental stanzas, the last three, it is said of the sea that it 'always begins again', or that it retains within it 'so much slumber beneath a veil of flames', or that it is 'the calm of the gods'. We could say that the sea is the surface of the world, reflecting its perennial nature, its fascinating Eternal Return. It is really 'the pure work of an eternal cause'. The sun is that facet of the world which the sea-surface takes as its fixed point, its undivided unity. Furthermore, it is from the place (the cemetery) that the relation between the sea-surface and the One-sun is rendered visible. In our terms (see Book IV), the marine cemetery is the exponent of the sea–sun relation. This is magnificently summed up in Stanza 10:

> Closed, hallowed, full of insubstantial fire,
> Morsel of earth to heaven's light given o'er—
> This plot, ruled by its flambeaux, pleases me—

> A place all gold, stone, and dark wood, where shudders
> So much marble above so many shadows:
> And on my tombs, asleep, the faithful sea.

We can see how the third object (the dead, the stones, the graves) is what comes to make legible the founding relation between the first two, the absolute light of Noon and the faithful sleep of the sea.

To begin with, the poem tells us that the complicity of the sun, the sea and the dead organizes an immobile world, devoid of transformation, a world in which appearing validates Parmenides' ontology. The images proclaim what is incapable of becoming. The inexistent term of such a world is consciousness, understood both as life and as thought. On one hand, we have the place where

> All is burnt up, used up, drawn up in air
> To some ineffably rarefied solution . . .

A place where the dead dissolve their living humanity into the immutability of being. This is the superb passage where—having noted that if its degree of existence were high, consciousness would change the sovereignty of Noon—one is obliged to conclude that consciousness is but the vain shadow of Noon and that the dead, ensconced in the earth, are the symbolic future of this 'change':

> Motionless noon, noon aloft in the blue
> Broods on itself—a self-sufficient theme.
> O rounded dome and perfect diadem,
> I am what's changing secretly in you.

And again:

> My penitence, my doubts, my baulked desires—
> These are the flaw within your diamond pride . . .

Nevertheless,

> But in their heavy night, cumbered with marble,
> Under the roots of trees a shadow people
> Has slowly now come over to your side.

> To an impervious nothingness they're thinned,
> For the red clay has swallowed the white kind [. . .]

This retroactively grounds the negative assertions about the power of change harboured by the consciousness of life. First of all, the poet is forced to confess 'I am all open to these shining spaces', thereby rejoining the complicity of the triad sea–sun–dead, which binds—like a pact—the 'just, impartial light whom I admire/Whose arms are merciless'. Then, appealing to interiority, he only finds in it the vacuity of the future:

> [. . .] I beseech
> The intimations of my secret power
> O bitter, dark, and echoing reservoir
> Speaking of depths always beyond my reach.

This seems to stabilize the initial features of a motionless appearing, in which the reflection of the sun by the sea incorporates all life to itself, cancelling it out.

This is a world where 'presence is porous' and where the poet's only duty is to celebrate the radiance of purity and serenity, of the Noon of the sea and the dead:

> Temple of time, within a brief sigh bounded,
> To this rare height inured I climb, surrounded
> By the horizons of a sea-girt eye.
> And, like my supreme offering to the gods,
> The peaceful coruscation only breeds
> A loftier indifference on the sky.

It is thus especially logical that the poem's final declaration is a confession of defeat at the hands of Eleatic philosophy, at the hands of Parmenides and Zeno, at the hands of those who refuted movement, subtly showing that the being of what appears as mobile is itself immobile, that Achilles never catches up with the tortoise, that the archer's arrow never leaves his bow:

> Zeno, Zeno, cruel Eleatic Zeno,
> Have you then pierced me with your feathered arrow
> That hums and flies, yet does not fly!

It is at this precise moment that one of the four components of the world, the sea, turns out to be an event-site. We appear to be dealing with a rhetoric of refusal, which gives rise to what we're looking for: a body.

> No, no! Arise! The future years unfold.
> Shatter, O body, meditation's mould!

But poetic reality is not to be found in this rhetoric. For what takes place—of which the 'no' of the poet, realized in the action of a body, is nothing but an effect—is an appearance of the marine place under its own differentiating norm, so that what was previously a shimmering acceptance of the reflection of Noon becomes fury, projection, pure movement. We could also say that, subjected to the sun, the sea was at its elementary place. Delivered over to itself it is instead a kind of self-overflowing, it is audaciousness, it is the creation of incalculable effects. The sea had colluded with a self-contented Noon, now it goes over to the side of the wind:

> And, O my breast, drink in the wind's reviving!
> A freshness, exhalation of the sea,
> Restores my soul . . . Salt-breathing potency!
> Let's run at the waves and be hurled back to the living!

Everything here is a staging of the event as the insurrection of the marine site. If the poet has ultimately been able to say 'no' to Parmenides; if his soul, which began as a 'dark reservoir', is restored to him; if his abolition, under the sign of the dead, is annulled by the new life ('The wind is rising! . . . We must try to live!'), it is because from the sea comes coolness, and not the stupor of Noon, because 'the wave/Dares to explode out of the rocks', and because what consciousness confronts, which a moment before was symbolized by the slumber of graves (this 'quiet roof, where dove-sails saunter by'), is now nothing less than the 'wild sea with such wild frenzies gifted', which one can ask to break with the solar immobility of the place ('Break, waves! Break up with your rejoicing surges/This quiet roof . . .').

It is crucial to note that the term 'sea' is ontologically invariable. What is modified or reversed is the transcendental value of its appearing. In metaphorical terms, the sea, which was on the side of the sun, goes over to the side of the wind. In abstract terms, the poem exhibits the two opposite meanings of the inaugural presentation of the marine site: 'The sea, the sea, forever starting and re-starting'. This 'forever starting and re-starting' can mean 'forever identical' but also 'forever different'. The final insurrection is the shift, with respect to the same term (the marine site), from a sovereignty of the same to a sovereignty of difference.

The entire process may be summarized as follows:

–The world of the poem comprises four objects: the sea, the sun, the dead and consciousness.

–The first three objects are bound by relations that are universally exposed in the poem, testifying to their immobile equivalence, their Eternal Return into the Same.

–The fourth term is the proper inexistent of the place.

–In the pure vanishing image of its 'elusive foam' the sea is abruptly revealed to be a site, which plunges into the furore of its own evaluation.

–This site is an event-site because among its consequences we find that the inexistent (consciousness, life) starts to exist maximally, that the ontologically vanquished becomes the living victor, that where the empty excluded of the place used to be there now stands a body capable of breaking the 'pensive form' of its submission. But what precisely is this body?

2. BIRTH OF A BODY: SECOND DESCRIPTION

Thursday, 18 January 1831, Évariste Galois delivers the first lecture of a 'Public Course in Higher Algebra'. Galois is 19 years old. He nonetheless announces that 'the course will comprise theories, some of which are new and none of which has been expounded in public courses'.

Let that introduce us into another world, that of 'algebra between Lagrange and Galois'. The features of this world are not overly esoteric. Displaying the thrust of his genius, Galois presents, as examples of the 'new' theories, the theory of equations that may be solved by radicals and the elliptical functions treated by pure algebra.

Let's concentrate on the first example. The general notion of equation gradually took hold once—in the sixteenth and beginning of the seventeenth century with Viète, the Italian algebraists and Descartes—it became possible to establish, in clear notation, the dependence of an 'unknown quantity' on parameters (supposedly known quantities), parameters that were named the 'coefficients' of the equation. The decisive step was to consider coefficients as themselves being, not fixed determinate quantities (numbers), but letters that may be replaced by such numbers. It is thus that the idea of a *general* form of equations came to prevail. To take a rudimentary example, $3x + 6 = 0$ is a first-degree equation which is particular (the coefficients are the numbers 3 and 6) and which admits of one solution ($x = -2$). The equation, $ax + b = 0$, is the general form of a first-degree equation. It admits of a formal or literal solution, namely $x = -b/a$, unless $a = 0$. It is clear that in the general case a solution is a value ascribable to x which is expressed on the basis of algebraic operations on the coefficients (in this instance, the division of b by a), a value that validates the initial equation: for the value $x = -b/a$, a value that exists as a number (unless $a = 0$), it is *true* that $ax + b = 0$.

The problem of equations 'solvable by radicals' is the following: for what types of equations, given in their general form, is it possible to establish the algebraic operations which, when applied to the coefficients, determine the value of the solutions? For example, we just saw that a first-degree equation is 'solvable by radicals' in an entirely elementary fashion: the literal combination of the two coefficients a and b, provided by the formula $-b/a$, expresses the value of x that counts as the (only) solution for the equation, and it also indicates the case of non-validity ($a = 0$).

The Arab algebraists already knew that second-degree equations—whose literal form is $ax^2 + bx + c = 0$—are solvable by radicals. The general formula which gives the two values of x that validate equality in function of the literal coefficients is the following:

$$\frac{-b \pm \sqrt{b^2 - 4ac}}{2a}$$

The Italian algebraist Cardan provided the formula for the solution by radicals of the general third-degree equation, and the one for fourth-degree equations was discovered subsequently.

This opened up the problem of knowing whether the fifth-degree equation (the one whose formula is $ax^5 + bx^4 + cx^3 + dx^2 + ex + f = 0$) and equations of higher degrees were solvable by radicals. At the end of the eighteenth century, Euler and Lagrange already had good reasons to think that the answer was 'no'. In 1826, the Norwegian Abel, aged (just like Galois when the latter inaugurated his algebra course) 19 years, demonstrated that fifth-degree literal equations are effectively not solvable by radicals: there does not exist a literal algebraic formula (roughly speaking: one that uses a finite series of operations such as addition, division, subtraction, multiplication and root extraction) that can provide—in function of the letters a, b, c, d, e and f—the values for which x validates equality.

Galois tackles the same problem in its general form. But we must understand that what is at stake for him is ultimately something completely different: nothing less than a new definition of algebra, which replaces the central consideration of calculations, whose terms are numbers, with the consideration of structures, whose terms are operations. That is why Galois brings forth a *new body* in the field of mathematics: the body that he names 'group', the first of a series of algebraic structures one of the most important of which was tellingly called, by French mathematicians, the *body* structure (in English, *field*—the difference is rife with consequences . . .).

The event around which the new incorporation crystallizes is the radical change in the status of combinatorics, the study of permutations. Just as the 'forever starting and re-starting' sea in Valéry's poem, visible at first as the metaphor of the immobile or the mirror of Noon, becomes the pure and violent difference that regenerates the possibility of life, likewise the theory of permutations, which for the towering Cauchy was still a local exercise, becomes with Galois the emblem of a formal revolution. Under the sign of the theory of permutations, a whole set of algebraic concepts are brilliantly gathered together, forming a new doctrinal body.

The very beginnings of the world that we're dealing with—in which the concept of group is born as the new body of the algebra to come—are to be found in Lagrange. Instead of labouring directly to find the formula that would give the solutions (or roots) of a general equation, Lagrange had the idea of going through the systematic study of the functions that link these solutions to one another. Following this path, he naturally encountered the role of permutations: given a function that links the solutions of an equation, if the solutions are permuted, does the function always have the same value or not? After all, given a literal equation, the fact that x and x' solve this equation means that, for the value x, you will indeed obtain the equation of the literal expression to zero, and if you replace x with x', you will still get zero. . . With this new technical idea, Lagrange achieved a limited result: he explained in an entirely formal and general way the reason why equations whose degree is less than or equal to four are solvable by radicals.

In the sequence of technical improvements, Cauchy's dissertation on what he called the 'theory of combinations' (1812) is undoubtedly fundamental. Cauchy had the idea of studying not just, like Lagrange, the effect of a permutation of the given quantities on the function that ties them together, but *the permutations themselves* (which he calls substitutions), *considered as possible terms for new operations*. That is how he defines the product of two substitutions (the implementation of one after the other, which in effect constitutes a third substitution), the 'identical' substitution, the nth power of a substitution, and the substitution that is the inverse of another (if you permute x and y, then y and x, you return to the 'identical' situation). In brief, he introduces the possibility of defining a calculus on something other than numbers.

Why does this possibility nonetheless fall short of the status of event-site? Why does it not authorize the formation of a body? Very simply, because the transcendental value of Cauchy's invention is not such as to 'maximize' its consequences, and in particular to sublate the inexistent of the (algebraic) world, which is the very status of the notion of operation. This status is still bound to the particularity of numerical givens, and is not thematized as such. Needless to say, Cauchy—and before him Gauss in a more arithmetical domain—provides examples of operations that do not presuppose a numerical field (for example the products and powers of substitutions). But they both do so within the existing theoretical framework, and to particular ends. They do not draw out the universal significance of these innovations for the algebraic world of their time. Accordingly, the concept of operation remains stuck in a kind of segmentation of domains, essentially prisoner to calculations— regarding which Galois will correctly remark that 'after Euler, they [calculations] have become more and more necessary, but more and more difficult, as they have come to be applied to ever more advanced scientific objects'.

A very interesting proof of this calculative restriction is that when Cauchy develops, in 1812 and then 1846 (after Liouville's study of Galois's manuscripts), the theory of substitutions, at no point does he concern himself with the question of equations. His work remains closed in upon itself, as if the theory of combinations were an autonomous domain at the margins of algebra. Were that so, the theory would remain, as Poisson remarked about the dissertation of 1812, of a relatively limited significance.

What Galois does pertains in fact to two registers:

1. He projects the theory of substitutions into a core domain of algebra, by attaching to each equation, through an entirely general method, a set of substitutions that characterize it (the 'group' of the equation).

2. He indicates very clearly that this projection decisively transforms algebra as a whole, since it accords a maximal value to the generic notion of operation by extricating it from the fetters of numerical calculus.

The first gesture (whose technical aspect we cannot convey here) allows him fully to clarify the problem of the solutions of equations by radicals (this solution is impossible for general equations whose degree is equal to or greater than the fifth); but it also allows him to show, in a construction that is as dense as it is enlightening, how the essence of this problem lies in structural configurations that demands to be examined in their own right (in the current vocabulary: base fields [*corps de base*], extension, associated group and normal subgroup [*sous-groupe distingué*]). It is to this end that Galois creates the concept of 'group' assigned to the substitutions of the solutions of an equation, engaging himself assiduously in its analysis. His most brilliant idea is certainly that of honing in on those substitutions (what today we would call 'permutations') of the solutions of an equation which leave the rational relations between the solutions unchanged. It turns out that these permutations form a subgroup of the total group of permutations. The existence and properties of this subgroup dictate the solution to the problem. But more profoundly, it is the first example of a notion that sheds a new light on the whole of algebra, the notion of *normal subgroup*. Why is this notion so important? Because it articulates the general ideas of operation and operational invariance. This articulation can be regarded as the matrix for the whole of modern mathematics.

Right before dying, in 1832, in a stupid duel (for, as he put it, 'a wretched coquette'), Galois brings to the attention of his closest friend, Auguste Chevalier, that all of his work aims to determine 'which quantities may be substituted for the given quantities without terminating the relation'. As Sophus Lie would declare much later:

> The great importance of Galois's oeuvre stems from the fact that his original theory of algebraic equations is a systematic application of the two fundamental notions of group and invariant, notions that tend to dominate mathematical science.

Through his second gesture, Galois creates the trace of the event, the sublation of the inexistent, by replacing calculative ontology (there are quantities over which one operates) with a structural ontology (there are operational difficulties that may be investigated in their own right, without making calculations). His awareness of this point is nothing short of astonishing. Let us consider some examples of what is truly the intellectual emergence of the possibility of a new mathematical body.

Galois knows that the upsurge of a new theoretical body, capable of historically bearing a new mathematician subject, demands breaks from which nothing can be deduced.

> It is generally believed that mathematics is a series of deductions. [. . .] If one could reliably deduce [the new theory] from known theories, it would not be new.

He also knows that what this break opens is a process, the duration of an inquiry, and not a given synthetic expression:

A new theory is the search for rather than the expression of truth.

Finally, he knows that the trace of this break (of this event in thinking) is very generally visible in language, in new notations, and that one shouldn't hesitate to thrust upon thought the surprise of new symbolizations:

The novelty of this subject-matter required the employment of new denominations, new characters. No doubt, this inconvenience may initially discourage the reader who finds it difficult to forgive authors whom he greatly esteems for now speaking to him in a novel language.

Galois is acutely aware that the significance of what thereby comes to writing is not reducible to limited domains or particular calculations. He perceives that the operators he's introducing signal the beginning of a new algebra, and that this algebra is the truth of the one that preceded it, the truth of the world 'algebra between Lagrange and Cauchy':

With regard to these kinds of equations, there exists a certain genre of metaphysical considerations which hover over all the calculations and often render them useless.

We will therefore expound, in some articles, the most general and most philosophical aspect of these investigations, which a thousand circumstances have prevented us from publishing earlier.

We undertake here the analysis of analysis.

The analysis of analysis: a remarkable formula, which institutes the new algebra as the truth-process of the old one, a process set off by the change in the meaning of combinatorics and by thought's new dedication to the disentangling of forms. It is from this standpoint that Galois perceives—not the least of the contributions that stem from his poetic lucidity about the development of mathematics—the role of the inexistent of a world as the trace of what happens to it, the mark of a site which unfolds for an instant. He effectively asks himself where the absolutely new ideas that visited him—but which also took a truncated form in Cauchy or an excessively circumscribed form in Abel—are to be located. His answer is superb: in the old world, among our predecessors, but under the form of non-knowledge, under the form of inexistence, of nil intensity:

It often seems that the same ideas belong to many, like a revelation. If we look for the cause of this, it is easy to find it in the works of those who preceded us, in which these ideas are present unbeknownst to their authors.

This presence 'unbeknownst to their authors' allows us fully to recapitulate the birth of the body that the new subject of algebra will take possession of—a body that depends on the trace of a site in the world instituted by Lagrange.

1. This world ('our predecessors', as Galois says) is dominated by a practice of algebraic symbolism which progressively impacts on all the dimensions of mathematical analysis. Accordingly, the discipline of this world is firstly that of very difficult calculations, which only 'the most profound geometers' can elegantly pull off.

2. In this world, the question of the solution of formal equations by radicals is a stopping-block, which is to say a real effect. It is clearly necessary to go through functional combinations of the solutions, but without extracting the structures that underlie this combinatorial dimension. Even the particular negative demonstration (it is impossible to solve by radicals the general fifth-degree equation) therefore remained beyond the reach of Lagrange, who nonetheless understood why it is possible to solve in this way equations of a lesser degree.

3. Though with Cauchy the theory of permutations took a decisive step forward, this progress remained disjoined from any overall vision of algebra.

4. Therefore, that which inexists in this world but is present, as it were, in its hollow imprint (with a nil intensity), is the idea that the 'philosophy' of algebra consists in operating on operations, in extracting structures, and not in linearizing calculations. Consequently, equations must be considered in a broader formal framework and associated to different albeit formally identifiable structures.

5. With Abel and then Galois, the theory of equations acts as a site in this world, to the extent that it appears within it as both central and maximally innovative, rather than merely as a stopping-block for calculations. It is through this theory that the 'analysis of analysis' will move, that is the beginnings of an algebra of structures, of their entanglements, their extensions, their isomorphism and so on.

6. The fundamental concepts put to work in this site, in particular those of groups, invariants and normal subgroups, sublate the inexistent, and this

sublation polarizes the constitution of a new theoretical body. These concepts put that which was either unknown or marginal in the period between Lagrange and Cauchy at the centre of the mathematics to come.

It remains to examine this body in its own right, as well as how it authorizes the entirely innovative treatment of algebraic problems that had been left in abeyance. In brief, how it authorizes the treatment of numerous *points* of the world in question.

3. THE BODY OF THE POEM

When the poet, overcoming the stupor of Being, escaping the Parmenidean fascination of Noon, exclaims 'Shatter, O body, meditation's mould!' [*Brisez, mon corps, cette forme pensive!*], where does this 'body' come from, which is capable of undoing the form of the One that had cancelled both conscience and life? In this entire affirmative peroration, the 'body' noticeably gathers together disparate elements, all of them drawn from the storm rising over the sea: 'the wind's reviving', the 'salt-breathing potency', the wave's 'reeking spray', the 'huge air', the 'blue flesh', the 'tumult'. . . In fact, concentrated in the figure of the body, we have a part of the marine site—the one which, counter to the 'quiet roof' and the 'sure treasure', is consistent with the inversion in the value of consciousness, which passes from mortal inertia to affirmative life.

We can therefore define the body: the set of elements of a site—in this case the sea—which entertain with the resurrection of the inexistent (consciousness and life) a relationship of maximal proximity. The function of appearing identifies as far as possible these elements (huge air, wind's reviving, exploding wave. . .) to what has become—as the measure of the event's force—the site's central referent: the inexistent suddenly raised to the maximal degree of existence, the metamorphosis of he who is 'all open to these shining spaces' into he who says 'No, no! Arise! The future years unfold'.

This former inexistent has become the key to the whole of existence. Accordingly, the maximal identity of the elements to it is achieved through the total unfolding of their own existence. It is because the wave 'dares to explode' that it enters into a positive relation with the imperative 'No, no! Arise!'. It is because the 'wind is rising' that it plays a part. It is because the huge air 'opens and shuts' the book that it is admitted into the composition of the body. We can thus say that the elements of the body—such as it is created by the poem within itself—are those whose identity with the becoming existent of the inexistent is measured by the intensity of their own existence.

Since the inexistent which is made incandescent is the trace of the event, we have a limpid abstract formula: a post-eventual body is constituted by all the elements of the site which invest the totality of their existence in their identity to the trace of the event.

Or, to employ a militant metaphor; the body is the set of everything that the trace of the event mobilizes. It is thus that the foam, the wave, the wind, the salt and the rocks themselves are required by the metamorphosis of the sea, the storm-event, whose trace is the vital upsurge of the poet and the poem.

It is clear that the trace of the poem opens onto a new present. Valéry puts it with precision: 'Fly away, my Sun-bewildered pages!' means that the old inscription is dead. 'We must try to live!' is the imperative of the present, grounded by the auto-appearance of the site. And waves, wind, foam and blue flesh are as though absorbed by this temporal imperative. In our vocabulary, we can say that these elements incorporate themselves into the eventual present.

A body is nothing other than the set of elements that have this property.

Among them, of course, the metamorphosed consciousness—the fascination of Noon transformed into a power of rupture—plays a central role. Poetic enunciation ('Shatter, O body!', 'Let's run at the waves and be hurled back to the living!') dominates, with its maximal intensity, all the other components of the body. Subjective movement is the point of existence that names all the others.

Separately distributed throughout the poem, these disparate elements turn out to be corporeally compatible. Gathered within appearing under the existential domination of the injunction ('Arise', 'Let's run', 'We must', 'Break'...), they are ultimately united in being (here, the being of language) by a poetic compatibility that allows them to hold together, authorizing the cohesion of a body. We perceive that the 'freshness, exhalation of the sea', the 'salt-breathing potency', the 'thousand idols of the Sun', the 'blue flesh', the 'huge air', the 'absolute hydra'—that all of this is the body educed by the site, which unifies, even in the intensity of the multiple, the sudden sovereignty of what did not exist.

4. ORGANS: FIRST DESCRIPTION

Let us take for granted the final existence of the body of the poem: the set of the elements of the marine site incorporated into the eventual present—foam, wind and waves—whose necessity of existence measures their identity to the injunction of awakened consciousness. We know that this injunction, which is itself a component of the body, dominates all of its elements and is the body's real synthesis, its ontological envelope.

Generalizing from our example, we can say that a body is the totality of the elements of the site incorporated into the eventual present. We can also call these the 'contemporary' elements of the event, meaning those elements which are as identical as possible, within appearing, to the trace of the event: the inexistent projected into existence, the inapparent that shines within appearing. Let me propose another formulation: a body is composed of all the elements of the site (here, all the maritime motifs) that subordinate themselves, with maximal intensity, to that which was nothing and becomes all.

Our aim now is to connect the capacity of a body to that which—in the site and even in the world—presents itself as the support for a decision. We want to examine the capacity of a body, with regard to a determinate choice, to affirm a point and hold it. As we know (see Book I), it is there that we find the zone of articulation between a body and the subjective formalism for which it serves as the support. Recall the analytic of the concept of 'point' developed in Book VI. Roughly speaking, a point is a 'projection' of the transcendental of a world onto the set $\{0, 1\}$, which is itself structured as a transcendental by the relation $0 \leq 1$. Conceptually, this means that the structure of a transcendental, which might be infinite, is made to appear before the tribunal of the decision (or the pure choice, or the alternative), which comes down to saying 'yes' (1) or 'no' (0). The subjective metaphor of the point can be expressed as follows: To decide is always to filter the infinite through the Two.

Valéry's poem concludes explicitly with this duality of the 'yes' and the 'no':

No, no! Arise! The future years unfold.

Yes, mighty sea with such wild frenzies gifted [. . .]

But there is a whole preliminary positioning of the points of the poem, that is of the pure dualities elicited by the place, dualities that will amount to a series of tests for the body engendered by the event. For instance, will the new body be capable of inducing the poet-subject of which it is the support to decide for desire?

> The eyes, the teeth, the eyelids moistly closing,
> The pretty breast that gambles with the flame,
> The crimson blood shining when lips are yielded,
> The last gift, and the fingers that would shield it—[. . .]

Or will he remain on the side of death?

> I pasture long my sheep, my mysteries,
> My snow-white flock of undisturbed graves! [. . .]

> The dead lie easy, hidden in the earth where they
> Are warmed and have their mysteries burnt away. [. . .]

Will he find the strength to escape the stupefying and immobile power of Noon, that incorruptible diamond?

> What grace of light, what pure toil goes to form
> The manifold diamond of the elusive foam!
> What peace I feel begotten at that source!

Or will he manage to uphold the complex virtuality of interiority and change, to be the secret corruption of the jewel?

> My penitence, my doubts, my baulked desires—
> These are the flaw within your diamond pride . . .

Will he be on the side of Zeno ('Achilles' giant stride left standing') or on the side of Bergson, of the melody of creative life ('The sounding/Shaft gives me life')?

A whole spectrum of instances of the Two thereby constitutes in language the points of the poem, before which the intricacy of the world is summoned to appear. When it 'shatters the mould', the final body must above all prove itself capable, in itself and through apposite organs, to answer 'yes' to the wind against Noon, to sexuality against death, to the exploding foam against the shimmering lull, to the singular wave against the void immensity, to presence against thought 'drunk with absence', to Bergson against Parmenides. There will thus be regions of the body, whose efficacy pertains to this or that point. There will be the region of movement ('Let's run at the waves'), the region of pure sensation ('O my breast, drink'), the region of command ('Break, waves!'). . . All of them will be efficacious with respect to a determinate point that the poem has made manifest in advance.

Consciousness alone or mere injunction is not enough for this regional specialization of the body, dividing and collecting itself as it is tested by points, by Kierkegaard's 'either/or'. Of course, that which in Book I we marked with the letter ε, the first declaration, is expressed in the logic of a subject of truth as follows: the event has taken place, I say 'yes' to it, I meld with the suddenly sublimated inexistent. And it is true that it is 'my book' (the poem itself) that the 'huge air opens and shuts'. Nonetheless, without the efficacious regions of the body, without the organs that locally synthesize these regions, we would be merely left with principles. I must really run at the waves, expose myself to the wind, break with Noon, explode on the rock and so on. All of this presupposes a local organization of the surging body, a ubiquity of regional syntheses, in sum that the body (self-)organizes.

A body, in its totality, is what gathers together those terms of the site which are maximally engaged in a kind of ontological alliance with the new appearance of an inexistent, which acts as the trace of the event. A body is what is beckoned and mobilized by the post-evental sublimation of the inexistent. Its coherence is that of the internal compatibility of elements, as guaranteed by their shared ideal subordination to the primordial trace. But the efficacy of a body, which is oriented towards consequences (and therefore towards the subjective formalism, which is the art of consequences as the constitution of a new present), is played out locally, point by point. A body's test is always that of an alternative. A point is what directs the components of a body to the summons of the Two. In order for this to happen, there must be efficacious regions of bodies, which validate the 'yes' to the new consequences against the inertia of the old world; there must also be, besides the brilliance of the trace, appropriate organs for such a validation. These organs are the immanent synthesis of the regional efficacy of a body.

It is only by working out an organization for the subjectivizable body that one can hope to 'live', and not merely try to.

5. BODIES AND ORGANS OF THE MATHEME

In a famous letter, written to his friend Auguste Chevalier on 29 May 1832, Galois declares the following:

> For some time, my main meditations have been aimed at the application of the theory of ambiguity to transcendent analysis.

This advocacy of the ambiguous, of the indiscernible, is the conspicuous sign of the birth of a new body, whose internal organization will take up more than a century.

This body comes together around what has served as the trace of the changed meaning of the theory of permutations, localizing in it the linked notions of group of operations and invariant. A mathematical entity is 'ambiguous' with respect to an operational field once an operation of this field leaves it invariant. In effect, if another entity is equally invariant, it will not be possible—in the operational field—to tell it apart from the first, since neither the one nor the other will be identifiable by the result of the operation, which leaves them both unchanged. Confronted with the performance of the operation, they are 'the same' because they do not register its effect.

The body that is born, after Cauchy, with Abel and especially Galois (it will later be called 'modern algebra'), is the one that replaces the linearity of calculations with a general theory of operations and invariants. Galois is explicit about this transformation:

> Analysts try to deceive themselves in vain: they do not deduce, they combine, they compose.

To the logic of simple deduction, which aims at a unique result, Galois opposes a logic of composition (bringing mathematics closer to music). The new algebraic body, the support of mathematical subjectivities to come, is in a sense spatial rather than linear: it tries to link together distinct forms and seeks—as though 'between' these forms—the new invariants. That is why one can provide a simple definition of the efficacious part of the body 'new algebra' with regard to a point of the mathematical world: it is a zone of correlation between forms, structures and operational fields which seem to be entirely separate. The great concepts that govern this zone and localize its invariants are the organs of the new body.

It is for this reason that Bourbaki's monumental treatise, which aimed to set forth the entirety of the structural implements (algebra, topology. . .), their zones of interference (groups and Lie algebras, algebraic geometry, the analytical theory of numbers, etc.) and their organs (great theorems of representation, of invariance, of natural isomorphy, etc.), was more akin to an anatomy of the mathematical body than to a dynamics of its creation. The real of the points, whose effective treatment in the world governed the becoming of the body, was effaced, so to speak, by a formidable cartography of efficacious parts. The example of Galois is far more transparent. The point that initiates the organization of the body is identifiable and it appropriately displays its binary logic: yes or no, are we ready to decide if equations of a degree higher than the fourth are solvable by radicals? In Abel's wake, Galois replies: 'Yes, we can decide. These equations are not solvable by radicals, the question is settled'. And the point is held.

To reach this decision, it is nevertheless necessary to stratify the body, defining within it a completely new link between previously separate, or even ill-defined, algebraic structures: the theory of the permutation of groups, on the one hand, and that of the extensions of operational domains, on the other. It is this link which circumscribes an efficacious part and admits of an organic synthesis.

It is philosophically rewarding to consider these matters a little more closely. We know from the Greeks that the operational domain of rational numbers admits of equations whose coefficients are rational, but which nonetheless remain devoid of a solution within that domain. Long after the Greeks, these equations will receive the name of 'irreducible'. The most historically famous of these, because it is linked to the problem of measuring the diagonal of the square, is the equation $x^2 - 2 = 0$. It is irreducible because $\sqrt{2}$ is an irrational number.

Ever since the birth in the sixteenth century of what is properly speaking literal algebra, but far more clearly since Gauss, we also know that if one 'adds' to an operational domain the solution of an irreducible equation, authorizing all of its calculable combinations with other elements of that domain, one obtains a new operational domain. The most famous of these adjunctions is the one that injects into the domain of real numbers the 'imaginary' symbol i, considered as the solution for the irreducible equation (for real numbers) $x^2 + 1 = 0$. Therein lies the origin of a domain of immense scientific significance, that of so-called complex numbers.

The procedure is actually a general one. Thus if you add $\sqrt{2}$ to rational numbers, and permit all combinations (such as $3\sqrt{2} - 17$, etc.), you obtain a new operational domain. It is called an algebraic extension of the rational numbers. If you introduce another solution to an irreducible equation, you will get an extension of the extension and so on. Galois's brilliant idea was to consider—as juxtaposed to the successive extensions of the operational domain by the solutions of irreducible equations—the sequence of groups of permutations defined over these solutions through the technique of normal subgroups. In fact, the efficacious part of the body capable of treating in a decisive manner the point 'equations solvable by radicals' is composed in the following manner: to each extension of the operational domain through the adjunction of solutions to an irreducible equation you make correspond a subgroup of the group of permutations of these solutions, namely the subgroup that brings together the 'indiscernible' or 'ambiguous' solutions, those that cannot distinguish the operations of the domain in question. Ultimately, to an ascending series of extensions of domains there corresponds a descending series of operational groups. As Galois says, it is the 'composition' of these figures that defines the efficacious part of the new body with regard to the point 'theory of equations'. Why? Because a descending series must perforce come to a halt on a non-decomposable or simple group. This in turn gives a meaning to the halting—which is as such indefinable—of the ascending series of extensions. This halting clause accounts for the general form of the problem and guarantees that the point (are equations solvable by radicals?) is definitively held.

As for the organ that synthesizes the efficacious part, it is composed of the link between the new algebraic concepts that make the entire construction thinkable. These are the two operators that make it possible to juxtapose the ascending series and the descending series: algebraic extension, which expands the domains through the injection of new literal symbols (such as i or $\sqrt{2}$); the notion of subgroup, which analyses the structure of permutations and—on the basis of the play of invariants and within a construction that contracts the field of investigation—distinguishes in that structure between what is simple and what is still composed.

It is in reflecting on these concepts and their usage—which is a matter of formal anticipation and composition rather than of calculation—that Galois is led to write the following:

I am only speaking here of pure analysis.

To plunge headlong into calculations, into group operations, to classify them in terms of their difficulties and not their forms, this is, to my mind, the mission of future geometers; this is the path I have undertaken in this work.

'Pure analysis', 'grouping of operations' and the definition of a new 'mission' for mathematics: this is a testament to Galois's awareness that he is in the grip of the subject-form of a new theoretical body. We can very clearly identify five conditions required for the effective existence of a body, and thus of a creative subject:

1. The mathematical world inherited by Galois is an active and dense world, teeming with new problems. It is the very opposite of an atonic world. Galois comes after Euler, Lagrange, Gauss and Abel. In the transcendental of such a world, there are points—in particular the point that concerns the question of knowing if equations are solvable by radicals, yes or no.

2. A site has come to be, which concerns the place of the abstract or formal study of operations in calculations and concepts. The trace ε of this site is the changed status of the study of permutations: from being a simple combinatorial pastime with no general significance, it comes to embody the paradigm of the concept of group in the mathematical world.

3. There exist elements incorporated to the trace, and thus a real body (a new algebraic thought) which is not reducible to this trace. Namely, Galois's sudden vision whereby the analysis of groups of permutations makes possible a kind of descending diagram of the extensions of numerical domains.

4. There exists an efficacious part of this body, made up of elements that decide the point—namely the form of the groups of permutations of solutions which are associated to different types of equations. It is this form which is associated to the extensions and which legislates over the general figure of the efficacious part of the body (the correspondences between distinct structures). In sum, from the fact that, for equations of a degree higher than the fourth, these groups are simple or non-decomposable, there follows the decision on the point: these equations cannot be solved by radicals.

5. There exist new concepts that envelop the efficacious part and thereby define a new organ of the body 'modern algebra'. For example, the concepts of group and subgroup, algebraic extension, invariant, simplicity. . .

These five conditions for the existence of a subjectivizable body can be summed up as follows: the world must not be atonic; there is a site-object and its trace, namely the maximal becoming-existent of an inexistent; elements of the object are maximally correlated to the trace and group themselves in a compatible manner; in the body constituted by all of its elements there are subsets which are its organs with respect to points.

Below, these conditions will be given a very clear and very striking formal expression.

The subjectivation of the new body will acquire the creative form of a constant broadening of structural correlations, of the 'visibility' of one structure in another. In particular, 'reading' algebraic structures in topological structures will become the key to contemporary mathematics. With the concept of sheaf, which synthesizes this type of correlation and serves as its general organ, there undoubtedly begins the history of a new body, for which Grothendieck arguably played around 1950 the same role that Galois played around 1830.

Be that as it may, let's hold on to the notion, which we have seen at work in both mathematics and poetry, that the sequence world–points–site–body–efficacious part–organ is indeed the generic form of what makes it possible for there to be such things as truths. This authorizes the materialist dialectic to contend that beyond bodies and languages, there is the real life of some subjects.

The night that democratic materialism announces to historical humanity, in the guise of a violent promise, is not an unavoidable night.

SECTION 2
Lacan

Contrasting the backward physiologism of many psychologists, Lacan can sometimes be found arguing for the signifier against the body, saying that 'its presence [of the subject] is constituted by the signifier more than by the body'; or establishing that the body is what resists the subject, so that—recalling Plato—the subject is negatively consigned to its body, rather than borne by it: 'It is not to its consciousness that the subject is condemned, but to its body, which resists in numerous ways against realizing the division of the subject'.

Lacan also notes that scientific truth is only attained at the price of completely forsaking perceptual information, and therefore everything that would connect the world to the organs of the body: 'Science only really took off went it left behind the presupposition, which it is appropriate to call natural, since it implies that the body's grips on "nature" are natural too'.

Lacan insists that the body, far from being that on the basis of which the subject identifies itself, its intimacy, its belonging or the natural 'sameness' of the self, is nothing but the receptacle for the impact of the Other, the place where the subject is constituted as exterior to itself: 'This place of the Other is not to be taken elsewhere than in the body, [it is] scars on tegumental bodies'. Or, in a decisive formula: 'The body paves the way [*fait le lit*] for the Other through the operation of the signifier'. It follows from this that the body is never an original given: the body 'comes second, whether it is dead or alive'.

Lacan often thinks of the body as an exposition to linguistic structure or as the inert mediation of the efficacy of that structure. As for the subject, for the psychoanalyst there is no causality that refers back to life as such, as absolutely as the body may be engaged in it: 'The fact that the biological substrate of the subject is fully at stake in the analysis does not in any way imply that the causality which analysis discovers is reducible to the biological'. If we think in terms of causal relation, the body is what this effect imposes itself upon, and not its living cipher: 'the language-effect imposes itself on the body'. No affection of the body can be simply corporeal. More radically, there is 'this body that I say is only affected by the structure'.

The word 'affected' is chosen with care. For Lacan, affect is the body, to the extent that structure operates within it. If we define (generic) man in Lacan's terms as the animal that inhabits language, affect names the effect of this habitation on the body: 'Affect comes to a body whose property would be to inhabit language'. There is a place of speech, and it is 'in flesh and bone, that is with all our carnal and sympathetic complexity, that we inhabit this place'.

In brief, the body is subordinated to the signifier. In this respect, it is for the subject the exposition to the Other; there is no action of the body, but only its being invested by the structure, and the sign of this investment is affect. It appears that we are as far as possible from the doctrine that we have been defending, which makes of the body an active composition, the support for the appearing of a subject-form, whose organs treat the world point by point.

In truth, the distance is not so great.

Some of the severity with which Lacan dismisses any constitutive power of the body, or even any immanent dynamic, is actually aimed at phenomenology, and in particular at Merleau-Ponty and Sartre, who describe the body as the presence of consciousness to the world: 'By wanting to resolve itself into presence-through-the-body, phenomenology [. . .] condemns itself both to transgressing its field and to making an experience that is foreign to it inaccessible'. If it is necessary ceaselessly to recall that it is from structure alone that the body draws the symptomal appearance of its effects, if at every opportunity it is necessary to repeat that 'knowledge affects the body of the being which only becomes a being by speaking', it is to the extent that the phenomenological vulgate, by separating the body from the letters that target it, institutes the presence-to-the-world of the body as the ontology of originary experience.

The repetition of the primacy of the signifier over physiological data is first and foremost a polemical thesis, which in no way excludes that the body is *also* the name of the subject. It is simply necessary to understand that it is so within the parameters of the materialist dialectic, which obliges the body to comply with the ideal exception of the True.

We can also grant Lacan that the body is the place of the Other, since for us it is only the evental becoming-Other of the site which commands the possibility of a body of truth.

Let us note in passing that Lacan goes rather far in this direction, since he accepts that the body thinks, and that it is precisely this body-thought which has been misunderstood by separating it under the name of soul. When he writes that 'the subject of the unconscious only touches the soul through the body, by introducing thought into it', we have no difficulty in recognizing something like a primitive formulation of our conviction that the body, gathered under the trace of the vanished event, sets out point by point, and organically, the thought-subject of a yet unknown eternal truth.

This is especially the case to the extent that the idea whereby the body affects (itself) under the goad of a trace was by no means foreign to the Master. It is not trivial to define desire as the 'signifier-effect on the animal it marks', if we understand that these effects *on* the animal are also the effects in the world *of* the animal, a marked body whose fate would then lie on the side of the True. One will also appreciate the fact that this effect of marking is described as the 'shearing effect' [*effet de cisaille*], a powerful image which I interpret in the following way: the becoming of a subjectivated body establishes the present in the perpetual danger that its ineluctable division—its 'shearing', one could not put it better—becomes that of its reactive negation, or even of its obscure occultation. This is the precarious equilibrium of the body under erasure as it resists the obliterated body and the vanished body. The consequence is that, when it comes to the subject-body to which we incorporate our fleeting animality, we are always tempted to say either that it exists (dogmatism, the temptation of the faithful subject) or that it does not exist (scepticism, the temptation of the reactive subject). Lacan chalked this oscillation up to the primacy of the sexual act, this psychoanalytic form of the latent process of the psychic True, when he wrote that 'the moment of the sexual act [. . .] is articulated in the gap between two formulae. The first: there is no sexual act [. . .]. The second: there is only the sexual act'.

We are steadfastly Lacanian with regard to the theme of the subsumption of bodies and languages by the exception of truths—even though Lacan himself would limit their impact, stopping at the threshold of their eternal power. This theme requires above all the recognition of the potential absoluteness of a trace, the trace of an event which absorbs disappearance in a deferred and maximal appearance. This trace marks out the only beginning that counts, including the beginning of the body. Lacan says it too: 'The primary, in its structure, only functions through the all or nothing of the trace'. It is then necessary that the truthful grasp of a subject over the world manifest itself in the regime of the cut, of the upsurge of a new present, and not in that of productive continuity: 'Only through the play of the cut is the world ready for the speaking being'. Finally, one must be persuaded that only through incorporation is there an effect of truth. Incorporation into what? Into this new body electrified by the impact of the trace. If, as we argued at the end of Book I, it is indeed by its affect that the human animal recognizes that it participates, through its incorporated body, in some subject of truth, we will say, with Lacan, that 'it is as incorporated that the structure makes affect'. More profoundly, if we accept that the body of truth comes to be through the incorporation of some available multiplicities—among which there may be 'bodies' in the ordinary sense of the term—we will penetrate the meaning of that enigmatic, and almost pre-Socratic, formula from *Radiophonie*: 'The first body makes the second by incorporating itself within it'. Here I can unhesitatingly communicate with Lacan's construction, which incorporates the natural body into the body conceived as the stigmata of the Other.

Where then can we find the point of dissension? At the very point of agreement, in the interpretation of the ambiguity of the theory of the 'two bodies', which is presupposed by every process of incorporation. In this aspect of his teaching, Lacan treats what I believe to be a sequence or a contingent becoming as a structure. For him, in effect, the marking of bodies stems from the fact that—note the Heideggerian style—the human animal is 'a living "being" (which) distinguishes itself from others by inhabiting language'. Under this axiom, the subject is effectively split into two bodies: the one which he 'has' and which, as an objective body or living object, bars access to the one which he uses, this body-place-of-the-Other where his speech makes him. If man has a body, 'he has no other despite the fact that, on account of his speaking-being [*parlêtre*], he has some other at his disposal, without managing to make it his'. This second body is generally a symptom for something Other and not a possession or the basis for a new subject. This is proven by the canonical feminine example: a woman 'is the symptom of another body'.

It follows from all this that the formal operations of incorporation into the place of the Other and of splitting of the subject constitute, under the name of Unconscious, the infrastructure of the human animal and not the occurrence—as rare as it may be—of the present-process of a truth which a subjectivated body treats point by point. We could say that Lacan's anticipation restricts its implementation to the truths of psychoanalysis, which are truths of structure. The act in which the cure sometimes resolves itself indubitably involves its application to the real, but it is marked by the scepticism with which every de-absolutization of what is created by chance shields itself.

When Lacan says that 'the object of psychoanalysis is not man, it's what he lacks', one will note that he has yet to separate this famous psycho-analysis from philosophy, since by 'eternal truths' we too understand what is lacking in the man of democratic materialism, and what can only be accessed by vitally incorporating oneself into the Other body—which Lacan too, as we have just seen, bears witness to.

But when he adds 'not absolute lack, but the lack of an object', he takes a step too far in the direction of finitude, which de-philosophizes him. This is of course to his great satisfaction, since he sees in the absolute what he does not hesitate to call 'an inaugural mistake of philosophy', which according to him would have always been busy 'suturing the breach [*béance*] of the subject', and in so doing 'bolting down truth'. Our defence is to situate the singularity of the human animal one notch further. Inhabiting speech does not suffice to found this singularity and the breach that results from the linguistic marking of the body is by no means the last word. Such breaches, which may be located in behaviours that reveal the body to be divisible (into 'my' body and the symptomal body, or body-place-of-the-Other), can be effortlessly observed in animals with small brains. Like the water-turtle which, as soon as it sees me, swims towards the glass of the aquarium, frenetically thrashing its feet, and looks at me with its shining yellow-green reptilian eyes, until, intimidated or culpable, I give it its ration of dried prawns.

It is only as a transhuman body that a subject takes hold of the divisible body of the human animal. The breach is then on the side of creation, not of the symptom, and I am not persuaded that the 'case' of Joyce—'Joyce-the-sinthome', as Lacan says—suffices to dissolve the one into the other. Rather, we observe the gap between, on one hand, the transcen-dental laws of appearing and, on the other, the present engendered by a subjectivizable body, a present that initiates an eternal truth. This is also the gap between the multiple-body of the human animal and its subjective incorporation.

But the crucial teaching bequeathed by Lacan remains the following: it is in vain that some, under the impulse of democratic materialism, wish to convince us, after the comedy of the soul, that our body is the proven place of the One. Against this animalistic reduction, let us repeat the Master's verdict: 'the presupposition that there is somewhere a place of unity is well suited to suspend our assent'.

SECTION 3

Formal Theory of the Body, Or, We Know Why a Body Exists, What It Can and Cannot Do

The purpose of the formal exposition is to elegantly show that the concept of body is a creative synthesis of the logic of appearing. The materiality of a subject of truth—a body—is what polarizes the objects of a world according to the generic destiny of a truth. In this respect, a body allows the onto-logical destiny of appearing itself to appear. As should be evident by now, this can only be done by 'treating' the points of the world. The exact con-ditions for the existence of a subjectivizable body are thereby elucidated, and the manifest rarity of truths becomes rational.

1. FIRST FORMAL SKETCH: DEFINITION AND EXISTENCE OF A BODY

The starting-point is obviously a world **m**, with its transcendental T, and an object, say (A, Id), which prescribes distributions of differences and identities to the elements of A. The world could be, for instance, Valéry's poem 'The Graveyard by the Sea', or the state of algebra between Lagrange and Galois. The object could be, in the first case a figural place, the marine cemetery of Sète, as recomposed in the poem on the basis of four elements (the sea, the sun, the dead, consciousness), in the second case, the singular question of the 'generic' equations that may be solved by radicals.

We obviously assume the fundamental results of the Greater Logic and the theory of change. In particular, every object possesses, as an element, a proper inexistent (an $x \in A$ such that $\mathbf{E}x = \mu$). Consider, for instance, the consciousness crushed by the immutable Noon in the poem, or the purely combinatorial interpretation (by Cauchy) of the group of permutations of the roots of equations at the moment when Galois is about to produce its matheme. Let us now suppose that (A, **Id**) is a site, and more particularly an event. Following the definitions from Book V, we therefore know:

– that **Id**(A, A), or **E**A, the fulgurating exposition of A under its own function of appearing, has the maximal value. For the time of its appearance/disappearance, the site A is such that **E**A = M. The same goes for the suddenly explosive role of the solution by radicals of equations in Galois's dissertation (at the same time that the question it bears, being entirely resolved, loses any interest), or for the figural place of the poem, suddenly borne away from the lethal ontology of the One towards the multiform affirmation of the 'deliriums' of the real;

– that, among the consequences of the vanishing maximality of the site, there is the passage of the transcendental value of appearance of the inexistent from μ to M, that is the integral existence within the object of what was previously its proper inapparent. Such is the case of the poet's consciousness—'O bitter, dark, and echoing reservoir/Speaking of depths always beyond my reach'—which becomes, under the effect of the liberated sea, of the gushing foam, a race towards life.

Let us agree to call ε the proper inexistent of the site-objects. The imposition of the event is manifested in the schema of maximalization.

$$[\mathbf{E}\varepsilon = \mu] \rightarrow [\mathbf{E}\varepsilon = M]$$

Let us now leave the examples and proceed in a purely formal manner. Consider any element, say x, of the site-object (A, **Id**). Within appearing, this element has a certain degree of identity with ε, the proper inexistent of (A, **Id**). Before (A, **Id**) comes to be as a site, that is 'before' the event, we have **E**$\varepsilon = \mu$, and therefore, **Id**(x,ε) = μ, given that (P.2) **Id**(x, ε) $\leq$ (**E**ε), hence **Id**(x, ε) $\leq \mu$, that is **Id**(x, ε) = μ.

What happens when, under the effect of the site, **E**$\varepsilon = M$?

We know that **Id**(x, ε) $\leq$ **E**x $\cap$ **E**ε, which, if **E**$\varepsilon = M$, means that **Id**(x,ε) $\leq$ **E**x.

It is thus clear that the degree of identity of an element of the site to the prior inexistent, now evaluated within appearing in a maximal manner, is at most equal to the degree of existence of that element.

We will therefore say that an x *incorporates itself into the evental present if and only if* **Id**(x, ε) = **E**x. *This means that* **Id**(x, ε) *is as large as possible. Or that x is as identical as possible to the consequences of the event.*

The theory of the ontological order-relation <, which can be found in Book III, tells us that **E**x = **Id**(x, ε) is exactly equivalent to the assertion which bears directly on the elements of A: $x < \varepsilon$. We can therefore say that, if x incorporates itself to the eventual present, it is ontologically related, in terms of order, to the inexistent that has come to exist. Inversely, if an element x is such that $x < \varepsilon$, it incorporates itself to the eventual present (since $\mathbf{E}x = \mathbf{Id}(x, \varepsilon)$). In other words, the relation $x < \varepsilon$ characterizes incorporation to the eventual present. It could serve as the definition for this incorporation, though it is less legible than the (basically identical) one which makes explicit the role of existential intensity in this affair.

A crucial remark is in order: all the elements that incorporate themselves to the eventual present are compatible with one another. Recall that compatibility is a relation in being, among elements of the multiple A, a relation established through the mediation of real atoms that are determined in appearing by the elements (in the ontological sense) of A.

To establish this, we first make use of Proposition P.3: $\mathbf{E}a \cap \mathbf{E}b \le \mathbf{Id}(a, b)$ is an algebraic expression of the compatibility between a and b. We then take two elements of a site, x and y, which incorporate themselves to the eventual present. By the definition of incorporation, we get

$$\mathbf{Id}(x, \varepsilon) = \mathbf{E}x \text{ and } \mathbf{Id}(y, \varepsilon) = \mathbf{E}y$$

But (Axioms 1 and 2 of the functions of appearing, II.2.3):

$$\mathbf{Id}(x, \varepsilon) \cap \mathbf{Id}(y, \varepsilon) \le \mathbf{Id}(x, y)$$

Therefore,

$$\mathbf{E}x \cap \mathbf{E}y \le \mathbf{Id}(x, y)$$

This shows that x and y are compatible.

We can proceed more swiftly, by using the synthetic definition of incorporation, $x < \varepsilon$, and passing through Proposition P.5: if, for the 'real' order-relation, two elements are both dominated by the same third element, they are compatible. Now, if x and y are incorporated into the eventual present, it is because we have $x < \varepsilon$ and $y < \varepsilon$. It follows that $x \ddagger y$.

This allows us to posit the fundamental definition of a body: *a body C_ε, relative to the proper inexistent ε of a site $(A, \mathbf{Id})$, is the set of the elements of A which incorporate themselves to the eventual present*.

On the basis of this definition, we can establish the principle of the *coherence of bodies*. We have just seen that the elements of a body are compatible in pairs. It follows, by the very important Proposition P.7, that a body admits of a real synthesis, that is of an envelope for the order-relation $<$, which operates not on phenomena but on the multiple composition that supports these phenomena in being. We will call S_c (for 'corporeal synthesis') the element that serves as the envelope for a body C_ε. The element S_c obviously endows the body C_ε with a special coherence. It is the guarantee of a certain unity in being, beyond its surge into appearing (into the world). Recall that, by definition, S_c is the element that prescribes the (real) atom $a(x)$ thus defined:

$$a(x) = \Sigma\{\mathbf{Id}(c, x) \,/\, c \in C_\varepsilon\}$$

In other words, S_c envelops the degrees of identity of all the elements of a body to all the elements of the site. It thereby carries out the corporeal synthesis of what happens to differences in the site. These differences are 'filtered' by the elements of bodies, which enjoy an eminent relationship to the consequences of the event. In effect, an element of the body which is maximally identical to the supreme effect of the event (to produce the existence of an inexistent) is in a certain respect one of the guardians of the event's power.

In actual fact, the corporeal synthesis S_c, the guarantee of the unity of a post-evental body, is nothing other than the inexistent ε, post-eventally brought to its maximal existence by the site.

We know that in the post-evental world $\mathbf{E}\varepsilon = M$ (see above the formula for the consequence for ε). But ε incorporates itself to the evental present, since $\mathbf{Id}(\varepsilon, \varepsilon) = \mathbf{E}\varepsilon$, directly by the definition of $\mathbf{E}$. Consequently, ε is an element of the body C_ε, which gathers together all the elements of the site-object which incorporate themselves to the present in the wake of the evental upheaval. We thus have $\varepsilon \in C_\varepsilon$.

We saw that for every $x \in C_\varepsilon$ we have $x < \varepsilon$. This simply means that the over-existent ε, which is internal to the body and greater than all the other elements of the body, is the (internal) envelope of that body. It immanently dominates all the elements. In fact, as we saw earlier, $x < \varepsilon$ characterizes the elements x of the body. We may therefore define the body by its envelope: everything that is dominated by ε, that's the body.

We can also make the following remark: save for the trace ε, no element of the body has a transcendental value of existence equal to the maximum.

Take in effect an element x of the body, and suppose that $\mathbf{E}x = M$. We know that $x < \varepsilon$. This means that $\mathbf{Id}(x, \varepsilon) = \mathbf{E}x$, and therefore that $\mathbf{Id}(x, \varepsilon) = M$. But we also know that $\mathbf{E}\varepsilon = M$. Finally, it follows that $\mathbf{Id}(x, \varepsilon) = \mathbf{E}\varepsilon$, which is equivalent to $\varepsilon < x$. Contrasted with the previous result, whereby $x < \varepsilon$, this relation, by dint of anti-symmetry, allows us to conclude that $x = \varepsilon$.

Such is the formal existence of the following descriptive statement: 'Unless the inexistent has become over-existent, the elements of a post-eventual body do not maximally exist in the site. They have yet to become'.

This pertains to the peroration in Valéry's poem ('We must try to live . . .') insofar as, save for the absolute conviction of the consciousness that says this—and which, just a moment before, was nil—life has yet to be secured for any component of the body engendered by the poem. 'Let's run at the waves and be hurled back to the living!'—yes, but this is an imperative, not a givenness.

The same may be said for Galois's declaration:

The time will come when the algebraic transformations predicted by the speculations of analysts will no longer find either the time or place to reproduce themselves. At that point one will have to rest content with having predicted them.

This 'prediction', the structural art of the new algebra, indicates that the components of the new mathematical theoretical body have yet to become.

Finally, with regard to the appearance of a body, we have the following eight formulas (A is the set that underlies the site, ε its inexistent), all of them post-eventual:

1. $(\mathbf{E}\varepsilon) = M$ (eventual consequence)
2. 'x incorporated to the eventual present' $\leftrightarrow \mathbf{E}x = \mathbf{Id}(x, \varepsilon)$
3. 'x incorporated to the eventual present' $\leftrightarrow x < \varepsilon$
4. $C_\varepsilon = \{x \,/\, x \in A$ and x is incorporated to the eventual present$\}$
5. $C_\varepsilon = \{x \,/\, x \in A$ and $x < \varepsilon\}$ (by 3 and 4)
6. $\varepsilon \in C_\varepsilon$
7. ε is the real synthesis or envelope, for $<$, of C_ε
8. It can be inferred from the statement 'x is an element of the body and x differs from the trace ε' that the degree of existence of x is strictly lesser than the maximum M.

2. SECOND FORMAL SKETCH: CORPOREAL TREATMENT OF POINTS

It is a matter of formalizing what it means for a body to *treat a point*. This basically comes down to formalizing the efficacy of a 'decision' for a determinate subject.

Let's start with the formalisms from Book VI.

Since a point is a filtering of the multiple by the Two, it is represented by a function, ϕ, that projects the transcendental of a world on the minimal classical transcendental, the Boolean couple $\{0, 1\}$.

We then posit that *an element x of a body C_ε affirms a point ϕ, if ϕ (Ex) = 1.*

Note that ε, the real synthesis of the body C_ε, affirms every point. In effect, $(\mathbf{E}\varepsilon) = M$, and since every point conserves maximality, for every point ϕ we get $\phi(M) = 1$, hence $\phi(\mathbf{E}\varepsilon) = 1$, and therefore ε affirms ϕ.

This universal efficacy of ε does not really indicate the existence of a coherent efficacious part of the body for a determinate point ϕ. It is in some sense an indifferent efficacy. In effect ε, the trace of the event, is a *general* condition for the existence of bodies. In this respect, it is devoid of a singular connection to a determinate point of the world. In order to formalize such a connection, we must consider what happens to elements of the body other than ε when they appear before the point. This leads to separating and gathering together those elements of the body that affirm the point. The definition of an efficacious part of the body (for a given point) naturally follows: *an efficacious part of a body C_ε for a point ϕ is the subset of the elements of C_ε, other than ε, which affirm ϕ.*

$$C_{\varepsilon\phi} = \{x \mid x \in C_\varepsilon \text{ and } x \leq \varepsilon \text{ and } \phi(x) = 1\}$$

Nothing guarantees that $C_{\varepsilon\phi}$ 'exists' for a determinate ϕ. It may be empty, if in C_ε only ε affirms ϕ. If $C_{\varepsilon\phi}$ is not empty, being composed of elements that are compatible in pairs (as are all the elements of a body), it admits of a real synthesis (an envelope for the relation <). We will write ε_ϕ the element that thereby synthesizes $C_{\varepsilon\phi}$.

Note that ε_ϕ may be ε itself. Nothing effectively prohibits the envelope of the subset $C_{\varepsilon\phi}$ from being exterior to that subset. It is clear that ε is always a candidate for enveloping a subset of the elements x of C, since we know that for every x, we always have $x < \varepsilon$.

This case (ε is the envelope of the efficacious part $C_{\varepsilon\phi}$) leads us back, outside of immanence, to an anonymous degree of efficacy. If the envelope of the efficacious part is effectively ε, it is because this efficacious part does not possess in itself, in the singularity of its connection to the point, the wherewithal to realize its own synthesis. If ε is the envelope of an efficacious part of a body relative to a point ϕ, we will say that this part is dispersed or inorganic.

We will instead call organ of the body C_ε for the point ϕ the envelope ε_ϕ of the efficacious part $C_{\varepsilon\phi}$, to the extent that it is distinct from ε. Only if it possesses an organ for ϕ will we say that a body C_ε treats the point ϕ.

We can make here a formal remark that goes somewhat in the direction of Deleuze (or Bergson): if there exists an organ ε_ϕ, then this organ is interior to the corresponding efficacious part $C_{\varepsilon\phi}$. We could say that every organ is immanent to its own region of efficacy in the body.

This is by no means obvious. The envelope of $C_{\varepsilon\phi}$ could perfectly well remain exterior to $C_{\varepsilon\phi}$. This is the case after all, as we've seen, when this envelope is none other than ε. What's more, it could even turn out that the envelope ε_ϕ is not even in the body C_ε. In effect, Proposition P.7 guarantees the existence, in the set A underlying the site $(A, \mathbf{Id})$, of an ontological envelope for every part whose elements are compatible in pairs. But it does not tell us that this envelope is in this or that subset. Nothing requires that ε_ϕ be in the body C_ε. It is only obliged to be an element of A.

We will nevertheless demonstrate that, if it is distinct from ε, ε_ϕ is indeed an element of C_ε.

Being an envelope of $C_{\varepsilon\phi}$, ε_ϕ is the smallest element of A to dominate, through the relation $<$, all the elements of $C_{\varepsilon\phi}$. In particular, it is smaller than ε, which also dominates all the elements of $C_{\varepsilon\phi}$, since it dominates all the elements of C_ε, of which $C_{\varepsilon\phi}$ is a part. We thus have $\varepsilon_\phi < \varepsilon$, which is a *characteristic* property of belonging to the body, as we saw earlier in the first formal sketch. Therefore, $\varepsilon_\phi \in C_\varepsilon$.

We will now show that if ε_ϕ is not ε, then it is necessarily not only interior to the body C_ε, but also interior to the efficacious part $C_{\varepsilon\phi}$.

Suppose in effect that it is not. This means that it does not affirm the point ϕ, since $C_{\varepsilon\phi}$ is the subset of the elements of the body that affirm this point. But this is impossible. That is because for every element x of $C_{\varepsilon\phi}$, we have $\mathbf{E}x \le \mathbf{E}\varepsilon_\phi$, as we saw in the demonstration of P.7. Now, every point ϕ conserves the transcendental order, and we therefore have $\phi(\mathbf{E}x) \le \phi(\mathbf{E}\varepsilon_\phi)$, which, since $\phi(\mathbf{E}x) = 1$ (x is internal to the efficacious part), implies that $\phi(\mathbf{E}\varepsilon_\phi) = 1$.

Accordingly, ε_ϕ affirms the point and we must rule out the notion that the organ ε_ϕ is exterior to the efficacious part $C_{\varepsilon\phi}$.

Given a point ϕ and a body C_ε, it is clear that there are three possibilities:

1. Only ε affirms the point. The efficacious part $C_{\varepsilon\phi}$ is empty; the point ϕ is not treated by the body.

2. The part $C_{\varepsilon\phi}$ is not empty, but its synthesis, which necessarily exists (the elements of $C_{\varepsilon\phi}$ are compatible in pairs), is exterior, meaning that it is none other than ε. There is no organ, and the point ϕ is not treated by the body.

3. There exists an organ $\varepsilon_\phi \neq \varepsilon$: the point ϕ is treated by the body. Consequently, the organ is immanent to the efficacious part of the body, meaning that it too affirms the point, without thereby having, like ε, the maximal degree of existence.

This gives us the following corporeal schemata (for a given point):

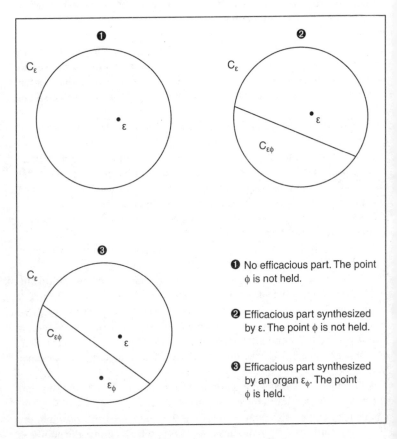

❶ No efficacious part. The point ϕ is not held.

❷ Efficacious part synthesized by ε. The point ϕ is not held.

❸ Efficacious part synthesized by an organ ε_ϕ. The point ϕ is held.

But what are the chances, supposing an event, that a body arise, which is capable of treating a point? We have seen that this question is of the utmost importance, since it is useless for a body suited to bearing the subjective formalism to exist if it is incapable of treating any point. In this case we would have either inert or inconsequential subjective forms. For things to be otherwise and for some point to be treated, the following conditions must be fulfilled, in an order of decreasing generality:

1. The transcendental of the world is such that there exist points ϕ. As we saw in Book VI, there are worlds without points (for example, in the case where the transcendental is a Boolean algebra devoid of any isolate), *atonic* worlds.

2. There must be an event (that is a maximally evaluated site, whose consequence is that an inexistent ε attains maximal existence). There are worlds where no event arises, just facts, or only mere modifications—*stable* worlds.

3. There must exist enough elements of the site which are incorporated into the evental present (x's such that $\mathbf{Id}(x, \varepsilon) = \mathbf{E}x$) in order for there to constitute itself—over and above ε itself—a coherent body C_ε. There are worlds in which ε alone bears the incorporation into the present, resulting in the almost instantaneous withering away of the consequences of the event. These are worlds without bodies, *inconsequential* worlds.

4. Given a point ε, there must exist elements x other than ε that decide ϕ (that is $\phi(\mathbf{E}x) = 1$). This means that the efficacious part $C_{\varepsilon\phi}$ of the body, C_ε, is not empty. There are worlds in which it is empty, and in that case the efficacy is anonymous, or without singularity. These are *inactive* worlds.

5. The envelope of the efficacious part $C_{\varepsilon\phi}$ must differ from ε. This means that in the body C_ε there is an organ for the point ϕ, and therefore that this body treats that point. Obviously, for a given point ϕ, which is to say for a place of decision, there are worlds in which the point is not treated. These are *inorganic* worlds.

This system of five conditions imposes very rigorous criteria. It decrees that the world be neither atonic, stable, inconsequential, inactive nor inorganic. This elucidates why the creation of a truth—which requires the treatment of at least one point—is rather rare.

But we should note the following: the x's that compose $C_{\varepsilon\phi}$—all of which differ from ε (which we have expressly excluded from the efficacious part $C_{\varepsilon\phi}$)—cannot have the maximal degree of existence. Accordingly, their envelope is not *forced* to have the maximum value M, which would dictate that it be equal to ε. The possibility that there exists an organ for the point ϕ is thus real. As rare as it may be, the effective treatment of a point by a body—the organicity of the body with respect to that point—is by no means determined not to be. When it comes to the body that bears their subjective form, some truths are therefore always possible.

SCHOLIUM

A Political Variant of the Physics of the Subject-of-Truth

Having completed the analysis of the constitution of a subject-body and set forth the system of conditions for its existence, we can revisit our argument synthetically, starting directly with the examination of the world as seen from the perspective of the points which are to be treated; that is, starting with the possibility of a body—under the assumption that the evental trace has already been attested. We will then endeavour, with regard to a determinate world, to answer the following question: 'Why can a body exist in this world?' Just as Mao, on 5 October 1928, asked in a famous report: 'Why is it that Red Political Power Can Exist in China?' The question of the composition of the body, of its efficacious parts, and finally of its organs will be unfolded through the programmatic question of its existence.

We will do this in seven steps.

1. *Given the evidence of a subject-body in a world, we can make our way back to its conditions of existence. Let us call this approach subjective induction.*

What is it that Mao calls 'red power'? It is the prolonged existence, in certain rural zones, of a revolutionary force led by a very small number of communist militants. We are clearly dealing with a body by means of which the revolutionary process starts to produce the truth of contemporary China.

Mao's approach is inductive. He begins with a paradoxical remark: there are small liberated zones in China. Now, as he'll put it:

The prolonged existence, in a country, of one or more small regions in which red power prevails, encircled by white power, constitutes an absolutely new fact in the history of the world.

It is necessary to elucidate this paradox by referring back to its historical conditions, to the world 'China', to the sites that appear within it. That is the nature of the question 'Why?' when it is applied to the existence of a body.

2. Subjective induction initially determines the transcendental characteristics of the world as favourable or unfavourable to the appearance of a new body.

Mao's qualification of the world 'China in the twenties' proceeds in terms of transcendental singularity. China is neither a stable imperialist country, where the prolonged existence of a local revolutionary power is obviously impossible; nor a colonized country, subject to the direct dictatorship of established predators supported by a military administration. China, according to Mao, is under the 'indirect domination' of imperialism, and thus finds itself disputed, divided, dismembered into zones of influence of imperialisms that are allied to different 'local despots'. We could say that the transcendental of the world China-in-the-twenties displays a disparate topology of imperial and national intensities, an almost infinite hotchpotch of territories traversed by forces opposed to one another. Whence the existence of intermediate non-controlled zones, refuges for dissidents—as the region of the Jinggang mountains will be for Mao and his troops in the years 1927–29.

This localization of political appearing in the China of the twenties is bolstered by the decentralized and anarchic character of agrarian production. As Mao says, there is 'a local agrarian economy, and not a single capitalist economy for the whole country'. This weakness of the market represents a great advantage for the insurgents. It also makes it possible, if one manages to enlist the local peasants, to find in politically and militarily poorly-controlled districts the means of subsistence.

A transcendental that strongly localizes intensities in a discontinuous manner; a world consigned to a kind of anarchy of political appearing—on condition that an event imposes its trace, this is what augments the 'chances' of the dialectical constitution of a subject-body.

3. Subjective induction identifies the trace of the event and thinks the space (or the place) of the new present.

Of course, the site that Mao localizes in the transcendental according to which China historically appears in the twenties depends on the great event of 1911: the collapse of centralized imperial power and the dawn of the republic. But it cannot be simply identified with this break. After 1912, under the name of 'Republic', we effectively have a long sequence of military anarchy, in which, as Mao writes:

> The different cliques of old and new warlords, supported by imperialists as well as compradors, local despots and bad landlords, ceaselessly fight one another.

This anarchy over-determines the positive factors of the environing historical world: in the midst of such a decomposition of reactionary authorities, the path of a revolutionary army is clearly marked out. Besides, by rousing all those who wish to reunify China and protect it from post-feudal banditry, it lies in the background of what Mao calls the 'democratic bourgeois revolution' of 1926–27, the true evental reference for the body in the making whose historical name will be 'Red Army'. The revolutionary cycle which makes up the site from which the question of a new subject-body is posed ('red power') stretches from 1924 to 1927. It includes the Canton insurrection as well as the peasant insurrections in Hunan. The trace of this site is without doubt the statement according to which 'The Chinese people can and must unify and entirely revolutionize its country'. This statement involves the conviction that the fate of the Chinese people cannot be left in the hands either of foreign powers—including of course the Japanese invader—or of military cliques, nor indeed of corrupt politicians or, finally, of the official direction of the national movement, embodied by Chiang Kai-shek.

But which elements of the world have a maximal identity with this trace and are virtually incorporable into the new body? Mao's response is unequivocal: in a massive way, these are the poor peasants, together with a certain number of workers from the central and southern provinces and some intellectuals won over to communism. They have proven their maximal identity to the new political path through 'potent uprisings' and the creation of 'an extended network of trade-union organizations and peasant leagues', so that in several districts in these provinces 'the political power of the peasants has existed'. In these districts it is possible to say, if ε is the political statement concerning the liberation of the Chinese people, that $\mathbf{Id}(x, \varepsilon) = \mathbf{E}(x)$, for many of the '$x$'s' of peasants, workers and intellectuals.

What we have here is a new localization of what, in the particularly non-classical world of twentieth-century China, will give an unprecedented political body its chance. Mao remarks that 'it is not in the regions of China that have escaped the influence of the democratic revolution [of 1926–27] [. . .] that red power appears and can maintain itself'. There, the value **Id**(x, ε) is generally too low to permit incorporation into a 'red power'. That is why, from October 1927 onwards, Mao will install his rudimentary army and the communist cadres that follow him in the Jinggang mountains, as an immediate acknowledgment of the many revolutionary episodes in the region (the insurrection in Nanchang in August 1927, the insurrection of the autumn harvest. . .).

Through a series of successive filterings, subjective induction allows us to think the place in which the new present is constituted, what we could call the space of the new time.

4. *Subjective induction takes account of the immanent heterogeneity of the body.*

Since the insurrections of 1927, from Canton to Nanchang, all failed—faced as they were with the bloody determination of the white generals, Chiang Kai-shek included—what Mao leads into the mountains is a collection of debris. The enumeration that Mao makes of the ingredients of what is nonetheless the embryo of the future Red Army, the one that will seize power in Beijing 20 years later, is rather picturesque:

(1) troops formerly under Yeh Ting and Ho Lung in Chaochow and Swatow, (2) the Guards Regiment of the former National Government at Wuchang, (3) peasants from Pingkiang and Liuyang, (4) peasants from southern Hunan and workers from Shuikoushan, (5) men captured from the forces under Hsu Keh-hsiang, Tang Sheng-chih, Pai Chung-hsi, Chu Pei-teh, Wu Shang and Hsiung Shih-hui and (6) peasants from the counties in the border area.

Faced with this court of miracles, Mao is worried and understandably so. He is well aware that one can find in it workers and peasants, but also dodgy figures, déclassé individuals and ex-thieves, what the Marxist tradition would call 'elements of the Lumpenproletariat'. He begs the Party Committee 'to send workers from the coal mines of Anyuan'.

But he also knows that, in the final analysis, these disparate elements can incorporate themselves into the Red Army, insofar as they are compatible with it. What guarantees that they are is the maximal value taken by their relationship to the evental trace, that is to say the statements that emerged from all of the localized revolutionary insurrections in China in the years 1924–27.

 5. *Subjective induction knows the sources of the compatibility between the elements of a body, and thus of its practical cohesion.*

How can we know the degree that evaluates the relationship between an element and the evental trace? And how can we consequently evaluate the consistency that a body is imputed to have? Mao answers: through permanent discussion, assemblies, 'political education'. What is decisive is that '(soldiers, whatever their origins) know that they fight for themselves, for the working class and the peasantry'.

But, more subtly, the cohesion of the body 'Red Army'—on which depends the fact that the new present is subjectivated to the point of attaining its immanent eternity (an entirely new idea of politics and revolution)—relies on the capacity of those who compose this body to exhibit its singularity to others. In other words, to work on new incorporations. The figure that emerges here is that of the soldier-militant, a figure suited to Mao's thesis according to which the Red Army—and not the Communist Party alone—is 'charged with the political tasks of the revolution'.

That is why the non-military organization of soldiers, which is named 'committee', has a twofold function: to represent the interests of those who have accepted, under the sign of an Idea of the country, to incorporate themselves into the new body; but also to enlighten all those who they encounter about the political subject of which this body is the body:

Each company, battalion or regiment has its soldiers' committee which represents the interests of the soldiers and carries on political and mass work.

Any compatibility of the elements of a body is thus subjected to the test of an internal evaluation (what are the links between an element and other elements of the same body?) and an external evaluation (what is the action of an incorporated element in the world in which the body surges up?). The unity of these two evaluations is the dialectical dynamic of the cohesion of bodies; it deserves the name of 'dialectic of the subject'.

 6. *Subjective induction takes into account the points that must be treated by the subject-body.*

The fact that transcendental political intensities are distributed in such and such a way—in the China of the twenties, according to a dispersive topology—concerns the local possibility of a body. That in such and such a place, such and such points are what must be treated by a constituted body concerns the real of that body: the subjective becoming of an eternal truth, and thus the appearing of this truth in a world.

In 1927, Mao localizes the body 'Red Army' in certain regions of China, namely the Hunan-Jiangxi border area, and within this small space he proposes a classification of points. There are in effect the 'military question', the 'land question', the 'question of political power', the 'question of party organization', 'the question of the character of the revolution' and 'the question of the location of our revolutionary base'. One can quickly see how these six chapter headings overlap with six points, all of which are the object of bitter debates. They are 'points' in the strict sense, that is matters about which there are two orientations, such that to choose one of them concerns the totality of the world in which the subject-body 'Red Army' advances.

For example, the 'question of party organization' filters the entire local situation—the world 'Jinggang mountains'—through the opposition between, on one hand, the hypothesis of a solid safeguarding of red power, rooted in the population and practicing strategic defence, and on the other, the alternation, when the enemy attacks, of propositions of the type 'fight to the death' and propositions (which in Mao's view are subjectively identical) of the type 'take flight'.

The 'character of the revolution' names the classic debate of the twenties about the Chinese revolution: is it a proletarian revolution as in Russia or a democratic bourgeois revolution?

The 'location of our revolutionary base' touches on the transcendental topology of the whole subjective process. Must the principal organs of red power, and its army in particular, hold the centre of the mountainous region, or go south, where the terrain is more favourable? This is the point around which Mao's first open rebellion against the Party will articulate itself. The Party Committee for the Hunan province decides for the second hypothesis. Convinced that subjective factors (the support of the peasants) prevail over objective benefits (the nature of the terrain), and facing the dilemma 'either disregard instructions or go surely towards defeat', Mao chooses disobedience.

Let us develop the structure of the first three points in greater detail.

Regarding the expression 'military question', it is important to understand the following point: in the periods of temporary stabilization of the enemy camp—of a lull in the civil wars between generals—is it necessary to persevere with the line of division of the red forces and of 'adventurous advance'? Or is it necessary to stick resolutely to strategic defence? Influenced by the insurrectionalism of the Stalinist envoys of the Comintern, some push for an offensive at all costs. Throughout his 20 years of life as a partisan, or as the leader of an insurgency, Mao will in point of fact privilege the organization of the defensive. Or, more precisely, having affirmed that 'the rules of military action all derive from a single fundamental principle: strive to conserve your forces and annihilate those of the enemy', Mao never stops noting that if the offensive decides the outcome of the war, defensive capacity determines its political consistency. The famous 'Long March' is itself an epic consequence of this perspective. It represents an immense strategic retreat, aiming to conserve what is essential at the cost of terrible sacrifices: the existence of a subjectivated body, of a political Red Army. It too only owed its existence to the very conflictual treatment of the 'military question', with Mao and his partisans opposing all those who refused the withdrawal. Mao proposed a striking formula in this regard: 'When we abandon the territory, it is in order to conserve that territory'.

By 'land question', we must understand the well-known political dilemma faced by revolutionaries in a rural milieu. One can—as the Central Committee of the Communist Party dictated in 1927—practice 'total confiscation and complete (egalitarian) redistribution of land'. But then one throws small landowners and middle peasants into the arms of the counter-revolution organized by the feudal forces. Or, in order to consolidate the besieged revolutionary base, one makes concessions to peasant landowners, but risks sapping the insurgent energy of poor peasants.

In the territory where the subject-body exists, 'political power' poses, albeit on a small scale, the question of the links between the state and the Communist Party—a decisive question throughout the history of the USSR and the People's Republic of China. In the liberated zones, executive committees are set up everywhere, 'elected in mass meetings of sorts'. Now, not only are these committees often made up of fine speakers devoid of real conviction (Mao says, and I know from personal experience how right he is, that 'in such meetings intellectuals and careerists easily prevail'), but what's more 'the organs of the Party, wishing to simplify their work, conduct a lot of their business above the heads of the committees'. The 'Two' form of this point is particularly clear: either one concentrates the totality of the capacity for decision in the hands of the Party leaders, or one endows popular power with a militant reality, in the form, as Mao conceives it, of 'councils of delegates from the workers, peasants and soldiers'. For forty years, from the Jinggang mountains to the Cultural Revolution, from the peasant mountain councils (1927) to the workers' Commune of Shanghai (1967), Mao, possessed by a profound distrust of Party bureaucracy, will ceaselessly—though without definitive success, it must be said—treat the point while avoiding the easiest choice: the concentration of power in the Party, the sovereignty of the cadres, the Stalinist maxim, 'when the line is fixed, the cadres decide everything'. That is why he looked for support from the peasant movement, the rebellious workers, the youth and also the army. Let's not forget that already in 1927, Mao wrote that 'democracy in our army is an important weapon for undermining the feudal mercenary army' and argued for military egalitarianism:

> Officers and men receive equal treatment, soldiers are free to hold meetings and to speak out; trivial formalities have been done away with; and the accounts are open for all to inspect.

In the point that is constituted, in the fabric of historical circumstances, by the contradiction between Party-State and popular movement in the world 'twentieth-century China', Mao most often tried to contradict Stalinist fatality.

7. *Subjective induction examines the organs of the body appropriate to the points.*

To each point there corresponds a meticulous examination, by Mao, of the resources available for its treatment in the subject-body to which he himself is incorporated: the People's Army, the Party and the peasants as components of the paradoxical survival of 'red power'. We can follow how this theory of the efficacious parts and organs is clarified, point by point, by looking at four examples.

I. In what concerns military power, the efficacious part of the body is composed on one hand by the regular army, on the other by so-called local forces: 'Detachments of the red guards and insurrectional detachments of workers and peasants'. It therefore possesses no immediate unity. The organ in the proper sense is the strategic capacity of articulation of the two components, since the singularity of this body (an army that is not that of a State, but of a politics) stems from not being reducible to the simple appearing of a unified executive power. The organ is thus a principle, for which Mao provides the following general formula: 'The principle of the Red Army is the concentration of forces and that of the Red Guard is the dispersion of forces'.

II. In the case of the land question, the efficacious part of the body is composed of poor peasants. Landlords are excluded and the subjective incorporation of small landowners and rich peasants is perennially in doubt. But an organic cohesion of poor peasants, capable of forcing the passage of the agrarian reform over to an egalitarian redistributive line, can never be taken for granted. In actual fact, it depends on the peasants' conviction that victory is possible:

The poor peasants take action against the intermediate class in the villages only when the revolution is on the upsurge, for instance, when political power has been seized in one or more counties, the reactionary army has suffered several defeats and the prowess of the Red Army has been repeatedly demonstrated.

The efficacious part only acquires its organ for treating the point when the power of consequences exceeds the simple localization of this part. The subject-body must be visible to everyone in the world as a continuous present.

III. We have seen that putting in place a new type of popular power makes a point of the fact that it is in balance with the easy authority of the Party. The efficacy for the treatment of this point is obviously on the side of popular actors, if needs be against the Party cadres. But it is generally inactive, for a reason that Mao identifies with great acuity and which has lost none of its force: the popular masses tend to turn to the authorities, they have little taste for a political commitment that would eat up their already limited time.

People want to resolve problems without excessive worries, and they don't smile upon the democratic system [the councils of delegates] with all of its complications.

Today the questions 'Why would I go to this meeting, to this assembly? Why should I be a militant, when my objective life is already so full of constraints?' still remain the principal obstacles to the worker and popular unfolding of a democratic politics from which electoral professionalism and the parties of Capital have been extirpated.

Mao's solution is a classical one: the efficacious part can only be organic-ally realized if the link between reunions and action is patent. There is an organ of popular power in the conditions of the movement:

[There will be a people's power] when this power will have proven its efficacy in revolutionary struggle, when the masses will have understood that it is capable of mobilizing to the best effect the forces of the people and to give them the greatest possible aid in their fight.

In short, in the Maoist vision, the political subject-body can only organ-ically treat the point people's power/Party power in the circumstances of mass movement, struggle and battle. Lacking an appropriate organ, it is incapable of treating this point positively in conditions of inertia or peace.

Perhaps we have not moved beyond this. In any case, it is in this point, which in its own terms remains unresolved, that Maoist politics en-countered the danger of its own reactive subject, and then of the becoming-obscure in which, in its extreme forms (the Khmer Rouge and Sendero Luminoso), it was shipwrecked.

IV. As we have said, the Party is confronted with an immanent scission: on one hand, the opportunistic tendency (if things go badly, one disbands, if they go well, one charges forward without reflecting); on the other, the difficult upholding of a line that articulates local offensive onto a strategic defence. That is its point. The efficacious part with regard to this point is the kernel of experienced revolutionaries. In effect, when the political body becomes visible and shares out the subjective present that it grounds, the Party, regarded as the most refined expression of the subject, grows exponentially. It is to the Party that people incorporate themselves en masse. But many of these joiners are careerists. As soon as the wind turns, they betray:

As soon as the White terror struck, the careerists defected and acted as guides for the counter-revolutionaries in rounding up our comrades, and the Party organizations in the White areas mostly collapsed.

It is therefore important that experienced revolutionaries oversee membership. Finally, the organ of the efficacious part, with regard to the point under consideration, is the purge, with its complement of clandestineness, ordeals, selections and rigorous education:

After September the Party carried out a drastic house cleaning and set strict class qualifications for membership. [In several districts] Party organizations [. . .] were dissolved and a re-registration was undertaken [. . .] underground organizations have been built up to prepare the Party for carrying on its activities when the reactionaries come.

Thus the organ is what is capable of allowing the efficacious part to concentrate on itself, in order to traverse the point on the side of the duration of the present, even if this is to the detriment of enthusiastic numerical enlargement: 'Though greatly reduced in numbers, the membership has gained in fighting capacity'.

All of these examples show that when it comes to a political body that carries a new subject (e.g. the Chinese Red Army), creating, through the consequences of its act, a new truth (e.g. Maoist politics as the paradigm of people's war), the treatment of a point ultimately requires corporeal constraints, which are tied to its immanent organicity: the principle of concentration/dispersion, the duration of local victories, 'movementist' subjectivity, purging.

Point by point, a body reorganizes itself, making appear in the world ever more singular consequences, which subjectively weave a truth about which it can be said that it will render eternal the present of the present.

CONCLUSION

What is it to Live?

0. We are now in a position to propose a response to what has always been the 'daunting' question—as one of Julien Gracq's characters has it—the question that, however, great its detour, philosophy must ultimately answer: what is it to live? 'To live' obviously not in the sense of democratic materialism (persevering in the free virtualities of the body), but rather in the sense of Aristotle's enigmatic formula: to live 'as an Immortal'.

To begin with, we can reformulate the exacting system of conditions for an affirmative response of the type: 'Yes! The true life is present'.

1. It is not a world, as given in the logic of its appearing (the infinite of its objects and relations), which induces the possibility of living—at least not if life is something other than existence. The induction of such a possibility depends on that which acts in the world as the trace of the fulgurating disposition that has befallen that world. That is, the trace of a vanished event. Within worldly appearing, such a trace is always a maximally intense existence. Through the incorporation of the world's past to the present opened up by the trace, it is possible to learn that prior to what happened and is no longer, the ontological support of this intense existence was an inexistent of the world. The birth of a multiple to the flash of appearing, to which it previously only belonged in an extinguished form, makes a trace in the world and signals towards life.

For those who ask where the true life is, the first philosophical directive is thus the following: 'Take care of what is born. Interrogate the flashes, probe into their past without glory. You can only put your hope in what inappears.'

2. It is not enough to identify a trace. One must incorporate oneself into what the trace authorizes in terms of consequences. This point is crucial. Life is the creation of a present, but just like the world vis-à-vis God in Descartes, this creation is a continuous creation. The cohesion of a hitherto impossible body constitutes itself around the trace, around the anonymous flash of a birth to the world of being-there. To accept and declare this body is not enough, if one wishes to be the contemporary of the present of which this body is the material support. It is necessary to enter into its composition, to become an active element of this body. The only real relation to the present is that of incorporation: the incorporation into this immanent cohesion of the world which springs from the becoming-existent of the eventual trace, as a new birth beyond all the facts and markers of time.

3. The unfolding of the consequences linked to the eventual trace—consequences that create a present—proceeds through the treatment of the points of the world. It does not take place through the continuous trajectory of a body's efficacy, but in sequences, point by point. Every present has a kind of fibre. The points of the world in which the infinite appears before the Two of choice are like the fibres of the present, its intimate constitution in its worldly becoming. In order for a living present to open up, it is thus required that the world not be atonic, that it contain points which guarantee the efficacy of a body, thus lending creative time its fibre.

4. Life is a subjective category. A body is the materiality that life requires, but the becoming of the present depends on the disposition of this body in a subjective formalism, whether it be produced (the formalism is faithful, the body is directly placed 'under' the eventual trace), erased (the formalism is reactive, the body is held at a double distance by the negation of the trace), or occulted (the body is denied). Neither the reactive deletion of the present, which denies the value of the event, nor, a fortiori, its mortifying occultation, which presupposes a 'body' transcendent to the world, sanction the affirmation of life, which is the incorporation, point by point, to the present.

To live is thus an incorporation into the present under the faithful form of a subject. If the incorporation is dominated by the reactive form, one will not speak of life, but of mere conservation. It is a question of protecting oneself from the consequences of a birth, of not relaunching existence beyond itself. If incorporation is dominated by the obscure formalism, one will instead speak of mortification.

Ultimately life is the wager, made on a body that has entered into appearing, that one will faithfully entrust this body with a new temporality, keeping at a distance the conservative drive (the ill-named 'life' instinct) as well as the mortifying drive (the death instinct). Life is what gets the better of the drives.

5. Because it prevails over the drives, life engages in the sequential creation of a present, and this creation both constitutes and absorbs a new type of past.

For democratic materialism, the present is never created. Democratic materialism affirms, in an entirely explicit manner, that it is important to maintain the present within the confines of an atonic reality. That is because it regards any other view of things as submitting the body to the despotism of an ideology, instead of letting it roam freely among the diversity of languages. Democratic materialism proposes to call 'thought' the pure algebra of appearing. This atonic conception of the present results in the fetishization of the past as a separable 'culture'. Democratic materialism has a passion for history; it is truly the only authentic historical materialism.

Contrary to what transpires in the Stalinist version of Marxism—a version that Althusser inherited, though he disrupted it from within—it is crucial to disjoin the materialist dialectic, the philosophy of emancipation through truths, from historical materialism, the philosophy of alienation through language-bodies. To break with the cult of genealogies and narratives means restoring the past as the amplitude of the present.

I already wrote it more than twenty years ago, in my *Theory of the Subject*: History does not exist. There are only disparate presents whose radiance is measured by their power to unfold a past worthy of them.

In democratic materialism, the life of language-bodies is the conservative succession of the instants of the atonic world. It follows that the past is charged with the task of endowing these instants with a fictive horizon, with a cultural density. This also explains why the fetishism of history is accompanied by an unrelenting discourse on novelty, perpetual change and the imperative of modernization. The past of cultural depths is matched by a dispersive present, an agitation which is itself devoid of any depth whatsoever. There are monuments to visit and devastated instants to inhabit. Everything changes at every instant, which is why one is left to contemplate the majestic historical horizon of what does not change.

For the materialist dialectic, it is almost the opposite. What strikes one first is the stagnant immobility of the present, its sterile agitation, the violently imposed atonicity of the world. There have been few, very few, crucial changes in the nature of the problems of thought since Plato, for instance. But, on the basis of some truth-procedures that unfold subjectivizable bodies, point by point, one reconstitutes a different past, a history of achievements, discoveries, breakthroughs, which is by no means a cultural monumentality but a legible succession of fragments of eternity. That is because a faithful subject creates the present as the being-there of eternity. Accordingly, to incorporate oneself into this present amounts to perceiving the past of eternity itself.

To live is therefore also, always, to experience in the past the eternal amplitude of a present. We concur with Spinoza's famous formula from the scholium to Proposition XXIII of Book V of the *Ethics*: 'We feel and know by experience that we are eternal'.

6. Yet it remains important to give a name to this experience [*éxperimentation*]. It belongs neither to the order of lived experience, nor to that of expression. It is not the finally attained accord between the capacities of a body and the resources of a language. It is the incorporation into the exception of a truth. If we agree to call 'Idea' what both manifests itself in the world—what sets forth the being-there of a body—and is an exception to its transcendental logic, we will say, in line with Platonism, that to experience in the present the eternity that authorizes the creation of this present is to experience an Idea. We must therefore accept that for the materialist dialectic, 'to live' and 'to live for an Idea' are one and the same thing.

In what it would instead call an ideological conception of Life, democratic materialism sees nothing but fanaticism and the death instinct. It is true that, if there is nothing but bodies and languages, to live for an Idea necessarily implies the arbitrary absolutization of one language, which bodies must comply with. Only the material recognition of the 'except that' of truths allows us to declare, not that bodies are submitted to the authority of a language, far from it, but that a new body is the organization in the present of an unprecedented subjective life. I maintain that the real experience of such a life, the comprehension of a theorem or the force of an encounter, the contemplation of a drawing or the momentum of a meeting, is irresistibly universal. This means that, for the form of incorporation that corresponds to it, the advent of the Idea is the very opposite of a submission. Depending on the type of truth that we are dealing with, it is joy, happiness, pleasure or enthusiasm.

7. Democratic materialism presents as an objective given, as a result of historical experience, what it calls 'the end of ideologies'. What actually lies behind this is a violent subjective injunction whose real content is: 'Live without Idea'. But this injunction is incoherent.

That this injunction pushes thought into the arms of sceptical relativism has long been obvious. We are told this is the price to be paid for tolerance and the respect of the Other. But each and every day we see that this tolerance is itself just another fanaticism, because it only tolerates its own vacuity. Genuine scepticism, that of the Greeks, was actually an absolute theory of exception: it placed truths so high that it deemed them inaccessible to the feeble intellect of the human species. It thus concurred with the principal current in ancient philosophy, which argues that attaining the True is the calling of the immortal part of men, of the inhuman excess that lies in man. Contemporary scepticism—the scepticism of cultures, history and self-expression—is not of this calibre. It merely conforms to the rhetoric of instants and the politics of opinions. Accordingly, it begins by dissolving the inhuman into the human, then the human into everyday life, then everyday (or animal) life into the atonicity of the world. It is from this dissolution that stems the negative maxim 'Live without Idea', which is incoherent because it no longer has any idea of what an Idea could be.

That is the reason why democratic materialism in fact seeks to destroy what is external to it. As we have noted, it is a violent and warmongering ideology. Like every mortifying symptom, this violence results from an essential inconsistency. Democratic materialism regards itself as humanist (human rights, etc.). But it is impossible to possess a concept of what is 'human' without dealing with the (eternal, ideal) inhumanity which authorizes man to incorporate himself into the present under the sign of the trace of what changes. If one fails to recognize the effects of these traces, in which the inhuman commands humanity to exceed its being-there, it will be necessary, in order to maintain a purely animalistic, pragmatic notion of the human species, to annihilate both these traces and their infinite consequences.

The democratic materialist is a fearsome and intolerant enemy of every human—which is to say inhuman—life worthy of the name.

8. The banal objection says that if to live depends on the event, life is only granted to those who have the luck [*chance*] of welcoming the event. The democrat sees in this 'luck' the mark of an aristocratism, a transcendent arbitrariness—of the kind that has always been linked to the doctrines of Grace. It is true that several times I have used the metaphor of grace, in order to indicate that what is called living always involves agreeing to work through the (generally unprecedented) consequences of what happens.

The advocates of the divine, rather than of God, have long strived to rectify the apparent injustice of this gift, of this incalculable supplement from which stems the sublation of an inexistent. In order to fulfil this task, the most recent, talented and neglected among these advocates, Quentin Meillassoux, is developing an entirely new theory of the 'not yet' of divine existence, accompanied by a rational promise concerning the resurrection of bodies. This goes to show that new bodies and their birth are inevitably at stake in this affair.

9. I believe in eternal truths and in their fragmented creation in the present of worlds. My position on this point is entirely isomorphic with that of Descartes: truths are eternal because they have been created and not because they have been there forever. For Descartes, 'eternal truths'—which, as we recalled in the preface, he posed in exception of bodies and ideas—cannot transcend divine will. Even the most formal of these, the truths of mathematics or logic, like the principle of non-contradiction, depend on a free act of God:

> God cannot have been determined to make it true that contradictories cannot be true together and, therefore, he could have done the opposite.

Of course, the process of creation of a truth, whose present is constituted by the consequences of a subjectivated body, is very different from the creative act of a God. But, at bottom, the idea is the same. That it belongs to the essence of a truth to be eternal does not dispense it in the least from having to appear in a world and to be inexistent prior to this appearance. Descartes proposes a truly remarkable formula with regard to this point:

> Even if God has willed that some truths should be necessary, this does not mean that he willed them necessarily.

Eternal necessity pertains to a truth in itself: the infinity of prime numbers, the pictorial beauty of the horses in the Chauvet cave, the principles of popular war or the amorous affirmation of Héloïse and

Abelard. But its process of creation does not—since it depends on the contingency of worlds, the aleatory character of a site, the efficacy of the organs of a body and the constancy of a subject.

Descartes is indignant that one could consider truths as separate from other creatures, turning them, so to speak, into the fate of God:

> The mathematical truths which you call eternal have been laid down by God and depend on him entirely no less than the rest of his creatures. Indeed to say that these truths are independent of God is to talk of him as if he were Jupiter or Saturn and to subject him to the Styx and the Fates.

I too affirm that all truths without exception are 'established' through a subject, the form of a body whose efficacy creates point by point. But, like Descartes, I argue that their creation is but the appearing of their eternity.

10. I am indignant then, like Descartes, when the True is demoted to the rank of the Styx and the Fates. Truth be told, I am indignant twice over. And life's worth also stems from this double quarrel. First of all against those, the culturalists, relativists, people preoccupied with immediate bodies and available languages, for whom the historicity of all things excludes eternal truths. They fail to see that a genuine creation, a historicity of exception, has no other criterion than to establish, between disparate worlds, the evidence of an eternity. And that what appears only shines forth in its appearance to the extent that it subtracts itself from the local laws of appearing. A creation is trans-logical, since its being upsets its appearing. Second, against those for whom the universality of the truth takes the form of a transcendent Law, before which we must bend our knee, to which we must conform our bodies and our words. They do not see that every eternity and every universality must appear in a world and, 'patiently or impatiently', be created within it. Since a truth is an appearance of being, a creation is logical.

11. But I need neither God nor the divine. I believe that it is here and now that we rouse or resurrect ourselves as Immortals.

Man is this animal to whom it belongs to participate in numerous worlds, to appear in innumerable places. This kind of objectal ubiquity, which makes him shift almost constantly from one world to another, on the background of the infinity of these worlds and their transcendental organization, is in its own right, without any need for a miracle, a grace: the purely logical grace of innumerable appearing. Every human animal can tell itself that it is ruled out that it will encounter always and everywhere atonicity, the inefficiency of the body or the dearth of organs capable of treating its points. Incessantly, in some accessible world, something happens. Several times in its brief existence, every human animal is granted the chance to incorporate itself into the subjective present of a truth. The grace of living for an Idea, that is of living as such, is accorded to everyone and for several types of procedure.

The infinite of worlds is what saves us from every finite dis-grace. Finitude, the constant harping on of our mortal being, in brief, the fear of death as the only passion—these are the bitter ingredients of democratic materialism. We overcome all this when we seize hold of the discontinuous variety of worlds and the interlacing of objects under the constantly variable regimes of their appearances.

12. We are open to the infinity of worlds. To live is possible. Therefore, to (re)commence to live is the only thing that matters.

13. I am sometimes told that I see in philosophy only a means to re-establish, against the contemporary apologia of the futile and the everyday, the rights of heroism. Why not? Having said that, ancient heroism claimed to justify life through sacrifice. My wish is to make heroism exist through the affirmative joy which is universally generated by following consequences through. We could say that the epic heroism of the one who gives his life is supplanted by the mathematical heroism of the one who creates life, point by point.

14. In *Man's Fate*, Malraux makes the following remark about one of his characters: 'The heroic sense had given him a kind of discipline, not a kind of justification of life'. In effect, I place heroism on the side of discipline, the only weapon both of the True and of peoples, against power and wealth, against the insignificance and dissipation of the mind. But this discipline demands to be invented, as the coherence of a subjectivizable body. Then it can no longer be distinguished from our own desire to live.

15. We will only be consigned to the form of the disenchanted animal for whom the commodity is the only reference-point if we consent to it. But we are shielded from this consent by the Idea, the secret of the pure present.

NOTES, COMMENTARIES AND DIGRESSIONS

The number headings refer to the canonical division into books, sections and subsections. P stands for preface and C for conclusion.

P.

Epigraph. André Malraux, *Anti-Memoirs*, translated by Terence Kilmartin (New York: Holt, Rinehart & Winston, 1968).

P.1.

You can find Antonio Negri's letter in the first issue, from spring 2004, of the journal *La Sœur de l'Ange*. Now in Toni Negri, *Art et multitude. Neuf lettres sur l'art* (Paris: EPEL, 2005). To my knowledge, the best and tersest critique of Negri's historico-political conceptions, namely of his recent bestseller *Empire* (co-written with Michael Hardt), is the one penned by my Argentine friend Raúl Cerdeiras. It can be found in issue 24–25 (May 2003) of the Journal *Acontecimiento*, under the title 'Las desventuras de la ontología biopolítica de *Imperio*' (The Misadventures of the Biopolitical Ontology of *Empire*).

P.1.

Althusser regarded Marxism as a complex ensemble because it contained two creations (that of a science, historical materialism, and that of a new philosophy, dialectical materialism) enveloped in a single break, a single historical discontinuity. This was a way of commenting upon and rectifying the (Stalinist) tradition of the communist parties. This tradition effectively postulated the opposite. Two breaks—one philosophical (dialectical materialism) and the other scientific (historical materialism)—were contained in a single intellectual *dispositif*, which took the form of a worldview: the proletarian ideology, Marxism–Leninism.

P.1.

It is the question of the 'pure event' that connects the Mallarmé of 'A Dice-Throw' and the Valéry of 'The Graveyard by the Sea': under what conditions can the poem capture what lies beyond what is, what purely happens? And what then is the status of thought, if it is true that such a happening strikes at thought's corporeal support?

P.1.

Phenomenology, in its German variant, is indisputably haunted by religion. This probably stems from the motif of a lost authenticity, of a forgetting of the true Life, of a deleted origin—a theme that traverses all of Heidegger's writings, but which is also fully established in Husserl's *Krisis*.

In this regard, if the late Dominic Janicaud was correct to detect a certain smell of the sacristy or the convent in the recent postures of this philosophical orientation, he was wrong to feign ignorance that such a turn was presaged in some of the most important propositions of phenomenology's founders. See Janicaud's brilliant essay 'The Theological Turn in French Phenomenology' (in the collective volume *Phenomenology and the 'Theological Turn': The French Debate*, New York: Fordham, 2001).

So as not to be unilateral, let us add that the democratic humanism of the so-called analytical tendency—which still largely dominates the academic closure of philosophy in England and the United States—poorly conceals, beneath its proclaimed but severely limited scientism, the maintenance of a pious frame of mind.

The greatest French representative of the connection between phenomenology and religion is Paul Ricœur. With regard to his last great book, *Memory, History, Forgetting*, translated by Kathleen Blamey and David Pellauer (Chicago: University of Chicago Press, 2006), I have shown how its intellectual strategy presupposes the indestructible latency of a Christian subject at the very heart of the text. See my 'The Subject Supposed to be a

Christian: On Paul Ricœur's *Memory, History, Forgetting'*, translated by Natalie Doyle and Alberto Toscano, *The Bible and Critical Theory*, 2.3 (2006).

Ricœur's humanist religiosity is clearer, more demonstrative, in short more *political*, than his German sources. His chief problem is not that of original authenticity. Rather, it is that of knowing to whom the spiritual direction of democratic legalism belongs.

P.4.

Within that astounding artist's atelier which the Chauvet cave represents, I choose the horses rather than the lions or rhinoceroses, not due to their intrinsic superiority, but because of the persistence over thousands of years of the motif of the horse in mimetic art. It remains beyond doubt, however, that the attempt at a perspectival rendering of a whole herd of rhinoceroses using the gradation in the size of their horns, or the air of attentive melancholy or tense disquiet in the gaze of the lionesses, testifies, together with what I have said about the horses, to the universality of the power of the line in these artists from more or less 30,000 years ago.

For the four images discussed in text, see the 'Iconography' section.

P.5.

It is widely recognized that what Malraux, in *Le Miroir des limbes* (Paris: Gallimard, 1974), presents in the guise of discussions with the crucial figures of the twentieth century (Mao, Nehru, de Gaulle. . .) is for the most part an effervescent and reconstructed monologue. Just as radically as Deleuze, from very early on Malraux practised the free indirect style, making children behind the back of everything on the planet which he deemed of any worth. The result is nevertheless at times so intense that its truth surpasses that of exactness. In *La Tête d'obsidienne* (Paris: Gallimard, 1974) in which Malraux dreams up some decisive dialogues with Picasso— in some parts more felicitously than others—the theme of an invariance of the arts spanning Lascaux and Picasso himself is put in the mouth of the painter, almost like a fable: there would be a 'little chap' [*petit bonhomme*], the same creator throughout history who, countering the production of applied artists of 'painter-artists', would allow the manifestness of painting, the manifestness of art, to episodically emerge. This is what Picasso-Malraux says:

And the prehistoric sculptors! Not really men? But they were. Definitely. And very happy with their sculptures. In no way painter-artists! But all of them wanted to paint and sculpt following their idea. [. . .] I think that it is always the same Little Chap. Ever since the caves. He returns, like the wandering Jew.

I love this comparison of eternal truths, advancing and being reborn in becoming, with the wandering Jew.

P.5.

Regarding this period of political life in China, allow me to refer to my text 'The Cultural Revolution: The Last Revolution', in *Polemics*, translated by Steve Corcoran (London: Verso, 2006). It is another possible example of the universals that are created in politics. For the sake of all of the world's revolutionaries, the Cultural Revolution effectively explored the limits of Leninism. It taught us that the politics of emancipation can no longer work under the paradigm of revolution, nor remain prisoner to the party-form. Symmetrically, it cannot be inscribed in the parliamentary and electoral apparatus. Everything begins—and here lay the sombre genius of the Cultural Revolution—when, by saturating the previous hypotheses *in the real*, the high-school and student Red Guards, and then the workers of Shanghai, between 1966 and 1968, prescribed for the decades to come the *affirmative realization* of this beginning. But their fury was still so enmeshed in what they were rising up against that they only explored this beginning from the standpoint of pure negation.

P.5.

For Mao's criticisms of the Soviet model, see the two texts on Stalin's *Economic Problems of Socialism in the USSR* in Mao Tse-tung, *On Practice and Contradiction*, presented by Slavoj Žižek (London: Verso, 2007). For the *Discourses on Salt and Iron* (the 'Yan Tie Lun'), see the edition translated by Esson M. Gale (Taipei: Ch'eng-Wen, 1967).

P.5.

To fully grasp the relationship between my philosophical endeavour and my political commitment, or, to be more precise, not to fall into the temptation of opposing them, we must begin from a precise and coherent conception of the relations between philosophy and its outside. This will also allow us to dispel the idea of some fatal contradiction between the philosophy expounded in *Logics of Worlds* and the inventions of thought, politics and anthropology set forth by my friend and political comrade of 35 years, Sylvain Lazarus, notably in his *Anthropologie du nom* (Paris: Seuil, 1997). For me, this outside operates as a system of conditions-in-truth for philosophy. Now, no result of any condition of philosophy is ever reproduced as such in the axiomatic field of that philosophy. In this sense, philosophy's appropriation and metamorphosis of its conditions cannot be distinguished from the philosophical act itself, which is why one can never object anything to philosophy that is purely and simply exterior to it. What must be considered instead is the degree of *compatibility* between a philosophical operation and a non-philosophical operation which, having been seized conceptually, has entered into the field of the philosophical operation. That is how we must understand Lazarus's thesis according to which philosophy is a 'relation of thought'. That which has been thought and invoked as a condition by a philosophy is reconceived in such a way that it becomes another thought, even though it may be the only other (philosophical) thought *compatible* with the initial conditioning thought.

In short, the relation of philosophy to other kinds of thought cannot be evaluated in terms of identity or contradiction, neither from its own point of view nor from that of these other kinds of thought. Rather, it is a matter of knowing what it is that—as an effect of conceptual sublimations (or speculative formalizations)—remains essentially compatible with the philosophy in question, and what is instead organically alien to it. For example, it is not in the least contradictory but, on the contrary, perfectly compatible that the Terror can constitute for Sylvain Lazarus a singular politics, relying on the body that bears it (as he says, from 1793 the state is weak, a mere administration dependant on certain places, like the Convention, the clubs, the army. . .) *and* that, philosophically speaking, as Hegel immediately thought, it is a projection of the egalitarian maxim. This is even, for the philosopher, a perfect example of the materialist dialectic between existence and being, or between the immanent protocol of the becoming of a truth in a world, and—once that truth has come to be—its trans-worldly eternity. Furthermore, it is entirely natural that in the labour of this compatibility, anthropology, which is strictly linked to the process of a politics and thus to the present of a truth, concerns itself with the first aspect, isolating and singularizing it, while philosophy turns to the second, whose concept it renews.

The same point can be made about the category of prescription, which was introduced very early on, in the eighties, by Lazarus (against the themes of expression, representation or the programme) and which then became fundamental in order to identify the politics of the Organisation Politique. The figure of the state revolutionary is certainly not *immediately* homogeneous to the separation between politics and the state imposed by the category of prescription (a politics prescribes the state, which is exterior to it, by identifying, with respect to a particular question, a new possible, which is in turn thought and practiced in immanence to a situation). I will come back to this. Nevertheless, this (philosophical) figure is entirely built on prescriptive statements. Moreover, it is quite obvious that Mao opposes the voluntary dimension of prescription to Stalinist objectivity, just as the Legalist adviser to the Chinese emperor opposes the inflexible will harboured by the law to the natural developments that the Confucians wish to submit action to. In the remainder of *Logics of Worlds*, these conceptual usages of a central political category will be generalized. In Book I, it is proven that the absolute precondition for a subject is a prescriptive statement. In Book VII, very precise examples of such prescriptions are deployed as immanent conditions for the consistency of subjective bodies. The access to a point (in the sense that I give to this word in Book VI) is entirely marked out by the complex which comprises the statement and the becoming of that which carries it. And so on. We must speak here of an essential *philosophical fidelity* to the central themes of a politics.

The same can be said for the category of 'historical mode of politics', which was also introduced very early on in Lazarus's thought, and which permitted the passage beyond the saturation of previous 'Marxist' representations. Because of how it elucidates their discontinuous and self-thought nature, this category still seems to me indispensable if different politics are to remain intelligible. It cannot in any way be opposed to the eternity of truths. Were we to imagine such a contradiction, we could just as well register it, in a purely intra-philosophical manner, as a contradiction between this eternity and the irreducible multiplicity of worlds in which truths make their way. But that would be absurd: in the materialist dialectic, what secures the eternity of truths is *precisely* the fact that they result from a singular process, in a world disjoined from every other.

In fact, *Logics of Worlds* proposes what could be termed a philosophical sublimation of the category of mode, a sublimation which is without doubt the most comprehensive form of the compatibility between philosophical concepts and non-philosophical givens. The category of 'historical mode' is an obvious condition, in the ambit of political typification, of what I rename—because philosophy is *always* (re)naming—the path of a truth in a world, which is accompanied by the constitution of its own contemporaneity (a new present). We could say that, by inscribing every truth-procedure in the sequence of a new present which *is* its appearance in the singularity of a world, *Logics of Worlds* not only validates but presupposes—in the guise of the heterogeneity of worlds and the precariousness of the present—the doctrine of the modes of politics.

Of course, this sublimation (or universal projection) introduces a whole strictly philosophical arsenal which is perfectly alien to the forms of intellectuality of politics or anthropology: truth, subject, body and so on. It is also true that it proposes its own figures, which are always transversal. Take the figure of the state revolutionary which, subsuming a Chinese emperor, Robespierre, Lenin and Mao, seems to straddle several historical modes that are irreducible to one another (revolutionary, Bolshevik, dialectical. . .). The idea that there exist subjective invariants (constituted here by the conjunction of four predicates: equality, confidence, will and terror) seems directly to contradict the nominalist discontinuity of modes. A careful reading will show that this is not at all how things stand. At no point can the difference be formulated as a contradiction. This integrative or conditional difference stems entirely from the difference between politics, anthropology and philosophy, or between the real conditioning and the conceptual conditioned. When the difference is conceived in this way, it is possible to see how the invariants, which are subordinated here to the speculative didactic of truths (and thus to the polemic against democratic materialism), emerge intelligibly on the background of the anthropological theory of modes, assumed as a contemporary condition of philosophy. In effect, what constitutes the trans-worldly subjectivity of the figure of the state revolutionary is indeed the fact that it tries to enact the separation between the state and revolutionary politics, with the added tension that *it tries to do so from within state power*. Consequently, the figure in question only exists if we presuppose this separation. Moreover, that is why it is only philosophically constructible today, after a new thinking of politics has made it thinkable and practicable to situate oneself, in order to think action, from the interior of a politics for which state power is neither an objective nor a norm.

I have said enough, I think, for it to be clear that, as far as I myself am concerned, attempts to oppose my philosophy to my organized commitment, or to the political and anthropological creation of Sylvain Lazarus, have no more chance of success today than they did in the past.

P.8.

This abrupt definition of mathematics is to be found in '. . . ou pire, compte rendu du séminaire 1971–1972' (*Autres écrits*, edited by Jacques-Alain Miller, Paris: Seuil, 2001). It is indexed to the inventions of Frege and Cantor.

Nothing ties me more to Lacan's teaching than his conviction that the ideal of any thinking is that aspect of it which can be universally transmitted outside of sense. In other words, that senselessness [*l'insensé*] is the primordial attribute of the True.

What may be called 'Platonism' is the belief that in order to come close to this ideal, it is necessary to mathematize, by hook or by crook. This is opposed by all the doctrinaires of sense or meaning, be they sophists or hermeneuticists—all of them, at bottom, Aristotelians.

P.9.

Jean-Claude Milner, *Le Triple du plaisir* (Lagrasse: Verdier, 1997). Though I did not notice it at the time—despite being treated in it as a sadist under the honourable, but transparent cover of Plato—with this little book begins Milner's very peculiar 'post-linguistic' trajectory, which I will not discuss here.

I.1.

In 1982, I published a book entitled *Theory of the Subject*. This goes to show that in the long-run, the theme of the subject unifies my intellectual undertaking, against those who define (post)modernity by the deconstruction of this concept.

The category of 'subject' has been criticized from the right, through its Heideggerian incorporation into metaphysical nihilism. But also from the left, through its reduction to a mere ideological operator. Althusser argues both that History is a 'process without a subject' and that the distinctive feature of ideology—opposed to science as the imaginary is opposed to the symbolic—is to 'interpellate individuals into subjects'.

Only pious phenomenologists or conservative Sartreans would have come to the defence of the subject if Lacan had not entirely refounded its concept, while taking on board the radical critique of the subject of classical humanism. That is why traversing Lacan's anti-philosophy remains an obligatory exercise today for those who wish to wrest themselves away from the reactive convergences of religion and scientism.

I.1.

I would like to mention Bruno Bosteels, who for some years has been defending two original theses about my work:

a. The dialectic remains a crucial question for me, even if *Being and Event* appears in this regard as a turn.

b. Theory of the Subject is a book that the further developments of my thought do not invalidate—quite the opposite.

While awaiting the appearance of his book *Badiou and Politics*, which will doubtlessly be decisive, the reader will refer to his article 'On the Subject of the Dialectic', in the collection *Think Again: Alain Badiou and the Future of Philosophy*, edited by Peter Hallward (London: Continuum, 2004).

I.5.

The anti-colonial sequence of the French Revolution is politically and historically fundamental. Its omission in most historical narratives only confirms the racist and colonialist repression which, up to and including the Algerian war, served as the basis for the spirit of the Third Republic, which today so many kind souls declare themselves to be nostalgic for. The best book on Toussaint-Louverture, the anti-slavery revolution in Saint-Domingue and the creation of the first state governed by former black slaves (Haiti), was written in 1938 by a man from the Americas, C. L. R. James (*The Black Jacobins: Toussaint L'Ouverture and the San Domingo Revolution*, New York: Vintage Books, 1989). But it is very striking that we had to wait for the writings of Florence Gauthier to elucidate the manoeuvres of the Caribbean colonial lobby and their crucial role in the fall of the revolutionary government, on 9 Thermidor 1794. See, for example, the collection of studies edited by the Société des études robespierristes in 2002: *Périssent les colonies plutôt qu'un principe* ('Let the colonies perish rather than a principle'—the phrase is Robespierre's).

Nevertheless, from the wild insurrection of the slaves of Saint-Domingue up until the devastating victorious war led by Dessalines and Christophe against Napoleon's troops, which had come to restore slavery, we have here one of the most astounding epics conceivable. It is not lacking in great Homeric scenes like the session of the Convention when, in the presence of a black delegate, the abolition of slavery is decreed without debate, since every 'discussion' of such a point is deemed to be shameful; or the peaceful organization, in 1796, under Toussaint's dictatorship, of the first interracial egalitarian society that humanity has ever known. The political friendships between men of towering stature also recall the ancient narrative. For instance, Toussaint's friendship with two white revolutionaries, the governor Laveaux and Sonthonax, France's representative in Saint-Domingue.

The most vigorous literary treatment of these episodes—besides, of course, what was made of them by our great black national poet, Aimé Cesaire (see *Toussaint-Louverture*, Paris: Présence Africaine, 1960, and especially *La Tragédie du roi Christophe*, Paris: Présence Africaine, 1963)—is, rather strangely, of German origin. I am thinking of Anna Seghers's *Karibische Geschichten* (Berlin: Aufbau, 2000 [1949]) and its theatrical adaptation in Heiner Müller's *The Mission: Memory of a Revolution*, in *Theatremachine*, translated and edited by Marc von Henning (London: Faber and Faber, 1995 [1979]). With regard to the last two references, the reader can also profitably refer to Isabelle Vodoz, 'Deux lettres de Jamaïque sur la Révolution. Anna Seghers, *La lumière sur le gibet*, Heiner Müller, *La Mission*', *Germanica*, 6 (1989).

I.7.

The young philosopher of post-situationist provenance, Mehdi Belhaj Kacem, tackling my work in a manner that is both systematic and 'wild', outside of any academic injunction, has endeavoured to enhance the importance of affect in the eventual constitution of a subject. He is thereby attempting a novel, unprecedented synthesis between my mathematized ontology (which he calls 'subtractivism') and an original theory of affect and *jouissance*, which he extracts and reorganizes on the basis of Deleuze and Lacan. We could also say that he is seeking a conjunction between the structuralist (and Maoist) generation of the sixties and his own generation, raised—as he himself affirms—on pornography, drifting and indolence. His highest aim is basically to invent, for this generation, a new *discipline*.

Two books put out in autumn 2004 by his faithful publisher (Éditions Tristam, based in Auch) attest to this work in progress: *Événement et repetition* (a diagonal, at once patient and impatient, drawn through *Being and Event*) and *L'Affect*.

I do not doubt for a second that what is at work today—with Mehdi Belhaj Kacem, as with others both in France and abroad— is the replacement of the philosophical generation of the sixties and seventies, many of whose representatives have already passed away.

I. Scholium.

For what concerns contemporary music as it may be grasped in thought, I refer the reader to the many texts by François Nicolas. These texts are structured by powerful conceptual arrangements (such as the opposition writing/perception, the extimacy of text and music, the function of the theme and so on) and characterized by impeccable analytical precision. Nicolas's complete bibliography can be found on the web (type 'François Nicolas' into Google). In passing, let me declare my particular liking for the book *La Singularité Schönberg* (Paris: L'Harmattan, 1998).

François Nicolas is a composer, first and foremost. Among his works, I will only mention here *Duelle* (2001), which blends singing, instruments and machines, according to a principle of inclusion-externalization so subtle and so strangely lyrical that the audience during its first performance was utterly divided. I think this work is prophetic, because it organizes an 'exit from serialism' (this is Nicolas's expression) which avoids reactive dogmatisms (the return to sound and melody) as well as the chief danger in the post-modern context: eclecticism.

On serialism, François Nicolas has written a very exhaustive and dense text: 'Traversée du sérialisme', *Conférences du Perroquet*, 16 (1988). There, he defines and periodizes serialism in a manner that differs from mine. For him, serialism properly speaking starts right after World War Two, and not with Schönberg's 'dodecaphonism'. To examine the reasons for this difference in approach would take us too far afield.

I. Scholium.

Charles Rosen, *The Classical Style: Haydn, Mozart, Beethoven* (London: Faber and Faber, 2005 [1970]).

I. Scholium.

It is in his *Seminar XVII: The Other Side of Psychoanalysis*, translated by Russell Grigg (New York: W.W. Norton, 2007) that Lacan, introducing the thinking of the truth-*jouissance* dis-relation, declares, for instance: 'The love of truth is the love of this weakness whose veil we have lifted; it is the love of that which truth hides, which is called castration'.

Foreword to the Greater Logic.

The wish to elucidate the exact position of logic in philosophical thinking and its history, and thus generically to define what a 'greater logic' might be, is particularly present in Claude Imbert's notable work. Her 1999 book, *Pour une histoire de la logique* (Paris: PUF, 1999), is magnificent. I particularly admire the way in which Imbert navigates between the two beginnings of her history, the Platonic and the Stoic, in what is an exemplary transcendental inquiry.

I should add here that many of Imbert's studies are in my view classics, from her introduction to Frege's writings to her latest contributions on Lévi-Strauss, by way of her analyses in the field of painting.

II. Intro.

At the beginning of World War One, demonstrating his sangfroid, the extraordinary *calculus of distances* that characterizes him, Lenin reads Hegel's *Science of Logic*. We have his notebooks, which were published in his complete works. Two points are worthy of attention. First of all, the immense importance that Lenin accords to this reading, the kind of stunning revelation it represents for him. He will go so far as to say that, if one fails to master this *Logic*, Marx will remain incomprehensible. Second, the repeated verdict according to which, grasped in his principal orientation, Hegel is a materialist. I interpret this idea in the following way: in dialectical materialism, it is the dialectic that sustains the novelty of revolutionary materialism, not the other way around. That is indeed why I argue that rather than opposing an emancipatory materialism to a putative bourgeois idealism, we should divide materialism itself. That is how, in opposition to democratic obviousness, I recover the constitutive virtue of the predicate 'dialectical': materialist dialectic against democratic materialism.

I should add that I too am filled with Lenin's enthusiasm. In effect, I think there are only three crucial philosophers: Plato, Descartes and Hegel. Note that these are precisely the three philosophers whom Deleuze is unable to love.

II. Intro. 2.

A possible polemical path for the exposition of the transcendental would involve confronting its concept with Foucault's rearrangement of what he calls the 'doublet' of the empirical and the transcendental. Should we view the great discursive *dispositifs* that Foucault sets up under the heading of *epistemes* as occupying the position of the transcendental of a world, in the sense that I understand it here? And is the relation between the surface of texts and their epistemic organization, as well as the relation between bodies or practices (things) and their seizure by the transcendental power (of words), akin to the materialist dialectic of appearing-in-a-world?

A particularly original examination of Foucault's presuppositions has been carried out by Cécile Winter in her unpublished thesis on the clinic. She reconstructs, segment by segment, what Foucault extracts as the conditions of statements relative to a body, which is taken as deployed in space, in the great epoch of the 'birth of the clinic'—this is the title of Foucault's book, perhaps his best—right after the French Revolution. This allows us to make an informed judgment and eventually conclude, as I have, that in Foucault there is no formal theory of the transcendental. And that in this sense empiricism prevails, an empiricism as subtle as Descartes's matter.

II.1.2.

The entire beginning of *Being and Event* is a philosophical commentary on the axioms of set theory, such as they have been gradually extracted from the ambivalences lent to them by their Cantorian creation. To activate the dialectic of my two 'great' books, the old and the new—that is the dialectic of *onto*-logy and onto-*logy*, or of being and appearing—it is certainly useful to (re)read the first two parts of *Being and Event*.

II.1.3

Having advocated in the Scholium to Book I—with reference to the music of the twentieth century—the hard lesson of the identifications of Truth,

I hope I can be allowed a concession to sheer personal taste. Of all the musicians active in the second half of the twentieth century, after Webern's death, Olivier Messiaen is my favourite. I believe it is because he obstinately maintains—by means of composite but original devices (less neo-classical in spirit than those of Dutilleux, so to speak)—an extraordinary affirmative virtue. Pierre Boulez, undoubtedly both more subtle and more rigorous, only conquers a restricted space and leaves music far too fettered by a kind of critical asceticism. Christianity certainly helps Messiaen to celebrate, in the music itself, the correspondence between music and world, a correspondence of which the 'brute' usage of birdsong is a symbol. But this is still only a subjective means. As the affirmationist that I am, I salute—in Messiaen's particular combination of overlapping rhythms, disparate harmonic modes and violent tonalities—a kind of conquering voluptuousness whose optimism I find enchanting.

(Regarding affirmationism, let me refer, for the second version of its 'Manifesto', to the collection *Utopia 3*, edited by Ciro Bruni and published by GERMS in 2002; and for its third version, to *Polemics*.)

The Messiaen-world can be said to invent a concerted sacralization of its own components. Like the cinema of Rossellini, it is a world haunted by the modern possibility of the miracle. Not for nothing is Messiaen's only opera called *Saint Francis of Assisi*, and one of Rossellini's most striking films is *Francesco, giullare di Dio* (Francis, Jester of God). The reference to this saint, defender of an open-handed and praise-filled link to the world, suggests that for both Rossellini and Messiaen the modern miracle is neither dominating nor triumphal. Rather, it is a discreet shift in the relations between existence and inexistence.

Unable to follow the Catholic figure of the saint, this is what I prefer to call 'restricted action'. Restricted action is the ineluctable contemporary form of the little political truth of which we are capable.

II.1.5

I take this opportunity to pay tribute to Étienne Gilson's marvellous book *Choir of Muses*, translated by Maisie Ward (New York: Sheed and Ward, 1953), since it features Georgette Leblanc, Maeterlinck's muse—alongside Laura, Petrarch's muse, Clotilde de Vaux, Auguste Comte's muse, and Mathilde Wesendonk, Wagner's muse. In the background, there is the luminous enigma that the figure of Beatrice represents, which is treated in another great book by Gilson (*Dante and Philosophy*, translated by David

Moore, New York: Harper & Row, 1963 [1939]). We could say that Gilson tries to measure the transcendental intensity of these feminine apparitions in the genesis of certain worlds-of-thought: *The Divine Comedy*, the *Canzoniere*, *Tristan and Isolde*, the *Discours sur l'ensemble du positivisme*, *Ariadne and Bluebeard*. . . The least that can be said is that Beatrice, Laura, Mathilde, Clotilde and Georgette are not there for nothing. But it is not at all simple to know what this means. What is their place, both maximal and (in)existent, in the final brilliance of the worlds which are thereby created? In the end, Gilson does justice to the transcendental power of these muses, be they discreet (Mathilde), strident (Georgette), entirely concrete (Clotilde) or difficult to identify (Beatrice).

II.2.1.

The reference here is to the *Science of Logic*, translated by A. V. Miller (London: Allen & Unwin, 1969) (some translations modified).

I have never ceased measuring myself up to this book, almost as unreadable as Joyce's *Finnegans Wake*. Already in 1967, in a study devoted to non-standard analysis, entitled 'La subversion infinitésimale', which appeared in *Cahiers pour l'analyse* 9, I relied on the enormous 'Remark' (about 30 pages) devoted to differential calculus which opens, in the dialectic of being, the developments on the quantitative infinite.

(This 'remark' by Hegel is painstakingly examined, in a manner both mordant and subtle, by Jean-Toussaint Desanti in his most severely scientistic book, *La Philosophie silencieuse* (Paris: Seuil, 1975), whose very explicit subtitle is *Critique of the Philosophies of Science*. In it, Hegel is the embodiment of a particular variant of the bad relationship between science and philosophy, the variant 'incorporation (of the sciences) to the concept'. I take this opportunity to pay homage to he who will have been, with respect to ontology, my immediate predecessor; or who would have even anticipated me, had he chosen to turn into an effective philosophical proposal—into a system—the astonishing promise represented by his only real book, *Les Idéalités mathématiques* (Paris: Seuil, 1968).)

Between 1970 and 1980, I refined the schemas of the dialectic almost incessantly, constantly interrelating Mao's canonical texts (*On Contradiction, On the Correct Handling of Contradictions among the People*) and Hegel. There are traces of this labour in a small collective book from 1977, *Le Noyau rationnel de la dialectique hégélienne* (Paris: La Découverte), in which I prefaced some Chinese studies on Hegel, as well as in *Théorie du sujet*

(1982), where the (objective) opposition between the 'splace' [*esplace*] (structural bond) and the 'outplace' [*horlieu*] (the advent of exception), like the (methodological or subjective) one between algebra and topology, is rooted in the exegesis of the beginning of the *Science of Logic*.

Of course, one will also consult the meditation in *Being and Event* (1988) where I cross swords with Hegel on the opposition between 'limit' and 'boundary', in order to explode the pre-Cantorian opposition between true infinite and 'bad infinite'.

II.2.3.

Two references with regard to this point: 'What is Love?', *Umbr(a)*, 1, 1996; 'The Scene of Two', *Lacanian Ink*, 21, 2003. I have also discussed this truth-procedure at length with regard to Samuel Beckett (see especially 'The Writing of the Generic', in *On Beckett*, edited by Nina Power and Alberto Toscano, Manchester: Clinamen, 2003).

Of course, there are also Lacan's considerations, which I rely on—save to contest his complicity with the moralizing pessimism which suspects that love is nothing but an imaginary supplement for sexual dereliction. The other discussion would be with Jean-Luc Nancy, who inscribes love into the border shared by a meditation on the other and a meditation on the flesh (see especially *A Finite Thinking*, edited by Simon Sparks, Stanford: Stanford University Press, 2003).

I have nothing but respect and admiration for Nancy. I have publicly declared as much, while discreetly pointing to the gulf that separates us, in the text entitled 'L'offrande réservée', included in the collection *Sens en tous sens. Autour des travaux de Jean-Luc Nancy* (Paris: Galilée, 2004).

But in the end I stand, in some isolation it seems, between psycho-analytic pessimism, on one hand, and neo-religious recuperation, on the other, while maintaining (as they both do) that to think love is a major task, and a difficult one. What sets me apart from the first is that I think it is entirely inexact to treat love as though it belonged to the order of failure; from the second, that my approach to love is not at all spiritual, but formal. What we need to invent is something like a mathematics of love, without thereby falling into the infinite classifications of Fourier, who only envisages a universal *erotic* order.

II.3.3.

Here begins the construction of the logical formalisms that will test the consistency of my thinking of appearing.

As we are dealing with the transcendental, whose paradigm is what mathematicians call a Heyting algebra, the foundational book is Helena Rasiowa and Roman Sikorski, *The Mathematics of Meta-Mathematics* (Warsaw: Panstwowe Wydawnictwo Naukowe, 1963), which broaches the question in terms of the order-relation and is preoccupied with topological models.

In what concerns the readings suited to the thinking of the object (Book III) and of relation (Book IV) that I propose hereafter (see note III.3.1), they naturally recall, at the beginning of our path, the initial givens about the order-structure, the minimum, the conjunction and so on.

It is important to note that in Bourbaki's great treatise the most general framework distinguishes—after pure logic and set theory—three kinds of structure: algebraic structures, topological structures and order-structures. There is an insight here about the irreducibility of the thinking of order both to algebra and to topology. In effect, the order-structure—which underlies the singularity of every world as the transcendental of the differences that manifest themselves in that world—cannot be placed under the rubric either of the calculable or of localization.

II.3.8.

It is this structure which is not just a Heyting algebra, but a complete Heyting algebra. 'Completeness' signifies the existence of the envelope for every part of T, including—and this is the essential point—a part containing an infinity of degrees. In fact, the envelope infinitizes the transcendental operations. That is why complete Heyting algebras lead us into topology. In truth, they have been constructed in such a way as to allow the opens of a topological space to serve as their model. This is without doubt why Anglophone mathematicians call them *locales*: they formalize the logic of places. We will return to this point, namely in Book VI. On all these issues, see the bibliography in note III.3.1.

II.5.1.

Para-consistent logics are logics that admit the excluded middle but not the principle of non-contradiction in its general form. These logics, studied especially by Da Costa and the Brazilian school since the beginning of the 1960s, obviously furnish a different interpretation of negation than the ones, differing among themselves, provided by classical and intuitionist logics. See Newton C. A. Da Costa, *Logiques classiques et non classiques*, translated from the Portuguese and completed by Jean-Yves Béziau (Paris: Masson, 1997); in particular Appendix 1, which clearly expounds a para-consistent formalism: the system C1.

Ultimately, it seems that the two great Aristotelian principles (non-contradiction and the excluded middle), as forwarded in *Metaphysics* Γ, condition three logical types (and not two, as it was long believed). In effect, one can universally validate both principles (classical logic), or the principle of contradiction alone (intuitionist logic), or the excluded middle alone (para-consistent logics).

Basically, the canonical model of classical logic is set theory, that of intuitionist logic is topos theory, and that of para-consistent logics is category theory. These models are progressively more general and negation becomes increasingly evasive in them.

II.5.1.

We are here close to the famous formulas of sexuation proposed by Lacan in his seminars (*On Feminine Sexuality, the Limits of Love and Knowledge: Encore, The Seminar of Jacques Lacan, Book XX, 1972–1973*, edited by Jacques-Alain Miller, translated by Bruce Fink, New York: Norton, 1998) and in the text 'L'Étourdit', in *Autres écrits*. These formulas famously inscribe the fact that Woman [*la* femme] (in)exists and that *a* woman is not-all. For our part, we will say that *a* woman (semi-) exists or exists for me [*(mi-)existe ou 'm'existe'*]. As for Woman, she over-exists.

III.1.2.

I cannot enter into the objective phenomenology of a painting without acknowledging the entirely unique enterprise, connected to my own, undertaken by François Wahl, in his book *Introduction au discours du tableau* (Paris: Seuil, 1996). Just as Hubert Robert allows me to unfold the logic of the transcendental constitution of the visible, so François Wahl traverses paintings and landscapes in order to construct an entirely new theory of the visible as discourse. Even if what we understand by this term may vary, or even oppose us to one another, we converge on the certainty that the problem of the consistency of the world is a logical problem.

Wahl remains in the generic element of the 'linguistic turn', which demands that perceptual organization be referred back to discursive categories. Consequently, he cannot accept that the logic of appearing orders qualitative intensities. For him, to the extent that they draw their effectiveness from the order of discourse, logical 'units' are devoid of quality. We could say that Wahl is both closer to phenomenology—since he maintains that an irreducibly 'human' dimension, language, is the entry-point for a thinking of the visible—but also closer to Lacan, insofar as it is ultimately around a vanished object that the energy of what is exposed to us is constituted.

The discussion will doubtlessly carry on following the publication of François Wahl's next great book, *Le Perçu* (Paris: Fayard, 2007).

III.1.4.

Not every *f* function of the underlying multiple *A* towards the transcendental *T* can claim to identify an object-component. A certain homogeneity with the organization of appearing by the transcendental indexing needs to be respected. In technical terms, it should be noted that

1. The function is 'extensional', meaning that for two elements x and y of A, the conjunction of $f(x)$ and $\mathbf{Id}(x, y)$ cannot be greater than $f(y)$. The interpretation of this point tells us that the degree to which y belongs to the component cannot be lesser than the degree to which x belongs to the same component, or than the degree which measures the identity of x and y. This is intuitively clear: if x belongs by degree p to the component and y is q-identical to x, the belonging of y to the component is certainly at least equal to the greatest degree which is simultaneously inferior to p and q, thus to $p \cap q$.

2. The function respects the norms of existence. It is clear that an element x cannot belong 'more' to a component of A than it exists in A as a whole. The degree to which x belongs to the component, that is $f(x)$, must therefore remain bounded by the existence of x in the set as a whole, that is $\mathbf{E}x$.

We thus have the following two axioms, which codify the fact that a function of A to T does indeed define an object-component:

$$f(x) \cap \mathbf{Id}(x, y) \leq f(y)$$

$$f(x) \leq \mathbf{E}x$$

III.1.5

I have chosen a philosophically striking formulation of the postulate of materialism. However, it poses some mathematical questions, due to the fact that the formula 'there exists an element that identifies the atom' obliges us to confront the twists and turns of identity (of equality, isomorphy, equivalence. . .), a familiar conundrum for formalisms.

Let us put it plainly: while it is in line with the conceptual evidence, the formal treatment of this definition (Subsection 5 of Section 3 of this Book) is not completely rigorous. At a very early stage, Françoise Badiou pointed out to me that there was considerable wavering in this respect.

Another sophisticated reader of one the first drafts of *Logics of Worlds*, Guillaume Destivère, diagnosed this deductive weakness and wrote to me a letter about this point for which I am very thankful. He spotted the 'mistake' and gave a version of the postulate of materialism that was less striking, more technical and, most importantly, which complied with the requirements of formal cohesion.

But, one will ask, why did you retain in the text this approximation which had been brought to your attention? Because, as important as the formal test may be, it is here only at the service of the concept, and my formulation of the postulate of materialism suited me. I kept it because the mathematical uncertainty had no consequences for the argument. The formal distortion—which basically replaces 'in biunivocal correspondence to' with 'prescribed by', and 'isomorphic' with 'identical'—does not in fact carry over into the consequences. I reproduce below the decisive moment in Destivère's intervention (note that this intervention relates to an earlier version, so that the vocabulary is not always the same—the idea is nevertheless perfectly clear):

> You precisely say: 'That every atom is real means that it is prescribed by an element of A. This does not entail that two ontologically different elements prescribe two different atoms'.
>
> But further on, you demonstrate the anti-symmetry of the relation < by affirming the opposite, namely that 'If the partitive functions *a* and *b* are the same, by virtue of the materialist axiom according to which every atom is real, there exists a *single* element of A which is the ontological substructure of A. This means that the elements *a* and *b* are identical, or that *a* = *b*.'
>
> If this anti-symmetry really is indispensable for you, you will be obliged to reinforce the axiom of materialism so as to place A in *bijection*

with the atomic components of $(A, \mathbf{Id})$. This requires that we have $a = b$ (in the ontological sense) if and only if $\mathbf{E}a = \mathbf{E}b = \mathbf{Id}(a, b)$. The 'philosophical commentaries' would then follow suit, since it suffices that three intensities are equal to one other in order for two beings to be confused with each other.

Besides, it seems that this reinforcement of the axiom of materialism has been surreptitiously but definitively admitted, once you explicitly confuse the partitive function $\mathbf{Id}(a, x)$ with a.

The axiom of materialism would then be as follows: For every object $(A, \mathbf{Id})$, the application that makes a function $\mathbf{Id}(a, x)$ of A towards T correspond to an element a of A is a bijection of the multiple A on the set of the atomic functions of the object.

We will again come across Guillaume Destivère later on (with regard to the inexistent, in Book IV) and the occasion will be far more dramatic.

III.2.

Quotations are from Immanuel Kant, *Critique of Pure Reason*, translated by Norman Kemp Smith (Basingstoke: Palgrave, 2007) (some translations modified).

Kant is the one author for whom I cannot feel any kinship. Everything in him exasperates me, above all his legalism—always asking *Quid juris?* or 'Haven't you crossed the limit?'—combined, as in today's United States, with a religiosity that is all the more dismal in that it is both omnipresent and vague. The critical machinery he set up has enduringly poisoned philosophy, while giving great succour to the Academy, which loves nothing more than to rap the knuckles of the overambitious—something for which the injunction 'You do not have the right!' is a constant boon. Kant is the inventor of the disastrous theme of our 'finitude'. The solemn and sanctimonious declaration that we can have no knowledge of this or that always foreshadows some obscure devotion to the Master of the unknowable, the God of the religions or his placeholders: Being, Meaning, Life. . . To render impracticable all of Plato's shining promises—this was the task of the obsessive from Königsberg, our first *professor*.

Nevertheless, once he broaches some particular question, you are unfailingly obliged, if this question preoccupies you, to pass through him. His relentlessness—that of a spider of the categories—is so great, his delimitation of notions so consistent, his conviction, albeit mediocre, so violent, that, whether you like it or not, you will have to run his gauntlet.

That is how I understand the truth of Monique David-Ménard's reflections on the properly psychotic origins of Kantianism (*La Folie dans la raison pure*, Paris: Vrin, 1990). I am persuaded that the whole of the critical enterprise is set up to shield against the tempting symptom represented by the seer Swedenborg, or against 'diseases of the head', as Kant puts it.

Kant is a paradoxical philosopher whose intentions repel, whose style disheartens, whose institutional and ideological effects are appalling, but from whom there simultaneously emanates a kind of sepulchral greatness, like that of a great Watchman whose gaze you cannot escape, and who you can't help fearing will entrap you into 'demonstrating' your speculative guilt, your metaphysical madness. That is why I approve of Lacan pairing him up with Sade (see 'Kant avec Sade', in *Écrits*). Sade is a laborious and compulsive writer, capable of turning blood-soaked eroticism into trite neo-classicism and sexual positions into botched acrobatics. Yet he abides, watching, surveying. He is the sad regent of debauchery, whose mandatory and sinister character he incessantly reveals.

I pay my tribute here to Kant's philosophical sadism. In vain I seek to draw from this quibbling supervisor, always threatening you with detention, the authorization to platonize, that is, with regard to the critical incarceration (O, the eternal 'limits' of Reason!), the saving *exit pass*.

III.2.

There exists in fact another Kant, a dramatized and modernized Kant, pushed in the direction of contemporary politics and the teachings of Lacan. A '*Kant avec Marx et Lacan*', who is a Slovenian creation. We must pay tribute here to the utterly original Slovenian school of philosophy, whose interlocutor I have had the pleasure of being for some years. Like every true school, it has experienced splits and animosities. But I, being far from Ljubljana, can at least once salute together Rado Riha, Jelica Sumic, Slavoj Žižek, Alenka Zupančič and all their friends. We owe to this school an entirely new vision of great German Idealism, a vision that brings it into line with a post-Marxist political theory (in their own way, all these Slovenian thinkers were involved in socialist Yugoslavia, and all were readers of Althusser), a political theory which itself depends on a reading of Lacan centred not so much on the force of language but on the unbearable shock of the real.

For Rado Riha and Jelica Sumic, see the German collection *Politik der Wahrheit* (Vienna: Turia + Kant Verlag, 1997).

For Alenka Zupančič, the essential book is *Ethics of the Real* (New York: Verso, 2000).

I will speak of Slavoj Žižek below (see the notes to Book VII).

III.3.1.

The serious (logical) business starts here. In these thirty pages or so, I set forth the crux of the formalism of the transcendental machinery, a machinery whose pieces we identified in the first section, on the basis of examples passed through the sieve of objective phenomenology (the protest and the painting by Hubert Robert).

The stakes of this kind of formal exposition are twofold. First, it is a question of elucidating the constitutive operations of appearing, so that doubt can no longer be cast on the rigorous manner in which these operations produce their effects. Second, it is a question of proving that the equation 'appearing = logic' is incontrovertible, once we can formalize all the conditions of appearing in the most modern treatment of logic possible (or nearly). This modern treatment no longer takes a linguistic or grammatical form. From the outset, we place ourselves amid far more general—I would even say ideal—constructions, which belong to category theory and one of its specialized branches: topos theory. Since my aim is purely philosophical, I have not attempted to reproduce the whole categorial context. I have cut straight to what I needed, which is in fact a special category: the category obtained by connecting sets to a complete Heyting algebra, that is to what I have renamed a transcendental. In short, what is philosophically treated here is a theoretical fragment of a vast and moving edifice: the categorial reformulation of logic. This fragment has a mathematical name: the theory of Ω-sets. Ω designates a complete Heyting algebra which is used to measure the degree of equality between two elements of a set. Its philosophical name is general theory of appearing. I transcribe Ω into T (for transcendental). Consequently, the function that relates the pairs of elements of a multiple-being (a set) to a transcendental T (to an algebra Ω) is simply the function of appearing, or transcendental indexing. Everything else follows, under the condition of the postulate of materialism (every atom is real) which, in its precise mathematical form, defines what mathematicians call a 'complete Ω-set', the formalization of what I call an object. The fact that the entailments are tightly packed together does not stop them from being, in the long run, very clear. What's more, I hold that the philosophical comprehension of the significance of this mathematical fragment greatly contributes to the mastery of its deductive transparency.

The mathematical bibliography should focus on accessible expositions of the theory of complete Ω-sets. Unfortunately, and contrary to my chosen angle, the majority of presentations remain prisoner to an often heavy-going examination of the entire arsenal of category theory. Accordingly, in the short bibliography that concludes this note, after having located the philosophical fragment that interests me in the books I mention, I briefly indicate the degree of autonomy of its presentation and, more generally, the breadth of mathematical knowledge that it presupposes.

In *Logics of Worlds*, the logico-mathematical equipment is self-sufficient: everything is defined and demonstrated. All that remains is to desire to understand, which is the only problem in mathematics.

The book with which I myself began is Robert Goldblatt's *Topoi: The Categorial Analysis of Logic*, 2nd ed (New York: North-Holland, 1984). The theory of Heyting algebras (or transcendentals) is expounded in Chapter 8. The rudiments of the theory of sets 'evaluated in a Heyting algebra' (the theory of objects), at the end of Chapter 11. The comprehensive theory (complete Ω-sets and their relations), in Section 7 of Chapter 14. In the main, one can follow these fragments without worrying too much about the details of topos theory (which is masterfully expounded in this book, no doubt because the model of sets is constantly taken as a conceptual and pedagogic guide).

The book in which I remain immersed to this very day is Francis Borceux's *Handbook of Categorical Algebra* (Cambridge: Cambridge University Press, 1994). It comprises three volumes, whose subtitles are *Basic Category Theory, Categories and Structures* and *Categories of Sheaves*. The fragment that is of particular interest for us takes up the first two chapters of Volume 3: 'Locales' (Heyting algebras), then 'Sheaves'. The theory of complete Ω-sets is presented in Sections 2.8 and 2.9 of Chapter 2. The fragment's independence is variable. In effect, the book makes moderate, but not negligible, usage of the categorial arsenal as it is presented in the first volume (functors, natural transformations, etc.). But it is a didactic manual which, though high-level (and of formidable complexity in its specialized chapters), retains a faultless immanent clarity.

The intermediary book is Oswald Wyler's *Lecture Notes on Topoi and Quasitopoi* (Singapore: World Scientific, 1991). The presentation of the vocabulary of categories is concentrated in Chapter 0. Heyting algebras are introduced in the first section of Chapter 2. The indexing of sets on such algebras, which here take the name of H-sets, is entirely laid out in Chapter 8, in a more 'probabilistic' version (the concept is that of 'fuzzy sets'). All of this is rather clear, but sometimes features unhelpful or forced generalizations.

An interesting, but often more elliptical book is J. L. Bell, *Toposes and Local Set Theories* (Oxford: Oxford University Press, 1988). Heyting algebras are presented (at some speed!) in the first chapter, under the heading 'Elements of Category Theory', as an example of a closed Cartesian category constructed on the basis of a partial order-structure. The fragment that interests us philosophically is found in Chapter 6 ('Locale-valued Sets'). The problem is that the treatment takes place almost invariably on the basis of *topoi* (special categories) considered in terms of their internal logic, or even identified with this logic, resulting in a formalism whose manipulation must be understood in advance (see Chapter 3).

The founding article for the mathematical fragment in question, namely the treatment of sheaves in the register of Ω-sets (philosophically, this is the construction of the transcendental functor, or the operator of the retro-action of being-there on pure being), is from 1979. See Michael P. Fourman and Dana S. Scott, 'Sheaves and Logic', in M. P. Fourman, C. J. Mulvey and D. S. Scott, *Applications of Sheaves* (Berlin: Springer Verlag, 1979).

III.3.7.

There exist in fact very close relations between transcendental structures and topological spaces. The concept of a complete Heyting algebra (of a locale) was forged with the aim of generalizing the properties of the opens of a topology, finite intersections (conjunction) and infinite unions (envelope). What's more, one could broach the question of appearing (the question of being-there) starting from more topological concepts and following the movement of their generalization in the direction of locales and Ω-sets (that is, in the direction of the logic of appearing).

All of this will be dealt with again in Book VI, as we try not to be devoured by the Minotaur of the matheme. The most important theorem establishes that the set of the points of a transcendental can be considered as a topological space.

III. Scholium. 2.

The Battle of Gaugamela, which serves here as my central example, is studied in a number of histories of Antiquity and treatises in military strategy, on the basis of those patchy, and undoubtedly approximate, sources which are the Greek historians of the period. A clear synthesis can be found in John Warry, *Warfare in the Classical World* (London: Salamander, 1998).

III. Scholium. 3.

Grothendieck was an outsized mathematician, so to speak, perhaps as profound as Riemann. I say 'was' because he retired decades ago—a little like the young chess genius Bobby Fischer. In any case, he retired from public mathematical activities. Loïc Debray, a mathematician friend (who in addition was also a disinterested defender of imprisoned or dead revolutionaries from the seventies and eighties, 'Red Army Faction' and 'Action Directe') tells an arresting story in this regard. In his initial thrust, at the beginning of the 1950s, Grothendieck was convinced that another way of doing mathematics was about to be invented, or better, a mathematics other than the one that had been unfolding ever since the Greeks. And then, in the wake of his staggering creations (a version of algebraic geometry which was entirely new), he would have concluded that, no, it was the same mathematics continuing. And he would have then preferred to preoccupy himself with sheepherding and anti-nuclear activism.

A Rimbaud-like legend? Commerce and the desert, because 'science is too slow'? I don't know. It remains that, when their true meaning is grasped, the idea which has received the name of 'Grothendieck topos' and the related idea of a sheaf shine in the sky of pure thought, like Sirius or Aldebaran.

IV. Intro.

Wittgenstein and Lacan are the two greatest anti-philosophers of the twentieth century, what Kierkegaard and Nietzsche were for the nineteenth. But in Wittgenstein's case this is due, in my mind, to the *Tractatus* alone. The further oeuvre—which is not really one, since Wittgenstein had the good taste not to publish or finish any of it—slides from antiphilosophy into sophistry. It is a risk that every anti-philosophy runs: in order to uphold the exorbitant privilege which it accords to its pure enunciation (it is true because it is me who speaks) and ultimately to its own existence (I break in two the history, if not of the world, then at least of what I'm dealing with), anti-philosophy often demands a rhetorical forcing which renders it indiscernible from the sophists of its time. This is true of Nietzsche's peremptory maxims or pastiches of the Gospels, Kierkegaard's biographical chatter, or Lacan's wordplays. The 'second Wittgenstein' is obsessed with urgent and preposterous questions, as if he were obstinately seeking some stupefied delirium. These volleys of question marks are at times surprising inventions, which pleasingly derail the mind, at other times trite acrobatics. The mortifying respect which they have garnered among academics might not have amused him (he seems not to have been easily diverted) but it would have elicited his aristocratic irony to find himself as a kind of mummified hero.

The *Tractatus*, written in the proud and formulaic style beloved of anti-philosophers (consider Pascal), is instead an undeniable masterpiece, even though its religious (or mystical) finality is perplexing. This perplexity is dispelled as soon as we explore the inescapable comparison: Wittgenstein and Saint Augustine. I have investigated this comparison in a long article on Wittgenstein published in 1994 in Issue 3 of the journal *Barca!*, under the title 'Silence, solipsisme, sainteté. L'antiphilosophie de Wittgenstein'.

IV. Intro.

I have dealt with sophistry and its difference from philosophy in my 1992 book *Conditions*, and with anti-philosophy in a pamphlet on Nietzsche ('Casser en deux l'histoire du monde?', *Conférences du Perroquet*, 1992; see also 'Who is Nietzsche?', translated by Alberto Toscano in *Pli* 11, 2001), as well as in the aforementioned article on Wittgenstein.

In what concerns sophistry, it is obviously necessary to be aware of the role it is accorded by Barbara Cassin, the very opposite of the one I reserve for it. See her great book *L'Effet sophistique* (Paris: Gallimard, 1995). Convinced that philosophy's inception is fettered by a specific rhetoric (the predicative rhetoric that Aristotle transforms into a general logic, or ontology, in Book I of the *Metaphysics*), Cassin makes Gorgias and his successors into the artisans of another path for philosophy, in which, since 'being' is exchangeable with 'being said', the function of non-being (ultimately, of silence) is constitutive, in the stead and place of that of being. Ontology is replaced with logology. We could say that Cassin attempts a synthesis between Heidegger (there is indeed a Greek inception that destines and traverses us) and the linguistic turn (everything is language, and the philosophy closest to the real is a general rhetoric). It is as the hero of this synthesis that Gorgias challenges the hegemony of Parmenides. As we know, this was also Nietzsche's point of view, which to my mind goes to confirm what I argued earlier: every anti-philosopher is a virtual accomplice of sophistry. Like everything else, this complicity was already discerned by Plato, when in the *Theaetetus* he articulated the 'ontological' complicity between the sophists and Heraclitus. For Heraclitus is undoubtedly the proto-founder of anti-philosophy, just as Parmenides is the proto-founder of philosophy. This is something that the anti-philosopher Lacan grasped perfectly in his Seminar XX: 'the fact that being is presumed to think—is what founds the philosophical tradition starting from Parmenides. Parmenides was wrong and Heraclitus was right. That is clinched by the fact that, in Fragment 93, Heraclitus enunciates "he neither avows nor hides, he signifies" '. The one who is right here is the one who replaces the alternative avowing/hiding or being and non-being—an alternative which Lacan had previously declared to be 'stupid'—with the ruses of signification. Lacan thereby clarifies the reasons why Plato treats Heraclitus as an adversary and Parmenides as a 'father'. I think these reasons are excellent ones, and I draw the same consequences from them as Plato did.

IV.1.1.

I spent part of the autumn of 1968—note the date!—in Montreal, to assist my friend Roger Lallemand, an outstanding Belgian intellectual as well as a top-notch lawyer, in his tasks as the delegate of the *Ligue des droits de l'homme* at the trial of two Quebecois independentists, Vallières and Gagnon. Vallières had written the great book, the great cry of Francophone Canadians: *Nègres blancs d'Amérique* (Montréal: Parti Pris, 1968; translated by Joan Pinkham as *White Niggers of America: The Precocious Autobiography of a Quebec 'Terrorist'*, New York: Monthly Review Press, 1971). I love Quebec, this strange withdrawn America, where a classical French is spoken. There, beneath the flag of the *gauchismes* of the time, I encountered warm-hearted friends, militants full of intelligence and vivaciousness. The trial, with its bewigged judge and its witnesses speaking in a sensuous and for me mysterious way (at last, a deep and striking French!), was like a melancholic fiction. But a fearsome one! The verdicts were unforgiving. This luminous Indian autumn, where the cobblestones of the Parisian May mingled with the Quebecois liberation struggle, was like a clearing in the forest of time. Perhaps this charmed voyage to Canada anticipated the fact that my most well-versed and ardent interpreter and critic is today a Canadian, Peter Hallward, Anglophone but Francophone, schooled in the United States but living in London, and fond like me of the Quebecois cause. I dedicate these pages to him. This does not exempt one from reading the book he has devoted to me, which is—and will long remain, I think—a kind of classic: *Badiou: A Subject to Truth* (Minneapolis: Minnesota University Press, 2003).

IV.2.

Leibniz! What virtuosity! What endless delight! What an appetite for knowledge and enjoyment! Leibniz inspires as much sympathy as his sour adversary, Voltaire, inspires antipathy. Besides, he is a very great mathematician, which in my mind counts for a lot. But he has an Achilles' heel: he would like to attain universal recognition by reconciling the most conflicting doctrines. He reminds me of Sosie, in Molière's *Amphitryon*, who, facing the night's threats, exclaims: 'Gentlemen, I am a friend of the whole world!' Moreover, just as it is difficult to take seriously the baroque churches of southern Germany, which resemble immense boudoirs for loose women, I can't take Leibniz entirely seriously. Let us not forget, by the way, the subtitle that Deleuze gave to *The Fold*, his brilliant 1988 study: *Leibniz and the Baroque*. Therein lies the whole problem. I have said what I think of Deleuze's text in a long review, translated into English by Thelma Sowley as 'Gilles Deleuze, *The Fold: Leibniz and the Baroque*', in *Gilles Deleuze and the Theater of Philosophy*, edited by Constantin V. Boundas and Dorothea Olkowski (London: Routledge, 1994).

Truth be told, Leibniz resembles Aristotle: an all-encompassing curiosity; the will to embrace, in a new synthesis, the unilateral viewpoints of his predecessors; the certainty that there exists an architecture of the universe; the ascendancy of finality over mechanism; a temperate conservatism in politics; but especially this: an essential vitalism, or organicism. Being (substance, the monad) is organized as an animal. Everything lives, 'everything is full of souls', as Victor Hugo put it. These thinkers have a master-enemy, the one they bitterly pay tribute to, from whom they originate but who they wish to dislodge from his pedestal. For Aristotle it is Plato, for Leibniz, Descartes. After the classical Master, the supple, baroque-like disciple. The disciple has to betray, he can't help it. Having said that, it is always with a certain tenderness that I reread the one who, like myself, practices a 'metaphysical mathematics'. As for the bibliography, see Gottfried Wilhelm Leibniz, *Philosophical Writings*, edited by G. H. R. Parkinson (London: Everyman, 1995).

IV.2.

Guy Lardreau is a Leibnizian with regard to a crucial point: he argues that applying thought to secondary, futile, commonplace objects is the proper task of philosophy. This necessarily means that these microscopic objects 'express' a general Sense. On this kinship, see Guy Lardreau, *Fictions philosophiques et science-fiction* (Arles: Actes Sud, 1988).

IV.2.

The most impressive contemporary meditation on the One is to be found in the work of Christian Jambet. Building on a refined knowledge of the contributions of Arab and Persian philosophy, in particular in terms of its Shi'a sources, Jambet proposes the concept of the paradoxical One, whose being [*être*] is essentially thought as not-being [*non-étant*]. The deepest drive which characterizes this strange oeuvre is to overcome that which in Henry Corbin, Jambet's teacher, remained dependent on Heidegger: the interpretation of the not-being of the One as a destiny of being. Through a kind of ideological 'revolutionism', Jambet assumes that the fact that being [*l'être*] is not the being [*étant*] that it is must instead be understood according to the One, or starting from the One.

For the detail of his argument, see his beautiful book *La Grande Résurrection d'Alamût* (Lagrasse: Verdier, 1990).

IV.3.3.

In this section, I am making use of the techniques of category theory (diagrams, the study of their commutative character, cones, universal position, etc.) in a simple and informal manner. Whoever wishes to take the occasion to practice these techniques further will refer to the initial chapters of the books cited in note III.3.1.

IV.3.4.

The thinking of the inexistent formalizes what I believe to be at stake in Jacques Derrida's sinuous approach. Ever since his first texts, and under the progressively academicized (though not by him) name of 'deconstruction', his speculative desire was to show that, whatever form of discursive imposition one may be faced with, there exists a point that escapes the rules of this imposition, a *point of flight*. The whole interminable work consists in localizing it, which is also impossible, since it is characterized by being out-of-place-in-the-place. To restrict the space of flight, it is necessary to force the signifiers of discursive imposition, to diagonalize the great metaphysical oppositions (being/beings, mind/matter, but also democracy/totalitarianism, state of law/barbarism or Jew/Arab) and to invent a language of decentring, or a *dispositif* of acephalic writing. Hence not only the deliberate friction between the most overtly literary prose and the harshest philosophical conceptuality, whose emblem is the Genet/Hegel pairing in *Glas*, but also the function of the dialogue (with Hélène Cixous, Élisabeth Roudinesco, Habermas, Nancy. . .) which, as in the young Plato, raise the stakes of the aporia.

All of this gravitates around the question of what is to come under the inexistent. Let us say that if A is any discursive imposition whatsoever, $\varnothing_A$ is the fleeting object of Derrida's desire. Its way of belonging to A—which is measured by nothing (by μ)—is to not be of it, or to inexist for it. Except that, simply by saying that it inexists, and thus confusing it with nothing-ness (that is with being), one misses out the fact that $\varnothing_A$ indicates the possibility of a full existence elsewhere. These alternating slippages organize Derrida's 'touch', his new proposition about the bonds between thinking and the sensible, which says that what gently evades us is what makes us think otherwise than here. This is set forth in detail in the book devoted to Jean-Luc Nancy, which is indeed entitled *Touching: On Jean-Luc Nancy*, translated by Christine Irizarry (Stanford: Stanford University Press, 2005). This book concludes with a formula which limpidly exemplifies what I mean: 'Greeting without salvation' [*Un salut sans salvation*]. This is truly $\varnothing$: the being of nothing, which is not some being [*l'étant de rien, qui n'est pas rien d'étant*].

In homage to Derrida, I write here 'inexistance', just as he created, a long time ago, the word 'différance'. Will we say that $\varnothing_A$ = inexistance = différance? Why not?

IV.3.4.

Since the writing of the aforementioned note, Jacques Derrida has died.

For two or three years, I had been in the process of patching up with him, after a very long period of semi-hostile distance and sundry incidents, the most pointed of which involved the colloquium *Lacan avec les philosophes*, in 1990. The documents relating to this quarrel can be found at the end of the proceedings published in 1991 by Albin Michel.

At the beginning of this new phase in our relations, Derrida told me 'In any case, we have the same enemies'. And we all saw those enemies, especially in the United States, scurrying out of their rat-holes on the occasion of his death. Death, decidedly, always comes too soon. This is one of the forms taken by its terrifying logical power: the power to precipitate conclusions. I count on paying homage again, and often, to Jacques Derrida, rereading his oeuvre, otherwise, under this emblem: the passion of Inexistence.

IV.3.4

It is here that Guillaume Destivère, of whom I spoke of earlier with regard to the formulation of the postulate of materialism, reappears on the stage of the writing of *Logics of Worlds*, in a manner which I at first believed to be entirely momentous. On 19 January 2005, at 1.50 am (which doesn't bode well: it was clearly urgent!), he sent me the following message, with the subject-heading 'Is the World of ontology really materialist?':

Pardon me for only dealing here with one point, which is perhaps derisory, but perhaps crucial, and which poses a problem for me, instead of telling you of the immense and magnificent vistas that your manuscript opens for me.

It can be put in a couple of words. It is a question of the World of ontology. There is a transcendental T with two elements, 0 and 1. If I read correctly, you do not give details anywhere, for a given set A, regarding what would be its function of transcendental indexing as an object of this World of ontology, but it is difficult to imagine that it would be something other than the Kronecker symbol over A, let us write it as k, defined over $A \cdot A$ by $k(x, y) = 1$ if $x = y$, and $k(x, y) = 0$ in the opposite case.

But, in that case, it appears that in general such an object (A, k) of the World of ontology *does not have its proper inexistent*. In effect, we may consider the h-function of A in T as constantly equal to 0, acknowledging that it is an atomic component of (A, k). But we will never be able to write it as the real atomic component in the form $h = k(a, x)$ for an element a of A, since we would then necessarily have $h(a) = 1$. In other words, in the World of ontology, the Kronecker symbol does not verify the axiom of materialism.

Is it serious, doctor? I thought this was the only somewhat urgent remark I had up to this point!

I confess to having experienced some very difficult moments after reading this message. Not only did it cast doubt on the generality of the postulate of materialism, but also on the entire theory of the event! After all, in Book V an event is defined by its capacity to 'sublate' the inexistent of an object. I started thinking of the terrible case of Frege, whose entire reduction of mathematics to logic, a theoretical edifice patiently constructed over a number of years, was brought down by a small proof by Russell (I allude to it at the beginning of Book II). The night between the 19 and 20 had me poring over my notes and the relevant literature. At last, on January 20, at 6.29 pm, I was able to send Guillaume the following blistering reply:

Let us agree to call 'canonical classical exposition' of a set A the following set: $A^* = [\varnothing, \{\{x\}/x \in A\}]$, that is the set constituted on the one hand by the void, on the other by the singletons of the elements of A.

We will then call 'canonical transcendental indexing of A^*' the function of $A^* \cdot A^*$ on $T_0 = (0, 1)$ so defined: $\mathbf{Id}(x, y) = 1$ if and only if the multiples x and y share a common element: $\exists z [(z \in x)$ and $(z \in y)]$.

We can easily recognize that $(A^*, \mathbf{Id})$ is an object. For every non-empty atom is real, since it is prescribed by the appropriate singleton, while the empty atom is prescribed by $\varnothing$.

The proper inexistent of this object is of course $\varnothing$. We have in effect $\mathbf{Id}(\varnothing, x) = 0$ for every x, and therefore also $\mathbf{E}\varnothing = 0$.

We can therefore say that, to the extent that one absolutely wants to represent a pure multiplicity A *as object*—which we could call an 'ontological objectivation'—this object is really A^*. Or, to put it in a different way: in ontology *considered as a world* (which mathematics does not oblige us to do, since it deals with being 'without appearance', or non-localized being), a pure multiplicity is objectivated in terms of its canonical classical exposition, which is in turn marked by its canonical indexing.

The more arcane aspects of this affair involve the existence of an isomorphism between the universe (the topos, in effect) of sets indexed with no regard for the postulate of materialism and the universe (the topos) of the sets indexed with the postulate of materialism. The clue to this isomorphism is contained in the above tactic.

Missed by a hair's breadth.

V. Epigraph

The epigraph is taken from the play *Endgame* (New York: Grove Press, 1958). Of all twentieth-century writers, Samuel Beckett is the one who has been my closest philosophical companion. What I mean by this is that thinking 'under condition of Beckett' has been, in the register of prose, the counterpart of what, for a long while, thinking 'under condition of Mallarmé' has been for poetry. To Mallarmé I owe a sharper understanding of what a subtractive ontology is, namely an ontology in which evental excess summons lack, so as to bring forth the Idea. I owe Beckett a comparable sharpening in my thinking of generic truth, that is the divestment, in the becoming of the True, of all the predicates and agencies of knowledge. Mallarmé recounts how a vessel's shipwreck summons, for the swallowed captain who inscribes lack at the surface of the waves, the imminence of the abyss. Then, the Sky receives the Constellation. Beckett tells of how a larval creature, crawling in the dark with its sack, wrests from another, encountered by chance, the anonymous tale of what it is to live. Then comes the sharing of what Beckett calls 'the blessed days of blue'. Perhaps the only goal of my philosophy is to fully understand these two stories.

In 1995, I published a small book, *Beckett, l'increvable désir* (Paris: Hachette), where I soberly declared my debt. But the best account of my relation to his prose is in an English-language book edited by Nina Power and Alberto Toscano, *On Beckett* (Manchester: Clinamen Press, 2003). All of my texts on Beckett, translated by the editors, are contained within it, along with some very fine studies, notably that of Andrew Gibson, a subtle delimitation of the resonances between literature and philosophy and of the ethical effect of these resonances.

V. Intro. 1.

Let us recall the basic parameters of the most important mathematical paradigm for *Being and Event*. In 1940, Gödel proves the coherence with the axioms of set theory of the statement according to which, if an infinite set has cardinality κ (it has κ elements), the cardinality of the set of its parts is κ +, the successor of κ. The excess of the parts of a multiple over this multiple can therefore be minimal (from κ to the quantity that comes right after κ). In 1963, Paul Cohen proves that it is equally coherent with the axioms of set theory for the set of the parts of an infinite set to have a more or less arbitrary cardinality, in any case one that is as large as one wants. The excess of parts over elements is ultimately *without measure*.

On all these issues, there now exists a clear and comprehensive book in French: Jean-Louis Krivine, *Théorie des ensembles* (Paris: Cassini, 1998).

V.1.1.

The example of the Paris Commune was the object of a talk in which I unfolded, with far greater precision than I do here, the whole labyrinth of interpretations of this brief but astonishing political sequence. The text of this talk is now included in the volume *Polemics*.

V.1.2.

Paying a 'visit' to Rousseau is an almost obligatory exercise for the contemporary French philosopher. This is for at least four different reasons; thinking through their convergence can provide us, as we shall see, with a key to our present.

1. Rousseau communicates with our epoch (after Nietzsche, let's say) through his inflexible anti-philosophy. He was persecuted by those who in the eighteenth century were called the *philosophes*. He railed against them, privileging, in opposition to conceptual architectures (Leibniz), as well as abstract ironies (Voltaire), a sensory evidence and political exigency that brought him close to popular consciousness and its organic intellectuals, as was blindingly clear between 1792 and 1794.

2. Rousseau is very close to us by dint of the diagonal approach to languages which he proposes, his advocacy of a complete de-specialization of knowledge. Abrupt, abstract and formulaic in *The Social Contract*, dramatic and elegiac in *The New Heloise*, enchantingly supple in the *Reveries*, the inventor of an intimate eloquence in *The Confessions*, insistent and

549

didactic in *Émile*, he adjusts his writing to the various registers of thought, thereby exhibiting, in the phrase itself, the multiple of Ideas.

3. Under cover of morality, Rousseau inaugurates the modern critique of representation. We must take entirely seriously—as Philippe Lacoue-Labarthe has done in his *Poétique de l'histoire* (Paris: Galilée, 2002; in English see 'The Poetics of History', translated by Hector Kollias, *Pli* 10 (2000))—his polemic against the theatre, namely in the *Lettre à D'Alembert sur les spectacles*. One of the strengths of this text, which Lacoue-Labarthe approaches in his own language (that of a history of mimesis) is that it puts forward an indissoluble link between political corruption and the spectacle (in this regard, Debord didn't invent anything new). But Lacoue-Labarthe profoundly recasts the significance of Rousseau's examination of the theatre. He deciphers in it the real reasons that led Heidegger to his scandalous underestimation of Rousseau's significance. And he shows why the conventional reading of this genius 'lays itself open to misrecognizing, to different degrees, that which makes for the absolute originality of Rousseau's thought, which is his thinking of the *origin*'.

4. Rousseau anticipated the modern dialectic between the private and the public. He understood that a self-exposition, a declaration, was inevitable the moment that politics concerned anyone at all, rather than a specialized class (nobles or politicians). The generic character of the general will, its anonymity, presupposes the personal commitment of all those who decide on its content. So there is no 'contradiction' between the Rousseau of *The Social Contract*, the living armature of the thinking of politics, and the somewhat wayward Rousseau, handing out a tract on the streets of Paris justifying himself against his *philosophe* persecutors.

Lacoue-Labarthe has woven all these motifs together. As a subtle and innovative Heideggerian, he has oriented them towards the historial function of Rousseau's verdicts on the connection between politics and representation, as well as towards his dream of a 'spontaneous' popular theatricality (the civic Feast) that would 'almost' no longer be theatre. Lacoue-Labarthe glosses on this 'almost', a gloss through which he continues, via Rousseau, his long peregrination through the arcana of the 'theatrical' destiny of the West.

If we instead wish to turn towards a theoretician (and practitioner) of the theatre who is entirely free of the perennial 'critique of representation' and thus free, if you will, of Rousseau and Heidegger (and Lacoue-Labarthe. . .), we will read the most recent writings of François Regnault, which I publicly discussed with him during one of my seminars. There are two variegated volumes which combine the experience of the man of the theatre (actor, director, dramaturge, author) with the penetration of the Lacanian, breadth of knowledge with the oblique luminosity of style. They present a sort of discontinuous, stellar history of the theatre of the last few decades. See François Regnault, *Écrits sur le théâtre* (Arles: Actes Sud, 2002)—volume 1: *Équinoxes*; volume 2: *Solstices*.

V.2.

All of the quotations from Deleuze are taken from *Logic of Sense*, translated by Mark Lester with Charles Stivale (New York: Columbia University Press, 1990 [1969]).

I recounted the hostile, amicable, aggressive and evasive nature of that absence-laden bond between Gilles Deleuze and me in the first chapter of my *Deleuze: The Clamor of Being*, translated by Louise Burchill (Minneapolis: Minnesota University Press, 2000). The remainder of that book elucidates, point by point, the affinities and brutal caesuras between our two metaphysical setups. One will complement this reading with 'Of Life as a Name of Being, or, Deleuze's Vitalist Ontology', in *Theoretical Writings* (see the note below). It is also possible, of course, to find other transcriptions of talks—notably in London and Buenos Aires—which tackle the idea of a 'Deleuzian politics', or do real justice to Deleuze's staggering and very paradoxical philosophical work on the basis of cinema.

Once again, it is necessary to pay homage to François Wahl for being the first, in his preface to *Conditions* (Paris: Seuil, 1992), to have constructed a pertinent parallel between Deleuze and Badiou.

V.2.

Ten years after the death of Deleuze, an entire generation of young thinkers takes inspiration from him. I myself am linked to this generation in several ways. I am thinking especially of a whole host of Anglophone friends. I think of the organizers of the excellent English journal *Pli*, an expression of the fact that, at the University of Warwick, potent consequences were drawn from Deleuzian axioms: Alberto Toscano and Ray Brassier, who later became, among a thousand other things, my translators and exegetes, without ever freezing into any posture of dependence.

In particular, I owe to them the edition of a collection of texts, some of them previously unpublished, all written by me between 1990 and today.

This collection, entitled *Theoretical Writings* (London: Continuum, 2004), is the most effective direct introduction to my work in English.

Incidentally, the best indirect introduction (via studies by several authors) to my work in French was put together in 2001 by Charles Ramond, on the basis of a colloquium held in Bordeaux, under the title *Alain Badiou: Penser le multiple* (Paris: L'Harmattan, 2002). In it, you can find all kinds of remarkable texts, in particular by Balibar, Lazarus, Macherey, Meillassoux, Rancière, Salanskis and Ramond himself.

I am thinking of Simon Critchley, who welcomed me several times to the University of Essex, then to New York, and who, in several subtle studies, tries to institute a kind of discordant union or pacific tension between Levinas and me. This exercise exposes him to harsh disputes with other interpreters, namely the leading figure among my Anglophone 'connoisseurs', Peter Hallward, of whom I have already spoken.

I am thinking of Sam Gillespie, who came from the United States to join my other friends in England, a particularly acute and occasionally mordant analyst (see *The Mathematics of Novelty: Badiou's Minimalist Metaphysics*, Melbourne: re.press, 2008), whose intense work was interrupted by his death.

I am thinking of Justin Clemens and Oliver Feltham, who edited and skilfully introduced the collection *Infinite Thought* (London: Continuum, 2003). The former taught me a few things about myself in his study 'Letter on the Condition of Conditions for Alain Badiou' (*Communication and Cognition* 36, 1/2), the former tackled an immense task: the English translation of *Being and Event*.

And I think of many others: Steve Mailloux, Ken Reinhard... They should all know, whether named or not, that they changed my image— which for too long was very French in its distance and abstraction—of everything that originates from the old British Empire.

V.2.

The Differend, translated by Georges Van Den Abbeele (Minneapolis: Minnesota University Press, 1988) represents, to my mind, the point of equilibrium or maturity of Jean-François Lyotard's enterprise. Someone else with whom, for a long time, I did not have an easy relationship! I often dubbed him a modern sophist, and he regarded me as a Stalinist. One day, at the beginning of the 1980s, coming out of a philosophy department meeting at Paris VIII, we drove back from François Châtelet's home towards Montparnasse. It was pouring rain, so we stopped the car for a while by the sidewalk. A long conversation ensued, both abrupt and trusting, in the narrow confines of the vehicle. Later Lyotard compared it to a talk under a tent among warriors from the *Iliad*.

In 1983, coming out of a session of the seminar 'The Retreat of the Political', organized at the École Normale Supérieure by Sarah Kofman, Lacoue-Labarthe, Lyotard, Nancy and others, to which I was kindly invited (the content of my two interventions makes up my concise 1985 book, *Peut-on penser la politique?*, Paris: Seuil), Lyotard told me that he was publishing 'his' (only) book of philosophy, *The Differend*, and that it was my commentary he was waiting for. I accepted without further reflection, read the book, and wrote my commentary. See my article 'Custos, quid noctis?', *Critique* 480 (1984).

The untimely death of Lyotard affected me deeply. I think I explained why on the occasion of the homage paid to him by the Collège International de Philosophie, whose proceedings were published in 2001: *Jean-François Lyotard, l'exercice du différend* (Paris: PUF). My contribution features in this collection under the title 'Le gardiennage du matin' (The Guardianship of Morning).

V.2.

The text of Lacan from which I draw the equation religion = meaning is none other than the letter in which he announced, in January 1980, the dissolution of the École Française de Psychanalyse, which he had founded sixteen years earlier. The entirety of Lacan's marvellous subjective style is contained in the opening lines of the two texts of foundation and dissolution. In 1964, 'I hereby found—as alone as I have always been in my relation to the psychoanalytic cause—the Ecole Française de Psychanalyse, whose direction, concerning which nothing at present prevents me from answering for, I shall undertake during the next four years to assure'. And, in 1980, 'I speak without the slightest hope—specifically of making myself understood. I know that I do so—by adding thereto whatever it entails of the unconscious'. Saint-John Perse comes to mind: 'Solitude! our immoderate partisans boasted of our ways, but our thoughts were already encamped beneath other walls' (*Anabasis*, translated by T.S. Eliot). The two texts by Lacan are included in *Autres écrits*. They were translated by Jeffrey Mehlman, under the respective titles of 'Founding Act' and 'Letter of Dissolution', in *October* 40 (1987).

V.2.

For a very different interpretation of the Deleuzian category of the event—appreciative and radically Spinozist, albeit absolutely modern—see the fine book by François Zourabichvili, *Deleuze, une philosophie de l'événement* (Paris: PUF, 1996).

V.3.

The axiom of foundation is a 'special' axiom in set theory, which is like a requirement of the heterogeneous (or of the Other) within every multiple. This axiom effectively demands that among the elements of a multiple, elements that are themselves multiples, there be at least one that contains an element that is not an element of the initial multiple. In other words, in the composition of that which composes a multiple, there is (at least) one element that is alien to the 'fabric' of this multiple, an element marked by alterity.

In formal terms, we will say that, given a multiple A, there always exists $a \in A$ such that one x of a does not belong to A:

$$(\exists a)\ [a \in A \text{ and } (\exists x)\ (x \in a) \text{ and } \neg(x \in A)]$$

This foreign element x will be said to *found* A. This means that a multiple is only founded to the extent that it depends in one point on the Other: on what does not belong to it.

The consequence of the axiom of foundation is the impossibility of self-belonging. In effect, if $A \in A$, the singleton of A, that is $\{A\}$, the set whose sole element is A, is not founded: the only element of $\{A\}$ being A, if $A \in A$, since we also have $A \in \{A\}$, no heterogeneous term appears.

VI. Epigraph

Taken from Natacha Michel, *Le Jour où le temps a attendu son heure* (Paris: Seuil, 1990) (The Day when Time Waited for its Hour). About this very beautiful novel, whose descriptive and metaphorical power weaves an enchanted matter (the book fastens the flux of the prose to something like a pure idea of summer), we could say that it is a novel of points. For its theme is that of knowing whether one can entirely superimpose the political conversion of the 'no' (revolt, strike. . .) into a 'yes' (the invention of a new idea of politics), on one hand, and amorous conversion (the declaration, through which a harsh and perpetual 'no' turns into an ecstatic 'yes'), on the other. So that these two crucial examples of the appearance of the infinite before the judgment of the Two—to concede and to consent—are entwined in the poem of an evening, on a terrace where the marine horizon amicably signals to those who, in the blue of summer, have committed their existence.

It's worth noting that that one of the nine novellas that make up *Imposture et séparation* (Paris: Seuil, 1986) is entitled 'The "No" of Charles Scépante'. It is the blade of the yes/no knife that is sharpened in writing by the patient grindstone, incrusted by diamonds, which Natacha Michel turns.

VI.1.1.

Sartre was like an absolute Master during my whole early life as a philosopher. The first more or less contemporary conceptual text that sparked my enthusiasm was *Sketch of a Theory of the Emotions* (London: Routledge, 2001 [1939]). During the *khâgne*, the preparation for the entry exam to the École Normale Supérieure, my professor, Étienne Borne, who thought me very gifted, regretted the fact that I indulged in pastiches of *Being and Nothingness*. During my years at the École Normale Supérieure, day after day, in between games of flipper (we used to call it the 'zinzin'), I debated with two convinced Sartreans, Emmanuel Terray and Pierre Verstraeten. The second became what he already was, an exacting and innovative 'specialist' of his teacher's thinking. His book on Sartre's theatre, *Violence et éthique* (Paris: Gallimard, 1972), remains a model of the genre. As for the first, having become an anthropologist, he mixed studies on Africa (among which his massive thesis on the kingdom of the Abron), with essays on our shared passion—politics—and more intimate writings that reflect his secret, consuming relation to literature and poetry, as well as an 'existential' sensibility even more difficult to divine. One should read the very singular books he has devoted to Germany: *Ombres berlinoises* (Paris: Odile Jacob, 1996), and *Une passion allemande* (Paris: Seuil, 1994).

I ask myself which of us three has remained faithful to those explosive and terrible years (the Algerian war was taking place), in which we scrutinized line by line the *Critique of Dialectical Reason*, published in 1960 (Paris: Gallimard; translated into English by Alan Sheridan-Smith, and introduced by Fredric Jameson, London: Verso, 2004), after having attended the 1959 premiere of *The Condemned of Altona*. Terray has always maintained that he read *Being and Event* as fully in line with, precisely, the *Critique*. Verstraeten instead lamented from early on that I was so attracted by 'hard' structuralism and the formalism of mathemes. As for me, it is especially in politics that I object to their attitudes. After the debacle of 'real socialism', Verstraeten rallied to the democratic order. To my great outrage, he approved the bombing of Belgrade by NATO's American planes. As for Terray, I find him so wedded to realism that in the end he seems to have given up on the heroic communist voluntarism whose spirit animated the Sartre of the 1960s. He resembles those temperate progressives, firm on a number of questions, but still internal to the dominant political logic (capitalist-parliamentarianism, right and left, 'movements', etc.). I see him, for instance, as occupying the same space as Étienne Balibar, who recently told me that the only important philosophical question today is that of right, or Yves Duroux, both of whom have always been convinced anti-Sartreans. See *La Politique dans la caverne* (Paris: Seuil, 1990). In this book, Terray explicitly takes sides with the sophists against Plato, in the name of democratic immanence against despotic transcendence. This goes to show that after almost fifty years of comradeship, friendship, remoteness, reunions, that which had been sealed by our common reference to Sartre has mutated into positions which are situated, at least philosophically speaking, on opposing sides. As Mao said: 'One divides into two'. This doesn't in the least impede friendship, which has no truck with the One.

VI.1.3.

I love the fact that in 2004, aged 97, Oscar Niemeyer, one of the two main creators of Brasilia (but not of the astonishing master plan in the form of a bird, dreamed up by Lucio Costa) declared: 'Once a communist, always a communist'. In the conception of Brasilia—and of almost all of Niemeyer's projects—there is a very potent inscription of signs, measuring up to the earth and the sky. I have always been struck in Greek temples by this desire to treat as equals the horizon, altitude, the air and the wind; above all in the Parthenon, whose appropriateness to its site—whose terrestrial exact-ness—is breathtaking. Niemeyer is like a Greek communist. Like Plato, after all.

Which brings me back to where I started. Niemeyer's architecture, egali-tarian as a matter of principle—like that of his teacher Le Corbusier—is nonetheless entirely alien to democratic materialism; it wants triumphal affirmations. This brings to mind the American philosopher Richard Rorty's declaration of the 'priority of democracy to philosophy'. It was by declaring the opposite that Plato—moving beyond the poetic speech of Heraclitus/Parmenides and the rhetorical relativism of the sophists— founded the singularity of philosophy. The unsparing critique of the Athenian democratic paradigm in Book VIII of the *Republic* is not an add-on, some kind of reactionary outburst. It participates in the construction of the very first philosophemes. Yes, philosophy is more important than every historical form of power, and therefore more important than any established 'democracy'. Today, it is far more important than capitalist-parliamentarianism, the mandatory form for the administration of phenomena in our 'West'. That is why, ever since Plato, philosophy is destined to communism. What is communism? The political name of the egalitarian discipline of truths.

VI.2.

Kierkegaard is the most garrulous among the anti-philosophers, but they all are, since they need to make the details of their existence count as proof of the deconstruction to which they submit the great edifices of philosophy. See in Rousseau, against the clique of the philosophers, the *Confessions*, or *Rousseau Judge of Saint-Jacques*; in Nietzsche, against Wagner, the last writings, *The Case of Wagner*, and all of *Ecce Homo*. To get the better of Hegel, Kierkegaard must turn the pitiful episode of his own betrothal to Regine into an existential feuilleton. In that monstrous outpouring which is *Either/Or*—a masterpiece nonetheless—'The Seducer's Diary' and 'The Aesthetic Validity of Marriage', three hundred very dense pages, are the speculative projection of microscopic vicissitudes. But Kierkegaard remains an unsurpassable master when it comes to choice, anxiety, repetition and the infinite. All quotations are taken from *Either/Or*, volume 2, translated by Walter Lowrie (Princeton: Princeton University Press, 1959) and *Concluding Unscientific Postscript*, translated by Walter Lowrie and David F. Swenson (Princeton: Princeton University Press, 1968).

VI.3.2.

The category of the interior allows us to obtain in a very intuitive manner the category of *open* set, which is used more generally in topology. Given a topology on a referential set E, a part A of E is an open (for the topology in question) if *A* is identical to its interior. That is, if **Int**(*A*) = (*A*). In other words, *A* is open because nothing separates its exterior from its interior. It is a part without a boundary.

In philosophy, the open is a major ontological category from Bergson to Deleuze—via Heidegger, of course. I do not intend here to undertake the examination that its metaphorical usage deserves, which can only attain some modicum of discipline if it is sifted through the matheme. The contemporary dossier on this question would need to be compiled, in my view, by scrupulously comparing the usage of the adjective 'open' (open morality, open religion, the Saint, the Mystic) in *The Two Sources of Morality and Religion*, trans. R. Ashley Audra and Cloudesley Brereton (Notre Dame: University of Notre Dame Press, 1977 [1932]) and Heidegger's critical discussion of the use made of the noun 'the open' (*das Offene*) in the eighth of the *Duino Elegies* by Rilke. See Heidegger's 1946 text 'What are Poets For?', in *Poetry, Language, Thought*, translated by Albert Hofstadter (New York: Harper & Row, 1971).

The most interesting point undoubtedly has to do with the rather flagrantly normative value accorded to 'opening'. Today, who would dare to flaunt—as many ancient Greeks and classics did—the virtues of the closed? Who doesn't claim to be open, if not to all winds, which is the case for the majority, then at least to the Other, to races, different sexualities, the youth, the sea air, abortion and the marriage of priests? 'Any more open than me and you'd be dead', says the petit bourgeois, who deep down is fearful, cosseted by his comfort and terrified by the first 'other' he runs into (a young woman with a headscarf, for instance). The somewhat closed attitude of some is to be preferred to this kind of convivial openness. But let us leave aside the discomfiting destiny of terms. A painstaking *disputatio* on the open could take its cue from Giorgio Agamben's *The Open: Man and Animal*, translated by Kevin Attell (Stanford: Stanford University Press, 2004). As usual, Agamben, taking all sorts of lexical precautions, carefully orients his thought towards his recurrent theme: being as weakness, as presentational poverty, as a power preserved from the glory of its act. His latent Christianity generates a kind of modern poetics, in which the open is pure exposition to a substance-less becoming. Likewise, in politics, the hero is the one brought back to his pure being as a transitory living being, the one who may be killed without judgment, the *homo sacer* of the Romans, the *muselmann* of the extermination camp (the expression was recorded by Primo Levi). The properly human community, communism, is what may come, never what is there. And Saint Paul, despite his foundational role, his assurance and his militancy is brought back—via a single opaque phrase from the *Epistle to the Romans*—to the tremblings of messianism, in a paradoxical kinship with Walter Benjamin. Without a doubt, nothing makes it easier to judge what sets us apart (notwithstanding our friendship) than the gap between our respective books on the apostle. This is already evident from the titles: *The Time that Remains*, translated by Patricia Dailey (Stanford: Stanford University Press, 2005) for Giorgio, and for my part *Saint Paul: The Foundation of Universalism*, translated by Ray Brassier (Stanford: Stanford University Press, 2003). Agamben, this Franciscan of ontology, prefers, to the affirmative becoming of truths, the delicate, almost secret persistence of life, what remains to one who no longer has anything; this forever sacrificed 'bare life', both humble and essential, which conveys everything of which we—crushed by the crass commotion of powers—are capable of in terms of sense.

VI.3.2.

Topological structures are generally defined by axioms that bear directly on open parts, or, more succinctly, on opens. The advantage of beginning with the notion of interior is that its axiomatization is very intuitive. Starting from the notion of interior, 'open set' is a natural consequence, as we saw in the previous note: it is a set in which nothing—no 'boundary'—separates its interior from its exterior. This means that it is identical to its interior. If we begin instead with the notion of open, we find ourselves in an operational field devoid of immediate clarity. And the concept of interior of A (the union of the opens included in A) also loses its self-evidence. That is why I follow here the exposition in Rasiowa and Sikorski's canonical book (see note II.3.3).

VII. Epigraph

These verses are taken from 'Maritime Ode' (1915), in *Poems of Fernando Pessoa*, edited and translated by Edwin Honig and Susan M. Brown (San Francisco: City Lights, 1998). In French, it was translated in 1943, and revised in 1955, by Armand Guibert (Montpellier: Fata Morgana, 1995). Whether we are dealing with Fernando Pessoa, or with that astonishing discoverer, transcriber, and donor, Armand Guibert, the canonical reference is Judith Balso, to whom I also owe the discovery—so late!—of the one who I now regard as the greatest poet of the twentieth century. Balso shows how Pessoa's poetic devices sublate a failing metaphysics, and how the cut of the language, split between several distinct poets (Campos, Caeiro, Reis. . .), aims to illuminate the intimate link between the poem's declaration and the fleeting multiplicity of being. This demonstration is encapsulated in her *Pessoa, le passeur métaphysique* (Paris: Seuil, 2006).

On Armand Guibert see, also by Balso, the article 'Le paradoxe du traducteur: un hommage à Armand Guibert', *Quadrant* 16 (1999).

VII.1.2

To get the real flavour of the abstractions that will follow, it is necessary to have an image of the period in mind, and to inscribe within it the young Évariste Galois. This has often been done, but generally to the detriment of a genuine grasp of his mathematical genius. Galois has been portrayed as a kind of Rimbaud of the sciences, without gauging the absolute difference separating the romantic flights of the years 1820–40 from the heroic despair which in 1870–72 permeates the Paris Commune and its repression.

It is true that in the background of Galois's creation, there are the Three Glorious Days of July 1830, the Republican banquets, the expulsion from the École Normale, the trial and imprisonment, the duel to the death. . . And all this before the age of twenty.

Nevertheless, the real historical basis of this adolescence is a profound social mutation, a major upheaval of the social fabric, as testified by the novels of Balzac, but also by the first 'proletarian' writings, utopian communisms, clandestine associations. . . These fascinating developments—whose most dazzling synthesis will be provided by Marx between 1843 and 1850—have been incorporated into contemporary philosophy by Jacques Rancière. Read *The Nights of Labor: The Worker's Dream in Nineteenth Century France*, translated by John Drury (Philadelphia: Temple University Press, 1989). But even better, that truly stunning book, *The Ignorant Schoolmaster: Five Lessons in Intellectual Emancipation*, translated, with an introduction, by Kristin Ross (Stanford: Stanford University Press, 1991), where Rancière puts his conception of equality to the test of Jacotot's strange notions of pedagogy. Rancière's conception of equality inspired me, and still does, because of its axiomatic power: equality is never the goal, but the principle. It is not obtained, but declared. And we can call 'politics' the consequences, in the historical world, of this declaration.

Of course, I cannot endorse Rancière's manner of examining the logic of consequences, that is of examining politics. It is too historicist for my taste.

I harshly criticized him on this point in my *Metapolitics*, translated by Jason Barker (London: Verso, 2005). But make no mistake: it is on the basis of a very real affinity that this unending dispute takes place. After all, who else can be mentioned, from this generation of philosophers, who has similarly maintained the founding categories of the politics of emancipation in all their speculative and historical verve? I would say the same for Rancière's writings on literature and cinema. As though I had passed through them in a dream, they are both familiar and remote. For example, I have nothing to object to his brief *Mallarmé* from 1996; it is simultaneously exact as to the letter of the text, plausible in its interpretation, and written—as always with Rancière—in a prose at once appealing and assured, like an essay emerging from some kind of inner eighteenth century. Having said that, 'my' Mallarmé (from *Theory of the Subject, Conditions, Being and Event, Handbook of Inaesthetics*. . .) is not the same. The difference is already patent in the subtitle chosen by Rancière: *The Politics of the Siren*. I would certainly have written 'The Ontology of the Siren', for I see no politics in the 'so white hair trailing' [*si blanc cheveu qui traîne*], no more than in the 'impatient terminal scales' [*impatientes squames ultimes*]. But then Rancière demonstrates, in a brilliant talk, that I am torn between two contradictory Mallarmés, that my current Mallarmé disowns the one of twenty years ago. . .

I think these complex crossing paths are governed by two very simple things. First, we have kept the same philosophical fidelity to the 'red' sequence that goes from 1965 to 1980, albeit with completely different references. Second, History separates us. Rancière still believes in it (while criticizing its current usage), and I not at all. Just like René Char, I can say that 'indifference to history' is one of the 'extremities of my arc'.

Have we strayed far from Galois? Not entirely. What sets Galois apart from Rimbaud—who decides point blank to stop writing, to bring to an end 'one of his follies', poetry—is his relentless optimism, the conviction, present until the very eve of the duel in which he will die, that everything remains to be done, that mathematics can be founded again, and that he himself is capable of doing it. He thereby channels the marvellous Promethean ideology of his epoch. So it is also necessary—perhaps Rancière is right?—to incorporate Galois into History, deciphering him in terms of that French version of romanticism, which was the rational activism of the partisans of Progress.

Having said that, we cannot leave Évariste Galois without mentioning the study that Jules Vuillemin devoted to him, under the heading

'Galois's Theory', in pages 222–330 of the monumental first volume of his *Philosophie de l'algèbre* (Paris: PUF, 1962). A first volume which, as often happens with such colossal philosophical endeavours, was never followed by a second.

Philosophie de l'algèbre gives the fullest expression to the virtues and shortcomings of this philosopher, at once unique and disappointing: murky technical expositions, forced speculative analogies, striking formulas, and a stubbornness that pays off in the end. Vuillemin's fundamental idea is that Galois provides us with the paradigm required to think 'the general notion of operation'. This makes possible an nth—but nonetheless fruitful—revisiting of the theory of abstraction in Kant and his successors.

Let's consider two characteristic passages. The first, on Galois's finding (by 'permutation' we should understand the literal results of the movements that replace certain letters by others, by 'substitution', these movements themselves, to the extent that they can be made out as movements):

> [In Galois's approach] the operation is as though abstracted from its result: as Galois puts it, permutations designate substitutions, but since I may combine any permutation with any other, this freedom indicates that in actual fact I operate with substitutions and not permutations themselves. In other words, it means that the elements of the group are always operations, even though these operations may be designated by their results.

The second, on the application of this finding to the examination of philosophical systems:

> To examine if the faculties of knowledge can give rise to a group structure is first of all to examine if they can be regarded strictly speaking as operations.

VII.2.

All the quotes from Lacan are taken from *Autres écrits*.

VII.2.

The Lacanian most prone to injecting the notions of the master into the most varied 'bodies' of contemporary appearing is no doubt Slavoj Žižek, whose lack of affiliation to any group of psychoanalysts grants him a freedom which he delights in abusing: jokes, repetitions, a captivating passion for the worst flicks, quick-witted pornography, conceptual journalism, calculated histrionics, puns. . . In this perpetual dramatization of his thought, animated by a deliberate desire for bad taste, he ultimately resembles Lacan. There are also in him precious residues of Stalinist culture. I too am rather familiar with that register, so we gladly articulate our relations in its framework. Together, we make up a politburo of two which decides who will be the first to shoot the other, after having wrung from him a deeply-felt self-criticism.

But as in Lacan, behind the modicum of infancy which language allows, there are urgent matrices of thought, modules of sorts that can be readily implanted in cinema: *The Art of the Ridiculous Sublime: On David Lynch's Lost Highway* (2000); in musical theatre: *Opera's Second Death*, with Mladen Dolar (2001); in the accidents of politics (essays on the Yugoslav conflict, on 11 September, on the Iraq war. . .) or in its essence (*The Ticklish Subject: The Absent Centre of Political Ontology*, 1999). Beneath all this lies the cement platform which holds up the entire spectacle: the incorporation of Lacan into great German Idealism, or the modern recasting of this idealism, via Lacan, in order to describe with virtuosity all the sexualizable symptoms of our factitious universe. See his fine book *The Indivisible Remainder* (London: Verso, 1996).

My debate with Slavoj Žižek concerns the real. Following Lacan, he has proposed a concept of it, which is so ephemeral, so brutally punctual, that it is impossible to uphold its consequences. The effects of this kind of frenzied upsurge, in which the real rules over the comedy of our symptoms, are ultimately indiscernible from those of scepticism.

Having said that, we are essentially united in the face of the crookedness which prevails in the academy. Along with many who have been mentioned in these pages, we both belong to the last faction of the antihumanists, of the partisans of desire at the risk of the Law. The future is in our hands.

VII. Scholium.

All the quotations from Mao Tse-tung are drawn from the two most important texts written in the initial sequence of the Red Army's existence, namely in Autumn 1928. The first is 'Why is it that Red Political Power can Exist in China?', the second is 'The Struggle in the Chingkang (Jinggang) Mountains'. They can be found in the first volume of Mao's *Selected Works*.

(Unless in common usage, such as Chiang Kai-shek, the romanisation of Chinese terms has been changed to pinyin.)

What memories of the year 1969, when we closely studied these magnificent texts! May '68 is an ambiguous episode, situated between the dismal festive and sexual ideology that still encumbers us and the far more original levy of a direct alliance between students and young workers. It is in the period between Autumn 1968 and Autumn 1979—from the creation of Maoist factory cells to the strikes at Sonacotra—that the truly creative consequences of the second aspect of May '68 work themselves out. As happens in practically all the becomings of a subject of truth, this set of consequences—which we can call 'Maoist politics'—strongly prevails, in terms of both thinking and universality, over the event 'May '68', which lends it its subjective possibility.

C.0.

In Julien Gracq's *The Opposing Shore*, translated by Richard Howard (London: Harvill, 1997 [1951]), this same old Danielo, of whom we spoke in VI.1.1, examines in his own way the question 'What is it to Live?' at the level of a city.

C.8.

The book by Quentin Meillassoux, begun several years ago, incessantly redrafted and transformed, will appear soon, or so I hope. Its title will certainly be *Divine Inexistence*. But Meillassoux has already published an excellent short book that can serve as an introduction to his thought: *After Finitude*, translated by Ray Brassier (London: Continuum, 2008). The title should not mislead: this is not some kind of prophetic fantasy. Meillassoux is the advocate of a novel and implacable rationalism, a rationalism of contingency. His norm is the clear argument: everything should be demonstrable. And everything can be inferred from a single principle, the principle of factuality: it is necessary that the existence and laws of the world be contingent.

C.9.

The Descartes quotations are taken from two famous letters, which also indicate his consistency when it comes to the doctrine of the 'creation of eternal truths'—which was so fiercely disputed by a number of his friends and so harshly mocked by his enemies, namely Leibniz. See the letter to Father Mersenne of 15 April 1630 and the letter to Father Mesland of 2 May 1644, in *The Philosophical Writings of Descartes*, vol. 3: *The Correspondence*, edited by John Cottingham et al. (Cambridge: Cambridge University Press, 1991).

C.10.

'Make yourself, patiently or impatiently, into the most irreplaceable of beings' is the maxim that can be found at the end of Gide's *Fruits of the Earth*, translated by B. A. Lenski (New York: Vintage, 2002 [1897]). This post-Nietzschean eloquence *à la française* enchanted me during my adolescence, all the more because my mother was very responsive to it. Through this kind of text, I traced a diagonal line between the fifties and the twenties, between two post-war periods, between the 'Zazous' of 1945–50 and the crazy years 1920–25. My youth resonated with that of my parents, the Charleston, silent cinema, convertibles, flappers, the new eroticism, surrealism, 78s. . . From the thirties onward, the clash between what Sylvain Lazarus has called the 'three regimes of the century'—parliamentarianism, fascism and communism—revealed the little real contained by these phenomena in comparison to the invention that, after 1914, dominated the century: total war, both inner and outer.

STATEMENTS, DICTIONARIES, BIBLIOGRAPHY, ICONOGRAPHY AND INDEX

The 66 Statements of *Logics of Worlds*

The first occurrences in each statement of a given technical term are followed by an asterisk indicating that the term is to be found in the 'Dictionary of Concepts', which is placed after the statements.

PREFACE. DEMOCRATIC MATERIALISM AND MATERIALIST DIALECTIC

Statement 1. Axiom of the materialist dialectic: 'There are only bodies* and languages, except that there are truths*'.

This axiom is disjoined from that of democratic materialism: 'There are only bodies and languages'.

Statement 2. The production of a truth* is the same thing as the subjective production of a present*.

Statement 3. Produced as a pure present*, a truth* is nonetheless eternal.

BOOK I. FORMAL THEORY OF THE SUBJECT (META-PHYSICS)

Statement 4. A theory of the subject* cannot but be formal.

Statement 5. A subject* is a formalism borne by a body*.

Statement 6. A subjective formalism* is conditioned by the trace* of an event*, which is written ε, and of the existence, in the world* affected by this event, of a new body*, written C.

Statement 7. A subjective formalism* is the articulation of operations drawn from a set of five possible operations: subordination (written—), erasure (/), consequence ($\Rightarrow$), extinction (=) and negation ($\neg$). These are the operations that take hold of a body*.

Statement 8. The result of the action of a subject* (or of a formalized body*) concerns a new present*, written π.

Statement 9. There exist three figures of the subject*: the faithful subject*, the reactive subject* and the obscure subject*. Their mathemes are the following:

Faithful subject:

$$\frac{\varepsilon}{\cancel{c}} \Rightarrow \pi$$

Reactive subject:

$$\frac{\neg\varepsilon}{\dfrac{\varepsilon}{\cancel{c}} \Rightarrow \pi} \Rightarrow \cancel{\pi}$$

Obscure subject:

$$\frac{C \Rightarrow (\neg\varepsilon \Rightarrow \neg\cancel{c})}{\pi}$$

Statement 10. There are four subjective destinations: production, denial, occultation and resurrection. In each case, we are dealing with a kind of present* π. Produced by the faithful subject*, denied by the reactive subject*, occulted by the obscure subject* and reincorporated into a new present by a second fidelity.

Statement 11. We can cross the three subjective figures, the four destinations, the four generic procedures*—love, politics, arts and sciences—and the affects that correspond to them. We thereby obtain the battery of twenty concepts required for a phenomenology of truths*:

	POLITICS	ARTS	LOVE	SCIENCES
Affect	*Enthusiasm*	*Pleasure*	*Happiness*	*Joy*
Name of the present	*Sequence*	*Configuration*	*Enchantment*	*Theory*
Denial	*Reaction*	*Academicism*	*Conjugality*	*Pedagogism*
Occultation	*Fascism*	*Iconoclasm*	*Possessive fusion*	*Obscurantism*
Resurrection	*Communist invariants*	*Neo-classicism*	*Second encounter*	*Renaissance*

BOOK II. GREATER LOGIC, 1. THE TRANSCENDENTAL

Statement 12. The Whole has no being. Or, the concept of universe is inconsistent.

Statement 13. No multiple, except for the void, can be thought in the singularity of its being without relying on the previously thought being of at least one other multiple.

Statement 14. A multiple is only thinkable in the singularity of its appearance to the extent that it is inscribed in a world*.

Statement 15. To think a multiple such as inscribed in a world*, or to think the being-there* of a multiple, presupposes the formulation of a logic* of appearing* which is not identical to the (mathematical) ontology* of the pure multiple.

Statement 16. A logic* of appearing*, that is the logic of a world*, comes down to a unified scale for the (intrinsic, subject-less) measure of identities and differences and for the operations that depend on this measure. It is necessarily an order-structure*, making sense of expressions like 'more or less identical', and, more generally, of comparisons of intensities. We call this order, and the operations associated to it, the transcendental* of a situation (or of a world). The transcendental is designated by T, and the order that structures T by the conventional symbol $\leq$. For a multiple, 'appearing' means being seized by the logic of a world, that is being indexed* to the transcendental of that world.

Statement 17. The transcendental* organization of a given world* makes it possible to think the non-appearance of a multiple within it. This means that there exists, in the transcendental order-structure, a minimal* degree*. It is written as μ.

Statement 18. The transcendental* organization of a given world* authorizes the evaluation of what there is in common in the being-there* of two multiples that co-appear in that world. This implies that, in the transcendental, given two degrees* of intensity there exists a third which is simultaneously 'the closest' to the other two. This degree measures what we call the conjunction* of two beings-there*. It is written as $\cap$.

Statement 19. The transcendental* organization of a given world* assures the cohesion of the being-there* of any part of that world. This implies that, to the degrees* of appearance in the world of the multiples which constitute that part, there corresponds a degree which both dominates them all and is the smallest degree to do so. This degree, which synthesizes, in the closest possible manner, the appearing* of a region of the world, is called the envelope* of that region. If the region is B, the envelope of B is written as ΣB.

Statement 20. In the order of appearing*, synthesis, which is global and capable of infinity (the envelope*), prevails over analysis, which is local and finite (conjunction*). Consequently, the conjunction of a singular apparent and an envelope is itself an envelope. In other terms, $\cap$ is distributive* with regard to Σ.

Statement 21. In the order of appearing*, there exists a transcendental* measure of the degree of necessary connection between two beings*. This measure is called the dependence* of one of the beings towards the other, or, more exactly, the dependence of a transcendental degree* of appearing with regard to another. The dependence of degree q with regard to degree p is written $p \Rightarrow q$.

Statement 22. Given a world* and a definite apparent* of that world—which is accordingly given with its degree* of appearance—there always exists another apparent whose degree of appearance is the greatest of all those which, in their appearing, have nothing in common with the first (or, whose conjunction* with the first is equal to the minimum*).

In other words, in the transcendental* of a world, every degree admits of a reverse*.

Statement 23. The conjunction* of a degree* and its reverse* is always equal to a minimum*. And the reverse of the reverse of a degree is always greater than or equal to the degree itself. This is written, for the first property, as $p \cap \neg\, p = \mu$; and for the second, as $p \leq \neg\, \neg\, p$.

Statement 24. There exists, in the transcendental* of any world*, a maximal* degree of appearance. This maximal degree is the reverse* of the minimal* degree. It is written M, and $M = \neg\, \mu$.

Statement 25. The reverse* of the reverse of the minimal* degree* is equal to this same degree. That is, $\neg\, \neg\, \mu = \mu$. By the same token, the reverse of the reverse of the maximal* degree is equal to the maximal degree. That is, $\neg\, \neg\, M = M$. In these particular cases, double negation is equivalent to affirmation. When it comes to double negation, the minimum and maximum behave in a classical manner.

Statement 26. For a given world*, ordinary logic*, that is formal propositional and predicate calculus, receives its truth-values and the signification of its operators from the transcendental* of that world alone. Accordingly, ordinary logic, or smaller logic, is a simple consequence of transcendental logic, or Greater Logic*.

Statement 27. The world* of ontology*, that is the historically-constituted mathematics of the pure multiple, is a classical* world.

BOOK III. GREATER LOGIC, 2. THE OBJECT

Statement 28. The transcendental* degree* which measures, in a given world*, the identity of one apparent* to another, also measures the identity of this other apparent to the first: the function of transcendental indexing* is symmetrical.

Statement 29. The intensity of co-appearance, or conjunction*, in a given world*, of the identity of one apparent* to another, and then of this other apparent to a third, cannot surpass the degree* of identity that can be directly evaluated between the first and the third. With regard to conjunction, transcendental indexing* obeys a condition of triangular inequality.

Statement 30. An apparent* in a world* cannot exist* in that world less than the extent to which it is identical to another apparent.

Statement 31. If an element of a multiple inexists* in a world*, it is only minimally identical to another element of the same multiple.

Statement 32. Take a world* and an apparent* of that world. Take a fixed element of the multiple which constitutes the being of this apparent. The function that assigns, to every element of this multiple, the transcendental degree* of its identity to the fixed element is an atom* of appearing. This atom is called the real atom* prescribed by the fixed element.

Statement 33. Postulate of materialism: 'For any given world*, every atom of that world is a real atom*'.

Statement 34. Every localization* of an atom on a transcendental degree* is also an atom.

Statement 35. The atoms* of appearing prescribed by two ontologically distinct elements of an object* are nonetheless identical if and only if the degree of transcendental* identity of these two elements is equal to their degree of existence* (which is therefore the same for both). Or: if and only if they exist to the exact extent that they are identical.

Statement 36. Two elements of an object* are compatible* if and only if their degree of identity is equal to the conjunction* of their existences*.

Statement 37. If we identify the elements of the support-set* of an object* with the atoms* they prescribe, there exists over every object an order-relation*—which is called onto-logical—written <. This order-relation can receive three equivalent definitions:

- *algebraic*: two elements are compatible* and the existence* of the first is lesser than or equal to that of the second;
- *transcendental*: the existence of the first element is equal to its degree of transcendental* identity to the second;
- *topological*: the first element is equal to the localization* of the second on the existence of the first.

Statement 38a. Fundamental theorem of atomic logic*. Appearing* in a world* as an object* retroactively affects the multiple-being which supports this object. In effect, every homogeneous region of this object admits of a synthesis for the ontological* order of the elements of the multiple in question.

Let B be an objective region*. If the elements of this region are compatible* in pairs, there exists, for the onto-logical* order-relation of statement 37, and envelope* of B, and, therefore, a real synthesis* of this objective region.

Statement 38b. Complete form of the ontology* of worlds*: Let A be a set that ontologically underlies an object* $(A, \mathbf{Id})$ in world* $\mathbf{m}$ whose transcendental* is T. We will write $\mathbf{F}A$, and call 'transcendental functor of A', the assignation to every element p of T (or transcendental degree*) of the subset of A comprising all the elements of A whose degree of existence* is p, that is $\mathbf{F}A(p) = \{x \mid x \in A \text{ and } \mathbf{E}x = p\}$. We will call 'territory of p', and write Θ, every subset of T of which p is the envelope*, that is $p = \Sigma\Theta$. Lastly, we will call 'coherent projective representation of Θ', the association, to every element q of Θ, of an element of $\mathbf{F}A(q)$, say x_q (this obviously gives us $\mathbf{E}x_q = q$), which possesses the following property: for $q \in \Theta$ and $q' \in \Theta$, the corresponding elements of $\mathbf{F}A(q)$ and $\mathbf{F}A(q')$, x_q and $x_{q'}$, are compatible* with one another, that is $x_q \ddagger x_{q'}$. Given these conditions, there always exists one and only one element ε of $\mathbf{F}A(p)$—p being the envelope* of Θ—which is such that, for every $q \in \Theta$, the localization* of ε on q is uniformly equal to the element x_q of the coherent representation, that is $\varepsilon \restriction q = x_q$. This element ε is the real synthesis* of the subset constituted by the x_q's, in the sense that it is their envelope for the onto-logical* order-relation written $<$.

Statement 39. Death* is a category of logic* (of appearing*) and not a category of ontology* (of being).

BOOK IV. GREATER LOGIC, 3. RELATION

Statement 40. Ontologically, the dimension of any world*, measured by the number of multiples appearing within it, is that of an inaccessible cardinal*. Every world is accordingly closed*, but from the interior of the world this closure remains inaccessible for any kind of operation.

Statement 41. Let us define a relation* between objects* as a function between the support-sets* of the two objects involved in the relation. To the extent that this function creates neither existence* nor difference—it conserves the degree* of existence of an element and never diminishes the degree of identity between two elements—it turns out to conserve the entirety of atomic logic*, in particular the localizations*, the compatibilities* and the onto-logical* order. If the two objects concerned are (A, a) and (B, β), and if the relation is ρ, with $a \in A$ and $b \in A$, this is expressed as follows:

$\mathbf{E}\rho(a) = \mathbf{E}a$	conservation of existence
$a(a, b) \leq \beta[\rho(a), \rho(\beta)]$	no creation of difference
$(a \ddagger b) \rightarrow [\rho(a) \ddagger \rho(b)]$	conservation of compatibility
$(a < b) \rightarrow [\rho(a) < \rho(b)]$	conservation of the onto-logical order.

Statement 42. Second constitutive thesis of materialism (for the first, see statement 33): Simply on the basis that every world* is ontologically held in an inaccessible closure, we can infer that every world is logically complete*. In other terms, the ontological closure* of worlds entails their logical completeness. Or, more technically, on the basis that the cardinality of a world is an inaccessible infinite, we can deduce that every relation* is universally exposed*.

Statement 43. Every object* of a world* admits of one, and only one, ontologically real element whose transcendental degree* of existence* in that world is minimal*. Or, every object that appears in a world admits of one element that inexists* in that world. We call this element the proper inexistent of the object in question. If (A, a) is the object, the proper inexistent is written $\varnothing_A$.

BOOK V. THE FOUR FORMS OF CHANGE

Statement 44. A site* may happen, but it cannot be. The appearing* of a site is also its disappearing.

Statement 45. Real change* (fact*, weak singularity*, event*) is distinguished from simple modification* by that ontological exception which is the appearance/disappearance of a site*.

Statement 46. In order to distinguish in real change* between the fact*, on the one hand, and the (weak) singularity* and the event* (or strong singularity), on the other, we must consider the intensity of existence* fleetingly attributed to the site* by the transcendental* to which it is associated in order to form an object* in a determinate world*. If the degree* of intensity remains lesser than the maximum*, it is a fact. If it is equal to the maximum, it is either a weak singularity or an event.

Statement 47. In order to distinguish a weak singularity* from a strong one (or an event*) we must consider consequences. An event makes the inexistent* proper to the object* in question pass from the minimal* transcendental value to the maximal* value. A weak singularity is incapable of doing this. We will say that an event absolutizes the proper inexistent of its place. The trace* of the event, often written ε, is the prior inexistent maximized (or absolutized, relative to the world* in question).

Statement 48. Every event*, every absolutization of the inexistent*, is at the price of a destruction (of a death*). This is because an existent must take the place of the sublimated inexistent.

Statement 49. An event* sets off the stepwise recasting of the transcendental* of the world*.

BOOK VI. THEORY OF POINTS

Statement 50. The set of the points* of a transcendental* has the structure of a topological space*.

Statement 51. There can exist worlds* without any point* (atonic* worlds).

Statement 52. There can exist worlds* that have as many points* as there exist transcendental degrees* (tensed* worlds).

BOOK VII. WHAT IS A BODY?

Statement 53. That an element of a site* is maximally identical to the trace* of an event* signifies that its degree* of identity to that trace is equal to its own intensity of existence*.

Statement 54. The elements of a body* are compatible* with one another.

Statement 55. For the onto-logical* order-relation written <, every body* admits of an envelope* (a real synthesis*), which is identical to the evental trace* itself.

Statement 56. That a body* is suited to affirming a point* presupposes that the efficacious part* appropriate to that point configures an organ*, that is a real synthesis* distinct from the trace*.

Statement 57. If there exists an organ* that allows a body* to affirm a point*, this organ is an element, not only of the body, but of its efficacious part* which is apposite to the point in question.

CONCLUSION. WHAT IS IT TO LIVE?

Statement 58. To live supposes that an evental trace* is given.

Statement 59. To live supposes some incorporation* into the evental present*.

Statement 60. To live supposes that a body* is suited to holding* some points*.

Statement 61. To live supposes that a body* suited to holding* some points* is the bearer of some faithful subjective formalism*.

Statement 62. To live supposes that some fidelity engenders the present* of an eternal truth*.

Statement 63. For the materialist dialectic, 'to live' and 'to live for an Idea' are one and the same thing.

Statement 64. The maxim of democratic materialism, 'live without Idea', is incoherent.

Statement 65. Several times in its life, and for several types of Ideas, every human animal is granted the possibility of living.

Statement 66. Since it is indeed possible, commencing or recommencing to live for an Idea is the only imperative.

Dictionary of Concepts

In each definition, the first occurrence of a word which also figures in the dictionary is marked by an asterisk.

In general, we have tried first to provide a definition that is as conceptual as possible, which is then followed by a more formal elucidation.

AFFIRMING (A POINT*)

A subjectivizable element of a body* is said to affirm a point of the transcendental* of the world* in which this body arises when the value of the point for the degree* that measures the existence*-in-the-world of that element is maximal*.

In other words, if ϕ is the point and x is the element, x is said to affirm the point if $\phi(Ex) = 1$.

APPEARING

A dimension of multiples which is not that of their being qua being (covered by ontology*), but that of their appearances in worlds*, or of their localization (or being-there*).

ATOM (OF APPEARING)

The instance of the One in appearing* and, therefore, the instance of what counts as one in the object*.

Take a world* whose transcendental* is T and an object of this world, written $(A, \mathbf{Id})$. We call 'atom' a function of the set A to the (ordered) set T such that at most one element in A takes the maximal value M in T. In other words, an atom is a component* of the object reduced to at most one certain element (that is, an element whose value of belonging is maximal). The atom is thus the instance of the 'no-more-than-One' in the object.

ATOM, REAL

An atom is a real atom when the instance of the One in appearing* is dictated by the instance of the One in being: the atom of appearing* is prescribed by an element (in the ontological sense) of the multiple which appears.

Let a be a fixed element of the support-set* A of an object*. Let there be a function that makes correspond to every x of this set the transcendental value $\mathbf{Id}(a, x)$, which measures the identity of the being-there* of x to that of a. It is possible to demonstrate that this function is an atom, and it is referred to as the real atom prescribed by a.

In atomic logic*, the atom prescribed by an element of the support-set of an object of the world is generally identified with this element itself.

BEING-THERE

Designates the multiple conceived according to its appearance in a world*, or as localized in a world; the multiple conceived as 'there' and not according to its strict ontological* composition. It is therefore synonymous with 'apparent', or at times, by Heideggerian custom, with being [*étant*], or even with support-set*. However, technically speaking, we generally use 'support-set' to designate a multiple A which enters into the definition of an object* $(A, \mathbf{Id})$. 'Being-there' is better-suited to designate the mode of appearing in the world of the *elements* of A. In other words, 'being-there' tends to be a category of atomic logic*.

BODY

In general, a multiple-being which, on condition of an event*, is the bearer of a subjective formalism* and makes this formalism appear in a world*.

In a more rigorous sense, a body is composed of all the elements of a site* which incorporate* themselves to an eventual present*.

BOOLEAN ALGEBRA

A transcendental* is a Boolean algebra when it verifies, for every degree* p, the law of double negation: there is an equality between the reverse* of the reverse of a degree and that degree itself ($\neg \neg p = p$). An equivalent property is represented by the law of the excluded middle: the union* of a degree and its reverse is equal to the maximum* ($p \cup \neg p = M$).

CARDINAL, INACCESSIBLE

We know that a cardinal number is the measure of the absolute numbers of elements of a given multiple. Thus the cardinal number which is written '5' measures the quantity of elements of every finite multiplicity comprising five elements. Cantor was able to define infinite cardinals through a procedure which we will not reproduce here. He also defined an order of infinite cardinals at the price of admitting the axiom of choice. Among the infinite cardinals, we will call 'inaccessible' those cardinals that cannot be obtained, on the basis of a smaller cardinal, by either of the two fundamental constructions of set theory: union, which allows one to move from A to $\cup A$ by considering all the elements of the elements of A (dissemination); and the collection of parts, which allows one to move from A to $\mathbf{P}A$ by considering all the parts of A (totalization). It is possible to say that an inaccessible cardinal is internally closed for the operations of dissemination and totalization: if one operates on a cardinal smaller than the inaccessible cardinal by applying these operations to it, one always obtains a cardinal smaller than the inaccessible cardinal. Note that the infinite cardinal $\aleph_0$, which is the smallest of the infinite cardinals, is nevertheless inaccessible (because the operations $\cup$ and $\mathbf{P}$, applied to finite cardinals, obviously produce finite cardinals). An inaccessible cardinal greater than $\aleph_0$ is instead absolutely gigantic and its existence is indemonstrable: it must be prescribed by a special axiom.

CHANGE, REAL

A real change is a change in the world* that requires a site*. It is therefore more than a modification*.

CLASSICAL (WORLD)

A classical world* is a world whose transcendental* is a Boolean algebra*. The logic of such a world is also said to be classical (it validates the excluded middle and the equivalence between affirmation and double negation).

CLOSED, CLOSURE (ONTOLOGICAL*)

A set is said to be ontologically closed when it is not possible to exit it by applying to an element of the set, however many times, the operations of the dissemination of elements or the totalization of parts. See the entry *Cardinal, inaccessible*.

COMPATIBILITY, COMPATIBLES

Two elements of the support-set* of an object* are compatible if the 'common' of their existence* is the same thing as the measure of their identity*.

Take any object of a world*, written (A, **Id**) and two elements a and b of the support-set of this object, that is of A. It is said that a and b are compatible, which is written $a \ddagger b$ if (this is the simplest form of the definition, but not the most 'originary') the conjunction* of their degrees of existence* is equal to their degree of identity (see the entry *Transcendental indexing*).

COMPLETENESS (LOGICAL), LOGICALLY COMPLETE WORLD

A world* is logically complete if every relation* within it is universally exposed*. This property is called the (logical) completeness of a world. The second constitutive thesis of materialism says that every world is logically complete (the thesis is inferred on the basis that every world is logically closed*).

CONJUNCTION

Given an order-relation* over a set T, we say that there exists the conjunction of two elements x and y of this set if the set of all the elements lesser than or equal to both x and y admits of a maximum*.

In a more approximate language, we will say that the conjunction of x and y is the greatest of the elements smaller than x and y (but 'greater than' and 'smaller than' subsume equality).

When the conjunction exists, it is written $x \cap y$.

DEATH

We call 'death', for an apparent in a particular world*, the passage from a positive value of existence* (as weak as it may be) to the minimal* value and therefore the passage to inexisting*. In other words, 'death' designates the transition $(\mathbf{E}x = p) \supset (\mathbf{E}x = \mu)$. Keeping in mind the definition of existence (as the degree of self-identity), we can also define the death of a singular apparent in a determinate world as the coming to be of a total non-identity to itself.

DEGREE, TRANSCENDENTAL

The elements of a transcendental* are often called degrees because they serve to 'measure' identities or differences or existences* relative to a determinate world*.

DEPENDENCE (OF ONE TRANSCENDENTAL DEGREE* ON ANOTHER)

The transcendental measure that synthesizes everything which, in conjunction with one degree, remains lesser than the other. In other words, the dependence of a degree is its capacity to be enveloping with regard to everything that entertains a non-nil relation with the degree on which it depends.

Formally, the dependence of q with regard to p, written $p \Rightarrow q$, is the envelope of all the degrees t whose conjunction with p remains inferior to q:

$$(p{\Rightarrow}q) = \Sigma \{t \mid p \cap t \le q\}$$

By a certain misuse of language, it is also customarily said that an element y of a world depends 'to the p degree' on another element x of the same world, if the transcendental value of the dependence of the existence of the one with respect to the existence of the other has the value p. In other words, if:

$$(\mathbf{E}x \Rightarrow \mathbf{E}y) = p$$

DISTRIBUTIVITY (OF THE CONJUNCTION* RELATIVE TO THE ENVELOPE*)

We say that the conjunction is distributive relative to the envelope (when these terms are defined with regard to an order-relation* over a set T) if the conjunction between an element x and the envelope of a subset B is equal to the envelope of the conjunctions of x with all the elements of B.

In other words, we have:

$$x \cap \Sigma B = \Sigma \{x \cap b \mid x \in B\}$$

EFFICACIOUS PART (OF A BODY*, AND FOR A GIVEN POINT*)

Set of the elements of a body which affirm* a point (with the exception of the evental trace*, which is present in every body and affirms every point).

Take a body in an event-site*, and take a point ϕ of the transcendental* of the world* in question. We call efficacious part of the body for the point ϕ that part of the body which comprises all the elements x of the body for which $\phi(\mathbf{E}x) = 1$.

ENVELOPE

Let us suppose that an order-relation* is defined over a set T. Let B be a subset of T. We say that there exists an envelope of B (for the order-relation) if the set of the elements greater than or equal to *all* the elements of B admits of a minimum*.

In a more approximate language, we will say that the envelope is the smallest of the elements greater than all the elements of B (but 'smallest' and 'greatest' subsume equality).

The envelope of B, when it exists, is written ΣB.

EVENT (OR STRONG SINGULARITY)

An event is a real change* such that the intensity of existence* fleetingly ascribed to the site* is maximal*, and such that among the consequences of this site there is the maximal becoming of the intensity of existence of what was the proper inexistent* of the site. We also say that the event absolutizes the inexistent. The event is more than a (weak) singularity*, which is itself more than a fact*, which is in turn more than a modification*.

EXISTING, EXISTENCE

The degree* of existence of a being is the transcendental indexing* of its self-identity. This degree is also called the 'existence' of the being in question (relative to its appearing* in a world*). Existence (like death*) is, therefore, a category of appearing and not of being. Formally, let $(A, \mathbf{Id})$ be an object* in a world and let a be an element of A. The existence of a is the value in the transcendental* T of $\mathbf{Id}(a, a)$. The existence of a is generally written $\mathbf{E}a$.

EXPOSITION (OF A RELATION), EXPOSED RELATION, EXPONENT

A relation* between two objects* is exposed (in the world*) if there exists a third object which is itself related to the first two objects in such a way that the 'relational triangle' is commutative. In other words, if A and B are two objects (we are simplifying the notation), and if ρ is a relation between A and B, we will say that ρ is exposed if there exists an object C, a relation f of C to A, and a relation g of C to B, relations which are such that the composition of ρ and f is equivalent to g. Or if we go from C to B passing through A, thereby linking up with f and then ρ, we are doing the same thing as if we went directly from C to B through g.

We then say that C is an exponent of the relation ρ.

EXPOSITION (OF A RELATION*), UNIVERSAL

Take an exposed* relation in a world*. We say that it is universally exposed if there exists an exponent* for it such that, for every other exponent, there exists, from the latter towards the former, a single relation which makes it so that all the relational triangles commute.

Formally, if A and B are the objects implied in a relation ρ (ρ 'goes' from A to B), if U is an exponent such that, for every other exponent C, the triangles UAB and CAB naturally commute (since U and A are exponents of ρ), but the triangles UCA and UCB also commute, we will say that U is the universal exponent of ρ.

FACT

A fact is a real change* such that the site* comes to be assigned an intensity of existence* that is strictly inferior to the maximum*.

FUNCTION OF APPEARING, OR IDENTITY-FUNCTION

See the entry *Transcendental indexing*.

GENERIC PROCEDURE

We call 'generic procedure' the ontological* process of the constitution of a truth, that is the production of a present* by a subjective formalism* of the 'faithful'* type, as borne by a body*. The word 'generic' stems from the fact that, as I established in *Being and Event*, the object* of the world* constituted by the ensemble of this production, or the set of the consequences of the evental trace*, is a generic set in the sense given to this word by the mathematician Paul Cohen: a set as little determined as possible, such that it is not discernible by any predicate.

To date, the human animal knows four types of generic procedure: love, politics, art and science.

HOLDING (A POINT*)

It is said that a subjectivated body* can hold a point if there exists in that body an organ* for that point.

INCORPORATION, INCORPORATING ONESELF
(TO THE EVENTAL PRESENT*)

An element of a site* incorporates itself to the evental present if its identity to the trace* of the event is maximal*.

Formally, it is clear that if x incorporates itself to the present of an event whose trace is ε, it is because the existence* of x is equal to its degree of identity with ε. We therefore have:

$$\mathbf{E}x = \mathbf{Id}(\varepsilon, x)$$

INEXISTENCE, INEXISTING, INEXISTENT

Inexistence is a mode of being-there* of an element of a multiple appearing in a world*, namely the 'nil' mode: this element exists* 'the least possible' in the world.

Given an object* $(A, \mathbf{Id})$ in a world, an element a of A inexists in this world if its degree of existence is minimal*. In other words, a inexists if $\mathbf{E}a = \mu$. We also say that a is the inexistent of the object. Every object admits of one (and only one) inexistent, generally written $\emptyset_A$.

LOCALIZATION (ON A TRANSCENDENTAL DEGREE*)

Take the real atom* prescribed by the element a of an apparent A. We call localization of this atom on a transcendental degree the function that associates to every element of A the conjunction* of its value for the real atom in question, on the one hand, and of the transcendental degree, on the other. This function is obviously a component* of the object of which A is the support-set*. It is possible to demonstrate that this component is still an atom.

The localization of the atom prescribed by a on the degree p is generally written as follows: $a \upharpoonright p$. But it is necessary to bear in mind that $a \upharpoonright p$ is an (atomic) function, which is none other than the function $\mathbf{Id}(a, x) \cap p$.

LOGIC, OR GREATER LOGIC

We call 'logic' the general theory of appearing* or of being-there*, that is the theory of worlds* or of the cohesion of what comes to exist* (or inexist*).

LOGIC, ATOMIC

Atomic logic is the logic that takes as its starting point the identification of the elements (in the ontological sense) of a being and the real atoms* prescribed by these elements. Atomic logic thus circulates 'between' ontology* and logic*. Its most important theorem is the identification of a real synthesis* for every sufficiently 'homogeneous' zone of an object*.

The fundamental relations of atomic logic are compatibility* between two elements (identified with the atoms that they prescribe) and the onto-logical order-relation*. It is by combining these two relations that we demonstrate the fundamental theorem of the Greater Logic, which concerns the characteristics of the transcendental functor (see *Statement 37*).

LOGIC, ORDINARY (SMALLER LOGIC)

Ordinary logic is a grammar of correct statements accompanied by a theory of deduction and a systematics of interpretations. Today, it is generally presented as the exposition of symbols and rules of entailment for symbols (syntax) and as mathematics of domains of interpretation (semantics, theory of models). We can show that when conceived in this way, logic is nothing but a small part of the Greater Logic*, or theory of appearing*, from which it is deduced.

MAXIMUM, MAXIMAL

Given an order-relation* over a set T, we say that it admits of a maximum, or of a maximal element, if there exists an element of T which is greater than or equal to every element of T. This element is written M, if it exists. We can then write that, for $x \in T$, we always have $x \leq M$.

MINIMUM, MINIMAL

Given an order-relation* defined over a set T, we say that it admits of a minimum, or of a minimal element, if there exists an element of T lesser than or equal to every element of T. This element is written μ, if it exists. We can then write that, for $x \in T$, we always have $\mu \leq x$.

MODIFICATION

We call modification every change in the world* that does not require a site*. A modification is therefore not a real change*. It is simply a temporal cut among objective successions, that is a set of transcendental indexings* which are constitutive of a temporalized object*. In what concerns the differential evaluation of their intensities, temporal differences have no unique features that would set them apart from spatial differences.

OBJECT

'Object' is the name of the generic form of appearing* for a determinate multiple. It is therefore, after 'world', the most fundamental concept of the Greater Logic*.

We can say that to be an apparent of such and such a world* comes down, for a multiple, to objectivating itself within it. Since in terms of the laws that localize elements within it, a world is largely defined by its transcendental*, it is easily understood that an object is the transcendental indexing* of a multiple. It is beyond doubt, therefore, that 'object' is a category of appearing (or of logic) and not a category of being (or of ontology*). It is a structure of being-there* in a world.

We must be careful at this point, so as to avoid idealist or critical interpretations of the notion of object. On the one hand, we must reaffirm an important result of *Being and Event*, namely that *what* appears (the pure multiple) is perfectly knowable (by ontological science, otherwise referred to as 'mathematics'). On the other hand, we must postulate that what is counted-as-one in appearing, its atoms*, is ultimately prescribed by the real composition of multiple-being.

Take a determinate world whose transcendental is T. An object is first of all the joint product of a set (termed the 'support-set'* of the object) and of a transcendental indexing of this object on T. That is why it is written as $(A, \textbf{Id})$ or (A, a) or (B, β), etc. Furthermore, the object is the submitting of this given to the postulate of materialism, to wit that every atom is a real atom*. Given these conditions, we say that an object $(A, \textbf{Id})$ is a form of the being-there of the multiple A (in the world in question).

OBJECT-COMPONENT

An object-component is a part of the object, in the sense that the word 'part' refers to appearing*, and not to the ontological* composition of the support-set*. This means that elements of the set belong 'more or less' to the component: there is a transcendental degree* of this belonging.

Take an object $(A, \mathbf{Id})$. For $x \in A$, a function $\kappa(x)$ of A to the transcendental T *defines* a component in the following sense: if $\kappa(x) = p$, we will say that x belongs to the component 'to the p degree' of belonging. In particular, if $\kappa(x) = M$, the belonging of p to the component κ is certain (that is, absolute). If $\kappa(x) = \mu$, the belonging of x to the component is nil.

OBJECTIVE REGION

Given an object $(A, \mathbf{Id})$, we call 'objective region' every subset B of A.

ONTOLOGY

Science of being qua being. Hence, science of multiplicities qua pure multiplicities, or multiples 'without One'. This science, which is indifferent to any localization of multiples, and consequently to their appearing* or being-there*, is historically identical to mathematics. It is distinct from fundamental logic*, or Greater Logic, which is the thinking of appearing as such, or science of being-there. If the fundamental concept of ontology is the multiple (mathematics of sets), the fundamental concepts of logic are world* (logics of worlds) and object* (atomic logic*).

ORGAN (OF A BODY*)

Given a body and point*, we call organ of a body for this point the envelope* for the onto-logical order-relation* of the efficacious part* of the body suited to this point, provided that it differs from the trace* ε. If the organ exists, it is written ε_ϕ.

PHENOMENON

The phenomenon of an element of a multiple which appears in a determinate world* is constituted by the set of the transcendental values that the identity-function* of the multiple assigns to the couple formed by this element and all the elements that co-appear with it.

Given a fixed element of A, say $a \in A$, we call 'phenomenon of a relative to A' (in the world **m** in question) the set of the values of the function of appearing $\mathbf{Id}(a, x)$ for all the x's that co-appear with a in set A.

POINTS (OF A TRANSCENDENTAL*)

A point of the world* (in fact, of the transcendental of a world) is the appearance of the infinite totality of the world (of the totality of degrees*) before the instance of the decision, that is the duality of 'yes' and 'no'. 'To hold* a point' means to hold this instance in the face of the world. Or, to have the subjective* (that is, corporeal and formal) wherewithal to submit the situation to the decisional pressure of the Two (I say 'yes' or I say 'no', I find and declare a point of the situation).

The notion of point 'filters' the nuances of the transcendental (the possible infinite of degrees) through the decisional and declaratory brutality of the 'either this or that' represented by the simple pair of the zero and the one. This pair is the most classical* transcendental there is. It is this pair which interprets ordinary logic*, namely the logic of the mathematics of sets (an element belongs to a set E, or does not belong to it, there is no other transcendental possibility). A point is a global correlation, which respects operations, between a complex transcendental and the basic classical transcendental which supports binary logic.

We can put this in formal terms: given a transcendental T, we call 'point' of the transcendental a function of T to the set $\{0, 1\}$ (itself considered as a transcendental, once it is provided with the total order-relation* $0 \leq 1$), to the extent that this function conserves the transcendental operations and draws its values from the totality of the set $\{0, 1\}$, and not from only one of its two elements. This means that if ϕ is the function (the point), if B is a subset of T, and if $\cap'$ and Σ' are the operations of conjunction and envelope in $\{0, 1\}$ considered as a transcendental, we have:

- $\phi(p \cap q) = \phi(p) \cap' \phi(q)$
- $\phi(\Sigma B) = \Sigma' \{\phi(p) \mid p \in B\}$
- There always exists in T at least one p such that $\phi(p) = 1$, and at least one q such that $\phi(q) = 0$.

There exist transcendentals that do not have any points.

PRESENT, EVENTAL PRESENT

A present is the set of consequences in a world* of an evental trace*. These consequences only unfold to the extent that a body* is capable of holding* some points*. What's more, this body must bear the formalism of a faithful subject*.

The present is written π.

RELATION (BETWEEN OBJECTS* OF A WORLD*)

A relation between two objects of the same world is a formal connection between these objects which conserves the structure of appearing*. In particular, a relation is not creative of existence, nor is it a radical deformation of the 'place' of the object.

Given two objects of the same world, say (A, a) and (B, β), we say that a function ρ of A to B is a relation in the world if this function conserves the degrees of existence* and the localizations of atoms* on the trans-cendental* degrees*.

In other terms:

$$\mathbf{E}\rho(x) = \mathbf{E}x$$
$$\rho(x \upharpoonright p) = \rho(x) \upharpoonright p$$

We can then show that a relation in fact conserves the entirety of atomic logic*.

ORDER-RELATION

A set T is said to be 'endowed with an order-relation' when:

1. It is possible to define a relation $\leq$ whose arguments are the pairs of elements of set T, a relation that is written $x \leq y$ and is generally read as 'x is lesser than or equal to y' or 'y is greater than or equal to x'.
2. This relation obeys the following three axioms:

    – transitivity: if x is lesser than or equal to y and y is lesser than or equal to z, then x is lesser than or equal to z;
    – reflexivity: x is lesser than or equal to x;
    – anti-symmetry: if x is lesser than or equal to y, and y in turn is lesser than or equal to x, then x and y are equal.

It is especially important to note that nothing, in this definition, requires (or excludes) that the relation exists for *every* pair of elements of *T*. If it is not the case, the order is referred to as partial. If it is, the order is said to be total.

ORDER-RELATION, ONTO-LOGICAL

It is possible to define, between two elements of the support-set *A* of an object* (*A*, **Id**), an order-relation*. This relation is said to be onto-logical, or real, and is written <. Its simplest definition is that *a* is lesser than or equal to *b* if the transcendental degree* which measures the identity between *a* and *b* is the same as the one which measures the existence* of *a*. In other words, we have:

$$(a < b) \leftrightarrow (\mathbf{E}a = \mathbf{Id}(a, b))$$

REVERSE (OF A TRANSCENDENTAL DEGREE*, OF AN ELEMENT OF THE WORLD*)

A transcendental generalization of classical negation. The reverse is what is maximally 'alien' to what is given, the synthesis of what is entirely exterior to it.

Given a transcendental *T* and a degree of *T*, say *p*, we call reverse of *p* the envelope* of all the degrees of *T* whose conjunction* with *p* is equal to the minimum*. The reverse of *p* is, therefore, the synthesis of everything whose conjunction with *p* is considered as nil in the transcendental. The reverse of *p* is written $\neg p$.

Formally, this gives us

$$\neg p = \Sigma \{q \ / \ (p \cap q) = \mu\}$$

By a certain abuse of language, we say that an element of a being of a world is the reverse of another element (or even its negation) if the degree of existence* of the one is the reverse of that of the other.

SINGULARITY (WEAK OR STRONG)

A singularity is a real change* whose site* comes to be assigned the maximal* intensity of existence*. So it is more than a fact. The singularity is weak (we also simply say 'singularity', without the adjective) if its consequences do not imply that the inexistent* of the site comes to take the maximal value. If instead this consequence exists, the singularity is said to be strong. We then also call it an event*.

SITE

A site is an object* to which it happens, in being, to belong to itself; and, in appearing*, to fall under its own transcendental indexing*, so that it assigns to its own being a value of existence*. A site testifies to an intrusion of being as such into appearing.

Take an object $(A, \mathbf{Id})$ in a world $\mathbf{m}$. It is a site once it comes to be affected by the ontological relation $A \in A$ (self-belonging) and, consequently, by a transcendental evaluation of existence* of the type $\mathbf{Id}(A, A)$, that is $\mathbf{E}A = p$.

SUBJECT

The mode according to which a body* enters into a subjective formalism* with regard to the production of a present*. Accordingly, a subject has as its effective conditions, not only an event* (and thus above all a site*), but a body*, along with the existence in this body of an organ* for at least some points*.

SUBJECT, FAITHFUL

Subjective formalism* whose operation is the production of a present*, which it does by holding* to some points*.

SUBJECT, OBSCURE

Subjective formalism* whose operation is the occultation of a present* through the imposition, on the body* of the faithful subject* and on the evental trace*, of a violent negation, dictated from the point of a supposed pure transcendent body.

SUBJECT, REACTIVE

Subjective formalism* whose operation is the denial of a present* by the imposition on the body of the faithful subject* of a subordination to the negation of the evental trace*.

SUBJECTIVE FORMALISM

We call 'subjective formalism' the different combinations through which a body* enters into a relation with a present* (and hence with the post-evental stages of truth*). These combinations employ the operations of subordination, negation, erasure and consequence. There are three subject-ive formalisms: faithful*, reactive* and obscure*.

SUPPORT-SET (OF AN OBJECT*)

The support-set of an object is its ontological* dimension, in other words, within it, the being [*l'étant*] or *that which* appears, that is a pure multiple. The other dimension is the identity-function* that relates it to the transcendental*—the logical dimension.

Given an object (*A*, **Id**) of a world* **m**, we call 'support-set' of this object the multiple *A* which enters into the identity of the object, and whose transcendental indexing* is the identity-function **Id**.

SYNTHESIS, REAL

The notion of real synthesis is crucial in the effort to think the retroactivity of appearing* on being, of logic* on ontology*. In effect, it designates the possibility, for some objective regions*, to be regulated by an order which is directly defined, on the basis of transcendental indexing*, over the elements of the appearing multiple. Moreover, under certain conditions, this order admits of dominant points that totalize on their hither side the region under consideration.

The real synthesis of a part *B* of a being *A* appearing in a world* is an envelope* of *B* for the onto-logical order-relation* <. We can demonstrate that every part *B* whose elements are compatible* in pairs admits of a real synthesis.

TOPOLOGICAL SPACE

A mathematical concept that aims to rigorously think what is the 'place' of a being, its environs (or neighbourhoods), its boundary, and so on.

A topological space is the conjoined product of a set E and a function **Int** (meaning 'interior of'). The 'interior' function associates, to every part A of E, another part (called 'interior of A') which obeys four fundamental axioms: the interior of A is included in A; the interior of the interior of A is nothing but the interior of A; the interior of E is E itself; and, finally, the interior of the intersection of the two parts A and B is the intersection of their interiors.

TRACE (OF AN EVENT*, OR EVENTAL TRACE)

We call trace of an event, or eventual trace, and generally write as ε, the prior inexistent* which, under the effect of the site*, has taken the maximal* value. In the post-eventual world*, we therefore have $\mathbf{E}\varepsilon = M$.

TRANSCENDENTAL (OF A WORLD*)

The concept of 'transcendental' is without doubt the most important operational concept in the whole of the Greater Logic*, or theory of appearing*. It designates the constitutive capacity of every world to assign to what abides there, in that world, variable intensities of identity vis-à-vis what also abides there. In short, 'transcendental' designates that a world, in which pure multiplicities appear in the guise of objects*, is a network of identities and differences that concern the elements of *what* appears. It is possible then to understand why the fundamental structure of the transcendental is the order-structure, which is the general form of what sanctions the 'more' and the 'less'.

In the end, every 'more' or 'less' concerns appearing, or existence*. And if there exists an onto-logical order*, it is in the retroaction, on multiple-being, of its worldly conditions of appearance.

In formal terms, given a world **m**, the transcendental of that world is a subset T of that world which possesses the following properties:

1. An order-relation* is defined over T.
2. This order-relation admits of a minimum* written μ.

3. It admits of the existence of the conjunction* for every pair $\{x, y\}$ of elements of T.
4. It admits of the existence of an envelope* for every subset B of T.
5. The conjunction is distributive* relative to the envelope.

TRANSCENDENTAL INDEXING, FUNCTION OF APPEARING, IDENTITY-FUNCTION

The transcendental indexing of a multiple relative to a given world* is what establishes the measure, in that world, of the identities and differences in the intensity of appearance of two elements of that multiple. In other words, it is what provides the mode of appearing for that which composes a pure multiple.

Transcendental indexing is a function which makes a transcendental degree* correspond to a pair of elements of the multiple under consideration. We say that this degree measures the identity of the two elements in the world where they appear.

Formally, let A be the set which is supposed to appear in a world. It only appears in that world to the extent that a transcendental indexing **Id** relates it to the transcendental T of the world in the following way: for every pair of elements a and b of A, we have **Id**$(a, b) = p$, where p is an element of T. We will say that a and b are, for the world in question, 'identical to the p degree'. For example, if p is the minimum* μ of T, a and b are 'as little identical as possible'. This means that the being-there* of a is—in this world—absolutely different from that of b.

We therefore call the function **Id** function of appearing, or identity-function, for self-evident reasons.

TRUTH

The set—which is assumed to be complete—of all the productions of a faithfully subjectivated body* (of a body seized by a subjective formalism of the faithful* type). Ontologically, this set results from a generic procedure*. Logically, it unfolds a present* in the world* by holding* to a series of points*.

UNION

Given an order-relation* on a set T, we say that the union of two elements x and y of T exists, if the set of all the degrees lesser than or equal to x and y simultaneously admits of a maximum*.

Speaking more roughly, we will also say that the union of x and y is the greatest of all the degrees which are smaller than both x and y. But 'greatest' and 'smaller' subsume equality.

The union, when it exists, is written $x \cup y$.

We can demonstrate that if T is a transcendental*, the union of two degrees* always exists.

WORLD

By 'world' we understand an ontologically-closed* set—that is a set measured by an inaccessible cardinal*—which contains a transcendental* T and the transcendental indexings* of all the multiples on this transcendental. We can thus say that a world is the place in which objects* appear. Or that 'world' designates *one* of the logics* of appearing*.

WORLD, ATONIC

We say that a world is atonic when its transcendental* has no point*.

WORLD, TENSED

A world is tensed if it has as many points* as there are transcendental degrees*.

Dictionary of Symbols

We provide here the list of the logical and mathematical symbols employed in Logics of Worlds, *in their order of appearance, with their usual meaning and an attempt at an 'oral' approximation, that is a possible way in which they may be said (rather than simply read). The Greek letters will be read in keeping with their canonical pronunciation (alpha, beta, etc.). For the precise definition of the symbolized notions, see the 'Dictionary of Concepts'.*

$\neg$ Reverse, and also negation. One will read $\neg p$ as 'reverse of p', or 'non-p'.

$\in$ Belonging to a set. One will read $a \in E$ as 'a belongs to E', or 'a is an element of E'.

$\leftrightarrow$ Logical equivalence. One will read $P \leftrightarrow Q$ as 'the proposition P is equivalent to the proposition Q'.

$\exists$ Existential quantifier. One will read $(\exists x)P$ as 'there exists an element x such that one can affirm the proposition P'.

$\forall$ Universal quantifier. One will read $(\forall x)P$ as 'for every element x, one can affirm proposition P'.

$\leq$ Inequality. One will read $p \leq q$ as 'p is lesser than or equal to q' or 'q is greater than or equal to p', or by a misuse of language 'p is smaller than q' or 'q is larger than p'.

$\rightarrow$ Logical implication. One will read $P \rightarrow Q$ as 'the proposition P implies the proposition Q'.

$\cap$ Conjunction. One will read $p \cap q$ as 'the conjunction of p and q'.

Σ Envelope. One will read ΣB as 'envelope of the set B'.

$\Rightarrow$ Dependence. One will read $p \Rightarrow q$ as 'dependence of q with regard to p'.

$\cup$ Union. One will read $p \cup q$ as 'p union q', or 'union of p and q'.

Id   Function of appearing, or transcendental indexing. One will read **Id**$(x, y) = p$ as 'x is identical to y to the p degree'.

E   Existence, degree of existence. One will read **E**x as 'existence of x'.

$\restriction$ Localization. One will read $a \restriction p$ as 'localization of a on p'.

$\ddagger$ Compatibility. One will read $a \ddagger b$ as 'a is compatible with b'.

$<$ Ontological inequality. One will read $a < b$ as 'a is of a lesser rank than b'.

$\varnothing$ Empty set. One will read $\varnothing$ as 'the void' [*le vide*] or empty [*vide*].

$\varnothing_A$ The inexistent of a multiple. One will read $\varnothing_A$ as 'the proper inexistent of A'.

Selected Bibliography

Badiou, A. (2009 [1982]) *Theory of the Subject*. Trans. B. Bosteels. London: Continuum.

—— (2006 [1988]), *Being and Event*. Trans. O. Feltham. London: Continuum.

—— (2009 [1992]), *Conditions*. Trans. S. Corcoran. London: Continuum.

—— and J. Bellassen, (1977), *Le Noyau rationnel de la dialectique hégelienne*. Paris: Maspero.

Belhaj Kacem, M. (2004), *Événement et répétition*. Auch: Tristram.

—— (2004), *L'Affect*. Auch: Tristram.

Cassin, B. (1995), *L'Effet sophistique*. Paris: Gallimard.

Char, R. (1995), *Feuillets d'hypnos*, in *Œuvres complètes*. 'Bibliothèque de la Pléiade'. Paris: Gallimard.

da Costa, N. C. A. (1997), *Logiques classiques et non classiques*. Trans. and ed. J.-Y. Béziau. Issy-les-Moulineaux: Masson.

David-Ménard, M. (1990), *La Folie dans la raison pure*. Paris: Vrin.

Deleuze, G. (1990), *Logic of Sense*. Trans. M. Lester with C. Stivale. New York: Columbia University Press.

Desanti, J.-T. (1968), *Les Idéalités mathématiques*. Paris: Seuil.

—— (1975), *La Philosophie silencieuse*. Paris: Seuil.

Euclid. (2002), *Elements*. Trans. T. L. Heath. Santa Fe, NM: Green Lion Press.

Gilson, E. (1953), *Choir of Muses*. Trans. M. Ward. New York: Sheed & Ward.

—— (1963), *Dante and Philosophy*. Trans. D. Moore. New York: Harper & Row.

Gracq, J. (1997), *The Opposing Shore*. Trans. R. Howard. London: Harvill.

Hallward, P. (ed.) (2004), *Think Again: Alain Badiou and the Future of Philosophy*. London: Continuum.

Hegel, G. W. F. (1969), *Science of Logic*. Trans. A. V. Miller. London: Allen & Unwin.

Huan, K. (1931), *Discourses on Salt and Iron: A Debate on State Control of Commerce and Industry in Ancient China, Chapters I–XIX*. Trans. E. M. Gale. Leyden: E.J. Brill.

Janicaud, D. (2001), 'The Theological Turn in French Phenomenology', in *Phenomenology and the 'Theological Turn': The French Debate*. New York: Fordham.

Joyce, J. (2000), *Finnegans Wake*. London: Penguin.

Kant, I. (2007), *Critique of Pure Reason*. Trans. N. K. Smith. Basingstoke: Palgrave.

Kierkegaard, S. (1959), *Either/Or*. Trans. W. Lowrie. Princeton: Princeton University Press.

—— (1968), *Concluding Unscientific Postscript*. Trans. W. Lowrie and D. F. Swenson, Princeton: Princeton University Press.

—— (1989), *Sickness Unto Death*. Trans. A. Hannay. London: Penguin.

Lacan, J., *On Feminine Sexuality, the Limits of Love and Knowledge: Encore, The Seminar of Jacques Lacan, Book XX, 1972–1973*. Ed. J.-A. Miller, trans. B. Fink. New York: Norton.

—— (2001), *Autres écrits*. Ed. J.-A. Miller. Paris: Seuil.

—— (2007), *Seminar XVII: The Other Side of Psychoanalysis*. Trans. R. Grigg. New York: W.W. Norton.

Lazarus, S. (1997), *Anthropologie du nom*. Paris: Seuil.

Leibniz, G. W. (1995), *Philosophical Writings*. Ed. G. H. R. Parkinson. London: Everyman.

Lyotard, J. F. (1988), *The Differend*. Trans. G. V. D. Abbeele. Minneapolis: Minnesota University Press.

Malraux, A. (1968), *Anti-Memoirs*. Trans. T. Kilmartin. New York: Holt, Rinehart & Winston.

—— (1974), *Le Miroir des limbes*. 'Bibliothèque de la Pléiade'. Paris: Gallimard.

—— (1974), *La Tête d'obsidienne*. Paris: Gallimard.

—— (1990), *Man's Fate*. Trans. H. M. Chevalier. New York: Vintage.

Mao Tse-tung (1967), *Selected Works*, vol. 1. Peking: Foreign Languages Press.

Meillassoux, Q. (2008), *After Finitude*. Trans. R. Brassier. London: Continuum.

Milner, J.-C. (1997), *Le Triple du plaisir*. Lagrasse: Verdier.

Nicolas, F. (1998), *La Singularité Schönberg*. Paris: L'Harmattan.

Pessoa, F. (1998), 'Maritime Ode' in *Poems of Fernando Pessoa*. Ed. and trans. E. Honig and S. M. Brown. San Francisco: City Lights.

Plato. (1993), *Sophist*. Trans. N. P. White. New York: Hackett.

—— (2000), *Timaeus*. Trans. D. J. Zeyl. New York: Hackett.

Rasiowa, H., and Sikorski, R. (1963), *The Mathematics of Meta-Mathematics*. Warsaw: Panstwowe Wydawnictwo Naukowe.

Ricœur, P. (2006), *Memory, History, Forgetting*. Trans. K. Blamey and D. Pellauer. Chicago: University of Chicago Press.

Rosen, C. (2005), *The Classical Style: Haydn, Mozart, Beethoven*. London: Faber and Faber.

Rousseau, J. J. (1997), *Julie, or the New Heloise*. Trans. P. Stewart and J. Vaché. Dartmouth: University Press of New England.

Sartre, J. P. (1965), *Lucifer and the Lord*. Trans. K. Black. London: Penguin.

—— (1989), *Dirty Hands*, in *No Exit and Three Other Plays*. Trans. S. Gilbert. New York: Vintage.

—— (2003), *Being and Nothingness*. Trans. H. E. Barnes. London: Routledge.

Spinoza, B. (2005), *Ethics*. Trans. E. Curley. London: Penguin.

Valéry, P. (1950), 'The Graveyard by the Sea' in *Selected Writings*. Trans. C. Day-Lewis. New York: New Directions.

Virgil. (2006), *The Aeneid*. Trans. R. Fagles. New York: Penguin.

Wahl, F. (1996), *Introduction au discours du tableau*. Paris: Seuil.

Iconography

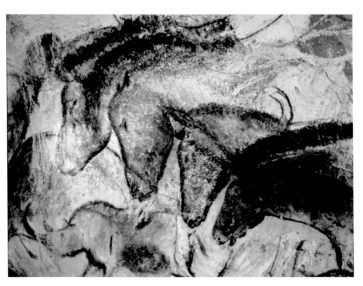

1. Panel of horses from the Chauvet-Pont-d'Arc cave, Ardèche.
Photo from the French Ministry of Culture and Communication, Direction régionale des affaires culturelles de Rhône-Alpes, Service régional de l'archéologie.

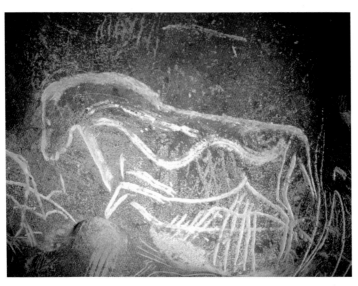

2. Panel of large engravings from the Chauvet-Pont-d'Arc cave, Salle Hillaire, Ardèche.
Photo from the French Ministry of Culture and Communication, Direction régionale des affaires culturelles de Rhône-Alpes, Service régional de l'archéologie.

3. Pablo Picasso, *Two Horses Dragging a Dead Horse*, **1929.**
Picasso Museum, Paris. © Succession Picasso 2006 / Photo RMN – Thierry Le Mage.

4. Pablo Picasso, *Man Holding Two Horses*, **1939.**
Ludwig Museum, Cologne. © Succession Picasso 2006 / Rheinisches Bildarchiv Köln.

5. Hubert Robert, *The Bathing Pool.*
The Metropolitan Museum of Art, New York. Gift of J. Pierpont Morgan, 1917.
Photo © 1987 The Metropolitan Museum of Art.

6. Masterplan of Brasilia

a. As drawn by Lucio Costa.

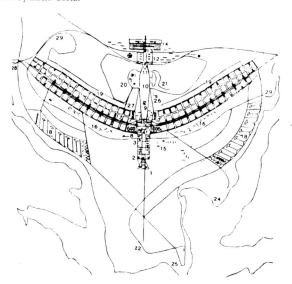

b. As implemented.

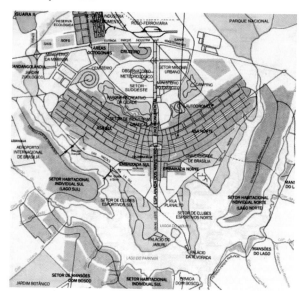

Index